CITY OF LONDON
THE HISTORY

David Kynaston was born in Aldershot in 1951.
After graduating from New College, Oxford, he
studied at the London School of Economics.
A professional historian, in addition to the four-
volume *The City of London*, his works include
*King Labour: A History of the British Working
Class, 1850-1914*, histories of the *Financial
Times* and the stockbrokers Cazenove & co., and
the first two volumes in a planned history of
Britain between 1945 and 1979, *Austerity Britain,
1945–51* and *Family Britain, 1951–57*.

David Milner, editor of this volume, was born in
1971. After postgraduate work at university he
became an editor for Secker & Warburg at
Random House. He now works as a freelance
editor for leading publishers, and lives in the
Cotswolds with his wife and two children.

DAVID KYNASTON

City of London

THE HISTORY

EDITED BY
David Milner

David Kynaston

VINTAGE BOOKS
London

Published by Vintage 2012

2 4 6 8 10 9 7 5 3 1

First published in Great Britain in 2011 by
Chatto & Windus

Vintage
Random House, 20 Vauxhall Bridge Road,
London SW1V 2SA

www.vintage-books.co.uk

Addresses for companies within The Random House Group Limited
can be found at: www.randomhouse.co.uk/offices.htm

The Random House Group Limited Reg. No. 954009

A CIP catalogue record for this book
is available from the British Library

ISBN 9780099554820

The Random House Group Limited supports The Forest Stewardship
Council (FSC®), the leading international forest certification
organisation. Our books carrying the FSC label are printed on FSC®
certified paper. FSC is the only forest certification scheme endorsed
by the leading environmental organisations, including Greenpeace.
Our paper procurement policy can be found at:
www.randomhouse.co.uk/environment

MIX
Paper from
responsible sources
FSC® C016897

Printed and bound by CPI Group (UK) Ltd, Croydon, CR0 4YY

Contents

Preface

This book is an abridgement of my four-volume history of the City of London published by Chatto between 1994 and 2001. The individual volumes comprise *A World of Its Own, 1815–90*; *Golden Years, 1890–1914*; *Illusions of Gold, 1914–45*; and *A Club No More, 1945–2000*. Back in 1987, when the idea of a history of the City began to take shape, I conceived it as a single volume – before the addictive properties of research changed the project's dimensions. So almost a quarter of a century on, it is appropriate to have it at last in the form that my very patient publishers originally (and understandably) wanted.

Why, to continue for a moment in autobiographical vein, the City? Why in 1978 did I sign up at the LSE for what would become a doctoral thesis on the London Stock Exchange (1870–1914) and the start of a long journey? Part political, part literary, I think: political in that I was well aware of the left's demonisation of the City following successive sterling crises since the mid-1960s, and was broadly sympathetic to this perspective, but intuitively felt that it was too abstract, with no really intimate understanding of the place itself and its inhabitants; literary in that as an adolescent I had been fascinated by the City clerk Mr Pooter, by Rex Mottram and his City friends in *Brideshead Revisited*, and above all by Henry Wilcox in *Howards End*, while more recently I had discovered George Gissing, who during the 1890s vividly pictured the City as the centre of a destructive whirlpool, sucking everyone in. There was also a personal element: an unsettled 27-year-old looking for a new direction, I was inspired by the example of E. P. Thompson, who in his 1976 book *Whigs and Hunters* had 'parachuted' into the eighteenth century. I knew no one in the City, had no family connection with it, and indeed had barely set foot there. It felt time to make my own leap.

Many all-consuming years followed before in 2001 that phase of my working life ended. Ten further years on, I am not the person to write a detailed account of the latest instalment of the City's fortunes – the asset bubble, the crash in 2008, that extraordinary but not unpredictable apparent wriggling free from punishment and correction for the often devastating consequences of its actions. (Recommended accounts include

Fool's Gold by Gillian Tett, *Whoops!* by John Lanchester and, for a historian's dispassionate, long-view analysis, *Crises and Opportunities* by Youssef Cassis.) Instead, I would like briefly to offer a handful of thoughts informed by an awareness of the City's two preceding centuries.

Starting with ecology and habitat. The old City was a heterogeneous place of thousands upon thousands of small or medium-sized firms, each satisfying particular, often niche demands; the new, supermarket-style City is far more homogeneous, dominated by vast conglomerates inevitably lacking 'touch' and responsiveness. So too with the habitat, where not only has the Square Mile progressively lost much of its idiosyncratic charm – not least with the ongoing erection of such overbearing, hubristic buildings as the Shard, the Cheesegrater and the Walkie Talkie, to name only three infantile, Americanised nicknames in the City of Wren and Soane – but two miles downstream Canary Wharf is like a latter-day version of Fritz Lang's *Metropolis*, conveying (to my eyes anyway) no humanity, no intimation of a continuum between past and present, and instead an overwhelming masters-of-the-universe syndrome, as it towers above some of the poorest, most deprived parts of London. Humans function better in an environment that is on a human scale: a simple truth, which we pay a high price for forgetting.

As comes across again and again in these pages, the old City was in many ways like a village, albeit a peculiarly important one. Many people knew each other; it was a place of countless chance encounters in an era before City workers spent whole days in large, self-contained silos; and, across a range of markets, there was the daily practice of face-to-face dealing, prior to the coming of the relentless, dehumanising computer screens. It may have been a strikingly unmeritocratic village, and it may have been riddled with cartels and restrictive practices, but crucially it was a way of life that encouraged trust and cohesion – the very qualities that were so palpably absent when the credit crunch struck. From the 1920s the village also had, in the person of the governor of the Bank of England, an acknowledged leader, keeping up standards, banging heads together and generally doing his best to avert or minimise any serious troubles ahead. The opening up of the City with the Euromarkets in the 1960s and deregulation in the 1980s made that role increasingly problematic, but the removal of supervision from the Bank in 1997 meant it was impossible. No institution is perfect – and there is plenty in this book critical of the Old Lady – but the prospect now of a restoration of the Bank's authority is welcome.

There is a further key contrast. 'The modern City is in many ways a cruel, heartless place, and its occupants work such cripplingly long hours', I wrote in my introduction to the final volume, 'that inevitably they lack much of the roundedness of earlier generations.' A decade on that would seem true in spades – and if so, it is a truth linked to a larger truth perceptively pointed out in 2010 by the Cambridge philosopher Simon Blackburn. In the context of a general lament for the 'loss of faith in the humanities as a whole' in contemporary British culture, he noted how

> it is well known that a large part of the financial meltdown of the last couple of years has been because young whiz-kids from mathematics and physics are flocking into grotesquely overpaid jobs in the City, and there, having had no smidgeon of an education in humanistic fields, making fantastical models and predictions in complete disregard of the real world.

To which I would add three things: that the City has indeed become a young person's place, with the virtual disappearance of more cautious, restraining 'grey-hairs' a crucial absence; that these unchecked models and predictions, not to mention ever more complex financial instruments, have been – and seemingly continue to be – predicated on arrogantly rigid efficient-market assumptions about human behaviour that also enslaved a generation of economists but have now been revealed as a case of the emperor's new clothes; and thirdly, that for an unforgettable portrait of a non-rounded City man as technical virtuoso wreaking terrible damage, see John Veals in Sebastian Faulks' *A Week in December* (2009), a novel comparable in its searing disgust to Trollope's *The Way We Live Now*.

This brings one to an unavoidable word: greed. Of course, people who worked in the money-making, incentivised parts of the City always wanted to do well for themselves, but what has changed in relatively recent years has been the hugely enlarged opportunity for being so much *greedier* than was ever realistically possible before. After all, American-style annual bonus rounds only came to the City in the mid-1980s, and it was not until 1997 that these bonus payments hit the £1 billion mark; whereas in the most recent round, unapologetically announced in early 2011 amidst vitriolic criticism, the total was a staggering £7 billion. There have been several reasons for this exponential jump, but arguably the most important is the arrival of the insidiously tempting one-way bet. Whereas in the old City the dominant partnership structure ensured that anybody indulging in risky activities (including proprietary trading) thought long and hard about it, given that it only needed one person's folly to bring down the whole partnership, the ludicrous situation that has emerged in the new City is that bonus-hungry investment bankers are essentially engaged in an unequal joint venture with their banks – unequal because those banks not only supply the financial ammunition for risky if potentially rewarding trading but take the bullet if that trading goes wrong. Yet as we now know, it is a very special kind of bullet, because 'too big to fail' has become the seemingly inescapable reality, with the state (aka the taxpayer) conveniently present as permanent long-stop. Greed was the particular bugbear of Siegmund Warburg, the great post-war City figure and a firm believer in the work being primarily for its own intrinsic satisfaction, with the role of a banker comparable to that of a doctor. We now have Niall Ferguson's groundbreaking biography, and in July 2010 there was something hopeful, even inspiriting, about the queues snaking outside St Paul's to hear him launch it with a coruscating attack on the new City values, or rather lack of them.

Ultimately, for the sake of a decently equitable society, for the sake of a more balanced economy, for the sake of the health of our democracy vis-à-vis the almighty markets and for the sake of the preservation of financial stability through proper regulation, we have only our politicians to look to – and they have let us down badly. This book details some of Labour's past tribulations at the hands of the City, so it was entirely understandable (if mistaken) that the Blair-Brown government of 1997–2010 should have wanted the City off its back, and to do so gave it such enormous leeway. After all, it seemed for so long a virtuous circle: London pushing ahead as the world's leading international financial centre; an ever-greater tax take from the City paying for schools, hospitals and so on; and never a sterling crisis, let alone a full-blown financial crisis, in sight. Yet when the moment of decision came in October 2008, and government saw no alternative but to bail out the British banking system, suddenly there was a unique opportunity for democratically elected politicians to retrieve some of the huge ground that had been lost to the financial markets – a loss of ground going back to the end of fixed exchange rates in the early 1970s and the abolition of exchange control in 1979, but accelerating after 'Black Wednesday' in 1992. The politicians, even if they identified the chance, failed to take it, and who knows when it will come again.

My optimistic guess is that if and when it does, it will be grasped. As a society we now at last recognise that the City – for all the majority of honest, well-intentioned people who work there, as indeed was always the case – has become an overmighty, unaccountable subject that needs to be tamed. During the 1990s, as I wrote my volumes, I came to realise that what I was trying to do was to de-mythologise the City: to see it true, and not to take it at its own valuation. That is what we must continue to try to do if we are belatedly to return the beast to the cage, so that it may in time play its full and productive part in the common weal.

David Kynaston
May 2011

PART ONE

1815–1914

I have seen the West End, the parks, the fine squares, but I love the City far better. The City seems so much more in earnest: its business, its rush, its roar, are such serious things, sights and sounds. The City is getting its living – the West End but enjoying its pleasure. At the West End you may be amused, but in the City you are deeply excited.

Charlotte Brontë, *Villette* (1853)

CHAPTER ONE

Outsiders

Picture the prosperous underwriter at home:

> We dined at 6 oClock. The dinner consisted of two Courses, viz: a Fine
> Turbot at the top, A Sirloin of Beef at the bottom & vermicelli Soup in
> the middle, with small dishes making a figure of dishes. The remove roast
> ducks at the top & a very fine roast Poulet at the bottom, macaroni, tartlets
> &c &c. afterwards Parmesan & other Cheese & Caviare with toast. –
> Champaigne & Madeira were served round during dinner . . . I observed
> that Mr Angerstein drank very little wine *after dinner.* – While the
> Conversation went on He for some time slept, – after He awoke He eat
> an orange with Sugar. – He appears to consider His Health but looks very
> full and well.

The appreciative guest was the diarist Joseph Farington, his host John
Julius Angerstein, in his late sixties in 1804 but still the best-known man
at Lloyd's. 'When his name appeared on a policy, it was a sufficient
recommendation for the rest to follow where he led without further
examination.' From uncertain beginnings, Angerstein's life had charted
an exemplary course. He was born in St Petersburg in 1735, nominally
into a well-known Hanoverian family recently settled there, though it is
at least possible that he was the natural son of the Empress Anna of
Russia and the merchant Andrew Poulett Thomson. Either way,
Angerstein was in Thomson's counting house in the City of London by
the age of fifteen; he was soon making his way as a marine insurance
broker and underwriter; and in 1774 he had a handsome country villa
built for him in Blackheath. There, at Woodlands, he was not only a
munificent and particular host but also such an acute collector of pictures
that after his death in 1823 the collection formed the nucleus for the
National Gallery. Yet always, requiring even less sentiment of judgement,
there was Lloyd's, and in 1810 we hear the authentic, dispassionate voice
of Angerstein giving evidence to a parliamentary committee. The question was nervous enough: 'Do not you believe, in point of fact, that
there are a great many Underwriters in the Coffee-house in Lloyd's,
though not among those with whom you deal, who have very little
capital?' His reply was unanswerable: 'I suppose this may be the fact,

but I cannot say; I go into the Coffee-house to do my business with those I have business to do with'.[1]

William Hancock also found the streets of London paved with the right stuff. The son of a Berkshire innkeeper, he entered in 1773 the service of Smith, Payne & Smiths, a leading bank in Lombard Street, and speedily rose to be confidential clerk. From 1780 he became a compulsive defalcator, robbing his trusting employers of enormous sums of money, until just before Christmas 1798, expecting at last to be uncovered at the annual balancing of books, he wrote them an almost boastfully wretched letter of confession:

> I shudder when I behold the enormity of my guilt but it would be a mockery of too detestable a nature to affect remorse while I have continued almost to the present moment to follow up a principle of such dishonourable conduct . . . I anticipate the inevitable necessity of self murder which guilt will force me to because altho' I have been base enough to turn your confidence to the most dishonourable purposes I cannot endure to meet you when you know me guilty, much less can I stand the infamy of a public stigma.

But Hancock's crimes were not discovered, the letter was not sent, and over the next eight years there took place an annual ritual of more defalcations, the remorseful missive composed and the losses not noticed. By 1805 he was expressing a wish to retire, which prompted a letter between partners: 'Mr Hancock's abilities, fidelity, long services & zeal are so great that in my opinion it will be very injudicious to suffer him to quit us. He hinted that he knew the Banking business was not so productive as formerly & that since our attention had been turned to the *expences* he had not presumed nor should he ever again give any orders which might incur expence.' At last, in January 1807, Hancock's nerve cracked. One Tuesday, instead of going to work, he travelled to Brighton, from where he sent the senior partner the key to his desk and an accompanying letter: 'When you open the desk, summon all your fortitude and self-command to prevent those who may be near to you suspecting the infernal confessions which the papers in the packet will place before you. It is beyond all of the worst systems of private treachery ever known. When this reaches your hand, mine will be lifeless.' So it was, and it transpired from Hancock's meticulously kept red leather pocket book that since 1780 his defalcations had amounted to £87,800, worth at least £5.5m in present-day values. No one knew what had become of the money or why he had done it.[2]

Hancock's death caused few ripples in the wider world, but perhaps the Goldsmid brothers, being of broad sympathies, nodded mutely. Benjamin and Abraham Goldsmid were the youngest sons of a Dutch merchant who had settled in London shortly before their birth in the 1750s; and after going into business together in 1776 they achieved an

4

astonishing ascent, so that by the beginning of the nineteenth century they were the dominant figures in the City. Their firm did all sorts of business – bill broking, money dealing, loan contracting, dealing in the Funds, merchanting, virtually the lot – and to each they brought dexterity, resource and attention to detail. Their fame grew, so did their fortune, and inevitably they acquired country houses. Abraham's was Morden Hall, while Benjamin built his own resplendent mansion at Roehampton, fervently described by a contemporary biographer: 'Every thing is here on a scale of magnificence and beauty equal to any Nobleman's country seat. Drawing, Music and Dancing Rooms furnished with the highest taste and latest fashions . . . Ice houses, hot houses, the whole forming an accommodation fit for the reception of a Prince.' Both men were also prominent philanthropists, Benjamin being the founder of the Royal Naval Asylum, and both were friendly with the royal family. Yet the end came with remarkable suddenness. Benjamin had become fat, gout-ridden and melancholic; and in 1808 he hanged himself, by the silk cord that he normally used for levering himself out of bed. It was a huge blow to Abraham, the gentler, less socially ambitious of the two. He seemed to recover, but in 1810 a loan for which he had contracted began to go badly wrong, an over-driven ox knocked him down in Lombard Street, and by the last Thursday in September he was in a strangely savage mood on the Royal Exchange, talking of revenge against his enemies in the money market. That evening at Morden Hall he played a distracted hand of cards and early the next morning he shot himself, in the part of his grounds called the Wilderness, given over to a rookery. News of his death caused intense consternation in the City, to the outrage of William Cobbett, who issued a characteristic blast in his *Weekly Political Register*:

> All this for the death of a Jew merchant! The *king* and the *heir apparent* to be informed of it by a royal Messenger! And, is it really true, that this man's having shot himself made the citizens of London forget almost every thing else? Is it really true, that such an event put business nearly at a stand? Is it really true, that it produced an effect equal to *peace* or *war* suddenly made? And is it true; is there truth in the shameful fact, that a Jew Merchant's shooting himself produced *alarm* and *dismay* in the capital of England, which is also called, and not very improperly, perhaps, the emporium of the world?

There may have been truth in these dreadful impeachments, but for Abraham and his brother, both interred in the Jews' burial ground at Mile End, it hardly mattered.[3]

Altogether more robust was the next great Jewish financier. The brewer Sir Thomas Buxton encountered him – a short, heavy figure with protruding lips and bulbous eyes – at a dinner party in 1834, and fragments of a life story spilled out:

There was not room enough for all of us in Frankfurt. I dealt in English goods. One great trader came there who had the market to himself. He was quite the great man, and did us a favour if he sold us goods. Somehow I offended him, and he refused to show me his patterns. This was on Tuesday. I said to my father, 'I will go to England.' I could speak nothing but German. On the Thursday I started. The nearer I got to England, the cheaper goods were. As soon as I got to Manchester, I laid out all my money, things were so cheap, and I made good profit . . .

When I was settled in London, the East India Company had £800,000 worth of gold to sell. I went to the sale, and bought it all. I knew the Duke of Wellington must have it. I had bought a great many of his bills at a discount. The government sent for me, and said they must have it. When they had got it, they did not know how to get it to Portugal. I undertook all that, and I sent it through France; and that was the best business I ever did.

The monologue was only briefly interrupted when someone at the dinner table expressed the hope that his children were not too fond of money and business:

I wish them to give mind, and soul, and heart, and body, and everything to business; that is the way to be happy. It requires a great deal of boldness, and a great deal of caution, to make a great fortune; and when you have got it, it requires ten times as much wit to keep it. If I were to listen to all the projects proposed to me, I should ruin myself very soon.

The speaker was Nathan Mayer Rothschild, a nonpareil figure in the City's entire history, and for once the recollections late in life of a successful self-made man bear some relation to historical fact. Rothschild was born in 1777 the third son of a Frankfurt merchant, was based in Manchester from 1799 and prospered as a textile merchant, and in 1808 opened a permanent office in the City, at first in Great St Helen's Street but moving to New Court in St Swithin's Lane shortly after. During the latter stages of the Napoleonic Wars he made his fortune through the audacious conduct of crucial bullion operations on behalf of the British government, in the course of which he was much helped by large credits from his four brothers, who were based in various financial centres on the Continent. That was the prime source of his initial great wealth; it was not (contrary to legend) a major killing on the stock market from being on the inside track over the Battle of Waterloo. The Rothschild of these decisive years was quite as masterful and single-minded as the relatively benign latter-day version, though not without a neurotic and self-aggrandising streak. Usually on the receiving end were his brothers, one of whom, Salomon, showed some letters to an Amsterdam associate, who in turn wrote to Nathan in June 1814: 'I have to confess sincerely, dear Mr Rothschild, that I was embarrassed for your own brother, when I found these big insults in your letters. Really, you call your brothers nothing but asses and stupid boys.' He went on: 'Now God gave you the good fortune to carry out large-scale transactions, such as, I think, no Jew has ever done. So you should be happy about it together with your brothers.' Six months later and Nathan, unabashed, was writing to brother Carl in Frankfurt:

> I have taken the firm resolution to put the Frankfurt House on a new basis . . . I would rather give up business in Frankfurt than to have you cry for money all the time . . . Speaking quite frankly your letters sometimes drive me crazy. They are written in such a crude way. You use some horrible expressions . . . I am risking wife and children and am content with a fifth, quite apart from the fact that I drive myself crazy.

He need not have worried, for 1815 was to be the year in which he netted about a million in connection with the payment of the British Army and its allies. 'I do not read books, I do not play cards, I do not go to the theatre, my only pleasure is my business', Nathan informed his brothers at the start of 1816, before adding astutely of the place he had made home: 'As long as we have a good business and are rich everybody will flatter us.'[4]

City houses rose, City houses fell, and in October 1812 an anxious clerk wrote to his mother in Scotland:

> The situation of this house is truly disastrous . . . You can have no idea of the Extravagance of both nay all the partners. They are men of the most generous, easy disposition imaginable – but all their friends are disgusted with their ridiculous stile which has resembled that of Princes more than Merchants. These things must have an end – a variety of unfortunate, ill contrived, ill advised, Speculations carried off in the last two years £50,000, a great property say £140,000 lies in Jamaica unsaleable. Mr Murphy's Brother a great scoundrel in Spanish America owes us £300,000 which he disputes & will not pay a halfpenny of. These things added to the Expenditure of the partners which may amount yearly to £25,000 have brought the house to its present state of humiliation wherein it cannot obtain credit for a £100 – after being thought the richest house in London. All are afraid of us – all have envied us – so all now laugh at us hate us & wait with impatience to see our ultimate fall . . . Yet so sanguine are the partners about their affairs that tho' we are struggling from day to day – they conceive themselves perfectly safe & think because they have large property in various hands that it must all be recovered & their distresses relieved & such is their infatuation that whilst at this moment one lives in a Gothic Castle on the Banks of the Thames & at Grosvenor Square the other is contesting the Worcester Election tho' absent in Spain.

The castle-dweller was Colonel Murphy, the parliamentary candidate Sir William Duff Gordon, the house Gordon, Murphy & Co. And the much-harassed clerk was John James Ruskin, who as a young man in Edinburgh had hoped to study law but had been overruled by his grocer father and compelled in 1801 to begin a commercial career in London. 'I cannot but say I have turned from my profession for moments repeatedly with disgust', he wrote in his apocalyptic letter home, adding that 'had I my life to lead over again, nothing should make me a Merchant'. For years he had been working fearsomely long hours, which were compounded by Sir William's habit of coming from the House of Commons to the City in the evening; and in August 1813, with the firm still staggering on, he took his first holiday in almost a decade. He later recalled it: 'I left by Coach for Edinburgh after being in Counting House till Midnight – totally exhausted & was seized with Typhus fever at Ferry bridge.' On Ruskin's eventual return to the City he left the firm and set up with two others a successful sherry-importing business.[5] In 1819 his wife gave birth to the Victorian prophet whose most abiding dictum would be that 'there is no wealth but life'.

Angerstein, Hancock, the Goldsmids, Rothschild, Ruskin senior – all outsiders who experienced intensely contrasting fortunes. Over the next two centuries the City would flourish inasmuch as it was susceptible to outside influences and the rise of new men, congeal inasmuch as it allowed itself to be dominated by dynastic conservatism. Clubs, like families, are capable of renewing themselves; but they still remain clubs. Such was to be the City's inner history until the late twentieth century.

CHAPTER TWO

The Whole Earth Emporium

Once upon a time the City was London, and by Tudor times at the latest it had established itself as a leading international trading centre. Thomas Gresham's successful establishment of the Royal Exchange in 1570 consolidated the fact. By the end of the seventeenth century London towered over the rest of the country in almost all types of trade (its population of half a million meekly followed by Norwich with 30,000). In the eighteenth century came the great surge in British commerce, which took three main forms: a growing domestic demand for American and Asian consumer goods (above all sugar, tea, tobacco and coffee) and North European raw materials (such as forest products like timber); a growing European market for re-exports of American and Asian consumables; and a growing protected market for British manufacturers in the American colonies and Africa.[1] The City of London was to the fore in servicing all three markets. This prosperity could not have been achieved without a growing naval dominance that brought Britain spectacular colonial gains in Canada, the West Indies and India, more than offsetting the subsequent loss of America, which anyway still left intact much of Britain's growing transatlantic commerce. It was this imperial thrust that gave a particular trading primacy in the City to so-called 'colonial goods', which included not only food and drink, but also cotton, dyestuffs and printed textiles. 'London is become, especially of late, the trading metropolis of Europe, and, indeed, of the whole world', asserted the banker-cum-economist Henry Thornton in 1802.[2]

The historic heart of this mercantile community remained the Royal Exchange, rebuilt after the Great Fire of 1666 and the single great meeting place for the City's merchants and the several hundred specialist brokers who acted as intermediaries between them. Defoe in the 1720s called it 'the greatest and finest of the kind in the world', while a few years later a revised edition of Stow's *Survey of London* explained how 'for the more easy expediting of their work the merchants dealing in the same Commodities have by custom fixed on these different Parts of the Exchange to meet one another, called Walks' – walks that included the Norway Walk, Virginia Walk, Jamaica Walk, Spanish Walk and Jews Walk. These walks, with their specialist implications, prefigured the ultimate decline of the Royal Exchange as a commercial assembly, but it was not a rapid process. During the eighteenth century, despite the emergence of the odd specialist exchange such as the Corn Exchange in Mark Lane in 1749 and the Coal Exchange in Thames Street in 1770, the celebrated heyday of the coffee house served to complement rather than rival the Royal Exchange in the daily rhythm of City life. Most of the main coffee houses were centres for trade with particular areas of the world, though Garraway's of Change Alley, for instance, was renowned for the length of its hours and the variety of its sales of commodities. Thus the Jamaica was largely frequented by those involved in the West Indies trade, the Jerusalem by those concerned with the East, the Virginia and Baltic (forerunner of the Baltic Exchange) by those whose merchandise came from either the American colonies or Baltic seaboard, and so on. What did these coffee houses provide? Partly working premises when offices were still rare, a place where merchants and others could do a certain amount of business as well as their paperwork either side of a session on 'Change; partly sustenance; but above all the very latest information, as 'the coffeemen vied with each other in maintaining the supply of a wide variety of domestic and foreign newspapers, news-sheets, journals, and bulletins, customs-entry forms, auction notices, price-current lists, &c, in addition to making known their particular brand of punch and other beverages'.[3]

And the merchants themselves? 'There is no place in the town which I so much love to frequent as the Royal Exchange', wrote Addison in the *Spectator*. 'It gives me secret satisfaction as an Englishman to see so rich an assembly of countrymen and foreigners making this metropolis a kind of emporium for the whole earth. Sometimes I am jostled by a body of Armenians, sometimes I am lost in a crowd of Jews or Dutchmen, sometimes Danes, Swedes or Frenchmen.'[4] It was of course no new thing for foreign merchants to settle in London in order to sell the goods of their home region and to buy return cargoes, but from the late seventeenth century there were successive waves of immigration. Huguenots, Dutch Jews and Germans handled much of the trade to and from northern Europe, while Portuguese Jews traded to and from the Iberian Peninsula, the Mediterranean and even beyond.[5] It was typical that during this third quarter of the eighteenth century the first members of the Cazenove family to make an impact in the City, the merchanting cousins John Henry and James, were grandchildren of a French Huguenot who had left France for Geneva in the wake of the Revocation of the Edict of Nantes. Or take Levi Barent Cohen: he was a Dutch merchant who settled in England in about 1770 and in due course became a great City patriarch, with Nathan Rothschild as a son-in-law.[6]

However, Addison gazed upon 'countrymen' as well as 'foreigners', and the City remained a strong pull to more homegrown mercantile talent. From Exeter (though his wool-merchant father had come from Bremen) was young Francis Baring, who after a suitably arithmetical education at Mr Fuller's Academy in Lothbury opened a merchant house at Queen Street, Cheapside in 1763. Forty years on and Farington was noting in his diary: 'Sir Francis Baring's House is now unquestionably the first Mercantile House in the City. He is a General Merchant. The Partners are respected. Other Houses, comparatively, only come in for gleanings.' It was a remarkable achievement and on his death in 1810 he was described by Lord Erskine as 'unquestionably the first merchant in Europe', being 'first in knowledge and talents, and first in character and opulence'.[7]

A strong international connection was virtually a prerequisite of successful merchanting, typified in the case of Barings in the late eighteenth century by its close links with the powerful Amsterdam house of Hope and Co. and its increasing ability to provide credit to leading merchants in North America. Credit was the crux, especially since many merchants, at home and abroad, began business with little or no capital. Systems of credit could be complicated things, but the basic mechanism on which they increasingly revolved was the sterling bill of exchange, a negotiable instrument through which a seller was able to receive payment for goods as soon as he had sent them on their way. Towards the end of the century a few of the leading London merchants, above all Barings, were taking on a 'finance' function and becoming what would eventually be termed merchant banks – or, more narrowly, accepting houses – to service the international trading community. It was a profitable business, done on a commission basis; but since it involved guaranteeing bills of exchange that would eventually be sold in the London bill market centred on the Royal Exchange, it was one that demanded the nicest possible judgement of clients, of trades, and of countries. So the substantial eighteenth-century City merchant was rarely a merchant pure and simple – he might easily do any number of other things, including dealing in bullion or negotiating foreign drafts and remittances.[8] Merchants *defined* the eighteenth-century City and would help to give it for long after a character that was as much 'commercial' as specifically 'financial'.

No merchant could be without insurance. Back in 1691 Edward Lloyd had moved his coffee house from near the river to Lombard Street in order to be as close as possible to the General Post Office, prime source of shipping intelligence, and over the next half-century Lloyd's Coffee House specialised increasingly in marine insurance, with *Lloyd's List* beginning publication in 1734. In 1769 a new, more morally upright Lloyd's Coffee House split from and superseded the old one, moving in 1774 into new premises on the first floor of the Royal Exchange, with Angerstein negotiating the agreement. Three aspects of the Lloyd's of the late eighteenth century stand out: that many of the underwriters were little more than speculators of slender means; that it was the brokers who during the eighteenth century largely held the market together and had to make correct assessments of risk on behalf of merchants; and that the small family firm was the norm, such as the insurance broking firm started by John Robinson in Birchin Lane in about 1800 that was the precursor of Hogg Robinson. Did it work? Angerstein certainly thought so, telling the 1810 inquiry into marine insurance that at Lloyd's 'every Insurance almost can be done with fair connections, and at a considerable advance of Premium'. Not everyone came out of the experience with roseate memories – 'the labour, the agitation of mind, the perpetual vexation, is not to be described', stated the experienced broker Thomas Reed, adding that 'I would rather begin the world again and pursue any other line' – but that was another matter. Some of the merchant witnesses complained that underwriters were too prone to take to the spas during the autumn and thus avoid winter risks, but the underwriter James Forsyth, an autumn regular, laconically remarked that 'it has not been in my own experience such a bad business at that time of the year, because I exact a high Premium'. Overall the select committee gave Lloyd's a clean enough bill of health, and the following year saw significant internal reorganisation, building on the introduction of a modicum of quality control in 1800 after which subscribers to the coffee house had to be elected.[9]

Another central pillar of the City now taking shape was the Bank of England, established in 1694 by opportunistic merchants in order to fund the war against France. Over the next century there were few pauses for peace, the national debt grew inexorably, and the Bank of England not only managed that debt but became a government bank, looking after the accounts of most of the departments of state. Moreover, backed by its considerable bullion reserves, it issued a large volume of notes, emerging as the dominant influence in the London money market. In the course of the eighteenth century it came to seem indispensable: in 1745, as the looming presence of the Young Pretender threatened a potentially fatal run on the Bank, a powerful group of merchants met at Garraway's and agreed to accept its notes as payment; in the financial crisis of 1763 the Bank for the first time acted as lender of last resort; and in 1781 the prime minister Lord North famously referred to it as 'from long habit and usage of many years . . . a part of the constitution'.

Yet what can be forgotten is that in the eighteenth century the Bank of England was essentially a profit-making bank run by merchants on behalf of the mercantile rather than the banking community, that 'rival' bankers were not allowed to be Bank directors, and that it saw itself fulfilling a private at least as much as a public function. There was certainly no continuous sense in which it was a central bank regulating a national financial system: indeed, it was still often called the 'Bank of London', a reflection in part of its aloofness from the emerging network of country banks and the fact that the use of its notes was more or less confined to London and the south-east. Yet what the Bank did exercise was a considerable degree of influence within the City, especially through its provision of short-term finance by means of discounting commercial bills. This increased rapidly from the 1760s and the main beneficiaries were City merchants and traders. 'Before the [French] Revolution our Bank was the centre upon which all credit and circulation depended, and it was at that time in the power of the Bank to affect the credit of individuals in a very great degree by refusing their paper', recalled Sir Francis Baring in the early 1800s.[10] It was a first step on the road to becoming village policeman, immigration officer and magistrate rolled into one.

There were plenty of other London banks – some fifty by the 1770s, nearly seventy by the end of the century – and at any one time at least half of these were City-based. Some firms, such as Barnett, Hoare & Co. or Willis, Percival & Co., both of Lombard Street, had been bankers in the City since the reign of Charles II. Others, like Smith, Payne & Smiths or Hanbury, Taylor, Lloyd & Bowman (the modern Lloyds) or Jones, Loyd & Co., essentially represented well-established provincial banking families (from Nottingham, Birmingham and Manchester respectively) who during the second half of the eighteenth century set up London offices and often moved their main interests there. What is most striking is the mercantile background of many of the private banks that were coming into existence. The firm of Barclay, Tritton, Bevan & Co. (the modern Barclays) derived partly from large-scale linen merchants trading in Cheapside; the three original partners of Vere, Glyn & Hallifax (the later Glyn Mills) were respectively the sons of a Paternoster Row mercer, a Hatton Garden drysalter and a Yorkshire clockmaker; or as Henry Thornton of Down, Thornton & Free put it, 'we are all City people and connected with merchants and nothing but merchants on every side'.

It is a key point, for whereas West End banks lent on mortgage and had many landed families as clients, City banks purchased bills of exchange and, broadly speaking, serviced the world of trade. The banks, for the most part tightly clustered in Lombard Street, were fundamentally deposit banks, and the note-issuing function gradually died out; many of them, especially the newer ones, not only facilitated mercantile credit by acquiring (as an investment) the bills of merchants, but also enjoyed a lucrative, expanding business by acting as London correspondent to banks in the country. This agency role included the clearance of payments with other banks through the London Bankers' Clearing House, established in 1773. But more important from the point of view of the larger economy, they functioned as a more or less benign conduit: rural banks would deposit in London the surplus savings of rural areas; banks in under-capitalised industrial areas, where the paramount need was for circulating capital rather than fixed capital, would secure short-term credit from their London agents. Altogether it was a virtuous circle that played a larger part in the financing of the Industrial Revolution than has often been recognised.[11]

The private bankers themselves comprised a distinctive breed of men who in time would come to represent the very bloom of the City.

One pillar remains. 'The Stock Exchange is a poor substitute for the Holy Grail', thought Schumpeter, and no doubt he had a point. The stock market's effective origins lay in the war finance of the 1690s, and during the next century and beyond it dealt primarily in British govern-ment securities ('the Funds'). Home to this market during most of the eighteenth century were the coffee houses of Change Alley, most famously Jonathan's and Garraway's. In a sense the modern organisation of the market began in 1734 when, over a decade after the stock manipulation that culminated in the South Sea Bubble, legislation introduced by Sir John Barnard, himself a merchant, sought severely to reduce the range of stockbroking business. In particular, it attempted to outlaw the highly profitable but speculative end of the business known as 'time bargains' – by which traders in effect gambled on future prices without actually buying or selling stock. Confronted by this hostile legislation, the brokers and jobbers of the day simply ignored it and developed their own self-regulating mechanism, in which the sanctity of the bargain was paramount. 'My word is my bond' became no idle boast. Economic logic was also on the market's side: holdings in the Funds were not just investments to merchants but the means by which they effected many of the loans between themselves; and for the property-owning nation at large, there was, following the introduction of Consols (British government stock) in 1751, nothing quite like 'the sweet simplicity of the three per cents'. It is clear from modern econometric historians that the capital market of the age was highly efficient and surprisingly well integrated with those of Paris and Amsterdam.

In 1773, with space increasingly at a premium despite the emergence of the Rotunda of the Bank of England as an alternative place for dealing in the Funds, the stockbrokers abandoned their coffee houses and found a home at the corner of Threadneedle Street and Sweetings Alley. The building had the words 'The Stock Exchange' inscribed above the door and an entrance fee was levied of sixpence a day. Payment of this tanner allowed a member of the public to pass through a waist-high bar, but his problems were not over: 'If he entered within the bar, either to watch his broker, or for essay, he was sure to be hustled, find lighted squibs put into his pocket, or his hat and wig canted out before him, until it was ascertained that he came for other purposes than espionage.'[12]

Until late in the eighteenth century there was little distinction between brokers (dealing on behalf of the public) and jobbers (making a market in securities in order to service brokers), and even then there were many who continued to perform both functions. Similarly mixed were the social origins of those who operated in the stock market: back in the 1690s a list of brokers included such names as Henry Contigno, Stephen Mahieu, Benjamin Nunes and Elias Paz. There was undoubtedly a strong Jewish element, and between the 1730s and 1750s there was no one more dominant at Jonathan's Coffee House than Samson Gideon. He made a fortune for himself, offered crucial advice to government over a series of war loans and other financial operations, and possessed a superbly sardonic touch: when during the crisis of 1745–6 the private banker Thomas Snow requested the repayment of a substantial loan, Gideon sent the money by return in bank notes wrapped round a bottle of hartshorn.[13]

What, though, was the stock market actually like? Although motivated by hostility, in 1761 Thomas Mortimer provided the closest description of the 'daily tumult' at Jonathan's, here shortly after noon:

Tickets – Tickets – South-Sea Stock for the opening – Navy-Bills – Bank Stock for the rescounters – Long Annuities – (*here the waiter calls*) Chance – Chance – Chance – *Mr Chance is not here, Sir, he is over at his Office* . . . Here Mr Full (*whispers a friend, but is overheard*) they are all BULLS by G—d, but I'll be d—d if they have any of my Stock, I'll go to Bath, and not come near them till the rescounters . . . I am a seller of five hundred, Sir – and I am a buyer, Sir, but pray at what price? – Why, as you are a friend, Mr Point-royal, I shall give you the turn, you shall have them at 14. The turn, Mr Mulberry, why do you think I do not know what I am about? they are all sellers at 13 – Well then, you shall have them at 13s. – I will take them at 12, and no otherwise – Well, you shall have them, put 'em down (for the drawing mind) but, d—n it, Tom, where did you get that paste wig? – Why, you son of a b—h, it is as good as your mop.[14]

Joining the lottery at about this time was Abraham Ricardo, a stockbroker in Amsterdam before moving to London. His son was David Ricardo, the leading economist who also doubled as an immensely successful jobber and loan contractor; and when in 1814 he was asked by a fellow economist which members of the market would be able to give advice on the thorny subject of circulation, his reply was objective:

The Stock Exchange is chiefly attended by persons who are unremittingly attentive to their business, and are well acquainted with its details; but there are very few in number who have much knowledge of political economy, and consequently they pay little attention to finance, as a subject of science. They consider more, the immediate effect of passing events, rather than their distant consequences.'[15]

Short-termism has a venerable history.

By the time Ricardo wrote, he and his fellow members had for over a decade been occupying their own purpose-built home in Capel Court, the first stone of which was laid in May 1801. Unlike its predecessor, the new Stock Exchange was a fully closed market, for 'instead of a breastwork barricado, as in the old house, they ran up high folding double doors, to prevent further interview from the outdoor stockholder, than with the porter at the porch, distinguished by a gold laced hat to call out by name any member wanted by his principal'. Members had to be elected (though the entrance qualifications were not formidable), these members in turn elected their own committee, and at last a modicum of respectability beckoned.

Banking would long have a social cachet denied to stockbroking, and a clue lies in the despairing tone of the Stock Exchange's first set of rules and regulations, drawn up in 1812: 'The Committee earnestly recommend, to the several members, that *order and decorum* which is so essentially necessary to be observed in all places of business, and that they forbear on their own parts, and discourage as much as possible in others, those rude and trifling practices which have too long disgraced the Stock Exchange in the estimation of the public, which would not be tolerated in any other place; and which, it is seriously apprehended, may have been injurious to the best interests of the House.'[16] Injurious yes, but to be tired of making butter slides or throwing paper balls was to be tired of Capel Court.

There was, of course, much else to the eighteenth-century City. For one thing there was the emergence by the 1770s, with the Goldsmid brothers to the fore, of specialist bill broking, further refining the process of mercantile credit; for another there were the bullion brokers headed by Mocatta & Goldsmid (Asher Goldsmid, an older brother) who conducted the business of London's increasingly important precious-metals market. Or take the specialist foreign exchange dealers: on Tuesdays and Fridays, between noon and three o'clock, they serviced with acute, competitive attention the merchants of the Royal Exchange, matching the needs of importers for remittances with the supply of bills from exporters. Bills were negotiated at the keenest rates and those rates were published immediately after the close of business in *The Course of the Exchange*. But there were many other types of dealing trades in the City, not least the drapers, mercers and silkmen who operated in London's extremely large textile and clothing market; while as for the City's many shops, a popular song called 'Country Commissions to my Cousin in Town' had the lively refrain 'a skein of white worsted from Flint's', referring to the well-known haberdasher near the Monument. There was also the traditional manufacturing sector: although there took place a general emigration during the century to the regions, where labour costs were lower, not only did London continue to provide much of the finance but significant manufacturing trades remained, such as coopering on the banks of the Thames. Perhaps an epitome of the variegated eighteenth-century City were the parents of Thomas Gray, born in 1716 in a house in Cornhill: his father was a money scrivener on 'Change, his mother with her two sisters kept a milliner's shop in the City; and between them they prospered sufficiently to send the young elegist to Eton.[17]

*

Outsiders were little enough impressed. 'Now Men seem vastly rich upon the sudden, set up for Greatness presently, and live profusely, and, in a little time, sink unaccountably, and carry their Acquaintance with them, to the Bottom', preached Bishop Fleetwood of Ely in a sermon in the City in 1718. By the 1730s there had emerged a clear 'country' critique of the City, depicting it as inherently unstable, parasitic and even treacherous. Dr Johnson defined in his dictionary the stock jobber as 'a low wretch who gets money by buying and selling shares in the funds', the 'cit' as 'a pert low alderman or pragmatical trader', and remarked to Boswell in 1778 that the wives of City tradesmen were 'the worst creatures upon the earth, grossly ignorant, and thinking viciousness fashionable'.[18]

Apart from the larger question of what did or did not constitute a healthy society and economy, there were two particularly sharp strands to the critique. One, as implied by the great cham, was almost a matter of taste, so that successive generations of social satirists and caricaturists made savage butts of City people, pointing up their corpulence, their mundane recreations, their general lack of elegance. The culminating example was Peter Pindar's depiction of the prominent, grossly overweight self-made merchant-cum-banker Sir William Curtis ('Sir William Porpoise'), with his 'nose as red as rose in June'. The other strand was even less benign and came out implicitly in 1785 when the Marquess of Lansdowne urged Francis Baring to stand for the House of Commons: 'It's the highest Injustice to consider every Merchant as a Jew, as if he were incapable of looking forward to anything but a Fraudulent Contract or a Line of Stockjobbing – the consequence of which is that their talents are left to prey upon the Publick instead of serving it.'[19] Anti-Semitism was a crude perspective on the City that had plenty of mileage left in it.

Whatever the emotional force of the critique from the country, the fact was that during the eighteenth century the landed came at least to some extent to accept that there existed an interdependence between themselves and the monied in the City. There was starting to crystallise that compact between the aristocracy and the commercial middle class: gentlemen were becoming capitalists, capitalists were becoming gentlemanly, and henceforth the twain would meet. Both sides seemed to have few qualms. 'It is gone into the city to look for a fortune', Dr Johnson flatly explained to a young nobleman in 1770 about where the gallantry and military spirit of the old English nobility had vanished; while from the point of view of the monied interest, there were several prominent examples of City men obtaining parliamentary seats, acquiring country estates and marrying their offspring into the aristocracy or gentry. This particularly applied to merchants – who on the whole made the real fortunes – and indeed as a pattern of social mobility became virtually a caricature in its own right. What, though, was the nature of the interdependence that shaped this compact? Essentially it lay in the City's crucial, highly profitable role in managing the national debt, thereby enabling the ruling landed class simultaneously to enhance national power through protracted warfare, consolidate the Hanoverian settlement and keep taxation not only low but also thoroughly regressive. The economic case was compelling for bringing the monied men on board.[20]

Nevertheless, it was in many ways a chequered, fractured sort of rapprochement. Even its strictly economic basis was somewhat patchy: thus research into who held stock in the East India Company has shown no significant scale of investment on the part of the landed interest; instead, it was fairly tightly held within the City. But it was at the social level that the key ambiguities lay, as exemplified by the painful ascent of Samson Gideon. From the late 1740s he was on the way up, acquiring a grant of arms, a country house in Kent and a collection of pictures; but in 1758 he was refused when he asked for a baronetcy in return for his considerable services to successive ministries, being mollified only when his fourteen-year-old son instead was created a baronet the following year. When in 1801 Sir Francis Baring's son, Alexander, became a member of a fashionable West End political dining club, the King of Clubs, Sydney Smith observed that it was only 'upon the express promise that he lends £50 to any member of the Club when applied to'.

Nor was integration entirely whole-hearted, let alone complete, on the City's part. Bankers tended to go into Parliament strictly in order to benefit the business; the average mildly prosperous merchant was at least as likely to acquire a cosy riverside villa within striking distance of the City as any sort of country estate proper; and during much of the eighteenth century the influence of the lesser merchants and tradesmen put the City into a state of quasi-permanent opposition to the government of the day. The City had its own culture, its own traditions, and altogether a pride that rendered it not entirely susceptible to aristocratic buyouts. Still, as Farington in 1803 noted shrewdly of his orange-eating host: 'Mr Angerstein might have been at the head of popularity in the City, but has chosen to associate chiefly at the west end of the town.'[21]

Who then did run the City? In one sense it is a meaningless question to ask – granted the inherently discrete, fragmented nature of the place – but it is clear that at any one time there existed a group of immensely wealthy merchants and financiers who had their fingers in most of the important pies. Overlapping directorships were rife, as is apparent from an examination of the directors of the Royal Exchange Assurance during the eighteenth century: twelve were at some time directors of the Bank of England, six of the East India Company and six of the South Sea Company. Most of the REA's directors were merchants (though with a significant minority of bankers), and there was a strong tendency towards dynasticism, especially on the part of those Huguenot merchant families who were on the REA's Court. Samuel Bosanquet, son of a Huguenot refugee from France who had come to London and built up a highly prosperous Levant trade, married in 1733 into the family of a leading Levant merchant who had helped to found the REA; and he subsequently enjoyed a seat on the Court for twenty years. His eldest son, Samuel II, not only in time became governor of the Bank of England but in the 1780s went into banking partnership (Forster, Lubbock, Bosanquet & Co.) with Edward Forster, governor of the REA from 1785 to 1812; while as for Samuel Bosanquet's second son, William, he was a successful merchant, deputy governor of the Levant Company and for many years a member of the REA's Court. But if the Bosanquets readily enough found their way into the charmed circle, not everyone was so fortunate. Particularly this applied to those of the City's Jews who, unlike Gideon or later the Goldsmids, were not manifestly the dominant financiers, through ability and force of personality, of their generation; and here one cannot ignore the anti-Semitic policy of the leadership of the Bank of England for most of the eighteenth century.[22] The Bank, with its power of refusing paper, for a long time made life very difficult for those merchants and others whose faces did not fit.

Yet approaching the end of that century the City was on the verge of momentous change. The catalyst was the state of almost continuous European warfare between 1792 and 1815 which severely blunted the activities of Britain's main trading rivals and greatly increased the proportion of world trade conducted by merchants based in Britain. Amsterdam declined as the leading international financial centre and was replaced by the City of London. There took place during these years a wholesale flight of capital to London; the French occupation of Amsterdam in 1795 was a final nail in the coffin for that city's financial future; and the transformation of Hope and Co. from a powerful independent house into a virtual subsidiary of Barings was eloquent testimony to the profound shift of fortunes. It was also in this period that for the first time foreign stock was marketed in London in significant quantity, though the grudging response to the Austrian loans of the 1790s revealed a certain innate prejudice on the subject. Nevertheless, taken together with the marketing of American securities pioneered in London first by Bird, Savage & Bird and then by Barings, the beginnings were at hand of what would become the City's historic role as exporter of capital.[23]

The City, moreover, similarly grew in *national* importance on the back of warfare. Three symbolic moments stand out: in 1793 a monumental commercial crisis was only avoided through Pitt, Angerstein and the directors of the Bank of England coming up with a timely issue of exchequer bills; three years later Pitt's ennoblement of the banker Robert Smith was a tacit recognition of the importance of financial advice, though Disraeli was right in spirit only when he famously claimed that the state's wartime dependence on the City had meant that Pitt 'caught them in the alleys of Lombard Street and clutched them from the counting houses of Cornhill', thus creating 'a plebeian aristocracy'; thirdly, in 1797, the beginning of Restriction (by which the drain on the Bank's gold reserves made it necessary to stop paying out gold in exchange for the Bank's notes) not only caused Gillray to draw his immortal, nickname-coining cartoon of 'Political Ravishment, or The Old Lady of Threadneedle-Street in danger!', but it also raised to near the top of the politico-economic agenda for the next half-century the whole question of the Bank's public responsibilities. In Walter Bagehot's later words: 'It was said to be the "manager" of the paper currency, and on that account many expected much good from it; others said it did great harm; others again that it could do neither good nor harm. But for the whole period there was an incessant and fierce discussion.'[24]

Wars were also fought, and during them Lloyd's found favour with the Admiralty thanks to the coffee house's unique news-gathering service; towards the end it was Rothschild who came up trumps in the task of keeping Wellington's army and its allies in the field. But above all what paid for the war was a series of government loans, amounting to a total borrowing of some £475m and creating a wider, even more permanent market in government securities. For the leading men of the City the potential rewards were enormous but the risks were great, and in practice a handful of loan contractors dominated the scene. The way was led by Walter Boyd, a resilient Scot who had served his mercantile apprenticeship in the Austrian Netherlands and Paris before coming to London in 1793; and during the intensely fluctuating years that followed he believed that he could ride the forces of rising interest rates, the drain of gold and restricted credit, but in the end they unseated him. Then it was the turn of the Goldsmids and, with increasing prominence, Barings, who in 1813 made a tidy £77,000 from two loans. Two years later, following Napoleon's return from Elba, Barings together with Smith, Payne & Smiths were responsible for a £30m issue in 3 per cent bonds, and at a critical juncture the house successfully placed large blocks of the loan with its correspondents in Amsterdam, Basle, Frankfurt, Hamburg, St Petersburg and Vienna – a harbinger of how over the ensuing decades it would often be on the strength of a firm's international connection that much of its City stature would depend.[25]

These were also the years when the City's specialist ability to service the needs of trade increased significantly and thereby set a pattern for the rest of the nineteenth century. Finance was even more than before the crux for trade, especially with the wartime growth of the consignment system; and here the City's emerging merchant banks (or accepting houses) held the key, not only enabling foreign producers to draw bills on London as soon as they had shipped their goods, but also, having provided those credit facilities, ensuring the safe warehousing of the goods, often in secure bonded warehouses on the banks of the Thames.

Credit was also at the heart of the increasingly sophisticated money market, where bill broking, building on the pioneering example of the Goldsmids, was starting to become an occupation in its own right. During the 1800s these brokers became increasingly effective in their role of sending bills for 'discount' (i.e. to be purchased) from bankers in industrial areas to bankers elsewhere looking for safe investments. The leading firm of bill brokers, following the demise of the Goldsmids, was Richardson, Overend & Co., of whom the four partners from 1807 were all Quakers, including Samuel Gurney from Norfolk. Another, smaller Quaker firm was started by William Alexander in 1810. He came from Rochester, where his father had been a schoolmaster, and worked for two City banks before starting his own bill-broking establishment in Lombard Street. For a time he quietly prospered, but in 1812 two City houses (one bank, one merchant) to whom he had lent money failed; and he was compelled to relinquish the services of his extremely able clerk John Allcard, who went to Richardson, Overend & Co. It was a great blow for Alexander, though in the end it was his firm that lasted the course rather than that of his more ambitious Quaker rivals.[26]

During these wartime years there arrived a host of new entrants in the City. They included (in chronological order between 1800 and 1809): Johann Friedrich and Johann Heinrich Schröder, sons of a wealthy Hamburg merchant who from their arrival in London concentrated, as both principals and agents, on commodity trade to Europe; Emanuel Henry Brandt, son of a Hamburg insurance broker, soon prospering through growing trade with Russia; Antony Gibbs, originally from the West Country but who had spent much of his mercantile life in Spain before coming to London to export textiles there and to South America; Nathan Rothschild, from Frankfurt via Manchester; and Frederick Huth, from Hanover via Corunna, specialising in exports to the west coast of South America. There were others, but the pattern is clear enough of a 'push' in the form of continental Europe becoming an untenable base for business and a 'pull' in the form of a critical mass of support facilities existing in London to maximise the trading or trade-financing potential of distinct areas of local knowledge. Often this knowledge was supplemented by extensive, far-flung family connections, and it is no coincidence that several of these new entrants were or would become genuinely international networks.

Equally crucial, however, to this creation of a more 'open' City was the weakening power of the Bank of England as, in effect, social and business arbiter. Sir Francis Baring in the 1800s described the Bank's traditional exercise of its power to refuse paper, and went on in a passage of fundamental importance: 'The Bank is still the pivot for circulation but no longer for credit and discount. In the distress of 1793, they committed a fatal error by deciding that all merchants and traders were entitled to their proportion of accommodation as the Bank was a public body and ought not to discriminate between individuals . . .' It may have been a fatal error from Baring's point of view, but the direct result was a City more open to merit, much of it Semitic, and judicious risk-taking.[27] There was no clearer sign of the changing times than the failure of the East India Company in 1813 to retain its monopoly of the India trade. With the chips down, and the maintenance of traditional Anglo-Indian mercantilism at stake, the merchants of the City failed to hang together, revealing a split not only between merchants of different trading interests but also between the older merchants and the new men. It was symptomatic when in 1812 one merchant wrote to the vice president of the Board of Trade referring almost hysterically to German and other alien newcomers who 'make their harvest now by perjury and fraud, thereby staining the character of England'.[28] The ill-mannered game would go on, but this time the new men held the winning cards.

CHAPTER THREE

A New Court

What was the City of 1815 actually like? A point of entry lies in the Post Office Directory for that year. To take part of a page at random is to get a flavour of a place that was so predominantly commercial, so little explicitly financial:

Thomas Nightingale, warehouseman, 26 Bucklersbury
N. A. Nilsen & Co., merchants, New Court, Crutched-friars
B. Nind, solicitor, 32 Throgmorton-street
J. Nind, paper-hanging manufactury, 10 Beech-street, Barbican
T. Nisbett, stock-broker, 11 Warnford-court, Throgmorton-street
James Nix, glover, 32 Bishopsgate-Street-within
J. Nixon, corn-factor, 33 Great Tower-hill
M. Nixon, grocer, 28 Red-lion-street, Spitalfields
J. Noakes, clock-maker, 24 Bishopsgate-within[1]

An awestruck spectator was Richard Rush, who, soon after arriving in London in December 1817 to take up the post of US minister, set out exploring:

Went through Temple Bar into the *city*, in contradistinction to the west end of London, always called *town*. Saw, by a hasty, exterior glance, the Bank, Royal Exchange, Lord Mayor's house, Guildhall, India house, the Excise buildings. If I looked with any feeling of wonder on the throngs at the west-end, more cause is there for it here. The shops stand, side by side, for entire miles. The accumulation of things, is amazing; it would seem impossible that there can be purchasers for them all, until you consider what multitudes there are to buy; then, you are disposed to ask how the buyers can all be supplied. In the middle of the streets, coal wagons and others as large, carts, trucks, vehicles of every sort, loaded in every way, are passing. The horses come so near to the foot pavement which is crowded with people, that their hoofs, and the great wheels of the wagons, are only a few inches from the people. In this manner the whole procession is in movement with its complicated noise; it confounds the senses to be among it all . . . I am assured that these streets present the same appearance every day in the year, except Sundays, when solitude reigns in them.[2]

Socially mixed, populous by night as well as by day, and still retaining its medieval street pattern, though now studded with the glories of Wren's

23

churches, the Georgian City was a place of much fascination. Moreover, already cramped to begin with, the City by the early nineteenth century was coming under severe pressure on space as the volume of its business increased; and the result was often multiple occupancy and the conversion of domestic property into a rabbit warren of tiny offices.

Nevertheless, despite this trend and the fact that many did commute daily to the Square Mile, there was still about the City in the pre-railway age a distinctly traditional and residential character. When Barings moved to 8 Bishopsgate in 1805–6, the firm took possession of a substantial house with an archway and open courtyard at the front, stables at the side and a garden at the back; and when in 1808 Jones, Loyd & Co. rebuilt its premises, there was still a separate entrance to the upper floors housing a partner, his family and servants.[3]

In 1815 the residential population of the City was some 122,000 (about a tenth of the population of London as a whole) and about 8,500 firms were operating there. The overwhelming majority of these firms were small, specialised and family owned. Glyns, for example, was one of the larger banks, but still had only thirty-six staff in 1815. The major exception was the Bank of England, where between 1792 and 1813 the number of clerks increased from 300 to 900. To cross the threshold of one of these firms was usually to enter an austere world. Take Prescotts in Threadneedle Street: massive oak doors opened into a dimly lit banking hall, as elsewhere known as 'the Shop', where clerks dealt with customers over an ancient oak counter and with quill pens and snuff boxes at hand to meet all needs; while beyond was the oak-panelled partners' parlour, directly above the strong room in the basement.

The new Stock Exchange in Capel Court was rather tucked away and with the only feature of note being the perhaps ironic one of a bust of Mercury on the keystone of the main entrance.[4] But the heart of the City remained that well-known, semi-circular triad of Mansion House, Royal Exchange and Bank of England. 'If it stood on elevated ground, with a fine area round it, proportioned to its magnitude, it would not be found deficient in magnificence', was how *The Picture of London* in 1815 damned with faint praise the cribbed and confined Mansion House built by George Dance in the 1730s. The same guide was more enthusiastic about the Royal Exchange: 'It has two principal fronts, one in Cornhill, and the other in Threadneedle-street . . . Each of the two fronts has a piazza, which gives a stately air to the building . . . In the centre of each front is a lofty gate, leading to a noble area, in which the merchants assemble.' Most contemporary eyes, though, were on the Bank of England, in 1815 approaching the end of its thorough, masterly rebuilding by John Soane. 'This immense pile of building is more extensive in its range of offices, and more eminent for its architectural ornament, and interior arrangement, than any single public office in the metropolis', asserted *Leigh's New Picture of London* soon afterwards.[5]

Soane's workmen were still busy when in about 1808 Robert Hawker, a clergyman from Plymouth staying in town with a merchant friend, agreed to accompany his host to the Royal Exchange. As Hawker continued to gaze at the 'busy multitude' before him, he realised after a while that there were 'many faces carrying with them the aspect of disappointment', and concluded his observations in a fine passage not without its lasting verities:

> The whirlpool runs round too rapidly, and drags into the vortex too powerfully, to allow attention, much less relief to such as are not within the tide . . . But what of that? Those that are out, and want places; and those that are in, and want none, by and by will all be upon a level. The most successful in the whole circle . . . what is the final upshot of his gains? He only dies somewhat richer than his neighbour; that's all; and his son, or heir, will take care to let the world know it. The enquiry at the Exchange, when his death is announced from every mouth, is, What did he die worth? . . . And it is for such ends as these, one generation after another is for ever projecting schemes of gain, pursuing the phantom to the very close of life, and dying in the very moment of grasping a bubble?[6]

The immediate post-war years were ones of appalling distress in large parts of Britain, agricultural as well as industrial, and fairly unrelieved depression in the City, characterised by restricted trade, restricted money and countless failures. Chancellor of the Exchequer was the hopeless Vansittart, who in a state of almost abject dependence on the City – above all the Bank of England and Nathan Rothschild – staggered through each financial year with an improvised mixture of loans and advances. Without the resource of an income tax, which City interests among others had repudiated, 'Van' by 1818 could muster a revenue for the year of only £56m, of which £54m was spent on servicing the national debt and providing for the sinking fund.

The most notable exception to post-war City gloom was in the area of foreign loans. Barings led the way and raised its name to new heights in 1817 by successfully bringing out three issues for the indemnity-laden French government that raised a total of 315m francs (over £12m). Tributes from back as well as front of the hand followed this massively lucrative operation. The Duke of Wellington: 'The fact is, that Baring having the French finances in his hands, and French loans being in fashion in England, has to a certain degree the command of the money market of the world.' The Duc de Richelieu: 'There are six great powers in Europe: England, France, Prussia, Austria, Russia and Baring Brothers.' James Rothschild: 'The Baring lot is and was well versed in the way of using influence, as we are.' In 1818 another French loan was less successful, but Barings had made its point.[7]

That same year Nathan Rothschild began the fight back, issuing a £5m loan for the Prussian government. The loan had been negotiated in the first place by a City-based merchant from Prussia called Barandon, but he lacked sufficient credit to bring it to the market and sold out to the opportunistic Rothschild for some £30,000. It proved a great success and, for the first time with a foreign loan, dividends were to be payable in London and in sterling.[8] The era of the foreign security as an attractive, readily marketable counter was under way.

It has to be said that the greater part of the money for the French indemnity loans was raised in France itself, and analysis of the Prussian loan shows that Rothschild distributed about two-thirds of it to his continental connections. In general at this time, and indeed for a very long time thereafter, London had little more than an agency role, giving its imprimatur to the loans being sought by foreign governments and using its manifold international connections to ensure the widest possible distribution.[9] To contemporaries, however, it did not seem quite like that. 'It exposes in its true light the base and wretched avidity of the Monied Interest, which, at the prospect of gain, is ready to forget all the claims of patriotism', declared the *Commercial Chronicle* in January 1817 about what Barings was doing, and other papers agreed. In the context of severe domestic trade depression, the notion of so much capital going abroad was, hardly surprisingly, repugnant.

Rothschild by contrast was wholly matter-of-fact: 'There is no doubt that the English people invest a part of their money in foreign securities on account of getting a better interest, besides its being a growing passion at the present time; we lay out fifty to sixty thousand pounds a week in the foreign funds for different English houses.' And when it came to the distinction between investment and speculation – that most agonising of nineteenth-century distinctions – Rothschild's reply was robustness itself: 'You may divide it in half, half speculative people and half for permanent investment, but in case a real rise takes place, which has been the case, they will all go out.'[10]

Helped by the Bank of England's return (albeit reluctant) to the gold standard in 1821, confidence picked up in the City during the early 1820s – confidence inevitably accompanied by widespread speculation, in which the Stock Exchange was to the fore. Late in 1821 a squall took place over the contentious question of option dealings, also known as puts and calls, where a speculator would pay an agreed sum for the right to buy or to sell a stock at a certain price on a given date in the future. The founding Committee of 1802 had unanimously condemned such dealings as injurious, but the first rulebook in 1812 had failed to distinguish them with sufficient clarity from the more acceptable (though still technically illegal) time bargains for the settlement. The row began with the Committee considering two rival requisitions from members. One demanded the outright abolition of puts and calls, 'which are now so frequent as to constitute the greater part of the business done in the House and which operate materially against the interests of those who do not comply with this practice'. The other took positive pride in 'the immense jobbing which is now consequent upon Options'. The Committee, conscious of the extremely dubious legal standing of such dealings, sided with the first petition and ruled that henceforth members would only be re-elected each March if they promised not to engage in them. Reaction was immediate, as members queued to express their outrage in person.

The turning point came on Christmas Eve, when some appeared who had signed the original requisition. Among them was James Capel, who stressed his individual support for the Committee's actions but then conceded that 'in the present temper of the House it would be better to try a mild measure first'. But it was John Hensley who gave the game away: 'Finding so many persons adverse to the regulation proposed, and that it was possible many might leave the House, he repented of having signed, as he was sorry to see dissension likely to take place.' That was indeed the danger, for the option dealers had already subscribed a considerable sum of money with a view to founding a rival stock exchange; and at this point the Committee backed down.[11] This pattern of surrender would frequently recur over the next century; after all, what is the point of a club unless it exclusively serves the interests of its members?

In 1822 came the year of the foreign loan. Nathan Rothschild established his dominance in this market by floating sizeable loans for Prussia, Russia (traditional Barings country) and the Neapolitan government, and above all there was widespread enthusiasm for making loans to the newly liberated countries of Latin America. Emissaries from Colombia, Chile and Peru all came to London, all were greeted warmly by merchants-turned-contractors who knew a handsome margin when they saw one, and all were ruthlessly exploited. The Peruvian loan was underwritten at 75 by Thomas Kinder, Jnr of Basinghall Street, but marketed at a price way above. Such was the popular capacity for self-delusion, and the appetite for higher rates of return than those provided by British government stock, that it even proved possible to issue bonds for an imaginary country, apparently somewhere in Central America, called Poyais.[12]

The Royal Exchange witnessed plenty of disturbances during these hectic months. Brokers and jobbers, unable to use the Stock Exchange itself because dealings there were still confined to British government stock, had already complained in vain to the Stock Exchange Committee about 'the want of an open and fair Market for Foreign Securities'. Having pointedly congratulated 'the Gentlemen from the Stock Exchange' on having 'behaved themselves this day in a peaceable manner on the Royal Exchange', a week later the same *Morning Chronicle* correspondent was complaining that 'the Royal Exchange has been numerously attended by pickpockets, and many Gentlemen have had their books cut out of their pockets'. Towards the end of October the following handbill, addressed to dealers in foreign stocks, was posted at the entrance of the Royal Exchange:

> Gentlemen – You have selected for the theatre of your operations one of the most frequented parts of the Exchange, particularly on foreign post days, of those whose habitual places you have usurped; you removing a few yards further to the north-east corner, a quarter always very thinly attended, will be considered as an act of courtesy for which the Merchants who frequent the French and Italian Walks will feel much obliged.[13]

The Stock Exchange eventually acquired a new room for dealing in foreign securities, which opened for business at the start of 1823. Connecting physically with the main house but separately organised and managed, it constituted a cumbersome, just about workable arrangement.

One man dominated the City of the early 1820s. 'You have beaten your antagonists so frequently that I am surprised there are any so hardy to be found in the Stock Exchange to oppose you in any considerable operation', Moses Montefiore applauded his brother-in-law Nathan Rothschild. Nathan's brother Carl, writing to another brother, was even more eloquent: 'We owe everything, really everything to him.' No one, extended family or otherwise, ever denied that Nathan Rothschild was a consummate operator; on the Stock Exchange, scene of some of his greatest coups, he invariably employed several brokers at any one time in order to ensure that the precise positions he had taken remained a matter of secrecy.

Inevitably some hated him in their hearts. In the spring of 1818 when the prime minister Lord Liverpool was considering a plan by the rising Tory politician William Huskisson to reduce government dependence on the City, he received two letters in quick succession from an anonymous member of the Stock Exchange:

> Let me inform you, the Capitalists of the Money Market . . . have set their faces against your Plan because it serves not their purpose or puts Money in their Pockets. The Jew interest alias Mr Rothschild are disappointed and straining every nerve to defeat your objects . . .
>
> If a Man asks Mr Rothschild, what is his opinion of the Funds, he answers they must be better & at the very same time he acts contrary. himself & sells to knock them down. It is a deplorable Circumstance that in so great a Country as this, Your Lordship & Colleagues should be the Sport [&] the caprice of a Jew Party, it is truly lamentable.

Rothschild was conscious enough of such anti-Semitism directed against him, but being a businessman first and foremost he showed himself perfectly willing over the years to enter into syndicates with leading Gentile houses.[14]

At least twice a week he was to be seen in the Royal Exchange, conducting his extensive foreign exchange operations:

> He never hesitated in fixing the rate, either as a drawer or a taker, on any part of the world, and his memory was so retentive, that, notwithstanding the immense transactions into which he entered on every foreign post day and that he never took a note of them, he could dictate the whole on his return home with perfect exactness to his clerks. His liberality of dealing was another conspicuous feature of these operations, and many merchants whose bills were objected to elsewhere found ready assistance from him, and his judgement was proved by the very small amount of loss which he incurred in consequence of such liberality.

If foreign bills were one speciality, so were bullion transactions. This systematic specialisation, which also included government stocks, was a way of maximising the potential of his high-level connections, which by 1815 were even better at home than they were abroad. His brother James wrote to him on one occasion from Paris, about not wanting to do anything in French Rentes without asking Nathan's opinion: 'One of the reasons is, that in respect of the English stocks, you always knew through H— what is going on, while here one remains always in the dark.' The reference was undoubtedly to J. C. Herries, the Tory minister. This specialisation paid off, for by the 1820s the capital of the London house alone was well over a million pounds, way ahead of all rivals, even Barings.[15]

Underwriting this ascendancy was the man himself, shrewdness and determination personified, day in, day out. Visiting Nathan at New Court in the summer of 1818 was the young diplomat Woodbine Parish, seeking to arrange banking facilities for the British party at the forthcoming Congress of Aix-la-Chapelle. After discussing the matter, Nathan handed Parish a letter of credit for £10,000:

> He then wrote a few lines to his brother, which he handed to me open to read, and then burst out laughing at my face on finding it was written in Hebrew!
> Business over he rang the bell and ordered coffee, which was brought in by a servant in gorgeous livery, upon a splendid silver salver, with all its appurtenances of the same, strikingly contrasting with his own appearance, 'en deshabille' in an old dressing-gown, with his black silk breeches loose and unbuttoned at the knee, his ordinary costume in the Counting House, as I was told, but cutting a very different figure to his appearance on Change, as I have seen him with all eyes upon him. What struck me very much was his correct information as to the details of our party and his knowledge of the persons likely to compose it, some of whose names I believe had not even transpired at the Foreign Office.[16]

A couple of letters give something further of the crisp flavour of Nathan in action. On 21 October 1817 he wrote to the Lords of the Treasury: 'Having about 150,000 oz of foreign bar Silver to ship to Hamburg, and there being no Court of Aldermen sitting at this time, nor will there be before 12 or 14 days, and the winter may set in, in a few days, I therefore humbly pray your Lordships order to pass the entry at the custom house without the certificate signed by the Court of Aldermen.' Or six years later, addressing the governor and deputy governor of the Bank of England: 'Gentlemen – An opportunity offering itself in which I could employ from One to Three Millions of Spanish Dollars, I beg leave to state the terms upon which I should be willing to receive from you the whole or any part of that quantity.' After briskly stating his terms, he ended with a characteristic sting in the tail: 'In the event of your compliance with these propositions, I must request that this affair may not be conducted through the agency of your Broker, who being himself a Merchant & Loan Contractor, it is desirable should not be apprised of the Arrangement.'

Although Nathan Rothschild would never lose his native toughness, by 1825 he not only possessed a country residence in Stamford Hill but had also moved into an elegant town house in Piccadilly, thus no longer living above the counting house in New Court. Many years later a relative recalled going to Stamford Hill at about this time to visit Nathan's sons during their school holidays: 'The two boys were surrounded by their father with every luxury. They had a miniature carriage with four white goats to drive about the grounds.'[17] An Anglicised dynasty was in the making.

What of 'Christian Baring', who according to Byron in 1818 held 'the balance of the world' alongside 'Jew Rothschild'? After the glory years under Sir Francis, Barings was entering a period of relative decline. The problem lay partly with one of the Bishopsgate partners, Swinton Holland, whose over-rigid control lost the firm its unrivalled ascendancy in Anglo-American trade. But the head of the house, Alexander, had a more harmful influence. Intellectually able but ultimately a vain dilettante, and far too distracted by matters of state and estate ever to concentrate on the more mundane aspects of business, he went a fair way towards undoing the work of his father. Such were the attractions of rolling acres and country houses that in the early 1820s the firm's capital dipped to about £250,000, more or less putting it out of contention in terms of contracting the major foreign loans. There is no doubt some truth in the argument that the partners of Jewish firms encountered, because of their continuing legal disabilities, far fewer distractions than their Gentile counterparts, but the heart of the matter surely lies in character. Nevertheless, one should neither exaggerate the decline nor underestimate those increasingly traditional Baring qualities of caution and sobriety. As the house wrote in June 1824 to an American correspondent, in the context of turning down a proposed operation in Philadelphian bank shares:

> In other times it might have suited us . . . to have entered into your views, but at the moment, being engaged in large financial operations in France, we do not feel disposed to divest ourselves of our own Capital, by placing it at a distance from us. Indeed, our object always is to have our Capital within reach that we may command it as necessary.[18]

Admirable sentiments, and indispensable for long-term survival.

Meanwhile, there were plenty of international houses – embryo merchant banks – starting to come through as significant City presences. Some were new, like Ralli Brothers, being Greek merchants forced abroad by Turkish persecution and reaching London in 1818. Others were longer established, but most derived from the migration to London towards the end of the Napoleonic Wars. Frühling & Goschen, for instance, was the 1814 combination of a wealthy merchant from Bremen and the son of a prominent Leipzig publisher. Also from Germany was John Henry (formerly Johann Heinrich) Schröder, who at the end of 1817 resigned his partnership with his elder brother and started his own merchanting firm, J. Henry Schröder & Co. It financed international trade, did a wide range of import–export business with St Petersburg and shipped large quantities of refined sugar to Hamburg, where Schröder himself concurrently ran another firm (J. H. Schröder & Co.) and lived for most of the year, leaving the London end in charge of a German confidential clerk. Another City firm originating from Germany was Frederick Huth & Co., its offices temporary home in 1822 to a wryly admiring French merchant:

> There is very little sociability, and, as in Holland, commercial interests are the dominant feature. You must not expect much friendliness from a John Bull who does not see his way to get something out of you. On the other hand, for learning commerce, London is without exception the best school. You are here in the centre of universal business, and you can know here what goods come from each country, and what goods they want in return.[19]

The attentive recipient of this letter was Daniel Meinertzhagen; a few years later, when his family house in Bremen met with disaster, he too came to the City.

A more indigenous, equally vigorous group were the textile merchants and warehousemen clustered to the east of St Paul's. There was no sector of British trade growing faster than textiles. City merchants, through their considerable working capital, enjoyed a control of credit and marketing denied to the disintegrated textile manufacturers of the north; this aspect of the Square Mile, linked closely to British industry, was more important than has tended to be recognised. The kingpin was undeniably James Morrison. He was the son of a Hampshire innkeeper, started at the Fore Street wholesale and retail haberdashery business of Todd & Co. in 1809, and within five years was not only a partner but also the son-in-law of Todd. Under his direct influence turnover rose phenomenally: £65,000 in 1813, £650,000 in 1817, over £1.5m in 1822, by which time Morrison was sole managing partner. (In 1818 he is said to have cleverly anticipated the death of Queen Charlotte and bought up most of the available crepe.) His business methods over a longer period are well described by his friend Sir John Bowring:

> Morrison told me that he owed all his prosperity to the discovery that the great art of mercantile traffic was to find sellers rather than buyers; that if you bought cheap, and satisfied yourself with only a fair profit, buyers – the best sort of buyers, those who have money to buy – would come of themselves . . . So, uniting this theory with another, that small profits and quick returns are more profitable in the long run than long credits with great gains, he established one of the largest and most lucrative concerns that has ever existed in London.

No wonder that Morrison himself wrote to a junior partner in the 1820s: 'None can approach us in the science of business, independent of success and profit. There is an intellectual pleasure in this.'[20]

By this time several of what would become the main stockbroking firms were taking shape. The future James Capel & Co. was called Marjoribanks, Capel & Co. James Capel had come from Worcestershire to the City early in the century to enter the office of John Capel, a stockbroking cousin who was also one of the Stock Exchange's original managers. He soon teamed up with two other brokers, whose most important connection was with Thomas Coutts; James Capel himself became a partner in 1813, and other partners, including Coutts connections like David Marjoribanks, followed. Connection was indeed everything: John Helbert Israel (he later dropped the 'Israel') and John Wagg were uncle and nephew; by the 1830s both were related by marriage to the Rothschilds. Both operated profitably as brokers to New Court, and eventually the two became partners, forming Helbert Wagg. In 1823, John Menet took into partnership his brother-in-law Philip Cazenove, who through his father's merchant business enjoyed a useful connection with Rothschild, and thus founded the modern Cazenove & Co. The future R. Raphael & Sons was a firm with a difference. Raphael Raphael was a Dutch Jew who as a young man had left Amsterdam to come to London as a merchant. He made a considerable fortune during the war, and from the 1820s with great deftness reshaped his business into a specialised mixture of stockbroking, foreign banking and bullion broking – creating for himself and his firm an exception to the rule that Stock Exchange members should not pursue outside business activities.[21]

These nascent figures and firms all had to rub along with the humour of Capel Court. The foreign loan boom of 1822 caused a few new japes, like the plausible creation of entirely fictitious bonds called Chinese Turnpikes, a favourite ploy on novice brokers ever after. Sometimes Stock Exchange humour was linked to Stock Exchange obstinacy, as the City report for 5 November 1824 explained:

> The Bank was shut today, and so was the Royal Exchange until twelve o'clock; but the British and Foreign Stock Exchanges were both open; the opening of the two Stock Exchanges, however, gave great offence to a large majority of the members, who claimed the right of a holyday upon the ground of immemorial custom; and these gentry appeared to be determined that no business should be transacted, for, from the opening to the close of the houses, one incessant discharge of fireworks, of all sorts and descriptions, was kept up, accompanied by loud and repeated cries of 'Holyday! Holyday!' &c; and, to enliven the scene, an effigy of Guy Faux was introduced, and conveyed through the Foreign Market, amidst loud uproar and laughter.

The particular grouse on this occasion was that the first payment of the Neapolitan loan (contractor, N. M. Rothschild) was due that day. 'And it was observed', the report went on, 'that if a contractor of a loan, for his own private convenience, chose to fix a day which is well known as being a holyday, such contractor should take the consequences of his own act.'[22]

Expansion was in the air in the specialised craft of bill broking, a slightly less boisterous area of the City. 'Has the business of your house, as bill brokers, increased since the year 1810?' the Commons committee on the resumption of gold asked in 1819 its principal exponent, Samuel Gurney of Richardson, Overend & Co.; he simply answered, 'Yes, very much.' Four years later his firm's annual turnover was up to a colossal £20m. Crucial to this prosperity was the continuance of cheap money after 1815, which meant that London banks were no longer able to make their customary turn of 1 per cent on the balances that their country correspondents lodged with them. Instead, much of this short-term money passed to the bill brokers, who employed it not only to buy and sell bills on a differential rates basis, but also to make their own short-term loans with it, whether to major capitalists like Rothschild, or to members of the Stock Exchange needing to carry over stock from one account to another, or to commission merchants temporarily requiring funds in order to meet acceptances. It was an attractive business on the face of it, and by 1822 there were some twenty-five bill-broking firms operating in the City, though in practice many failed to last the course.[23] One that did, by the skin of its teeth, was the firm immortalised by Jos Sedley's boast in *Vanity Fair* that 'Alexander will cash my bill down on the counter, sir.'

When its founder William Alexander died in 1819, the business of Alexanders was in a poor way.[24] His widow Ann was determined to keep it going until their son, George William Alexander, came of age in 1823, and this she succeeded in doing. The boy had been working in the firm since he was thirteen, showed a businesslike cast of mind from the start, and on attaining his majority was made a partner. Appropriately, the style of the firm now became Ann & G. W. Alexander – one of the very few instances ever of a woman being the senior partner in a firm doing business in that male bastion, the City.

CHAPTER FOUR

Il Est Mort

'The abundance of money has led to a variety of speculations in England, and scarcely a week has passed but some new company was founded to direct a world projected adventure. What must be the cure of this mania time only can show.' Thus the private thoughts of the merchant Samuel Thornton on New Year's Day 1825. By March the person providing the answers was the Duke of Wellington, as recorded by his good friend Mrs Arbuthnot: 'He thinks the greatest national calamities will be the consequence of this speculating mania, that all the companies are bubbles invented for stockjobbing purposes & that there will be a *general crash*.' So it proved; during the second half of the year a combination of circumstances came together to produce arguably the most severe financial crisis of the century. The collapse of the absurdly overblown boom in foreign loans and company promotions, speculative overtrading in imported commodities, rashness on the part of the country banks, Bank of England policy that veered between complacency and an over-sharp contraction of credit – all these things, in hotly debated proportions, played a part.[1]

On 18 November, in correspondence to the Norwich Bank, a concern intimately bound up with the great Norfolk family of Gurney (from which Samuel Gurney came), J. J. Gurney reported back from London in critical mood:

> There is a tremendous pressure upon this town, & I suppose almost *all* the Bankers are more or less distressed . . . The root of the difficulty is in the Bank of England, where they are extremely restricting their discounts with a view to producing a favourable effect on the exchanges, so as to prevent their being run upon for gold . . . It seems strange that the pecuniary facilities of the whole realm should thus depend on the management of a small despotic Committee.

By 1 December the head of the family, Hudson Gurney, was at the front line. Calling in at Barclays, London agents to the Norwich Bank and fellow Quakers, he found 'Jno Tritton's face very long, & Bevan running about the office and refusing Bill upon Bill offered for Discount'.[2]

In fact, by the start of December, the Bank of England had reversed its policy and begun to discount largely. But, as one young private banker now discovered, the change came too late. Henry Sykes Thornton, 25-year-old son of Henry and nephew of Samuel, had been a partner for only a few months in the family bank (Pole, Thornton, Free, Down & Scott), but it was long enough for him to realise that Peter Free's management had left the bank in poor shape to cope with the run on it that began on Thursday the 1st. The bank narrowly survived the very hefty withdrawals made on the Saturday through a timely loan from a rival bank, Smith, Payne & Smiths, one of whose partners, John Smith, had a family link. Smith then arranged that those directors of the Bank of England who were in town should gather the following morning.

First thing on Sunday the Bank directors met, including the governor, Cornelius Buller, who was connected by marriage to Henry's elderly senior partner, Sir Peter Pole. After examining the books, and insisting that Free leave the business, they agreed to lend £400,000. For a moment it looked as though the house was saved, but it proved a false dawn. City hopes were raised by the rumour that Pole's, with its extensive country banks agency, had been bailed out, before on Thursday the 8th news came of the failure of Wentworth & Co., a leading Yorkshire bank. An almost tidal run on the country banks began on the Saturday, which made up Henry Thornton's mind that there was no alternative but for Pole's to stop payment.

Henry took his decision (bringing down over three dozen country banks) calmly enough, but when the City found out on Monday morning its reaction was very different. Tuesday was no better, as news came that Williams & Co. of Birchin Lane was in trouble, and an impassable crowd gathered outside their door. The *Morning Chronicle* reported that '"Never were such times", cried many of the oldest visitors of the 'Change, while others exclaimed, "If this state of things continues, we must ask not who is gone, but who stands? for unless something is done to relieve the pressure, and to restore confidence, few can resist so overwhelming a torrent of distrust."' Wednesday was a day of further stoppages and panic, during which 'the Royal Exchange was thronged long before the customary hour of assemblage, and Corn-hill, Lombard-street, Nicholas-lane, and all the streets in which banking-houses are situated, were crowded to such a degree, as to impede the progress of passengers', so much so that police were called in. Gloom pervaded the Stock Exchange, where 'in the Foreign Stocks all were on the decline, and of Home Shares nothing was said except a hearty wish that they were all in a very warm place'. The only positive development of the day was a meeting that afternoon at Mansion House of about a hundred merchants and bankers, who passed a resolution expressing confidence in the Bank of England's attempts to stem the crisis.[3]

It was on the whole a justified confidence, for since the start of the week the Bank had been making every effort to bolster the market. Several years later Jeremiah Harman (a former governor) would recall with pride the assistance rendered:

> We lent it by every possible means, and in modes that we never had adopted before; we took in stock as security, purchased exchequer bills, we made advances on exchequer bills, we not only discounted outright, but we made advances on deposits of bills of exchange to an immense amount; in short by every possible means consistent with the safety of the Bank; and we were not upon some occasions over nice; seeing the dreadful state in which the public were, we rendered every assistance in our power.

With Buller more or less out of the frame because of his connection with Pole, the deputy governor, J. B. Richards, took charge. A key moment came on Thursday, when the Cabinet gave its sanction to the Bank issuing £1 notes for the first time since the resumption of gold payments over four years earlier – on the condition that such issue was 'understood to be strictly temporary'.[4] By the next day these notes were in circulation.

Yet on Friday the 16th the situation was as grave as at any stage. That morning Mrs Arbuthnot and her husband (Joint Secretary of the Treasury) were put in the highly fractious picture by Herries, the member of government closest to the City:

> Mr Herries told us that such had been the extraordinary demand for gold to supply the country bankers & to meet the general run upon them that the Bank of England was completely drained of its specie & was reduced to 100,000 sovereigns . . . The Bank expects to be obliged to suspend cash payments [i.e. gold] tomorrow, and they want the government to step forward to their assistance & order the suspension . . . Rothschild has made most gigantic efforts to assist the Bank & he told Mr Herries that, if he had been applied to sooner, he wd have prevented all the difficulty. As it is, if they can hold out till Monday or Tuesday, he will have enormous sums over in sovereigns from Paris, & the pressure will be entirely relieved.[5]

Rothschild may not have been averse to the prospect of suspension, but clearly he was also mindful of larger responsibilities. The *Morning Chronicle*'s City correspondent reported that, in the course of the Friday morning, 'we were informed that 150,000 sovereigns had arrived from the Continent, which were immediately paid into the Bank of England by the house of Rothschild'; while according to Canning's private secretary half a century later, it was on the Friday night that 'the Rothschilds poured into the Bank £300,000 coin'.

Whatever Rothschild's contribution, the Cabinet met that Friday evening and, in five acrimonious hours, hammered out a political compromise. The central figure was Wellington, who reluctantly accepted the insistent demand of Huskisson and Canning that the Bank must not be allowed to use the crisis as a device for once more going off gold, but convinced his colleagues that Huskisson's notion of depriving the Bank of its Charter should it be forced to stop payment was preposterous. The Iron Duke held firm, as Mrs Arbuthnot admiringly recorded: 'He told Lord Liverpool that while there was life there was hope; that there was a chance of the Bank standing & while that chance remained, he wd not despair; that the government were bound to support them to the very utmost of their power . . . for that their interests were those of the country.'[6] The Bank was not compelled to stop payment on the Saturday; over the weekend it ran out of £5 and £10 notes but then in the nick of time received a fresh supply from its printers; and by Tuesday, courtesy of Rothschild, major infusions of gold were arriving from France. A mild run on the Bank's gold reserves continued until Christmas Eve, but by then that precious intangible – confidence – had been at least partially restored.

Who, in a larger sense, deserved credit for averting catastrophe? Historians have usually given the award jointly to the Bank and to Rothschild – the latter accolade no thanks to Alexander Baring. He sought to downgrade the contribution of French gold by putting about an inherently as well as circumstantially implausible story to the effect that what had really saved the day was the fluke of Bank officials happening to come across a box of unissued pound notes.[7] Yet perhaps accolades were hardly to the point. Thomas Love Peacock, the son of a London glass merchant, was not only a poet and novelist but also from 1819 an official of the East India Company; after the worst of the crisis was over, he reflected on the whole crazy phenomenon he had witnessed:

> Now curst be the projects, and curst the projectors,
>   And curst be the bubbles before us that rolled,
> Which, bursting, have left us like desolate spectres,
>   Bewailing our bodies of paper and gold . . .
>
> For what is a man but his coat and his breeches,
>   His plate and his linen, his land and his house?
> Oh! we had been men had we won our mock riches,
>   But now we are ghosts, each as poor as a mouse.[8]

1826 was not the year of the silver lining. February was the worst month for failures and attendant dramas, and even in late April money remained scarce and the mood was still very downbeat. As the summer wore on there was no full restoration of confidence, and in particular a notoriety attached to the now thoroughly discredited sphere of foreign loans. In September one member of the Stock Exchange accused another of having exploited inside information about Chilean default; fisticuffs ensued, and after an exchange of cards it was very nearly pistols for two and coffee for one.[9]

Early next month Prince Hermann Pückler-Muskau, inveterate and impecunious traveller, spent the night anchored just below London Bridge, at the start of a tour of England in search of an heiress. In the morning he 'hastened as quickly as possible out of the dirty City, swarming like an ant-hill', and headed for the West End. But a few days later he was back, visiting first the Royal Exchange:

> The imposing statues of English sovereigns, combined with the antique and stately architecture, excite a poetical feeling, to which the thought of the boundless commerce of which London is the centre gives a still deeper significancy. The men, however, who animate the picture soon draw one back into the region of common-place, for selfishness and avarice gleam but too clearly from every eye. In this point of view, the place I am describing, and indeed the whole City, have a repulsive sinister aspect, which almost reminds one of the restless and comfortless throng of the spirits of the damned.

While at the Royal Exchange the prince took the opportunity to look in on 'the celebrated Lloyd's Coffee House, the dirtiest place of the kind in London, which exhibits few traces of the millions daily exchanged in it'. There followed brief glances at the Bank of England – 'the vast and beautiful building' where 'hundreds of clerks . . . mechanically conduct the gigantic business' – before he 'reached an extremely dark and mean-looking coffeehouse, called Garraway's, where estates and houses of enormous value are daily put up to sale'.

Finally, he could not resist making a call on Nathan Rothschild. 'I found him in a poor obscure-looking place, and making my way with some difficulty through the little court-yard, blocked up by a waggon laden with bars of silver, I was introduced into the presence of this Grand Ally of the Holy Alliance.' Speaking 'in a language quite peculiar to himself – half English, half German – the English part with a broad German accent but with the imposing confidence of a man who feels such trifles to be beneath his attention', the host 'did not stand much on ceremony' and 'broke out into bitter complaints that every poor devil who came to England had something or other to ask of him'. A courteous visitor could only pay the compliment that Europe was unable to manage without him, prompting the riposte from Rothschild: 'Oh no, you are only jesting – I am but a servant, whom people are pleased with because he manages their affairs well, and to whom they let some crumbs fall as an acknowledgement.' At which point exit Pückler-Muskau, discouraged from fortune-hunting in that particular direction.[10]

It was a pity he failed to penetrate the Stock Exchange, where he would have found plenty to amuse him. Many years later a veteran member recalled benignly the atmosphere of the 1820s:

We were only a few hundred strong then, and everybody knew everybody else. We had some fine games. At 2, Capel Court, Mendoza had a boxing booth, where, instead of knocking prices about, a member could go and knock somebody about or get knocked about himself, if things did not suit him inside. An old woman had a stall *inside* the House, close to Capel Court door, where those who had not quite outlived their earliest tastes could feed on buns, cakes, etc. Sometimes, in the afternoon, a jobber used to give us a tune on a cornet, and I reckon we had plenty of fun when things were dull. Almost over every bargain a glass of sherry used to be drunk.

'Who pays?' he added, was a very common expression.[11]

*

In the immediate aftermath of the 1825 crisis, with much blame being attached to inadequately capitalised country banks, legislation was passed permitting the establishment of joint-stock banks outside a radius of sixty-five miles of London, thus ending the Bank of England's monopoly of joint-stock banking. As for the conduct of the Bank itself, widely criticised for having allowed the crisis to reach the proportions it did, public attention now turned away from the question of gold and towards the less emotive area of how it could function more effectively, above all in terms of an effectively controlled note issue that in practice would operate as a national currency.[12] The Bank was fortunate at this stage to have someone capable of grasping the intellectual nettle, in the person of John Horsley Palmer, deputy governor from 1828 to 1830 and governor from 1830 to 1833. His origins were impeccably mercantile – he took over from his father the running of a prominent East India house – but unlike most merchants he had a keen interest in monetary questions, theoretical as well as practical. For six years from 1827 he was the key figure at the Bank: first he blocked Huskisson's plan to introduce a limited form of bimetallism, effectively arguing that the Bank already possessed adequate silver bullion; then he evolved his own currency principle, by which note circulation would fluctuate in relation to the Bank's holding of specie, a principle that in effect sought to further the Bank's independence of government; and in 1832 he cogently enunciated this doctrine to the Bank Charter Committee, so that it became known as the 'Palmer rule'. It was at that parliamentary committee, whose purpose was to consider the renewal of the Bank's Charter the following year, that the City's leading figures closed ranks around the Bank. 'It is exceedingly well managed', insisted Samuel Gurney, while Nathan Rothschild echoed the sentiments: 'I feel the management, and I know that it is good.'[13]

The Bank's Charter was duly renewed – but at a price. Henceforth joint-stock banks would be allowed in London itself, though without the power to issue notes. The new dispensation touched keenly on private bankers, whose heyday was drawing to an end with the inexorable rise over the rest of the century of the City-based joint-stock bank, drawing its capital publicly, answerable to its shareholders, and not based on the traditional, quasi-hereditary system of a private partnership.

It was not only the banking system that was being reshaped in the decade after the high drama of 1825.[14] The crisis had revealed all too palpably that the Bank of England's resources were not infinite, and the pragmatic response of the London banks was to cease relying on being able to discount bills there and instead to build up their own liquid cash reserves. The question then, faced in time by joint-stock banks as well as private, was how to make the most profitable use of those reserves; and the answer, from soon after 1825, was to put out such balances with the City's bill brokers, in effect as call loans secured on first-class bills. The implications of this were considerable, for the bill brokers in effect became bill dealers, holding their own portfolios of bills and dealing in them as principals. 'The business remained unchanged in character for some years after I became a partner', G. W. Alexander was to recall, 'but gradually it became a deposit business, money being left at call, the rate being ½ per cent below that of the Bank of England. Any bills sold were guaranteed by the broker.'[15] From the point of view of the banks, confidence about these short-term loans took two main forms: that the bill dealer's reputation depended on using only unimpeachable bills as security; and that, should that not be the case, the Bank of England would be willing (on a selective basis from 1830) to discount the bills, in effect acting as lender of last resort to these embryo discount houses and thus ultimately to the financial system as a whole. Put another way, the modern London money market was starting to emerge, discount houses now gained the City's acceptance in a way that had not been the case for bill brokers prior to 1825, and the Bank had taken up what would become its permanent position of sometimes recalcitrant long-stop.

The four leading firms to whom the Bank granted this discounting facility in the course of the 1830s were Overend, Gurney & Co. (as that house was called from 1827, following the death of Thomas Richardson), Sanderson & Co., Alexanders (where Ann Alexander was gradually taking a back seat), and James Bruce. The dominant figure at Sandersons – a rising force partly on account of its extensive connection with the wholesalers of the Cheapside area – was William Morris. As a young man in 1820 he had come to the City from Worcester; after securing a berth via a distant family connection he became a partner in 1826; seven years later he moved from above the Lombard Street office to the village of Walthamstow, travelling daily to the City by stage coach; and in 1834 his wife gave birth to another William Morris, one who eventually would excoriate everything the City stood for.[16]

But without a doubt the leading discount house post-1825 was Overend Gurney, from 1833 based at the corner of Lombard Street and Birchin Lane, or the 'Corner House' as it was invariably called. It was run as a very commercial, unsentimental operation. The firm profited greatly from the new banking strategy, and continued to build up its traditional business with the country banks. Judgement was all, and in 1842 one of the partners of Overend Gurney put down on paper the following summarising dictum: 'The one cardinal point for the employment of money to be repaid to the Public at call (especially in our scale of figures) is to have nothing fluctuating in value, nothing of a lock-up character, and if possible nothing insecure, and these have been our governing principles for many years past.'[17]

The author of those timeless criteria may well have been Samuel Gurney, for many years the leading bill broker. He lived at Ham House in Upton, where he was an almost Dr Dolittle figure, one of his daughters recalling how before breakfast 'he used to take us about, the animals clustering round – the very tame kangaroos and peacocks, the dogs, as well as the horses and cows'. Then it was off to Lombard Street, where he tried his best to apply his Quaker principles. The story goes that on one occasion, after a large forgery upon the firm had been discovered, he said to the trembling culprit: 'By the law we must hang thee – but we will not do that; so, be off to the Continent, and beware of ever returning.' The portrait painter George Richmond used to say that his face was a most extraordinary mixture of shrewdness and benevolence: each, in Gurney's case, demanded the other.[18]

However, for another decade after 1825 it was Rothschild who remained the indispensable man, always on the lookout for appropriate new business: in the first half of the 1830s he acquired a monopoly of the Spanish quicksilver industry and arranged loans for (among others) Belgium, Greece and Portugal as well as the West India planters requiring compensation after the abolition of slavery in the colonies. 'The influence of Mr Rothschild is so great, that if much money should be wanted for any operations in which he is deeply engaged, there will be but little chance for other speculators to obtain the requisite accommodation', commented in 1835 the *Circular to Bankers*, the well-informed City organ of the country bankers and no friend of Rothschild. That same year Thomas Raikes, diarist brother of a recent governor of the Bank, paid due tribute to Nathan and his brothers:

The Rothschilds have become the metallic sovereigns of Europe. From their different establishments in Paris, London, Vienna, Frankfurt and Naples, they have obtained a control over the European exchanges which no party ever before could accomplish, and they now seem to hold the strings of the public purse. No sovereign without their assistance now could raise a loan.[19]

Yet there persisted, in society at large as well as in the City, a powerful undertow of prejudice against him, caught in Macaulay's description of a formal evening in 1831 at 'the Jew's': 'I did not see one Peer, or one star, except a foreign order or two, which I generally consider as an intimation to look to my pockets.' The attitude of politicians varied greatly: Huskisson was paranoid, Wellington was unashamedly dependent, and Althorp when he became Chancellor in 1830 'boasted of ordering his door to be shut against Rothschild'. Nathan himself could take or leave them, as Mrs Arbuthnot recorded in 1828: 'I asked him what was thought of the Duke in the City. He said they had unbounded confidence in him. I asked what they thought of Mr Peel, and he said they did not think about him at all.' Like most City people he probably assumed that politicians overrated their own importance, important though the course of politics could be to the City. Ultimately it was money, not legislation, that made the world go round. And in the context of a minor spat in 1830 between government and Rothschilds, it was a salutary lesson taught to Althorp by the governor of the Bank, Horsley Palmer: 'Of this I am sure, that Mr Rothschild never drew a Bill without his receiving in one way or another ample remuneration, and the probability is, that what government saved in Agency, they fully lost in the exchange.'[20]

And Barings? After its spell in the semi-doldrums, that still prestigious house was now fully restored by the distinctly unpatrician figure of Joshua Bates, who at Alexander Baring's instigation became a partner in 1828 and was for the next three and a half decades the dominant day-to-day presence at 8 Bishopsgate. Bates came from Boston and, entering his forties, already possessed wide mercantile experience in Europe and America. Above all he had the appropriate personal qualities for the job. A handful of contemporary estimates suggest something of the man. No one knew him better than the firm's American agent Thomas Ward, and after a visit by Bates he noted in his diary how he did not 'look very far ahead, nor understand general principles clearly', but had 'great nerve, and self possession and self confidence'. On another occasion he wrote directly to Bates: 'You are the most uniformly laborious man I know.' Ward's son also got to know him, and in 1836 wrote to his father: 'I never saw a more busy, calm and dry man than Joshua Bates . . . His tone was dry, his words few.' Finally, there was the verdict of a compatriot who called on him in London: 'The man was illiterate and ignorant but possessed a strong mind and much business ability.'[21]

It is through his diary that one really begins to understand Joshua Bates. An entry at the end of 1832 evokes the dour underlying puritanism with which he sought to run Barings:

43

Having been generally successful in business, we have become too free and open in our conduct and have incurred risks that it will not be wise to repeat. A system of secrecy should be encouraged in our office and none but clever persons admitted into the office. A rigid economy should also be enforced as much as in less prosperous times, avoid all pride & ostentation & unnecessary show.[22]

Under the watchful direction of Bates, and serviced by some forty clerks who dealt with up to 200 letters a day, Barings by the mid-1830s was engaged in an extraordinarily wide range of transactions. The staple acceptance business, in effect lending credit on commission, enabled a host of correspondents in Europe, America and the Far East to use bills on Barings and to facilitate the transport of raw materials and manufactured goods; while the firm itself not only bought and sold merchandise, securities, specie, bullion and bills of exchange for account of its many international trading clients, but also provided the credit for exchange accounts, received remittances and made collections and payments for those who required such services, and negotiated insurance and assembled passengers and freights on behalf of shipowners. The firm also acted on its own account – dealing in merchandise, specie, securities or whatever came to hand – and by 1834 had even become shipowners. For Barings, in contrast to Rothschilds, almost anything was fair game, provided there was sufficient certainty attached to it. That indeed was the crucial consideration, and comes out most clearly in the well-ordered approach that Bates, in tandem with the excellent Ward, adopted to the key question of the granting of credits. The golden rule, in Bates' words, was not to forget that 'by being too liberal we lose our money and not being sufficiently liberal we lose our business', and therefore 'the middle course is the one it should be our aim to follow'. What this meant in practice was trying to know the most possible about the individual houses requiring credit, with credit ratings based as much as anything on personal assessments of prudence and honesty, and never granting credits that exceeded a firm's total capital. Bates was also adamant that if a correspondent required credit from Barings, then it was a condition of supplying it that the correspondent should not also seek credit from anywhere else. 'It should always be a condition of granting credits', he wrote in 1832, 'that the parties keep their account entirely with us.'[23]

Control, above all quality control, also permeated the area of choosing and marketing securities, which were at this time usually American and with a bias towards states rather than corporate or municipal issues. 'It has been our invariable practice not to offer any stock which we did not ourselves deem good' was the guiding principle, enunciated to Ward some years later. The marketing of the $7m Louisiana loan of 1832 stands out, and prompted an interesting letter from Bates to Ward:

We shall all make money, and pretty easily too. At one time . . . Rothschild gave out that he should take the loan. When he found out we had got it he said he hoped we would give him a part of it. We told him we would gladly do so at the same price that we gave it to the public, which he declined.[24]

There was no doubting the profitability of the business as a whole: £98,000 in 1832 and £119,000 in 1833, with the volume of acceptances outstanding by the end of that latter year running at £2.3m. But had the firm expanded too far, too fast? John Macvicar, a London correspondent of Jardine Matheson, was a warm admirer of Barings, writing in November 1832 that 'nothing can be higher than the Credit they enjoy'; but by the following spring he was reporting a certain City scepticism:

Baring Bros are extending themselves greatly as a commercial house – their Credit is beyond any question of doubt – but some people say, they don't like their extending their business to such a great length as they are doing – the amount of their engagements of one kind and another must be enormous. In the money market here their Bills are as current as Bank of Eng^d paper.[25]

But the City did not yet properly know the Bostonian in its midst.

*

1831 was the year of the Reform Bill and all the feverish excitement attached to it. 'It is impossible to describe, in adequate terms, the degree of interest felt by all classes in the City, as to the propositions which are to be brought forward by Ministers. On the Royal Exchange, scarcely any other topic meets with any attention.' Thus the *Morning Chronicle* in February. There ensued over the rest of the year a round of meetings, petitions and so on, generally in favour of reform, befitting the fact that since 1818 the City's parliamentary allegiance had been almost wholly Whig. Yet in the reform crisis itself, there is little evidence that *haute finance* – as opposed to the ranks of City shopkeepers who looked to the liverymen for political leadership – felt any enthusiasm for political democracy. Nathan Rothschild throughout maintained the closest relations with the obdurate Wellington; Alexander Baring (recently retired from business but still a significant City figure) actually moved over to the Tories, declaring that 'liberty for all' was his goal; and Joshua Bates confided to his diary in August that 'the reform bill will cause great uneasiness as to the value of property & if it pass there is no calculating its consequences'.[26]

To a degree the Whig government managed to tone down the City's aversion when it presented a revised bill in December, although there was one intense drama to come. These were the 'May days' when King and

Lords refused to back down, Grey resigned, and Wellington attempted to form a ministry. Nothing augments doubt and apprehension more than a run on a bank, especially if it is the Bank of England, and the Radical tailor Francis Place carried the day with his famous placard 'To Stop the Duke, Go for Gold'. As the City's leading bankers and others reluctantly yielded to the dictates of common sense over gut prejudice, Rothschild inevitably took the decisive initiative. He did his best to prop up the Funds, but after a few days was compelled to report to Wellington, through the person of Arbuthnot, 'that among the monied men there is an alarm lest there should be such an opposition to all Reform as would cause commotions'. With Rothschild's rider being that Wellington must grant some measure of reform, the duke preferred to let Grey do the work and so the Whig ministry was reinstated. Even then some regret lingered. 'The power of the King & Lords appears to be gone', Bates noted later in the month, 'and the only chance for good gov^t lies in the hope that people will find more profit in attending to their business than to politics.'[27]

The City's inherent conservatism was typified in the post-1815 years by the sluggish custom given to the splendid new London Commercial Sale Rooms in Mincing Lane; the overwhelming preference remained for continuing to hold sales either in coffee houses (above all Garraways', often by candlelight) or in the rooms of the brokers themselves. By the mid-1830s the pattern began to change and by the end of the decade some twenty sales by auction were being held daily at the LCSR. If one wanted skins – whether 65,000 of raccoon or 52,000 of mink or a mere 10,200 of chinchilla – it was necessary to go to the LCSR on Monday, Tuesday or Thursday.[28]

It was a niche market that many on the Stock Exchange might have envied towards the end of May 1835, as in the context of war Spanish stock fell in one week from 72 to 50. The 'Spanish panic' seriously affected at least half the membership. It was memorialised by a contemporary account that transcends journalism and explores the collective psychology of a market under the severest pressure:

> The ruin was so comprehensive, both in its actual and probable results, that scarcely an individual could be found whom it did not reach, or fearfully threaten . . . It was painful to witness the inroads which this state of suffering was making upon the habits and feelings of individuals. The usual hour for closing the business of the day was no longer a signal for returning home. Home had ceased to be the source of those serene delights, the expectations of which sustain a man through the toils he undergoes. Alas! what is home to him, who carries thither a vulture-secret gnawing at his heart, which it is mercy to keep from others while he can, but to do which, he must deceive those whom he has never yet deceived. Is that a home, to which its master knows he is the messenger of sorrow, if his tongue speak the tidings that are upon it?[29]

The author of this feeling narrative was William Heseltine, one of the principal jobbers in Spanish stock. Like many members he defaulted at the end of May, but in July managed to secure his readmission to the Stock Exchange. Things would probably have been even worse but for an emergency whip-round in the City. Writing to the Bank of Liverpool on 28 May, the banker George Carr Glyn noted that 'the exertions which have been made (in which we have felt it a duty to contribute to the utmost with prudence) will I trust prevent much further mischief'. Joshua Bates meanwhile could not resist drawing a moral on the Stock Exchange's behalf: 'I hope they will take a lesson from Experience and never carry their Speculations so far again. My House has nothing to do with it – we have never touched Spanish or any of the speculative stocks, and never intend to do so.'[30] The inhabitants of Capel Court paid little or no attention to such austere moralisers.

Were they interested in events nearer to home than the Iberian Peninsula? Conventional wisdom would suggest not. Undoubtedly it is true that through most of the nineteenth century British industry had, in a direct sense, relatively little to do with the City; it preferred to rely on a mixture of self-finance and local finance in order to raise long-term capital. Instinctively, and not without reason, provincial industrialists tended to regard the City as a remote, rather baffling place where they would surrender control and probably be charged heavily for the privilege. The Stock Exchange for its part concentrated heavily on government stocks, whether home or foreign. An analysis of the stockbroking business of Marjoribanks, Capel & Co. in 1830 reveals that hardly any transactions at all were done in British non-government issues. Inevitably this orientation led to charges of ignorance as well as indifference.

It is perhaps typical that David Ricardo apparently never visited either the industrial Midlands or the North. Yet one should resist the temptation to caricature. Bates, for instance, made a fact-finding tour of Liverpool, Manchester, Birmingham, Leeds and Sheffield in 1833. In general, not only was the City's textile quarter intimately involved with the rest of the country, but the London money market continued to act as an effective conduit of short-term funds between the rural and manufacturing districts. Nor were all the Bank of England directors of the 1830s remote from industry: in particular, several had close links with metal and mining. To take a figure like William Thompson – MP for the City, director of the Bank and chairman of Lloyd's, but also leading ironmaster in South Wales – is to dispel simplistic notions of the City (at this stage anyway) as an offshore island.[31]

Railways were a great case in point of City involvement that was crucial but not always beneficial. In the 1820s the pioneer Stockton and Darlington Railway borrowed heavily from Richardson, Overend & Co.; in 1833 the first London meeting of the Great Western Railway took place at the fine old Jacobean house in Lime Street then occupied by the firm of Antony Gibbs, with the firm's head, George Henry Gibbs, becoming a director and a loyal supporter of Brunel; in the same year George Carr Glyn joined the London board of the projected London to Birmingham railway (eventually the London and North Western), becoming chairman four years later. Then in 1835 came the City's first railway boom, as the number of officially listed companies (twenty-one in July 1835) almost trebled in the next twelve months. 'The whole active interest of the Stock Exchange have lately directed their almost exclusive attention to Shares in Railways', noted the *Circular to Bankers* by February 1836. What is significant, though, is the extent of misgivings felt by those most closely concerned with the new railways, or at least the respectable, non-speculative ones. 'I have done everything to stop the gambling in our shares not to the satisfaction of the Stock Exchange here or of the share brokers elsewhere', Glyn himself wrote in October 1835. But even though the line was not yet built, he was unable to restrain extreme bullishness in the Birmingham shares, a phenomenon analysed the following February by George Gibbs, the cousin of George Henry, senior partner of the merchants Gibbs Son & Bright of Bristol and Liverpool, and himself until recently on the GWR board:

> The advance in these shares has been at least £55 in the last twelve months and yet for my life I cannot discover one fact bearing upon their value on which any rise can reasonably be built, that was not as well known before it commenced as it is now, with one single, and that to my mind alarming, exception – the patronage of the Stock Exchange.

Bates of course condemned the boom out of hand, but for the Stock Exchange itself there was a greater good, even after the boom collapsed in 1837. This was the creation of a major and permanent market in non-government securities, sustained over the years by the high volume of shares issued by the railway companies, thereby ensuring ready marketability. 'Home Rails', in short, were set to become a feature of City life.[32]

In the mid-1830s, though, the main buzz came from across the Atlantic. Partly it was a case of London firms like Barings acting as intermediaries in the private placing of American securities; but essentially it was a question of American trade and its financing, with a particular emphasis on the cotton boom then being enjoyed by the southern states. No house exploited the opportunity more effectively than Barings, who seemed to hold all the aces: no shortage of capital; the capacious knowledge combined with fine judgement of Bates in tandem with Ward; and a Liverpool office, opened in 1832, that did most of the actual importing and exporting. It was an opportunity that for the most part Liverpool's own merchants failed to take, lacking the requisite financial and banking resources; the major exception, William & James Brown & Co., was the Liverpool branch of an American merchant house. It was in London that new rivals to Barings in the financing of American trade emerged.

One merchant now turning himself into a 'foreign banker' was Timothy Wiggin, an American who earlier in his career had made a fortune in textiles in Manchester before coming out of retirement in 1825 to take over the London business of the failed American merchant Samuel Williams. By the mid-1830s, based at 7 Tokenhouse Yard, he was flourishing more than ever before. 'If I had to choose between Baring Bros and him', Macvicar even declared in 1833 to Jardine Matheson, 'I should under all circumstances give him the preference.' Timothy Wiggin & Co., however, was but one of the 'three Ws,' a trio of Anglo-American houses now seeking to gain market share in the financing of transatlantic trade. The other two were Thomas Wilson & Co. and George Wildes & Co., and of the latter firm Overend Gurney wrote in 1834 that 'we are always informed that their connections are very respectable which gives us great confidence in their acceptances'. By the beginning of 1836 there was one other major contender, Morrison Cryder & Co. Morrison was James Morrison, the immensely wealthy textile merchant, Cryder was John Cryder, an American merchant introduced to Morrison by Sam Gurney; and together their ambitions were such that from the start the City's jocular nickname for the new house was 'Over-Baring'.[33]

However, even Morrison, one of the shrewdest businessmen of the age, underestimated the dangers involved. Three were paramount: dependence on the continuing buoyancy of American trade; the problem in the pre-telegraph era of granting acceptance credits to traders beyond the realm of personal knowledge; and the increasing tendency of London houses to grant 'open credits', in other words accepting bills of exchange unsecured by invoices or bills of lading, a tendency that could not but produce undue speculation in the American trade itself. In July 1836 Glyn was reporting the Bank of England as getting 'very fidgetty' about 'the American houses'.[34]

One house anyway should have reassured the Old Lady. Bates indeed felt moved to record on 25 July:

> Commerce seems prosperous & the comfort of mankind more general than at any former period during the memory of man or than has been recorded in History. Emigration seems the natural cure for excessive population in old countries & if Peace continues there is no counting the increased wealth of this Country. Religion and Temperance seem to be on the increase also. Thank God for all these.

On that same day Lionel de Rothschild in Frankfurt wrote to his brother in London: 'Yesterday evening he was in danger, but today is a little

better. He has this instant called me to tell you re Exchequer Bills, &c.'
The patient was Lionel's father, taken ill several weeks earlier while in
Frankfurt to attend Lionel's wedding. Three days later, on 28 July, Nathan
Rothschild died at the age of fifty-nine. For a week afterwards the City
was bombarded by rumours and contradictory reports – of his death, of
his miraculous recovery – but at last (the story goes) a pigeon was picked
up on the south coast, bearing the words '*Il est mort*'. And on 6 August
there was published what became a famous lithograph, 'The Shadow of
a Great Man', showing a silhouette of Nathan standing in front of his
favourite pillar on the Royal Exchange. Two days later, a funeral procession of seventy-five carriages left St Swithin's Lane, and such were the
crowds that it took over a quarter of an hour to pass through Cornhill,
on its way to the Jews' burial ground in Whitechapel Road.

Among the many tributes paid, one of the most telling was by the
Circular to Bankers:

> He had a clear and comprehensive view of weighty matters of business, a
> strong and unfettered will, a promptitude of decision, and a punctuality
> in execution unexampled, in their combination. To this were superadded
> a confidence in the success in any thing he undertook, a pride of temper
> resulting from his high new position which made him bear down at any
> personal risk all opposition, and a dexterity in working the unseen
> machinery requisite to his operations, that rendered his brief and brilliant
> career so remarkable.

Present at the interment was William Heseltine, who two days later
published from the Stock Exchange his *Reflections at the Grave of N. M.
Rothschild, Esq.* Most were to the effect that a shroud has no pockets, but
one verse has a more satisfying roundness, last words from one City man
to another:

> Upon thy struggling path of life
> Strong lights and shades were cast,
> Which led through toil, suspense, and strife
> To triumph at the last!
> In the continued conflict then,
> With selfish, artful, flattering men
> Through which thy spirit pass'd
> What wonder though some stains of earth
> *Were* blended with thine inward worth![35]

CHAPTER FIVE

Nae Luck Aboot the Hoose

The recently ennobled Lord Ashburton (the former Alexander Baring) was still by September 1836 offering words of instruction to his old partners: 'The variations of all stocks & their wild fluctuations seem to arise much from Nathan's death. In the end the emancipation of the money market will be a benefit, but the sudden cessation of a despotic rule is apt to exhibit such symptoms.'

In fact, for reasons wholly unconnected with Rothschild's death and instead everything to do with the rapid and alarming downturn of the American economy, the City's latest round of monetary disturbances was only just beginning. The Bank's immediate response was to take ostentatious disciplinary action against all the leading firms engaged in American trade and finance, including even Barings. Bates was not amused: 'The Bank of England has been playing some shabby tricks. Refused to discount the Paper of seven Houses . . . This made it necessary for us to offer to discount our own acceptances.' The manoeuvre lasted only a few weeks, but in October the governor, James Pattison, called in partners of each firm and formally told them that 'the extensive Credits hitherto given to the Bankers of the United States and others, either as open Credits or in anticipation of the Sale of States Securities in this Country, are objectionable so far as the Bank of England is concerned'. Undoubtedly the most over-extended of the houses were the 'three Ws', and that same month it required joint action by Overend Gurney and Jones, Loyd & Co. to carry Wiggins over its difficulties. 'A very disastrous state of things is expected in New York & every one seems alarmed', Bates noted in mid-November, and he added without exaggeration: 'On the whole everything wears a gloomy aspect, with a prospect of failures.'[1]

As events unfolded in 1837, against the background of an unnervingly steady flow of bad news from across the Atlantic, the sharpest commentary was that provided by George Carr Glyn to the Bank of Liverpool. One of Glyn's main concerns was that too many of the Bank of England's directors were, in his own words, 'impregnated with political economy doctrines'; and during these anxious months he placed great reliance on the 'practical knowledge' of Horsley Palmer (who was still a director) to overcome these insufficiently pragmatic tendencies. There was a particularly nasty moment early in March, when the three Ws were under the cosh:

> I may tell you that had it not been for the firmness of Horsley Palmer & the Deputy Governor, the Governor and his party in the Court would have brought down every American house . . . I really think the Governor is mad upon this subject. He and I have been brought into disagreeable collision.[2]

Over the next few weeks, with the City straining on every rumour and Bates working closely with Palmer on the detailed arrangements, the Bank reluctantly agreed to a rescue package for the beleaguered Ws. Was the laissez-faire Pattison – who in 1835 had become one of the City's Whig MPs – swayed by provincial pressure? Two directors of the Bank of Liverpool came down to London to see what they could do, stayed at St Paul's Coffee House, and while there wrote to the governor in the strongest possible language of 'the great embarrassment which prevails in Lancashire both in the Mercantile and Manufacturing interests, arising chiefly from the want of confidence occasioned by the doubt and discredit thrown upon American paper', adding that 'unless immediate steps are taken to restore confidence and mercantile credit, we must soon inevitably witness the most awful crisis ever known in this or any other Country'.[3] Pattison was indeed about to vacate the governor's chair, and Glyn was hopeful that henceforth a larger view of the Bank's responsibilities would more readily prevail.

By May remittances from the United States were still obstinately invisible, many bills were arriving only to be dishonoured, and even those bills accepted were difficult to discount. Bates believed that it now would not be so disastrous if the three Ws did stop, that the worst had been averted; but three days later Glyn more accurately reflected the City's mood when he wrote that 'we all entertain the strongest hopes of the Bank taking the decisive step and determining to carry these houses', adding the next day that 'every thing is progressing very satisfactorily with the Americans'. By Tuesday the 30th the crunch was imminent, as Wilson & Co. and Wiggin & Co. formally asked the Bank for further assistance, blaming 'the temporary and almost universal suspension of credit throughout the principal commercial Cities of the United States'. Morrison's diary was graphic enough: 'News from U.S. horrible. The Bank deliberating on the W's – and all consternation. Dismal forebodings – no sleep all night.' Wednesday brought no relief, as the Bank continued to delay its decision, 'and from what Mr Palmer tells me', wrote Glyn, 'I fear the result'. Glyn was confident of the governor, Timothy Curtis, and his deputy, Sir John Reid, but not of most of the rest of the Court.[4]

Thursday the 1st saw a stately but pointed minuet between merchants and politicians. The Court requested the governor and deputy governor to lay before the prime minister and Chancellor of the Exchequer the Wiggin/Wilson application for further relief and to state to them 'the apprehension of many of the Directors, from the character of the accounts received from America, of the eventual solvency of the Houses in question'. They duly waited upon Melbourne and Spring-Rice, and later in the day returned to Threadneedle Street to present to their colleagues the following buck-passing minute:

> It appears that unless further assistance be given to certain houses in the American Trade their failure will ensue and very great and extensive commercial and manufacturing distress will inevitably follow. Lord Melbourne and the Chancellor of the Exchequer also collect from the statement made to them that less of eventual loss is apprehended by the Governors from taking this course than if further assistance were now to be refused.
>
> Lord Melbourne and the Chancellor of the Exchequer are deeply impressed with the public inconvenience which would result to the manufacturing and commercial interests from a suspension of the houses engaged in the American Trade, and are most anxious if it can be done with safety that these calamities should be mitigated if not averted.
>
> But they do not possess either the data or the knowledge by which the solvency of commercial houses can be ascertained, and they feel that it is not within their province to direct or influence the decision of the Bank of England.

Was there an embarrassed pause before 'the Governor informed the Court that the opinions referred to in Lord Melbourne's Letter were stated as his own and the Deputy Governor's, and not of the Court, except as relates to the Solvency of the Houses'? Now at last the decision had to be made; and a furious Glyn reported soon afterwards that the proposal to extend relief was defeated by a single vote.[5] Curtis and Reid had fatefully overplayed their hand, the three Ws would never trade again.

Various small firms fell in their wake, but attention soon turned to Morrison Cryder and Browns of Liverpool, both of whom were also putting in for assistance. 'I believe that Morrison has taken his deeds & parchments to the Bank. It must have been a bitter step.' So Glyn recorded on the 8th, when in fact it became clear that the Bank was willing, on the security offered, to lend £325,000. Morrison's own feelings were mixed, and he wrote to his agent in the States the next day:

> The last ten days has been like a horrid dream! All the Ws are gone and with them many others, indeed, as far as respects the American Houses, one looks about to see who is left standing, not who has fallen, the list is a brief one now! All who had not resources out of business like myself or opulent friends like Barings are gone . . .
>
> We shall of course lose & that I fear considerably, but we shall soon make it up. A few of us must have all the business hereafter.

A week later, to general City relief, the Bank also bailed out Browns, and the worst of the crisis was over. Only one major Anglo-American house had weathered it more or less unscathed. 'Probably in one way & another we may lose one year's commissions, which considering the nature of the crisis & the little warning to allow us to get out of it ought to convince people of our prudence & of our means.' Thus, with justified satisfaction, Joshua Bates later in the summer.[6] In a year of knockouts and long counts, Barings had fought canny and won through conclusively on points.

*

On a Wednesday the following January, despite a temperature below zero and streets almost impassable with snow, the timber broker Charles Churchill and his family enjoyed a night out:

> Mr Ernst Wolff & Mr Selby drop in to Dinner, wch leads to a Box at the Olympic, with young Todd, Mama, Charles, & the Girls. The Bengal Tyger & Puss in Boots.
>   The same night on coming out we learn the Conflagration of the Royal Exchange wch with all its attached Buildings becomes a heap of Ruins in a few Hours. Obliged to hold our Exchange at Guildhall.

It was horribly true – the Royal Exchange was no more, apart from its clock tower and some of its walls, left standing and covered in great icicles. The Gresham Committee, responsible for the building, held an immediate inquiry, and at least one of its witnesses lacked nothing in descriptive eloquence:

> John Alley states that he left the Auction Mart Coffee House at ¼ before II returning home to Wood Street where he resides, perceived a strong light proceeding from the Northern Windows of the Captain's Room in the Royal Exchange, and smoke issuing through the Roof above – the windows below were perfectly dark – immediately assisted in breaking open the Iron Gates and padlock leading to the North Staircase and to Lloyds, and was first to ascend, he was followed by some of the fire Brigade – went immediately through the passage, turned to the right examined the Door of the Captain's Room found it in flames on the inside and also the Door of the Kitchen or Bar of the Captain's Room – had I knocked it, it must have fallen – returned to the Door of the Washing Room attached to Lloyds – the Skylight over was on fire – attempted to force the Door and while in the act was knocked down by one of the fire Brigade (into the burning embers which fell from the Skylight) who insisted that no doors should be forced. Notwithstanding the threat went to the apartments of the Secretary of Lloyds, forced open the Door and entered – the whole of the cornice of the inner room was on fire – saved many of the books which he gave to the Broad Street Watchman, Croker – returned for more books but found it impossible to enter the Secretary's Office without danger – turned his attention to the Subscriber's Room and assisted in removing the Drawers until it was considered unsafe longer to remain in the room.

The seventeenth-century Royal Exchange had long been a building waiting for its terminal conflagration, the weather badly hindered the brave if ill-organised attempt to save it, and the last tune rung out by the bells in the tower was 'There's Nae Luck aboot the Hoose'. London had known no worse fire since 1666 itself.[7]

The late 1830s and early 1840s were not easy times in the City – though not as grim as they were in the British economy at large – and in the summer of 1839 the Bank of England found itself in what can only be described as a pretty pickle. For a variety of reasons, among them lax management and the drain on sterling caused by the need to pay for wheat imports, the Bank's bullion by the last week in July stood at barely £3.7m, just over a fifth of the circulation and palpably inadequate. The Bank's initial reaction seems to have been to look to the house of Rothschild, but Nathan's son Lionel, still finding his feet, received the most cautionary advice from his more experienced cousin Anselm on the Continent:

> Do not take any rash step in a large operation. Your mother tells me that Herries told your good father in her presence to mind and not trust the Bank without any guarantee . . . as the Bank being involved in difficulties may *stop* suddenly . . . Mind, you are not your good father and do not have his influence, and he was capable of acting in other ways than prudence would direct you.

So much for the Bank of England's rock-solid reputation. Instead, finding no joy at New Court, it turned elsewhere, as Bates recorded on 20 July:

> The Bank applied to my House yesterday to assist them in negotiating a Loan from the Bank of France which Tom Baring & I said there could be no hesitation about our entering on but Mildmay was violently opposed to. I went to the House of Lords to see Lord Ashburton & get his opinion, which was the same as that of Tom & myself.

Humphrey St John Mildmay was the over-cautious son-in-law of the former Alexander Baring; Tom Baring was the very able (if too often absent) grandson of Sir Francis Baring, and was mainly responsible for international loans. In tandem with Timothy Curtis from the Bank, Tom Baring went to Paris and, though encountering considerable hostility from the Rothschilds there, successfully organised a banking syndicate, under the Bank of France's auspices, to put up the loan. For Barings it was a great triumph, as well as an important marker in its relations with the Bank.[8]

The Bank and other City institutions had embroiled themselves in the affairs of the Bank of the United States, whose charismatic London agent, Samuel Jaudon, had been marketing whole rafts of American securities since 1838, on the back of an apparently recovering economy. Over the next few years the Bank of the United States suspended specie payments in October 1839 and finally folded early in 1841, while in the course of 1841 and 1842 no fewer than eight American states defaulted. There developed in London an unbridled anti-American mood, and by June 1842 Bates was writing as much in anger as in sorrow that 'there never was a Country so disgraced in point of Credit as the United States of America'.

This wretched story concealed two important trends for the future. One, in terms of the finance of Anglo-American trade as a whole, was the speed with which the shock of 1837 was soon forgotten and the sway of Barings was again disputed. Huths and Schröders each established branches in Liverpool, Rothschilds became more active in the field through the impatient urgings of its US agent August Belmont, and Brown Shipley of Liverpool (as Browns there now became) vigorously pursued a policy of opening as many small credits as possible, involving an aggressiveness and willingness to take risks that Barings under Bates no longer countenanced.

There was also the establishment in London of a permanent market for American securities, involving that remarkable figure George Peabody, merchant, financier and philanthropist.[9] He had been born in 1795 of fairly humble Massachusetts origins; by 1815 he had become a partner in a Baltimore-based firm which imported dry goods from Britain; by 1837 he had made five trips to Britain; and from 1838 he was a permanent resident, occupying offices at 31 Moorgate. Over the next seven years he moved decisively from merchanting to finance, above all marketing American securities and then trading heavily in them, soon becoming the City's acknowledged expert on the subject. Inevitably he found himself in an invidious situation as one state after another defaulted; quite apart from the strain it put on his own resources, he was even denied admission to the Reform Club on account of his nationality. Peabody, however, had a long-term faith in the United States: ultimately it would be rewarded.

The City's two dominant merchant banks – the reality existed even if the term had not yet been coined – remained Rothschilds and Barings. Lionel de Rothschild (formally Baron Rothschild from 1838, in belated recognition of the title granted to his uncles by the Austrian Emperor in 1822) lacked the genius of his father but was no fool. He had been educated at the University of Göttingen, spent apprentice years in London, Paris and Madrid, and essentially perceived his task as one of consolidation. Much more of a conformist than Nathan, he was disinclined to speculate on the stock market or indeed take major risks of any sort; in 1843 he closed his firm's account at the Bank of England, marking a break from Nathan's policy of large-scale borrowings there. Other houses, however, were on the rise, among them Huths, which by this stage was in active contact with almost all the leading commercial centres.[10] The key emerging figure was Daniel Meinertzhagen, who had married Frederick Huth's daughter in 1833.

Meanwhile, the joust continued between the City's old private banks and their new joint-stock rivals, of which by the end of the 1830s there were five. The long-term future lay with the upstarts – adequately capitalised, paying interest on current as well as deposit accounts, and not dependent on the caprices of a dynastic system producing satisfactory partners. No one was more aware of continuing social inferiority than J. W. Gilbart, general manager of the London and Westminster from its 1834 inception. In January 1838 he explained to his directors why the bank's City office had advanced less rapidly than its branches elsewhere:

> 1. The City Bankers have more influence over their customers than the Bankers in the Western parts of London. The City customers have occasion for discounts and loans which the Bankers most liberally grant. When they leave their Bankers to come to us they come to a Bank where they are less well known and where from that circumstance alone they might not be treated with the same degree of confidence. Hence we have drawn but few accounts from other Bankers and those few have been chiefly of an inferior class to whom their former Bankers have refused accommodation.
>
> 2. Our exclusion from the clearing-house. I need not say that this operated to our disadvantage in the City.
>
> 3. Our Influence is less powerful in the City. In the City of London the power of swaying the actions of other men and the opportunities of exercising this power are possessed chiefly by those who are extensively engaged in mercantile pursuits. Not many of our Directors and none of our large proprietors are thus engaged.[11]

Despite the efforts of Smith, Payne & Smiths – which in its 1836 set of rules governing the admission of new London partners had continued to state, as in the 1788 deed, that partners were forbidden to win or lose more than £50 in a day 'by play or betting at Cards, Dice or any other Game of Chance or by another species of Gaming whatsoever' – the writing was on the wall for the private banks. By 1841, only twenty-nine remained of the fifty-two which had been members of the clearing house in 1810.[12] It is tempting to argue that it was arrogance that proved their undoing. Barnett, Hoare & Co. of Lombard Street were masters of the ostensibly courteous yet cool and haughty tone, as in a letter to the Leith Bank in July 1841:

> We are favoured with your letter enclosing the Draft of a Bond for our approval, and proposing an Annual payment of £105 for our Conduct of your business. With reference to this sum we desire to call to your recollection your former proposal to keep £5,000 as a Cash balance in our hands, as our remuneration, which we did then and do now consider by no means

excessive. The lowest sum therefore we can name for annual commission is £200 and we beg leave to add, without intending any disrespect, that even on those terms, we are not anxious to retain your account, subject to a call for £10,000, which we fear is likely often to be made upon us.[13]

*

The political allegiance of the City remained predominantly Whig/Liberal. It was not, in terms of the City of London constituency itself, a passionate conviction: George Grote in 1837 only scraped in above Horsley Palmer by a handful of votes; four years later, when Grote decided not to stand, Lord John Russell became his successor only because no leading City figure was prepared to come forward, and the support given to Russell by the Rothschilds and their satellites in that election owed less to larger political questions than to the willingness of Russell to champion political privileges for Jews.[14] Similarly clouded, as in the 1820s, was the question of the City and free trade, firmly back on the agenda by the early 1840s. Once again debate was polarised along the lines of sectional interests.

In general terms, the City gave credit to Peel for financial and commercial competence – certainly in comparison with the preceding Whig ministries – but essentially felt that not necessarily wise policies of economic liberalisation were being thrust upon them. Bates for one was disgruntled, declaring in 1843 that 'all the doings of Sir Robert Peel in the Tariff etc by which he inclines towards the free trade system have been wrong, not only wrong in the abstract but wrong in reference to the condition of the country, its debt, poor laws etc'.[15]

The truly divisive question, of course, was the Corn Laws, the repeal of which would denote the final triumph of free trade. In the autumn of 1843 there took place a celebrated City by-election fought almost wholly on that issue. James Pattison, the prominent merchant and Bank of England director, was the candidate supported by the Anti-Corn Law League; while Tom Baring was the protectionist. The eventual result was close but decisive – Pattison 6,532, Baring 6,367 – and the *Circular to Bankers* (supporters of Baring) acknowledged it to be 'a victory of money over land, of cosmopolitism over country, of democracy over aristocracy'. Nevertheless, the City electorate was hardly representative of the monied interest as such, the League had proved far more adept than the protectionists at mobilising the popular vote of the City, and according to Bates 'many Conservatives were out of Town', presumably because it was a Saturday. Yet for all that, there does seem to have been an emerging mood in the City by this time that, whether or not desirable, the movement towards free trade was becoming inevitable – and that therefore it was better to adjust to it than to fight it.[16]

The following year saw one of the cornerstones of nineteenth-century legislation: the Bank Charter Act of 1844, whose immediate antecedents lay in two pamphlets published early in 1837. The first, by Horsley Palmer, blamed the joint-stock banks and excessive speculation in foreign securities for the recent heavy pressure on the money market; the other, written in explicit repudiation by the private banker Samuel Jones Loyd, blamed the Bank of England itself, and in particular called for a rigid separation of the Bank's issuing and banking functions. Over the next few years two clear schools of thought crystallised: the pro-Palmer 'banking' school that wanted bankers to have discretionary powers over the volume of currency; and the pro-Loyd 'currency' school that explicitly refuted such powers. Unfortunately for the former, the Bank of England's track record remained such as to inspire little general confidence. Indeed, even at the time of the war of the pamphlets, James Capel was reporting to the Royal Bank of Scotland that 'there is a growing feeling in the commercial world (at least amongst those we are acquainted with) against the Bank . . . and many persons go so far as to aver that should their Charter be renewed, it will be on much less favourable terms than the present'. In particular, the 'Palmer rule' of 1832 was openly discredited, Daniel Hardcastle in 1842 bluntly declaring that 'it is effective against a Bank of issue, but not effective against a Bank of deposit also'.[17] By 1844 the Bank of England's Charter was liable for renewal, the prime minister was Sir Robert Peel, and having become a convert to the 'currency' school he was determined to put through a fundamental overhaul of the Bank's working practices and its position within the national monetary system.

During the early months of the year he and Henry Goulburn, his Chancellor, engaged in a round of negotiations with William Cotton the governor and Benjamin Heath the deputy governor. They involved plenty of give and take but were harmonious enough, and both sides put forward fruitful suggestions. 'I must declare', Peel remarked to the Commons with apparent sincerity in May, 'that I never saw men influenced by more disinterested or more public-spirited motives than they have evinced throughout our communications with them.' Peel's main measures were separation of the Bank's note issue from its banking operations, restrictions on other banks of issue, a fixed ratio between notes and bullion, and a fixed fiduciary issue of £14m (i.e. the amount of notes that might be issued against securities). 'Peel has gained immense credit by his measure (and speech) about the Bank', recorded Greville, while the Bank's proprietors met and, encouraged by a typically capable speech from Loyd, gave their almost unanimous support to the bill. Opposition in Parliament was similarly muted, and it seemed that Peel and Cotton between them had created a very satisfactory consensus.[18]

Then came the revolt of Lombard Street, triggered by a belated realisation that an extension of issue on securities beyond £14m would only be permitted in order to replace the issues of country banks that were being withdrawn. On the last day of May, Horsley Palmer (still a Bank director) wrote to Peel asking him to increase the fiduciary limit to £16m, but to no effect, as Peel explained to Cotton on 4 June:

> My confidence is unshaken that we are taking all the precautions, which legislation can prudently take, against the recurrence of a monetary crisis. It *may* occur in spite of our precautions – and if it does, and *if it be neces-sary* to assume a grave responsibility for the purpose of meeting it, I dare say men will be found willing to assume such a responsibility.
>
> I would rather trust to this, than impair the efficacy and probable success of those measures by which one hopes to control evil tendencies in their beginning, and to diminish the Risk that extraordinary measures may be necessary.

Three days later, on Friday the 7th, the senior partners of the City's private banks held a meeting to consider the following memorial:

> We are apprehensive that the absolute limitation of the issue to £14,000,000, without any power of expansion being reserved, whether that amount be in itself a proper amount or not, will create a general feeling of uneasiness throughout the country, and, by preventing the satisfactory reception of the measure, will deprive the scheme of many of the advantages it possesses, and interfere with its success. We respect-fully submit that the effect of such an absolute limitation will be to restrict the business of the country by leading to a general withdrawal of legitimate accommodation, unless some power be reserved by the bill for extending the issue.

Almost all the bankers signed, but then, as a clearly rattled Cotton explained to Goulburn the following Monday, there occurred a hiccup:

> If you have not yet received the resolutions from the Bankers I think I can explain the cause.
>
> Raikes Currie, Henry Thornton and some others did not approve of the proposed alteration of Sir Rob' Peel's measures but their partners assented as did old Mr [Lewis] Loyd on part of Jones Loyd & Co. Prescott Grote & Co. refused to sign just as the document was about to be forwarded to you. Mr Loyd came in great alarm and said the name of his house must be struck out as his son [i.e. Samuel Jones Loyd] would not allow it to remain if he was to continue member of the Firm, that he was willing to retire and would do so unless the name of his House was withdrawn.
>
> I strongly suspect that Mr Palmer is very much at the bottom of this movement. He has been trying to influence members of the Court and I shall not be surprised if he brings forward some resolution which may probably place me in a Minority, but I will make the best fight I can and I shall be supported by the intelligence if not by the members of the Court.

A suggestive letter: Samuel Jones Loyd successfully terrorising his vener-able father, Horsley Palmer trying to snatch victory at the last from his old theoretical rival, the governor outnumbered as he sided with Peel, and most of the great banking names of the City up in arms. In the event, Palmer did not seek to mobilise malcontent Bank directors; but on 11 May, West End and City private banks came together to sign and present to government the previous week's memorial. There were seven City refuseniks (including Prescotts and Jones Loyd), but twenty-one City banks signed. The reply from Peel, however, was couched in terms of the flattest refusal, and over the next few weeks the bill smoothly became law.[19]

Precisely as with the resumption decision a quarter of a century earlier, the City had been powerless to prevent itself being imposed upon. Yet, exactly as with the return to gold, the Bank Charter Act eventually became entrenched as one of the great Victorian orthodoxies. Not only did the Act confer exclusive issuing rights upon the Bank, but in the very *narrowness* of its remit lay the possibility of a technical mastery over monetary affairs that henceforth few outside critics would be able to challenge. Peel's legislation may have been excessively inflexible and mechanistic, yet there are few things less susceptible to lay control than an esoteric machine. Moreover, it was a machine imbued with a powerfully moralistic character, capable of resisting merely technical arguments. To listen to the certain, unfaltering voice of Samuel Jones Loyd, the ultimate architect of the Act, as in July 1844 he published a pamphlet refuting the weak-kneed wish of his fellow bankers to have a get-out clause in times of heavy monetary pressure, is to realise with a vengeance how the City too was being called upon to play its part in the emerging, thoroughly stern-minded Peelite-cum-Gladstonian dispensation:

> To accede to such a request would be virtually to destroy the efficacy of the measure. The commencement of a drain of bullion, and consequently of pressure on the money-market, is the period at which the provisions of the Bill become practically important; and unless they are then strictly adhered to, the whole measure becomes a nullity. A general conviction that they will not be suspended on such occasions is essential, for producing throughout the community that cautious forethought and that healthy tone of self-reliance, upon which the safety and utility of the measure must materially depend.[20]

CHAPTER SIX

Horrid, Horrid Panic

The Bank Charter Act was designed partly to curb speculation, but its framers could not be blamed for failing to take into account the lure of the iron monster. The railway mania, as it became known, was under way even before Peel's measure became law, and in 1845 it reached its height. The grotesque bubble was about to burst. 'The Crisis in the Share Market' was the main headline by the end of October in the *Railway Monitor*, the newly started weekly supplement of *The Economist*, and over the next few months premiums turned to discounts, members of the Stock Exchange were hammered, and new railway lines stopped being projected. 'Oh! the horrid, horrid panic!' lamented *Punch*, 'What a – what a dreadful bore!'[1]

The main speculative interest came not from the City but from the regions where the railways were actually being constructed, and though by October 1845 some 121 railway securities were being actively dealt in on the London Stock Exchange, this was a lower total than in either Liverpool or Manchester. Moreover, powerful elements of *haute finance* kept a cautious distance. 'The mighty loanmongers, on whose fiat the fate of kings and empires sometimes depended, seemed like men who, witnessing some eccentricity of nature, watch it with mixed feelings of curiosity and alarm', wrote Disraeli in *Endymion* many years later. He was clearly referring to Rothschilds, probably discouraged by the experience of its Paris house in relation to new French railways, and Barings, where Bates in April 1845 argued that since 'the rage for railroads is great' and 'much swindling is going on in the Share market', it plainly followed that 'a crash is looked for sooner or later'.[2]

It was now that there began the systematic practice of stagging – applying heavily for the shares in new companies with a view to selling them immediately at a premium – and *Punch* that year had plenty of fun satirising 'Stag-hunting in Capel Court'. Services were required in many and different ways as the mania raged and then messily expired, and it was no coincidence that new firms of solicitors emerged, including one founded in Leadenhall Street by the Linklater brothers, sons of a provision merchant in Wapping High Street: there was no shortage of work for them and other legal gentlemen. After all, as the Stock Exchange's Edward Callow was to recall, 'a solicitor or two, a civil engineer, a Parliamentary agent, possibly a contractor, a map of England, a pair of compasses, a pencil, and a ruler, were all that were requisite to commence the formation of a railway company'.[3]

In the short term, the rollercoaster nature of the railway boom played its part in the major commercial and financial crisis of 1847, but it was not the main cause. Arguably as important was the Bank of England's unexpectedly aggressive discounting policy in the immediate wake of the Bank Charter Act, prompting the *Bankers' Magazine* to remark in April 1845 that the Bank's directors were 'now anxious to push their business, as bankers, to an extent hitherto quite unknown to their system of management'. This policy, perhaps at root a cussed response to the prevailing notion that the Bank was now no more than a mechanical instrument of parliamentary legislation, was one of the reasons why money was such a drug on the market in the mid-1840s and indeed why the railway mania flourished as excessively as it did.

The crux, though, was the corn situation. Following the failure of the Irish potato crop in 1845, Peel the following summer pushed through the repeal of the Corn Laws, a measure that divided the City (and even individual City families such as the Barings) quite as much as it did the Conservative Party. Then not only did the Irish crop fail again but the European crop failed; the English harvest was poor; and that winter saw rising imports of ever more expensive wheat, causing a massive drain of gold. By April 1847 the atmosphere was one of crisis and an anxious Chancellor of the Exchequer, Sir Charles Wood, looked in vain for guidance to the great mercantile names of the City, as he admitted to his banking confidant, Samuel Jones Loyd: 'I saw at Lord John's, Lionel Rothschild & Bates this morning & (low be it spoken), I am utterly confounded at the ignorance they displayed, of facts & circumstances which I should have thought every merchant in the City must have known. They really had little or nothing to say for themselves, & admitted that things were proceeding rapidly.'[4]

They were at least correct in that respect, especially as the 'company of merchants' had just performed a disconcertingly abrupt U-turn in its monetary policy, abandoning cheap money and, through temporarily restricting discounts, inducing a sense of panic about the lack of available credit. The pressure on discount houses like Overend Gurney became intense, even the bills of Coutts being refused in Lombard Street, and trade at large was more or less paralysed.

Loyd was determined to keep the Whig government on the straight and narrow, and in a letter in June to Wood he with some justification put the blame on the Bank's failure to protect its banking reserve of notes during the enforced outflow of bullion; but the City as a whole knew where to pin the blame, and in early July there was presented to government a 'Petition of the Merchants, Bankers, and Traders of London against the Bank Act', essentially a protest against credit rationing but with larger implications:[5] the Peelite cornerstone was starting to look shaky.

In August there were numerous failures in the trade, and on the 19th there fell to the partners of Prescotts a task of the utmost delicacy:

> The Committee were occupied nearly the whole of this day, in closely inspecting the affairs of Messrs W. R. Robinson & Co., who through imprudent operations in Corn have found themselves in embarrassment . . . The great personal esteem they entertained for Mr W. R. Robinson, the head of the house, and the present Governor of the Bank of England, and the desire they felt of averting from the commercial body so severe a blow, as the failure of a house in their high position, would have led them to have incurred considerable inconvenience and even hazard, if they could have found themselves in any way justified after inspection of their accounts. It is therefore with the utmost regret that the Committee were compelled to inform Mr Robinson, that they could not assist him, as they took an unfavourable view of his affairs . . . the stoppage of the House we fear is inevitable.[6]

The governor of the Bank had failed, and most people in the City were profoundly shocked: in the words of one correspondent on the 24th, 'it has created an extraordinary sensation, in consequence of the head of the firm occupying the prominent position of Governor of the Bank of England'.[7] The new governor was James Morris, head of the merchants Morris, Prevost & Co.

The crisis deepened during September as a whole series of mercantile firms went down. Gower, Nephews & Co., merchants over-committed in Mauritius sugar estates, failed on the 11th, and that meant another member of the Bank of England's Court, Abel Lewes Gower, having to leave it; as did the failure on the 18th of the East and West India merchants Reid, Irving & Co., whose senior partner Sir John Rae Reid had not long since been governor of the Bank and who had vainly led commercial opposition to the Whig policy of equalising duties on foreign and colonial sugar. Between these two failures there occurred the stoppage with liabilities of over £2.6m of the discount house Sandersons, within days of the sudden death of its managing partner, William Morris senior.

An intense frustration by now existed that there was in the Bank's Issue Department a large reserve rendered inoperative by what *Punch* aptly termed 'The Obstruction in Threadneedle Street', in other words the Bank Charter Act.[8] Early on Saturday 23 October, ten leading City figures, including Samuel Gurney and George Carr Glyn, waited on ministers and requested a suspension of the Act. Later in the morning, James Morris and another Bank director, G. W. Norman, also knocked on the door at Downing Street, and once again the ball was lobbed over the net:

> Lord John Russell and the Chancellor of the Exchequer considered any restrictions in the way of Discount &c &c to be highly inexpedient and expressed a strong wish, that the Bank should act liberally today, with an emphatic assurance that happen what might, the letter authorising a possible deviation from the Law of 1844 should be sent to the Bank on Monday morning.[9]

News of the meeting leaked to the City, and the evening edition of the *Morning Chronicle* reported that 'Consols have improved today, and a better feeling is prevalent in the Stock Exchange'.

'The deed is done; and I hope it will succeed, but, I never did anything so unwillingly in my life. I am very curious to know the effect in the City. I am afraid that it will be too much approved.' Thus Wood, in all financial matters a strict Peelite, to Loyd on the Monday morning. Gurney later recalled that historic day as it affected him in the very nerve centre of the City:

> We had again a very heavy demand upon us; and we applied to the governor, and said that, to supply Lombard-street with what was wanted, we should require £200,000 more . . . The governor postponed a decision on our application till two o'clock. At one o'clock, however, the letter from the government authorising relaxation was announced. The effect was immediate. Those who had sent notice for their money in the morning sent us word that they did not want it – that they only ordered payment by way of precaution. And after the notice we only required about £100,000 instead of £200,000. From that day we had a market of comparative ease.[10]

So easy that ultimately the Bank did not have to exceed the fiduciary issue of notes as laid down by the Act: instead, it was the fact alone of the letter having been issued, potentially allowing such a relaxation, that turned the crisis. Disraeli, in the witty speech that he afterwards claimed made him party leader, compared the suspension of the Act to the lique-faction of St Januarius' blood ('the remedy is equally efficient and equally a hoax') and he was not far off the mark.[11]

Peelite free trade was about to become one of the City's cardinal orthodoxies, and so too, if more tentatively at this stage, was adherence to the Bank Charter Act. Why should this have been, granted that it was said in 1847 that only three people in the City supported it? One of those three (the figure was surely an underestimate) was Loyd, and in the immediate wake of the crisis he did an extremely effective job in ensuring the Whig government followed his line of blaming the Bank of England

for the turmoil rather than the Act, a piece of legislation he continued
to couch in terms of the higher morality. Wood was willing to be imbued
and wrote to Loyd shortly before Christmas: 'Take Glyn for instance. Is
not his judgement warped by the difficulties in which he was placed?
Can you expect men who believe that an issue of paper would have saved
them, to think so much of general good as of their own?' Yet it is arguable that the very *suspension* of the Act in 1847 crucially blunted City
opposition, for it was hard not to feel that it mattered much less now
that it was apparent the government would relax its stringency in an
emergency.[12] One way and another a holy trinity was being created – gold
standard, free trade, Bank Charter Act – and it would take more than
reason to shake it.

Out of the cumulative mercantile wreckage of 1847, Joshua Bates and
his house once again came up smelling of roses: 'We do not hold on our
own account £20,000 worth of goods, and our consignments, which are
also moderate, will sell for enough to cover our advances', he smugly
informed his American agent early in November.[13]

*

Within months of the crisis, France and much of the rest of Europe was
convulsed by revolution. Some London houses with intimate continental
connections (notably Rothschilds) were temporarily hit as a result of the
turbulent European events of 1848–9, but in general the City benefited
from the marked capital flight, totalling some £20m by the summer of
1849.[14]

London in 1848 had its own moment of threatened revolution. The
Chartists gathered on Kennington Common on Monday 10 April, and
the City, as the *Morning Chronicle* explained, took no chances:

> The Bank of England was not only defended by an extra garrison, but its
> parapets were surmounted with a breast-work of sand bags, so placed as
> to defend and cover the besieged, but allowing apertures sufficiently large
> to permit him to take deadly aim upon his assailants. The Royal Exchange
> held within its area 200 pensioners; and the Mansion-house was also
> supplied with a strong guard. In fact, this was the case with the Mint, the
> Custom-house, the India-house, and many of the private banks and
> warehouses.[15]

The route of the main Chartist procession was from Fitzroy Square via
Holborn, Farringdon Street and Blackfriars Bridge, thereby missing the
City proper; but there were also eastern gatherings of Chartists, who
met each other in Finsbury Square and, about 12,000 strong, marched
down Bishopsgate Street and Gracechurch Street on their way to London
Bridge.

Meanwhile, at 10.45 in the committee room of the Stock Exchange, there were anxious discussions, with William Hichens in the chair in the absence of the chairman and deputy chairman, both on duty as special constables in the Royal Exchange:

> The Chairman said the Bankers in Lombard Street were sending over their Securities to the Bank of England, and recommended to confine all business today within the narrowest possible limits; and the present meeting was convened to consider the propriety of closing the House.
>
> Mr Mullens suggested that such a Step might occasion serious and unnecessary alarm, not only throughout the Country, but all over Europe, and most exaggerated conclusions would no doubt be drawn as to the State of the Metropolis, if the Stock Exchange was to be shut.

Outside the Bank of England a large crowd of spectators 'most vociferously cheered' whenever soldiers entered the building; but inside the Stock Exchange a nervous trading floor awaited developments south of the river:

> About two o'clock . . . the news arrived that the procession had been abandoned, and that the Chartists at Kennington were fast dispersing. The intelligence was received with much gratification, and the national anthem was universally called for. The members instantly acted upon the suggestion, and being uncovered sang 'God save the Queen' in the most enthusiastic style. Consols immediately went up.

It was a turning point of British history, and the jubiliant tone to the *Morning Chronicle*'s 'Money Market and City News' written the next day caught the City's mood:

> The triumph of the people over the mob, the victory of peace and order against violence and intimidation, which was so happily obtained yesterday by the loyal conduct of the citizens of London, is indeed a subject for great thankfulness, and should fill every honest heart with joy. The benefits arising from so happy a termination to those agitating disturbances will be speedily felt throughout the land . . . Our energetic suppression of disorder will also tell to advantage in all parts of the world, and its effects will be speedily manifested in the confidence which foreign nations will have in directing their produce to this country, which is now almost the only one in which they can feel the security necessary to induce business: England has only to be quiet, and the trade of the world must centre in her.[16]

CHAPTER SEVEN

The Fatal Day

'The world', Joshua Bates reflected on his sixty-fifth birthday in October 1852 (though at the time he believed he was only sixty-three), 'seems very prosperous since the discovery of Gold in California & Australia, & the extension of railways & navigation by Steam are working great changes in the world.' He could not have been more right, for in the early 1850s the international economy was in the process of taking off spectacularly, so that by 1870 the volume of international trade would be five times what it had been back in 1840.

Indeed, in retrospect the 1860s marked a unique decade: capital, goods and labour flowing almost unhindered round much of the known world in unprecedented quantities, the nearest we would ever come to a fully liberal, free-trading system. And at the heart of that system lay the City of London, providing not only unrivalled entrepôt facilities in terms of physical trade but also credit accommodation on a worldwide basis. Moreover, as a concomitant of this, the London money market found itself becoming increasingly sophisticated, increasingly international, with domestic bills of exchange gradually starting to give way in importance to foreign or external bills as London's great contribution to the provision of short-term commercial credit – bills guaranteed by the City's growing array of accepting houses. The pattern was similar in long-term finance. British overseas investments, some £200m in the mid-1850s, increased about fivefold over the next twenty years and, in conjunction with the permanent effects of the railway boom, a fully-fledged rentier class was born.[1]

There was one other crucial component to all this global activity, and that was the profound transformation taking place in the world's communications. In 1851 a submarine cable was laid between Dover and Calais; and a year later Bates was noting that 'the Electric Telegraph is used more & more', adding that 'news is transmitted from Vienna in 12 hours, from Paris in half an hour'. Other European cities soon followed, and by 1860, in the context of negotiations over a Russian loan, he was able to record with satisfaction: 'Rec^d a Telegram that the Contract for the Loan had been signed & despatched per mail, so that we shall have it in 5 days.

The Telegraph is beginning to be much used and very usefull.' Six years later a cable was successfully laid under the Atlantic. One should not exaggerate the pace of change in practice – at Barings indeed, the twice-weekly foreign post day remained the fulcrum of business – but there was no denying the larger trend towards the City as hub of a global commercial wheel.[2] Mid-Victorian Britain is still remembered as the workshop of the world, Isambard Kingdom Brunel still holds imaginative sway, but it was in the under-publicised accounts department that the long-term future lay.

*

The lot of the solvent Capel Court population was to man the floor during the not very onerous trading hours of eleven to three. Sometimes there was frantic activity, but very often markets went quiet, even for days at a time. That was when elderly or frail members knew to beware. Towards the end of June 1851 the Managers of the Stock Exchange called upon the Committee to do something about 'the disgraceful scene which occurred in the Stock Exchange yesterday afternoon, a football having been introduced and between one and two hundred members engaged in the play for a considerable time'. One of these unmuddied oafs was identified as Henry Brown, and the Committee duly grilled him:

> The Chairman pointed out how derogatory it was to the character of the Stock Exchange that such disorderly conduct should be pursued, and expressed his surprise that the son of a member of the Committee so much respected as Mr Chas Brown should set so bad an example to the junior members of the House, and as the Committee were determined to suppress those disgraceful practices, he hoped Mr Henry Brown would aid them in so doing and would now give them an assurance that he would not only refrain from them himself but discourage the practice whenever it was in his powers. Mr Henry Brown said he was afraid to give an absolute pledge, because on the impulse of the moment he might be led away to forget it, but he said he would endeavour to control any such impetuosity, and restrain himself as much as possible and avoid play for the future.

But if football was sidelined – though only temporarily, for in 1858 one of the Managers (James Capel) was 'grossly insulted' when he tried to blow for time – there was plenty of other work for idle hands. In January 1852 the Committee read a letter from William Hartridge complaining of the conduct of three members, who then appeared in person:

> Mr Mendes said that seeing Mr Hartridge going out of the House, with a blotting paper cap on, he could not help laughing but had no intention of giving offence.
> Mr Eykyn said he was going into the Stock Exchange, he met Mr Hartridge in New Court followed by several members, he turned round

too, but had nothing to do with putting the cap on, and he denied that he made any noise, nor did he dance before him, as alleged by Mr Hartridge.

Mr Pawle said that seeing Mr Hartridge leaving the House with a paper cap on, he followed to enjoy the fun.[3]

It was a place where, as in any school at any time, it was no fun being the odd person out.

There were few such japes in Lombard Street, where a certain gravitas remained the leading characteristic of the best sort of private banker. It was a quality epitomised by Robert Bevan, the senior partner at Barclays for many years: a keen evangelical and prominent supporter of the YMCA, he was the severest of taskmasters towards any clerk who strayed in any detail. In general, it was still bottom that counted. 'He is not a brilliant man but perhaps not the worse banker on that account. I have a high opinion of his integrity and good sense.' Thus Loyd to his father in January 1850 about Henry Norman, a new recruit to the family bank, shortly before he himself was elevated to the peerage as Lord Overstone and left active business in Lothbury.[4]

In the end, of course, it was an inherently unsustainable system. The age of steam now demanded something more than the traditional clip-clop. The joint-stock banks – in the City, the London and Westminster, the London Joint Stock, the Union Bank of London, the London and County, and the Commercial of London – provided it with a vengeance. In the ten years after the 1847 panic, they not only broadened the range of their activities but increased their deposits from almost £9m to over £43m – a phenomenal expansion of banking and credit by any yardstick and in turn reflecting the thriving national economy. 'It is impossible to foresee the consequences of the failure of one of these large establishments', warned Thomas Weguelin, a Bank of England director, in 1856.[5]

Contemporaries were slow to realise, however, that the real danger of this rapid growth of deposits turned on the accompanying growth of the call loan system, by which the joint-stock banks employed an increasing portion of their reserves at call with the City's bill brokers (or dealers); and these bill brokers, headed by Overend Gurney, in turn used that money in order to finance bills and thus make a profit on it, keeping perilously low reserves in cash while they did so. But for the joint-stock banks themselves these were golden years, above all once the private banks in 1854 at last agreed to admit them into the clearing house in Abchurch Lane. The joint-stock banks could now compete on equal terms for the country agency business and, quite apart from the symbolism of the climb-down, there was no doubt which way the contest was going.[6] The dictates of economic logic had gone against the private bankers.

Pride as much as avarice motivated the City's top merchant bankers by the 1850s. 'Half my pleasure is to work for a house which we intend to be perpetual', asserted Tom Baring in 1849, matched a few years later by Bates: 'I do not any longer work for money but having arrived at that age when it would be impossible for me to arrive at any other distinction than that of a Merchant I feel that it *is* something to be at the head of the first commercial House in the World.' Beneath this comfortable sheen of self-congratulation, there were considerable problems and tensions within the Barings partnership. They began in 1853 when Baring told Bates that he intended to devote less time to business. The reaction was typical: 'I told Mr Baring that I did not think it would answer for him to be much more absent than he is at present, that it would not look well for me as I should be supposed to be working for money which I should be sorry to have thought of me.' It was also decided at this time that young Edward ('Ned') Baring should enter the firm, in effect as the house's designated Baring of the future; and this likewise unsettled Bates, who while admitting that he was 'clever' also found the young man 'vain and desirous of playing the first fiddle'. There was also the disconcerting fact that most of the firm's capital came from himself and Tom Baring, and after totting up his personal fortune at just under £750,000, Bates decided in 1855 that despite advancing age there was no alternative but to stay in the partnership for at least another two years: 'If I go out the House must be dissolved and liquidated which would be a great folly. It would take 100 years to get up another House that would enjoy such unlimited confidence throughout the world.'

Bates continued to grumble:

> I ought to retire, but who is there to succeed? The Junior partners have not £20,000 capital amongst them . . . Besides the present generation of young men appear to be educated very superficially. There is a great desire to get rich without the study of labor necessary to qualify them for business. They fancy they know all about it while they have not discovered that they know nothing.[7]

That was in January 1857, but it was another seven years – complaints about extravagance, wistful talk of leaving the firm one day – until at last Bates died in harness; and perhaps he would not have wished it otherwise.

What about the business itself? There remained at Barings a significant adherence to its general merchanting tradition, supplementing the firm's financing of trade which was its bread and butter and in which it was still the City's dominant house. In 1851 its volume of acceptances ran at over £2m, by 1855 they were over £4m. Rothschilds dominated the field of foreign loans. Placing most of a £4.4m Austrian government loan in 1851, contracting for a Brazilian government loan of almost £1.5m in 1851, organising the conversion of the Belgian state debt in 1853 – all this was immensely profitable work carried out at New Court.[8] There was at this time no underwriting in the state loan business, and therefore a house needed substantial resources in order to become a permanent player in that market, quite apart from the range of quality contacts needed to secure the business in the first place.

Nevertheless, as so often with the second generation, there was not quite the same verve there once had been. John Francis (a permanent official at the Bank of England who also wrote books) was a shrewd commentator on City matters, and in 1849 he had this to say of Nathan's sons:

> His children inherit his business; but they do not inherit his position in the stock-market. They are competitors for government loans; but though with the name remains a certain amount of its former power, they do not appear willing to entertain the extensive and complicated business in which their father delighted.[9]

Amongst other merchant banks, increasingly powerful operators were R. Raphael & Sons, under the astute leadership of Henry Lewis Raphael from the mid-1850s. Schröders was also making solid if somewhat anonymous progress mainly in international trade finance, though in 1853 it undertook its first foreign bond issue, for the Matanzas and Sabanilla Railroad Co. of Cuba.[10] A fellow countryman of John Henry Schröder was Alexander Kleinwort, who had served a lengthy mercantile apprenticeship in Havana and come to realise that the serious money was to be made not in the physical trade of sugar and other commodities but in the *financing* of that trade. Kleinwort & Cohen was in business by 1855, and within three years, now as Drake, Kleinwort & Cohen, it had a capital of £200,000 and was poised for future prosperity.

But perhaps the most striking success story around this time was Hambros. Coming from a well-established Copenhagen mercantile family, Carl Joachim Hambro was permanently based in the City from 1839 and, despite a tendency to lengthy periods of depression, managed to expand the business steadily; other City houses were slow to pick up on Scandinavian accepting business. The successful management in 1851 of a Piedmontese loan (against ferocious Rothschild attacks) was the crucial breakthrough, and the rest followed. His son Everard was educated at Trinity College, Cambridge, and in 1866 married a daughter of Martin Tucker Smith, partner at Smith Payne & Smiths of 1 Lombard Street. The antisocial Carl Joachim never became a City insider, but his son would more than make up for it.[11]

Finally, of these rising merchant bankers, there was the American George Peabody. A bachelor of miserly personal habits, he scrutinised newspapers with the greatest care but had no interest in literature; he once confessed that during all his time in London he had never visited either the Royal Academy or the National Gallery; in 1851 it was twelve years since he had been absent from his office for two consecutive business days; and not long afterwards he expressed his fear that 'we are all making money rather too fast, and not altogether by the "sweat of the brow" as stated in the Scriptures, as the lot of man'. Yet Peabody was also a great host, one of the acknowledged centres of American social life in London, and (in later life anyway) prone to considerable acts of philanthropy. During the summer of the Great Exhibition he held on 4 July a vast, much talked-about dinner and ball at Willis' Rooms, and among the guests was the aged Duke of Wellington. But not everyone in the City appreciated him, and in July 1853 Bates recorded some remarks recently made to him on 'Change by Daniel Meinertzhagen, by now the leading partner at Huths:

> 'Your countryman Peabody is a great boaster & does not do it cleverly. I was there the other day when he opened his book & said there my payments this month are £500,000'. This adds Mr M is out of proportion with his means, for in 1851 he invited me to the opera [one of Peabody's favourite forms of entertaining] & after to take a glass of negus with him, when P said, how much do you think I am worth? Mr M said, I suppose you may have over £100,000. Yes replied Mr P, rather more. I had considerably more but lost some of it & which I have now newly recovered.

Towards the end of his life, Bates himself would reflect that Peabody was one of the few people with whom he had ever quarrelled, and referred to his 'want of sincerity' and 'fondness of show'.[12]

Huths as well as Barings were well established in the Anglo-American trade by the early 1850s, and there is no doubt that George Peabody & Co. was emerging fast as competition, being an especial irritant to the other firms in the field through its practice of actively seeking accounts at a lower than usual commission rate. What really seems to have motivated Peabody was the desire, following the ignominious demise of the three Ws in 1837 and the collapse of American credit soon afterwards, to establish a permanent American presence in the City. 'It has almost become a by-word among the English that no American House in London can long sustain their credit, that sooner or later all must fail', he reflected in 1851, adding that 'we not only, from self pride, but from feelings of Patriotism wish and intend with the smiles of Providence and the exercise of our best judgment and discretion, to refute hereafter such remarks'. But permanence demanded the exercise of foresight, and during the early 1850s he was much preoccupied by the search for a suitable American partner who could be trained to take the firm on beyond his own retirement or death. At last in 1854 he hit on Junius Spencer Morgan. He was forty-one years old and an established, highly regarded merchant in New

England who had impressed Peabody by his demeanour at a dinner for the new American Minister in London. That same year the firm moved to more commodious premises at 22 Old Broad Street, its capital stood at almost £500,000, and the all-American future seemed assured.[13]

Then in October 1857 the City braced itself for another full-blown financial and commercial crisis, largely the result of the collapse of banks and railroads in the United States. As much in the firing line as any of the bill brokers was George Peabody & Co., whose correspondents were either failing or finding it next to impossible to remit payments:

> I hope my house will weather the storm. I *think* it will do so even though so many in debt to me cannot pay. If I fail I will bear it like a man. In my conscience I know I never deceived or injured another human being . . . Nearly all the American houses in Europe have suspended operations and nothing but great strength can save them. It is the loss of *credit* of my house I fear.

Peabody's problems, as admitted in this letter to a favourite niece, were not helped by the attitude of Barings, which had extended him credit of £150,000 and during the crisis was relentless in pressing for repayment. He was compelled to go to the Bank of England to ask for assistance, some hard bargaining ensued, and after several days during which Peabody trawled the City for appropriate lenders and guarantors it was eventually announced that the Bank of England would advance his firm £250,000 and other banks (headed by the Union Joint Stock, with the London and Westminster refusing) £550,000. In the event Peabody needed a total of only £300,000, and that was soon repaid, as American credit recovered surprisingly quickly from the crisis.

Nevertheless, it had been a traumatic episode, and over the next few months he gradually eased out of business, so that by the spring of 1858 it was Junius Morgan who effectively headed the firm. That left him free to concentrate on philanthropy for the rest of his life, and in March 1862 Bates recorded without comment that 'Geo Peabody has given 150,000 pounds for the benefit of the poor of London.'[14] So were born the famous model dwellings, fortress-like monuments to one of the City's more admirable adopted sons, even if he did occasionally boast over a glass of negus.

Others also suffered during the autumn of 1857. Francis Bennoch was head of the firm of Bennoch, Twentyman & Rigg, who operated as wholesale silk dealers in London and manufacturers in Manchester. The previous year he had struck up a friendship with Nathaniel Hawthorne, the well-known novelist now doubling as American consul in Liverpool, who had found him 'a kindly, jolly, frank, off-hand, very good fellow', in his mid-forties and living prosperously at Blackheath. Hawthorne had lunched convivially with him at the premises in Wood Street ('a very narrow street, insomuch that one has to press close up against the wall, to escape being grazed when a cart is passing') and afterwards been given a tour of the extensive establishment, being shown 'innumerable packages of ribbons, and other silk manufactures, and all sorts of silks, from the raw thread to the finest fabrics'. Now, on 9 November 1857, Bennoch's firm failed for just over £250,000. 'Of all men on earth I had rather this misfortune should have happened to any other; but I hope and think Bennoch has sturdiness and buoyancy enough to rise up beneath it.'

A week later Hawthorne was asked to pay a visit to Wood Street. 'The interior of the warehouse looked confused and dismal; two or three clerks seemed to be taking an account of stock . . . Then appeared Mr Rigg, the Junior partner, looking haggard and anxious.' Rigg escorted Hawthorne upstairs to the dining room: 'Everywhere the packages of silk were piled up, and ranged on shelves, in paper-boxes and otherwise; a rich stock, but which had brought ruin with it.' Upstairs, Bennoch 'looked paler', while Twentyman, the middle partner, 'appeared as much or more depressed than his fellows in misfortune, and to bear it with a greater degree of English incommunicativeness and reserve'. The four of them, however, ate a hearty enough dinner: 'It was roast beef, and a boiled apple-pudding, and – which I was glad to see, my heart being heavy – a decanter of sherry and another of port.'

There was to be a happy ending to this mercantile story. The firm did repay its creditors, it did get going again, and Bennoch himself flourished into old age. But for Hawthorne at the time, the episode caused a sharply diminished pleasure in London life. A fortnight later he found himself walking down Cheapside, a prey to the darkest thoughts:

> It is really an ungladdened life, to wander through these huge, thronged ways, over a pavement foul with mud, ground into it by a million of footsteps; jostling against people who do not seem to be individuals, but all one mass.[15]

*

Another American, Henry Adams, many years later recalled the world capital, almost in spite of itself, that he encountered in 1858: 'London was still London. A certain style dignified its grime; heavy, clumsy, arrogant, purse-proud, but not cheap; insular but large; barely tolerant of an outside world, and absolutely self-confident . . . Every one seemed insolent, and the most insolent structures in the world were the Royal Exchange and the Bank of England.' The Old Lady was indeed long renowned for a certain haughtiness, and after 1857 she was particularly frosty towards the discount houses, which were widely blamed for, if not causing the crisis, certainly exacerbating matters. These houses now included a joint-stock company, the National Discount formed in 1856, but the temperature truly dipped in relation to Overend Gurney. Not only was Samuel Gurney no more, but his capable if unpopular deputy David Barclay Chapman (known in the City as 'Gurney's Liar') had also departed the scene, retiring at the end of 1857 with a handsome payoff following a blistering attack upon him by *The Times* for his irresponsible conduct during the crisis.[16] Control passed to the younger generation, chiefly in the persons of the over-ambitious Henry Edmund Gurney and the extravagant David Ward Chapman, and the traditional Quaker virtues began to recede.

It was undoubtedly with Overend Gurney in mind that the Bank in March 1858 made it clear that it would no longer offer discount facilities to the City's bill brokers – a controversial policy from the start, being carried only by the casting vote of the governor. It was intended to make the discount houses more self-reliant, but *The Economist* was not alone in expressing concern about its inflexible implications in times of monetary strain. Inevitably the Bank, with Bonamy Dobree as governor from 1859 after two years as deputy, came under pressure to reverse it; and by the beginning of April 1860, with Bank rate up to 4½ and the onset of a certain tightness, *The Economist* (by this time under the notable editorship of Walter Bagehot) was calling for a truce. It did not deny that before the new rule the bill brokers had been 'perpetually competing with the Bank' and 'reducing its profits at the very time that they were relying on it for their safety', but it wanted a compromise, on the grounds that the credit of the bill brokers was being affected, potentially very damaging in the event of a crisis.[17] They were wise words, but Overend Gurney at the Corner House by now felt that words alone were not sufficient to concentrate minds.

The story of a momentous episode unfolds in Dobree's diary, begin-ning with a flat but meaningful entry on Thursday 12 April: 'Barclays, Overends & Barnetts with Sheppard & Pelly & Co. took away on the 9, 10, & 11th £1,600,000 in 1,000 Notes which Notes have not returned to the Bank.' In other words, Overend Gurney had mobilised its (largely Quaker) connections, including the stockbrokers Sheppard, Pelly & Allcard, to make major withdrawals from the Bank, all in £1,000 notes. By the end of the week Daniell of Mullens (the government brokers) was telling Dobree 'that on the Stock Ex Messrs Gurney & Co. avow that they took from the Bank a very large Amount of Bank Notes early in the Week with a view to reduce the Bank's Reserve to the lowest possible Amount'. The stakes of the game became clear on the Monday, when Dobree was informed through an intermediary that 'if the Rule excluding the dis Houses should be modified, the Notes withdrawn & still locked up in Lombard St shall be returned to the Bank "*tonight*"'. However, Dobree recorded, 'the Governors refuse to entertain any such proposal'.

The next morning there arrived on his desk a sinister anonymous message: 'Overends can pull out every note you have, from actual knowledge the writer can inform you that with their own family assistance they can nurse *seven* millions!!' But such threats were too late, for that same day Dobree heard that the game was over: 'Overend, Gurney & Co. have told Mr Masterman [John Masterman, a prominent banker and Tory MP for the City] that if it would be considered a conciliatory Step on their part, they will at once return to the Bank the Million, Five Hundred & Fifty Thousand Bank Notes locked up in Lombard St. They are sorry for what they have done.' The penitent bill brokers may have been affected by the imminence of a parliamentary question to be asked on the subject of the sudden sharp drop in the Bank's reserve, but in any case the notes were duly returned to Threadneedle Street on the Wednesday, 'identical but all cut into Halves'. The following day a relieved Court 'approved of the Course pursued by the Gov^rs in this disreputable Affair'. It had been quite a run-in, showing the Old Lady's mettle in a trial of nerves as much as strength, and auguring ill for a particular discount house should it ever come running to that elderly female for help. 'I do hope you will remain obstinately firm against these tricksters', one of the Bank directors had written to Dobree during the episode, and no one on the Court would have disputed the epithet.[18]

How, as it endeavoured to reconcile the functions of commercial and central banking, was that Court chosen? If old-style personal recommendation still counted for everything, nevertheless, partly following reforms in 1848, the system tended to produce a more able, usually university-educated Bank director than had once been the case. None was abler, at least on paper, than the director whom the City quickly tagged 'the fortunate youth'. Dobree in January 1858 recorded how 'Mr W. Goschen called to ask if there would be any objection to his son being considered a candidate for the Bank direction'. George Joachim Goschen, educated at Rugby and Oxford and a partner in the family firm of Frühling & Goschen, was twenty-seven when he became a director. Three years later he published *The Theory of the Foreign Exchanges*, an overnight City classic which went into its fourth edition in as many years. His commercial and intellectual reputation made, he was returned unopposed as a Liberal MP for the City in 1863, having been put forward by two fellow directors of the Bank; and two years later he became vice president of the Board of Trade, which compelled him to retire from business and relinquish his directorship of the Bank and where he nobly refrained from grumbling that he had been set to govern packages. Goschen's relationship with the City would remain intimate if not always happy.[19]

Few of the mid-Victorian directors of the Bank of England had more than tenuous links with the aristocracy, and the great majority were solid, socially unpretentious members of the London and Home Counties *haute bourgeoisie*.[20] Nor were they on the whole stunningly wealthy: of the twenty-three elected between 1833 and 1847, over half left fortunes of under £100,000. Nevertheless, these directors were significant figures in the national picture, for quite apart from their seats in the Bank direction and their individual mercantile bases a fair proportion of them were also MPs, no fewer than ten of them in 1863. Some no doubt sought parliamentary seats for reasons of social prestige, but others were highly conscious that, with monetary matters so often high on the political agenda, it was important for the Bank to be adequately represented in the Commons. These MPs were predominantly on the Liberal side, yet it is a striking fact of the period that easily the worst relations between Westminster and City were those between Gladstone and the Bank.

The man who embodied the financial conscience of the Victorians first became Chancellor at the end of 1851, and by 1854 he was displaying what Morley called 'a toughness, stiffness, and sustained anger that greatly astonished Threadneedle Street'. The bone of contention was recondite enough – involving certain well-enshrined conventions allowing the Bank to profit through the timing of payments to it of dividends on the national debt – but for Gladstone the abuse symbolised the continuing existence of 'old corruption' at the heart of the financial system. And though he won this particular battle, thereafter he never forgave the Bank for what he regarded as its obstructive attitude. By 1859 he was back at the Treasury, the object of considerable personal mistrust in the City. 'There never was a Chancellor of the Exchequer whose course it was less easy to predict', W. G. Prescott wrote to Overstone, while Overstone himself declared that 'surely Gladstone is a most dangerous finance Minister'. During the winter of 1860–1 he waged another fierce conflict with the Bank, this time over the price paid by government for the management of the public debt, and once again the Bank gave way amidst much thinly veiled animosity. At the same time Gladstone also succeeded, again against Bank opposition, in establishing the Post Office Savings Banks. In a late fragment he would recall his ulterior motive: 'I had an object of first-rate importance, which has been attained: to provide the minister of finance with a strong financial arm, and to secure his independence of the City by giving him a large and certain command of money.'[21]

Ultimately, though, the irony of Gladstone's intervention was to be writ large. The Huskissonian return to gold became a City sacred cow; the Peelite Bank Charter Act in practice, if not by design, gave the Bank a permanent and unchallengeable pivotal role; and now the Gladstonian pursuit of balanced budgets, a pursuit aimed in part at freeing governments from dependence on the Bank, would become a hallowed orthodoxy that in time the City even believed was its own creation and certainly was prepared to defend at all costs. Gladstone may have regarded the Bank of England parlour as like a university common room – narrowing the point of view – but over the years successive governments could hope to escape from a certain subserviency to the City only if they were able to fight the good fight on the City's own ground, however 'narrow' and technical that might be.

*

May 1866 – a date forever associated with Overend Gurney. Back at the start of the decade, not all country bankers had been impressed by the rock-like foundations of that house, and the Liverpool Union Bank was particularly sceptical, pressing its London agents, Barnett, Hoare & Co., to make enquiries. Lombard Street breathed reassurance:

> We have had constant and most confidential interviews with Messrs Overend & Co. during the last few weeks.
> We believe they have exercised great prudence in their management, that they have very materially reduced their liabilities and are prepared for a much heavier pressure than it seems possible should come upon them.
> We know they are keeping a very large reserve (as much as a million and a half at least) so placed that it is at hand any hour.

That was on 15 February 1861. Soon afterwards, amidst false rumours sweeping the City that Overend Gurney had stopped payment, Dobree (in his last weeks as governor) tried to give another anxious correspondent as precise a picture as possible:

> The house referred to has made, it is said, heavy losses during the last 18 months, – to the extent of £300m [i.e. '*mille*', the old-fashioned term for thousand] @ £400m, – and is considered to have as much more locked up in inconvertible securities: it does a rather reckless business and is continually incurring losses. It is however believed at the same time, that the *profits* are commensurate, and that the capital is ample enough to meet any contingency. The uncertain mode in which the business is conducted is the subject of general censure.[22]

Dobree, for one, had clearly not yet heard of the return to prudent management at the Corner House.

Over the next few years, the business there continued to be conducted by Henry Edmund Gurney and David Ward Chapman, and someone who encountered them both was Frank Wilde, operating in a tiny office in Mincing Lane on behalf of a firm of Liverpool tea brokers. Gurney he judged 'the most thorough man of business', but 'Chapman I don't think anything of at all and never did'. In August 1864 he found himself reporting a dispute, involving 'not the pleasantest' of interviews with Chapman:

They were evidently precipitate and I conveyed to them that it would only have been within the bounds of courtesy of commerce for *us* to offer to take up our bills . . .

Chapman distinctly gave me to understand that they wanted the drafts taken up as they were a dead lock to them. There is no doubt that their course has been most unusual and I told them so. It was however no use to cut off one's nose to spite one's face and they volunteered that if we sent in acceptances of ours for £40,000 they would discount them.[23]

The sensible minnow knows when to cease protest, but it was all far removed from those standards of conduct once inculcated by old Sam Gurney.

The following July, encouraged by the recent example of the Morrison textile business successfully transforming itself into the Fore Street Warehouse Company, the firm of Overend Gurney went public. The new company was to pay £250,000 in goodwill, the capital was to be £5m, and Chapman was to retire from the business. The prospectus promised prospective shareholders that 'the Directors will give their zealous attention to the cultivation of business of a first-class character only'. Details of past profits, or of assets and liabilities to be transferred, were conspicuously absent.

City reaction was mixed. The partners of Prescotts declared that they had 'no intention' of applying for any shares, but expressed satisfaction that 'the family of Chapman is to be expunged from the concern', not least since 'the present Gentleman of that name is considered to want steadiness of character'. Another private banker, Robert Fowler, was just about sanguine: 'It is an extraordinary change. They have lost a good deal of money, but they must have a splendid business at bottom.' *The Economist* had its silent qualms, and laid implicit stress on the fact that accounts would at last be available; but to the uninitiated reader there was comfort in that eminent journal's assertion not only that 'Overend's must have much money left with them', but that 'as to the management, there ought to be, and must be, great traditional knowledge and skill in a concern which has been so very profitable so very long, and where such vast sums have gradually been made'. The *Bankers' Magazine*, the great proponent of joint-stock enterprise in all financial matters, was wholly enthusiastic: 'Without laying any claim to the gift of prophecy, we may confidently anticipate that the position of the new company will be relatively as high as the standing of the house to whose business it succeeds.'

The terms of the issue were attractive, the name was a great one, and the shares went quickly to a premium. In August 1865 the customary question arose of settlement and quotation by the Stock Exchange Committee. Usually a formality, on this occasion the company's broker,

Samuel Gurney Sheppard, was required to give evidence about some aspects of the flotation:

> The managing directors [two of them, including Henry Edmund Gurney] were to receive £5000 per annum between them, and also ⅕th of the residue of the nett profit after 7% was obtained. It could not be supposed that they would undertake the duties for £5000 a year alone . . . Any one could have seen the articles of association before subscribing, in fact he – Mr Sheppard – had shown them to a great number of persons.

There ensued 'a very long discussion' before James Bury Capel (son of James Capel) moved that the application be granted, and this was carried by eight votes to one.[24] *Caveat emptor*, but had the buyer been adequately warned?

It was during the winter that Gurney proposed to borrow money from Glyns at a special rate on some securities which seemed to that firm's Bertram Currie of doubtful value. Currie dared to express misgivings, to which Gurney retorted indignantly: 'Do you presume to question the credit of Overend, Gurney, and Co.?' By early 1866 the City as a whole had the shakes, not just about Overend Gurney but about the whole mesh of finance companies created during the 1863 boom. Several had intimate connections with Overend Gurney, including one, the Contract Corporation, that went into liquidation at the end of March. War on the Continent also threatened, and by mid-April Mathesons was reporting serious 'want of confidence in monetary circles' and 'stocks of all descriptions being eagerly pressed for sale'.

The moment of truth soon came. On Wednesday 9 May, the City report for *The Times* began starkly: 'The panic continues to increase in intensity, and this has been one of the worst days yet experienced.' Thursday the 10th paid for all. 'Very fine & hot,' noted the young Richard Biddulph Martin of the private bank Martins, as he found himself gratifyingly close to the centre of things:

> Usual work. Not much doing till about ½ past 2. Birkbeck came in to say that Overend Gurney & Co. had stopped. K. Hodgson came in & said it was for £10,000,000, with £3,500,000 unsecured. We had £50,000 with them . . . They could get no assistance from the Bank.

The first informant was presumably Robert Birkbeck, the other managing director of Overend Gurney; and the second Kirkman Hodgson, a recent governor of the Bank and senior partner of the merchants Finlay, Hodgson & Co. The formal announcement of the failure was made soon afterwards, probably waiting on the closure of the Stock Exchange, and another private banker, Currie, wrote in laconic style to his father: 'The fatal day, the long expected day has come & O. G. has put up his shutters. For some weeks I have ventured to predict this event . . . The panic is pretty smart &

beats 47 or 57 . . . I think some of the new Banks will have a hard time & financial companies & contractors must go right & left.' It was indeed the third big crisis in twenty years, and all shared the immediate fear of Mathesons that 'the failures will not stop here, so many houses all over the Country depending upon that Company for their supplies'.[25]

Two retrospective questions at once arose. Why had the mighty Overend Gurney failed? Why had the Bank of England let it go down? The answer to the first did not publicly emerge for another three and a half years, when the directors of the company stood trial for having published a false prospectus – false in the sense that the firm had been bankrupt *before* it went public. Prosecuting counsel's opening speech contained a memorable and revealing passage:

> Whether stimulated by zeal or enthusiasm, or whether actuated by that insane cupidity which was too largely a characteristic of the present day, instead of adhering to the plain, honest, and rational system which had been adopted by the old members of the firm, they plunged into the most extravagant speculation . . . Not content with being mere money dealers or bill discounters, they became partners in various undertakings. They covered the sea with their ships, ploughed up the land with their iron roads.

It was all true. Back in 1859 the new generation holding the reins at Overend Gurney had transformed the firm's business beyond recognition, becoming shipbuilders, shipowners, grain traders, ironmasters, railway financiers, and seemingly much else besides. These were lockup investments, often poorly judged, and by 1861 the firm was in deep trouble. Undoubtedly large doses of vanity, ambition and greed played their part in this fateful diversification; but perhaps there was also some sense, as one of its partners had told Dobree at the end of 1859, in which the Bank of England's new, restrictive policy affected the firm's core business sufficiently to give such diversification added appeal. After 1861 the firm tried to recover, but its management was not up to the task, and problems were further compounded by an over-speculative approach to financing the new finance houses thrown up by the boom. Conversion in 1865 to a limited liability company, following the failure of merger talks with the National Discount Co., was a final desperate throw – a bold and in a way honest attempt by Gurney to shed extraneous commitments, return to the straight and narrow of discounting business, and end the whole Chapman era. It was implicitly recognised as such by the jurors in 1869, who acquitted Gurney and his fellow directors, but the attempt itself came too late to save the Corner House in the troubled monetary conditions of 1866.

Should the Bank have stepped in? Once it became clear that spring that Overend Gurney required assistance to survive, it appointed a committee (Hodgson and two private bankers) to scrutinise the books. The three wise men determined that the business was rotten beyond redemption, and no helping hand was held out.[26] Yet remembering the intensely strained relations between the Bank and Overend Gurney between 1857 and 1860, culminating in the infamous £1m gun held at the Bank's head, it is hard to feel that the Bank in 1866 was making a strictly financial decision. Overend Gurney had once very much been members of the club – by this stage far from East Anglian upstarts – but it was a club that would never condone such bare-faced tactics directed against its ex officio chairman. *That* in the end was the new generation's most grievous misjudgement.

Their transgression of these unwritten rules was a mite academic as Black Friday dawned and City commuters read the confident prediction in *The Times* that the shock of Overend Gurney's failure 'will, before this evening closes, be felt in the remotest corners of the kingdom'. Among those travelling in from south of the river was Charles Churchill, Jnr, a timber broker like his father, and on arrival he somewhat breathlessly found 'City great excitement, Lombard S^t in uproar, talk of runs on nearly all the banks, the English Joint Stock stops'. Diarists and commentators vied with each other. 'Great confusion all day, the streets were crowded and almost impassable', recorded Martin, while according to the partners of Prescotts (who were falsely rumoured to have sold their business to a joint-stock bank), it was 'a day of most intense excitement and panic in the City, in fact such a day has never been experienced in the memory of any one'. *The Economist* thought Lombard Street 'looked more like a country fair than its usual self', *The Times* described 'throngs heaving and tumbling about' as by noon 'the tumult became a rout' and 'the doors of the most respectable Banking-Houses were besieged'. In the course of the day several stoppages were announced, rumours of many others gathered credence, and so seriously was the situation taken that 'even at Lady Downshire's ball', according to Charlotte de Rothschild, 'everybody spoke of the immense City failures'.[27]

Help, as was becoming the custom on these set-piece occasions, was already at hand. 'A complete collapse of credit in Lombard St and a greater amount of anxiety than I have ever seen', scribbled Bagehot that morning in a hasty note to Gladstone (nearing the end of a seven-year stint as Chancellor), and Gladstone stilled his Peelite doubts and took the cue. His diary entry for the Friday characteristically records the process:

> From 2¼ till past midnight I was except 20m. occupied in receiving a stream of City magnates and deputations on the panic, in considering with Cardwell, Goschen, Ld Halifax [the former Sir Charles Wood], the Gov. & Dep. Gov., & Mr Hodgson, the proper course to take, & after obtaining all requisite information, arranging the letters & making the necessary

announcements in the H. of Commons. Although the case was perplexing at the onset, & will be so in the *hereafter*, yet when we obtained the facts of the operations of the day our course became at once perfectly clear.

The paramount operational fact was that on a day of the severest credit panic, the Bank of England lent to banks, discount houses and merchants the phenomenal amount of £4m; but it is clear that the pressure on Gladstone to authorise suspension yet again of Peel's Act came not from the governor, a linen manufacturer called Lancelot Holland, but from the successive deputations, which included country bankers as well as 'City magnates'. Again as usual, it was essentially psychological relief that was craved, and once more the trick worked.

The next morning began in a mood of watchfulness rather than fear, and by the end of the day Martin was able to record that 'the government allowing the Bank to issue Notes at 10% gave relief & the panic subsided to a great extent'.[28] The worst of the crisis was over. Things gradually returned more or less to normal, but it was a long haul: Bank rate stayed at 10 per cent until August (partly in the context of war between Prussia and Austria, partly also against a background of agitation at home for further parliamentary reform), and there was a handful of major banking stoppages. Several new firms arose from the ashes of Overend Gurney, but all agreed that, for good or ill, there would never be another Corner House.

In September occurred a significant postscript to the crisis. Addressing the Bank's proprietors, Lancelot Holland looked back with pride:

> This house exerted itself to the utmost – and exerted itself most success-fully – to meet the crisis. We did not flinch from our post. When the storm came upon us, on the morning on which it became known that the house of Overend and Co. had failed, we were in as sound and healthy a position as any banking establishment could hold, and on that day and throughout the succeeding week we made advances which would hardly be credited . . . We would not flinch from the duty which we conceived was imposed upon us of supporting the banking community, and I am not aware that any legitimate application made for assistance to this house was refused.

In a leading article headed 'The Great Importance of the Late Meeting of the Proprietors of the Bank of England', Bagehot at *The Economist* pounced on this statement as a welcome acceptance of the doctrine that the Bank was lender of last resort and thus responsible for maintaining 'the sole banking reserve of the country'. It was not a reading of the governor's remarks that found favour with Thomson Hankey, a West India merchant who had been on the Court since 1835, was governor in the early 1850s, and besides being a member of the Political Economy Club was MP for Peterborough:

The 'Economist' newspaper has put forth what in my opinion is the most mischievous doctrine ever broached in the monetary or banking world in this country; viz. that it is the proper function of the Bank of England to keep money available at all times to supply the demands of bankers who have rendered their own assets unavailable. Until such a doctrine is repudiated by the banking interest, the difficulty of pursuing any sound principle of banking in London will be always very great. But I do not believe that such a doctrine as that bankers are justified in relying on the Bank of England to assist them in time of need is generally held by the bankers in London.

Hankey was mistaken, for in the keen debate that ensued the balance of banking opinion came down on Bagehot's side.[29] There had been too many crises in too short a time for a 'purist' interpretation of the 1844 Act any longer to be tenable: the banking department of the Bank of England could not, in short, behave like any other bank. For a quarter of a century the moral rigour of the old currency school had been a perhaps noble attempt to evade inexorable banking realities, and now at last its insidious sway was unofficially declared over and out.

CHAPTER EIGHT

Ties that Bind

Detached observers were conscious by the early 1870s that the City was entering a new phase. In January 1872 the *Quarterly Review* sought to pin down and explain what was happening. After referring to 'the great expansion of the trade of the country during the last fifteen, but particularly during the last ten, years, and the rapid way in which, for political and mercantile reasons, London is becoming the financial centre of the Old and New World', it went on:

> Political distrust and revolution in France, the absence of unity and coherence between North and South Germany, and the want of a great Teutonic financial metropolis, combine with the unquestioned stability and credit of English institutions, the benefit of firm and equal laws, and the facilities and inducements of the freest ports, the lowest tariff, and the cheapest manufactures in the world, to render London the place of ultimate settlement of the largest part of the business of both hemispheres. Hence the accumulation here of foreign capital and the growth of a powerful class of banks and financial houses.

This analysis rightly if only implicitly identified the Franco-Prussian War of 1870 as a turning point. Its effects were manifold: the non-convertibility of the franc for eight years confirmed sterling as the unrivalled medium of settlement; the Bank of France's suspension of specie payments left London as the only world bullion market; the Paris Bourse's sharp loss of business; a flow of 'hot money' to London; and a human drain that included the ambitious, not always scrupulous international financier Baron Émile d'Erlanger, who took offices from the London and Westminster at 43 Lothbury and proceeded to lay the foundations of the firm Émile Erlanger & Co. Following the pattern of the 1860s, many other foreign houses were also establishing a foothold in the City, notably Crédit Lyonnais and Deutsche Bank.[1]

However, there were two other dimensions to the story. One was the importance of the continuing communications revolution, so that by 1872, for example, the City was in instant telegraphic contact with Tokyo and Melbourne as well as Europe and the States. Related to this was the increasing – and rapid – internationalisation of the money market, the waning of the inland bill (particularly from the 1880s) and the rise of the foreign bill on London, by which the City's discount and accepting houses financed ever-greater volumes of international trade.[2] More than ever, then, the City of London had become by the early 1870s indispensable. More thoughtful observers wondered what the implications of this seemingly gratifying development might be.

No one faced these implications more squarely than Walter Bagehot, the man whom G. M. Young would designate as *Victorianum maxinte*, 'most Victorian of the Victorians', the man 'whose influence, passing from one fit mind to another, could transmit, and can still impart, the most precious element in Victorian civilization, its robust and masculine sanity'. In May 1873, six years after the appearance of *The English Constitution*, Bagehot published his classic treatise *Lombard Street*, subtitled *A Description of the Money Market*. Its tone from the start was memorable and authoritative: 'The briefest and truest way of describing Lombard Street is to say that it is by far the greatest combination of economical power and economical delicacy that the world has ever seen.' Underlying all the detached analysis of that phenomenon was an almost passionate argument that the case of Overend Gurney and developments since then, above all the demise of Paris as a counterweight to London and the sheer volume of the City's liabilities as well as assets, meant that 'we must examine the system on which these great masses of money are manipulated, and assure ourselves that it is safe and right'. However:

> It is not easy to rouse men of business to the task. They let the tide of business float before them; they make money or strive to do so while it passes, and they are unwilling to think where it is going. Even the great collapse of Overends, though it caused a panic, is beginning to be forgotten. Most men of business think – 'Anyhow this system will probably last my time. It has gone on a long time, and is likely to go on still'. But the exact point is, that it has *not* gone on a long time. The collection of these immense sums in one place and in few hands is perfectly new.

Or put another, even more ominous way: 'Money will not manage itself, and Lombard Street has a great deal of money to manage.'

In a series of pithy, often wounding sentences Bagehot trained his particular guns on the Old Lady herself: 'No one in London ever dreams of questioning the credit of the Bank, and the Bank never dreams that its own credit is in danger. Somehow everybody feels the Bank is sure to come right.' Moreover: 'The Bank directors are not trained bankers; they were not bred to the trade, and do not in general give the main power of their minds to it. They are merchants, most of whose time and most of whose real mind are occupied in making money in their own business and for themselves.' And:

> We have placed the exclusive custody of our entire banking reserve in the hands of a single board of directors not particularly trained for the duty – who might be called 'amateurs', – who have no particular interest above other people in keeping it undiminished – who acknowledge no obligation to keep it undiminished – who have never been told by any great statesman or public authority that they are so to keep it or that they have anything to do with it – who are named by and are agents for a proprietary which would have a greater income if it *was* diminished, – who do not fear, and who need not fear, ruin, even if it were all gone and wasted.

What was to be done? In the core of his book, Bagehot suggested 'three remedies'. Firstly, that 'there should be a clear understanding between the Bank and the public that, since the Bank hold our ultimate banking reserve, they will recognise and act on the obligations which this implies'. Secondly, that in terms of improving the government of the Bank, 'we should diminish the "amateur" element; we should augment the trained banking element; and we should ensure more constancy in the administration'. Thirdly, that 'we should look at the rest of our banking system, and try to reduce the demands on the Bank as much as we can'.[3] Bagehot did not expect a warm reception for his arguments. 'In the *street* itself I fear I shall be sent into financial exile as neither the Directors of the Bank of England nor the Private Bankers nor the Joint Stock nor the Bill brokers will much like my remarks on them.' In fact the book was speedily reprinted, though it seems to have inspired little or any public discussion on the part of the City, nor even elicited a review in the *Bankers' Magazine*.

On the question of public acceptance of the Bank's public duties, it is extremely difficult to be precise about the effect of Bagehot's stirring words, though most historians of the British financial system have agreed that in some sense they did mark a turning point, that thereafter it was not possible even to pretend that the Bank was like other banks and could, when it came to it, evade its role as lender of last resort in time of crisis. Nevertheless, neither within nor without the Bank was this formally articulated at the time, and only future responses to specific contingencies would reveal how far the Bank was really moving along the road towards what would be called central banking. As for ending of the cult of the amateur in the Bank's direction, with an attendant wish for a permanent deputy governor and a willingness to break the taboo of not allowing commercial bankers (as opposed to merchant bankers) on the Court, Bagehot seems to have met a brick wall. If the Bank of England considered his reform proposals, we do not know about it. Certainly there was no City agitation along these lines.

What we do have, however, is the reaction to *Lombard Street* of one of the more independent-minded Bank directors, William Lidderdale. He wrote to his partners at Rathbones in Liverpool in October 1873, against a City background of alarm and despondency caused by bad news from both America and Europe:

> That our Banking and Monetary system in this Country is of an over-complicated & interdependent nature which makes difficulties in any important quarter a serious matter for every one, is a fact upon which none of us are likely to differ. The system of taking enormous sums on deposit at call or short notice, on which interest has to be paid & which there is almost a necessity to employ if serious losses are to be avoided, is one which carries risk on its face. Mr Bagehot says things *are* so & that it is useless trying to change the system, & then throws upon the Bank of England the onus of providing a reserve adequate to the needs of all its competitors as well as regular customers.

According to Lidderdale, however, the system was perfectly capable of taking the strain; he asserted that 'so far as concerns the big Joint Stock Banks, they most undoubtedly have remembered their lesson & materially improved their practice in the last 6 years'. Crisis, what crisis? When the Bank raised its rate to 7 per cent soon afterwards, prompting a certain raising of the moral eyebrows from his Liverpool correspondent, Lidderdale returned to the defence of the status quo with a robustness of language which suggested that it would be a while yet before meritocratic reform of Bank direction featured on the Threadneedle Street agenda:

> You have a very curious notion about the action of the *Merchants* who occupy seats at the Bank Court – the effect of alterations of rate is gener-ally much less felt in their business than in Banking arrangements, & people who do the latter on a large scale are much more constantly face to face with questions of self interest . . . Then many Directors, men like Morris, Latham, Hankey, Hubbard, Huth, Campbell, the present governor Greene, & Gibbs are personally in a position so little touched by anything which goes on in the Bank that it cannot be a matter of material interest what the rate is. Certainly no body of men have a right to claim superiority to even unconscious promptings of self interest, but I am bound to say that I have never seen more honest endeavours to decide in the true interest of the Bank, even when I have differed with the majority.[4]

'In the true interest of the Bank': it remained a private institution with, as Bagehot deplored, only muffled, semi-acknowledged public responsibilities.

Of Capel Court, many shared an evidently cool opinion at this time. 'Without taking a specially gloomy view of the world in general', declared *Blackwood's* in September 1876, 'we see that at least in its financial depart-ment and on the Stock Exchange, the powers of evil for the time are decidedly in the ascendant.' Many honest merchants in the City would not entirely have disagreed, perhaps among them Lidderdale, who back in 1868, following an invidious legal case involving Foster & Braithwaite, had come to the conclusion that 'the things practised daily for convenience on the Stock Exchange will rarely stand the light'. Lidderdale continued to do business through Foster & Braithwaite, but four years later was describing that firm as 'brokers whom it is necessary to keep in order, or you find yourself let in with the highest price in purchases & the lowest in sales'.

Fittingly, it was one of Foster & Braithwaite's most experienced partners, Charles Branch, who towards the end of 1876 took up the public cudgels in 'A Defence of the Stock Exchange' published in *Fraser's Magazine*. His attitude to the public was thoroughly robust: 'We, the Stock Exchange, never asked you to buy a bad security. If you thought fit to venture your money, and have lost it, so much the worse for you and your advisers.' Put another way: 'The Stock Exchange is a channel, not a filter. It argues no fault in the construction of an aqueduct that the water it conveys is often dirty.' And on this theme of what one might call a stringent passivity: 'We afford you every facility for buying what you want, and for getting what you have bought, and for selling it again if you are tired of it . . . But our duties, responsibilities, and powers end there.' There was a pleasing lack of cant about Branch's piece. He argued, as one might expect, that 'the trust confided to the members is but rarely abused', that 'principals seldom suffer loss by the failure of brokers'; but he also made the memorable assertion that 'a Stock Exchange restricted to investment business [i.e. as opposed to speculation] would be as useful and as popular as a public-house licensed only for ginger-beer'.[5]

On 20 March 1877, J. R. Yorke proposed in the House of Commons that the affairs of the Stock Exchange be scrutinised by a Royal Commission. In the course of his speech he made much of how the Stock Exchange 'encouraged speculation by admitting a low class of members with small security'. Yorke was a Tory backwoodsman, as was the seconder of the motion, Sir Charles Russell, who reserved much of his ire for the contractors of recent disastrous foreign loans to Honduras, San Domingo, Costa Rica and Paraguay, which had been characterised by the creation of artificial premiums and the unloading of stock on the public just before the price fell like a stone – behaviour that itself had led to a parliamentary select committee and inspired Anthony Trollope to write his great novel of disgust, *The Way We Live Now*, serialised during 1874–5: 'A few years ago', declared Russell, 'they would not have been allowed to put their foot within the pale of respectable society, but now-a-days respectable society not only tolerated, but toadied them, and enabled them to carry on their sinister practices.' The country gentlemen needed the support of a political heavyweight, and it came from Robert Lowe, a tough-minded former Chancellor of the Exchequer:

The point was not that people gambled on the Stock Exchange; it was that the Stock Exchange, having rules, did not act upon them in many cases, and that in others they wilfully abstained from inquiry, where they well knew if they had inquired they would have found that a syndicate had been organised, and that the whole thing was a deception, and a fraud upon the public. It was not that people had lost their money foolishly, not that they had been deluded – for that would happen as long as human nature remained the same – but it was in order that we should not have a body receiving certificates and acting upon them, and who, knowing them to be false, and knowing that the loan had not been allotted, yet proceeded to give it all the vogue it could, just as if it had been allotted, that inquiry was needed.

The Conservative government agreed to establish a Royal Commission – a decision, however, that immediately produced a hostile response from the two most eminent organs of the fourth estate. *The Economist* called it 'an attempt to give effect in a halting and hesitating manner to the vague feeling which prevails among the outside public that the Stock Exchange is primarily responsible for most of the great frauds upon investors which have been perpetrated in recent years, and that such frauds may be prevented for the future by legislation of some kind'. While as for *The Times*, it argued root and branch that the Stock Exchange machinery itself 'does not make the deceits and frauds, nor can their cure be found in a re-adjustment of the machinery', adding unequivocally that 'the remedy for fraudulent ventures is the punishment of those who concoct them'.[6]

Chairman of the Royal Commission was Lord Penzance, while those sitting on it included a significant cluster of high-level City insiders: Nathaniel (Natty) de Rothschild; Henry Hucks Gibbs; Benjamin Buck Greene, a recent governor of the Bank; and Septimus Scott, chairman of the Stock Exchange Committee itself. Evidence was taken from June 1877 to April 1878, mostly on Saturday afternoons, and over fifty witnesses faced almost 9,000 questions.

Predictably, the elephantine scale of evidence produced a mouse of a report. There were, when it came to it, only four significant recommendations put forward on a majority basis by the Royal Commission: that legislation was required in order to prevent pre-allotment dealings; that 'some public functionary' should determine certain questions relating to settlement and official quotation; that the Stock Exchange should be incorporated, as opposed to continuing as a voluntary, self-regulating institution; and that the public should be allowed to watch the members going about their business. 'Some minor proposals may be adopted', thought *The Times*, 'but they are certainly not of a kind to transform the Stock Exchange.' In particular, it saw the question of incorporation as more or less irrelevant, while as for a proposed ban on pre-allotment dealings, 'it is obvious that the prohibition would extend to honest transactions as well as to those that are dishonest, and in thus becoming offensive to the morality of the Stock Exchange would prove a dead letter'. To the even more laissez-faire, non-interventionist *Economist*, the whole thing showed once again that 'it is impossible to establish a tribunal whose verdict should effectively sift out the false from the true, and separate the doings of the honest man from those of the thief'.[7] In practice, the report elicited an almost entirely negative response from both government and the Stock Exchange itself. Pre-allotment dealings remained the norm; settlement and quotation remained wholly within the Committee's jurisdiction; the Stock Exchange remained a self-regulating, decidedly unincorporated body; and would-be public spectators remained excluded for another three-quarters of a century. The club, in short, preferred to stay just that, and the contrary trend of outside opinion was not yet strong enough to do anything about it.

It was a club, however, whose prestige in the larger world had hardly risen as a result of the events and successive inquiries of the 1870s. Such anyway was the judgement of T. H. S. Escott, leading journalist as well as author of an incisive survey published in 1879 on *England: Its People, Polity, and Pursuits*. His assessment of stockbroking is a reminder that there was a way yet to go before the stereotypical mid-twentieth-century image of the pinstriped paragon of boring respectability:

> Roughly it may be said professions in England are valued according to their stability, their remunerativeness, their influence, and their recognition by the State. These conditions may partially explain the difference which English society draws between the callings of the merchant and the stockbroker. Stockbrokers make immense fortunes; but there attaches to them a suspicion of precariousness infinitely in excess of that which, in some degree or other, necessarily attaches to all fortunes accumulated in commerce or trade.

Escott then discussed the noble heritage and the stability of being a merchant, before continuing in a delightfully malicious passage that may or may not have been pinned on the walls of Capel Court:

> It is different with the stockbroker, whose social position is so sudden that it cannot yet be looked upon as assured – whose wealth, though great, has the garish hue of luck, and the glories associated with which may dissolve themselves at any moment into thin air . . . He has acquaintances in the highest circles, and congratulates himself on being in society. But the blissful experience is not one in which his wife shares. She has to be content with all the talk, stories, and scandal of society which she hears retailed at her husband's table by the young guardsmen and other patrician guests who readily accept the invitations to a house where cook and cellar are both excellent, where the hostess and such other ladies as may be present are pretty or attractive. As a consequence of this, there is a copious stream

of male visitors at the residence of the fortunate speculator in scrip and shares, while the lord and master of the household is occupied in the City. Perhaps an uncharitable world begins to talk; at any rate, the glitter and show of the *ménage* acquire a certain flavour of Bohemianism, between which and the animating spirit of English society the only sympathy that exists is of a purely superficial kind.[8]

*

Early in 1868 a minor stir had been caused when Lord Walter Campbell, nineteen years old, decided to try his luck in the City, starting at the bottom. The possibility emerged of a junior clerkship at the London branch of Rathbones, and Lidderdale, in sardonic vein, gave his reluctant approval:

> I presume it is hardly needful to explain to the Duke of Argyll that his Son will meet in our Office with no respect of persons but what is due to merit & faithful service – that he will have to begin at the lowest step, copy letters, go out with messages, prepare tea samples for tasting, run to the Post Office & fulfil every duty required of other junior clerks. This is not very agreeable especially to young men of Ld Walter's age, but unless he is prepared to take business *ab initio* he had better try another career.

For Lord Walter and almost everyone else in the vast clerical army, daily life in the City remained manual and laborious. It is true that in 1873 the first typewriter was spotted in the Square Mile, but it would be many years before it became a standard feature of office furniture – not least because of an innate reluctance to employ women typists, eventual super-seders of the traditional male copying clerks. Barings recruited its first female member of staff in 1873, and by the mid-1880s there were ten of them, with the architect Norman Shaw thoughtfully providing a separate entrance. In general, though, they were still a somewhat *rara avis*. This conservatism was encouraged by the continuing small size of most staffs: fewer than thirty at Kleinworts by 1871, despite the firm's increasing prosperity, while five years later at Heseltine Powell, leading stockbrokers specialising in American issues, there were only seven on the books.[9] Put another way, these firms were small, self-contained worlds in which complete, indeed arbitrary power rested in the hands of the senior partner of the day, usually abetted in the fine detail by his office manager or (in the case of rather larger concerns) his departmental heads.

In 1874 the Civil Service Inquiry Commission quizzed William Newmarch, the robust and well-known secretary of Glyn Mills, about how he managed things:

> *Do you think that any system of increase of salary by seniority merely would be likely to answer?* – We could not carry on our business upon that plan at all. It would not answer. The state of efficiency at which the establish-ment has arrived (and its efficiency is generally admitted in the City) has

arisen in the largest degree from every man knowing at the end of the year he will be dealt with according to his merits; that if he has turned out inefficient his salary will either not be increased, or will very likely be temporarily reduced, or that in an extreme case the man will be sent away altogether.

And they feel a sense of justice, and know that they will be promoted if they are worth it? – That sentiment is most entirely felt, and it operates in the strongest manner.[10]

Yet it was rarely a thoroughgoing internal meritocracy, if only because of the strong element of paternalism that often obtained in practice. Nowhere did personal ties matter more than in the City's most rarefied circles, where the stakes were at their highest, the demands of trust at their most pervasive. Without a doubt one of the most prominent figures in those circles was Bertram Currie, by the 1870s the main man at Glyn Mills, which was still regarded as the leading City non-merchant bank after the Bank of England itself. Not everyone fully appreciated his qualities: 'He was extremely clever, intellectual and agreeable . . . He was an avowed and mocking Atheist, extremely satirical and cynical, and I have never dined there without hearing him pass bitter and ironical remarks upon people.' This verdict was passed after his death by the wife of a former governor of the Bank and she could have been dining at any one of three residences – in Whitehall, in Coombe near Kingston, or in Minley Manor on Bagshot Heath. Currie's intellectual authority was massive, he was regarded as a pillar of monetary orthodoxy, and in the words of Gladstone, in a rather differently couched tribute, 'he was so entirely first among the men of the City, that it is hard to measure the distance between him and the second place'.

Currie himself, as one might guess from such warmth, was a committed Liberal in his politics, but declined to take the seat in the Commons that was his for the asking – it would, he said, 'have diverted my mind from money-getting'. In the City, his closest personal tie was with Ned Baring, in the 1870s the rising but not yet dominant force at 8 Bishopsgate, the man whom Joshua Bates twenty years earlier had found 'clever' but 'unattentive' and 'fond of society'. As young men they had often rented a summer house together on Wimbledon Common; by this time they were neighbours at Coombe; and it was only natural that Baring should have been godfather to Currie's eldest son.[11] It was an imperishable connection, the sort that ensured one friend's willingness always to go the extra mile on behalf of the other.

But if Baring was 'old' City, who was 'new'? None has quite the claim of Ernest Cassel, the most remarkable presence in the Square Mile since Nathan Rothschild and a financial genius who would no more have thought of standing on 'Change than of trying to force his way through the doors of Capel Court. Biographical legends grew apace even in his lifetime, but this much seems more or less certain:[12] he was born in 1852, the son of a small-time banker in Cologne, and after serving a brief banking apprenticeship in that city, he arrived in Liverpool at the age of sixteen with only a bag of clothes and his violin. For a year he worked for a firm of grain merchants there. In April 1870 he secured a clerkship with the Anglo-Egyptian Bank in Paris. Then came the Franco-Prussian War and a speedy evacuation to London, where Cassel managed to obtain a berth with the issuing house Bischoffsheim & Goldschmidt, then at the height of its energetic, thoroughly cosmopolitan, not always scrupulous powers. Cassel quickly made a mark: he not only was instrumental in saving a Jewish firm in Constantinople in which Bischoffsheims was interested but also managed to pull some crucial legal irons out of the fire in relation to the house's notorious Central American loans. By 1874 he was manager at an annual salary of £5,000; and soon he was poised to begin his career as an independent financier owing allegiance to no one but himself. In an age of instant communications across the world and ever more mobile capital, his rapid ascent would reveal piquantly how leaden-footed the traditional arrangement of a family-based network had become. Such an ascent relied utterly on personal qualities. Not many found Cassel a likeable man – for all his undoubted integrity, he had little grace and less humour – but only a fool would doubt his judgement or his willingness to back that judgement.

Elsewhere in the City the decline of the commission merchant helped to accentuate the century's underlying shift from 'merchanting' to 'merchant banking', though that latter term itself was hardly in use until the 1890s. It was this problem of semantics that prompted Francis Hamilton to write to the Marquis of Salisbury in 1871 in the context of Sir John Lubbock's impending Bank Holiday legislation: 'There are many Houses, such as Messrs Rothschilds, Baring Brothers & Co., and my own firm Brown, Shipley & Co., who are not legally Bankers, but Merchants, tho' their transactions in Bills of Exchange, Home and Foreign Monetary operations are on a much larger scale than many Bankers.' Barings had by this time almost stopped trading in goods on its own account, though there remained for many years a house tradition that the firm was still willing to deal in anything provided that the operation was likely to yield a profit – despite the unsuccessful purchase in 1874, on behalf of the Chinese, of an iron-clad frigate from the Danish government, an exotic manoeuvre that should have stayed on the drawing board. Morgans was also more or less moving out of commodities, with the decision in 1873 to stop dealing in iron rails.[13]

For most merchant banks there was, of course, the daily bread-and-butter business of accepting. A host of City firms, large and small,

performed an accepting function, almost invariably relating to the particular part of the world with which they traded, and there was no special
mystique or splendour attached to the term 'an accepting house' until
after the First World War. Between them these firms were responsible in
the mid-1870s for guaranteeing trade bills amounting at any one time to
some £55m, a volume of acceptances outstanding which was some £20m
greater than the comparable figure forty years earlier. It was a volume
that made London the trade capital of the world and reflected partly
sterling's status as a world currency, partly the efficiency of the service
provided, but above all the simple fact that the sheer international breadth
and depth of people and firms gathered together in the City far exceeded
those of any other financial centre. It was also a competitive market –
increasingly so in the last quarter of the century – and at this stage the
market leader was far and away Barings, with Schröders and Kleinworts
very much the houses on the way up. In 1871, for example, Kleinworts'
acceptances stood at just under £3m (more than Hambros and Rothschilds
combined), providing a commission income of £94,135. The countries
responsible for the majority of that business were the United States,
Britain, Cuba, Brazil and China, but ten other parts of the world each
provided over £1,000 of commission. In all these countries many of the
clients were of German origin and favoured a 'German' firm for trade
credit. But how did Kleinworts itself decide to whom to give credit? The
firm's founding father, Alexander Kleinwort, offered an incontrovertible
axiom to his American agent not long before his death: 'It is most important to do a profitable safe business, to avoid reckless speculation and all
parties who do not deserve and inspire full confidence.'[14] Joshua Bates
could not have put it better, and in truth these qualities were always
needed: local knowledge or access to local knowledge, sound judgement,
and an infinite capacity to take pains. Some in the City had those qualities, most had not.

Accepting must have seemed an attractively profitable field to get into,
and by the late 1860s those reputed iconoclasts of the Square Mile, the
joint-stock banks, were tempted to dabble. *The Economist* was less than
satisfied: 'The commercial public view with great and justifiable anxiety
the growth of the new system under which London Bankers undertake,
for a commission large or small, engagements which properly belong to
a merchant.'[15] For another quarter of a century or so the City's leading
joint-stock banks continued to hold back from mounting a significant
challenge to the merchant banks. Undoubtedly the risk argument carried
great weight; so too did a feeling that the established accepting firms,
with their mercantile origins, international connections and linguistic
skills, were inherently better suited to the business. Yet at some level this
diffidence also reflected the culture of the City as a whole, a culture of

specialist businesses fulfilling 'niche' roles – a culture that would have viewed with horror the late twentieth-century concept of so-called 'integrated' houses operating across the whole financial waterfront. In a City of alleys and courts that Dickens would still have broadly claimed as his own, small remained beautiful.

That said, there was in the merchant-banking sphere little *glamour* attached to accepting, which remained for many years the poor cousin (in terms of status) by comparison with the variety of tasks that these firms undertook for foreign governments, above all the key role they played in floating loans on the London market. Not all of these loans were profitable – though some were immensely so – but provided the country concerned was more or less reputable, they had the great attractions of enhancing or entrenching a house's position within the City pecking order, and creating the strong possibility of future spin-off business from the foreign government concerned, ranging from payment of dividends and operation of sinking funds to the undertaking of exchange operations and provision of short-term credit. But how could firms break into the magic circle, above all in relation to high-profile European loans? As Morgans found in the 1870s, it was one thing to become a regular member of syndicates: this it was able to do partly through the ripening friendship of J. Pierpont Morgan (son of Junius) and Everard Hambro, the two men being neighbours in Roehampton each summer.[16] However it was quite another matter to be asked to take the lead in the most prestigious loans, and as yet Rothschilds, Barings and to a degree Hambros were the only London houses that consistently had that standing.

As for actual profits, we have runs of figures for the 1870s for six merchant banks. They show Rothschilds making a very sizeable average net profit of £520,000 a year – sizeable certainly for a firm of a handful of partners and a staff of well under a hundred – followed by Barings (£242,000), Morgans (£154,000), Schröders (£144,000), Gibbs (£85,000) and Kleinworts (£50,000). Anecdotal evidence suggests that another merchant bank, Huths, was making at this time a net profit of between £50,000 and £80,000 a year.[17]

What about capital? Taking 1875, Rothschilds was way out in front, with the London house alone possessing a capital of over £6.5m, part of the total capital of the Rothschild banks of over £34m. Then (in terms of the figures and best guesses readily available) came Schröders on £1.68m, Barings on £1.62m, Morgans on £1.46m, Brown Shipley on £1.2m, Kleinworts on £840,000, Hambros on £630,000 and Huths on £500,000.[18] It is arguable[19] that historians have made too much of this question of capital – after all, the real trick is matching capital to business requirements, rather than building up capital for its own sake, and indeed Rothschilds' return on capital of 9.8 per cent during the 1870s was less than that of Barings (11.9 per cent) or Morgans' (15.1 per cent) – but there is no doubt that City men themselves were much preoccupied by the subject, especially when the constituent elements of a partnership changed for any reason.[20]

There existed a gulf between the Capel Court fraternity (with probably only a few exceptions) and the leading houses which every day employed its services. It was a gulf epitomised by the almost dog-like relationship that the stockbrokers Helbert Wagg endured for the best part of a century with its main patrons, N. M. Rothschild & Sons. 'On the fortnightly settlement days', Alfred Wagg was to relate feelingly, 'my grandfather or father would go over to New Court with a statement of the position across which Baron Lionel would write £500 or £1,000, being an arbitrary fee which he fixed as our remuneration, varying in amount according to the humour he was in.' Running the fortnightly gauntlet in 1879 was Edward Wagg, and it was he who was summoned by a very ill Baron Lionel to his bedside at 148 Piccadilly. 'I have been looking at my fortnightly account', the great man managed to say, 'and you have made a mistake in the addition.' Less than twenty-four hours later he was dead.[21]

Within Capel Court itself, communications were changing even more rapidly than elsewhere in the City – in 1868 pneumatic tubes were introduced to link the market floor with the telegraph office, while four years later the conservative Managers reluctantly allowed the coming of the ticker-tape machine, by which Stock Exchange offices were kept in touch with the very latest market prices as collected on the floor by officials of the Exchange Telegraph Company – but the underlying club-like code of morality remained constant. It was communications that revealed the code in action at the end of 1874. The occasion was the railway smash at Shipton-on-Cherwell, near Oxford, just after midday on Christmas Eve, killing over thirty people. 'The overturned carriages, the heartrending shrieks of the injured, the dead bodies seen in all directions, and the scattered luggage combined to render the spectacle horrible in the extreme,' reported *The Times*, adding that 'the more slightly injured at once set to work with praiseworthy alacrity to help their distressed fellow travellers'. But did they all? Within days, and possibly hours, a story passed into circulation that a stockbroker on the train had, on emerging unscathed from the debris, instead attended first to the speculative possibilities of the disaster. Apparently he had hied to the nearest telegraph office, wiring his authorised clerk to sell 5,000 of the railway (the Great Western) on which the accident had happened. Over the years this outrageous example of insider dealing became firmly embedded in Capel Court mythology.[22]

Manning the London market, and setting the tone for the whole institution, were the jobbers, those little-known men whose activities have been so largely effaced from the historical record. Few in the outside world comprehended the art of jobbing and probably not many stock-brokers did either. It was an art that Bagehot, in one of his *Economic Studies*, made a valiant effort to evoke if not to explain:

> The trade in which Ricardo spent his life, and in which he was so successful, is of all trades the most abstract . . . There is a story that some dealer made very many thousand pounds by continued dealings in the shares of some railway, and then on a sudden asked where that railway was. The whole thing had been a series of algebraic quantities to him, which called up no picture, but which affected a profit and loss account. In most kinds of business there is an appeal of some sort to the senses; there are goods in ships or machines; even in banking there is much physical money to be counted. But the Stock Exchange deals in the 'debts', that is the 'promises', of nations, and in the 'shares' of undertakings whose value depends on certain future dividends – that is, on certain expectations – and what these expectations are to be, is a matter of nice calculation from the past. These imponderable elements of trade cannot be seen or handled, and the dealing with them trains the mind to a refinement analogous to that of the metaphysician.[23]

No one doubted there was a fundamental difference between brokers and jobbers, and the company promoter H. Osborne O'Hagan drew a sharp distinction between their respective qualities: 'Those who have much experience of the Stock Exchange will have found out that – there are, of course, exceptions – stockbrokers are generally honest but not particularly brilliant individuals, especially if they confine themselves to invest-ment business; there is little scope for the development of the brain. On the other hand, stock jobbers and dealers who are actively working for themselves have a very different reputation.' Jobbers, in other words, were different animals, not necessarily possessing the social graces so desirable in a broker, and it was not until the 1890s that the first Etonian became a jobber, in the person of C. T. 'Pubbles' Barclay.[24]

Strictly speaking in Stock Exchange terminology a jobber was a jobber, whatever the somewhat murky historical connotations of that word and whether he maintained merchant-style a large open-ended book in particu-lar stocks or whether he was always concerned to go home square at the end of each trading day. But even if 'dealer' sounded more acceptable, among the 1,800 or so jobbers there was enormous segmentation, and at least several hundred of them were not part of firms or partnerships as such, operating instead as one-man outfits on their own account with little more at their back than the proverbial book and pencil. Often they did not have offices, even though (for reasons of space) there were no longer desks available on the market floor for the purpose of settling accounts.

The classic defence of the jobbing system was that it provided ready marketability in the widest possible range of securities, but it was by no means clear to the Royal Commission into the Stock Exchange that this was necessarily the case. Whereas Consols, Egyptian stock, and English railways were relatively marketable types of securities, problems arose with, for instance, 'National Provincial and Bank of England shares, East and West India Dock stock, the shares of water companies, gas companies, of insurance companies (almost all of them)'. The former stockbroker Charles Branch examined the Official List and estimated that some 285 of the securities on it were in practice marketable, representing about £610m in nominal value, and that some 1,082 securities were not marketable, representing about £563m. In consequence, the jobber was often a redundant figure, and 'many brokers spend very much time in trying to find a broker who has the business the other way, and they sometimes succeed and often fail'.

Branch, unconstrained because no longer a member himself, further elaborated on the plight of the brokers when they attempted to take independent action: 'We have in the Stock Exchange what is called a notice board, but it is in fact not a wall space at all, but it is on part, not even the whole, of a supporting pillar; a part of this pillar is supposed to contain the notices from brokers as to the stocks which they wish to buy or to sell, and the part of it which is devoted to that purpose is kept under lock and key, and is jealously supervised by jobbers, who exclude notices upon what have appeared to me to be the most idle pretences.' In short, said Branch, the whole thing was 'a farce'.

What unfortunately the ten jobber witnesses before the Commission failed to provide was significant insight into the psychology of their very specialised craft. Near the end of the inquiry, George Medley, a member for twenty-seven years and for the last dozen a jobber in the American market, gave some clue. 'There is nothing a man dreads so much as meeting another man the same way as himself. If two or three meet together it amounts to a chicken panic, that is to say, we get afraid of one another.' Not long after that vivid expression, discussion turned to the question of public access in order to counter charges of the public being kept deliberately in the dark:

> It has been suggested that it would be much better if the Stock Exchange were open like any other market is? – They would not see the business done, although they might fancy that they would, because important business is done in a whisper. No dealer would allow what a broker does with him to be known. It must be kept secret. That is the essence of the business . . .
> It would lessen the confusion which exists on the Stock Exchange if the markets were separated so that the business might be done in different rooms? – But the confusion is not a hindrance, it is not inconvenient. We want to hear what is going on in other markets. Our markets move as it were

by electricity; if we hear a shout in one market we want to know how things are going on there, one market affects another . . . There is a shout, and it is most important for us to hear it in other parts of the House. It is telegraphed all over the country immediately. If I was in another room I could not hear it. I certainly cannot see that anything would be gained by that.

Medley, however, was no blind defender of existing practices, and he argued that admission to the Stock Exchange should be made more restrictive: 'I should be most inclined to make a man pass an apprenticeship. I do not think that the mere possession of a certain sum of money qualifies a man for the practice of such a business.'[25]

The Royal Commission apparently failed to appreciate that there was an important vested interest involved concerning the whole question of admission. Whereas Lloyd's was an institution which since the 1770s had been owned by its members, who therefore had a natural inclination to keep a lid on numbers in order to minimise competition, the situation was different at the Stock Exchange. There it was the shareholders who owned the building, and these proprietors had an equally natural wish to keep the Stock Exchange as open as possible to new members, in order to maximise their income through entrance fees and annual subscriptions. The proprietors elected the Managers, the members elected the Committee, only about a quarter of members were also proprietors, and inevitably there was a certain underlying tension between the two ruling bodies. Francis Levien on behalf of the Committee may have emphasised to the Royal Commission the continuing tradition of a stock market open to all the talents, but essentially it was a policy supported by the proprietors rather than the membership as a whole. That it *was* a relatively open market, in terms of admission and by comparison with either Lloyd's or the New York Stock Exchange, there is no doubt. It is true that the level of sureties was raised in both 1872 and 1874 – so that by the autumn of 1874 a prospective new member without a clerical apprenticeship on the Exchange was required to find three sureties for £750 each – but entrance fees remained low at a maximum of 100 guineas, as did annual subscriptions at no more than 20 guineas. In 1850 there had been well under 1,000 members; by 1877 there were over 2,000; and the only future limitation seemed likely to be shortage of physical accommodation.[26]

But if it was relatively easy to become a member of the Stock Exchange, it was another matter to flourish there. Family ties often remained of paramount importance – almost two-fifths of firms had at least two members of the same family amongst their partners – and indeed in 1867 Isaac Braithwaite drew up a new deed of partnership ensuring that for ever and a day his firm's full partners would come from three families only (Braithwaite, Barkworth, Savory), with any outside recruits to Foster

& Braithwaite having to make do as salaried partners. Wealth and connection were also crucial ingredients of success, especially in relation to broking firms. Here the new, much-criticised West End intake particularly made its mark, and in July 1874 Charlotte de Rothschild was writing a little waspishly to her children in Trouville about what had been 'our chief topic of conversation at dinner yesterday' and would soon be causing an even bigger splash in the world beyond 148 Piccadilly:

> The confidential clerk of Arthur Wagg is on the point of leaving him, and on account of the work which cannot be left undone on the Sabbath, the successor of the valuable employer must also be a Christian. Mr Bisch [presumably Henri Bischoffsheim?] knowing the complexity of the young Jewish broker, has recommended to him, during one year as a confidential clerk, and afterwards as a partner, the scion of a noble house, no less a person than the Duke of Argyll's son, Lord Walter Campbell, who puts ten thousand pounds in the business, and is to receive ten per cent on the amount the first year and after that a proportion of the profits to be determined by Mr Bisch and your father. This is the proposal, very liberal on the part of Arthur Wagg, who is delighted, and who by his liberality gives great satisfaction to Lord Walter. Your father, however, has advised Lord Walter to go and speak to the Duke, as that proud nobleman might not like his son to enter into partnership with an Israelite. The Waggs will be overjoyed, if the partnership should really take place, to be connected in business with the brother-in-law of Her Royal Highness the Princess Louise.

Three days later Charlotte reported that 'one of the Bank directors, Mr L in the house of Rathbone, says that the red-haired young gentleman is very clever and has excellent business habits'. The journey to Inverary proved fruitful, and the following year, when the young aristocrat became a member, it was widely seen as a landmark in the Stock Exchange's history.[27]

For another sort of Stock Exchange experience, however, we should turn to the words of Francis Carruthers Gould. He was born in 1844 the son of a Barnstaple architect and, after being educated locally, became a member of the Stock Exchange for over twenty years. There he found ample fodder for his gift for caricature, and collections of his sketches of fellow members were published for private circulation. Eventually he decided to leave Capel Court and during the second half of his life he became a prominent political cartoonist, of Liberal sympathies, as well as assistant editor of the *Westminster Gazette*. In old age he looked back on the place with some fondness. 'A more generous and kindly community of men it would be impossible to find', he wrote, asserting also that nowhere in the City did there exist 'a higher standard of personal honour in all the relations of business'. Nor did it worry him that the atmosphere had been 'like a big school where all the boys knew each other's peculiarities or eccentricities, applied nicknames with uncanny accuracy, and occasionally "ragged" unmercifully'. Yet he had no regrets about having left the Stock Exchange. And in a passage going close to the heart of that institution's peculiarly unsettling and febrile collective psyche, he tried to explain why:

> I cannot say that it was ever a congenial occupation that suited my temperament. It was like living on a tropical volcanic island; when the sun shone and things went smoothly it was pleasant enough but there were too many sudden and unforeseen bolts from the blue . . . It was a life of alternations. Some men made fortunes swiftly, some plodded on cautiously, content merely to make a living, whilst others fell by the way. Some were fortunate or skilful enough to weather all the storms and even to profit by them, but there were others whose tragic fate it was to work all their lives only to fail at the end.[28]

CHAPTER NINE

Playing the Game

'If England be the heart of international trade and cosmopolitan finance, and London be the heart of England, the City is the heart of London.' So affirmed Escott in 1879, and he convincingly depicted the Old Lady herself as lying at the *very* heart of the matter:

> Along with the joint stock and private banks by which it is surrounded, and with which its relations are close and intimate – for as the central institution it keeps the reserves of the other banks as well as its own – it represents the banking of the metropolis, and therefore, in the final issue, of England. Owing to England's world-wide commercial relations, this same banking system, and the subsidiary agencies by which it is buttressed, acts as the general international Clearing House; and bearing in mind the duties that further devolve on it from the fact that London is the great bullion centre, we can form some faint idea of the multiplicity and complexity of its operations, and the vastness of the weight which presses on the central pivot around which the entire commercial and financial system revolves.[1]

A pressing and universal weight indeed, as not only did most of Europe in the course of the 1870s move to a gold standard, but the sums of money flowing through London became ever greater. The logic was irresistible: sterling, backed by the Bank's undeviating adherence to the gold standard, was *the* international currency; London was where the world's trade was financed and settled; and there existed in the City a short-term money market of unrivalled liquidity and security.[2] Could the Bank of England, still predominantly run by merchants, cope with its ever-more demanding role as 'the central pivot'? Bagehot was not alone in having his doubts.

The real problem was one of resources. The Bank's clout in the money market was by the early 1870s becoming palpably weakened by the rival impact of other banks, especially joint-stock ones, whose deposits were continuing to rise at a far greater pace than the Bank's; this in turn led to an ever-wider divergence between the actual, competitively determined market rate and the official Bank rate. In December 1874 there appeared in *The Economist* a bold letter, probably written by Newmarch of Glyns,

asserting that 'it is felt on all sides that the old system of paternal government is passing away' and that 'the Bank of England, which once distanced
every competitor, is now only *primus inter pares*'. Newmarch even advocated that the London banks should keep their own cash reserves (as
opposed to the single-reserve system, accepted by Bagehot as a fact of
life) and settle the rate of discount themselves, without reference to Bank
rate. The proposal set all Lombard Street talking, but next month the
Bankers' Magazine came down on the side of the sceptics. In part it argued
that the plan 'does not in any way connect the proposed reserve with the
supply of bullion or of gold coin, which should form the basis of every
banking reserve'. Its main thrust, however, was the key role that the Bank
of England had played, 'by pledging the resources of the nation', in the
still vividly remembered crises of 1847, 1857 and 1866. And: 'If "Lombard
Street" is prepared to face any storm that may arise without requiring
this aid, then, and then only, it is strong enough to carry the proposed
plan successfully through.' The journal was also doubtful if the government would come to the aid of the new joint-stock banks in the event
of a crisis.[3] Over the next few months the debate fizzled out, but it had
been a clear sign that the Bank could not, even after vanquishing Overend
Gurney, take its authority in the City wholly for granted.

In fact, conscious in best Bagehot fashion of the importance of
protecting its reserve, the Bank had already started to refashion its
monetary policy. This was the so-called Greene–Gibbs policy – Benjamin
Buck Greene was governor from 1873 to 1875 and Henry Hucks Gibbs
was deputy governor, before becoming governor himself over the next
two years – and what in effect it entailed was that when money was lent
at home, Bank rate was simultaneously raised, so that gold came in from
abroad and thus fortified the reserve. Or in the sanguine words of Gibbs
himself, writing to a less than convinced Oxford economist in 1877: 'The
Bank of England has but one weapon, the rate, wherewith they defend
their own position, and make those who want to borrow money pay a
little more for it, inducing, by the rise of interest, the foreigners to
minister to the provisions of the Act of '44, and send more note-producing
gold into our coffers.' The trouble was, however, the continuing difficulty
of making Bank rate effective; unrealistic levels of Bank rate, geared to
potential foreign drains of gold, had the invidious domestic effect of
making the banks pay over the odds in their deposit rates; and in 1878
there was more, quite serious talk of an independent rate and an independent reserve. But it seems that once again Lombard Street failed to
speak with one voice, and plans for what would have been little less
than a unilateral declaration of independence were quietly shelved.[4]
There, in a somewhat unsatisfactory state, matters remained for another
decade, awaiting a strong, tough-minded man to come to the Bank's

helm and try to assert in a more thoroughgoing way the dominance of Threadneedle Street.

That dominance would have to be asserted over a banking system that had been undergoing rapid change and was beginning to take something like its modern, mature shape. 1878 was an important year. The spring saw the failure of Willis, Percival & Co., and according to John Biddulph Martin (Richard's brother) in his year-end review, this 'caused a very bad feeling at the time, & was felt to be discreditable to private Banking'. Willis Percival was one of Lombard Street's oldest banks and, having failed with liabilities of over £500,000, was absorbed into the Hampshire and North Wilts Banking Company. That joint-stock bank, which had recently tried to secure a seat on the London Clearing House but had been rejected by the private bankers who still controlled it, now renamed itself as the Capital and Counties Bank and, after a further wait, at last got its prized seat. Meanwhile, in the autumn of 1878, there had taken place what Martin referred to as 'the scandalous failure of the City of Glasgow Bank'. There was no doubt that it was a scandal – involving over £8m of depositors' funds – and inevitably it shook the City profoundly.[5]

The City's mood remained apprehensive for several months, and the story goes that shortly before Christmas one of the Rothschilds (presumably Alfred, being a Bank director) went to the Chancellor, Sir Stafford Northcote, and asked him if, before he went out of town, he would leave a signed letter suspending the Act, the letter to be used on the moment should necessity arise. It is unclear whether this request was granted, but in the longer term the City of Glasgow crash proved, in two specific ways, a turning point in banking history. One was that it led to legislation providing for compulsory publication of balance sheets on the part of joint-stock banks; the other was that, to an extent still a matter of historical debate, it made banks increasingly preoccupied by the question of liquidity and as a direct result increasingly less likely to adopt a liberal approach in their lending policy.[6] The upshot was undoubtedly a more stable banking system – but arguably at the expense of overall British economic development.

By the early 1880s the City was increasingly the magnet to the provincial joint-stock banks, which by this stage had close, regular links not only with its discount houses but also the leading stockbroking firms. There could have been no clearer indication of how times were changing when in 1884 Lloyds of Birmingham, a bank hitherto confined to the Midlands, attained for itself a presence in London, and with it a seat on the London Clearing House, by the simple expedient of buying up Barnett Hoares and Bosanquets, two of Lombard Street's more venerable private banks. The new bank – called, for the time being, Lloyds, Barnetts and Bosanquets – fundamentally represented a takeover, and it was symbolic that within a few years the dignified old premises of Bosanquets were being knocked down in order to allow the construction of a grand London office for the newcomer.[7]

One of the private banks' major problems, now acute in the wake of the recent legislation, was that they were mistrusted because of their continuing refusal to publish balance sheets. Yet quite apart from an instinctive reluctance to do so, they knew all too well the consequences of publicising the fact that, with very few exceptions, their capital and reserve were both negligible in comparison with most joint-stock banks. One of those exceptions was Glyn Mills, and in January 1885 it took the bull by the horns, issuing a circular that aroused much attention. 'The plan upon which they have hit', asserted the *Statist* (a relatively new, would-be rival to *The Economist*), 'does credit to their enterprise and forethought. They have decided to retain all the advantages which private banking offers, while giving to the public the information which is so highly prized in the case of joint-stock banks.' After noting the existing partnership's determination to retain private banking's traditional advantages of accumulated skills and unlimited liability, the *Statist* predicted that 'under the new arrangement there seems no reason why private banking should not hold its own against joint-stock banking'.

There was no denying that it was a clever compromise, but this optimism was misplaced, for in the long run capital was always going to be king as far as deposit banking was concerned (even if the same did not always apply in merchant banking), and that factor alone meant that private banking was ultimately doomed. Yet equally important was the human factor. Only a few weeks earlier, John Biddulph Martin had noted somewhat caustically in his review of 1884: 'Richard took his holiday principally in Scotland, but at the best was very little in Lombard Street.'[8] Richard Biddulph Martin, by now senior partner of the family bank, was an able banker and a far more attractive, 'rounded' figure than the average joint-stock banker; but no joint-stock banker remained on the payroll unless he put in the hours. That, in the end, made the difference. Among those who regretted the Glyn Mills initiative of 1885 was Gladstone. 'Mr G says he is a Tory and old-fashioned enough not to wish to see the entire break up of the private bank system', recorded one of his private secretaries. But as he well knew, and sometimes acknowledged, the world was changing in all sorts of ways, not least in the conduct of British foreign policy – from the mid-1870s far more 'forward' than it had been for many years, and finding in the City an increasingly willing helpmate and ally.

The decisive moment, of great symbolic as well as substantive importance, came in November 1875 when Disraeli's Conservative government was alerted to the possibility of buying a 44 per cent share in the Suez Canal Company and responded to it with alacrity. Disraeli decided not to consult Parliament, bypassed the Old Lady, and turned instead to his long-time friends in New Court. 'They alone cd have accomplished what we wanted, & they had only 4 & 20 hours to make up their minds, whether they wd, or could, incur an immediate liability of 4 millions.' So the prime minister reported to the Prince of Wales almost immediately afterwards.

In reality Baron Lionel had a little longer to make up his mind, but the gist was true: the British government needed £4m virtually at once and Rothschilds agreed to advance it, making from the transaction a profit of almost £100,000. The Chancellor of the Exchequer later admitted privately that 'we took their offer on their own terms without looking too closely into them'. Disraeli, however, was jubilant ('You have it, madam'), the price of Egyptian stock rose sharply, and it was not until the following February that Parliament debated the purchase and its terms. A well-intentioned stockbroker suggested to Alfred de Rothschild that Disraeli should deflect criticism by publicly stating that Rothschilds had given its services gratis. Alfred passed the suggestion on to his father, who summoned the stockbroker and did not mince words: 'Arthur Wagg, you're a young man and will learn better. I've made £100,000 out of the deal, I wish it had been £200,000.' Baron Lionel, with all the insouciance of his own father, was unconcerned about any parliamentary censure and did not believe he had broken any unwritten City code. As Disraeli's secretary, Monty Corry, noted at the time:

> As to the question whether the government should not have applied to the Bank of England, Baron Rothschild – giving no opinion as to the Bank's *power* – says that he understands the authorities to be about equally divided (even now) on the point of their *willingness* to have acted as the agents of the government in this transaction. It is a point, moreover, which could only have been determined by the full Board, at the obvious sacrifice of despatch and secrecy. Mr Hubbard, for one, is clear that the Bank could not, and would not, have acted, while Mr Gibbs and Mr Thomson Hankey take the other view.

Corry added that Rothschild 'declares without hesitation that the Bank of England could not have found the required sum without grave disturbance of the money market'.

Altogether it was an episode destined for the history books, and it further cemented the close relationship between Disraeli and the Rothschilds, nominally Liberal though that family still was. 'The greatest man in England', Baron Lionel once called him, to which Natty is said to have added, 'In Europe, Papa'. What of the larger consequences? 'We have now', *The Times* solemnly intoned on 27 November 1875, 'an abiding stake in the security and welfare of Egypt.' City opinion was divided, but the aged Overstone probably spoke for the majority when he sought to reassure G. W. Norman three days later: 'I admit the difficulties which you suggest as attaching to the Suez Land purchase. Nevertheless I believe it to be a wise step – indeed almost an inevitable step.' While as for the prospect of an increased British influence over Egyptian affairs, 'from this I think we cannot shrink'.[9]

It was Gladstone who seven years later, as prime minister, earned the ungracious thanks of the City through his reluctant decision to occupy Egypt. The City's involvement with that country had been long and intimate: in trade from the late 1830s, mainly in cotton, so that by 1880 four-fifths of Egypt's exports went to Britain, which in turn supplied almost half her imports; and in finance from the 1860s, with loans issued by Frühling & Goschen under the most onerous terms to the debtor nation helping to cause almost permanent Egyptian financial crisis. In 1876 it was George Goschen who on behalf of the British bondholders designed the plan that effectively led to Anglo-French supervision of Egyptian finances; and two years later it was Rothschilds which issued an £8m Egyptian loan on the security of the khedive's domain lands. In 1879 the khedive (Ismail Pasha) was deposed, European informal supremacy was further reasserted, and in the early 1880s British invest-ment poured into Egypt. This in turn led to a nationalist reaction, and eventually revolt, and so to the fateful occupation of 1882. What precisely were City attitudes, and what was the extent of City influence on this turning point in Gladstonian Liberalism as well as the evolution of British imperialism? No precise evaluation is possible, but there is some suggestive evidence.[10]

By late March, Natty Rothschild, with an apparently threatening nationalist revolt well under way, was reported as being in a deeply anxious state, paying daily visits to the Foreign Office. It was also reported that half of the domain loan was still in the hands of Rothschilds, which perhaps explains the anxiety. It seems clear that, from late spring, Natty was helping to create a climate in which occupation appeared the only answer. By mid-June a British fleet was poised outside Alexandria and riots there had killed fifty Europeans. 'England has greater interests in Egypt than any other European Power, and those interests must be defended', declared *The Economist*, no knee-jerk imperialist.

The Times in its City report of 26 June anticipated difficulties at the impending Stock Exchange settlement: 'Egyptian securities have always been a favourite medium for speculation, and large accounts are known to have been open for the rise when the Egyptian imbroglio commenced.' Significantly, though, the same item referred to Gladstone's comforting statement 'a week ago' that 'the bondholders' interests would be protected'. By 5 July, Egyptian securities were going up on what transpired to be false rumours that Admiral Seymour's fleet 'had actually commenced a bombardment of the works that have been erected to command the harbour', while in the words of another market report soon afterwards, 'the prospect of an early intervention has certainly been well received in the City'. In short, 'the general feeling' at Capel Court was 'a wish for "some decisive action", the present suspense being regarded as intolerable'.[11]

That decisive action came on the 11th, as Alexandria was bombarded. The stock market itself waited on further events, but there is no doubt that the City as a whole was firmly behind Gladstone's action. *The Economist* would have been in danger of alienating its natural constituency if it had not toed the line and, with riots starting to spread inland, declared that 'whatever may have been the case a few days ago, it is no longer possible to speak of our action in Egypt as opposed to legitimate national aspirations'. And: 'Our interests in the Suez Canal, which it has all along been acknowledged we are bound at all hazards to maintain, are now distinctly threatened.' On 20 July the government decided upon a military expedition to Cairo, and Capel Court approved: 'There is nothing which the Stock Exchange apparently dreads so much as delay.'

In August the *Bankers' Magazine* backed government policy, making much of the importance to British economic interests of the Suez Canal and arguing rather tortuously that while 'we do not say that because we have great commercial interests in Egypt we are therefore entitled to interfere by force of arms in the settlement of her internal affairs', nevertheless 'what we have a perfect right to maintain is, that as there exists a trade route over which we have a right of way, we cannot allow that right of way to be interfered with and our passage stopped'.[12] On 13 September at Tel-el-Kebir the British Army defeated the Egyptian insurgents; in the battle's immediate wake there began the de facto British occupation of the country, pending the return of full security to the canal and satisfactory stability to Egyptian finances; and few dissenting voices were raised in the City.

Historians have long debated the causes of the occupation of Egypt. Clearly the Suez Canal was thought to be at risk and thus the safety of India, that jewel in the imperial crown; clearly the internal disorder in Egypt was perceived as serious, even if it was somewhat overestimated; and clearly there were anxieties as to what the French might do if there was no British initiative.[13] Yet it is equally clear that the economic dimension was also very important, and that the well-vocalised interests of the Egyptian bondholders were no negligible concern. There existed a conjunction of interests, and their exact weighting will doubtless remain a matter of debate. Conjunction, not conspiracy. 'The bondholders are now in possession of Egypt', declared the Radical writer and thinker Frederic Harrison on 26 June to the Anti-Aggression League; and five days later, in an open letter to Gladstone published even as Seymour awaited his orders, he further activated a historical hare that would run and run:

> Turn it which way you will, it comes back always to this – that we are to go to war really for the money interests of certain rich men in London and Paris . . . Does it necessarily follow that, because certain Englishmen hold large sums in Unified bonds, and because they have invested much capital in Egyptian works, that Europeans are to be guaranteed as a domin-ant caste; and that, if the Egyptian people make any effort to displace one rivet of the dominion, there is instant appeal to war, ending in virtual conquest?

No, it did not *necessarily* follow – but it helped . . . And when Harrison made his final, vain, magnificent appeal – 'the permanent exploitation of Egypt by Western speculators and adventurers is an object which it is worthy of your career formally to repudiate as a national concern' – perhaps even Gladstone in the watches of the night would have conceded the point to that extent.[14]

*

It was around this time that arbitrage business in the more popular American railroad stocks – in other words, exploiting the difference in price at any one time on the two sides of the Atlantic – began to take off. The question of whether or not to enter this field was facing all the leading Anglo-American houses, and in October 1882 Brown Shipley had addressed it with due circumspection:

> It will not suit us, with our Credit & Exchange business making such large calls as they do at present upon our time strength & resources, to embark in Arbitrage business to anything like the extent that such houses as for instance Raphaels do it . . . But there are firms who like Hambros do a certain limited amount of Arbitrage business & seem to find it profit-able, & we have thought that to do something of the kind in a moderate way if it were only as an experiment might be well worth our while.

Brown Shipley, however, made it clear to Brown Brothers, who had recently acquired a seat on the New York Stock Exchange and were pressing to go into arbitrage, that it had serious reservations. After outlining the continuous application required if such arbitrage business between the two houses was to prosper, the letter went on:

> We may as well say at once, that no one of our existing partners in London can spare the requisite time nor are we any of us fitted by training, taste, or temperament to undertake it, besides it would be a new departure for us to discount & to borrow & might prove detrimental in other ways.[15]

In the event Brown Shipley failed to become significant arbitragists, while neither Barings nor Morgans made the attempt. In fact it was a thoroughly tricky, 'nimble ninepence' kind of business that does not seem to have suited the stolid Anglo-Saxon temperament – an Achilles heel on the part of the City that perhaps also explained why, from the late 1870s, it was Vienna and Berlin, not London, that made the running in the evolution of futures markets for foreign exchange dealing. Or as a senior partner of Robert Benson & Co. was subsequently to put it, 'Nobody understands arbitrage and foreign exchange unless born a Jew or an Armenian.' The partners of Raphaels and Samuel Montagu both fell into the former category, possessing a combination of aptitude, resources and capacity for sustained work that made their success in these demanding fields assured.[16] Was it a way in which a gentleman would choose to make a living? The silent implication was clear enough, and it did not flatter Armenians.

There were no such qualms about foreign government loans, even though they could involve some distinctly covert operations. Between 1877 and 1890 almost a quarter of the business (measured by value) still went to Rothschilds, while Barings and Hambros vied for second place, with the American houses of Morton Rose, Morgans and Seligmans in hot pursuit. For the really big loans, involving an international syndicate, it was significant that it was no longer a London house that invariably took 'the lead'; and when in 1880 the Russian government authorised a £20m loan, not only was it floated in Paris, but only two of the fifteen banks who participated in the syndicate were British.[17] Nevertheless, London still maintained an overall edge over other capital markets.

Following Lionel's death, at the helm in New Court at this time was Natty Rothschild, who had no great analytic intelligence, but made up for it with strength of character, sense of duty, and unwavering determination to hold what he had. 'Yes, by selling too soon': such was his typically blunt reply when asked if he had a secret for making money. As for imagination not being his long suit, implicit testimony came from his hero Disraeli, who once remarked that 'whenever I want to know an historical fact, I always ask Natty'. Natty, however, could also be very affectionate, even sentimental; he had little interest in the trappings of wealth; he abhorred unnecessary letter writing; and he possessed what a descendant would call 'enormous, almost ruthless vitality and drive'. He may not have been quite the man to advance the Rothschild position, but nor was he someone who would squander a unique legacy.

We have glimpses of life in New Court under Natty and his two brothers. Carl Meyer had come to London in the 1870s, and by the 1880s this extremely able native of Hamburg was the rising man at Rothschilds, in effect acting as trusted confidential clerk. Of the three brothers, Alfred was Meyer's particular benefactor, and it was not unusual when, in March 1886, Meyer dined with him: 'We chatted till very late, so I did NOT go to Asch (where I hear Cassel was the matador & won everybody's money).' The reference to Cassel is significant, for not only did he prosper exceedingly in the 1880s – making a fortune out of backing the mining of Swedish iron ore, getting increasingly involved in Mexico and Turkey, and formally leaving Bischoffsheims in 1884 – but he also in time became very friendly with Meyer as the latter's unconditional loyalty to the Rothschilds eventually waned. But that lay ahead when, on 10 August 1886, the confidential clerk, with justifiable aspirations to a partnership, wrote a letter to his wife that serves as an eloquent reminder that, however dubious the reputation of the place itself, the Stock Exchange was more than ever where the daily pulse of the City beat most strongly:

> Nothing fresh politically but la Bourse simply mad, I hardly ever remember such times, things jump up before you can say Jack Robinson, today Mexican Rails were all the rage, also Atlantics and other exotics . . . I am sure and try to get a few crumbs off the table of the rich. Today I made £100 in the twinkling of an eye, by buying only £2000 of a stock in the morning and selling it 5% higher in the afternoon. Nit schlecht![18]

Meanwhile, the firms that would help mould the twentieth-century Stock Exchange continued to take shape. In 1882, the story goes, Henry Rudolph Laing and Fletcher Hayes Grant Cruickshank were on their way to a poker game when they decided to start their own stockbroking firm. Two years later, P. Cazenove & Co. was in danger of falling apart on the retirement of its senior figures, but recruited two experienced brokers, John and Swainson Akroyd, to join the young Arthur Philip Cazenove, the firm becoming Cazenove & Akroyds. On the jobbing front, one young member, Fred Durlacher, after obtaining banking experience in Hamburg through a friend of his father's and spending a year as a broker, started on his own as a jobber in 1881 before teaming up with his brother Neville three years later, the new partnership dealing in breweries as well as railways; while in 1885, a well-established jobber called George Wedd set up in partnership with Harry Jefferson, the new firm soon becoming a significant presence in the Consol market.[19]

Although he once described himself as 'an ardent disciple of Schopenhauer', Harry Panmure Gordon was the extrovert par excellence of an extrovert community, and by the 1880s he had already had a very full and varied life. He was born in Perthshire in 1837, the only son of a well-known City figure who was a director of the Union Bank of London; he was educated at Harrow, Oxford and Bonn University; there followed four years in the 10th Hussars, before his spendthriftness may well have played a part in his father's bankruptcy; he thereupon resigned his commission and went to China, joining a trading firm in Shanghai; and shortly after his arrival the Taiping rebellion broke out. This gave Panmure Gordon the chance to organise and command the Shanghai Mounted Volunteers, part of the 'Ever Victorious Army' that suppressed the Taipings. This military prowess won him a great reputation as well as a personal connection with Li Hung-chang and other Chinese notables. He returned to England in 1865 and, becoming a member of the Stock Exchange, joined the firm of J. & A. Scrimgeour, and in 1876 he established his own stock-broking firm.

Over the next quarter of a century Panmure Gordon flourished not only as an extremely successful practitioner, especially in the new-issue sphere, but also as one of the most talked-about men in the City. The attention focused on a unique lifestyle. His homes (at Adelaide Crescent, Brighton and in time at Carlton House Terrace and near Rickmansworth) were lavish affairs in which he entertained freely; his penchant was to drive four-in-hand into the City; he was reckoned to have the best private collection of carriages in the world; his sartorial tastes were such that he possessed over a thousand neckties alone; and in *Who's Who* he listed his hobbies as salmon fishing, breeding collies and running his estate. All this cost money. 'Well, I shall live a rich man and die a poor one,' he once remarked, computing that his minimum expenditure was £2,000 a month. But, as he well knew, there was a pay-off, for his way of life, added to an attractive personality, enabled him to mix freely with the cream of society and gave him an entry into the best City parlours; altogether he was probably the most enviably connected of all late-Victorian stockbrokers.[20]

The Capel Court climate in which 'PG' and others prospered in the 1880s was generally an invigorating one. In November 1884 *The Economist* described the inexorable increase 'in recent years' of the 'speculative element' in the House:

> The field for speculation afforded by the Stock Exchange is so various, the *rationale* of its methods has become so easy, and the initial credit or capital required is so small, that its popularity is easily explained . . . Firms with a large investment business, subsisting chiefly by that alone, are gradually diminishing. In fact, the number of first-rate houses of this description could almost be counted on one's fingers. The process by which they are dropping out – to be seen in all directions – is a perfectly natural one, and none can grow up to take their place; for it took in most cases fifty or a hundred years under the old order of things to build up a great investment house, with its connection of, perhaps nominally, three or four thousand clients. The most pretentious of the newer houses are very different, even the soundest of them. In their case, speculative business is the main thing, and apart from it many firms, with a very different reputation, could by no means exist.

Inevitably, the newer members of the Stock Exchange tended to be speculative in their orientation. And, looking back over the past ten years or so:

Social reasons had begun to make the 'House' fashionable, owing to the apparent ease with which large fortunes were realised, and also the club-like nature of its life, when the Clearing House became firmly established [from 1880], and the necessity for a considerable degree of technical skill was largely swept away. As a consequence, a great influx took place, but the new element rather made up for want of business instincts by a greater liking and desire for business of a highly adventurous type.

In short, asserted the august journal, the Stock Exchange 'has undergone a greater permanent transformation than is generally recognised'.[21]

Its great problem by the early 1880s was one of *Lebensraum*. By 1883 the membership was over 2,500 (compared with less than 1,500 in 1870), while the following year the amount of space per person admitted to the House (members and their clerks) was down to an oppressive 2.08 square feet. Inevitably the poor clerks were blamed for the congestion – one year for crowding out the Foreign market on settlement days, another for loitering in general, yet another when the Hercules Passage entrance was deemed to be 'always obstructed by a crowd of clerks and foreigners'. Relief, however, was at hand. The Stock Exchange's architect, J. J. Cole, was commissioned to design a new building that would link with the existing one. In March 1885, soon after the new wing – with its dominant feature, a great dome – had been opened for business, the Prince of Wales made a tour of inspection. Hearty cheers followed by enthusiastic renditions of the national anthem and 'God Bless the Prince of Wales' were the inevitable accompaniments to the royal visit.[22]

The Stock Exchange no doubt liked to think that it was becoming an accepted part of national life – those eighteenth-century outlaw days long gone – but the fact that the veining of the marble in the new wing caused it to be known as 'Gorgonzola Hall', as the financial journalist Charles Duguid reported, was a gratifying reminder that its denizens could never take themselves quite seriously. In that hermetic, often hothouse world, plenty of other nicknames were in everyday use.[23] Many referred to securities, and the schoolboy logic behind the tag was readily apparent. Thus 'Ducks' were Aylesbury Dairy Co. shares, 'Haddocks' were Great North of Scotland ordinary stock, 'Matches' were Bryant & May shares, 'Sarah's Boots' were Sierra Buttes Gold Mine shares, and so on.

Similarly cerebral were some of the other terms frequently swapped between members. A 'turn' was well understood (even outside Capel Court) as the profit on a bargain, but few outsiders realised that a 'rasper' was a particularly big turn. 'Jam tart' meant exactly the market, in other words with buyers and sellers at the same price. A 'picker-up' was that unmentionable cad who not only tried to get a fellow member to make a wrong price but then dealt with him. To 'bang' was to offer stock loudly with the intention of lowering the price, to 'puff' was to bid for stock loudly with the intention of raising the price. A 'squirt' was someone who hung about the market with a paltry order, not dealing fairly. To 'read' was to try to tell by a man's face or manner what he wanted to do, to 'shoot' was to make a man a close price in a stock without knowing if there would be a profit or loss on the bargain. A 'sweater' was a broker who undercut the competition by working for small commissions, a 'poacher' was a jobber who dealt out of his own market or continually changed markets. There were plenty of other slang expressions, but probably the classic of them all was the cry of 'Fourteen hundred!' – for some mysterious reason the shout that would go up whenever a stranger was spotted in the House, invariably prompting a vigorous, even bruising 'rat-hunt' to flush him out of the sacrosanct place.

In the mid-1880s a junior called Murray Griffith sought to penetrate this mysterious, compelling temple. He joined a firm of dealers in the Home Rails market, served a rather turbulent apprenticeship checking bargains, and then his big moment came:

> Quite early, I was admitted to the precincts of the Holy of Holies, the House, and then at once I realised that I had fallen amongst a lot of men who were always kind and helpful . . . when I became an authorised clerk all the big men acted more like fathers to me than competitors . . . All this struck me as true sportsmanship to help along a youngster. This kind of schoolboy comradeship in the hard battle for success, established in my mind the fact that the Stock Exchange was full of human beings. The only standard to live up to being that you 'play the game'.

'Forty Years in the Best Club in London', Griffith called his fragment of memoirs. And as memoirs, they serve as a necessary antidote to the recollections (written at about the same time) of Carruthers Gould. Neither man denied the volatile, even seismic character of Stock Exchange life: but whereas the artist found it an existence unbearably ruthless in its practical working out, for Griffith it was an exciting, even exhilarating way of life fortified by the good fellowship of the club to which he was proud to belong. There is little doubt with whose view most members would have empathised. And, in a rather wonderful passage, the by now very successful jobber laid his faith on the line:

> I have always considered that the Stock Exchange is the real and true example of a socialistic institution, inasmuch that it gives everyone a chance of getting on, if he has the energy and brains so to do. Again, I say they ask no questions; you do not require a banker's reference, etc, all you have to do is to 'play the game'; and even if a man is unfortunate and comes to an end financially, it is not a question of how he came to grief, 'but did he play the game?'[24]

CHAPTER TEN

Gentlemen Capitalists

The relationship between the City and Gladstone had long been difficult, but in the mid-1880s it attained a new pitch of animosity. 'We want Gladstone turned out before any good can come to this country d—n his eyes.' That was the private view of the Hong Kong and Shanghai Bank's David McLean in June 1884, and the events of the next two years compounded it, as the City became in every sense a Tory stronghold. In the 1885 election, fought mainly on Joseph Chamberlain's Radical programme but also offering a verdict on Gladstone's second ministry, both City seats (their number had been reduced by the recent Redistribution Act) fell comfortably to the Conservatives. Then, in a state of electoral deadlock, came Gladstone's suspiciously sudden conversion to Irish Home Rule. The City had always taken a very strong line against violation of property in Ireland, and on this most fundamental of issues it made its views clear at a mass meeting held at the Guildhall on 2 April 1886. 'It was a great success', noted the strongly Tory private banker (and former Lord Mayor) Sir Robert Fowler in his diary. 'The hall was crowded and enthusiastic, though a few held up their hands against us. The great thing was getting the leading City Liberals to take the stand they took against Gladstone.' Among those Liberals who spoke against Home Rule were Sir John Lubbock, Richard Biddulph Martin, and the prominent copper merchant and former governor of the Bank, H. R. Grenfell. Grenfell was unequivocal: 'If there was one thing the City of London would not stand it was the disintegration of the Empire – (*loud cheers*) – and the separation of this country from Ireland (*renewed cheering*).'¹ Some City Liberals remained faithful to Gladstone, most notably Bertram Currie and Samuel Montagu, but most did not, including Natty Rothschild; he had long been unhappy with Gladstone's foreign policy (his family had always been Palmerstonian in outlook), and now at last he made the formal break. The ordinary City man fully shared the views of his betters.

In June Gladstone's Home Rule Bill was defeated in the Commons, in July he went down to a crushing electoral defeat – an election in which the Liberals did not even put up a candidate for the City. There was one final twist to 1886. Chancellor of the Exchequer in Salisbury's new Tory ministry was Lord Randolph Churchill, a man renowned for his contempt for middle-class, suburban Conservatism, what he called the 'pineries and vineries'. Late in the year, in an ill-judged move, he resigned; but Salisbury called his bluff, accepted the resignation, and replaced him with George Goschen, who, like so many City men, had broken with Gladstone over Ireland.

Perhaps inevitably, much nonsense has been written about the City's historical influence on politicians and the political process. Of course, it did exercise *an* influence – and one should hardly be surprised, for by the late nineteenth century, as Britain's visible trade deficit widened, the well-being of the economy was increasingly dependent upon the 'invisible' earnings provided by the City. Successive generations of politicians appreciated that it would be counterproductive deliberately to antagonise the City. Even Gladstone toed that particular line: when at the outset of his third ministry it was suggested to him that Chamberlain should go to the Treasury, he discounted the idea on the grounds that, in his secretary's words, 'the City would be terrified at his views'. Some of the City's leading figures, usually either merchant bankers or private bankers, also moved freely in the same social world as the leading politicians of the day, meeting as a matter of course and more or less as equals at clubs, dinner parties and country-house parties. There are two examples of particularly close relationships. One was between Gladstone and Bertram Currie, the former invariably turning to the latter whenever he needed advice on financial subjects. The other was on the Tory side. 'Churchill and Natty Rothschild seem to conduct the business of the Empire in great measure *together*', Reginald Brett recorded in 1886 during Lord Randolph's brief chancellorship. And two years later, Hamilton was noting that 'R. Churchill turns to N. Rothschild for everything, according to N. R.' There is no doubt that Natty loved being in the political know. Edward Hamilton described him as 'an infallible retailer of political as of all other news', with 'a wonderful knowledge of what is going on'. Hamilton himself, as a significant presence at the Treasury and on good personal as well as business terms with Natty, was very conscious of the importance of ensuring that Whitehall was not seen to be unduly influenced by the City. And in April 1889, in the context of consulting the Rothschilds about an imminent issue of Exchequer bonds, he wrote the most telling of entries in his diary: 'Though I always think it well to keep clear of them in the East End I actually lunched in New Court.'[2]

All that said, there are two powerful negative points to be made. Firstly, it is arguable that there existed an underlying conflict of interests, in that successive British governments naturally pursued national interests, whereas the City by definition pursued international interests.[3] That was a conflict, though, that would surface more in the twentieth than

nineteenth century. Secondly, *if* a leading City figure did go into Parliament
– and, increasingly, the leading City men did not – it was as likely to be
for social as political reasons, and often he had little to say for himself
once there.[4] Few bankers (if any) possessed any great global vision or
unusual prescience about the future course of events.

However, Natty Rothschild himself exemplifies the phenomenon that
has been called 'gentlemanly capitalism', or alternatively 'integration'.[5]
This is the phenomenon by which, in the late nineteenth century, the
upper reaches of the City moved increasingly close to the traditional
landed governing class, thereby achieving an intimate and privileged access
to power denied to their industrial counterparts in the provinces. Such
access, the argument runs, was in no sense conspiratorial, but rather the
natural outcome of shared values and assumptions in turn deriving from,
as much as anything, shared lifestyles. 'Manufacturers and merchants as
a rule seem only to desire riches that they may be enabled to prostrate
themselves at the feet of feudalism.' That dispirited verdict of Cobden as
early as 1863 was echoed a quarter of a century later by Engels, who
lamented 'the political decline and abdication of the bourgeoisie'.[6] Or
put differently: W. G. Prescott's foray into the Scottish Highlands may
have been ill-judged, and a cause of surprise to his thoroughly middle-
class banking partners, but it pointed the way to a plutocratic, grouse-
shooting future.

Why did the British aristocracy, a notoriously closed caste, let in the
men of finance? By the 1880s, a specific economic motive was that the
rent rolls of the aristocracy were falling and thus many of its members
needed to find not only a new investment strategy but also alternative
sources of income. Both necessities brought them into close and continuous contact with the City, which offered well-paid, light-duty jobs as
well as investment portfolios to suit every taste and pocket. Sometimes
these jobs took the form of partnerships within City firms, usually stockbroking; sometimes it might be a half-commission arrangement with a
stockbroker, in effect touting for West End custom; and sometimes, if
an impecunious aristocrat was very lucky, it might be what was called
with delightful accuracy a 'guinea-pig' directorship. E. C. Grenville
Murray, in his *Side-Lights on English Society* published in 1881, described
how peers were 'at a premium for directing companies':

> If a Noble Lord's character can bear anything like the test of scrutiny – and
> so long as he is not on the turf it generally can – he may command good
> terms for letting his name be put on a prospectus. His patronage means
> success. What a peer offers for sale the public will buy; and if they are
> ruined it will console them greatly to hear that his lordship is a fellow
> sufferer in pocket. Noble Lords always pretend to be heavy losers by joint-
> stock directing.

As company promotions boomed in the last two decades of the century, the opportunities were there for the taking; and by the mid-1890s about a quarter of the entire nobility were company directors.[7]

On the other side of the compact, the City's great moment came in June 1885 when Natty Rothschild and Ned Baring were made peers, as Lord Rothschild and Lord Revelstoke respectively. 'It is thought desirable at this moment to give an addition of commercial strength to the House of Lords', explained Hamilton, little guessing that within a year both men would abandon Gladstone over the Irish question. There were, not least due to royal prejudice, few precedents for these new peers: Robert Smith, who in 1796 had become Lord Carrington; Loyd who became Lord Overstone; and, in 1869, George Carr Glyn who became Lord Wolverton. 'I did not know that you would be allowed to remain in business', wrote Glyn's partner, Sir Charles Mills, in his letter of congratulation, reflecting a traditional view of the nature of aristocracy. In 1885 itself, neither Rothschild nor Revelstoke had any intention of leaving the counting house, though for both men it was an honour gratefully received. Natty in particular was flourishing as never before, and Hamilton's diary entries vividly convey the sense of him at the very centre of the social-cum-political elite:

> *27 May 1886.* Dined last night at the Rothschilds (Lord) – a big dinner – the German & Spanish ambassadors, both new, the Duke & Duchess of Wellington, Curzons, C. Beresford, W. Caringtons, Sir W. White, R. Spencer, Mrs Leo R & others. It was followed by an evening party, at which the house is always seen to great advantage.

> *16 July 1888.* I wound up my season last night with a dinner at the Rothschilds – a large party . . . After dinner there was an evening party – first, music . . . and then a recitation or two from Sarah Bernhardt.[8]

Capel Court was infamous for its noise and dust and acrid sweat, but sometimes its rewards could be beautiful. What in base terms were the City's rewards? It is clear that, among those active in business in the late nineteenth century, few provincial industrialists left fortunes of the same magnitude as those accumulated by the City's leading operators.[9] There were, for instance, fewer cotton millionaires than merchant banker million-aires – millionaires who included Natty Rothschild, the three Raphael brothers, Herman de Stern and Baron Schröder. In the mid-1890s the *Statist* published some invaluable wealth statistics, compiled on the basis of deaths since 1887. They by no means claimed completeness, but they showed that thirty-eight 'foreign bankers and merchant bankers', presum-ably all based in the City, had left an average of £512,578 and that ninety-three 'English bankers and money dealers', presumably many of whom were based in the City, had left an average of £211,450. By comparison, to take some occupations outside the financial sphere, 110 'coalowners and merchants, ironmasters, machinists, engineers and contractors', *some* of whom would have been City-based, left an average of £240,487; 193 'manufacturers, merchants, and warehousemen in the textile trade', which again would include City men, averaged £209,063; 119 brewers averaged £167,637; 101 judges, barristers and solicitors (again, a minority City component) averaged £84,933; and sixty-seven physicians and surgeons could manage only £50,614. Significantly well down this league table were eighty-four members of the Stock Exchange, whose average was £95,685 – though it is worth bearing in mind that one has to multiply by about sixty times to get a rough modern-day equivalent.[10] There was little doubt, then, where the serious money was to be made. Saving lives was all very well, even making things, but the world of issuing, accepting and exchange was what truly buttered the parsnips.

The successful City man had, therefore, something tangible to offer when he sought a marriage partner, and by the late nineteenth century it was no longer rare for that partner to be a daughter of an aristocratic family. There exists a heroic sample of leading bankers (including merchant bankers), 413 in all, who flourished in the City between 1890 and 1914, and by definition the great majority of these were also active in the 1880s. For the generation in the sample born between 1800 and 1820, only about 5 per cent married into an aristocratic family. But for the next generation, born between 1821 and 1840 and accordingly well-established City figures in the 1880s, the proportion rises sharply to at least 24 per cent – by any reasonable criterion, a proportion denoting significant upward mobility. That ratio of a quarter, moreover, applies to the next generation, those born between 1841 and 1860 and presumably the bankers who were actually getting married in the 1880s. If intermarriage was a crucial part of the 'integration' between land and finance, so too was education. The 413 again tell an interesting story, the sample showing an increasing tendency, culminating in the generation born between 1861 and 1880 but already well established by the 1821–40 cohort, for leading bankers to be educated at a public school followed by Oxbridge – precisely the education that was becoming a *sine qua non* in the political elite at large.[11] And in terms of the values inculcated by that education, few would deny that they were more 'gentlemanly' than 'capitalist'.

But of course, there are other perspectives on the whole phenomenon, beginning with the long-run assertion that there was nothing new about close links between the City of London and landed society. The copper merchant and Bank of England director Charles Pascoe Grenfell (1790–1867) married the daughter of the Earl of Sefton; while his son Charles William (1823–61), elder brother of Henry, married the granddaughter of the second Earl of Harewood. One has only to examine the composition of the Phoenix Assurance board from 1840 to see there a strong cluster of City merchants and others whose *fathers* had actually had country seats. Nor, in terms of the accelerated integration that undoubtedly did take place in the late nineteenth century, should one be naive about the process. The country life may have had its inherent attractions, but for an astute operator like Ernest Cassel the motivation for learning to hunt was that the value of the contacts he thereby cultivated, along with assiduous attendance at the card table, the racecourse and the shoot, more than outweighed the pain and embarrassment of an unfortunate tendency to fall off his horse. Not quite in the Cassel class, but impressive nonetheless, was Robert Benson, who in the last quarter of the century systematically utilised a socially deft marriage and a brother-in-law relationship with the 4th Earl Grey to build up for his house a select circle of well-heeled investors, who in effect employed him as a congenial financial consultant. It can even be argued that there was a specific business motive in the buying of land, despite the fact that rent rolls were falling: in the case of the Gibbs family, for instance, it is clear that there was a conscious strategy to acquire land partly as a way of preventing the firm from over-extending itself into riskier investments.[12]

Moreover, it seems extremely implausible that anti-City animus on the part of landed society could have died away overnight. Sir Gorgius Midas, that nouveau riche vulgarian in the pages of *Punch*, was an immortal creation of George du Maurier that rang many bells; while Hamilton in 1885 noted that 'some people are turning up their noses at the Rothschild Peerage'. Or consider what was in one sense the cardinal act of integration, the marriage in 1878 between the 5th Earl of Rosebery, a future prime minister, and Hannah Rothschild, a niece of Baron Lionel. Perfection, however, was marred by the attitude of the respective families: his mother strongly opposed the union, her male relatives stayed away in droves from the wedding. The barriers could go up, in other words, on either side of the social divide.[13]

There is further evidence of Rothschild reluctance unconditionally to cross that divide. 'It is curious that all the Rothschilds (with one exception) should have preferred building their own houses & making their own places to buying old family seats with ready made parks which no amount of money can produce', remarked Hamilton in 1886, adding that 'it is moreover remarkable how clannish they are, & how they have all settled down in the same country' (referring to the Vale of Aylesbury). And two years later Hamilton listened to Natty speaking 'with all his natural *class* prejudices' about the 'harm which a few of the aristocracy do to their class by frequently displaying a want of sense of honour in money affairs and by resorting to gambling in these days'. Such, even among Rothschilds, was the tenacity of City culture, which was essentially of a middle-class, non-aristocratic character. Or take the notable tribute paid to Tom Baring on his death in 1873. 'He was certainly a proof, if any were wanting,' wrote Bertram Currie to his father, 'that a merchant may be as good a gentleman as an acred lord or squire and he was wisely content with and proud of his trade.'[14]

In terms of non-integration, the classic case was surely Kleinworts, the merchant bank on probably the steepest ascent. The firm's founding father, Alexander Kleinwort, who continued living in Camberwell until his death in 1886, insisted that his two sons, Herman and Alexander, be educated on the Continent rather than going to an English public school. Thus equipped with fluent French and German, they then received a thorough commercial grounding, not an Oxbridge gown in sight, before finally becoming partners in the early 1880s. These younger Kleinworts both married women whose first language was not English; they continued to work extraordinarily hard and had little or nothing to do with aristocrats or aristocratic pursuits; and when they eventually did buy country estates, they were on a fairly modest scale. Other successful Anglo-German houses, most notably Schröders, followed this pattern to at least an extent, as did the Anglo-Greek houses like Rallis. They all avoided wasting time being a director of the Bank of England; yet contrary to what one might expect, given the prestige of the institution, those who were Bank directors were, for the most part, distinctly non-integrating. Of the twenty-seven (still mostly merchants) elected as directors between 1848 and 1873, only ten of whom left fortunes of over £300,000, we have information about nineteen of their wives: they comprised the daughters of five clergymen, five City merchants, two MPs, two lawyers, two admirals, one ambassador, one landowner, and one banker – but no aristocrats. Charlotte de Rothschild in 1869 recorded with some bewilderment these tacit parameters: 'The governor of the Bank called at New Court yesterday and told the Gentlemen he had been offered a Baronetcy, and had declined it; the reason of such a refusal I cannot comprehend; Mr Crawford thinks that a man in business ought not to be Sir Robert.'[15]

*

Members were at first reluctant to inhabit the new part of the Stock Exchange with its great dome, but then, in 1886, came the momentous discovery of gold on the Witwatersrand, and soon the New House was filled by the jobbers and raucous noises of what would become known as the 'Kaffir Circus'. By May 1887 *The Economist* was writing of 'A Mining Promotion "Boom"'; while two years later the *Statist* was detailing 'The South African Fever' and estimating that since 1886 the London capital market had channelled at least £50m into ventures like (to name some registered in January 1889) the Anglo Transvaal Prospecting

Company, Madeline Witwatersrand Gold Mining Company, West Battery Reef Gold Mining Company, and so on. In many parts of the City, however, even in New Court at times, there remained an underlying scepticism about gold mines that would prove hard to shift. In 1888 *The Economist* described mining shares as traditionally 'the happy hunting-grounds of organised gangs of promoters, who, together with their associates – low-class advertising agents, &c – care nothing about the value of a mine, provided only that it can be made a means of fleecing the public'. Or as an adage, beloved of the Stock Exchange, ran from about this time: 'A mine is a hole in the ground owned by a liar.'[16]

An important episode was the successful flotation in the spring of 1887 of Cecil Rhodes' Gold Fields of South Africa (later Consolidated Gold Fields). Rhodes himself was still an unknown force in the City; the person who secured the support for the flotation was his right-hand man, Charles Rudd, upper middle class, with a brother who was a director of the London Joint Stock Bank and now chairman of Gold Fields. Between them the Rudds obtained influential backers, including the well-connected East India merchants Arbuthnot Latham and several leading operators on the Stock Exchange. Control at this stage stayed firmly in the hands of Rhodes in South Africa, but he would have conceded that it was the London flotation that gave his company the critical mass it needed.[17] Another key episode, which concerned diamonds not gold, came soon afterwards and also involved Rhodes. This was the convoluted establishment during 1887–8 of what became De Beers Consolidated, in effect the amalgamation of the Kimberley diamond mines. Rhodes came to London in July 1887, passed the informal test of an interview with Natty Rothschild, and was lent £500,000 by Rothschilds in order to effect one of the critical mergers in the process. Soon after De Beers was formed there arose the question of a debenture issue, and in August 1888 Rhodes wrote plaintively to Natty about the problem of getting adequate security for the loan:

> The whole case depends whether you have any confidence and trust in myself. Perhaps someone else can do it better, I really do not know; you know my objects and the whole case is a question of trust. I know with you behind me I can do all I have said. If, however, you think differently I have nothing to say.[18]

Much turned on that word 'objects', and over the years there would be a significant divergence between the Empire-driven Rhodes and the commerce-driven City, whatever the latter's imperial sympathies. While as for 'trust', Natty's man on the De Beers board was Carl Meyer, in whom he invested somewhat more of that rare commodity than he ever would in Rhodes himself.

By 1890 the South African gold-mining boom was temporarily over – awaiting a technological solution to the problem of non-remunerative pyritic ore below a certain level of the reef – but in the thriving City of the late 1880s, there took place an upsurge of home industrial issues, and these included the advent of smaller share denominations, a diminution of uncalled liabilities, a need for external capital on the part of more technologically driven industries, and (not least important) a natural wish by families owning businesses to reap the considerable material fruits of converting to a public company.

One such family was Guinness of Dublin, which offered its inimitable business to Barings in 1886, having had it turned down a few years earlier by Rothschilds. The total size of the issue was £6m, and Edward Hamilton that October recorded the outcome: 'There has been nothing within the recollection of the City like the rush for shares in the Guinness Co. . . . It seems pretty clear that the Barings put the rate of interest on the preference & debenture shares 1% too high.' Whatever the truth of that charge, there were some sensational scenes at 8 Bishopsgate, as the merchant bank was besieged, desperate applicants hurled through windows their forms wrapped around stones, and (in the words of the *Daily News*) 'special policemen kept back the pushing crowd of clerks, agents, messengers and City men'.

But that was not the only thing that the City would remember about this flotation: for it eventually emerged, partly as the result of assiduous digging by the *Financial News*, that despite, or perhaps because of, the phenomenal over-application for above all the £4.5m ordinary and prefer-ence shares, Barings had kept back almost £1m of them for itself, set aside handsome portions for favoured City houses, and made available barely a quarter of the shares for the public at large. 'One of the most disgraceful Frauds on the Public that in my experience has ever been concocted': that was the view of Robert Cecil, addressing Barings from his writing desk at the Carlton Club. The firm itself took it all stoically on the chin, finding solace in a profit of over £500,000; but it had been an illuminating experience, with the pros finely balanced against the cons.[19]

For the two great rivals, there was an immediate sequel to the episode. On the same day that he noted the rush of applicants for Guinness shares, Hamilton added intriguingly: 'Apropos of the success of this undertaking and the failure of the Manchester Ship Canal which was in the hands of the Rothschilds, an invidious comparison is drawn between "Rothschild's water" and "Barings' beer".' The following year, 1887, the two houses came together in July to offer jointly to the public a £4m issue to try again to enable the canal to be built. It proved a miserable flop, with the public applying for less than a fifth, little interest being shown outside Lancashire, and the City remaining indifferent. It was an awkward baby to hold, with Barings and Rothschilds each being left with over 40,000 shares, and it may well have been the moment when New Court anyway decided that British industrial promotions were not for it. Revelstoke perhaps had his moment of revelation the following year, in the course of negotiations for the conversion of a Liverpool brewery, Messrs Walkers, into a joint-stock company. 'During the discussion', the *Bankers' Magazine* related soon afterwards, 'some strong words were used in Lord Revelstoke's presence. He pointed to the door, and the firm lost the quarter-million or so which might have accrued from the business'. But for whatever cultural and commercial reasons, Guinness and the Manchester Ship Canal would for many years stand out like sore thumbs in the issuing history of Barings and Rothschilds, where the foreign remained firmly their home patch. For the Ship Canal itself, however, there was a surprisingly happy outcome to its relations with the City. An issue in 1889 proved appreciably more successful, while much of the financial initiative passed to Glyns and Alexander Henderson, who between them helped to ensure that the canal could be opened by Queen Victoria in 1894.[20] British industry was coming by fits and starts to need the City, but as yet the City in return was hardly giving British industry its best shot.

Perhaps there was an excuse in the overheated late 1880s, with so much going on. One of the most striking developments was the rapid growth of investment trusts. These trusts were quoted on the London Stock Exchange and spread their assets across a wide range of investments, being designed, in the words of the prospectus in 1868 of the pioneer Foreign and Colonial trust, 'to give the investor of moderate means the same advantages as the large Capitalists'. That at least was the theory, though in practice they were found most attractive in the late 1880s by existing investors who felt they were no longer obtaining an adequate return on British government securities.[21]

At this stage 'old' City had relatively little to do with investment trusts, if only because they were new. Few in the City – on the financial side at least – were now 'older' than Natty Rothschild, and very soon after the Guinness affair he was asked by the journalist Frank Harris if he was jealous of the large profit made by Barings:

> I don't look at it quite in that way . . . I go to the House every morning and when I say 'No' to every scheme and enterprise submitted to me, I return home at night carefree and contented. But when I agree to any proposal, I am immediately filled with anxiety. To say 'Yes' is like putting your finger in a machine: the whirring wheels may drag your whole body in after the finger.

Was his firm already entering upon a slow but inexorable decline? One might think so, to judge by a remark in January 1887 from Morgans in

London to Drexel Morgan in the States: 'Since failure in Manch Ship Canal issue & small success in one or 2 other enterprises their name does not carry with it that persuasion to the public w^h it used to do.'[22] Of course one can exaggerate, for not only did the house continue to bring out a steady stream of foreign government issues but in 1889 it was responsible for the phenomenally successful Burma Ruby Mines issue, when the crowd in St Swithin's Lane became so great that Natty reputedly had to climb up a ladder to get into the bank. Yet even that venture was double-edged, for it caused plenty of trouble as well as profit and may have played a part in persuading Natty that all company promotions, foreign as well as domestic, were simpler eschewed.

An increasingly pivotal figure inside New Court was Carl Meyer – 'the ever industrious C.M.', Cassel called him – and in January 1890 he wrote a formal letter to Alfred de Rothschild requesting to be relieved of his duties unless he be transformed from a salaried clerk into a financial adviser. Meyer's terms included 'that my name should be removed from the list of clerks under the control of the worthy Allard'; that he should receive a minimum yearly income of £6,000 to replace his salary; and 'that, if at any future time you should determine upon conferring the procuration of the house (as is done at Vienna and Frankfurt) upon any of the members of the staff, I should be one of those entrusted with that mark of confidence'.

Though some changes were made to Meyer's position, he never became a partner. Instead, over the years, he became increasingly close to Cassel, while Rothschilds remained an autocracy. In February 1890 two great autocrats came together, as Revelstoke was a guest at a house party held by Natty at his country home near Tring. The inevitable Hamilton (an almost Jamesian figure) watched closely: 'It is rather amusing to see the heads of the two great rival financial Houses together. They take stock of each other with jealous eyes, the jealousy being somewhat ill-disguised.'[23] The two men, temperamentally so different, knew each other well, and both may have wondered whether the ultimate spoils would go to the hare or the tortoise.

Hamilton's diary also makes it patently clear how, by the late nineteenth century, no Chancellor of the Exchequer could get very far in a financial operation without, in his words, 'taking the financial "bigwigs" into confidence', none of whom was bigger than Revelstoke and Rothschild. This certainly applied to Goschen's enormous operation in 1888, when he sought to convert £500m of British government 3 per cent stock to 2½ per cent. On paper everything was in his favour, helped by the cheapness of money, the dearness of securities and his own high reputation in the City, not least after his recent political switch; but for any Chancellor a major conversion was a severe test of nerve. 'I am more & more convinced that the right way to set about a conversion is by persuasion

rather than by force', wrote Currie to Goschen on 11 January, as preliminary discussions began, and a week later Hamilton was reflecting along
the same lines: 'The Chanc of the Exchequer must nerve himself into
giving the stock-brokers some consideration, if he is to succeed with any
conversion on a large scale. I am glad to say he has taken into his confidence men like Lord Revelstoke, Rothschild & B. Currie. Without their
co-operation he will embark in a hopeless task.'[24]

In March Goschen formally put forward his scheme in Parliament,
and *The Economist* declared that 'Mr Goschen has every reason to be
gratified with the reception his Debt Conversion scheme has met with',
that 'probably, indeed, he was just a little astonished at the enthusiasm
with which it was first greeted on the Stock Exchange'. Goschen's conversion was the great triumph of his chancellorship, though Gladstone, whose
own attempted conversion of 1853 had not come off, growled afterwards
that the whole thing was no more than a 'magnificent swindle'.[25] But if
so, it was a swindle which the City, properly remunerated, was prepared
to countenance.

Early in 1889, however, as Goschen and the Treasury prepared the
rather technical endgame of the conversion operation, all was not such
sweetness and light. Hamilton again:

16 January. The most formidable financial job ahead is the redemption of
the balance of old Consols & Reduced threes . . . I am convinced it ought
to be done *en bloc*, & if we go the right way to work I don't believe it
will be as formidable a business as many people think. The way to do it
is to get certain big houses like Barings & Rothschilds to form a syndicate
which would take at a given price such amount of new stock as will be
required to replace the old stock . . .

31 January. In consequence of a talk I had with Lord Revelstoke in the
autumn, he has made an informal proposal through me. It is that he would
take 20 or 25 millions of stock at par . . .

I have impressed upon him [Goschen] the importance of taking the
Rothschilds likewise into confidence; and he will give them a hint that he
has had a 'nibble'. We must have the co-operation of both houses, between
which there is a considerable amount of jealousy.

7 February. Revelstoke & Rothschild are in communication with one
another, & the Revelstoke proposal seems to have elements of success in
it; but the terms originally proposed will have to be materially modified.
Rothschild won't look at them: the possible margin of profit being considered wholly out of proportion to the risk run.

13 February. Agreement with financial houses has broken down; they opened
their mouths a deal too wide. They would not take the new Stock (20 or
25 millions), running all risks, higher than 97½, as against present price
of 98¾ to 99 and Revelstoke's original offer of £99.13.6.

Perhaps the two houses were simply too greedy, perhaps Natty was once again displaying his excessive caution, or perhaps Goschen at his end of the negotiations was unduly anxious about criticism from Gladstone if he made his terms too generous. In any event, the government was left with no alternative but to turn to its faithful retainer, the Bank of England, to help it redeem the old stock.[26]

Conversion, let alone redemption, would not have been possible without the blessing of the Stock Exchange, where *la vie spirituelle* continued. In 1889 there was the scandal of members defying the Committee by openly smoking all day long, as a way of protesting against the House's inadequate sanitation in the context of prevalent enteric fever. Early in 1890 the Committee considered a complaint from the Managers about 'a sudden rush made by a crowd of persons at the main entrance on the 23rd of December whereby a pugilist named Slavin was carried, or forced, into the House', but decided it would not be politic to interfere. And in October 1890 the *Rialto* reported a lively episode: 'The Stock Exchange was much excited by a bet made by one of its members – that he would go from the House to the top of the Monument and back inside 15 minutes. As a matter of fact he did it in a little over 8 minutes, and a good deal of money changed hands over the event.'[27]

But sometimes there was business too, and for the Stock Exchange as a whole these were marvellous years. James Capel & Co. was probably typical in enjoying annual profits over the next two years of well over £50,000; and in 1890 the *Bankers' Magazine* asserted that 'the stockbroker who kept a modest man-of-all-work in the year 1885, perhaps now has two gardeners, a coachman or "tiger", and even a footman or two, in place of the factotum'. Probably not employing a nursemaid was a member called Hugh Stutfield, who some years later, in an article memorably entitled 'Celibacy and the Struggle to Get on', recalled the heady late 1880s:

> About five years ago [*c.*1889] there was quite a rush of gilded youth within the portals of Capel Court. Nearly every firm of standing could boast of one or more sprigs of nobility on its staff of clerks, and smart cavalry officers were glad to act as 'runners' [half-commission men] if they could not become partners . . .
>
> Financial houses and firms of old standing vied one with the other in foisting unmarketable rubbish on the guileless investor, who, through the medium of trust and other companies, fell a victim to various ingenious devices to part him and his money.[28]

CHAPTER ELEVEN

A Friend in Need

In October 1889, not long after the London Dock Strike, William Lidderdale (the new governor of the Bank of England) pondered 'the present tendency of finance':

> Too much capital is being forced into industrial developments, financiers are taking larger & larger risks in securities which require prosperity & easy money to carry without becoming a burden . . . People are now attracted only by the promise of profits beyond interest. On the basis of 20 years ago we have most of the elements of a Crisis, with the additional danger that our collective liabilities are enormously increased with but a small increase in the central cash reserve of the country.

So, was a crisis inevitable? He thought not, placing his faith in the current mode of 'financial operations':

> No great loans are taken without the issuing firms taking in numerous associates who share the risk for a consideration. London & Paris, London & N York, London N York & Berlin or Hamburg, combine to carry out the operation thus greatly lessening the dangers of unsuccessful issue by a division & spreading of the liability . . . so great has become the solidarity of Finance that it seems to me it would need something like a sudden outbreak of war, under present circumstances, to produce a crisis.[1]

Even so, at the start of December 1888 the *Statist* had published a well-informed, highly critical article on 'Messrs Baring Brothers' Issues'. It itemised the firm's thirty-one principal issues since 1882 (of which all but two, Guinness and the Manchester Ship Canal, had been foreign) and then proceeded to accuse Barings of not fulfilling its moral duties as an issuing house:

> Their prospectuses too frequently are not merely meagre, but quite insufficient to enable anyone to judge of the character of the security. The Messrs Baring, moreover, never state what compensation they receive for bringing out either a loan or a company, though surely this is a material circumstance.

The paper concluded on a frankly ominous note: 'It is much better, in the long run, that bad business should not be embarked in than that insecure loans should be foisted on the public by one of the greatest of our houses.' The *Bankers' Magazine* had only recently, and justly, cited this household name as the prime case of a firm that had 'never known, during the present century, anything but first-class credit, into which enters the elements of dignity – moral, personal and commercial alike'. Solid, deeply respectable and rather unimaginative, there was on the face of it no more English house in the City.[2]

What was going on?[3] The answer lies primarily with one man and one country. The man, inevitably, was Revelstoke, who may well have had his head turned by the phenomenal success and profitability of the Guinness issue, even to the extent where he came to believe that simply to have the name of Barings attached to an issue was sufficient to guarantee its favourable reception. And the country to which from the mid-1880s he devoted ever more of his firm's resources was the Argentine, into which British capital was pouring at an astounding rate, totalling up to £150m (about £9bn in present-day terms) by the end of the decade. That seductive land of rich pampas had long held a fatal attraction for the City, and amidst considerable competition from other houses Barings was responsible for about a quarter of the funds now flowing to it. The main conduit was the Buenos Aires firm of S. B. Hale & Co., examined and given a clean bill of health by Brown Shipley in November 1887.

Less than a year later Revelstoke was paid a visit by the firm's leading director, C. H. Sanford, who had recently obtained from the Argentine government the much-sought concession to develop the sewerage and water system of Buenos Aires. Was Sanford a man to trust? Barings had had at least one unfavourable report on him, yet Revelstoke not only agreed to bring out the Buenos Aires Water Supply and Drainage Company but also, with his propensity for double-or-quits, decided against the increasingly common custom (as he no doubt saw it, but which so reassured Lidderdale) of having the issue fully underwritten. The flotation took place in November 1888 and, as the *Statist* noted with grim satisfaction, flopped. The implications for Barings, left with a vast number of unmarketable shares, were dire: it had agreed to operate on joint account with Hale & Co. and it was committed to finding further capital for a massively expensive project as well as stumping up the rest of the purchase money to the Argentine government. Judgement was all, and Revelstoke's had deserted him.

Matters got worse in 1890, fuelled by a lethal Argentinian combination of financial maladministration and political turmoil. With large holdings in other South American securities likewise locking up the firm's capital, Revelstoke and his partners had placed themselves in a position of appalling exposure. During September the situation remained on hold, though Barings achieved some temporary alleviation through borrowing some

£500,000 from its good friends at Martins. On 7 October, Hamilton dined with (among others) Natty Rothschild, who 'confessed to being very uneasy about the present state of things in the City'. And Hamilton glossed: 'Nobody knows exactly why an uneasy feeling should prevail: beyond that there is a sort of general apprehension that certain big houses are not in a very comfortable or easy position, mainly due to the Argentine crisis & the general fall in securities which causes their lock-up to be so enormous.' Within a few days Goschen, still Chancellor, was recording a similar mood in his diary: 'Went to the Bank, things queer! Some of the first houses talked about. Argentine, etc, have created immense complications. Uncomfortable feeling generally.'

Then, on the 13th, Bertram Currie of Glyns received the first intimation that his old friend and neighbour was in serious trouble. The intermediary was Sidney Brunton, a partner with the stockbrokers Brunton, Bourke & Co. and a leading figure in the money market:

> He came with a message from Lord Revelstoke to say that the firm required a large sum of money, and that it was difficult for them to appear in the market as borrowers. Before replying to this proposal, I told Mr Brunton to ask Lord Revelstoke for a statement of the bills payable and receivable. He returned with the answer that the acceptances of the firm amounted to ten millions sterling, and the bills in portfolio to nine millions sterling.[4]

The upshot was that Glyns advanced £1m, and later in the month another £250,000. All was intensely secretive, no one could yet name names, and the City's perturbed frame of mind was accurately reflected in an out-letter of the Imperial Ottoman Bank written on the 24th:

> We are going through peculiar times in London just now. Money is not so scarce, otherwise we would have a panic, but it is almost impossible to sell stock of any class from Consols downwards. 'The Market' won't buy excepting to close a/cs, and none of the 'big houses' here are free to buy, their commitments being already as much as they can carry.[5]

The impossibility of selling securities compounded the problems of Barings, as did the policy of the Russian government of steadily withdrawing its large-scale deposits from the house, with another major withdrawal (£1.5m) due on 11 November. The probability is that, by the end of October, Revelstoke had sufficiently swallowed his pride to take into his confidence perhaps a handful of leading figures, who in turn realised that something must be done.

The next sighting in a largely invisible process occurred at 8 a.m. on Saturday 8 November, when Everard Hambro – second only to Currie as a close friend of Revelstoke – caused some raised eyebrows by calling at such an unusual time of the week on Natty Rothschild in New Court.

Their discussions were inconclusive, but Hambro pressed on and saw Revelstoke himself, who said bleakly that he would be able to say on Monday whether Barings could go on or would have to stop. The two men were both directors of the Bank, and Hambro told Revelstoke that the only man who could help him now was the governor; he arranged that Lidderdale should come to Hambros in the afternoon so that he could discreetly see Revelstoke. At that meeting – before which Lidderdale scribbled a note to Goschen asking him to come to the Bank first thing on Monday – Revelstoke and a fellow partner laid before Lidderdale and Hambro 'a preliminary statement of their affairs', in Lidderdale's words soon afterwards, 'which rendered it uncertain whether the Firm would have any surplus after payment of their liabilities'. Inevitably the atmosphere was strained. Lidderdale, who had probably learnt only that day that Barings was in such trouble, contented himself with saying that he needed more precise information and would wait until Monday to see whether Barings could go on. Hambro had already passed on to Lidderdale his earlier conversation with Revelstoke, and all the evidence is that the head of Barings was in an emotional state.[6]

Lidderdale whiled away the next day by taking his small son to London Zoo. Perhaps even at this stage he saw the crisis as an opportunity as well as a challenge, for already that summer he had acted decisively to achieve for the Bank a greater degree of control over the money market than any governor had managed for a long time. As a good merchant, he was inherently hostile to bankers as a breed – 'a less public-spirited class . . . I do not know', he declared – and in particular resented their tendency to remove at a drop of the hat their already inadequate balances from the Bank. His words to Sir Reginald Welby at the Treasury, a few weeks before the crisis, were heartfelt:

> I don't think any one who has not sat for 2 years in the governor's chair during the last decade can realise fully – the dependence of the English Banking system upon the Bank – the difficulty that this dependence creates in our management. Banking liabilities have enormously increased, not so Bankers' reserves, and this makes our burden much heavier than before and leads to fluctuations in rates quite out of proportion to actual movement of currency.

His special ire was reserved for the joint-stock bankers, but on this Sunday he also felt considerable contempt for Revelstoke's gross mismanagement. He later told Hamilton that Revelstoke 'did not seem the least to know how he stood' and that 'it was haphazard management, certain to bring any firm to grief'.[7] Still, personal feelings aside, there was no getting away from the almost unthinkable consequences should Barings go down: not only would the failure of the City's leading accepting house inevitably bring down a host of other firms, including all the discount houses, but the very status of the bill on London would be threatened and thus the pre-eminence of the City as an international financial centre.

Yet what could the Bank do? The post-1873 intellectual legacy of Bagehot's *Lombard Street* meant that indisputably it would have to do *something*, but the equally indisputable fact was that a private institution, responsible to its shareholders and with reserves roughly half the size of Barings' estimated liabilities, could not hope to act as sole lender of last resort. It was all very difficult, and at this particular juncture in its affairs the Square Mile was extremely fortunate to have at its helm someone described by Welby as 'a model of a calm shrewd bold Scotch man of business'. Or as Hamilton, ear ever to the ground, had noted not long before the crisis broke: 'It is said that Lidderdale is considered in the City to be the best governor the Bank has ever had (not excepting Collet). He always knows his mind, & his judgement is very good.' Now that judgement was to meet its supreme test.

Goschen kept his Monday morning appointment in Threadneedle Street, and years later Lidderdale recalled that his first words were 'You gave me an unhappy Sunday, Mr Governor.' Goschen himself recorded the course of the interview in his diary:

> To the governor of the Bank. Found him in a dreadful state of anxiety. Barings in such danger that unless aid is given, they must stop. — came in while I was there; almost hysterical. Governor and he both insisted that the situation could only be saved if government helped . . . All houses would tumble one after the other. All credit gone. I entirely understood their reasoning, but remembering action taken in France when [in 1889] Comptoir d'Escompte was in difficulties, I said the great houses and banks in London must come together and give the necessary guarantee. This was declared impossible if the government didn't help.

The Chancellor then went to see two other (unnamed) bankers, both of whom insisted that government help was necessary. And he noted tartly: 'Both quite demoralised. Lidderdale much more of a man and keeping his head, though certainly he pressed me hard.' Goschen returned to the Treasury in mid-afternoon and informed Hamilton of the plight of Barings. 'Every effort will have to be made to keep them on their legs', Hamilton wrote later in the day, though adding that Goschen 'does not at present see his way to doing more than giving every support to the Bank'. And: 'I gathered from Goschen that poor Revelstoke seems to have well nigh lost his head, which is not to be wondered at. Though the City is very uneasy, depressed, & excited, they have not yet got word of the immensity of the storm that is brewing.'[8]

That evening, there was little sleep for Goschen as he wrestled with himself as to what his policy should be. 'If I do nothing and the crash comes I shall never be forgiven: if I act, and disaster never occurs, Parliament would never forgive my having pledged the National credit to a private Firm.' Eventually, his 'night thoughts' convinced him that it was impossible as well as undesirable to carry direct aid in Parliament: 'How defend a supplemental estimate for a loss of half a million! And would not immediate application put the whole fat in the fire?'[9] Goschen, like all Chancellors of the era, was a finance minister formed in the Gladstonian mould; and at the heart of Gladstonian Liberalism was an immutable belief in laissez-faire. The City, it seemed, would have to stand or fall on its own.

Between Tuesday and Thursday, as rumours flew with ever greater velocity, there were four main developments. The first was that Goschen continued to insist to Lidderdale that the government could offer no tangible help, while Lidderdale for his part was adamant that the Bank could act only within a larger umbrella provided by the government. Secondly, the Bank managed to persuade the Russian government not to make its £1.5m withdrawal from Barings. Thirdly, Natty Rothschild emerged as a constructive figure, not only persuading the Bank of France to lend £3m in gold to bolster the Bank of England's badly stretched reserves, but applying discreet pressure on his good friend Lord Salisbury (the prime minister) to adopt a more interventionist attitude to the crisis. Significantly, 'he said that if the catastrophe came', Salisbury recorded after their conversation, 'he thought it would put an end to the commercial habit of transacting all the business of the world by bills on London'. Rothschild seems to have been sceptical about the chances of Barings' long-term survival as a significant business, even if it did not sink immediately, but as Hamilton noted with pleasure after a dinner party on Wednesday, 'N. Rothschild spoke very nicely & unboastfully about the situation.' The fourth development was probably the most important – Lidderdale's decision to appoint Bertram Currie and the octogenarian Benjamin Buck Greene to determine between them whether Barings was solvent in the long run; in other words, whether it was worthy of rescue. It was an appointment that on the Wednesday brought forth the most pitiful letter from Revelstoke to Currie: 'I don't like to come & see you & hardly think I ought to write, but I cannot help sending one line in my wretched agony to implore you to do what you can. I know you will & I am sure you feel for us all in our nightmare.'[10] Pitiful, yes, but aimed at an old friend's heart with deadly effect.

Friday the 14th was the crunch. In the course of a trying morning it became clear that, in the eyes of Currie and Greene, the assets of Barings did show a substantial surplus over its liabilities, despite the firm's pressing need for an enormous cash advance of up to £9m, mainly in order to meet acceptances falling due over the coming weeks. Some ten years later

Greene wrote to Lidderdale about his memories of that morning: 'I must frankly say that as the amount required was so large . . . I considered the shutters must go up soon after I reached The City, instead of which on delivery of the report to my surprise you instantly said "They must be carried on."' Meanwhile, it was also becoming clear that, after almost a week of astute news management, including a degree of self-denial on the part of the press, the City at large was starting to succumb to outright panic. At about noon John Daniell, senior partner of Mullens the government brokers, burst into the Bank, crying to Lidderdale with his arms aloft: 'Can't you do something, or say something, to relieve people's minds? They have made up their minds that something awful is up, and they are talking of the very highest names – the very highest!'[11] During the next hour, Barings' bills started to pour into the Bank at an alarmingly rapid rate. With the entire credit of the City at peril, the moment was nigh for Lidderdale to earn the greatness that was being thrust upon him. At about two o'clock he slipped quietly out of the Princes Street door.

He took a roundabout route until he secured a hansom, which drove him to Downing Street. There he did not meet Goschen, who was committed to a speaking engagement in Dundee that evening and felt that he had to fulfil his programme to avoid panic. Instead his place was taken by W. H. Smith, first lord of the Treasury and widely known as 'Old Morality', and he was soon joined by Salisbury. For at least an hour neither side would back down from the positions taken at the start of the week. At one point Salisbury offered authority to break the 1844 Bank Charter Act, but this Lidderdale (he was to recall) 'emphatically refused', telling the prime minister that 'reliance on such letters was the cause of a great deal of bad banking in England'. And, 'after a short pause', Salisbury replied, 'I believe you are right.' Eventually, with stalemate looming, Lidderdale played his highest card:

> I told Lord Salisbury I could not possibly go on with the matter at the Bank's sole risk; that the Bank had been taking in Baring's Bills all the week, pending the investigation; that they were probably coming in fast now that alarm had set in, and that unless government would relieve us of some of the possible loss, I should return at once and throw out all further acceptances of the Firm.[12]

This threat prevailed. The two politicians in effect gave Lidderdale just under twenty-four hours to save Barings, promising that the government would bear half the loss resulting from taking in Barings' bills up to early afternoon on Saturday. By five o'clock, mercifully unhindered by the notorious traffic jams of late-Victorian London, the governor was back in the City.

Currie was among those waiting for him, as Lidderdale called an immediate meeting in his room at the Bank and announced his intention of starting a guarantee fund for Barings, with the Bank itself putting up the first million pounds. Currie at once declared that Glyn Mills would contribute half a million on the condition that Rothschilds did the same. Moments later Natty Rothschild arrived at the meeting. Would he agree? To quote Currie's subsequent, carefully measured account: 'He hesitated and desired to consult his brothers, but was finally and after some pressure persuaded to put down the name of his firm for £500,000.' What pressure? According to Hamilton the next day, it needed Lidderdale to say bluntly to Rothschild: 'We can get on without you.'[13] What would have happened if Rothschild had called Lidderdale's bluff is another question. But he did not, and the success of the guarantee fund was assured: over the next half-hour the City's inner circle rushed to contribute. Subscribers to the first list included Raphaels (£250,000), Antony Gibbs and Brown Shipley (£200,000 each), and Smith Payne & Smiths, Barclays, Morgans and Hambros (£100,000 each). In the evening, Lidderdale met representatives of the five leading joint-stock banks, who put themselves down for an impressive total of £3.25m. Effectively the fund guaranteed the Bank against any losses arising out of advances made to Barings to enable it to discharge its liabilities; and the happy consequence was that, in some form still to be determined, Barings was saved. 'We will do our best not to be unworthy of what has been done', wrote Revelstoke to Lidderdale on Saturday morning.[14]

The existence of the fund remained secret most of that day, as it steadily grew to almost £10m by mid-afternoon, eventually reaching some £17m by the following week. And, until news of it did leak out towards the end of Saturday, the mood of the City as a whole was encapsulated by the *Financial Times'* graphic leading article that morning on what it could only call 'The Agony':

> The City is becoming enveloped deeper and deeper in a baleful, mysterious crisis. Day by day thick clouds gather over the Stock Markets, and where they come from, and who is responsible for them, no one has a definite opinion. All who have financial interests at stake feel as if they were standing on the brink of a volcano which at any moment may open up and swallow them. This slow-killing agony has been going on now for about two months without coming to a head. The worst kind of fever would reach its climax in less time.

Meanwhile, from those in the know, there were a couple of instant verdicts on the dramatic solution of the previous day. 'It appeared to us that it was to the interest of our joint account to come forward, not only to diminish our loss on Barings' bills but to avoid the danger of losing by other firms stopping', explained Raphaels to its New York agents. Baron Alphonse de Rothschild in Paris, given the news of the guarantee fund by his London cousins, concurred: 'Evidence indeed that the English houses perfectly understand their responsibility and by preventing the catastrophe threatening the house of Baring they are shielding their self interest in as much as the house of Baring just now is the keystone of English commercial credit.' By Sunday the outlines of what had taken place were generally known, and Hamilton reported the very revealing reaction of the West End:

> Nobody talks of anything else but of the Barings . . . There is a strong feeling of sympathy for them. This is not unnatural for more reasons than one: everyone is relieved that the catastrophe has been averted, there is no suspicion of fraudulent intent, the House has always been popular & greatly respected, poor Revelstoke himself is known to have been the most generous & large-hearted man, there is the feeling ingrained in John Bull for the fallen, and moreover not a few are sorry to think that the downfall of Barings means the undisputed supremacy of the Jews in the commercial world.

Still, they were not universally shared sentiments. 'What a time you must have had in the City', wrote Lord Randolph Churchill to Alfred de Rothschild the next day from Monte Carlo. And he went on as only he could have: 'Fancy those Barings being brought so low . . . Lord Revelstoke will not be able to ride the high horse so much as he used to.'[5]

'Saved' was the *FT*'s bald headline on Monday the 17th. The following evening, at Reginald Brett's, Natty Rothschild was emphasising that (in words reported by his host) 'had Barings been allowed to collapse, most of the great London houses would have fallen with them', adding that 'about 6 millions' worth of Bills are drawn daily upon London, and an enormous proportion of this business passed through their hands'. In fact, the atmosphere of crisis did not pass quite so abruptly as these affirmations of relief might suggest. On Wednesday the 19th, Harry Gibbs wrote to his brother Vicary in Athens and mentioned that, over the past few days, all important firms, 'except possibly Huths', had been 'talked about'. His explanation showed a good understanding of City psychology: 'Of course the fact is that Barings having collapsed so fearfully, people are saying "Who then is safe?" & the Stock Exchange having received a tremendous shock & having no "business" to occupy their minds with, are simply talking wildly about the great houses, no matter how strong they may be.' Indeed, for a few hours that same day it seemed in Capel Court as if the guarantee fund had never been. John Biddulph Martin, in his retrospective account of the Baring crisis, related a sharp encounter:

> A rumour, more or less well founded, that the joint stock banks had announced that they would call in all loans from the Stock Exchange, caused almost a panic in the morning; it was certain that the governor of the Bank of England called the managers in and told them that if they

would not give their customers reasonable accommodation, they must not themselves look to the Bank in case of need. Thereupon they let it be known that they would make advances as usual, and a general improvement all round took place immediately. This seemed to be the turning point, and the crisis was at an end.[16]

Quite why the joint-stock banks lost their nerve at this thirteenth hour is unclear, but undeniably there was a touch of the triumphant central banker as Governor Lidderdale sent them on their way.

And Barings itself? 'A great Nemesis overtook Croesus', one partner at the time famously described the humiliation, adding that 'the line has never been out of my head since the Guinness success'. By Saturday the 22nd arrangements were well in hand for the old partnership to be wound up and replaced by a new company, called Baring Brothers & Co. Ltd, with capital of £1m subscribed by many of the leading City houses as well as members of the family. 8 Bishopsgate remained in a state of shock, and one visitor that day was John Biddulph Martin: 'Went to Barings about prospects of keeping the a/c. Painful interview with Ld Revelstoke, he almost broken down.' There was plenty of pain to come, for over the next few years the winding up of the old partnership involved the selling of all assets; and these included the private property of the partners, whose liability was (in the best City tradition) unlimited. None suffered materially and emotionally more than Revelstoke himself, who before his death in 1897 lost not only his country estate and his wonderful collection of French furniture and pictures, but also his position in the City and much of his self-esteem. In the depressed financial climate of the early 1890s, liquidation proved a protracted business, but eventually, in 1895, the Bank of England's loan was paid off and the long-suffering guarantors were no longer on risk.[17]

The greatest plaudits went to Lidderdale, who at the end of 1890 received a deputation and address of gratitude from the Stock Exchange Committee. His reply was wholly in character: 'I shall always remember with pride and satisfaction that, in the opinion of such a body as yours, in a moment of danger I was able to do my duty.' He had done so in an intense, peculiarly British crisis, played out almost entirely behind closed doors. It was a crisis that, through the device of the guarantee fund, had fully reaffirmed the Bank's authority within the City. As never before, the leading houses of the City had come together in conscious, collective action to rescue one of their own – a club to which the main joint-stock banks now clearly belonged, though arguably as second-class members being charged double for the privilege. Certainly there was some resentment on their part that they had not been taken into the inner councils of the Bank and had not featured on the initial subscription list.[18] But pehaps above all the crisis showed the importance of the personal touch. Almost a quarter of a century earlier, it would have been perfectly possible to save Overend Gurney, which in time did pay its creditors; but the firm had made the fatal mistake over the previous decade of antagonising the rest of the City elite. Whatever the dislike in some quarters of Revelstoke's rather arrogant personality, the same did not apply to Barings in 1890. 'The House has always been popular & greatly respected': Hamilton's words hit the nail squarely on the head. Barings, supremely, was the Establishment's – political, social, financial – *inside* house; and in Bertram Currie and Everard Hambro it had two exceedingly well-placed, powerful allies. This is not to deny that there was a more generalised fear for the future of other firms and the future of the City should Barings go down. But in the end, the lesson of the crisis, a lesson applicable not only in 1890, was that it will always pay to be fortunate in one's friends.

CHAPTER TWELVE

Small Reserves

In the mid-1880s the French traveller Paul Villars, taking notes for a new book to be called *London and its Environs*, stopped for a moment at a famous spot:

> From London Bridge the prospect is superb. The River, two hundred and fifty yards wide, rolling its yellow and glittering waves along, is covered with vessels from all parts of the globe, and so packed, so pressed one against the other, that it is difficult for those going out or coming in to push their way through the crowd of boats of all kinds which dart across the narrow channel left in the centre of the stream. In fact, as far as the eye can reach, extends a forest of masts, a network of cordage, a labyrinth of yards and rigging which seems inextricable: a lace of a thousand patterns, of which the threads are ropes and chain cables . . .
>
> The continued rolling of the cabs, the sound of horses' hoofs on the stones, the puffing of many steam engines, the blows of heavy hammers, the grinding pulleys, the groaning capstans, and, above all, the voices of a million of men, unite in forming a loud roaring, which is like the roaring of the sea.
>
> The noise as of waves envelopes you; you are clasped in its shadowy embrace, and lulled to sleep; the ear too rapidly struck by the multiplicity of sonorous vibrations, no longer transmits any sound. You are deafened; you feel the noise, but no longer hear it.

On the small scale as on the great, the late-Victorian City remained a world of its own, right down to its unrelentingly monochrome dress code. Herbert de Fraine, who began work at the Bank of England in 1886, recalled that code almost three-quarters of a century later:

> Everyone without exception carried either an umbrella or walking-stick. There were several large shops round the Bank where every sort and description of stick, tens of thousands of them, from malacca cane to natural ash, were on sale.
>
> We wore stiff-fronted shirts with stiff cuffs, and stiff white collars (not wing). We also wore tail-coats, for the short coat with the silk hat did not come in until shortly after the First World War.

The black-coated worker stepped out into an intensely crowded street life. Costers' barrows, fixed stalls and street-sellers of all kinds took up much of the kerb space; the dense traffic of carriages, omnibuses, cabs, carts and wagons often ground to a complete halt; and such was the general grime that it was common practice to protect the snowy cuff in business hours by a half-sheet of notepaper folded and fitted over the edge. Even the urbane Villars was disconcerted: 'There is nothing more curious than the appearance of the City streets. Here everyone seems to run rather than to walk. The City man goes straight forward like a shot from a cannon. He takes the shortest cuts: his minutes are valuable. Do not stop him to make any inquiry, you will not succeed.' The Frenchman could not have known it, but the showing of a clean pair of heels was all part of a wider code. Take that quintessential figure Walter de Zoete, a member of the Stock Exchange from 1867 to 1909, renowned for his conservatism, his phenomenal memory, and his refusal to use the telephone, on the grounds that personal contact was sacrosanct. De Zoete's advice to his son could not have been simpler: 'In the City as a young man you never walk but always run.'[1]

As for the City's buildings, the physical framework for this perpetual scurrying, the pace of change had slackened somewhat after the large-scale reconstruction of the 1850s and 1860s that had been typified by new railway stations like Cannon Street, new bank buildings like John Gibson's magnificent National Provincial in Bishopsgate, and new blocks like the eight-storey Mazawattee Tea Warehouse. *Building News*, looking back in 1889 over the past twenty years, reckoned:

> Within the bounds of the City the changes have been chiefly confined to straightening, here and there widening, and in rebuilding old premises. Fenchurch-street, Gracechurch-street, Cornhill, have almost been transformed architecturally, and the neighbourhood of London Bridge has put on quite a new aspect with the completion of the line of street from Cannon-street to the Tower.

A year later saw the demolition of that Tudor relic, the Sir Paul Pindar tavern in Bishopsgate, along with adjacent old houses. Were the new buildings up to the mark? 'Architecturally it has all the latest improvements,' enthused the *Bankers' Magazine* about the new building at 39 Cornhill, into which the Union Discount moved in October 1890, adding that 'it is fitted up with the electric light, has first-rate strong rooms and altogether is as airy, convenient, suitable and pleasant a building as can be wanted for the transaction of banking business'. It is doubtful, though, if it would have passed the Loftie test. W. J. Loftie, BA, FSA, was the author of an imposing volume called *London City*, published by the Leadenhall Press in 1891. His text was largely antiquarian, but in his closing pages, on 'The City as It Is', he decided to let rip:

The brief survey here attempted of some of the great thoroughfares of the City leaves an impression of sadness on the mind. London has been practically rebuilt since the beginning of the present reign, yet how little is there of good architecture to be seen anywhere. Some of the new houses would be a disgrace to any city. The designs of costly structures, covered with coloured marbles and polished granite, are often unworthy of a gin palace.[2]

Subscribers to Loftie's book included the Queen, the Lord Mayor and Lord Rothschild, but one suspects his words fell on deaf ears.

On Herbert de Fraine's first day at the Bank, thirty-five minutes were allowed for luncheon; and, 'a little way up Cheapside, on the right, I found a small court in which was a genuine old coffee-house with pew-seats built back to back'. No doubt on another day he tried one of Wilkinson's famous à la mode beef shops. Their menu was strictly limited – boiled beef served with soup, carrots and suchlike, all washed down by porter. Alfred Wells, who joined Freshfields as a clerk in 1889, was a keen patron: 'You entered the shop and found on either side wooden pens containing a centre table with two fixed forms, fully-dressed waiters served you, and at the end of the shop was the open kitchen with the chef. The only sweet was suet pudding and jam. These shops were so popular that at luncheon time you sat eating whilst there were three or four men at each pen waiting to take your seat when you had finished.' The experience sounds reasonably civilised, if not altogether relaxing, but elsewhere in the City a mildly horrified Villars observed feeding time at the human zoo:

> At one o'clock in the afternoon the streets are crowded with working men and clerks who hurry towards the nearest chop-houses and taverns to snatch a hasty but substantial meal . . . Standing around the counters is a crowd of men, with their hats on, hastily swallowing a few mouthfuls of food: and then, throwing down a piece of money, they rush away again, leaving their places to be filled up by new-comers as hungry as their predecessors. This manner of eating – standing, like animals from a rack – has something lowering in it, something that is repugnant to the French taste and instincts; but it is the custom, and that word explains everything.

There was still a significant shortage of cheap eating places in the City, and many clerks brought their own sandwiches and went out for a drink. 'Our clerks' old desks were chisled, cut about and worm eaten,' recalled Wells, 'and each contained all sorts of unconsidered trifles, and it was in these desks they placed their lunch when they arrived and generally consumed it furtively under cover of the lid.' And he added: 'The desks were never or seldom tidied up and when a colleague had occasion to look for a rubber or maybe a little pounce or other office material in an absent clerk's desk, he was often assailed with an aroma enough to spoil his own lunch.'

Better by far to be the son of a prosperous merchant, as the young Francis Oppenheimer discovered in the late 1880s when his father took him for the first time to the Gresham Club: 'Right across the further end of the dining room stretched a sideboard laden with the cold dishes in season: lobster, dressed crab, Dublin prawns, cold salmon, roast chicken and other birds, joints and a ham, meat pies, brawn and salads; jellies, fruit tarts and creams.'[3]

In the end, and not just with food, it all depended – usually on birth. Take two documents. The Sassoons were acknowledged merchant princes of the City, intimate with the Prince of Wales; and in about 1890 one of them, Arthur, reported to his nephew a visit that he and his brother had just paid to the Leadenhall Street office of David Sassoon & Sons:

> We went to the office (i.e. Reuben and I) yesterday at 11 and remained there till 1, while we signed the Hebrew and Arabic letters. While we were there, Bishop called and offered some Persian opium and he said there was a margin of more than $100 between the price here and that in Hong Kong, so we thought we might as well buy a small lot and make a little money. We went afterwards to Sandown with the Prince and Rosebery in a special and were grieved to see Ladas beaten. I had a plunge on him £40 to win £70. Better luck next time!

In contrast, on 1 July 1890, Edward Clodd, secretary of the London Joint Stock Bank in Princes Street, just opposite the Bank of England, recorded the following entry in his diary: 'My 50th birthday, spent as all my birthdays, except when they fall on a Saturday, at the Office till past 10.'[4] Clodd, a self-made man, was a well-known writer, especially on matters of rationalism and evolution, yet his diary is almost entirely mute about his life at the bank, despite the many, many hours that he spent there. And that, for the historian of the City, is the larger problem: muteness. What do we really know of the 301,000 people who, by 1891, were working daily there? Of that street-seller remembered by de Fraine, 'an old lady, plentifully pock-marked, who always sat in the same doorway with a large basket of very clean pink pigs' trotters that had a pathetically human appearance'?[5] We read *The Diary of a Nobody* and think we know, but it is an illusion.

*

Despite many fluctuations, the years between the Baring crisis and 1914, when all the certainties vanished, were indubitably the City's golden age. Only later did they seem to be dream days.

Nevertheless, the crux remained: most of the industrialised world financed its trade through sterling-denominated bills drawn on London – and it did so because it knew that such bills, suitably guaranteed, could (in the words of Ronald Gillett, a latter-day bill broker) 'always be discounted in the London discount market at the finest rate of the day, the proceeds converted into gold and the gold taken out of the country to any part of the world'. The bill of exchange drawn on London continued to be a three-legged stool: firstly, it had been accepted by a merchant bank, which in effect promised to pay at maturity, usually three months; it had, secondly, been acquired by a discount house or bill broker, the wholesaler in the operation; and now, thirdly, it was sold by the discount house to a bank, which valued the bill as a self-liquidating investment.[6] Altogether it was a virtuous circle, responsible for financing the bulk of world trade, only some of which passed through London or had anything to do with Britain.

By the late nineteenth century the City was also renowned for exporting capital to every quarter of the globe, yet for all its ever-increasing financial importance, it still retained in the late nineteenth century a strongly manufacturing-cum-commercial character. In 1891 up to two-thirds of all the firms in the City either made things or were essentially commercial in purpose.[7] Contemporaries naturally tended to identify the City with the Bank of England and the Stock Exchange, but most had never set foot in the Square Mile.

By this time it was clear that London's future in physical trade lay not in bulky, low-value goods, but in a mixture of re-exports, where it still enjoyed an ascendancy over other British ports, and in high-value imported goods such as fur, feather and diamonds, where specialist expertise and marketing skills made all the difference.[8] Overall, however, it was office trade that would now give London the international edge, as the City utilised London's place at the hub of the world's telegraphic and telephone systems, as well as increasingly rapid transport. To quote Ranald Michie, the historian of this key shift:

> It became possible to conduct a global trading business from an office in the City, maintaining constant contact supplemented by rapid visits and the receipt and despatch of samples and catalogues . . . The office in London was now responsible for the details of assembling cargoes, the ship's loading and unloading, bunkering, provisioning and manning, arranging passage, handling customs, organising insurance, etc. Specialist firms emerged in the City concentrating on particular types of ships, particular cargoes or particular routes.[9]

It was not only the international shipping market that London controlled, but also the trade in most of the world's leading commodities and precious metals. This the City did partly through its communications facilities; partly through its access to high-quality, continuous commercial intelligence; partly through its adaptability and accumulated expertise; partly through its ability to continue to attract talented incomers; and partly because the increasingly complex nature of international commerce meant that there was a global need for a single centre – London, as it happened – to act as fulcrum and mediator of the whole process. The City had, in short, the necessary critical mass, human as much as technological.

A host of back-up services helped to oil the intricate machine, such as company liquidators, ship brokers and auctioneers. Three were especially important: accountancy facilities, legal facilities, insurance facilities. These served a wider client base than just the City itself, but without them it would have been almost impossible for the City to have functioned. In a world of systematically concealed or distorted financial information, above all in annual reports or the launching of new companies, the role of the respectable but obliging accountant was crucial. According to the 1891 day-census, there were 701 accountancy firms operating in the City, and it was generally a rewarding occupation, not least when a company failed. Indeed, during the winding up of Overend, Gurney & Co., a protracted process that took no less than twenty-six years from 1867, Whinney, Smith & Whinney pocketed fees of £43,205, the equivalent of £2.5m in modern-day terms.[10] There was also useful money to be made – if, on the whole, less serious money – if one was a partner in one of the City's 2,026 firms of solicitors, especially if the firm was involved in the company-promoting process, where profit margins were notoriously wide. Ashurst Morris Crisp & Co. was such a firm, acting by the late 1880s for an enormous range of companies and maintaining the closest of relationships with a leading company promoter, H. Osborne O'Hagan. It was even strong enough to allow an amicable spin-off firm in the shape of Slaughter and May, established in 1889 by William Slaughter, who had worked for eight years for Ashurst Morris Crisp and whose father, Mihill Slaughter, had been a major administrative figure on the Stock Exchange. He took as his partner a young solicitor of county background called William May, and soon they too were specialising in new issue work, enjoying an especially fruitful connection with the leading international financiers Émile Erlanger & Co. 'A variety of matters turn up, something new almost every day and one comes in contact with numerous folk of all classes and degrees, rogues and otherwise, all engaged in the great melee of seeking wealth', noted May a few years later.[11]

As for insurance, despite the rise of individual companies such as the Alliance and the Commercial Union, the single great focal point remained Lloyd's on the first floor of the Royal Exchange. There, following long periods of sluggishness during much of the century, there were new signs of life by the 1880s. Three figures stand out. One was Colonel (later Sir) Henry Hozier, autocratic secretary from 1874 to 1906 at a time of mostly figurehead chairmen, and responsible for developing the system of coastal signal stations that gave Lloyd's an unrivalled grasp on the shipping intelligence of the entire world.[12] Then, on the business side, there was Frederick Marten, a marine underwriter who more than anyone pioneered large underwriting syndicates, increasing their size from the conventional two or three 'names' to up to a dozen.[13]

But the most important was Cuthbert Heath, as major and innovative a figure in his field as Nathan Rothschild had been in merchant banking.[14] Born in 1859, Heath was the son of a naval officer, was educated at Brighton College, and spent two years in France and Germany studying languages. At eighteen he joined a firm of insurance brokers, before he was elected a member of Lloyd's in 1880, backed by a £7,000 loan from his father. Within a year he was underwriting marine risks, but the truly seismic shift took place from the mid-1880s, when, in an opportune response to the late nineteenth-century depression in world shipping, he began to underwrite non-marine risks, something which had hardly happened in living memory at Lloyd's. Fire risks in 1885, burglary in 1889 and earthquakes in 1895 were three of the landmarks, while by the 1890s he was also pushing hard the idea of credit insurance, to protect trading firms against defaulting creditors. Like any pioneer he encountered a certain entrenched conservatism – for instance, when the Committee declined to allow non-marine underwriters to offer security to policy-holders comparable to that given by marine underwriters – but the long-term implications of what was on his part a very remunerative business were profound. Heath was a commanding, rather austere figure, possessed the highest standards, and was never to be seen in the market without the black box in which he kept his hearing aid. Moreover, unlike many pioneers, Heath had the interests of the institution to which he belonged close to his heart – something for which, in time, Lloyd's would be more grateful than it could express.

The practical as well as symbolic pivot of the whole financial system, and increasingly perceived as lender of last resort in times of financial crisis, remained the Old Lady of Threadneedle Street. Above all, the Bank of England was responsible for defending the country's gold reserve and thereby maintaining the gold standard, than which successive governors knew no higher duty. This was done primarily by judicious manipulation of Bank rate – in effect, raising interest rates whenever there was a need to attract gold to London – but also by a variety of more or less open operations on the gold market. One can, though, easily exaggerate the Bank's power. For one thing, its own resources were becoming steadily smaller in relation to those of the leading joint-stock banks, and as a result the Bank often found it difficult to impose its will on the money market. For another, by this time fundamental, essentially *impersonal* forces buttressed the gold standard, not least the fact of fixed exchange rates made possible by a world of broadly open economies in equilibrium with each other. Moreover, if the Bank's powers of monetary management were limited, so too was the potential of its moral suasion, or what a later generation would know by shorthand as the governor of the day raising his eyebrows. Certainly the resolution of the Baring crisis gave a perceptible short-term boost to the Bank's authority; but over the 1890–1914 period as a whole, the larger perception in the City was that the Bank was run along distinctly backward, old-fashioned lines and that it did not always recruit men of the highest calibre to be directors and, in turn, governors. 'It is difficult enough to get good men', conceded the governor himself in 1891, and few informed observers would have disputed the point.[15]

In mid-November that year, Hamilton of the Treasury dined at the Bank to discuss Goschen's currency proposals, put forward in the context of historically small bullion reserves and the fact that London, as the world's only free gold market, was peculiarly exposed:

> I had talk with sundry Directors about the Chancellor of the Exchequer's currency scheme; the main features of which are (1) to increase the central store of gold by extracting gold from people's pockets and substituting therefor one pound notes . . . and (2) when that central store has been increased, to give the Bank Charter Act some elasticity, which will dispense with the rude necessity of breaking the law [i.e. by periodically having to suspend the Act in time of crisis] and will give the Directors a discretionary power on payment of a high rate of interest to issue excess notes. Notwithstanding that the measure has the cordial approval of the governor himself, the majority of the Court appears to be very lukewarm about it, if not hostile to it. It is a case of 'laissez nous faire'. 'We have got on well enough up till now, why not leave us alone?' The unfortunate part of it is that Goschen admits that he is not very 'sweet' upon the plan himself. He thinks his own judgment has been a little warped by the views of Lidderdale, Welby [of the Treasury] & myself.

In fact, Lidderdale informed Goschen that fifteen directors were in favour of the revised plan and eleven against; but it is clear from individual letters to the governor, written during October, that most of those opposed were extremely hostile, typified by H. R. Grenfell's emphatic protest 'against the idea that Bankers should rely either on the government or the Bank to protect them from the results of their own want of perception'. A future governor, the merchant Samuel Gladstone, took an even stronger line: 'So long as speculation exists, and over-trading is possible, we may expect times of panic and pressure, and Mr Goschen's proposal would have as much effect on foreign exchanges as King Canute's orders had on the waves of the sea.' As for those reckoned in favour of the scheme, fairly typical of their lack of warmth (with few exceptions) was the seasoned verdict of Benjamin Buck Greene: 'Though, on the whole, I should perhaps prefer that matters remained as they are, yet I cannot but approve the object the Chancellor has in view in proposing to establish an independent and tangible reserve of gold from which to meet any temporary, though rare, emergency.' There was, in short, an understandably wan tone as Lidderdale reported back to Goschen on his soundings: 'Do you expect enthusiastic support from the Bank to anything? We are not a very youthful body of men, though wonderfully youthful in spirit, – considering.'[16]

Inevitably, much would turn on the response of the bankers themselves, for historical reasons not represented on the Court of the Bank of England. They had mostly lain low, waiting for more definite proposals than Goschen's to be formulated. The notable if pseudonymous exception had been Currie, and few would have been surprised when, early in November, at a meeting of the Institute of Bankers, his right-hand man at Glyns, A. S. Harvey, broke cover. After acknowledging without reservation that the Bank of England had acted correctly over the Baring crisis, he went on:

> The effect that this crisis has had upon us as bankers has undoubtedly been, that we have been subject to a vast amount of criticism; criticism which, to some extent, has resulted in intensifying the prudence which, so far as I can see, bankers have generally been conspicuous for exhibiting; and I dare say on the whole, the criticism will be beneficial to all of us. But I think I may venture to say, that if we want anything, it is rest. I think bankers should be left alone for a little while.

'A very shrewd, hard-headed fellow' was Hamilton's estimate of Harvey (once of the Treasury himself), and in such a gathering Harvey's words would strike a sonorous chord; it was also apparent that Lidderdale commanded less than unanimous support to his immediate rear, while poised to pounce from the Opposition benches was Gladstone, ever ready to denounce what he liked to call 'quackery'.[17] Altogether, it was little wonder if Goschen, never the most resolute of men, was starting to waver.

Nevertheless, he stood and delivered ably enough on 2 December to a meeting of the London Chamber of Commerce held at the Merchant Taylors' Hall in Threadneedle Street. About 750 were present, including many leading bankers, and the well-known private banker Sir John Lubbock took the chair. 'The end which he has in view is admitted by all to be of paramount importance: it is the means – the £1 note issue – which is regarded with some suspicion and doubt', Hamilton noted anxiously in his diary that evening. Press reaction the next day was mixed. Among those broadly in favour was the *FT*, which did however criticise Goschen on the grounds that 'there was throughout the address a tone of appeal for support from the banking interest which, though no doubt flattering, was perhaps rather overdone'. It was a point Lidderdale took up. 'I think', he wrote to Welby on the 3rd, 'the Chancellor should insist upon his proposals being considered from the point of view of Public advantage, not of individual inconvenience.' And he added, with his words underlined: 'Let the Bankers justify their opposition.' [18]

Shortly before Christmas the situation turned decisively. On the 17th, *The Times* came out strongly against the scheme; within hours Gladstone was denouncing it as a charter for speculation; and by the 19th Hamilton was starting to bow to defeat: 'Goschen's currency scheme gains no support; & it looks as if its abortion is inevitable.' Operating powerfully behind the scenes, and seemingly inspiring a whispering campaign against Lidderdale, was Currie. 'As far as I could gather before I left London,' he wrote to the Shadow Chancellor, Sir William Harcourt, on about the 17th, 'the feeling of the Bank directors and of the authorities generally, was not encouraging to the scheme of Goschen.' Currie insisted that the idea of £1 notes was doomed to unpopularity ('Fancy asking a hansom cab-driver for change for a £1 note') and took his customary tart line on the question of reserves: 'Mr Lidderdale is very eloquent upon the burden and cost to the Bank of maintaining the reserve, but, as I have ventured to point out to him, the dividends on Bank Stock continue to increase, and the rate of profit, as shown in a recent article in *The Economist*, is double that of any other Bank.' Harcourt took the bait, and in his usual forthright way wrote to Hamilton on the 21st:

> I don't find that the City at all share your admiration of Lidderdale. Indeed since it has been apparent that his confident predictions as to the favour-able issue of the Baring settlement are not well founded his reputation has fallen as quickly as it rose. I have had letters from persons whom you would recognise as being of the highest authority who regard the recent scheme as a mere Bank of England job to increase the profits of the Bank of England . . . From whatever cause it may arise it is clear to me that at present Lidderdale's authority will anything but strengthen currency pro-posals in the City.[19]

Harcourt's second sentence was an intriguing one, a reference to how long, in falling markets, the Baring liquidation was taking, thereby keeping the guarantors uncomfortably on the hook.

The early weeks of 1892 merely confirmed that Goschen would not be putting his proposals before Parliament. 'That the central gold reserve of the country needs enlarging is true', conceded a negative editorial in the *Bankers' Magazine*, 'but the right method of augmenting it is by steady accumulation, and not by tampering with the system on which our currency is based.' On 21 January a general meeting of the London Chamber of Commerce to consider Goschen's scheme was at best incon-clusive; soon afterwards, a questionnaire sent out by the Institute of Bankers to its fellows, about half of whom were City-based, produced a three-to-one ratio against the proposals. Hamilton was usually prepared to yield to the City's superior understanding in monetary matters, but by late January he felt himself little less than a prophet spurned:

> Natty R. has become more & more hostile to Goschen's currency scheme; & he won't argue the case quietly. He insists that the proposals are rotten in principle & would not work. I suppose I am prejudiced; but I confess I am much struck with the total absence of substantial or even plausible objections to the scheme. Indeed, I think the best objection I have heard yet raised to the introduction of the £1 note is that you could not toss with it as you can with a sovereign.

A Rothschild would never toss a sovereign for England, but Hamilton should not have been so surprised by the City's deep-seated conservatism and failure to put an intellectual spin on its instinctive, even atavistic objections. 'The sovereign is a general favourite', the long-headed Harvey had written to him in the course of 1891, adding presciently that 'patriotic fervour would induce the nation to surrender its gold coins, but I doubt if abstract financial considerations will'.[20] On this the sentiments of the City and of the public were as one, grinding down between them the suddenly rather ill-appreciated custodian of the nation's central store of gold.

It was an irony of the situation that the proposals had intended to introduce a greater degree of elasticity in the working of the Bank Charter Act, which was precisely what many City bankers had demanded in vain back in 1844. Now, however, such was the hallowed aura of Peel's masterpiece, that most bankers considered it tantamount to heresy to suggest remoulding it. Nevertheless, out of the chequered reform process following the Baring crisis there had come two major changes to the banking system.[21] Firstly, it had given a further push to the banking amalgamation movement, especially through the effect of monthly published balance sheets heightening awareness of competition between banks, and this in turn produced a more concentrated system that was easier for a central bank to attempt to control. Secondly, in the course of the 1890s the general level of bankers' cash reserves did increase appreciably.

Moreover, the failure of the plan to introduce £1 notes had the important if unintentional consequence of focusing attention in a less distracted way on the whole question of the central reserve. During the 1880s there had been little disposition to challenge Bagehot's conclusion that there was no realistic alternative to a single-reserve system; but it was a significant straw in the wind when the *Bankers' Magazine* asserted in March 1892 that instead of banks concentrating all their reserves at the Bank of England, 'we shall have to revert to the older methods – to causing each bank to maintain an adequate cash reserve of its own'. Or, as the inveterate Currie privately put it some months later, 'the time for living under the patronage of the Bank of England seems to be passing & the other Banks would act wisely in recognising this fact & in making provision for future troubles before they arrive'.[22] Over the next two decades the question of the reserve and its whereabouts would not go away, and it came to symbolise the shifting balance of power not only between the Bank of England and the rapidly growing joint-stock banks (capital of over £50m by 1891, compared with £35m ten years earlier, and almost 1,000 more branches), but also in some sense between an entrenched City establishment and a group of unwelcome, muscle-flexing upstarts from the provinces.[23]

CHAPTER THIRTEEN

The Circus

'I tried to talk City a little, but we did not get far. We agree in rejecting Bimetallism! – perhaps that is our only point of agreement.'[1] So reported Sidney Webb in March 1892 to his future wife Beatrice, one of whose older sisters was married to Daniel Meinertzhagen VI, a partner in the merchant bank Huths. Sidney was staying with the Meinertzhagens and it is unlikely that, in his awkward conversation with Daniel, he related his own experiences in the Square Mile, as a one-time clerk in the office of a small colonial broker. Still, to agree on bimetallism was something, for during most of the 1890s that arcane subject remained, as it had since the mid-1880s, high on the political economy agenda, even if not always uppermost in the daily thoughts of busy practical men.

Against a long-run background of falling prices and a more or less depressed world economy, the basic premise of bimetallism was that the introduction of a double monetary standard – silver as well as gold – would check the fall in silver prices. This would make it easier for countries not on the gold standard to import goods, thus benefiting trade as a whole. The argument made an obvious appeal in Lancashire, heavily reliant on the cotton export trade with India, while in the City it was a highly charged, even emotive question, granted the widely held assumption that the return to the gold standard in 1821, though enforced on a reluctant Bank of England, had in practice laid the foundations of London's nineteenth-century prosperity and international dominance. Over the years the bimetallists and their gold-standard opponents brought up armies of statistics to help wage their unyielding campaigns, but there were also gut instincts at work.[2]

These instincts represented an immovable force. Hamilton acknowledged as much in May 1892 after a bimetallic deputation, largely comprising Lancashire merchants, had been received in Downing Street: 'How is it possible that bimetallism should make way against the rooted monometallic convictions of every influential City man, bar two – H. Gibbs & H. Grenfell? It may be all very well in theory; but it is absolutely impossible in practice.' Hamilton exaggerated the absence of bimetallic support in the City, but his central point was in tune with that of the *Bankers' Magazine* the following month, in the context of an impending, American-inspired international conference on the silver question: 'In this country we are strictly mono-metallic on a gold basis, and we cannot believe that any suggestion will be made to our government for any change in that respect. Such a suggestion would certainly not be acceptable in banking circles here.' By the end of the summer, however, a decision as to where that conference should be held was becoming urgent, as was the question of who should be the British delegates. 'We cannot put ourselves in the position of receiving a report more or less Bimetallistic signed by a majority of British Commissioners', was the clear view of Gladstone on 21 August, soon after beginning his fourth term of office; and in this he was backed to the hilt by his Chancellor, Harcourt, who had lost little time in stressing to Hamilton his unequivo-cally monometallist views, unlike the recent electoral flirtation with bimetal-lism on the part of Salisbury and Balfour. A comfort was the support of a third Liberal believer, Bertram Currie, who had agreed to be a delegate, albeit reluctantly, telling Gladstone that 'no good can come out of the conference'.[3]

Who would be the City's other representative? On 31 August Hamilton noted that 'Harcourt is going to insist on a Rothschild . . . He says they can't refuse. "England owes something to the Rothschilds; but the Rothschilds owe a great deal to England."' Currie was unimpressed – 'Lord Rothschild bears no doubt a name of weight but that is about all' – though in the event it was Natty's younger brother Alfred, recently retired as a Bank of England director, whom a suitably flattered New Court put forward. 'Alfred is most anxious to meet your views', Natty wrote to Harcourt on the 31st, 'and help you in your "dilemma". Although he would very much prefer London he will consent to go to the Hague if you wish it.' By early October the venue had been definitely decided – not The Hague, but Brussels – and Alfred now took it in his stride: 'The selection of Belgium certainly augurs well; it was there that the great Duke of Wellington raised the standard of England to the zenith of military glory, and you may rest assured, my dear Harcourt, that as regards my own humble efforts, they will be strenuously devoted towards main-taining our financial standard to which England owes her overwhelming mercantile supremacy.'[4]

Henry Hucks Gibbs, writing to a fellow bimetallist two days later, was unimpressed by Harcourt's deliberate weighting of the British delega-tion as a whole, though he took sardonic pleasure in the choice of the new Iron Duke: 'Things look ill. Our fat friend has pickeyed us . . . Alfred Rothschild!! Well! he will have the satisfaction of having found the man of all those East of Temple Bar who knows least of the matter & has the most decided opinion.' Over the next few weeks, perhaps to relieve his frustration, Gibbs engaged in vigorous debate on the whole question with the equally combative Harcourt, whose overall position was:

> I desire London to remain what it is, the Metropolis of the Commerce of the World to which all nations resort to settle their business. This I believe and I think all those who have practical knowledge of the money market (with the striking exception of yourself) believe to be owing to the soundness of our monetary system, London being the only place where you can always get gold. It is for that reason that all the exchange business of the world is done in London.

After stressing the great increase over the past twenty years in the volume of trade, the national wealth and so on, Harcourt directed his final gibe against someone who had recently been Conservative MP for the City: 'I am not such a reckless radical as you are – I don't desire Revolution even in precious metals.' Soon after, on 14 November, Gibbs exploded:

> The money market! There is your error! You take the money market to comprise the whole of the Commerce of England; and therefore listen only to Bankers Home and Foreign – of whom Currie and Alfred Rothschild are good examples – who think (some of them) that they and their class have an interest in the maintenance of the present system. It would be not unnatural if the Rothschilds & the Banking interest generally should look upon the Money Market, and the dealing in Bills of Exchange, and in Foreign Securities, as the Be-all and End-all of Commerce. It is their own particular 'leather' . . . I am on the other side. I look upon those things as the handmaids, the very useful handmaids, of Commerce.

Claiming that not all bankers were in fact hostile to bimetallism – even that Natty Rothschild was 'not afraid' of it – Gibbs made a last rhetorical thrust: 'You have chosen your side. You have elected to march with the Drones, and against the Working Bees. I take the other side, and – I shall win.'[5]

On 17 November, with the Brussels conference imminent, Harcourt gave a dinner to the British, Indian and American delegates. Afterwards he kept behind the four British monometallist delegates (two City, two non-City) 'and gave them their final instructions'. The phrase was that of Harcourt's son and private secretary 'Loulou', who in his wonderfully gossipy diary revealed the last-minute dispositions:

> A. Rothschild has a plan of his own which he wishes to develop and with which he means to startle assembled Europe but will I expect only succeed in boring them. However happily we do not know what the plan is and are not responsible for it. B. Currie is a brutal monometallist and means to treat all bi-metallists with very scant courtesy and wants to 'have it over' & get back to England as soon as possible.

Their private instructions are to discuss no abstract questions, to be civil to any definite plan for bi-metallism but to disagree . . . & generally to give a civil attention to the currency faddists. [6]

The conference began on the 22nd. Alfred's right-hand man at New Court, Carl Meyer, was with him, and he reported to his wife the interminable round. 'We have endless small meetings, discussions, visits, &c. The worst of it is that Alfred won't go to see anyone & always sends others which with some of the swells produces a certain friction and coolness. As usual the French are the most disagreeable but our worst enemy is Bertram Currie . . . who is jealous of Alfred and tries to thwart his plans.' That was on the 27th, and the next day Currie, in a thoroughly bad mood throughout these weeks, listened with ill-disguised impatience as Alfred outlined his compromise plan designed to prevent the conference from sundering. Although distancing himself from the bimetallic position, he proposed an international agreement for purchasing silver, in order to keep up silver prices. It was never really a runner. On the 30th, Currie wrote to his wife that Ernest Cassel, the acute international financier, was in town for a day or two: 'He takes a very sensible view of the silver question, and has had nothing to do with the Rothschild proposal.' Or, as Welby at the Treasury noted the next day, 'we are much amused at the Rothschild proposal'.[7]

Alfred himself wrote Harcourt a letter on 5 December, from the Hotel Bellevue, which was a virtual admission that the plan was dead. Harcourt's reply – shown in advance to Natty and Leo Rothschild, who said that Alfred's trouble was that he was 'so excitable and nervous' – took the line that the failure of the conference had at least demonstrated 'that the Bi-metallic theory is generally repudiated' and 'that there is no material for an agreement upon subsidiary measures for the support of a silver currency'. In short, 'this result may be regarded as a *settler* for Bi-metallism'. Nevertheless, Harcourt declined to hand Rothschild and Currie their demob papers, saying, 'you know as well as I do the importance of *the form* in these international transactions'. And, with a conscious historical echo: 'I pray you therefore have patience yet for a little time and then you shall return bringing back "Monometallism with Honour".' Even as Harcourt wrote, Alfred's proposals were being formally withdrawn, it being clear that there was no support from either the French or the American delegates. 'He has done his best,' Harcourt with rare tact wrote to Natty on the 7th, 'but the situation was hopeless from the first. Since the days of the Tower of Babel the world has made up its mind not to agree. A monetary compact is as impossible as a Tariff concordat or a disarmament project.'[8]

The conference slowly wound to an inconclusive halt, and a week before Christmas one of the last speeches was given by Currie. 'It was', a less than admiring British delegate told Harcourt, 'spoken over the head of the Conference for English instruction – appealed to Bimetallists to return to their senses & consider the question closed – offered a remedy for increasing the Bank of England reserve – and finished up with some satirical remarks.' Still, the great thing for Currie and those who thought like him was that the world had apparently been made safe for mono-metallism; and when Loulou Harcourt jotted down on Christmas Day an entry conveying the fearless digestion of youth ('A magnificent turkey from Natty Rothschild full of great foie gras – excellent'), he would have had no worries about unwonted silver coins popping out of Christmas puddings.[9]

*

One of Goschen's last achievements as Chancellor was the Bank Act of 1892, under which the Bank of England found itself being distinctly 'squeezed' by the Treasury in terms of how much the government paid for the day-to-day conduct of its financial business.[10] Inevitably this attack on the Bank's income created strains. By August 1893, following a visit to Threadneedle Street, Hamilton was sounding an ominous note: 'The Bank will, I see, need to be carefully handled: they have not got over (what they consider to be) the hard bargain which we drove with them last year, and there is not a single Director who is politically friendly towards the government.' To perform this careful handling, there could not have been a worse Chancellor in situ than Sir William Harcourt – Liberal, abrasive, and spoiling for a fight with what he regarded as one of the last great unreformed vested interests. In the opposite corner was Lidderdale's successor as governor, a rather unimaginative, obstinate merchant called David Powell.

In September, Harcourt wrote to Hamilton about 'the scandalous conduct of the Bank which I shall not forget', accusing it of having, despite his best bargaining efforts, 'practically robbed the public of ¾% on £2,000,000'. Therefore, 'I shall have as little dealings as I can help with these gentlemen in the future . . . We have been made thorough fools of.' And, in a postscript, Harcourt declared with apparent sincerity that next time he really would borrow from Rothschilds '& show up these Bank gentlemen to the public for what they are'.[11]

The same gentlemen had, earlier in 1893, considered a report on the Bank's internal administration. One of the report's three authors had been the Bank's chief cashier, Frank May, who controlled almost as a personal fiefdom the cashier's department, employing more than half the Bank's staff of over 1,000 and responsible not only for the management of the note issue, but also the Bank's discounts and advances as well as its regular operations in the gilt-edged and money markets. 'Mr May', a profile a few years earlier in the *Bankers' Magazine* had asserted, 'is said to despise what is known as popularity, and, still more, the insincerity of word and manner sometimes laid to the charge of men who flinch from what may be their strict, although unpleasant, duty to their fellow workers.' It was later to be also said that May's 'military stiffness' had been 'much resented' outside the Bank, but on that matter the typically deferential profile was silent.[12]

The more critical retrospective tone was occasioned by a scandal, which was the discovery of 'certain irregularities', as the recurrent phrase went, in the chief cashier's office. A subcommittee comprising Lidderdale, Benjamin Buck Greene and James Currie reported to the Bank's Committee of Treasury on 8 November 1893, revealing that for several years past it had been May's practice to make large unauthorised advances. The chief cashier did not seek to justify himself and resigned almost forthwith.

Hamilton's thoughts were that:

> What struck one most was that there must be some very weak spot in the management of the Bank to have made it possible for May to act in the way he had, without being detected sooner. What had evidently been May's principal cause of ruin was his son's being in a firm of speculative brokers, through whom May had speculated on his own account with the result that he had on his own admission been completely cleaned out.[13]

For Harcourt the whole episode was a wonderfully opportune stick with which to beat the Bank, and a few days later Loulou recorded a further twist:

> The Bank business gets worse, the more one hears of it. It appears that May advanced Bank money to Crump the City Editor of the 'Times' without security & when the Trust Co.'s began to topple over May told Crump he must repay the loan. Crump replied 'You can't squeeze blood out of a stone. I am stone broke & have not a penny in the world.' May said he must raise the money so Crump went to the Proprietor & Editor of the Times & they dismissed him on the spot without a pension.[14]

Many investment trust companies, products of the late 1880s boom, had indeed perished amidst the protracted fallout from the Baring crisis; while as for Crump, his name was not to feature in the official history of the Thunderer. By early 1894 rumours of the exact nature of May's misdemeanours were starting to surface in the public prints, along with broader attacks on the Bank itself.[15]

An important effect was to bring out into the open again the whole question of who ran the Bank.[16] Back in January 1891, Hamilton had asked Lidderdale 'whether he favoured the idea of a permanent governor. He said, on the whole "No". It was difficult enough now to get good men to serve as Directors, and if you deprived them of the chance of occupying the *chair*, which to many was a coveted distinction, you would probably get even less good men to enter the Bank.' It was hardly, from one of the most capable governors of the century, a ringing endorsement of the calibre of the current direction. A more outspoken critic was Bertram Currie, who wrote privately in February 1893 that 'the old type of director has become extinct, and they are now recruited from iron-masters, ship builders, brewers, – in fact from every class except bankers'. By early January 1894, Currie's thoughts were focusing on the Committee of Treasury, tradition-ally more influential than the Court of Directors itself. 'He thinks it essential', Welby reported to Harcourt, 'that the governor's Council should be enlarged, & that the Octogenerians always excepting Greene should be shunted.' Nor was Currie alone in desiring this major reform. Hamilton, by 25 January, discovered that Everard Hambro, supported by Charles Goschen (the former Chancellor's younger brother) and some of the junior directors, were proposing to change the Committee of Treasury from an ex officio body of past governors to one elected from the general body of directors. 'It is believed', he noted, 'that the present ex-governors are too averse to so radical a step to admit of its being taken.'[17]

Henry Hucks Gibbs was one ex-governor decidedly averse. On the 27th he wrote to Powell to express his opposition. Without attacking Hambro personally, he identified him as the representative of 'Directors below the Chair' – that is, those who had not yet had a turn as governor – and poured scorn on them as a group:

> Some have shown more interest in the daily working of the Bank than others; but not a tithe of the active interest which used to be taken by their predecessors of 20 years ago.
>
> As a body – I hope I may say it without offence – they have neglected their own duties; and now they propose to assume ours.

Gibbs, a seasoned controversialist, then gave what one can only call the grand bum's rush to the nascent reform movement:

> Whence has all this agitation arisen? There can be no doubt I think that it grew out of the unhappy misconduct of Mr May, and of the comments of the press to which that gave rise. Now I must say, Mr Governor, that it is wholly beneath the dignity of the Court that any of its members should be influenced by the ignorant comments of the Press.
>
> It would scarcely be more indecorous if they themselves were to influ-ence such comments.

Powell made sure to circulate Gibbs' letter, and on 1 February the Court voted against Hambro's initiative, by an unspecified margin. The decision was too much for that thrusting young meritocrat the Earl of Leven and Melville, who had been a director since 1884 but now resigned.[18]

So, reform was officially off the agenda, but the fundamental issue remained: to what extent was the Bank still a private body, to what extent had it become a public institution? In practice, this conflicting balance of interests tended to be played out in the money market, and on 6 October 1893, a day after Bank rate had changed and a month before the May scandal broke, the *Financial News* squared up to the question:

> The Bank of England is trying to serve two masters. One of these masters is the body of its own shareholders, whose dividends depend upon the amount of discount business done by the Bank, and who do not like to see their prospects injured by the successful competition of the open market; and the other is the vast interest of British credit, represented in the City mind by the amount of gold in the Bank's vaults. The policy of the directors, as exemplified in their latest exploit of reducing the minimum official rate to 3 per cent, is too obviously the policy that animated Mr Facing-both-ways in Bunyan's allegory. They want to get some of the business which now drifts into other channels, and they do not want to encourage withdrawals of bullion by foreign customers. As usual in similar attempts, they have adopted a compromise course which is not at all certain to achieve either of the desired ends.

The *FN* went on to analyse the Bank's conflicting relationships with the government and its own shareholders, and concluded by calling in strong terms for the Bank's responsibilities to be more clearly defined.[19] That, however, over twenty years after Bagehot had addressed the subject, was something that few people inside or outside the City yet had the vision or will to attempt to do – not least in the 'company of merchants' itself, to use Ricardo's scornful but in some ways still apposite phrase.

*

On the last day of January 1894, the *Pall Mall Gazette* announced in flaring type that Gladstone was about to resign. When news of this reached the Stock Exchange, business came to a temporary halt, as members broke out in loud, enthusiastic cheering. Then, the cheering over, 'they began to bid lustily for stocks at a sixteenth under the market price, to express their feelings without adding to their holdings'. For the moment the rumour proved false, but it refused to go away. On 14 February Natty Rothschild paid a visit to Harcourt, 'evidently wishing' (Loulou wrote) 'to "fish" about the Gladstone reports'. However, 'Chex turned Natty off on to the subject of the revival of trade & business in the City.' At last, early in March, the GOM did go, and the *FT* appreciated the choice of Lord Rosebery (as opposed to Harcourt) as his successor: 'A Radical, yet an Imperialist, he is fully in touch with the progressive spirit of the times, but not with the advanced fanatics who would rush headlong to perdition.' He was also, the paper did not add, linked by marriage to the Rothschilds and had a certain City reputation.

Nevertheless, the *FT* did go on: 'On all accounts the speedy advent of the Conservatives to what is likely to prove a long spell of power is to be looked for. From a financial point of view the change is one that will be heartily welcomed, for it will doubtless help to hasten the long delayed revival of public confidence.'[20] With those sentiments few figures of substance in the City would have disagreed.

By the closing months of 1894 all eyes were increasingly turned to the South African mining market, otherwise known as the Kaffir Circus. In September, following a record gold return from the Rand in August, *The Economist* reported sceptically on 'Witwatersrand Mining Progress'. It argued that 'continued purchase by continental operators' was causing such a high level of Rand share prices, and that that level was 'too high, in view of the fact that in many cases the outcrop deposits are being rapidly exhausted'. Besides which, 'the deep-level claims have, for the most part, yet to be proved'.[21] The mood of the market, however, was progressively more bullish over the next few weeks, and by mid-November a boomlet was becoming a boom.

One place and one man epitomised it. The place was a new 'club for financial men' in Angel Court, off Throgmorton Street. Formally called the City Athenaeum, it was known to everyone as the Thieves' Kitchen, and its proprietor was Ernest Wells, hoarse-voiced, immaculately dressed and nicknamed 'Swears'. 'In the interval after lunch and from the closing of the "House" onwards until it was time to go West for dinner, the "Club" would be noisy with the rattle of dominoes . . . And what sums used to pass across the domino tables at the end of the game!' So wrote the *FN* many years later, adding that brokers' clerks would run to and fro executing the commissions of their masters sitting in the Kitchen. An early member of the club, but never of the Stock Exchange, was Barney Barnato, perhaps *the* man of 1895, whose visiting card was overprinted with the convivial statement, 'I'll stand any man a drink, but I won't lend him a fiver.' His life was already the stuff of legends: born Barnett Isaacs in the East End in 1852, and completely uneducated, he had made his fortune on the diamond fields of Kimberley, where quick wits counted for everything, breeding nothing. Now, like the other diamond magnates, he was concentrating mainly on gold mines, and at this stage his chief financial vehicle was Johannesburg Consolidated Investment, which in the twelve months up to February 1895 issued 623,000 shares. With his ready tongue and ability to move share prices, he acquired during the course of the boom a strong Stock Exchange following, which believed with some justification that if Barney flourished in his shameless booming of selected stocks then there would be lucrative pickings for them too. Against that, what did it matter if he dropped his h's?

1895 was a golden year, or so it seemed for much of the time. '*On dit*', noted the *FN* on 12 January, 'that Mr B. I. Barnato has bought the lease of Lord Dudley's house in Park-lane, and will make his future home there.'[22] By the middle of March, with Kaffir prices still rising inexorably, Barnato was back from a brief holiday in Monte Carlo – a great City favourite at that time of year – and was personally directing operations during after-hours dealings in Throgmorton Street. 'Was there ever a spectacle illustrating the race for gold more drastically than the seething, shouting, maddened crowd in the South African street market? And how long can this mad boom last? We feel inclined to say just as long as our French neighbours continue to send buying orders.'[23] Almost certainly there was much truth in this analysis by the *Citizen*, emphasising the continental dimension to the Kaffir boom. But wherever buying orders were coming from, come they did in phenomenal quantities, and the week beginning 18 March proved to be one of the more remarkable in the Stock Exchange's history. It began late on the Tuesday afternoon, when four members were arrested in Throgmorton Street during after-hours dealings, taken to the police station in Moor Lane, and charged with obstruction, disorderly conduct and resisting the police. Many other members gathered at the police station to protest, led by the jobber Harry 'Packy' Paxton, towering head and shoulders above everyone else. The following morning, at the Guildhall Police Court, one member was fined £10, another £5, and Mr Alderman Phillips 'said it was quite clear to him that the police were quite right in endeavouring to clear this thoroughfare'. Reaction that Wednesday was swift:

> The accusations brought by the police against the Kaffir crowd caused bitter feeling in the House, and the word was passed around to 'turn out' in force after four o'clock. Throgmorton Street at a quarter past four was simply impassable, although about thirty constables and three inspectors were on duty . . . Several times a rush was made by the crowd, carrying constables and inspectors off their feet. At about twenty minutes past four several empty cabs passed along, but the drivers refused to take fares. Mr Paxton, however, took possession of one, and, with Mr Leo Harward, drove up and down Throgmorton Street, to the great delight of the crowd, who cheered vociferously. On the second return of the vehicle an inspector boarded it, but withdrew when Mr Paxton ordered him off. It was not until 6.30 that Throgmorton Street resumed its ordinary aspect. No arrests were made.

The next morning, at a regular meeting of the Stock Exchange Committee, attention was drawn to these disturbances; but, 'after discussion, further consideration of the matter was deferred'.

In fact, the climax was at hand, for at five o'clock that Thursday afternoon the hugely popular Packy found himself under arrest. The police took him away with difficulty, through a crowd of turbulent dealers, as their comrade 'courteously acknowledged the salutations by raising his hat'. Charged with disorderly conduct, he was released after an hour or so. The next morning the outsize jobber appeared before Mr Alderman Bell at the Guildhall Police Court, who declared that Paxton and his fellow members had turned Throgmorton Street 'into a bear garden', that they 'had no more right to the place than any other person in London', and that the police must be upheld. He declined, however, to punish Paxton, and the defendant 'left the court in the company of his friends, who, on getting outside, cheered heartily'.

Later that day the Stock Exchange Committee voted by twelve to four 'to caution members against countenancing by their presence the scandalous disturbances which take place in Throgmorton Street after the closing of the House'. Writing to his correspondent in Melbourne, the merchant banker Harry Gibbs retailed the episode, accused the police of having been 'very rough', and added that Paxton had been described to him as 'an enormous man with a face like an elephant'.

Over the next few months, after-hours dealings in Kaffirs did continue, but there were no more outright confrontations; and soon the events of March 1895 became fixed in the collective memory as the Battle of Throgmorton Street. A last word on them goes to the protagonist himself and one of the thin blue line, in an exchange related by the financial journalist Charles Duguid in his history of the Stock Exchange published in 1901: 'It is told of Mr Paxton, who frequently refers jocularly to his experiences at the police court, that quite recently he playfully pushed his huge form against a policeman, saying, "Out of the way, I'm bigger than you." "Yes, sir," was the constable's respectful, ready reply, "I know you are. I saw you measured, you know, sir!"'[24]

Although never an occasion for pitched battles, the bimetallist issue was something that stubbornly refused to go away, and in January 1895 Chamberlain had sounded out Goschen as to whether the Conservatives might commit themselves to proposing a new bimetallist conference, presumably comparable to the one at Brussels. Goschen, however, replied that the existence in the City of a 'fanatical' monometallic clique – backed by the London press, including *The Economist* and the *Statist* – meant that bimetallism was not a viable electoral issue. Still, perhaps the City *was* shifting. 'I dined last night at Alfred Rothschild's', noted Hamilton on 14 February, and those present included 'Harry Chaplin [a prominent Tory politician], who declared that he should win on bimetallism in 5 years' time. He felt sure he had now Natty Rothschild on his side, who has long been wobbling. The brothers – Alfred & Leo – did not deny it.'[25]

Early in April the controversy began to come to the boil. Addressing the annual meeting of the Bimetallic League, held on the 3rd at the Mansion House before 'a large attendance of members and friends', the Tory politician

Arthur Balfour sought to reassure the City that bimetallism in no way threatened its prosperity:

> London's financial supremacy depended upon three facts: – First, our insular position as a nation rendering us less liable to risks of war than other less favoured countries; (2) through many generations the bankers of this City had proved themselves men whose credit could be relied upon; and (3) the fact that England was the greatest manufacturing country in the world. Not one of these facts was endangered. London, as the financial centre of the world, must gain, rather than lose, by anything that placed our currency upon a sounder basis than at present. (*Applause.*)

Two days later, at Glyn Mills at 67 Lombard Street, Bertram Currie assembled over twenty leading lights, mostly from the City, in order to form what became known as the Gold Standard Defence Association. They included Bank of England directors, such as those close friends Everard Hambro and Hugh Colin Smith; merchant bankers like Daniel Meinertzhagen of Huths, Henry Tiarks of Schröders, and Herman Kleinwort; and clearing bankers like Francis Bevan of Barclays and R. B. Wade of the National Provincial.[26]

On 20 May the GSDA presented its monometallic memorial to the Chancellor of the Exchequer, still Harcourt in what were the dying days of the Liberal government.[27] Merchant banks to sign up included Brown Shipley, Frühling & Goschen, Hambros, Huths, Kleinworts, Robert Benson, Raphaels and Schröders. Notable absentees were Barings, Morgans and Rothschilds. A few days earlier Natty had sent a decidedly disingenuous reply to Currie's request, stating that he did not propose to sign on the grounds that 'the movement abroad in favour of bimetallism appears to have quite died out now'. Currie himself lamented the fact that 'there are so few Bank of England signatories'. Both the clearers and the discount houses were, however, very well represented on the memorial. Two days after presenting it, Currie gave a full-scale speech at the London Institution in Finsbury Circus. He played down the current commercial depression as very different from the mid-century disasters he had known as a young man in the City; asserted as usual that an international agreement on silver 'belongs to the region of dreams and not of realities'; described his fellow adherents to monometallism as 'considerable in numbers and not wholly unprovided with the world's goods'; and concluded by cautioning Balfour and his party, likely to be in power very soon, not to tamper with the gold standard:

> The benefits to be derived from such a course are speculative and imaginary, while the possible dangers are real and palpable, sufficient to appal the stoutest heart and shake the nervous and disturb the slumbers of the most solvent trader in the City of London.

It was no surprise when Harcourt on the 27th replied to Currie in the most approbatory terms: 'I concur entirely in the opinion expressed in your Address that the experience of well nigh a century has proved that our present system of Currency is suited to the wants of this great Commercial Country and that to depart from it would be disastrous to the trade and credit of the United Kingdom.'[28]

Sir William was still in office on 22 June to field yet another missive from Henry Hucks Gibbs, who emphasised that in the list of bimetallism's supporters were 'included not only Merchants and Bankers in the City of London, but representatives of nearly every Industry in the Country, besides well known leaders of the Working Classes'.[29] Undoubtedly there were some leading City figures and institutions among the memorial's signatories; even so, there was not quite the same depth of solid City names as on the rival list – names such as Smith, Payne & Smiths, Alexanders and Robarts, Lubbock, as well as most of the leading merchant banks below the big two. Rothschilds and Barings (and indeed Morgans) continued to stay aloof from memorialising, though Thomas Baring did sign for the bimetallists in an individual capacity. All in all, despite his obvious prejudice in the matter, Harcourt's assertion to Currie that the monometallist memorial bore 'names amongst the most weighty which could be found to represent the judgement of the Merchants and Bankers of the City of London' was broadly correct – though perhaps one should add that it was a judgement that was coming to place greater weight on the financial than the commercial.[30]

Crucially, and for all his personal bimetallist sympathies, Salisbury appointed Sir Michael Hicks Beach, a diehard monometallist, as his new Chancellor. By November 1895, the Institute of Bankers' new president, the Hon. Dudley Ryder of Coutts in the Strand, was able to claim that the monetary question had receded since 'this time last year'. He referred specifically to 'the greatly increased production of gold' as well as the government's ultimate unwillingness to move in a bimetallist direction, whatever the views of some individual ministers. The following March the highly able Henry Raphael wrote in confident vein to the secretary of the GSDA: 'Bimetallism is only a form of discontent, when trade is bad & the country not prosperous. The reverse being now the case, I have for months past not been anxious about the excited activity of our adversaries.' Practical City man had, it seemed, triumphed completely. Or, as another merchant banker, Robert Benson, later in 1896 assured the Oxford economist Edwin Cannan, the GSDA had 'behind it %ths of the firms whose acceptances facilitate the trade of the world'. And he added, with an assurance that it would have needed a Cambridge economist to dent: 'There are no economic phenomena with which these men are not conversant.'[31]

*

1895 was not without its *haute finance*. On 17 April the signing of the treaty of Shimonoseki brought to an end the Sino-Japanese War, leaving China with a massive indemnity to pay, estimated by early May at up to £50m.[32] Over the previous twenty-one years China's regular loan-maker had been the Hongkong and Shanghai Bank, and on 11 May the bank's London manager, Ewen Cameron, informed Sir Thomas Sanderson of the Foreign Office that he wanted to raise £15m immediately in London, with a further £35m to be raised in due course. 'He seems to think it could be floated', minuted Sanderson. Two days later Cameron paid no fewer than three visits to the FO, during the third of which he showed to Sanderson the memorandum of a recent conversation between his stockbroker – Harry Panmure Gordon, the renowned China expert – and Natty Rothschild. Following two conversations of his own with Rosebery (still prime minister), Natty had told Panmure Gordon that, in the interests of China, it would be a mistake to achieve a diplomatic triumph over France and Germany by bringing out the loan on a solo basis. Instead, Natty proposed (in the words of Sanderson's own memorandum):

> That the loan should be divided in equal parts between the three countries: that Rothschilds would join the Hongkong & Shanghai Bank in bringing out the English portion. That if any attempt were made by France & Germany to exclude us, the British market should be closed to the loan . . . the best advice we had been able to get was that a loan of so considerable an amount as China would require could not be floated on the mere security of an engagement in the contract to an English firm. I told him in strict confidence that that was the opinion not only of Lord Rothschild but of Mr B. Currie. If it could not be done, we must take the next best alternative, and Lord Rothschild's proposal was such as we could openly write for.[33]

It soon emerged that the French had broken away to form a financial alliance with the Russians; and though over the next few weeks the Anglo-German group battled away under Rothschild leadership, victory went to St Petersburg, where on 6 July it was formally announced that a £16m loan, guaranteed by Russia and issued in Paris by a French syndicate, would be made on China's behalf.

'Russia has won the toss', commented the *FT*, 'and gone in first on a good wicket, with France as a partner to make the boundary hits. But we are to have our innings after the turf is worn.' There would indeed be future Chinese indemnity loans – on who knew what sort of wicket – and perhaps lessons would be learned from the first. 'This is England's opportunity. It will not remain open long. Have we a statesman who can see it and seize it?'[34] That was what a fairly young banker called Charles Addis, working for the Hongkong Bank in Shanghai, had written to his father shortly before the signing of the peace treaty. The events of the early summer showed that England did not have that statesman; but they also showed, perhaps more importantly, that in the context of keen international rivalry for influence in China it would no longer be possible for the FO to pretend that loan-raising finance existed in a virtuous void. Henceforth the worlds of finance and diplomacy were entwined – increasingly so over the next twenty years, and not only in China.

There was a significant coda to the story of the first Chinese indemnity loan. On 2 July, shortly before the ratification of the £16m Russo-Chinese loan, the prospectus appeared in London for a £1m loan to China.[35] The formal issuer was the Chartered Bank of India, Australia and China, but the man behind it was Ernest Cassel, emerging as the City's foremost international financier. The detailed background to this loan is shrouded in mystery; but it seems clear enough that Cassel over the previous few months had been working closely with the FO, and that once it became clear that the Rothschild-led initiative was doomed to failure, then there was official encouragement for the much smaller Cassel loan as a way of maintaining British face. Cassel was someone whose activities historians have struggled to trace precisely, not least because of his temperamental disposition to operate as far as possible as a loner.[36] 'A partner', he once remarked, 'is a man who can commit you to things and I don't mean ever to be committed to anyone.' There was quite a lot to be said against this self-made German Jew (and many said it): little sense of humour; few social graces; and the thinnest of skins when it came to any slights, real or imaginary. But there was much to be said on the other side, and one of the best pen pictures of Cassel comes from another German, Saemy Japhet, who was based in the City from 1896 and became a relatively close associate:

> He hid an innate modesty under what seemed coldness, and however kindly and almost affectionate he could be to those who were far below his own station in life, he could be very distant, even haughty towards those whom he suspected of snubbing him. He never gave them a second chance. As he was a true friend, in the same way he was a good hater; he never forgot an insult.
>
> His leading characteristic was his power of concentration and his directness. His 'yes' was 'yes' and his 'no' was 'no'. All who had dealings with him, whether they came to a successful end or not, were struck by the straightforwardness of his methods. He was a good listener, never interrupting, but his answers came out at once, well-formulated, clear, logical and full of common sense. Where others hesitated he acted, and many a proposition was already approved – or rejected – long before others had grasped the essential points. His perception was quick as lightning. He used to think of the smallest details while doing the biggest things.[37]

Cassel completely avoided the Kaffir boom, still raging by August 1895. 'Within the recollection of the oldest member of the Stock Exchange there has been no speculative movement at all comparable', declared *The Economist* on the 17th, adding that it 'shows as little sign of abatement as ever'.[38] Barney Barnato was by this time pulling strings with obvious pleasure. In the course of the month he revealed his plan to bring out what he grandly called the Barnato Bank Mining and Estate Company – in theory a holding company for his various ventures, in ill-disguised reality a gambling machine.[39] Barney himself was always available for interview, and on Saturday the 31st the *City Recorder* carried his boast that he was 'followed and backed by the best bankers in London, and practically by the whole of the Stock Exchange'.[40]

Monday 2 September was, according to the *FT*, 'Saint Barney's Day':

We have reason to believe that business was done yesterday in other stocks than 'Barney's Bank', but it was very difficult to discover it . . . In the market the morning scene was wonderful, and the excitement intense. Brokers had orders at limits based on one or other of the conflicting rumours as to the price at which the market would open; but the work of these was simple compared with that of the brokers who had orders to buy 'at best', and who had to fight their way through a crowd to get the opportunity of asking a jobber to make a price . . .

About the concern the public knows comparatively little, except that Mr Barnato has given his name to it, and that that name is associated with successes of the most brilliant kind. There is nothing succeeds like success, it is said, and yesterday's market is a notable example of the weight of this aphorism.

After almost a year of bucketing along regardless, the market was now being flooded with a vast quantity of watered stock based on gold-mining properties that for the most part were either marginal or undeveloped.[41]

On 14 September *The Economist* noted that 'the settlement in mining shares which has taken place within the past few days was about as little like the usual condition of things in the Stock Exchange during the "dead season" as it is possible to conceive'. On 1 October, Hamilton referred in his diary to 'the extraordinary boom in S. African gold shares, than which people can talk or think of little else, and out of which many are making their kills'. But the turning point came on 3 October, a Thursday, when massive sales in Paris led to prices slumping in London. In both the Paris and London markets, according to the *FT*, 'sales produced the greater effect from the fact that the Jews were again absent [following the Day of Atonement the previous Saturday], the day being one of their special celebrations, and thus a great deal of sustaining power, which might otherwise have been forthcoming, was wanting'. Over the next week the relapse in prices continued more or less unabated, with the *Statist* on the 12th blaming 'the refusal of the London banks to take such bills drawn upon the London branches of continental banks as had a financial appearance', an acceptance that much of the protracted Kaffir speculation had been Paris-led. The Circus continued to have the jitters until the 18th, when some of the leading South African houses quietly, and Barnato Bros noisily, agreed to take up stocks they had issued and for which no buyers could be found in the market. 'Barney to the Rescue' was the *FT*'s headline, with the paper praising Barnato for having 'loyally and pluckily supported the market' and seeing his bank as the target of a systematic, very determined bear raid. Subsequently, it was stated that Barnato had laid out £3m in supporting the shares in which he was specially interested; and *The Economist* commented darkly that 'if this be the case', then it proved 'that the market had got into a more serious condition than had been generally supposed'.[42]

Soon afterwards, on 7 November, in the closing days of his controversial tenure as Lord Mayor with reputedly close connections to various companies, Sir Joseph Renals returned unspecified favours by giving Barnato an official Mansion House banquet as formal recognition of what he had done to avert a catastrophe in the stock market. It was, Hamilton exclaimed that day, a dinner 'to thank this gentleman for supporting his own over-valued speculations and to advertise him more than he is already advertised'. He went on: 'It is said that it has been a costly affair – this dinner I mean – to Mr "Barnie" himself. I call it down-right prostitution of civic hospitality. Fortunately all respectable people with very few exceptions declined their invitations.' Hamilton was right, and it was a thin turnout (though including Carl Meyer) to hear Renals and Barnato pay mutual compliments.[43] The City, in short, remained sceptical about the merits of the Randlords and their loyal acolytes in the Kaffir Circus.

Meanwhile, another drama – wholly private and unreported – had been going on. Richard Meinertzhagen, second son of Daniel Meinertzhagen of Huths, was seventeen years old and due to leave Harrow at the end of the year. Daniel wanted him to follow family footsteps, Richard's deepest desire was to go to university to study zoology, and on 6 October son wrote to father:

> Money is not everything and I hate the City. If I can get a good degree in zoology I shall yet be a credit to the family. I know that both you and mother think I am no good but neither of you really know me or have seen my serious side. You know, Father, I do get things done, I think a lot and am not a complete ass nor have I earned the epithet 'black sheep' which has been bestowed on me. If I cannot do zoology may I do geography? A financial future has no attraction for me. I would sooner be penniless and doing congenial work than a millionaire living in and loathing the City.

Daniel remained adamant, and Richard wrote again on 4 November, saying that 'the idea of entering Huths fills me with loathing'. To which Daniel replied on the day of Barney's banquet:

> You have been well educated and enjoy a certain standard of living which is high. You must always try and live up to that standard and keep your place in the world. I think you should give the City a chance for you cannot enjoy life without money . . . After all, you have commerce in your blood and I can help you a great deal in the City. In the scientific world I should not be of any assistance to you. I am quite sure that if you worked hard in the City for a few years you will never regret the many advantages which would accrue.

At last, on the 9th, the would-be zoologist gave way:

> Money! I would sooner be a penniless scientist with successful research to my credit than be a senior partner in Huths, my soul blighted by gold and ripe to die of cancer in the stomach at the age of 55. Alright, I'll start in the City but the day I'm 21, if I hate it, you must let me go.[44]

CHAPTER FOURTEEN

A Very Cheerful War

Another victim of the Mine 'slump'. An inquest was held yesterday concerning the death of Frederick Oliver Heath (38), a member of the Stock Exchange, who was found with his throat cut in a train at Grosvenor-road Station on Tuesday. It was stated that he had been unable to sleep for the past three weeks owing to trouble caused by heavy monetary losses.

Heath slit his throat on 19 November 1895; it was clear that the recent market support operation by Barnato and others had failed to reverse the sharply downward trend in a notoriously overvalued sector. Gloom was not confined to the City. The new play at the Criterion was *The Squire of Dames*, including a scene where Miss Zoe Nuggetson, an American heiress, presses Mr Kilroy to marry her. He explains that she is too rich, to which she replies, 'We could speculate.' According to the *FN* on the 23rd, 'when this remark was made the other evening, after the collapse in the stock markets, a subdued but audible groan was heard from various parts of the stalls.'[1]

Far worse, though, was soon to afflict those interested in Kaffirs. The ill-conceived Jameson Raid at the end of the year plunged the Circus into a state of crisis, marking a long step on the road to eventual war between Britain and the Transvaal, with all the attendant consequences for the South African mining industry. Rhodes was certainly implicated in the raid, with a question mark hovering over other Randlords. There was, at this stage, little rational assessment of whether the policies of the Kruger government represented a fundamental obstacle to the future development of the gold-mining industry. On 14 January 1896, there took place a notable set-piece occasion, encapsulated by the *FT* as 'Barnato at Bay':

Seldom has the City of London manifested greater interest in a public meeting than was shown at that of the shareholders of the Barnato Bank. Although the meeting was not arranged to take place until mid-day, many persons secured seats as early as 9 a.m., and a number of shareholders were unable to obtain admittance at all. The Great Hall at Cannon-street was crammed almost to suffocation.

Barnato's speech lasted a full hour, and in the course of it he offered an upbeat assessment of the bank's assets, declared that he could sympathise with the grievances behind the Jameson Raid but not with the action itself, and expressed regret that the shares in his bank, currently standing at 1¹¹/₁₆, had initially gone to a £4 premium, against (he insisted) his wishes. Finally, the peroration:

> I am absolutely your guardian and your trustee, and I shall do all I can for the best interests of your property. (*Cheers.*) If I fail I cannot help it; I am only mortal, but I have done my best. In conclusion, I can tell you this, that the name of the Barnato Bank will not die out whilst the name of Barnato Brothers lives. I have every hope, and I trust that I shall be able to support these words – that the Barnato Bank will be one of the most successful of the many successes I have made in South Africa. (*Loud and continued cheers.*)

Altogether it had been a tour de force, well received on the Stock Exchange, where Barnato Bank shares closed on the 14th at 1⁵/₁₆. Yet, for all his bold assertions, Barnato himself was now on a rapid downward slide, his resources battered by the amount he had been compelled to pour into the market, his assets far stronger on paper than in reality. He still retained a loyal following in Capel Court, but by the end of 1896 his cherished bank was in liquidation. And as the *Citizen* had presciently wondered aloud in February that year, 'who will live in Mr Barnato's house in Park-lane when it is finished?'[2]

Other, more significant aspects of the Raid likewise reverberated in the City, including the enforced resignation of Rhodes as managing director of Consolidated Gold Fields, a move that signalled a fresh assertion of City authority over the company. The British South Africa Company was also affected, with Rhodes and the mining financier Alfred Beit both being compelled to resign from the board. 'Poor Horace [Farquhar] has been badly put out about the Chartered Company business', noted Hamilton on 7 May of a particularly well-connected banker. There were still some flurries of intense activity in Kaffirs, but on the whole the market did not prosper, not least because by the second half of 1896 it became the established conventional wisdom – owing more to febrile invention than detached analysis – that deep-level mining on the Rand was not going to be as successful as had generally been assumed. There was also the larger political situation, and when Barnato in October sent Kruger a placatory gift of two marble lions, the jaundiced view in the Circus was that 'a "stoney" bull and a cheerful-looking bear would have been more appropriate supporters for the President's roof-tree'. No wonder that the powerful jobber Tom Nickalls had returned by the autumn to the American market, a move that he can hardly have regretted the following spring as Anglo-Transvaal relations hit yet another rocky patch. 'There is a very general feeling in the City that trouble is brewing in South Africa', reported the *Citizen*'s resident Stock Exchange columnist in March 1897, and for once the City had got it right, even if the time-scale remained uncertain. For Barnato, things quickly came to a head: having been in the Cape, he left in early June to return to London to give a party on Jubilee Day, the 22nd, at the Park Lane house in which he still had not lived. When the ship was south of Madeira, he jumped overboard. On hearing the news, Carl Meyer wrote to his wife: 'Poor Barney! What a tragic end to the career of a gigantic humbug but an amusing one.' That, in the end, was the City's verdict on the meteor that had passed across its firmament.[3]

*

Booms came and went, but nothing affected the sobriety of the money market report. 'Money was in fair demand today', intoned the *FT* at the end of business on 14 November 1895, but almost certainly all sorts of arcane dramas were being played on that and subsequent days, including at the bill brokers Smith St Aubyn:

> By far the hardest day we have had for many months. £230^m [i.e. thousand] called . . . After the greatest exertions & aware that I could not afford to risk anything I went to the Bank for 50^m. Not a shilling anywhere at 2.30 and over £400^m on each side of the book. Discount varies between 1$\frac{3}{16}$ and 1$\frac{1}{8}$. Having no Stock prevented us getting Money from Stockbrokers.
>
> Money was again very much wanted and at one time it looked like the Bank. Eventually however we got in money and finally at half past one we took 50^m fine running February from McIver at 1$\frac{1}{2}$.

'The Bank' was of course the Bank of England. Governor for two years from the spring of 1895 was Albert G. Sandeman, a wine merchant with no very clear banking expertise, but who still controlled an institution whose lightest word could make or break.[4]

In fact, the Bank was an increasingly competitive force in banking at large by the mid-1890s. The determining context was partly the Goschen settlement of 1891 having squeezed its regular income, partly the long period of cheap money (Bank rate at 2 per cent from February 1894 to September 1896) further reducing income, and partly a wish to do something to redress the balance in relation to the ever vaster resources and thus potential muscle power of the joint-stock banks. The main form that this new competitive attitude took was much-increased discounting by the Bank's provincial branches, which during most of the 1880s had run at a loss but during the first half of the 1890s returned handsome profits of up to £80,000 pa.[5] In May 1896 Beckett Faber of the Leeds bank Beckett & Co. complained to the Central Association of Bankers that the Bank's instructions to its provincial agents had become "'Get business at fair rates if you can, but get business"', and he went on:

> We do not complain about fair competition but this is fostered by free money costing the lender nothing at all. How can we country bankers who pay well for our deposits meet such competition as this? Our loans are taken from us; our bills no longer exist in our cases and our current accounts are 'touted' for . . . The time is already arriving, if it has not already arrived, when the Bank of England must choose whether to be the banker for the government or a commercial bank. It cannot be both.

At the meeting of the Association a few days later, Faber's views were strongly supported by other country bankers; but talk of the banks keeping their own independent reserves was swiftly dispelled by other, City-based bankers, including Felix Schuster of the Union Bank of London, who successfully argued that a more prudent course was discussions with the Bank. On 3 June the Association held its annual dinner, and among those present were Sandeman, the deputy governor, Richard Biddulph Martin, and a country banker called Rowland Hughes, Liverpool manager of the North and South Wales Bank. Hughes noted: 'Martin twitted the Bank of England upon its new departure in competing against its neighbours. He charged the "old Lady" with having adopted the role of the "new woman".'[6]

A week later, Messrs Barclay, Bevan, Tritton, Ransom, Bouverie & Co. of 54 Lombard Street issued a circular announcing the creation of Barclay & Co., Ltd, an amalgamation of twenty private banks and capitalised at £6m. All but two of the twenty were situated outside London, with a heavy bias towards the eastern side of England, and the family ties between the partners of these banks were extensive, with (historically at least) a distinctly Quaker character. 'The Directors', announced the circular, 'have been selected from among the existing Partners, and the local management will remain in the same hands as heretofore, the private character of the Banks being thus preserved.' It was a claim made in implicit contrast to existing joint-stock banks, and to a large extent it was fulfilled, as Barclays over the next thirty years maintained a notably decentralised structure, putting a banking premium on local knowledge. Reaction at large, to an announcement that caused a considerable stir in the City, was probably summed up by the assertions of the *Bankers' Magazine* that 'the spirit of the age cannot be resisted' and that, for good or ill, 'amalgamation is the order of the day'.[7]

It was hardly surprising if many in the City disliked these new joint-stock creations, for not only did a high proportion of their leading figures come from the provinces, but the very way in which they were organised seemed to undermine the personal basis on which the City had traditionally conducted its business.

The middle of May 1897 saw Rowland Hughes back in London, and he spoke to the bill broker Whitburn of Reeves, Whitburn & Co., who gave crisp judgements on two major institutions. The first was the London and Westminster Bank, by now, some sixty years after its controversial beginnings, becoming a pillar of the City. 'They are', said Whitburn, 'the only Bank in London who keep a bona fide reserve of gold. They have had for years £500,000 in gold locked up in their vaults and I have not heard of its being disturbed. It is the first Bank in London after the Bank of England.' His other assessment was of that venerable pillar itself: 'The feeling is general in the City that there is a want of competency in the management of the Bank of England. What they require is a strong man with a large salary who would be above suspicion. They do some very queer things there.'[8] The governor by this time was Hugh Colin Smith, who in his favour was not a wine merchant – but instead, a wharfinger.

Was Smith the man to nurture a new spirit of concord between Bank and banks? In practice peace failed to break out in 1897, as it took several years for the Bank's theoretical policy of drawing in its competitive horns to be translated into action, above all in the provinces. This may have been because Smith's commercial instincts got the better of him over the remaining almost two years of his governorship, but perhaps more plausibly it was a case of the men on the ground finding it more convenient to make their own policy. If so, a key figure was undoubtedly Ernest Edye, in overall charge of the branches from March 1897, producing from them an annual average profit of £145,400 in his first seven years, almost double what it had been over the previous nine years. 'This business has grown up,' wrote Edye in 1904 in a typically combative retrospective report, 'in spite of what I may, at least, term lack of encouragement on the part of the Court – which is rather depressing. One Director, for instance, has more than once expressed his opinion that Branch Deposits had better be invested in Consols.' Such sentiments were anathema to Edye, who, especially in his early years in charge, seems to have sought business without apparent compunction. However, as he frankly admitted:

> The other Bankers, keeping accounts with the Bank of England, view with extreme jealousy any activity in the Bank's Banking operations – more particularly in the provinces, where the bulk of business in any individual place being less than that of London, particular operations are more easily identified. Bankers know that in the total 'private deposits' [i.e. of the Bank of England] their own deposits bulk very large, and from their point of view it is not unnatural that they should think it unfair that the Bank, holding their money free of interest, should compete with them in discounts, advances and the general Banking facilities which attract Drawing accounts.

Resentments, in short, were being stored up – and would linger long after Edye's money-making drive had been forcibly suppressed.[9]

Palpably short of competitive drive, in City matters anyway, was Richard Meinertzhagen, by January 1896 in reluctant situ at 12 Tokenhouse Yard:

> I was installed in a small windowless room and was given all sorts and conditions of Bills of Lading, Accounts, Letters of Credit, Acceptances and Cheques which I did not understand and did not want to understand. I loathed the whole business and was miserable . . . I never felt so out of place. Nobody seemed to pay much attention to me, in fact for days nobody would come near me or try and explain things I had no wish to understand.

After eight dismal months Meinertzhagen was sent by his father to Göttingen, from where he wrote at the end of September: 'I shall never make a City man, but learning German will be useful to me whatever I do.' And he went on: 'I want to see the world and not moulder away in a London fog. How can I justify my life to the Almighty if I have frittered away my time trying to make money, whereas if I can say I have done something to benefit humanity, I might get a good mark.'[10]

To outsiders, though, the money-making experience could seem thrilling. Part of the attraction derived from a reluctance over the years to explode the popular myth that jobbers on the Stock Exchange were somehow omniscient, possessing the gift of rapid, authoritative insight denied to other mortals. The truth about these extrovert and noisy but strangely inarticulate men was altogether more humdrum. It comes through strongly in a snippet from the *Statist* in 1896:

> *5 September.* It was perhaps a mercy that the telegram announcing the death of Prince Lobanoff [Russia's foreign minister] appeared in only one morning paper – the *Daily Telegraph* – which does not happen to have much vogue on 'Change. Three-fourths of the men in the House at Monday's opening knew nothing of the Kieff sensation, and even in the Foreign market it was not generally credited till confirmed by Reuter. When it did get known, many had to ask who Prince Lobanoff was; and a jocular reply, that he was only the Czar's brother-in-law, helped to still the troubled waves.

The real position was neatly defined by Lawrence Jones, a merchant banker who came to the City just before the First World War. He wrote in his memoirs: 'The idea that stock-jobbers have secret sources of information and know what a Poincaré is going to say next Sunday before he says it, and mark the prices of their wares up and down accordingly, is of course moonshine. They take the same interest in public affairs as the rest of us, no more nor less, and have the same sources of information, which is usually the press.'[11]

Richard Meinertzhagen was back in London by 1897. His father had arranged for him to join the highly respectable stockbrokers Laurie, Milbank & Co., which he did as a clerk in May. 'I loathed the whole business, did not understand the work, nor did I wish to understand it', was Richard's usual biddable attitude, even though his father Daniel 'did his utmost to raise my enthusiasm by asking large firms to give me orders on which I received fantastic commissions'. For instance: 'On one occasion, old Charles Goschen asked me to go round and see him. We had a pleasant conversation which ended in him asking me to buy him £75,000 worth of a South American investment. I did so and got a commission of over £80.' It made not a halfpenny of difference, as he recorded in his diary later that summer: 'I do not think I can stand this life much longer. I am wasting my life and my youth. A stuffy office, no exercise, complete slavery and a future ruined by an atmosphere in which gold is the sole aim.' The end of this wretched phase came with merciful swiftness. The following February his elder brother Dan died suddenly of appendicitis, and both his father and Frederick Huth Jackson pushed for Richard to take Dan's prospective place in Huths; but his mother insisted that he was unsuited, Richard himself remained adamantly against, and instead the berth went to his younger brother Louis, leaving Richard free to hunt for bigger game than sordid commissions.[12]

Did the soul of Bertram Currie nod mutely as young Meinertzhagen made his great escape? Who knows? The hammer of the bimetallists was operated on for cancer in December 1895, but was back in the City by the end of the following month. In August 1896 he found out from his doctor that his cancer had returned, and at once he wound up his affairs at Glyn Mills and said farewell to Lombard Street. 'From the moment . . . that the sentence was pronounced,' his widow would write in a memorial letter addressed to her dead husband, 'you steadily faced the near prospect of death, and ceased to feel any interest in the business that had hitherto engrossed you.' A renowned and sardonic atheist, he was now, in the words of his widow, 'most desirous to do all that he could to make amends for his neglect of religion in the past', and that autumn he was received into the Catholic Church. Currie died on 28 December 1896. His old admirer Sir Edward Hamilton wrote in his diary a warm appreciation – 'I shall always regard him as the longest-headed man in the City of his day' – that ended, however, on a melancholy note: 'He was a striking instance of the irony of wealth. His wife was a hopeless invalid & he had only two children, one of whom died and the remaining boy is sickly; while he was himself overcome by the direst of all complaints. How little can riches do to redress such a balance!' Many public tributes were paid, including of course from Gladstone, but the last word on a notable career belongs to Currie himself, on whose lips there was often the following favourite jingle:

> A City banker born and bred,
> Sufficient for my fame,
> If those who knew me best have said
> I tarnished not the name.[13]

*

In the 24 June 1898 issue of his *Investors' Review*, the tough-minded A. J. Wilson launched a full-scale broadside entitled 'Is the Stock Exchange Rotten?' Seeking to explain the current stagnation in Capel Court, especially in speculative dealings, Wilson took the line that this was in large part 'the direct offspring of stock market habits of business'. He claimed that the 'fair and honourable traders' who comprised the majority of members were 'at the mercy of the dishonest and unscrupulous minority'; and argued that Capel Court's invariable, all-purpose defence – to the effect that most swindles did not *originate* in the Stock Exchange – was inadequate. In fine, such was the modern sophistication of inside cliques and syndicates that the writer 'would as soon think of deliberately putting his hand into the fire as of perpetrating "a time bargain on open account" on the Stock Exchange in any security, so fully persuaded is he that the odds are bound to be against his success'.[14]

Wilson could fairly claim the moral high ground. Back in 1875, while on the *Pall Mall Gazette*, he had knowingly turned his back on a fortune by refusing to use his knowledge of the intention of Disraeli's government to buy a large stake in the Suez Canal Company; he founded the *Investors' Review* in 1891; and a contemporary was to describe him as 'the knight, without fear or reproach, of City Editors'.[15] However, with a very few honourable exceptions, led by Wilson's paper and *The Economist*, the probity of the financial press (and financial editors generally) left an enormous amount to be desired in the 1890s.[16]

Against this background, of a rising tide of criticism of all things to do with company promoting, the Stock Exchange and the financial press, came the Hooley revelations, *the* event of 1898. Having in the space of three years promoted twenty-six companies, only a handful of which were not now in serious financial difficulties or bust, Ernest Terah Hooley was declared bankrupt in the summer. Hooley's evidence before the London Bankruptcy Court began in late July, focusing at an early stage on the celebrated Dunlop promotion of May 1896 that had made his name. Hooley conceded that it had netted him somewhere between £100,000 and £200,000.[17]

In further evidence, the name of Harry Marks (founder-editor of *Financial News*) continued to crop up, and in all he seems to have received from the promoter a grand total of £31,110 in cash and shares. Hooley at one point was pressed to explain one of the larger payments, in connection with a Harry Lawson cycle flotation, which for £25,000, of which a third was to go to Marks, he had agreed not to oppose:

> He did not give the money to Mr Marks to abstain from writing in the *Financial News*. He would not say whether the payment was in virtue of a preconcerted arrangement. As a fact Mr Marks did about this time cease to publish unfavourable comments. The only reason why he gave Mr Marks this money was that Mr Marks was a friend of his. (*Laughter.*)

Even the name of the *FT*'s Douglas MacRae was mentioned, in connection with a cheque for almost £2,000, though Hooley added to further laughter that MacRae was 'the honestest man of the lot'. However, Hooley's evidence went well beyond the financial press. From the wider point of view his most damaging revelation was of a donation of £10,000 to the Conservative Central Fund as the price for his election to the Carlton Club and, he hoped, an eventual peerage. Though the party offered to return the money, the damage was done.[18]

'The now famous Mr Hooley' (in Hamilton's phrase) had in fact almost half a century of relative obscurity ahead of him, but his place in the history books was secure. Even before the bankruptcy proceedings ended, the Lord Chief Justice, Lord Russell of Killowen, took the opportunity of his address at the Law Courts on Lord Mayor's Day, on the occasion of the new Lord Mayor taking the customary oath of office, to inveigh against 'fraud which is rampant in this community, fraud of a most dangerous kind, widespread in its operation, touching all classes, involving great pecuniary loss to the community . . . fraud blunting the sharp edge of honour and besmirching honourable names'. Hugh Stutfield also had his say, contributing a perceptive, well-measured piece ('The Company Scandal: A City View') to the December *National Review*. If Hooley-style abuses were not to be repeated, the public must be educated, for 'the confidence investors display in the honesty as well as the ability of financiers to make money for them is quite touching in its *naïveté*'. Stutfield did not exonerate the Stock Exchange, but blamed 'a small minority' of members for making false markets and called on the Committee to take firmer action, above all to prohibit dealings before allotment. He also warned that 'the power and importance of the Stock Exchange are so great nowadays that the due performance of its functions is a matter almost of national concern, and if some of its members do not mend their ways we may witness some day the appointment of another Royal Commission and, possibly, the establishment of some form of Government control over its proceedings'. Stutfield then addressed the wider implications of the whole Hooley episode:

> The opponents of company law reform lay great stress on the danger of impeding enterprise by too stringent legislation. They seem to overlook the

fact that the dishonesty fostered by our existing limited liability system is a still more serious drag upon industry: firstly, owing to the squandering of vast sums on promoters' swindles; and, secondly, by deterring the public from embarking their money in undertakings which, though possibly speculative, are yet perfectly legitimate and useful. One is always hearing complaints in the City of the difficulty of obtaining capital to develop good properties. The joint-stock frauds of the last few years have rendered investors over-suspicious; they cannot distinguish what is honest from what is fraudulent.[19]

The pity was that few others in the City recognised, let alone accepted, the exercise of quality control by its financial intermediaries as crucial to a flourishing economy. Instead, a seductive mix of 'animal spirits', *caveat emptor* and promoters' slush funds continued to carry all before it, as the City's Establishment – the Bank of England, the great joint-stock and private banks, the merchant banks, the most reputable stockbroking firms – looked on more or less unconcerned.

*

The prospect of war between nations is never agreeable to cosmopolitan men of *haute finance*, and Carl Meyer, who early in 1899 had toured Egypt with Cassel ('a little dictatorial'), was no exception. During August, operating from his new City base at the National Bank of Egypt, he wrote almost daily to his wife, noting on the 28th, two days after Joseph Chamberlain's public warning to Kruger that the sands were running down in the glass, he was still hopeful: 'I persist in believing that Kruger will at the last moment cave in . . . The City has only been slightly affected by the acuteness of the situation but will become more nervous should an EXPEDITION be sent out.' As for the mood in the Kaffir Circus itself, the *FT*'s Mining Market report for 5 September summed it up: 'The generality of the dealers at the close still inclined to the opinion that war would be averted by the Boers giving way, though most of them seemed less pronounced in this judgment than hitherto. They were, at the same time, rather disposed to welcome a conflict, as the only likely means of clearing the situation.'[20] The atmosphere in the City remained turbid for the rest of September, amidst mounting press hysteria and a perpetual volley of rumours; by early October few doubted that, at last, war had become inevitable.

Perhaps the clinching moment came on Tuesday the 3rd, as Bank rate was suddenly raised from 3½ to 4½ per cent. Just over a week later, at three o'clock on the afternoon of the 11th, the Boer ultimatum expired. War had begun, and Charles Duguid, in his history of the Stock Exchange written not long afterwards, described the scene:

> Two great flags – the Royal Standard and the Union Jack – were unfurled from the bench in the Rhodesia Market, drawing all the members present to the spot. The singing of the National Anthem suggested itself. 'Where's

the conductor?' yelled a voice. Mr Charlie Clarke made his way to the front and mounted the bench, walking-stick baton in hand. The dead silence which followed the clearing of throats might have proved suggestive even to a less witty member, recalling the similar silence which ensues sometimes after settlement days, when the waiter mounts the rostrum with his hammer [i.e. to declare a member's failure]. It inspired Mr Clarke to make one of the most effective remarks ever heard within the Stock Exchange. 'Gentlemen!' he cried, having dealt the three dread blows. 'Mr Kruger has not complied with his bargains!' The effect was electrical; roar after roar of laughter and applause greeted the sally.

According to another account, it was a penny hammer that Clarke used, at what was arguably, for good or ill, the Stock Exchange's all-time supreme moment.[21]

'It was such a very cheerful war. I hated its confidence, its congratulatory anticipations, its optimism of the Stock Exchange. I hated its vile assurance of victory.' Such indeed was the prevailing mood in October 1899, caught by the incorrigibly dissenting G. K. Chesterton. Can one, though, go all the way and agree with J. A. Hobson's famous verdict, pronounced soon after the event, that the Boer War was 'the clearest and most dramatic instance of the operation of the world-wide forces of international finance'?[22] There is no doubt that Britain had formidable economic interests at stake in South Africa – not only gold, but also trade in general;[23] nor that, as far as the gold-mining industry itself was concerned, it had become an *idée fixe* that 'good government' in the Transvaal could get working costs down to 22/- a ton, six shillings less than they were in 1898 and the sure route to higher dividends;[24] nor indeed that by this time the attitude of the Randlords was generally warlike. Was there also some connection made, in the City and in the official mind, between London's continuing role as the world's only free gold market, the less than happy state of the bullion reserve, and the perceived need to ensure in the long term a regular supply of gold from South Africa? The connection or otherwise has been much debated, on remarkably slender evidence, and it is only instinct that tells one that there was some such connection.[25] South Africa meant gold, gold had become the very pivot of the City's existence, and to deny the connection surely goes against the grain.

Yet it would be still more foolish to deny the dimension of political autonomy involved in government policy. Two key assertions were made by Salisbury, dragged into war by Chamberlain and Sir Alfred Milner, High Commissioner in South Africa, almost against his better judgement. Justifying the conflict, he said it was in order to teach the Transvaal 'that we not the Dutch are boss'; and this, he emphasised, was a sufficient justification even if it involved fighting 'for people whom we despise, and for territory which will bring no profit and no power to England'.[26]

Natty Rothschild was more ambivalent in his attitude to the Randlords. He laboured long and hard, but to no avail, to prevent war.[27] He failed not because others in the City were more successfully manipulating the politicians, but because the politicians were – for a variety of reasons, some of them economic – prepared to go to war, knowing that they had public opinion behind them. It was a popular support in which, when all was said and done, the City was firmly in the vanguard.

On 1 November 1899, three weeks into the war and with much-exaggerated fears starting to be expressed about London's gold supplies now that South African mines were being shut down, Lord Hillingdon of Glyn Mills gave his inaugural address as president of the Institute of Bankers. He noted that, whereas twenty years previously the Bank of England had been easily pre-eminent in terms of its deposits (over £38m, with the National Provincial coming second on just £26m), now the Bank of England's £43m was surpassed by the National Provincial and the London and County, with two or three other banks poised to overtake. Hillingdon, with an implicit nod to the recently formed bankers' committees, then considered the implications:

> We have now to face a situation in which the Bank of England has admittedly lost a certain power of control in many ways. In many quarters, for instance, as you will have seen from the papers, there has been some anxiety as to the amount of our national reserve of gold, as this has not increased in anything like the same degree as the development of our credit. The Bank of England is, of course, the custodian of this reserve, and how far it is desirable to assist, and how we can best assist in augmenting this is a problem worthy of the keenest thinkers in the City . . . We should always bear in mind that we are not starting, as it were, with a clean slate, but are living and doing our business under a system which has worked fairly well for more than half a century.

Hillingdon's assessment was very much that of a City insider, the eminent private banker instinctively unwilling to upset the existing order of things.

In sharp contrast was the perspective of John Dun of Parr's Bank, who lamented the general failure to take action so far over the question of the inadequate bullion reserve, attributing that failure to 'a deal of apathy in the British mind'. However, Dun pointed out with satisfaction that 'many bankers, feeling that they ought not any longer to hang upon the skirts of the Bank of England, have begun to provide independent reserves for themselves – they have locked up bullion, sovereigns, and Bank of England notes in their strong room, so that when a period of pressure does occur, the strain should not be exclusively on the Bank of England'.[28] Everyone accepted that there was a problem, but whether the leading joint-stock bankers were capable of coming up with a solution that was financially and politically acceptable – financially to their

Mr. Rotchchild

Drawn Etch Pub by R. Dighton. Oct 1817

London Pub by Thos M Lean, 26 Haymarket 1824

A View from the Royal Exchange.

Nathan Rothschild in his prime.

Cheapside in 1823.

Corner of Bishopsgate and Threadneedle Street, just before demolition, 1862.

The same site, Threadneedle Street in 1865: suddenly the City of Dickens has become altogether less human.

The Bankers' Clearing House in Lombard Street, 1847.

G. E. Hicks, *Dividend Day at the Bank of England*, 1859.

Black Friday, 11 May 1866: the closed doors of Overend Gurney.

London Bridge *c.*1875.

"SAME OLD GAME!"

OLD LADY OF THREADNEEDLE STREET. "YOU'VE GOT YOURSELVES INTO A NICE MESS WITH YOUR PRECIOUS 'SPECULATION!' WELL—I'LL HELP YOU OUT OF IT,—FOR THIS ONCE!!"

Barings Crisis: *Punch*, 8 November 1890.

shareholders, politically to the rest of the City and its influential friends – was another matter entirely.

For the moment it seemed they were not, but the question remained on the agenda and in April 1900 a paper on 'Banking Reserves' produced a surprisingly frank discussion at the Institute. It was led by Dun, who in effect revealed why the twin initiative launched the previous summer had been a damp squib:

> It is a fact which is no longer a secret that many – I cannot say all, because we do not know – but many, and I think I may say most, of the large Joint Stock Banks, have accumulated in their own vaults, cash reserves beyond their daily requirements for till money. That is an admirable thing. That we should be able to fall upon some scheme whereby such private reserves on the part of the larger banks should be regulated, is another matter, and a very, very difficult matter indeed. The banks may be, and are, very friendly, but there is a good deal of latent jealousy, and not very latent competition amongst them, and Bank A would not brook that Bank B or Bank C should know the amount that it possesses deep down in its vaults in the shape of gold coin to meet an emergency. Therefore, although the subject is one on which I should like to preserve quite an open mind, I fear that we cannot fall upon a general scheme whereby the maintenance of such reserves can be regulated.

Inevitably, the other main contributor to the discussion was the Union Bank of London's autocratic Felix Schuster:

> What we require is co-operation, and not legislation . . . I should think some means could be devised by which the Bank of England, instead of holding itself rather aloof from other banks, should periodically meet us and tell us what their views of the situation are, and that we should from time to time discuss a common policy, and act harmoniously with one another, instead of acting in the dark, as we are doing now, quite unaware of what may be in the minds of the Bank of England.[29]

In short, put less tactfully, the time had come for the company of merchants to accept, at last, the City's foremost joint-stock bankers as first-class citizens.

*

Following considerable speculative losses at the tail-end of 1899, with the war going badly, business in the Stock Exchange ground almost to a halt during the early weeks of 1900. One way and another, it was a somewhat febrile City that the government had to deal with as it prepared to raise £10m with which to fight the Boers. Hamilton conducted preliminaries on the Treasury's behalf, while the governor's chair at the Bank of England was occupied by Samuel Steuart Gladstone, senior partner of the East India merchants Ogilvy, Gillanders & Co. and a first cousin of the great man.

'Unfortunately very self-opinionated, and will have his own way' was the unflattering estimate of one leading bill broker, but it was probably a just verdict. On 6 February he reported to Hamilton that 'the prevailing opinion' in the City was 'in favour of an addition to Consols', as opposed to the creation of a separate stock; and it soon became clear that this was also the Bank's own opinion, backed by Rothschilds and the government broker J. H. Daniell, largely on the grounds of the unrivalled liquidity of Consols. The advantage of a separate stock, though, was that it would appeal to a wider public, something Chancellor Hicks Beach naturally wanted, and two significant City figures supported that alternative. One was Cassel, who saw Hicks Beach on the 6th and objected to Consols partly because (in Hamilton's summarising words) 'there were large *bear* accounts open, and the speculators might put down the price against us as soon as they got wind of a large issue'. The other was Revelstoke, who as John Baring had succeeded to the title of his ill-fated father and was striving hard to restore the house to something like its old eminence. By the end of February the decision was made to go for a separate stock, and Hamilton on the 26th, after a visit to Threadneedle Street, even persuaded himself that the Bank was 'coming round to the idea of a special war loan in lieu of Consols'.[30]

Then, early on 1 March, a Thursday, came the news that Ladysmith had been relieved. Sidney Webb at the time wrote to Beatrice: 'All day long, in the City, there appears to have been a pandemonium of joy and shouting'.[31] The news was a marvellous fillip to the prospects of the imminent War Loan, but the enthusiasm seems barely to have infected Gladstone at the Bank. Writing to Hamilton on the 2nd, in response to a draft prospectus, his mainly technical letter ended on a thoroughly sour note: 'In conclusion I feel regret that the loan is not to be raised by an addition to Consols and would have preferred a terminable 3% annuity at par to a 2¾% one at a heavy discount and I hope that in pricing the price of issue the Chancellor will not aim too high.' Also in the band of doubters was Natty Rothschild, who was being overriden not only in his wish for Consols but also in the notion that the issue should be backed by a Rothschild-led guarantee, a plan that Hicks Beach shortly rejected. Writing to Hamilton from Tring Park on Sunday the 4th, Natty referred with foreboding to 'a financial Maggersfontein' (one of the Boer War disasters) and went on:

> It is no use living in a fool's paradise. The operation will have to be very carefully managed and everything done to insure success. The Germans are already trying to place a large loan and will no doubt offer very tempting prices to under-writers here and in America . . . The Chancellor told me he would send for me when he is ready.

In fact, Natty and his brothers were in the process of being moved sideways in the consultative process. A memorandum written by Hamilton on the Monday revealed who was entering centre stage:

> I had a talk with Sir E. Cassel last night. (He returned from Rome on purpose to render assistance.)
>
> He agreed cordially with me that it would be better to dispense with a guarantee altogether, if possible. If the price was fixed at (say) 98, he believed that the loan would be certain to go; and it would be much more dignified for the government to appeal direct to the public who would respond.
>
> At the same time there could be no harm & it might be a satisfaction to the Chanc of the Exchequer to sound a *few* big persons as to what they would be good for – he would be responsible for 2m himself.
>
> The Bankers might be summoned by the governor on the eve of the issue, and their co-operation invited.[32]

In essence Cassel's plan was adopted, though the eventual price was 98½, a full point above what most City people had been pressing for.

Even so, the issue proved a roaring success and was massively oversubscribed. 'Scores of clerks', reported the chief cashier at the Bank itself, 'are here every night until 10, 11, 12 and even ½ past one o'clock.' A satisfied Hamilton noted in his diary on 16 March: 'The loan, which the Stock Exchange with their love for slang have nicknamed "Khaki", was closed on Wednesday evening. It was subscribed more than 11 times over.' Arguably, City anxieties about overpricing had led to the loan being underpriced, as Revelstoke against the trend had feared. Hamilton, however, preferred to turn his attention to the question of allotment: 'Cassel who dined with me this evening thought that we were giving the big folk too much and not allotting enough among the small applicants. We can easily remedy this.' His word was becoming law, and Hamilton a few weeks later referred to 'the jealousy with which the Rothschilds regard Cassel'.[33]

On the evening of Friday 18 May, news reached London that Mafeking also had been relieved. 'The war has been hateful to us from the outset but the pluck and example of that little garrison is legitimate grounds for pride and enthusiasm.' That was the reaction of Gaspard Farrer of Barings, but relatively few in the City shared that sense of hatefulness, least of all on Mafeking Day. A memorable Saturday – and for the City, the high point of the war – was described by the *FT* in its daily stock-market report:

> So far as business was concerned, the Stock Exchange might just as well have been closed today, but it provided a useful purpose in providing a gathering place for some 5,000 City men who had gone crazy over the news of the relief of Mafeking . . . A few minutes before eleven Mr Charlie Clarke announced that on the stroke of the hour photographs would be

taken of the House, and asked members to stand steady and cease cheering at the time . . . After the photographs had been taken 'God Save the Queen' was sung with fine enthusiasm, followed by 'Rule Britannia', 'God Bless the Prince of Wales' and 'For He's a Jolly Good Fellow', rousing cheers being given for Baden-Powell, Roberts and the Queen. The House then degenerated into a somewhat riotous condition, members marching about in cheering columns, waving flags and blowing trumpets, while the note of the inevitable coaching horn was heard over all.[34]

As the summer wore on it became uncomfortably clear that the Boers were not going to curl up, close their eyes and think of Capel Court. Everyone knew that more money was going to be needed to wage the war. Gladstone was still governor, and on 23 July he wrote solemnly to Hicks Beach: 'I deprecate the issue of a further War Loan on the lines of the previous one, for it could only now be made at a considerably worse price than the former issue . . . I do not hesitate to say that an issue of Consols would be more popular with the City and the public than any other form.' Next day the Bank, already lending the government some £8.5m, formally declined to lend a further £0.5–1m, thereby forcing Hicks Beach's hand; also that day, Hamilton conveniently found himself in Threadneedle Street. After 'a talk with the Bank people' – still adamantly pro-Consols, anti-Khaki – he went on to New Court, and later in the afternoon 'got hold of Sir E. Cassel'. This time, to Hamilton's relief, the two great authorities were in agreement: both Rothschilds and Cassel insisted that Consols were out of the question and instead plumped for Exchequer bonds. Their word proved decisive, as Gladstone's advice was again spurned.[35]

A complicated week ensued as rival priorities vied with each other.[36] One was the government's need for money, the other was the Bank's need for gold in order to bolster its flagging reserve; and it quite quickly became government policy that the best way to square this pressing circle was to ensure that a substantial proportion of the new loan was placed in America, which would have the almost automatic effect of attracting considerable quantities of gold to London. In the end it was agreed to an advance placing in America, largely through the Morgan houses, of just over half the £10m issue. Hamilton reflected on 2 August that this was something that ought to be stated in the prospectus. However, 'the Bank of England are averse to this, and think we can arrange the matter by closing the list as soon as the sum required has been applied for'.[37]

Hamilton's concern was amply justified, and in due course the *Statist* told the story of a sore episode in relations between Chancellor and Square Mile:

> He has certainly not dealt very fairly with the City. He brought out the loan on one of the most unfavourable days of the whole year. It was known by very few on Friday afternoon [the 3rd]. It was publicly announced on the Saturday morning preceding the August Bank Holiday, when the Stock

Exchange was closed, and when, owing to the great heat that had prevailed previously, everybody that could was anxious to get away for a few days. The list was opened at 10 o'clock on Tuesday morning. Fifty minutes later it was closed, when it ought to have been known to everybody concerned that the day after the Bank Holiday the trains would all be late, and intending applicants would therefore not be in a position to apply early. As for the provinces and the Continent, they were entirely shut out. Lastly, the Chancellor of the Exchequer, in announcing the loan, did not state that more than half of it was already disposed of . . . If the British government holds back such a material fact as this, how can we expect anything better from the private promoter?

Not surprisingly, the language at New Court, as Carl Meyer reported to his wife later that day, was 'the reverse of complimentary'; while elsewhere, 'others threaten lawsuits against the Treasury – in fact, there is a h--- of a row and the papers will be full of it tomorrow'. So they were ('the government has gone in for stag hunting before the grouse shooting has begun' was the *FT*'s wry comment), but Hamilton took the larger view: 'We have got our money easily subscribed; and the London market is relieved at not having to find the whole of it itself.'[38]

Of course, what really rankled at New Court was the muscling in of the Morgan houses on an important British government issue, an eloquent testimony to their ability to offer a high-class transatlantic distribution service. It was with the purr of a cat that has got the cream that J. S. Morgan & Co.'s Clinton Dawkins, barely three months in the City, wrote to his mentor Alfred Milner on the 16th:

> You may have observed that we placed half, really more than half of the new ten million loan in the US.
>
> The Treasury were quite right in their general policy, and the gold we are bringing over will avert what would have been a 7 pc Bank rate and considerable trouble. But, of course, the Treasury went hopelessly wrong in details owing to the colossal stupidity of the Bank.

Dawkins then explained how the Bank had struck out from the draft prospectus the crucial 'material fact' and how Hicks Beach had 'weakly consented', thereby 'exposing the Govt to violent abuse'; and later in his letter he could not resist groaning, 'But the Bank of England! If that old institution is not reorganised on some better basis it will bring us into trouble yet.'[39]

*

In the early months of 1901, Finance's main concern remained government's heavy borrowing requirements in order to wage the war.[40] On 23 January, the day after the death of Queen Victoria, Barings wired to Baring Magoun in New York: 'Very important negotiations should not be suspected. We recommend caution, specially Rothschilds. Chancellor of Exchequer very anxious negotiations to be kept private.' The context was the intention of Hicks Beach to issue £11m of Exchequer bonds, once again using Morgans and Barings in both London and New York, with a substantial American placing. 'We will not be popular here, but it is the only way of getting a good price *and* of helping the gold situation here,' Dawkins wrote to Milner on the 25th. On 6 February, Hicks Beach came to the conclusion that there was no alternative but to seek guidance from the most traditional source. 'I am inclined to put the thing straight to the Bank people', he wrote to Hamilton. 'If they assure me that they believe the market here will take the bonds, and can themselves help *largely*, if necessary, to secure this, then I w^d try a free issue here. If they can't, then US.'[41]

Hamilton recorded the outcome:

> *11 February.* I hear the Exchequer Bonds have been subscribed for more than twice over, in spite of the prophecies of the croakers that the London market would not find the money. I am glad we have kept clear of America on this occasion.

The City as a whole was also pleased that there had been no repeat of the previous summer's manoeuvre, but the *FT* on the 13th was less than enamoured by other aspects of the latest War Loan. It declared that 'a subscription of less than 2½ times over' for an issue offered on attractive terms was 'not overwhelming'. It pointed out that 'the average price obtained is only £97 5s 4d, as compared with £98 2s 10d for similar bonds last November'. And it sounded a warning note: 'The public has shown that it does not like borrowing by pinches in the case of a big war; that it does not like the form of security changed every time, and that it does not like the principle of tender. We trust the Treasury will learn these lessons, but we imagine its great pride is that it has succeeded in "muddling through".'[42] By mid-March peace negotiations had collapsed, and it was obvious that there would soon be opportunity for further muddle and acrimony.

The new loan was to be for £60m, ensuring that it would be the last of the year. City opinion, as relayed to Hamilton at the end of March and beginning of April, was unanimous in favour of an issue of Consols, with a strong preference for a fixed price. 'We must try & get the general investor in', he summarised as Cassel's view, adding that 'an issue by tender [i.e. as opposed to fixed price] leads to so much cornering, & to favouring of syndicates'. So Consols at a fixed price it was, but £60m was a huge amount, enough to make Treasury and Bank distinctly nervous, especially at a time of considerable strain on the money market. At this stage the determining factor was the presence in Britain of the world's most renowned financier. Hamilton, as usual, is the invaluable guide:

17 April. Mr [Pierpont] Morgan came to see me yesterday. Dawkins brought him to pay his respects on the Chanc of the Exchequer. He impresses one at once as a strong man; but the appearance of his nose, poor man, is a terrible drawback to his company. He is quite open to a deal in connection with the new loan.

Same day [later in the entry]. In view of the immensity of the sum the Chanc of the Exchequer has practically approved the placing of 10 millions firm with Morgan and twenty millions with Rothschild. I think we shall be able to get 94½ for our Consols.

18 April. After seeing Cassel & Dawkins as well as Natty Rothschild & Daniell, I came to terms for the government . . . I believe 94½ is on the whole good; and that as 30 millions have been placed the other 30 will be greedily subscribed for. In the City there is always a 'sheep-like' tendency to follow the lead.

19 April. Consols have fallen. So the terms accepted yesterday are turning out good. The City people won't 'get fat' upon the loan.

Half the £20m placed firm with Rothschilds in turn went to the Bank of England, while a further £2m went to Cassel, who as ever had his finger closely on the City pulse. 'I have done my best', he wrote to Hamilton on the 18th, 'to impress upon the Rothschilds that the banking element should be taken care of . . . If there should be a strong demand and the bankers are left out there will be a great deal of ill feeling which may easily be avoided.' The next morning Hamilton passed on this opinion to the new governor, Augustus Prevost, who replied almost at once:

Curiously enough just as your letter of today arrived Lord Rothschild had only left the Bank a few minutes.

We had a thorough discussion on the very matter about Bankers & Joint Stock Banks to which you refer and came to the conclusion that there would be no advantage in including them in the amount taken firm. One of the great difficulties is what Banks to include & where to draw the line: they will subscribe if they want the Loan just as willingly as they would join in the amount taken firm.

'A member of a declining firm which is doing no good, and he has never shewn any grasp', was how a member of the discount market had recently described the new governor; and even if Prevost did feel any love for the joint-stock banks, which he presumably did not, he was hardly the man who was going to dissuade Natty in this particular matter.[43]

By Monday the 22nd, with the public portion of the loan starting to go live following the publication of the prospectus, it was, the *FT* reported, 'freely rumoured on the market that a syndicate composed of certain prominent London, New York and continental financial houses (the names of Rothschilds, Morgans, Sir Ernest Cassel and Wernher Beit and Company were mentioned) had made themselves responsible for the moiety of the loan'. Such rumours were like a red rag to the stockbroker Granville Farquhar, who from his office at 3 Drapers' Gardens despatched to Hamilton a grand remonstrance suffused with the xenophobic strain of anti-Semitism shared by many, outside as well as inside the Stock Exchange:

> When the British government issues a National Loan we do not expect in the *English Circles* in the City that the German Jew element are alone to be considered. With such people as Alfred Beit, [Henri] Bischoffsheim [for whom Cassel had once worked], Cassel, Carl Meyer in, and 10 millions to America, no wonder that the premium is a vanishing one, and that the feeling amongst all Banking Circles is wonder and indignation at the way things are managed . . . Is it to be wondered at that they are furious at finding every dirty German Jew in, and themselves left out?[44]

On 5 May, with the loan successfully if controversially accomplished, the impugned Meyer was in cynical vein. 'I hear the West end is gambling like mad in Yankees,' he wrote to his wife, 'so the crash is sure to come.' While the next day, less flippantly: 'City cheerful and the Yankee market still booming, for some particular shares – no collapse yet but all the serious people here regard the situation as fraught with great danger.'[45] Among those particular shares was Northern Pacific Common, which opened at 114½ and closed almost twenty points higher. There had begun on Wall Street a titanic battle for control of the Northern Pacific Railroad, with J. P. Morgan & Co. on the one hand, and Kuhn, Loeb & Co. on the other, representing the rival railroad interests. The battle – severe but inconclusive – was essentially an American story but with dramatic implications for London, by far the principal external market for American securities. By the 8th the price of Northern Pacifics was fluctuating wildly on both sides of the Atlantic, far too wildly for an old campaigner like Meyer: 'I am NOT making any money as it is much too dangerous to operate in the Yankee market in either direction – so I sit quite still and await events.'[46]

The following day, Thursday the 9th, proved one to remember. 'Panic Stricken Yankees: The Market Demoralised by the Northern Pacific Deadlock: Sensational Break in the Street' ran the *FT*'s headline, while according to the *FN*'s market reporter, the shares of Northern Pacific Common 'oscillated in a manner that was devoid of intelligibility'.[47]

Because of the extraordinary situation on Wall Street – in effect, the creation of an artificial corner in Northern Pacific stock – the underlying position in London was that some of the main Yankee dealers found themselves heavily over-committed and in no position to deliver the actual stock. According to one estimate, they had unwittingly sold the rival bidders some 150,000 shares more than actually existed. Over the weekend they called on the Stock Exchange Committee to grant a moratorium, thereby enabling those who were short of stock to postpone indefinitely the time of delivery. First thing on Monday morning, at a special meeting, the Committee agreed to do so, the motion being carried without dissent, after personal representations from R. Raphael & Sons, Leon Bros and others. There is no doubt that the moratorium, which in the event lasted for five weeks, was a key reason why the drama did not turn into a crisis. However, it was not the only reason, as was clear from some pointed remarks in the June issue of the *Bankers' Magazine*:

> When settling-day arrived, although bankers as a rule grasped the situation, and were generous in the matter of advances, a few concerns, instead of assisting in the relief of the Stock Exchange, stubbornly refused aid except where long connection and powerful influence rendered such proceedings impossible. Money was drawn in from all quarters, and a huge sum obtained from the Bank of England. With such ample supplies available, it would have been easy for all the banks to have been generous in their treatment; instead, they strengthened themselves and allowed the Stock Exchange to find a way out of its own difficulties. That it did so is now history, and it was enabled to come through the ordeal by the spontaneous 'open-handedness' of the Morgans and the Rothschilds and of certain of the foreign and colonial banks.

On 23 May, one of the Raphael partners was full of gratitude as he 'detailed his efforts to get Messrs Morgan & Co. and Messrs Kuhn & Loeb to assist in the settlement of the account and read a letter from Lord Rothschild'. Yet for Raphaels itself, one of the City's leading arbitrage houses, it had been a chastening experience, as a confidential report a year later made transparently clear: 'It came as such a shock to the market that a firm of such standing and repute was doing a business that was capable of landing them in such an awkward position, that their eyes are now open to contingencies that they never dreamed of before the unfortunate incident occurred.' The effects lingered, even by late 1904, when Kleinworts next reported to its New York correspondent on the standing of Raphaels: 'The great reluctance to purchase this name has to a material extent passed away. At the same time it is generally considered that there is not the same amount of money there that there used to be. This is as you are aware due to their Northern Pacific entanglement.'[48] Still, Raphaels lived to fight on.

As did the British and the Boers, for almost exactly another year, until at last on 1 June 1902 the War Office released Kitchener's telegram announcing that he had signed peace terms with the Boer delegates, and in the evening a copy was posted at the Mansion House, causing much enthusiasm. Also that Sunday, King Edward VII wrote to Cassel, his financial adviser: 'You will have doubtless heard that Peace is signed, which is the greatest blessing that has been conferred on this country for a long time! "Consols" are sure to go up tomorrow. Could you not make a large investment for me?'[49]

*

At eight o'clock the roar of the City has gathered strength and fullness, approaching the din of noonday. At nine o'clock every man, woman, and child in the Metropolis seems to be going somewhere. Crowds bubble intermittently from the underground stations. 'Buses in endless procession converge upon the Bank. The pavements are black with people. The scene from the Mansion House steps beggars description. You look upon a very maelstrom of men. They are not only 'going' to business! They seem to be rushing there! . . .

For a full hour it continues. Then, as the clock points to ten, there are gaps in the ranks. The tide of life suddenly slackens. The reinforcements grow weaker. Traffic once more moves freely in opposite directions; for the invasion of the morning is consummated. Business has begun.[50]

This spirited rendition of 'Going to Business in London', by P. F. William Ryan, was one of many such genre sketches that comprised *Living London*, an enormous anthology compiled by George R. Sims and published in magazine form from 1903.

How did one get a berth in one of the 40,000 or so firms (quite apart from joint-stock banks, insurance companies and investment trusts) that comprised the Edwardian City?[51] The short answer was, seldom by formal qualification (least of all by university degree, even in the Bank of England), sometimes by linguistic prowess, and usually by personal connection. A five-minute interview for a fifty-year career was about the going rate. Take the case of Albert Martin, for whom a long City stint lay ahead. In 1899, as a fourteen-year-old, he was interviewed for the job of office boy at the stockbrokers Cazenove & Akroyds and given some sums to do. He performed so well that he was told by Swinny Akroyd that he was 'too good for us'. Martin, however, insisted that he wanted the job and was given it – his first task being to empty the chamber pots kept by the Akroyds in the partners' room.[52]

Hours were long, though not ferociously so. At Kleinworts, one of the hardest-working outfits in the City, the stipulation was ten o'clock until work was finished or six o'clock, whichever was the later. But there was also, everywhere in the City, compulsory Saturday working, when clerks rarely left before the middle of the afternoon. In many firms (mainly less well organised than Kleinworts) the working day began at half-past nine or even nine. As for clerical pay, it varied greatly according to age, experience and duties, as well as type of firm. We tend to know about the higher-class firms – such as the stockbrokers Heseltine Powell, whose twenty clerks and office boys had an average annual salary of some £225 by the turn of the century – but in many, many firms in the City pay was worse and prospects uncertain.[53] Pensions still tended to be paid on an informal basis, if at all, and the long-serving clerk who died in harness remained a reality as well as a tradition. In short, to be 'something in the City' was not necessarily that gilt-edged proposition that many on the outside assumed it to be.

Office atmosphere varied as much as remuneration. 'Ten years ago,' wrote the stockbroker-cum-financial journalist Walter Landells in 1912, 'it was no uncommon thing to enter an office in which four different jobbers occupied as many corners of the room and shared the services of a single clerk-and-office boy, who spent most of his time smoking cigarettes and arguing questions of high topical interest with another over the way or across the passage.'[54] At the other end of the scale was the Bank of England, employing an army of clerks for whom monotony was the price of security.

In the City at large, most firms and companies, certainly the more important ones, were run along stern, strongly hierarchical lines. At the Union Discount, a letter to its staff from the manager implied a degree of putative control that extended well beyond 39 Cornhill:

> Subordination being absolutely necessary for the good order of an establishment where so many persons are employed, you are required to pay strict obedience to your superiors in office, and you are expected to be civil and obliging in your deportment to the public and to your fellow clerks.
>
> Your salary should be prudently and judiciously expended. Remember that if you omit carefully to regulate your expenditure you will become involved in pecuniary embarrassments, disqualify yourselves for any office of trust, and render yourselves unfit to be employed in the Company's service . . .
>
> I desire also most seriously to impress upon you that you are held responsible for your conduct as well when absent from the Office as when employed upon your duties here. You are therefore warned against contracting habits of dissipation, and you are strictly enjoined to be careful in the selection of your companions and to maintain for yourself a respectable character in all the relations of life.[55]

Telephones, typewriters and adding machines tended to lead to the employment of women; but though they were usually paid less than men, many employers were determined to resist for as long as possible. It was not until the First World War that the floodgates really opened, and until then the City remained a male bastion inhabiting a male culture exuding male pride and male prejudice. Before 1914 there were no women at Mullens or the Hongkong Bank, and only two at Schröders, while at Kleinworts the first female typist had to work with a screen surrounding her desk, since one of the partners would consent to her being employed only if he never had to see her.[56]

CHAPTER FIFTEEN

Big Players, Bit Players

'I am celebrating this very day another anniversary of my appearing into this odd world. I suppose I ought to be more cheerful. I am happy enough in the City, but there is *not* enough to do there.' So Clinton Dawkins complained to Milner in South Africa on 2 November 1900, not long after he had started at 22 Old Broad Street. The following spring, with Dawkins waving before Milner the prospect of a partnership at Morgans if he wanted one, he elaborated on his feelings:

> Much of the work is interesting. In connection with it comes the whole question of transforming the banking arrangements of this country. To put it briefly: if the rapid rate at which we are surrendering our foreign investments so reduces our invisible exports and dividends that they do not cover the excess of imports can we continue the free market for gold?
>
> Per contra; much of the work is dull, and it is intermittent.
>
> But it is a jealous mistress. The City does not involve long hours or much fatigue. But it means incessant presence and attention. You never know when you may not be called upon. You would not like this after the continuous excitement and prestige of high office.
>
> Coming from India – and striking a dull moment – I hated it at first. I like it now.

By November 1902, returning to London from an American trip, Dawkins had entirely changed his tune:

> I came back to find considerable bustle in Old Broad Street, not all of it of an agreeable character. But the rough must be taken with the smooth. The bustle is steadily increasing there, and it is enough to absorb one's whole energies the deeper one becomes involved. However Sundays in the country are a great resource.

Or as he wrote the following March, again to Milner and in words that anticipated his early death, 'we are driving away in the City'.[1]

One of Dawkins' initial problems was adjusting to the distinctive culture of merchant banking, far less bureaucratic than the higher reaches of the Civil Service, far more based on personal relationships, trust and instinctive decision-making seldom formally rationalised or articulated. It was a culture still wedded to the family-based private partnership rather than the joint-stock form of organisation, its terms of reference were essentially private rather than public, and it placed a deliberate emphasis on eschewing anything that smacked of the flash, the modern or conspicuous consumption. Small staff sizes were a vital part of this culture – at the turn of the century, some thirty-five at Schröders, forty-eight at Hambros, seventy-one at Barings.[2]

Was it also a culture that engendered a deep-lying and damaging business conservatism? Certainly it is tempting to argue that case, not least on the basis of missed opportunities by merchant banks in this period: arbitrage and foreign exchange; industrial finance; South African gold mines; Chinese loans.[3] There was also a palpable sense in which the City's senior merchant banks, fortified by the shared experience of having survived the Baring crisis, now grouped themselves into an exclusive club, reluctant to admit outsiders and intensely respectful of each other's spheres of influence.[4] 'It is understood, of course, that the preserves of Brazil and Chile will be respected as belonging to our noble friends in New Court': Revelstoke's caveat to Alfred Mildmay in 1902, in the context of Barings forging a continental alliance for the purpose of new South American loans, was hardly redolent of tooth and claw. The system of underwriting, now virtually mandatory for state loans, further strengthened the club by offering mutual insurance.[5] It was, on the face of it, a cosy existence, arguably made possible by the fact that, offsetting the private partnership structure and relatively small capital at their command, many merchant bankers possessed tentacles which reached deep into where the City's real money was: the joint-stock banks, the insurance companies, the investment trusts. Directorships were the crux, including of course of the Bank of England, still off-limits to clearing bankers; and in this period a major joint-stock bank like the London and Westminster (the London County and Westminster from 1909) had at varying times on its board partners from Arbuthnot Latham, Brown Shipley, Frühling & Goschen, Hambros and Huths.[6] If a merchant bank enjoyed an unimpeachable reputation, and if it had the right connections, there was usually little difficulty in raising large sums of money very quickly.[7]

In practice, it was not quite so *gemütlich*. This was a period of enormous business opportunities, and no merchant bank could have stayed in contention unless it took at least some of them. Analysis of the balance sheets of Barings and Schröders shows how, between 1895 and 1910, these merchant banks became increasingly 'bank-like' in their conduct of business, relying not just on their own capital to back their acceptances but also on ever-increasing volumes of deposits and client balances.[8] 'We have a desire to get more into the general banking business,' a partner of Morgans in London wrote to the Paris firm of Morgans in 1907, 'and to accomplish that end we should be quite willing to consider a reduction in the charges we have hitherto made to our clients, provided that by

doing so we could secure a considerable increase in Banking accounts.'
Moreover, a host of newcomers had been entering the merchant banking
arena, the total number of firms rising from thirty-nine in 1890 to sixty-
six by 1897. A few of these new entrants were actively interested in issuing,
but for most the great attraction was accepting – profitable but, by the
1900s, increasingly competitive, with the competition coming from not
only rival merchant banks but also joint-stock banks and foreign banks
with a base in London.[9]

Reputations only partly depended on figures, which anyway were usually
kept top secret. Nevertheless, inasmuch as they can be prised out, they have
their own interest. In terms of capital towards the end of the Edwardian
period, Kleinworts and Schröders were clear leaders, with over £4m and
£3m respectively; while of other merchant banks, probably only Antony
Gibbs, Morgan Grenfell (as Morgans became in 1910), Barings, Hambros,
Rothschilds, Lazards and Brandts had a capital of at least £1m.[10] As for
profits, probably the most reliable runs are for Barings and Schröders, which
between 1893 and 1903 made an average annual net profit of £142,000 and
£98,000 respectively, between 1904 and 1913 of £342,000 and £318,000
respectively.[11] To get those figures into some perspective, the profit of £208,000
that Schröders made in 1905 was the equivalent of some £12m in today's
terms. In the case of both merchant banks, the sharp rise in the second half
of the period was a direct reflection of the growing volume of world trade,
its annual rate of growth rising from 3.1 per cent per annum in 1893–1904
to 4.1 per cent in 1905–13.[12] Acceptance figures told the story (even though
rates were being squeezed because of competition). At the end of 1903, the
league table for outstanding acceptances was Kleinworts (£8.6m), Schröders
(£6.7m), Morgans (£5.3m, a 1901 figure), Barings (£3.8m), Hambros (£1.9m)
and Rothschilds (£1.1m), with Brown Shipley's not available. Ten years later
the top two were unchanged, but there were changes below: Kleinworts
(£14.2m); Schröders (£11.7m); Barings (£6.6m); Brown Shipley (£5.1m);
Hambros (£4.6m); Brandts (£3.3m); Rothschilds (£3.2m); and Morgan
Grenfell (£2.8m).[13] What one cannot conclude, however, is that Kleinworts
and Schröders emerged in this period as the City's foremost merchant banks.
Quite apart from the whole question of the issuing side of the business,
there remained larger imponderables such as personal wealth, political influence, social standing and general City clout.[14] In the City as elsewhere, league
tables give only part of the picture.

Dawkins, trying to entice Milner in February 1901, had no doubt who
the big three were: Morgans, Rothschilds and Barings.[15] He and other
City men, who had rather longer experience than Dawkins, agreed that
Rothschilds was a declining force. 'Absolutely useless & not remarkable
for intelligence' was Cassel's crisp verdict later in 1901, while according
to Revelstoke two years later, 'they refuse to look into new things . . .

and their intelligence and capacity is not of a high order'. Even Hamilton, a loyal friend to the firm, admitted as much, noting in 1905 that though Rothschilds 'have a sort of prescriptive right to be consulted by the government', they were 'being rather left behind in the great race'.[16]

In most eyes the main responsibility for the firm's increasingly manifest timidity rested with Natty, though Cassel remarked to Hamilton in 1902 that it was Alfred 'to whom the brothers defer' and the problem was that 'he would hardly take anything up now that had not the British government guarantee behind it'. Natty himself worked hard, and had plenty of common sense if not brilliance; but, undeniably, his gruff manner did not inspire confidences, as evidenced by the experience of the broker Alfred Wagg, still feeling his way in the City and, towards the Rothschilds, as instinctively canine as his father Arthur:

> Lord Rothschild sat at a desk at the end of the room. As I approached – the last of some dozen brokers who had probably all bored him by telling him a list of prices which he already knew – he sat facing the door sideways to his desk, puffing a huge cigar. I had barely got the first word out of my mouth, when he whisked his chair round and began writing. Nothing left for me to do, but to retreat, feeling like a whipped hound.

Natty undoubtedly had his merits, as Balfour rather touchingly acknowledged after his death in 1915: 'I was really fond of him; and really admired that self-contained and somewhat joyless character. He had a high ideal of public duty and was utterly indifferent to worldly pomps and vanities. Moreover he was perfectly simple.' But, from a business point of view, he was seriously flawed – by his offputting manner, by his residual dislike of the underwriting system that in turn made him intensely reluctant to bring out new issues, and above all by an almost paralysing fear of taking any unnecessary risks. 'He does not like trusting his own judgment', Hamilton observed in 1904.[17] It was a sad comment to have to make on a grandson of Nathan Rothschild.

But, as Dawkins intimated, the real problems came with the next generation. Neither of Natty's sons (Walter, born 1868, and Charles, born 1877) took to finance with any relish, and Walter in particular was an almost perpetual worry to his father.[18] His great passion was zoology. The only aspect of the City that does seem to have attracted Walter, during weary hours at New Court, was private speculation on the stock market. In 1908 Lord Balcarres recorded in his diary a somewhat exaggerated version of the outcome:

> Walter Rothschild is on the verge of bankruptcy. Papa has already paid his debts once or twice: now, he has speculated, he has expended huge sums upon a rather indifferent book about extinct birds, and they say that a lady friend has absorbed many shekels.

Anyhow poor fat Walter has raised money on the post-obits of papa and mamma. The former is furious: most of all that for the first time in history a Rothschild has speculated unsuccessfully. It is a great blow to the acumen of the family.[19]

His debts approaching a million pounds, Walter now left New Court: a relief to himself but no reassurance for the long-term future of N. M. Rothschild & Sons.

The firm's traditional great rival was more fortunate.[20] Ned Baring's son, born five years before Walter, was the subject of a telling entry in Hamilton's diary in 1901:

> Cromer came to see me this morning . . . He came to speak about John Revelstoke, who had had without much choice to take the chairmanship of the Royal Com^n sitting on the London Port, and to whom the work had caused very considerable loss owing to its involving so much absence from the City. Revelstoke, Cromer said, was anxious to get right to the front in the City – and so he will – and nothing would help him more than a Privy Councillorship, if his Royal Com^n work could be held to justify it. We must see what can be done when the Report is out.

Revelstoke, already a director of the Bank of England, did get his privy councillorship, and he did rise to the front in the City. He was honest, industrious and did much to restore the position of Barings; but with his self-importance, his distaste for most of mankind and his vestigial sense of humour, he was not someone to whom people readily warmed. 'He has the mind of a haberdasher who reads the social column in the *Daily Mail* every morning before retailing second-hand trowsers and "Modern Society" and Browning on Sunday afternoons', was the harsh verdict of one contemporary.[21] A far more attractive character was Gaspard Farrer, who came to Barings from H. S. Lefevre & Co. in 1901 while still retaining a partnership in the latter merchant bank.[22] Between them, Revelstoke and Farrer went a long way to giving a more competitive edge to Barings during the 1900s. 'The old practice here was to sit and wait for applicants', Farrer wrote in 1905 to Hugo Baring in New York in relation to the accepting business, adding that 'of recent years we have reached out to encourage old friends and get new ones, and the results so far seem highly satisfactory'. But in the end, Farrer's creed was a conservative one, as he had spelled out to an impatient Baring some months earlier:

> Our *credit* is the only asset which the firm of Baring Brothers & Co. possesses, that and character which is part and parcel of credit . . . we must be content to work slowly and build up the business to its former pre-eminence, and if I am content to do that, I am sure anyone of your name should be willing to follow the example . . . the least lapse into speculative finance, even if successful, would immediately raise a storm of criticism.[23]

Farrer could hardly have written a more cardinal text for the Barings ethos in the twentieth century (until the fateful February 1995).

The third of Dawkins' big three was of course J. S. Morgan & Co. itself.[24] The firm came out of the Boer War with much-enhanced prestige, following its intimate involvement in the transatlantic dimension of British government loans. Over the next decade it concentrated increasingly on issuing rather than accepting business, partly on the grounds that competition for acceptance business was reducing commission rates to the point where it was no longer a sensible deployment of capital. But it was also a reflection of the firm's unrivalled American connection, at the highest level of *haute finance*, as well as the personal preferences of the London partners.

In the early 1900s, however, the problem was the London partnership. Jack Morgan was always destined to succeed his father in New York; Walter Burns junior was fairly described by Dawkins in 1900 as, 'though quite capable', nevertheless 'young, fat & lazy'; and Dawkins himself was not quite the dream ticket he imagined himself to be. Essentially, he saw his time with Morgans as a necessary and rather irksome money-making prelude to his entry, later in his forties, to the world of politics; and even while with Morgans, he spent a large chunk of his time away from the office chairing the Committee on War Office Reorganisation, winning a knighthood, but not a reputation as a City heavyweight. In the event Dawkins' failings did not do Morgans permanent damage, but served to illustrate the risk of high-level recruitment of someone not trained in the sordid world of commercial finance.

Montagu Norman's City credentials by contrast could not have been more impeccable.[25] His grandfathers were George Warde Norman, a long-serving director of the Bank of England, and Sir Mark Collet, a governor in the 1880s; his father was Frederick Henry Norman, a partner (and then director) in Martins Bank. Norman himself (born 1871) was educated at Eton and Cambridge before going to Martins in 1892, moving after two years to Collet's firm, Brown Shipley. During the second half of the 1890s he spent much of his time in the States, acquiring an intimacy with American business methods. On his return to London he became a partner in Brown Shipley at the start of 1900. There soon followed active service in the Boer War, and in turn illness, and it was not until 1903 that Norman began properly to establish himself at Founders' Court. Brown Shipley was a merchant bank that had become entrenched in increasingly conservative ways during the late nineteenth century, its main business being the granting of acceptance credits to American customers of Brown Brothers in New York.[26] Norman swiftly emerged as the leading figure among the new generation of partners, broadening the acceptance business to include Europe and the Empire as well as the United States, but doing his best to discourage his fellow partners from overmuch foreign exchange business, on the grounds that it encouraged speculation. In general, if not the man to raise Brown Shipley to the top of the merchant-banking league, he gave the firm a degree of renewed vitality. 'A sort of merchant' he described himself to the wife of Charles Ashbee, and in truth the main interests of his life lay outside the City. In 1904 he acquired Thorpe Lodge on Campden Hill and transformed it into a house owing much to the ideals of William Morris. He read widely in philosophy, theology and psychology, endeavouring (in the words of his first biographer) 'to work out a coherent view of life which would allay the restlessness of his mind and meet a need which his work did not satisfy'.[27] In 1906 he grew a beard, in 1907 he became a director of the Bank of England, but for several more years the search for a spiritual equilibrium continued to preoccupy him.

*

Clearing (or commercial) banking itself was becoming ever less private, ever more joint-stock. Lombard Street's last wholly private bank, Brooks & Co., was absorbed by Lloyds in 1900; that same year the death of the recalcitrant Samuel George Smith II paved the way to what was in effect a takeover of Smith, Payne & Smiths (and the other Smiths banks) by the Union Bank of London in 1902; in 1903 the Union of London and Smiths Bank absorbed Prescotts Bank, where once George Grote had been senior partner. Robarts, Lubbock & Co. survived for the moment (eventually absorbed into Coutts & Co. in 1914) but was not a dynamic force, any more than were two banks, Glyn Mills and Martins, that had gone some way but not all the way towards shedding the private form of organisation: in both these last cases there were succession problems and a lack of full-time, focused leadership. Glyn Mills, moreover, squandered the opportunity of developing a defensive block of private banks. 'In my opinion,' Martin Ridley Smith of that famous banking dynasty acknowledged to the Institute of Bankers in 1903, 'private banking has not proved equal to the largely increased wants of the community, and it has naturally enough, therefore, been superseded by larger and more powerful institutions.' These institutions included the Union of London, for whom Schuster, also present, insisted that 'every endeavour in our case is being made to preserve all the old traditions in every way', adding tactfully of the partners of the old private firms he was so busy absorbing that, 'I hope that they will be useful, and that they will always justify their existences, not alone in business, but in their social position also.'[28]

All the leading joint-stock bankers kept a watchful eye on the various league tables. In terms of branches, Lloyds was ahead in 1897 with 248;

by 1913, after a period of phenomenal countrywide expansion, the London City and Midland led with 725. In the case of both banks, there was a shift from Birmingham to London as the centre of operations. In terms of deposits, the top six at the end of 1903 were: Lloyds (£54.5m); National Provincial (£50.4m); London City and Midland (£45.4m); London and County (£44.1m); Barclays (£34.6m); and Union Bank of London (£33.9m). Ten years later the leading trio were London City and Midland (£93.8m), Lloyds (£91.5m) and London County and Westminster (£85.4m); there was then a large gap until National Provincial (£67.9m) and Barclays (£60.8m); and a further sizeable gap to Union Bank of London (£41.3m) and Parr's (£41.2m). By this time the Midland and Lloyds both had deposits greater than either the Deutsche Bank (£79m) or Credit Lyonnais (£89m), the leading commercial banks of Germany and France.[29] As for specific City clout, at least of one type, an interesting measurement is the number of accounts held by members of the Stock Exchange: easily top in July 1901 was Parr's (858), followed by London Joint Stock (731), London City and Midland (643) and London and Westminster (617). Tying on fifth with 342 members was the curious pair of the Bank of England and the London and County Bank, popularly known as 'the farmers' bank' until its merger with the London and Westminster later in the decade.[30]

By the turn of the century the English banking system was starting to be criticised for its lack of ambition and its determination to confine itself largely to deposit banking, and was being compared unfavourably with the less specialised systems that prevailed on the Continent.[31] Taking comfort from the recent turmoil in the German money market, William Cole of the Maidstone branch of the London and County Bank drew an obvious lesson in an article published in the *Journal of the Institute of Bankers* in October 1899:

> The German banks try to foster and assist the industries of their land, and end by becoming shareholders and speculators in industrial companies. British banks, on the other hand, look only to their own stability; and by doing this they are, in the end, doing more for the cause of industry than their German rivals.

It was a historic fault line, one that would persist as generations of mainly home-grown bankers resisted the temptation to become so-called 'universal' bankers – a concept of banking that, in the challenging terrain of industrial finance, would have meant taking long-term stakes in industrial companies and issuing their securities.

Whatever his views on industrial banking, Felix Schuster was becoming by the 1900s one of the giants of the City.[32] 'He occupies a high position in the banking community, being a very intelligent and shrewd man', wrote Hamilton in 1902.[33] Significantly, his background was more 'City' than that of most of the leading joint-stock bankers. The family firm of Schuster, Son & Co., cotton merchants and foreign bankers, had traded in London since the early nineteenth century; and Schuster himself (born 1854) had, after being brought up in Frankfurt and doing his early training there, been based in London since 1873. After fifteen years working at Schusters in Cannon Street, for most of them as a partner, his life was transformed when the Union Bank of London bought out his firm and he became a director of the bank. In 1895 he was elected governor, and for almost thirty years he ran the bank – both day-to-day *and* high strategy – with an iron hand, the very model of the professional joint-stock banker. In July 1902, following the somewhat stressful negotiations that led to the Union Bank's takeover of Smith, Payne & Smiths, he wrote to one of the partners of that bank a personal letter that conveyed something of his banking credo. After declaring that his aim now was 'to further the interests of the combined institution . . . not merely from a money making point of view, but mainly with the desire of making the Institution as you say the strongest & most respected Bank in London & in the Country', he went on: 'the dividend I always tell my people will take care of itself as long as we keep free from doubtful or speculative business'.

None the less, Schuster believed passionately in the intrinsic merits of joint-stock banking; and in an address he gave in 1904 to the Students' Union of the London School of Economics, on 'International Commerce and Exchange', his peroration included a personally revealing passage on the rise and rise of the phenomenon:

> It is too often thought that these large undertakings are mere huge machines. No greater mistake could be made – behind all the machinery must be human life and energy, must be the living active brain, and the greater the advance of science, the greater will be the need for well-trained, well-educated minds, not only in what are called the learned professions, but also for those engaged in commercial pursuits. There will be openings and careers for those who are willing to study, willing to learn and go on learning as they grow older, willing, above all, to work.

A meritocratic profession for an increasingly meritocratic world was, in short, how Schuster saw joint-stock banking. It was typical that he should have taken the time to speak at the LSE, for during this period he emerged as the unrivalled intellectual among joint-stock bankers – 'a financier and economist of conspicuous ability', as the *Bankers' Magazine* put it, for once without exaggeration.[34] At a time when most joint-stock bankers preferred to keep their heads below the parapet, leaving the expression of 'opinions' to their betters, Schuster was an outstanding exception.

CHAPTER SIXTEEN

An Old Bank Song

'Chamberlain has been presented this afternoon with the freedom of the City, & got a great reception. He is the idol of the City.' Thus Hamilton's diary entry of 13 February 1902. Thirteen months later, with the war won, the Secretary of State for the Colonies returned from South Africa to receive another congratulatory address at the Guildhall. All of the Cabinet was present, and Chamberlain was 'received with prolonged cheering'.[1] More than any other top politician before or since, Joe was the City's man.

On 15 May 1903 – against the long-run background of perceived British economic decline since the late nineteenth century, a decline made painfully obvious by the military humiliations of the Boer War – Chamberlain made his historic speech in Birmingham in which he proposed the abandonment of free trade and its replacement by a system of tariffs loaded in favour of colonial imports.[2] Early reactions from the financial press were mixed: *The Economist* passionately against any form of protectionism, the *FN* under Harry Marks even more vehemently for, and the *FT* sitting on the fence. On 3 July Eddy Hamilton dined with Natty Rothschild: 'He is evidently rather taken by Chamberlain's plan. So I fancy is the majority of City folk. But City folk have done badly of late.' Two days later Hamilton was staying with Cassel at Moulton Paddocks: 'He is decidedly protectionist but fair-minded. His main arguments are (1) that he does not like the country should be so dependent on other countries, and (2) too much thought here is given to the consumer.' What Cassel did not tell Hamilton, nor anyone else for that matter, was that he had recently sent Chamberlain a cheque for £5,000 to help him launch his campaign. 'I have felt for some considerable time', Cassel's accompanying letter ran, 'that the present commercial situation differs widely from what it was in Cobden's time and may call for different treatment on our part. I greatly admire your action in bringing this matter up for discussion.' On 29 July there took place the first set-piece City response in the form of Schuster's address to the annual general meeting of the Union of London and Smiths Bank at the Cannon Street Hotel:

No issue of such gravity and of such importance in its consequences had been placed before the nation for several generations . . . The prosperity of banking must depend on the prosperity of the nation at large, but as bankers, perhaps, they might approach the subject from a different, possibly a wider, point of view, for they were not engaged in any particular trade – all trades, all interests, coming under their survey.

There followed the key passage in Schuster's speech, the classic defence from a City point of view of unfettered economic liberalism:

London was admittedly the banking and financial centre; go where they would, a bill of exchange on London was the one medium of exchange which always had a ready market. Continental and American bankers held their reserves in bills on London. Many of the larger foreign banking institutions had found it necessary to establish their own agencies in London in order to deal with the business which inevitably flowed there. Why was this? . . . The principal reason was that a bill on London was created in every part of the globe. There was always a seller because goods were shipped here, there was always a buyer because goods were obtained from here, because our ports were free, because our doors were open to the trade of the whole world. It was through being the centre of the world's commerce that we had become the world's clearing house.

Schuster knew his own mind and was not afraid to express it, which could hardly be said for the collective wisdom of the London Chamber of Commerce, already starting to be embarrassingly divided on the issue. 'The feeling amongst commercial men is certainly in favour of a searching inquiry being made into the whole question of our trade relations,' declared the August issue of its *Journal*, using that bland formula over the coming winter to disguise its inability to make a firm pronouncement either way.[3]

Chamberlain's resignation from the Cabinet on 17 September, in order to pursue his campaign unhindered by the constraints of office, did not unduly perturb the City. The *FT* – probably the surest guide to mainstream, middlebrow City opinion – continued to back the prime minister as he sought to hold together a badly divided party, though without writing off the hero of the City:

Let us divest our minds of cant, political and otherwise. It may be that Mr Chamberlain's policy is a little in advance of public opinion and Imperial necessity, but it might also be as well to learn precisely what the policy is before we finally make up our minds on the subject. On the other hand, the economic position taken up by Mr Balfour is clear enough. He simply desires that we should regain that power of negotiating for concessions from foreign countries which we have voluntarily abandoned. We have reason to believe, moreover, that the balance of commercial opinion in this country is beginning to turn decidedly in this direction.

Chamberlain began his countrywide campaign with a major speech in Glasgow on 6 October. The *FT* on the 9th complained that the pace he was setting was, 'to use a sporting phrase, "a little too hot" for those who wish to thoroughly examine the various sides of this most complex problem before they definitely range themselves for or against so momentous a change'.[4]

It was as if the City, with its overwhelmingly Conservative loyalties, was waiting for the power battle to be resolved in that party before showing its hand. Albeit passively, then, the City retained its predominantly free-trading allegiance – an allegiance that arguably owed as much as anything to its innate preference for the status quo. It was a deep-rooted conservatism cogently summed up by the *Bankers' Magazine* in January 1904: 'If there is one thing true in a commercial as in a monetary system, it is that sudden and frequent changes are detrimental to the activity and stability of commerce.'

Inasmuch as tariff reformers in the City looked beyond their own immediate situation, it was almost certainly the imperial dimension to Chamberlain's programme that appealed to them, rather than the opportunity to modernise British manufacturing industry. Chamberlain himself, who had been brought up in the City and never lost a certain emotional allegiance to it, seldom appeared to threaten the free flow of capital, as opposed to goods. Nevertheless, as the various exchanges during 1903–4 showed, there was an implicit and fundamental conflict involved: did the prosperity of finance depend upon industry's wellbeing, or was it the other way round? Schuster himself would remain sensitive to the charge of selfishness on the part of bankers, emphasising to the Institute in November 1904 that 'the banker can only be prosperous if the country, if trade generally, is prosperous'. All the same, the underlying logic of his position was that London's continuing dominance as the world's clearing house was necessarily part of the larger national good. It was a position that the experienced financial journalist W. R. Lawson, writing in the *Bankers' Magazine* in March 1904, explicitly challenged: 'Activity in bill business and in foreign exchange may not always coincide with public prosperity . . . Bill discounters may be making money when the creators of the bills are losing it. In no case can banking operations by themselves be accepted as conclusive signs of general well-being.'[5]

Coming from inside the citadel, its whole rationale scarcely challenged for over half a century, this was a startling admission. The battle lines were emerging, in rhetoric at least, between the national interest on the one hand, cosmopolitan finance on the other.[6] For the young Winston Churchill, that dogmatic free-trader, the choice was simple. Beatrice Webb, who had sat next to him at dinner the previous summer, recorded his views then: 'Looks to *haute finance* to keep the peace – for that reason objects to a self-contained Empire as he thinks it would destroy this cosmopolitan capitalism – the cosmopolitan financier being the professional peacemaker of the modern world, and to his mind the acme of civilization.' But the Birmingham economist W. J. Ashley, whose incisive book on *The Tariff Problem* was published in the autumn of 1903, saw things differently. His fourth chapter dealt with 'The Outlook under the Present Policy', concluding with a less than enchanted vision of a post-industrial future:

> More and more of our capital will probably be invested in the establishment of manufactures abroad. And while London and a few other great towns will become even larger agglomerations of labouring population, the rest of England will remain an agreeable place of residence for rentiers, big and little, and will flourish on the 'tourist industry'. And – though with some new features – the history of Holland will have been repeated.[7]

*

In November 1903 that hardy perennial the gold reserves question, in temporary abeyance since 1900, had returned to the agenda – though, in comparison with the tariff reform controversy, at a distinctly rarefied level. J. Herbert Tritton of Barclays, in his presidential inaugural to the Institute, called on his fellow bankers no longer to look to either government or the Bank of England, but instead to take the matter into their own hands. His plan was that they should increase their capital by one-fifth through an issue of 3 per cent preference stock, thereby raising £15m in cash. This they should devote to the accumulation of gold into a special fund to be known as the 'bankers' reserve of gold', to be physically deposited at the Bank of England but not merged in the figures of that institution. 'The boldness of the suggestion is apparent to all', the *Bankers' Magazine* noted, before going on to doubt its feasibility:

> The whole cost of the reform would fall upon the banking community, and, taking all things into account, the cost would not be light. If Mr Tritton's own bank is taken as an example, it would mean that the net profits would be drawn upon to the extent of about £16,600 per annum in order to pay the dividend upon the preference capital, the raising of which would fall to its share . . . We are afraid that there would be great difficulty in persuading the general body of bank shareholders to recognise the virtue of the step.

The *BM* was also doubtful whether the Bank of England would agree to manage the new fund, presumably involving some cost to itself; wondered how easy it would be to accumulate £15m in gold; and predicted that the Bank's existing reserves would inevitably suffer. The debate broadened in January 1904 when, at the half-yearly general meeting of the Union of London, Schuster told his shareholders 'that it was not on the shoulders of bankers alone that the responsibility should fall, although they should do their utmost to co-operate with the Bank of England in the attainment of the object in view and to impress on the Chancellor of the Exchequer that he also was conducting a banking business much larger than any of them'.[8] Almost certainly this was what his anxious shareholders wanted to hear.

Three weeks later, on 17 February, the Institute heard a paper from Alfred Clayton Cole called 'Notes on the London Money Market'. Cole was a merchant (the family firm was W. H. Cole & Co. of 85 Gracechurch Street), a director and future governor of the Bank of England, and would be remembered in his obituary as 'a man of great ability, of strong convictions, with fearless courage in expressing them'. Even though W. R. Lawson would later claim that he had watered down his remarks under pressure from the Institute's 'editorial committee', there was nothing timorous about Cole's tone to the assembled bankers:

> As regards the proposal to increase the capital of the banks, my reply is that the floating of a loan in this market of £15,000,000, or of £100,000,000, will not add one single golden sovereign to the bankers' cash reserves. We can only increase our stock of gold in this country by getting it from abroad. To do that we must offer to holders of gold abroad something that they will take in exchange for their gold. A loan in this market to increase the capital of the banks, to be subscribed for by the public who have deposits with them, is merely transferring a liability now existing on the part of the bankers to the public from their depositors to their shareholders. The only way the bankers can increase their cash in hand, or balances at the Bank of England, is by following the method now pursued, namely, calling in their short loans so that the market has to borrow at the Bank of England. To put their position permanently on a sounder basis they must agree that, instead of calling in their loans temporarily, they must all keep permanently larger balances at the Bank of England. Then the gold reserves of the country will be increased.

It was an old Bank song, most eloquently sung in the old days by Lidderdale, but the question remained as to who would most immediately benefit from these 'permanently larger balances'. No wonder that the *Bankers' Magazine* commented wearily in its report of the meeting that 'it seems hopeless to expect a satisfactory solution of the reserves question'.[9]

The question was not one that would go away, especially as the gold reserve averaged only £33m between 1903 and 1906 – hardly reassuring, granted that the wellbeing not only of the British banking system but also of the international gold standard in effect rested on the Bank's stewardship.[10] Resources and responsibilities were clearly out of kilter, far more worryingly so than they had been at the time of Goschen's ill-fated currency proposals. In practice the Bank could accumulate gold only if it was able to make Bank rate effective in the money market; this in turn meant that it depended, in order to stiffen the market at such times, on borrowing funds from the big joint-stock banks that would otherwise have been lent there; the uncomfortable long-term implication of this dependence was power-sharing between the Bank and the banks.[11] At the Bank, proud of its traditions but embarrassingly naked at the putative conference table, the inevitable suspicion grew that the large banks were using the whole gold reserves question as a convenient handle to advance their own power and influence. Thus Schuster's plea in November 1904 for more dialogue ('I think a great deal more could be done if we were in closer touch with one another. We all mean the same thing, but we have not the opportunities of really understanding one another') must have seemed to the Bank the thin end of the wedge. Yet for the big joint-stock bankers, thoroughly conscious of themselves as the arrivistes of the City, resentment was equally sharp. The oft-repeated complaint that the Bank was using bankers' balances to compete commercially against them was arguably as much symbol as substance.[12] Two cultures were in conflict, and during the decade before the First World War the conflict intensified, especially once Edward Holden decided to enter the fray.

*

Having endured five largely downbeat years, most of Capel Court's inhabitants stuck to the foothills during 1904. In January, 'Midas', the *FN*'s well-informed House columnist, put matters plainly:

> The truth is that there are too many men trying to make a living out of the Stock Exchange. In normal times, taking the good with the bad, there is not enough in the business to go round . . . It is clear that, in some way, the membership must be restricted. One may admire the tenacity and pluck of small men without capital, who plod on with big hopes and small bank accounts; but it certainly does not tend to the dignity of the Stock Exchange as an institution that it should number among its members a large body who are perpetually on the raw edge of circumstance.

By early March, following extensively signed petitions to the Committee, it was clear that at least half the members were in favour of membership restrictions. Much was made of the shortage of the space in the House, but *The Economist* was wholly on the money when it argued that 'the kernel of the demand for limitation . . . is the advantage of a pecuniary nature that would accrue to members'. The campaign for a ceiling on numbers was led by the stockbroker Ferdinand Faithfull Begg. Scottish, a former Conservative Unionist MP and an active supporter of Chamberlain's tariff campaign, he was renowned for his loquacity and was one of life's inveterate letter-writers to the press. According to one rather hostile profile, 'he regards himself as a public man, and affects the exclusive, though nobody is anxious to hear his opinions a second time'.

Begg now assured his critics that there was 'no proposal to limit the membership for all time', and later in March his party triumphed at the annual Committee election. *The Economist*, hostile to restriction, claimed 'a mass of authoritative opinion inside the Stock Exchange remains strongly opposed to limitation of membership'; but popular opinion among the small brokers and, above all, the small jobbers was running the other way.[13]

The newly elected Committee, moving slowly, had its detailed proposals ready by the autumn. In essence, a new member would have to find the money not only to pay for three shares in the Stock Exchange itself but also to acquire the nomination of a retiring or deceased member. 'Nearly everyone in the House maintains, and with surprise at the bare sugges-tion,' *The Economist* noted, 'that the public have no interest in the matter, and that it is a purely domestic affair, affecting the Stock Exchange alone.' The new rules were confirmed by the Committee on 14 November, and during a hectic fortnight before they were implemented some 664 clerks of almost certainly very mixed resources took advantage of the breathing space to become members under the old, less expensive dispensation. One member of the Committee, the leading Westralian (i.e. West Australian mines) jobber Edward Ridsdale, resigned in order to test the wider waters, but in the subsequent by-election was defeated (1,107 to 925) by a pro-restriction candidate. It was a result that had the effect of, in the words of the *FN*, 'proclaiming with no uncertain voice the deter-mination of members of the "House" not to have their reform scheme interfered with'.[14]

It took some time for the legislation to work through, and member-ship hit an all-time high of 5,567 in 1905 before declining to 5,078 by 1908 and 4,855 on the eve of the war. The actual expense of the new mandatory qualifications fluctuated according to the fortunes of the Stock Exchange as a whole: the price of a single Stock Exchange share during the ten years from 1904 tended to be between £150 and £250, while the going rate for a nomination varied from as high as £170 in March 1910 (and at other times perhaps higher) to as low as £15 in June 1907 and even reputedly, on the outbreak of the war, a packet of Players. In 1910 a member computed that the total cost of entrance amounted to about £1,315.[15] The contrast with the comparable 1870 figure of £60 was certainly quite stark – though at no point, in comparison with, say, Lloyd's or the New York Stock Exchange, could the required sum be termed gargantuan. Nevertheless, an ostensibly open market had given way to the closed shop.

The year 1905 also saw a wrangle over the 'constitutional' implications of the new membership qualifications. The managers had sanctioned with the utmost reluctance the rule that new members were henceforth to be shareholders in the Stock Exchange; they now sought to safeguard the power of the biggest shareholders, proposing that the voting system be changed to one vote for each share up to fifty shares. Their argument was the essentially self-interested one that if the present system remained in force, in other words one vote per shareholder, a future plethora of shareholders might well decide to make substantial reductions in the annual subscriptions, since they stood to lose relatively little by a cut in income and therefore dividends. Under Begg's leadership, championing the small man, considerable opposition built up against this proposal, and eventually the managers with fairly poor grace gave way.[16] The writing was on the wall – in the long if not the short term – for the system of dual control that had governed the affairs of the Stock Exchange for over a century.

In 1904 only a quarter of members were also shareholders in the Stock Exchange, a proportion that rose to about half by the eve of the war. It was an aggravating situation, granted that the managers were supposed to provide a service to the membership as a whole, and yet were answerable only to their shareholders. Few believed it was a satisfactory service. 'Had not the question of paying huge dividends to the proprietors of the Stock Exchange shares been a pressing consideration, the London Stock Exchange would before now have been in possession of a building equipped with every imaginable facility for the expeditious transaction of business, and worthy to house the largest, wealthiest, and most important Stock Exchange in the world.' That was the view of *The Economist* in November 1904, and it returned to the attack the following May, accusing the managers of having 'in some measure departed from the original objects of its founders'.[17]

In 1904 ten firms doing large-scale arbitrage business in the American market had vainly asked the managers for pneumatic tubes to be provided from the offices of the Anglo-American Telegraph and Commercial Cable Companies into the Stock Exchange; in 1907 the managers gave their usual niggardly response when the Exchange Telegraph Company sought improved facilities in order to speed up the process of transferring price changes to the tape, which, the company stated, compared unfavourably with the swiftness of the 'ticker' service on the New York Stock Exchange; over the next two years the managers agreed with only the greatest reluctance to erect more telephone boxes; and in 1911 a member made a futile complaint to the powerless Committee about the poor telegraphic facilities between the Stock Exchange and the continental bourses, stating that he had been 'informed by the late Secretary of the Post Office that if the Managers could give them more room they could greatly increase the number of operators'. Against the background of an increasingly integrated global market for securities, nine stubborn old men continued to be more preoccupied by the conspicuous consumption of blotting pads and other stationery – 'the waste in slips, particularly squares which are used for cuff paper, is enormous', one report gravely noted – than London's place as an international financial centre.[18]

CHAPTER SEVENTEEN

Across the Herring Pond

By the summer of 1905 it was clear not only that the Russo-Japanese War would end shortly but that Russia, in the midst of severe internal convulsions since the start of the year, would need funds sooner rather than later. Revelstoke sounded out his good friend Lord Lansdowne, the Foreign Secretary, first in June and then, with peace signed, on 11 September: 'I should be infinitely obliged if you could see your way to send me one word by telegraph. "Revelstoke – London" will always find me.' Lansdowne's telegram was satisfactory – 'I have not in any way modified my view' – as the British government, starting to look to a diplomatic alliance with Russia, lined up behind the international loan. It was never going to be the most popular of causes, with 'Bloody Sunday' in St Petersburg still a vivid memory.

Revelstoke travelled to Paris, where there took place on 10–11 October major international conferences on the prospective loan – a reminder that, when it came to Russian finance, London's relationship with Paris remained strictly subordinate. For one of nature's autocrats it was not an ideal scenario. Farrer on the 14th reported to Hugo Baring in New York:

> The whole of the Paris backers assembled and representatives from Hopes [of Amsterdam] and Mendelssohn [of Berlin]. I gather that the state of jealousy and hatred between the various French credit institutions is indescribable, and you probably know better than I what these French men are when they get together on any subject – talk, talk, talk and nothing accomplished. John got sick of it at the end of two days and returned Wednesday night, and has this morning left for Petersburg with Everard.

Everard was one of Revelstoke's younger brothers, and the two men had entrained on the Nord-Express, going via Ostend. They arrived in St Petersburg on Monday the 16th and put up at the British Embassy.[1] Revelstoke kept Farrer posted on the 22nd:

> I write these few lines after days of the hardest and most complicated work I've ever experienced . . . I can assure you that the work, bother, and responsibility is out of all proportion to the profit we may make in this affair, and that I only continue here from a sense that the presence of England in the matter is felt to be so vitally important by all concerned

that the whole affair would at once break up should we refuse to lend our co-operation. You see the French and Germans are as ever at each other's throats.

By Wednesday the 25th, with no trains leaving for the frontier and talk of a general strike, Revelstoke's discontent had switched to the locals:

It is evident that if things get worse we shall have something uncommonly like a revolution, in which case it will obviously not be the moment to embark on a public issue . . . M. Witte is named Prime Minister, as he probably will be, and if he grants at once a constitution, things may improve. But at the moment there is no real government, and I fancy these people are often apt to do things 48 hours too late.

There ensued a flurry of urgent wires:

26 October, Barings to Revelstoke, despatched 10.35 a.m. It cannot be right for us to appeal to public for money while strikes prevail throughout the country verging on revolution – no dispassionate onlooker could approve our action and nothing could justify us if accident occurred . . .

28 October, Revelstoke to Barings, despatched 5.48 p.m. Entire Syndicate expressed Russian Minister of Finance this morning loyal unanimous desire rally round him recognising supreme importance maintaining complete cohesion with view unhesitating action when moment favourable. Russian Minister of Finance expressed full appreciation our good will and strong sense undesirable annul international arrangement to which government attaches special value. He suggested we now draft project contract in which we can agree with him all detail omitting only price and date issue with view signature contract later when possible. Shall do this and leave soon as circumstances permit.

30 October, Barings to Revelstoke, despatched 11.55 a.m. We recognise value of complete cohesion and congratulate you on your success in maintaining it, but think that project contract should not bind us positively to issue in London even if Paris wish to issue unless we feel sure of success with our general public.

30 October, Hugo Baring to Barings. What is the news Lord Revelstoke?

30 October, Barings to Baring Magoun & Co. Lord Revelstoke still Russia – We have no anxiety – All quiet this morning.

31 October, Revelstoke to Barings. Sailing today German steamer 'Trave' for Lübeck.

The senior partner of Barings had made his getaway, paying the captain £100 for the exclusive use of his cabin. 'John and Everard got home Sunday evening', Farrer reported to Hugo Baring on 7 November, adding that 'John in good spirits and health, but poor Everard seems to have had a baddish time on the Baltic, four days without a meal.'[2]

The postponement of the Russian loan to 1906 opened the way to another international loan on behalf of Japan, some eighteen months after its tumultuous, massively popular 'chrysanthemums' loan of May 1904.[3] With French investors at last able to enjoy a slice of the Japanese action denied them during the war, it was not surprising that Paris offered the most attractive terms and took the lion's share – £12m of the £25m loan, leaving £6.5m for London and £3.25m each for Berlin and New York. Business on the Stock Exchange was slack towards the end of November, but when the prospectus of the new loan was published on the afternoon of the 27th 'there was the usual large crowds of applicants for the precious documents outside the premises of the various banks of issue', the *FT* adding that 'no doubt is entertained about the success of the loan'. Any doubts would have been foolish, for London's tranche was oversubscribed by almost thirty times. The novelty of this loan was not just the leading role for Paris but the fact that the usual London issuing group of Parr's, Yokohama Specie and Hongkong and Shanghai was now supplemented by Rothschilds, in turn a reflection of the part played in Paris by Rothschild Frères.[4]

To those same cousins in Paris, Natty wrote at the start of 1906 that 'on the whole, I think it is the heaviest 1st of January I ever recollect.'[5] In the Square Mile at large, the tone early in 1906 was generally muted. Farrer, hoping to persuade Gwinner of the Deutsche Bank in Berlin to visit him in London, took the usual *haute finance* line: 'If you can come, you will find Englishmen who can still sleep soundly in their beds without fear of waking to the boom of German guns and the news of German warships in the Thames. Can anything be more ridiculous than the fuss our newspapers have been making?' It was the Kaffir Circus that as usual attracted the most attention. 'Just inside the main entrance to the Stock Exchange, and where the Kaffir Circus drags out its dismal days,' noted *The Economist* towards the end of January, 'there is stretched a substantial expanse of canvas, designed to exclude the draught. The canvas is thickly studded with little paper darts, which stand out like so many quills upon the fretful porcupine.'

By mid-February, boredom was starting to give way to consternation, culminating on Wednesday the 21st, a day of outright panic. *The Economist*, often in this period unfriendly to Capel Court, found something admirable in 'The Philosophy of the Stock Exchange':

> Well-known names inside and outside were mentioned as being in distress, the owners, whispered rumour, flinging over every share they possessed, the gold industry described as ruined, while the market fell prostrate under incessant sales. The flatness filtered through to other markets; all the talk ran upon possible failures at the settlement, and a broker dealing in the American market probably voiced the opinion of a good many when he described the Kaffir slump as child's play in comparison with what would

be seen when the real fall in Yankees commenced. Yet through it all the Stock Exchange retained a good humour and cheeriness in vivid contrast to the state of prices . . . The sweepstakes on the Waterloo Cup were organised, the practical joking continued . . . Even at one or two of the private meetings, unhappily rendered necessary by the fall in prices, there were quips and jests – the risks run in helping a fellow member over his troublesome settlement treated as a joke.

The situation was grim enough, as the mining financier Julius Wernher remarked to a colleague on the 24th: 'Losses are terrible. I know a jobber who sold for £21,000 what cost him £82,000; even big and hitherto quite undoubted firms are in a sore plight.'[6] And when a few days later a prominent Kaffir speculator called Whamond killed himself in a West End hotel and had his accounts closed, gloom was further compounded. The *Investors' Review*, now edited by A. J. Wilson and Son, took a grim satisfaction at the turn of events. It argued that the unfortunate man had been 'lured into the purchase of Kaffir shares' and was merely 'one of the multitude which was beguiled about the time of the close of the Boer War by the calculating share peddler and by his tipster press into a belief that peace was to bring a "boom"'. The lesson was clear: 'There is but one way to peace of mind . . . the way of complete abstention from any speculative dealing on the Stock Exchange in these mine shares.' A diatribe followed against Kaffir shares, culminating almost biblically: 'It has been an abomination from first to last, this African market, and for all that has been suffered and lost retribution has yet to come.'[7]

In April 1906, with revolution having being forcibly suppressed, Russia returned as supplicant to the international capital market. Negotiations as usual took place in Paris, Germany dropped out for local reasons, and it was eventually agreed to make an £89m issue, with London's share under the leadership of Barings amounting to a little over £13m.[8] Rothschilds never even contemplated getting involved in the loan, leaving it to Farrer at 8 Bishopsgate to inform Windham Baring on 11 May that 'at the moment of writing we are popular in this market, having made money for everyone in the Russian loan'; and it did not need a cynic to discern that that was the surest way to popularity.[9]

Perhaps inevitably, the City was less concerned about the iniquities of the tsar and Count Witte than with those of the unwelcome new Liberal administration at home. 'The result of 3 months of C.B. [Campbell-Bannerman] government', the adventurous financier Arthur Grenfell wrote on 13 May to his father-in-law Lord Grey, 'has developed a state of nervousness in financial circles which though in my opinion exaggerated shows no signs of improving.' That government's finance minister was equally unimpressed, Asquith writing to Hamilton twelve days later in the context of his early attempts to wrestle with the intractable reserves question:

It is quite true I have spoken to 2 or 3 City men about the gold inquiry, always however with the double reservation, that I had come to no decision in the matter, and that what I said must be treated as strictly confidential.

In what other way one is to get any independent opinion of any value, I fail to see. The truth is all these people, & not least the Bank directors, are as jealous of one another as a set of old maids in a Cathedral town.

At this stage Asquith was apparently thinking of setting up a Royal Commission 'about various matters connected with finance', as Natty Rothschild put it in a letter of 6 June to the cousins in Paris. But, as Natty went on: 'I learn at the Bank of England they have told the Chancellor of the Exchequer that this Commission would be ridiculous & might be mischievous.' Asquith's thoughts then turned to more specific reform, and in a speech at Mansion House later in June, he argued that it would help the debate, in terms of assessing the cash balances on which the banks were working, if the banks were to publish their accounts even more frequently than they had started to do following Goschen's promptings of fifteen years earlier:

The Bank of England was obliged by statute, and conformed to that obligation, to publish returns every week. Why should not the joint-stock banks do the same? Dead silence seems for the moment to have followed that suggestion. To use a slang term which sometimes appeared in the vocabulary of the City, 'window-dressing' as he understood it, was an easy thing to practise at the end of every six months; it was conceivable that it might be practised at the end of every month; but he thought that window-dressing would be difficult to a point of impossibility to the joint-stock and private banks if they published their returns every week.

Governor Alexander Wallace was thoroughly conciliatory: 'There could be no question of the Bank of England's competing with the other banks'; and he described the Bank as 'the one institution in the country whose main aims were anything but that of serving its own interest', granted that 'the interests of the proprietors or shareholders had invariably to give way when national or more important issues were at stake'.[10] Between them it was a strong demarche on the part of Chancellor and governor, but the 'dead silence' was ominous.

Almost immediately, the City bigwigs had much else on their minds. Late on the afternoon of 13 July, a Friday, Morgans in London received a telegram from Jack Morgan in New York. 'Speyer & Co. NY have heard important Banking house is in trouble in London. Do you hear any rumours if so what. Cable as soon as possible.' Within the hour Teddy Grenfell (Arthur's more circumspect cousin) had wired back:

A few brokers are in trouble and the losses of South African houses have been very large. The idleness of markets and depression in prices gilt-edged has given rise to the wildest rumours of difficulties affecting even Baring Bros & Co. on account of fall in Russians & Speyer Bros on a/c of undergrounds. From Bank of England & from other sources I believe no important house in difficulties.

The Russian loan had come back to haunt Barings, as the situation in Russia once again deteriorated, the price of the loan stock went to a discount, and 8 Bishopsgate was believed to be a large holder. At the start of the following week Charles Goschen was sent by Wallace to New Court to reassure Rothschilds that none of the rumours about City houses had any foundation; while Teddy Grenfell the next day wrote along similar lines to Jack Morgan about the absurd rumours which, according to him, had touched on every major City house with the exception of Rothschilds.

'Something serious must be happening,' noted Smith St Aubyn's somewhat baffled diarist on Thursday the 19th. 'Forced sales of gilt edged stocks continue, & all sorts of names are mentioned as being in trouble. Barings, Speyers, even Morgans & more especially Erlangers. Nobody seems to be able to trace where the selling is coming from.' The next afternoon, under renewed interrogation from New York, Morgans sent back a further reassuring cable: 'We consider there is no foundation for the rumor whatever. Barings still talked about and on very best authority know them exceptionally strong. Speyer Bros have withdrawn their new scheme for financing underground which created comment.'[11] Two days later the Duma was dissolved, the Russian loan slumped to as low as 11 discount, and all the fine spring words about the loan paving the way to a more democratic future seemed at best fatuous.

The rumours about other houses gradually died down, but it was now that Revelstoke underwent what must have been a somewhat humiliating experience, described by Farrer in a letter to New York early in August:

> John went round to the Bk of England with our figures & by good fortune found the head of the discount department with the governors [i.e. the deputy governor was also present]. One Search by name, a real croaker but far the ablest of the Bank's permanent officials. The Governor commented that there cannot be another house in London in so liquid a position: & Search added 'no nor any other two put together Mr Governors' and his interview ended.

In another letter Farrer added the detail that when Revelstoke had arrived in the governors' room he had asked for Search to remain – a wise tactic. Farrer's colleague Alfred Mildmay, in his regular despatch to Buenos Aires, offered a perceptive overview on the whole unpleasant episode:

I am not altogether surprised that rumours regarding our affairs reached Buenos Aires. We heard here that our name was 'mentioned', principally, I think, in the west end of the town; I suppose people thought that the Russian loan had not really been taken up by investors and that we had been left with more of it than we could afford to pay for. We think, or rather we hope, that the better informed people realise that in the issue of loans our position is that of intermediaries between the public and the borrower. Our resources are not nearly large enough to enable us to retain any considerable portion of any loan we may happen to bring out, and we should much prefer making the underwriters take up a proportion of their liability, disagreeable though that would be, to hampering our own position in any way. The Russians we hold, taking into account our profit on the issue, stand us in at next to nothing.[12]

Sancho Panza rather than Don Quixote, perhaps, but even if the City remained its usual credulous, rumour-ridden self, there was no doubting that the lessons of 1890 had been fully learned and digested at 8 Bishopsgate.

*

The flow of the yellow metal around the world continued to determine Bank rate and thus the mood of the City. On 16 January 1907, a Wednesday, Natty Rothschild informed Paris that 'there is some idea that the rate of Discount may be lowered tomorrow, but of course it will all depend how the Bank's accounts read at the last moment, but we should not be at all astonished if some reduction were made'. And, with the suggestion of being on the inside track, he added that 'anyhow we know that some of the Directors will advocate a movement in this direction'. As usual a large crowd of members gathered in the Consol market, and this time the government broker obliged:

Relief at the actual receipt of the 5 per cent declaration was profound. It found vent in cheers, which are usual, and in the clapping of hands, which is so uncommon as to deserve comment . . . But the thankfulness met with a cold check. There was much shouting; there were no shouts to buy.

Five per cent, in other words, was hardly a comfortable rate, and on the last day of the month the Smith St Aubyn diary noted that it had been 'a horrible day – money was tighter than ever – the whole market was short and the Bank did a big business'.[13]

The situation did not improve in February, and in March a marked reaction set in, itself a response to the way in which prolonged over-trading and over-speculation in the United States was beginning to lead to palpable signs of weakness. Consols were at their lowest since the Overend Gurney crisis in 1866, and this despite renewed buying by the government broker amidst rumours of 'a leading Anglo-American house' in difficulties.[14] By the end of the month the air was poisonous with the darkest whispers and allegations.

Bank rate stayed at 4 for most of the summer and by 12 June Farrer was able to report to Windham Baring that 'we have had distinctly more cheerful markets . . . Not that there is any business to speak of, but every broker who comes into the room is not now prophesying the end of the world.'[15]

Nevertheless, London remained under a cloud, with America – as was becoming dismayingly familiar – the problem. There was trouble on the New York Stock Exchange, Yankees in London tumbled, and again there was the looming worry of autumnal gold flows across the Atlantic.[16] 'I am afraid we are in for a severe storm in the City', Arthur Grenfell wrote to Grey on Saturday 12 October after a week in which gold drained steadily from the Bank. 'We have had more anxious times than any since the Baring crisis. The American crisis was probably bound to come but Roosevelt has started the machine downhill before anyone had time to adjust the brake.'[17]

'I confess I am quite unable to describe that crisis accurately,' Natty Rothschild wrote to Paris about what was taking place on Wall Street, 'to account positively of what has taken place and still less in any way to forecast the future.'[18] A severe drain of gold from London to the States began on Monday 28 October, when 'as expected', the *FT*'s Money Market report noted, 'New York was a keen bidder for the bar gold offering in the open market today, and . . . secured £1,000,000, or practically the total available.' Natty Rothschild believed that the directors would be 'wise' to raise Bank rate from 4½ to 6, with gold withdrawals from the Bank that day totalling over £1.6m, of which all but £40,000 was on American account. Wednesday 30th was pay day on the Stock Exchange and, although no firms were hammered, there was an abundance of rumours, so much so that according to the *FT* 'names of firms alleged to be in trouble were bandied about with such freedom as to provoke the remark from one leading member that "not to be talked about is proof that you are a Stock Exchange nonentity"'. Bank rate went up on Thursday, but only to 5½. Few in the money market, however, believed they had seen the last rise, 'having regard to the energy with which New York is still striving to get further facilities for importing gold'.[19]

Friday 1 November was a Stock Exchange holiday, and when the governor, William Campbell, walked into the Bank on Monday the 4th, he looked at the figures and did two important things. The first, wholly off his own bat, was to raise Bank rate from 5½ to 6 – a decisive 'governor's rise' that much impressed the newest director, Montagu Norman. The money market 'expressed no surprise' and partly interpreted the action as 'a hint to houses here to guard against further facilitating the flight of eagles by extending loans to New York'. On the Stock Exchange, by contrast, the news caused 'a rude upset', as 'a rush of selling ensued which carried prices down all round'. Campbell's other action that morning was to send for Natty Rothschild and ask him to arrange with the Paris house to secure a major tranche of gold from the Bank of France – a request made plausible by the new, more attractive rate. With the reserve rapidly approaching the previous year's low point of just over £18.1m, the news on Tuesday late afternoon that the Bank of France had agreed to supply £3m of gold was warmly greeted in the City, and the thoroughly unwelcome prospect of a rise to 7 per cent began to be discounted, at least on the Stock Exchange, always the most volatile of bellwethers. By Wednesday evening even the money market was relatively sanguine – 'the market apparently regards the coming shipments of gold from France as doing away with the necessity of a higher official minimum' – but not so Natty Rothschild. Not only was he disturbed by the prospect of continuing large withdrawals of gold by New York, but he continued to be exasperated by the failure on the other side of the pond to take decisive action about resolving the American crisis.[20]

Arthur Grenfell was for once on the side of the pessimists:

We have had a very nasty week here & I am afraid have worse ones before us. The banks here have rather got the funks & have been calling in loans right & left, so that one has had a difficult job financing . . . Though I saw the Americans were drifting into troubled waters, it was impossible to foresee such an utter collapse of credit & it has been impossible to withdraw altogether from markets. The position here is sound & except for America we should have had fair markets. The American position has however plunged us into the worst crisis since the Overend Gurney smash in 1866. It is absolutely impossible to sell anything or even borrow from one's bank. Such a state of affairs has not been seen by many people.

That same day, Thursday the 7th, Bank rate rose from 6 to 7 – its highest level since 1873. On the Stock Exchange the announcement was a 'decided blow', causing 'a general reaction in prices'. Any sense of surprise, however, wore off in the afternoon when the Bank return was issued, showing that the reserve had fallen to the perilously low figure of £17,695,000. Natty Rothschild expressed full agreement with the Bank's step: 'They had no choice and were bound to act in that way, the accounts were low and it was absolutely necessary to give those on the other side of the Atlantic a serious warning.' And the next morning, in a leader headed 'Soaring Bank Rates', the *FT* conceded that 'for the moment all is gloom', but reiterated its usual stern line at such moments that 'so long as London remains a free market for gold, and so long as the exigencies of affairs in the States causes importers there to override ordinary exchange considerations by paying a premium upon gold, just so long will the flight of eagles across the herring pond continue'.[21] There was, in short, no alternative; and few ruled out the possibility of the rate going above 7.

Over the following week, with money exceptionally tight, the City became increasingly critical of the American failure to take effective action about what was after all a home-grown crisis. The Rothschilds, Vivian Hugh Smith of Morgans reported to Jack Morgan on Wednesday the 13th, were voicing 'a pretty general sentiment here by saying they could not understand why the American government should be absolutely powerless or unwilling to do anything to relieve the crisis except to say "thank you" for the assistance they receive from other governments'. The Stock Exchange two days later was racked by rumours that, in the context of continuing gold outflows, the Bank's directors were thinking of going to 8 per cent; while on Saturday the 16th, according to Arthur Grenfell, there were fears of an imminent rise to 9 per cent, even of the Bank Charter Act being suspended for the first time since 1866. 'Bankers have been pressing for loans,' he added on the Monday, '& as it was impossible to realise securities, the position has been much worse than it has appeared on the surface.' However, even as Grenfell wrote, news came through that, in Smith St Aubyn's words, 'the United States government has at last moved to help the situation', this action taking the form of the issuing of Treasury securities. 'The Yankee Relief' was the expressive title of the *FT*'s leader the next morning, and the worst of the crisis was over, especially as gold flowed into London over the next few weeks, attracted by the 7 per cent rate.[22]

Many had been scarred by the experience, among them Arthur Grenfell. 'I have not had an easy time in the City,' he wrote to Grey on the 25th, '& like nearly everyone else I have had to face big losses. I saw the crisis coming on from the first & had pretty well cleared my decks last year.' But Grenfell's boldness had been thwarted, and he went on to lament how, since his wife's death, 'I have found it so difficult to pull myself together that matters have drifted'. Then came the breast-beating, the blaming of others, and the final late flurry of self-confidence:

> However it is my fault. I deserve all I get. I have had to get a loan from my bankers & in normal times this would be considered quite right. But times are not normal & one never knows whether one's banker won't get frightened & call it in. Otherwise I am in a fairly strong position – & as soon as the American position rights itself, we may look for a good recovery here.[23]

*

'Prosperity to Trade and Finance' was the toast that Goschen had proposed at the National Discount Co.'s jamboree at the Ritz in July 1906:

> I denounce any theory which would dissociate the prosperity of finance from the prosperity of trade. (*Cheers.*) I denounce any theory which would say that in the City of London they may be driving a fine business, the profits of the bankers may be great, they may be raking in the means for increased dividends, and at the same time over the great area of the country there is depression. No, gentlemen, I hold in the strongest degree – I hold still more the theory, since the system of limited liability has developed, that there is a community of interests – an inalienable community of interests – between the finance of the City of London and of the great towns and the prosperity of the country at large. If there is prosperity in the country there will be prosperity in the City of London.

After a lengthy disquisition on the gold reserves question, Goschen returned to his main theme in a pointed peroration:

> You have no doubt a sense of the great responsibility which rests upon you. Let it not be thought that the City is composed simply of a group of rich and grasping men who are endeavouring to accumulate those vast fortunes which figure in the annals of some other countries. You are doing your best in order to promote the prosperity of trade and finance in the country at large. By your wisdom as you are wise, by your prudence as you are prudent, by your capacity as you have that capacity, you will help to mould to a great extent the course of business in the country at large and to maintain, by sound and orthodox and unfantastic methods, that great structure of British trade and finance to the prosperity of which I now ask you to drink. (*Loud cheers.*)[24]

The complacency was striking, but so also was the need to justify the City's activities to the nation at large. A debate was beginning that henceforth, sometimes to the City's ill-disguised exasperation, would never quite go away.

It was a debate related to that about the harmfulness or otherwise of capital exports. In January 1906 – just as there gathered force a new, astonishingly powerful wave of such exports that would last more or less up to the war – the *Statist* offered a broad defence:

> This country has to draw from abroad a large part of its food and of the raw materials of its industries. A revenue from investments abroad affords a very convenient means of paying for such imports. Again, the countries which need foreign capital for their development usually pay a higher rate for that capital than is paid at home. Consequently, foreign investment is generally more profitable than home investment. Moreover, foreign investment is generally made in the form of commodities, and therefore gives immediate employment to British capital and British

labour. And if the investment is judiciously made, it increases the purchasing power of the country where it takes place, and thus helps to increase the world's trade.[25]

When Chamberlain, in the course of the 1906 election, apparently suggested that the holding of large foreign investments was not necessarily helpful to British trade, he was jumped upon by Schuster, who insisted that 'the placing of our capital in foreign countries leads to the export to such countries of ships, railways material, and innumerable other articles, and thus creates employment for our working population'.[26] Schuster's arguments were far from unanswerable – but, as yet, only a muffled challenge was heard to these nineteenth-century tenets. One could hardly have expected otherwise. Despite some fluctuations, the Edwardian City was doing extremely well out of its predominantly international orientation; most leading members of the Stock Exchange were far more at home in Monte Carlo than Manchester; the merchant banks for the most part held aloof from domestic industry; the clearers on the whole stuck to their unambitious remit; and altogether, liquidity and profit taking were the name of the game, rumour and clubbiness the language of the market.

As to how that market made up its collective mind about the merits or otherwise of new issues, some passing remarks by the *Investor's Monthly Manual* in 1910 conveyed a wealth of meaning:

> Much of the present-day underwriting is done on the Stock Exchange, and a member will approach another with sometimes little more than a slip of paper, upon which are jotted brief particulars of the people connected with the matter, the proposed capital, profit estimates, etc. The names on the paper are what really count, and if first-class people are connected with any concern, underwriting will present no difficulties.[27]

The Victorian precept may have been that 'servants talk about people, gentlefolk discuss things', but in Capel Court the residents clung steadily to the socially inferior, conceptually less demanding way of interpreting the world. The future was tomorrow, the next account a remote contingency, and the long-term potential of new technologies rather less relevant than a Wellsian fantasy. 'Beating the gun', the Americans called it, and it was nice work if you could get it.

CHAPTER EIGHTEEN

Dread Nought

The year 1908 marked a turning point in the history of two of the City's great markets: Lloyd's on the first floor of the Royal Exchange; and the Stock Exchange in Capel Court.[1] The consequences proved beneficial in the case of the former, pernicious in the case of the latter. The contrast is both instructive and piquant.

Calls for internal reform at Lloyd's had been heard since a scandal in 1902 involving the failure of Percy Burnand, part of a famous Lloyd's family and a member since 1885; but the institution had chuntered on more or less untroubled, fortified in its self-regard by its strong, stoical response to the heavy losses incurred by the San Francisco earthquake of 1906. Matters, however, started to come to a head in the summer of 1908, against a background of generally lean business and several members of a large syndicate finding themselves in financial trouble. On 17 July the Financial and Commercial Supplement of *The Times* published a main leader on 'Troubles in the Marine Insurance Market' that was designed to cause a stir and did so. The anonymous author was a journalist called Harcourt Kitchin, who specialised in insurance matters. Having stressed the lack of centralised control exercised by Lloyd's over its members' operations, he argued that the existing system of deposits of £5,000 payable by each underwriting member of marine risks had become badly outdated:

> The largest syndicates have a premium income of from half a million even up to a million pounds a year, and although the 'names' no doubt receive accounts from their leading underwriter, yet no policy-holder has any knowledge at all as to how this large premium income is used . . . As compared with the large sums which should be readily available to meet liabilities of large syndicates for unexpired risks, it must be owned that the amount of the official deposits is insignificant.

Then came the posited remedy:

> What really is needed is not so much an increase in the amount of deposit, but a system of audit of underwriters' accounts . . . We believe that the public would be satisfied if the underwriting syndicates had properly audited balance-sheets prepared every year, and submitted them privately to the Committee of Lloyd's. The mere fact that such a balance-sheet had

to be submitted would automatically compel underwriters to make sure that all their liabilities for unexpired risks were provided for and their funds properly invested . . .

We believe that the credit of underwriting members would again become practically invulnerable, if they took the necessary steps to secure a semi-private audit.[2]

Almost certainly Kitchin was writing at the instigation of Sidney Boulton, a reform-minded member of the Committee; and only a week after the article appeared, a meeting of underwriters approved the establishment of a special joint committee to put forward an audit scheme.

Cuthbert Heath, who for the last two years had demanded an auditor's certificate before guaranteeing any of his fellow members, predictably dominated the committee's proceedings. He also, shortly before the meeting of underwriters early in November to consider the committee's proposals, played a tactical masterstroke. In the context of quite a strong tide of opinion swelling against what were seen as inquisitorial, continental-style innovations, he persuaded over forty underwriters – more or less the leading men of Lloyd's – to declare themselves to the Committee as willing to submit to an audit. In the event the well-attended meeting on the 3rd agreed not only to the introduction of the audit, but also to the principle of 'premiums in trust', in other words the device for not allowing a future Burnand to use underwriting money for outside purposes. 'In thus keeping pace with the times Lloyd's underwriters have achieved for themselves probably the greatest reform on record' declared the *FT* with perhaps a touch of hyperbole, while *The Times* added to its enthusiasm about 'The Strengthening of Lloyd's' some perceptive analysis: 'The acceptance of this plan by every member is voluntary, but as the names of all those who comply with its requirements will be marked on a board, members who do not see their way to agree to the audit will, no doubt, soon find themselves left out in the cold.'[3] Lloyd's remained very much a club, but the rules of the club were changing for the public good as well as its own.

The ultimate club, though, was still Capel Court: governed by the creed of private faces in private places and lacking a commanding figure like Heath. The question of capacity – enmeshed with brokers taking double commissions through bypassing jobbers, and jobbers bypassing brokers by dealing direct ('shunting') with provincial stock exchanges – came to the surface decisively in 1908. During January and February the Stock Exchange Committee was treated to a series of submissions and counter-submissions. Samuel Gardner, a well-known broker, 'said that our fathers had built up a sound system by which the broker as an agent kept the dealer who made prices at arm's length'. The campaigning Herbert Blyth, a leading jobber, declared that 'members of the public living near provincial exchanges were dealing year by year more with the provincial and less with the London brokers, because the former boasted that they could do as well or better for their clients', in other words by dealing with London jobbers. And the Westralian jobber Bernard Moore got close to the heart of the aggrieved feelings about shunters when he declared that the existing single-capacity rule 'was loyally kept by 90% of the members', but that a privileged minority 'had obtained private telephones, which their fellow members were unable to obtain'.

The more compelling if less popular arguments ran all the other way. Particularly cogent was Cecil Braithwaite, emerging as a leader of the lobby to abolish the distinction between brokers and jobbers. His letter to the Committee, backed by 903 signatures, stressed the economic logic of the situation:

> Brokers have no doubt lost some of their business owing to shunting, but, on the other hand, a very large number of members have gained a considerable amount by the present facilities in the way of being able to deal in such shares as cotton descriptions, cycle and motor shares, at close prices, where a few years ago the provincial exchanges were the only market . . . The shunter has made it possible to deal in anything in which there is a market anywhere, often at a moment's notice and within a very short space of time . . .
>
> The market in all securities will follow the money and those who control the stock, and it is impossible for any rule to make it otherwise . . . The whole tendency of all classes of business is to go to the men who can serve you best, i.e. the shop, and, what is more, the public demand it. If you deal with a man who makes his price outside the shop quotation you soon hear about it.

In person he 'drew attention to the fact that although his petition had been signed by a minority of the members, it had received the support of the great majority of the biggest firms'; and he even pointed out that his own stockbroking firm, Foster & Braithwaite, 'had suffered from the "shunting" business, because these firms had had the pluck to acquire the facilities at great cost which his firm might have had'.[4] It was a remarkably objective way of looking at the situation, but in the numbers game small was beautiful.

The issue of capacity and related working practices was effectively settled in March by the annual Committee election.[5] The organisation that mobilised opinion to defeat Braithwaite and his followers was the Stock Exchange Members' Association, in which Blyth was a predictably prominent figure. Significantly, whereas the twenty-five successful (and all SEMA-backed) candidates in that election who were still in active business belonged to firms that had an average of 3.5 partners, the nine

unsuccessful candidates (including Braithwaite) still in active business
came from firms with an average of almost five partners. Blyth, the day
after the election, 'received quite an ovation in the Kaffir Circus' – justifying Braithwaite's subsequent observation that 'the question of double
commission was originally raised by certain members of the South African
market' and that indeed 'the whole agitation emanates from inside the
House'. Following the election, the new Committee enacted in July 1908
what was in effect a trade-off to come into force from the following
February. On the one hand brokers were specifically forbidden from
making prices or taking a second commission, on the other hand jobbers
were equally specifically forbidden from dealing directly with non-
members. An exception to this latter restriction was made in the case of
arbitrageurs dealing with members of foreign stock exchanges. A House
correspondent of the *FT* convincingly explained the inconsistency:

> Logically, nothing can be said in favour of allowing arbitrage dealings with
> foreign bourses and tabooing the 'shunting' between London and the
> provinces. But from the average English broker's point of view, and that
> of most jobbers too, there is a very great difference. The fact of the matter
> is that most of them neither know nor care to know anything about the
> mysteries and movements of exchange, hence arbitrage dealings are outside
> their ambitions, as well as beyond their scope. But however insular alike
> in his language and his knowledge of foreign moneys, the House broker
> can see quickly enough that if, say, a Glasgow broker buys 10,000 'Caleys'
> through a jobber in London, there is no commission for the London
> broker thereon.

It was not only in Capel Court that this nimble ninepence business across
the international securities markets remained largely a mystery. 'Nothing
in the world would induce me to undertake an arbitrage business', Farrer
at Barings wrote a few years previously to Hugo Baring. 'It requires a
very special training and mind to do it successfully – John thinks someone
born in the Ghetto at Frankfort.'[6] For the moment they were allowed to
continue their incomprehensible activities in peace.

The new rules received a poor press, typified by the *Investors' Review*
accusing the Committee of 'behaving like a parish vestry, whose members
are anxious that none of the "perks", sacred through old usage, shall go
past them'. The hardening of capacity certainly did nothing for the Stock
Exchange's marketability. According to the financial journalist Henry
Lowenfeld in 1909, there was at any one time a genuinely free market in
only about 400 out of the 5,000 or so officially quoted securities, less
than half of the proportion estimated by the stockbroker Charles Branch
in 1877 as fully marketable. Among those minority members of the
Committee who resigned in March 1909 in protest against the new rules
which had just come into force was the stockbroker Gerald Williams.

His letter of resignation included this alternative vision of the market's future:

> To make it worthwhile for men possessing capital, brains and enterprise to be dealers on the Stock Exchange, and to make it possible for brokers to deal for a living wage without undercutting one another to a ruinous extent, I am therefore desirous of inducing brokers to deal on the floor of the House, if by so doing they do not prejudice the interests of their clients, and I am equally desirous that the only competition which brokers shall be allowed to use is that consisting of energy, honesty, and intelligence. There is no need to say a word in favour of wealth, which has always and will always command special advantages.[7]

The giveaway, as far as his opponents were concerned, was the final sentence. Certainly, the theme of a sacred barrier between jobber as principal and broker as agent, a barrier acting in some time-honoured way as a safeguard to the investing public, was at best only marginal in a campaign conducted for quite other reasons to harden the distinction between the two capacities. As numerous as they were undercapitalised, the small brokers and the small jobbers had combined forces to lock the Stock Exchange into an ossifying, thoroughly short-sighted institutional structure that would survive for another three-quarters of a century.

*

Few could guess how soon the world at large would change utterly. Winston Churchill, defending (as the new president of the Board of Trade) the Manchester seat that he had held since the 1906 election, expounded to his constituents in April 1908 what most people would have unquestioningly accepted as the immutable verities of the gold standard:

> In the transactions of States scarcely any money passes. The goods which are bought and sold between great Powers are not paid for in money. They are exchanged one with the other. And if England buys from America or Germany more than she has intended to buy, having regard to our own productions, instantly there is a cause for the shipments of bullion, and bullion is shipped to supply the deficiency. Then the Bank rate is put up in order to prevent the movements of bullion, and the rise of the Bank rate immediately corrects and arrests the very trade which has given rise to the disparity. (*Hear, Hear.*)
>
> That is the known established theory of international trade, and everyone knows, every single business man knows, it works delicately, automatically, universally, and instantaneously. It is the same now as in January 1906, and it will be the same as it is in 1908 when the year 2000 has dawned upon the world. As long as men trade from one nation to another and are grouped in national communities you will find the differences of free trading are adjusted almost instantaneously by shipments of bullion corrected by an alteration in the Bank rate.[8]

Such confidence, and in 1908 apparently such justified confidence. In the event, his relationship with the yellow metal was to blight this ambitious politician's career.

Churchill was speaking in the aftermath of the successful resolution, from the English point of view, of the 1907 American crisis. Early in 1908, J. Spencer Phillips of Lloyds told his shareholders that as a result of that crisis 'the open market in gold has been brilliantly vindicated'; but as far as the clearing bankers' committee set up to consider the general question of gold reserves was concerned, he was unable to 'give much hope of any conclusion being voluntarily arrived at, or anything being done in this matter beyond what each individual bank sees fit in its own eyes'.

Soon afterwards, responding to wider business concerns about high levels of Bank rate, the London Chamber of Commerce set up its own Gold Reserves Committee, and the deliberations of the other seem to have been suspended. Amongst those on the new committee were Schuster, his great rival Edward Holden (the pugnacious, fiercely driven Lancastrian largely responsible for the rapid growth of the London City and Midland Bank from the 1890s), and Tritton of Barclays; while the governor of the Bank of England declined to serve or to nominate any of his colleagues.

Proceedings were rather sporadic, but the nub began to be reached in the winter of 1908–9 when Tritton formally proposed the establishment of a secondary reserve, 'to be held by the Bank of England not as bankers but as warehousemen'. Schuster was broadly supportive but not so Holden, who insisted that 'he had not met one Bank Manager who would consent to have his reserves taken from him and kept in another place'. Tritton tartly responded that it would have been better if Holden 'had done me the honour of reading my remarks a little more carefully'. The eventual outcome was that the report, presented to the Chamber in July 1909, included as possible solutions *both* the approaches – Tritton's proposed visible secondary reserve physically based at the Bank, Holden's preference for a detailed public statement by each bank of its gold holding. With more hope than conviction, the report described the two schemes as 'not being altogether incompatible'.[9] What would be the next step? Asquith had already made it pretty clear that government was not prepared to intervene in order to bang heads together; while the Bank had offered precious little leadership in the matter since the end of Lidderdale's governorship seventeen years earlier. The new governor was the coffee merchant Reginald Johnston and there was minimal hope of a radical new initiative from that quarter.

Accordingly the question remained in a state of more or less animated suspension. The policy of the Bank seems to have been little more than hoping that somehow the whole matter would miraculously go away of its own accord; while the bankers did not yet have either the cohesion or self-confidence to alter the power relationship. In November 1909, as the new president of the Institute of Bankers, 'Fritz' Huth Jackson gave his inaugural address and called for unanimity from the clearers over the question. Jackson, as a merchant banker, was also a director of the Bank; and in his vote of thanks, Walter Leaf of the London County and Westminster (the merger had taken place earlier in the year) was tact itself – some might have thought servility – as he dwelt on the 'peculiar relation in which Joint Stock Banks stand to the Bank of England':

> It is very largely a sentimental relation, and one is continually learning how large a part sentiment plays even in the dryest financial business of the City of London. In some respects it might be called a filial relation; in some respects it reminds us of the relations of the Colonies to the Mother Country. But in any case I am sure that the attitude of the banks of England to the Bank of England is one of the highest respect and extreme admiration for the manner in which they have dealt with the difficult task which has been laid upon them.
>
> The keeping of a gold reserve is, as we all know, a very expensive, and in some ways an uneconomical process. It is one which we are very glad to have done for us by the Bank of England, and it is only the pressure of public opinion which would drive the large proportion of the Joint Stock Banks into using their own strong rooms for the purpose.

The Old Lady's representative was suitably self-deprecating in reply. 'As Dr Leaf says, the Bank of England holds a peculiar position in the banking world, and whether the directors of the Bank of England would be competent to conduct the affairs of the other banks in the country I do not pretend to say.'[10]

Holden's letter of March 1909 to the Liberal minister Reginald McKenna was a pointer to the urgency the gold reserves debate was starting to assume against the larger international backdrop:

> I am sure the people of this Country, be they Liberals or be they Conservatives, will applaud you if you will follow up without hesitation public opinion which says 'give us eight Dreadnoughts or even more'. There is one fact, however, which you ought to put before your Chancellor and your Prime Minister, and that is, while practically every Country has a War Chest, we have nothing. We ought to set about at once to accumulate gold.

It also reflected the sharpening anti-German mood in the City – a mood that had become notably apparent during the German loan episode a year earlier, in April 1908. In fact the loan comprised two issues in one: a Prussian loan of £10m, proceeds to be devoted to improving Prussia's railway system, and an imperial loan of £12.5m, for what the *Statist* bluntly described as 'warlike purposes only'. Both issues had a 4 per cent coupon and neither was to be redeemable or convertible until 1918. The Stock Exchange nicknamed it the 'Dreadnought loan' (treated as one because the issues were not brought out separately) and the City as a whole blew a less than cordial raspberry. H. A. Gwynne, editor of the *Morning Post*, writing soon afterwards to the Canadian prime minister, described the outcome:

> The recent German loan that was launched at a very low price and a high rate of interest, was regarded by the City as a war loan, and word was given by all the big houses that on no account was money to be invested . . . So high was this feeling that a single individual who sold £50,000 of consols to invest in the German loan was forced by City opinion to withdraw his application for money, it being put pretty plainly to him that he might be boycotted in consequence . . . A few insurance companies did give a little money, but they, too, under the same pressure have sold out.

The Economist, least bellicose of organs, sought to argue that pragmatism had also played a part ('with the prospect of more borrowing in the autumn, German credit will suffer still further depreciation'), but was unable to deny that 'people here naturally do not care to invest their money, even at a high rate of interest, in German battleships', or in short that the mighty operative force of 'sentiment' had been at work.[11]

As Germany pushed on with its shipbuilding programme, naval matters increasingly preoccupied the City – by March 1909, with the Germans believed to be secretly speeding up their programme and the jingoistic rallying cry 'we want eight, and we won't wait' passing into the English language, in a state of extreme agitation. 'In the City today', Natty Rothschild wrote to Paris on the 17th, 'the Public was much more interested in the Debate which took place yesterday on the Naval Estimates, & general dissatisfaction was expressed at the government proposals which only deal with 4 Dreadnoughts at present.' A fortnight later the Guildhall was the scene for another display of City ritualism, as the ancient building was packed out for a meeting – summoned by the Lord Mayor but initiated by the Naval and Military Defence Standing Committee of the London Chamber of Commerce – 'to consider the state of the Navy'. *The Times* wrote glowingly how 'men stood in serried ranks around and beyond the seats, surging about the statues of Nelson and Wellington and Pitt, filling the distant corners and recesses, and even content with precarious foothold upon a staircase'. The Lord Mayor, flanked by Balfour and Natty Rothschild, noted in his opening remarks how 'numerously and influentially signed' had been 'the requisitions from the banking interests, the Stock Exchange, the Baltic, the Commercial Sale Rooms, the Mincing-lane houses, the metal and timber trades, the London Chamber of Commerce, and merchants and traders generally'. There followed a long, rapturously received speech by Balfour, before his fellow

Tory and City MP, the stockbroker Sir Frederick Banbury, successfully moved that four further Dreadnoughts be built. Natty Rothschild then equally successfully moved that all necessary support be given to attain that end:

> He felt convinced that all of those present, in advocating a very strong Navy, had no intention of urging an aggressive policy. (*Hear, hear.*) To them it mattered not whether foreign Powers built up navies; all they wanted was that the British Navy should be predominant and strong . . . Looking round that great hall and seeing the memorials the citizens had put up to great men, he could only trust that the feeling which had inspired the citizens of London to erect them would continue. He was sure he was only voicing the feelings of the citizens of London when he said that they called upon the present government or their successors to keep the Navy of this country as strong in the future as it had been in the past. (*Loud cheers.*)[12]

Natty lacked the demotic touch, and his house may have been slipping in the ratings, but he remained the City's spokesman.

Cassel was almost certainly not present that boisterous afternoon at the Guildhall. Since 1908 he had been actively mediating between the two countries, doing his best to ease Anglo-German tensions. Inevitably he left himself open to criticism. 'Of course he takes the German and Semitic point of view of it all,' Lord Esher privately reflected. 'That is only natural. After all, *we* are fighting for our lives, for our Imperial and possibly National existence, which will be at stake ere long. The Cassels are at home in all lands – equally rich, equally composed.' Yet the truth of the matter was that Cassel, with his essentially cosmopolitan outlook, had a far more acute understanding of where the City's fundamental long-term interests lay than had the serried ranks who wanted eight and would not wait. And, of course, he was not alone. When, a few days before the Guildhall meeting, Teddy Grenfell wrote to Jack Morgan about the current Balkan crisis that 'I still cannot believe that the five Great Powers will be at each other's throats for such a rotten little country as Servia', he was expressing the same deep-rooted commercial conviction that, as Gladstone said on another occasion, 'the resources of civilisation are not exhausted'.[13] This tension between on the one hand an almost crude patriotism, and on the other an earnest desire not to destroy the wonderful global money-making machinery built up over the previous century, remained the City's most profound paradox, rarely explored by contemporaries at a conscious level. In 1899 there had been a certain economic logic to buttress gut instincts; this time round that logic was much more tenuous.

*

Lloyd George, in a nicely judged presidential speech in 1896 to the annual music festival of Welsh Nonconformist choirs, described the English as 'a nation of footballers, stock exchangers, public-house and music-hall frequenters'. In the City, if not necessarily on the terraces, the disapproval was mutual. Lloyd George's first Budget was the subject of a host of rumours during the months before he delivered it, Natty Rothschild reporting to Paris in January 1909 that the government's financial intentions 'are said to be predatory, certainly spiteful and very revengeful'. The following month J. Spencer Phillips, addressing the shareholders of Lloyds, attempted to get his retaliation in first:

> I am told every day by leading brokers in the City that there is quite a respectable amount of money coming forward for investment, but the invariable instructions are, you must invest it either in foreign stocks or foreign railways. (*Hear, hear.*) Rightly or wrongly, the trend of home politics, the uneasiness with regard to future legislation, and the fear of what this year's Budget may produce, is driving our capital every day more and more to other climes. (*Hear, hear.*) Please don't misunderstand me – I am only stating bare facts; I am no political partisan; I have never touched politics in any way; and in a bank board room politics are never discussed, except only so far as the political horizon may affect the money market. (*Hear, hear.*)

'Everybody is on tiptoe of expectation with regard to Thursday's budget', Carl Meyer wrote to his wife from the City on 27 April; two days later the anxious wait was at last over.[14]

The 'People's Budget', as it soon became known, involved increased licence and death duties, super-tax on large incomes, tax on unearned increment – and, generally aimed at the landed rather than manufacturing interest, was never likely to appeal to many gentlemanly capitalists. 'A patent and deliberate determination to use the machinery of finance to establish schemes and systems which, for want of a more specific term, may be called Socialistic' was the immediate appraisal offered by the *FN*, and Natty Rothschild on 3 May fully concurred, describing the Budget to his cousins as 'a vindictive one', with its most malevolent feature being 'the proposed taxation in connection with land' and in general its proposals 'most socialistic and remarkably unfair'. Two days later that austere financier Arthur Grenfell remarked to Grey that the Budget was 'very dangerous' and that 'the general result seems to be to discourage thrift'; while by the 10th the City was preparing to make its grand remonstrance. 'A petition is being drawn up which will require a good deal of skill and attention, a petition which will be largely signed and then presented to Parliament', Natty informed his cousins, adding that he did not anticipate the petition doing much good in the Commons but surmising that 'it may have a great effect in the country'. On the

14th he formally presented to Asquith a memorial from 'Bankers, Merchants and others largely interested in the trade and commerce of London and of the Country':

> We feel that the prosperity of all classes has been greatly due to the fact that this country has afforded indisputable safety for Capital, and we should deeply regret if this conviction were in any way weakened.
>
> In conclusion we would point out that though the taxes to which we have taken exception will in the first instance fall with excessive severity on Capital, they will also in our opinion tend to discourage private enterprise and thrift, thus in the long run diminishing employment and reducing wages.

Arthur Grenfell's younger brother Rivy took a more iconoclastic line about the City's unprecedentedly outspoken reaction to Lloyd George's proposals: 'They have hit the rich from every corner, and so everyone is crying out. Personally I think there is a great deal to be said in favour of these socialistic Budgets. Old Rothschild will not eat any less *foie gras* because he has to pay a little more for his motor cars.'[15]

Lloyd George declined to withdraw his proposals, so on 23 June, in the crowded great hall of the Cannon Street Hotel, there took place a big City protest meeting. Natty was in the chair, and those present included the usual range of suspects – Lords Avebury, Goschen, Milner and Revelstoke; Sir Alexander Henderson and Sir Everard Hambro; Herbert Gibbs, Leopold de Rothschild, Carl Meyer and Robert Benson; a resolution condemning the Budget was 'enthusiastically received and adopted'.[16]

The next day Lloyd George spoke at a lunch at the Holborn Restaurant. He poured scorn on the City's best efforts:

> You might have expected in a meeting of that sort to have sound financial criticism and at any rate some sound financial suggestions. I look in vain through the reports to find one such suggestion. You have simply the same old drivel about Socialism, and, of course, 'the thin end of the wedge' – which is becoming very thin by constant use – which you can find any morning in the columns of the 'Daily Mail' . . .
>
> Really, in all these things we are having too much Lord Rothschild. We are not to have temperance reform in this country. Why? Because Lord Rothschild has sent a circular to the Peers to say so. We must have more 'Dreadnoughts'. Why? Because Lord Rothschild has told us so at a meeting in the City . . . Well, I should like to know, is Lord Rothschild the dictator of this country? Are we really to have all ways of social and financial reform blocked? 'No thoroughfare, by order – Nathaniel Rothschild'? Now, there are countries where they have made it perfectly clear that they are not going to have their policy dictated merely by great financiers. And if this goes on this country will join the rest of them. (*Loud cheers.*)

Natty Rothschild could afford to smile. 'I have been very much amused today', he wrote to Paris after reading the papers. 'Mr Lloyd George did not appreciate the meeting in the City and he indulged in a violent diatribe against myself.'[17]

In fact the government was not without friends in the City as the crisis consequent upon Lloyd George's Budget gradually unfolded. Towards the end of the year Alexander Kleinwort was made a baronet soon after writing out a cheque for £20,000. There was also the support of Cassel, who in November stressed to his son-in-law his 'absolute loyalty to whatever government I happen to be serving, and if whoever happened to be in power could not be certain of that he would not give me, and I certainly would not wish, his confidence'. Even among unswerving Conservatives there were some, like Teddy Grenfell, who felt that the City's sustained outrage was overdone. 'In my opinion the Budget is an ill-considered measure but it does not justify the excitement and bad feeling which has been exhibited during the past 6 months,' he asserted to the senior partner of Bleichroders on 30 November 1909, as there drew to an end what was, from a City point of view, one of the more remarkable parliamentary debates.[18]

It began on Monday the 22nd, as the Lords debated the Finance Bill, and in the course of that first evening Revelstoke made his maiden speech. The City, he explained, 'daily – I may say hourly – in various ways, and mainly through its quotations of public securities, focuses the judgement of experts, which usually become finally the judgement of the entire people, concerning the welfare of the country'. He produced figures showing that over the past three years Consols had depreciated by over 6 per cent and English railways by over 10 per cent. 'This is a steady and hopeless depreciation of the securities in which the most conservative of us have been brought up to pin our faith.' And Revelstoke blamed not just the Budget but the fact that 'we have had speech after speech from our legislators of which the purpose has been to set class against class and to represent the interests of capital as antagonistic to the welfare of the people' – a novel doctrine, he concluded, that 'ignores the extent to which the prosperity of this nation has been due to its great capital resources, its heritage of financial supremacy, its unshaken credit'.

The following evening, Earl Russell specifically addressed himself to Revelstoke's speech:

> The noble Lord showed us all the columns of the Temple of Mammon – *totus teres atque rotundus* – with its swept courts, its strong walls and protecting fences, and asked whether it was right that anything should be done to disturb the security of this temple. Are you justified, he asked, in doing this by your Budget? That explained to me more fully than I have ever understood before why it is that the City as a whole is always found

in the rear of social progress and advance, because although the view was clear cut, it was a view which was obviously a narrow and a limited one. It was cut off at one point. It by no means embraced the country or the inhabitants of this country as a whole.

To some of us, hypocrites though the noble Lord may think us, there also arose a vision, not only of these slightly-disturbed financiers, of these unfortunate people who make a quarter per cent less on their money, and whose securities have fallen by so much per cent, but of those people who are to be seen homeless every night on the Embankment, of those who are unemployed up and down the country, of those who are starving, of those who are being sweated and are unable to compete on fair terms for a livelihood in the labour market of the world; and some of us felt that a slight disturbance in the temples of high finance is worth while if something is done to alleviate the lot of those unfortunate people, and to bring stability and enjoyment of life to a larger portion of the population of this country . . . There is as much to be learned on one side as on the other.

Russell's tour de force got under the City skin, as was clear on the 29th when Natty Rothschild made his long-awaited, typically brief contribution. 'When I talk of the City,' he emphasised, 'I do not mean only the members of the Stock Exchange and those who noble Lords opposite seem to think frequent Capel Court and Shorter's Court, but I am talking of men who are associated with the trade and commerce of this great country, without which trade and commerce England could not exist.' So too the second Viscount Goschen (chairman of the London County and Westminster Bank), in words his father would have approved:

> The City is not only composed of a number of financiers who are thinking of their own profit. It is the financial nerve-centre of this country, to which flow the savings and earnings of all classes of the community . . . And surely, if not from the highest motives, at least from their business instincts, those who are responsible for the use and custody of this money might be credited with a recognition of the fact that it is upon the mutual dependence of their own interests upon those of their customers and of their clients that the stability of credit rests. It is upon the character of their policy that really depends the credit of this country.[19]

It was not a particularly able defence of enlightened self-interest, but that defence was one that the City was not yet practised in expounding.

The Lords rejected the Budget by 350 votes to 75 and Natty the next day informed Paris that 'the majority has been welcomed in the City by very firm markets'. The inevitable general election followed in January 1910, earning headlines in the *FN* like 'Lloyd George Finance; or the Gentle Art of Robbing Hen-Roosts'.[20] The City itself was a contested constituency during the election, but the Tory candidates, Balfour and Sir Frederick Banbury, won comfortably, receiving over 17,000 votes each.

By this stage the City had moved firmly into the protectionist camp, testified to by the failure of a Conservative free-trade association to develop there in any meaningful way.[21] Why had the City made this shift? Mainly out of instinctive allegiance to the now protectionist Conservative Party; partly as an intellectual response to the problem of how to pay for increased expenditure – above all increased naval expenditure – granted that dramatically raising direct taxation was wholly unacceptable; and very little out of convinced adherence to Chamberlainite precepts of industrial regeneration. Or put another way, a liberal economic world order remained the City's ideal, the free flow of goods and capital continued unfettered until 1914, and the City prospered as never before or since. [22]

Lloyd George's Budget had become history, as had a phenomenal rubber boom on the Stock Exchange, by the time the constitutional question led to a second general election in 1910, held at the end of the year. In November the Stock Exchange Committee considered a letter from G. S. Pawle, indomitable veteran of the Stock Exchange's London to Brighton walking race:

> In view of new Rule No 17, the Committee may censure or *suspend* any member who in his conduct may act in a manner detrimental to the interests of the Stock Exchange.
>
> Seeing that at least five-sixths of the members regard His Majesty's present government and administration as 'detrimental to the interests of the Stock Exchange' I shall be obliged by a formal letter from the Committee giving or withholding their consent to my accepting an invitation to contest the Eastern Division of Hertfordshire as a supporter of the present ministry.

Pawle's letter, which may or may not have provoked a smile, was 'allowed to lie on the table'. To the City's disappointment the second election barely altered the political landscape, and in the course of 1911 the constitutional crisis, turning on much-truncated powers for the House of Lords, slowly moved to a resolution. Ultimately the City seems to have lined up with the 'hedgers' rather than the 'ditchers'. Natty Rothschild was certainly in the former camp, while the Stock Exchange greeted the passing of the Parliament Bill with palpable relief. Better a Conservative-dominated upper chamber, even without any authority over money bills, than 500 new Liberal peers, seems to have been the general feeling. The putative 500 included Thomas Hardy as well as Edgar Speyer, Bertrand Russell as well as Edward Holden, and for Revelstoke at least it would have been a mind-broadening experience.[23]

CHAPTER NINETEEN
Nibelheim

In 1911 the dog days of August were dominated by the heat (excessive), and a generally nervy, jumpy atmosphere in the markets. 'Very uneasy feeling on Stock Exchange & Yankees come over weak', noted the bill brokers Smith St Aubyn on Wednesday the 16th. That same afternoon there occurred what *The Economist* called 'a unique incident in the House', as one of the day's defaulters in the Stock Exchange met his fate:

> Upon the fall of the hammer a great hush ordinarily comes over the whole House when the waiters rise in their stands to perform the unpleasant duty of hammering a member. But the American market happened to be singing a lusty chorus to a well-known man, and did not notice the signal for default. Consequently the hammering was carried out to the accompaniment of song by the unconscious Yankee market, which did not realise that anything untoward was about until it was practically over. It was tragedy and comedy brought more closely together than most members can recollect in the course of their City life.

The young John Braithwaite, son of Joseph and a partner in Foster & Braithwaite only since 1908, was not among those in singalong mood. Just over a fortnight later, on holiday with his wife and baby son, he wrote to his father:

> I think we have made a great mistake in regarding the bringing out of companies as a definite branch of our business . . . We have suffered great financial loss and still worse we have ruined our reputation with those who followed us into Oil. We know nothing about [it] yet we presumed to pose as competent advisers. What induced us to do it? . . . I could kick myself when I think of how we sat in our office last year and were fooled by the specious show of one promoter after another into putting our names to enterprises of questionable integrity – which in the event have brought profit only to their promoters and vendors.

Braithwaite then dwelt on the likelihood of one of those oil companies going into receivership, with the possibility that that might lead to the smash of Foster & Braithwaite itself:

You may perhaps be surprised that I have spoken of the possibility of failure. It is because it has been before my mind like a nightmare day and night more or less continuously for the last month and more – I have suffered it all mentally over and over again – when the hammer has gone in the House it has sounded like a knell in my ears – I have thought of the long list of our names and the awful staggering hush afterwards – in a sense the bitterness of it seems past having realized it so – [illegible], and anything would be a relief.[1]

In fact the firm survived, and Braithwaite would remain a partner for another sixty years. Most City men know fear at one time or another in their careers, but hardly anyone has expressed it so vividly.

Montagu Norman of Brown Shipley was undergoing a rather different sort of personal crisis, one that the firm described on 4 October to Brown Brothers in New York:

Mr Norman, as you know, has had a good deal of business to attend to lately, and apparently has not been in very strong health for some months past: of this, however, his Partners had little suspicion, as, on any enquiry being made, he himself was so sensitive that it was impossible to insist on it.

About ten days ago, however, things came to a climax, and he felt compelled to leave the office under the impression that he had contracted a severe chill. Fortunately he went down to his Father's (Moor Place), and after arriving there (from all we understand) he had a serious collapse, and for 3 or 4 days was quite incapacitated with acute pains in his head and a high temperature. The family Doctor was called in, and at once pronounced it a case of nervous breakdown.

The illness continued, and in November he was seen by a London specialist. 'He says M. is like a sick animal who has gone away into a corner alone,' a relative reported, 'and he doesn't want us to poke him into activity of mind or body.' What had happened? It is clear that Norman by 1911 was increasingly at odds with at least one of his partners over Brown Shipley's recent emphasis on issuing securities and underwriting other issues, often of a speculative nature (several of them Canadian land issues), a trend that he saw as alien to the traditional and much sounder virtues of accepting; but in such a complex, elusive character it is unlikely to have been business alone that caused the breakdown. Norman himself professed bewilderment. Having been advised to take a long voyage to recoup his health, he wrote on Christmas Eve to an American partner:

I remember, tho' not very clearly, that I had a letter from you on the very day that my machine stopped working. That letter has vanished, and I don't know what it said, and from that time until now I have neither read nor written a letter. Indeed I have been a close prisoner and to me it seems that the Prison was constructed on the lines of Hell! . . . Anyhow I want no better imitation![2]

*

In the winter of 1911–12 the Committee of Imperial Defence conducted an inquiry into the financial and commercial implications should war break out between Britain and Germany.[3] Chaired by the Earl of Desart, a subcommittee quizzed various City eminents, including Huth Jackson. He argued that the creation of an earmarked war reserve of gold would work only if it was a secret one; insisted that, in the event of war, 'to suspend the export of gold even for twenty-four hours might be to jeopardise our position as the principal bankers of the world'; and generally took the line that if London could get through the first few days of war then all would be fine, because by lifting the Bank rate it would be able to call in gold from all quarters of the globe.

Governor Alfred Cole also gave evidence and, like Huth Jackson, strongly deprecated any notion of a wartime embargo on the export of gold. Inevitably he trotted out the familiar argument that it was the 'free market for gold' that more than anything had made London 'the international banking centre of the world'. Anyway, he went on, in the event of war 'probably failure would be confined to one or two accepting houses, and the City as a whole would escape any great financial disaster'. And in terms of defending the gold reserve, he concluded not unportentously, 'the adjustment of the discount rate to meet the ever-varying circumstances of each moment' was an instrument that 'had never failed us in the past' and 'might be relied on in almost any conceivable eventuality, so long as we retained command of the sea'. Schuster, equally inevitably, was unconvinced and continued to plug his idea of a special war reserve of actual gold. 'The Bank of England is so circumscribed', he told the subcommittee. 'In ordinary times the system works admirably; but directly there is abnormal pressure, such as is bound to arise on a great war, the Bank of England cannot meet all the commercial needs. There is no doubt about that in my opinion.' In short, the experts could not agree.

Other figures from other parts of the City also gave evidence. The most striking testimony was provided by Robert Ogilvie, a leading underwriter at Lloyd's. He confirmed that there was a large amount of German marine insurance placed in London; and related how in 1905, after German propaganda to the contrary, Lloyd's had emphasised that all claims would be met, even in wartime. There ensued an exchange of views that encapsulated the gulf between economic nationalism and economic liberalism:

Desart. I want to put to you the particular case of a German ship which has been insured in England, captured by a British cruiser and either destroyed or condemned; do you consider your honourable obligation extends as far as paying in that case?

Ogilvie. If we had insured her before the outbreak of war I think so, certainly.

Desart. Just consider the meaning of that.

Ogilvie. Of course bargains are very often unpleasant, or fulfilling them may mean something very unpleasant.

Desart. We are at war with Germany; the navy of your country is endeavouring to put pressure on the Germans by destroying their trade, and in pursuance of that has captured a ship and destroyed it or condemned it, whichever it may be; do you not see that you destroy the whole effect of that act of war by compensating the German owner for the loss he has experienced?

Ogilvie. I quite see that point, and I saw it all through; but that is rather governed, from our point of view, by the honourable carrying out of our bargain.[4]

Elsewhere in its investigations, the subcommittee found that much of Germany's flourishing foreign trade relied on the financial mechanism provided by the City of London; and the same fundamental dichotomy presented itself. Ultimately, British strategic considerations were incompatible with London's continuing role as the world's great financial and commercial clearing house. Not surprisingly then, remarkably few preparations were made over the next two and a half years about what to do with that fine-tuned machinery if war broke out.

Instead, for all their lurking fears, City men preferred to believe that, in the last resort, the worst would not happen. It was a belief that drew much comfort from Norman Angell's highly influential treatise *The Great Illusion*. On 17 January 1912, not long after it had gone into its sixth edition and a few weeks before Ogilvie's evidence, the author delivered a paper to the Institute of Bankers on 'The Influence of Banking on International Relations'. Angell 'drew a crowded audience' and 'his arguments were followed with marked attention and evident sympathy'. At the core of those arguments was the thesis that the world's finance and commerce were now so inextricably entwined, crossing all national boundaries, that the price of war between nation states must be so high as to make the prospect inconceivable. Angell concluded by seeking to refute the often-made charge 'that it is sordid that the conduct of men and nations should be guided by what they are pleased to call money considerations':

This condition of commercial interdependence, which is the special mark of banking as it is the mark of no other profession or trade in quite the same degree – the fact that the interest and the solvency of one is bound up with the interest and solvency of many; that there must be confidence in the due fulfilment of mutual obligation, or whole sections of the edifice crumble, is surely doing a great deal to demonstrate that morality after all is not founded upon self-sacrifice, but upon enlightened self-interest, a clearer and more complete understanding of all the ties which bind us the one to the other. And such clearer understanding is bound to improve, not merely the relationship of one group to another, but the relationship of all men to all other men, to create a consciousness which must make for more efficient human co-operation, a better human society.

The financial journalist W. R. Lawson observed that 'it is very evident that Mr Norman Angell has carried this meeting almost entirely with him', but Huth Jackson at the very end sounded a note of caution: 'It is all very well to get the bankers on your side, but that is not sufficient. What you have to do is to get the whole body of all the peoples in the world on your side.' And he concluded: 'But, gentlemen, bear in mind one thing, and that is that until you get that thing done, there is, I am afraid, little prospect of any change in the international position – that is to say, war will still remain a possibility.'[5] The Institute's president was only a moderately successful senior partner of Huths, but more than most of his fellows he had a grasp of the big picture.

*

Alan 'Tommy' Lascelles was a nephew of the 5th Earl of Harewood and, after coming down from Trinity College, Oxford, tried and failed for the diplomatic service. In September 1911 he had a long talk with Patrick Shaw-Stewart 'on careers, so far as I remember, and the effect of the City on the Soul'. Shaw-Stewart himself, after a glittering undergraduate career at Oxford, had recently migrated to Barings. Two months later a rather doom-laden diarist heard the bell tolling:

> I went early to see Ronnie Norman, who had to tell me of a job which he thought might suit me. It proved to be City, as I expected. Gerry Bevan, a partner in Ellis's, wants men to go into the office on half-commission. I went round to see him at 1 Cornhill, and liked him, and he said I could think about it to the end of the year. Which I shall do. I have always told myself I would never go into the City. But it might be a good thing, temporarily at any rate. Bevan did not disguise the fact that the first eighteen months are hell.

Over the winter Lascelles half-heartedly tried to get a job on *The Times*, but by January realised that journalism was not for him. And at the end of February 1912, admitting defeat, he 'went down to Ellis's, where Bevan introduced me to one of his partners, Tritton, a rather repellent young man, but said to be very successful'. Still, he had made a sound choice. Ellis & Co. was, the company promoter H. Osborne O'Hagan would recall in his memoirs, 'one of the leading firms of London stock brokers, old-established and prosperous'. The firm enjoyed an excellent connection, with Tritton and Bevan both coming out of the Barclays family stable.

Gerard Bevan also had talent on his side. 'Rarely, if ever, have I known a man able to explain a business in a clearer and more concise form than he did', Émile d'Erlanger would recall, adding that 'his command of figures and memory were exceptional'.[6]

Lascelles began at 1 Cornhill on 1 April, not long before his twenty-fifth birthday: 'My first day in the City. I was bored and bewildered, understanding little of what I saw and nothing of what I heard.' The next day, 'Tritton started me off in the Transfer Department, the lowest rung in the ladder. I want to go through the office thoroughly and comprehensively.' Two days later Lascelles was smitten by the romance of finance: 'My fellow clerks are perfectly charming to me, and love me. They spare no pains to explain everything, and in return I think I am beginning to make myself quite useful. It excites me very much. Both sides of this elementary office work appeal to me – the dashing-about with stock to deliver against time, and the book-keeping.' That was on Thursday the 4th. A week and a half later, on Monday the 15th, stock-delivering and book-keeping suddenly seemed unimportant:

> About noon the streets were full of posters announcing that the *Titanic* had struck an iceberg, half-way across the Atlantic on her maiden voyage. She got into touch with the mainland by means of her wireless installation, and hour by hour we were kept informed of her movements. There was something extraordinarily dramatic in the thought of this great overgrown monster wallowing about in mid-ocean, while we in Cornhill could almost watch her flounderings. Then suddenly the messages became blurred and ceased altogether; it was put about – no one yet knows by whom – that all the passengers were saved and that the ship was being towed into Halifax by one of the rescuing liners, and we all went to bed regarding it as a good joke.

Press reports endorsed Lascelles' account. 'Business on the Stock Exchange was again very brisk yesterday, and few departments were without a share in it', began the *FN*'s market résumé compiled on Monday evening. And: 'Consols were made a little easier by way of precaution induced by the alarming reports concerning the "Titanic"; but second thoughts dispelled this anxiety, and the apparition of the government broker in the market sufficed to harden the quotations.'[7]

By Tuesday morning the awful truth was known and, again in the *FN*'s words, 'members came to the City with the one thought uppermost in their minds, and some time elapsed before transactions actually commenced upon anything like a normal scale'. Over the next few days rumours and counter-rumours swelled about the fates of individual City men. Among those who had booked berths but in the end did not undertake the voyage were Vivian Hugh Smith and Robert Benson's son Guy ('very well groomed, quite the young man in the City' was one verdict as he began his career). At least two members of the Stock Exchange drowned. One was Austin Partner: he had become a member on 1 April and joined the broking firm of Meyers & Robertson two days later; the managers were informed that 'he left a widow and children poorly provided for, and it was unanimously resolved under the very exceptional circumstances to return the entrance fee'. The other was J. H. Loring, a partner in the brokers Rose, van Cutsem & Co. Refusing to jump after the boats had gone, 'he was brave to the end, and his farewell words were an expression of love and devotion to his wife and two children.' The Lord Mayor at once set up a *Titanic* relief fund and early donors included the King (500 guineas), the Queen (250 guineas), Speyers (a showy £1,050), Rothschilds (£525), Barings (£500) and the Bank of England (a sober £262 10s). Lloyd's inevitably bore the business brunt, and it was said that the only prominent underwriter who had declined to accept the *Titanic* was Edward Mountain, justly renowned for his intuition. It was an event that acquired, in the City as elsewhere, an instant momentousness. To Natty Rothschild it was 'one more proof, if it was wanted, how natural forces baffle human ingenuity'; while to Lascelles it was 'Nature's most effective *tour de force* since Sodom and Gomorrah', the ill-fated boat having been 'the last word in ostentatious luxury, and the very embodiment of our insolent claims to have conquered the elements'.[8]

Life, however, went on, and later that month the apprentice broker moved from Bedford Court Mansions to Egerton Gardens in South Kensington. May brought an invitation – hardly to be refused – to dine with Bevan at his home in Upper Grosvenor Street:

> His walls are hung with Corots, Raeburns, Hoppners, his wife with strings of pearls – everywhere evidence of excessive wealth. She is a gaunt, slouching woman whom I didn't take to, and who began by asking me if I had found my way all right – as if I had walked from Balham. It was a Dinner-Party of the sort I rarely see, but which I suppose I shall know only too well in middle age. I took a plump, mature sister of Nigel Playfair, the actor, in to dinner.

Later that week Lascelles allowed himself 'a day's respite' from what he now called 'Nibelheim': the short-lived romance was over.[9]

*

The British government and the Marconi Company began negotiations in 1910 over the construction of a chain of long-distance wireless stations round the Empire. They were difficult negotiations, conducted on the company's behalf by Godfrey Isaacs, managing director of the English Marconi Company and brother of Sir Rufus Isaacs, the Attorney General.

At last, on 7 March 1912, the Post Office signified its acceptance of the general terms of Marconi's tender. As the negotiations went on, theoretically in secret, so the shares of English Marconi boomed, from around ¾ at the beginning of 1911 to 9⅞ by 19 April 1912. On that latter date, on which much would turn, dealings were formally begun in London in the shares of the American Marconi Company, seeking to raise its capital from $1.5m to $10m. The natural place to float the issue was indeed London, where in the spring of 1912 Marconis of all descriptions, shares in the Spanish and Canadian companies as well as the English, were booming wildly – especially after details of the *Titanic* disaster and ensuing rescue of survivors began to come through, giving striking proof of the value of wireless telegraphy. In these auspicious circumstances American Marconis were introduced on the London Stock Exchange on 19 April at a considerable premium.[10]

The Marconi boom proved short-lived, and within weeks rumours were rife in the City that Liberal ministers, including the Attorney General, had made use of privileged information to get in on ground-floor terms, sell at the top and thereby make a handsome killing for themselves. On 20 July, in a weekly called the *Outlook*, the intrepid W. R. Lawson came out: 'The Marconi Company has from its birth been a child of darkness. Its finance has been of a most chequered and erratic sort. Its relations with certain Ministers have not always been purely official or political.' Referring to Godfrey Isaacs by name, Lawson went on:

> All the world knows that a similar surname exists among the members of the Asquith Cabinet . . . It is also a matter of common knowledge that the Postmaster-General for the time being bears the honoured name of Samuel. Here we have two financiers of the same nationality pitted against each other, with a third in the background acting perhaps as mutual friend. If expedition and equity could be looked for anywhere, it was surely in such a combination of business and political talent.

During the rest of the summer the investigative and rhetorical running, of an increasingly explicit anti-Semitic character, was made by another weekly, the *Eye-Witness*. Its founder and until recently editor was Hilaire Belloc, whose family history had been moulded by ill-advised stock-market speculation back in the 1870s and who dreamed of an England not only returned to the old faith but expunged of Jewish cosmopolitan finance.[11] By August the phrase 'The Marconi Scandal' was starting to stick, and in October the Commons voted to appoint a select committee of inquiry, which began sitting later that month. Its first few months were concerned mainly with technical matters regarding the contract between the government and Marconi, and it was not until early 1913 that the affair returned to the boil.

Isaacs remained the number one target, and on 25 March 1913 the Attorney General gave evidence to the select committee. He admitted that he had bought American Marconis for himself and other members of the government. 'There was absolutely nothing wrong in the transaction,' Natty Rothschild remarked to his cousins that evening, 'but it was a very stupid thing to do.' That in general, though it is hard to be sure, seems to have been the attitude of the City. A few weeks later *The Economist* described the mood in the Stock Exchange:

> It goes without saying that the House bears little love to the Government. Those, however, who blame some ministers complain not that they had a deal in American Marconis, but that they did not admit it in the House of Commons long ago. Rightly or not, the Stock Exchange appears to see little harm in the fact of ministers having a flutter, like the rest of the world, in American Marconis; and there is a feeling that had they frankly said so when the question first arose nobody would have thought a penny the worse of them after the inevitable newspaper storm had blown itself out. The Stock Exchange critic objects to even a similitude of evasion, and the almost pathetic earnestness with which American Marconis were defended as an 'investment' has enabled the jesters to use that word 'in its Cabinet sense'.[12]

It no doubt helped Stock Exchange spirits that, though Isaacs had shown some business sense, the same could not be said of Lloyd George. From his evidence it was clear that, after an initial profitable deal, he had bought too late, sold too soon, and altogether shown little grasp of how to play the market – even allowing that it was permissible for him to have attempted to do so in the first place. His fumblings were in painful contrast to the cool mastery displayed by Percy Heybourn, the jobber at the centre of the American Marconi market operation. He gave evidence on 9 and 10 April 1913, almost exactly a year after that operation, and proved at least a match for his inquisitors.

He began by describing, albeit with minimal circumstantial detail, how in March 1912 he went over to America with Godfrey Isaacs and agreed to take from him 250,000 American Marconis at 1¼, in other words just over par. Then, on 18 April, as it was clear that there was a boom on his hands, he took from Isaacs first another 50,000 shares at 2⅛ followed later in the day by a further 50,000 at 2⁷⁄₁₆. He then circulated, for the start of business the next morning, a market slip introducing the shares at 3¼. At which point in the narrative Leo Amery, a Tory member of the select committee, asked Heybourn how many of the 250,000 shares he had placed among his friends at 1½ before the 19th – that is, *before* the shares were generally available. 'That is a question I am afraid I cannot answer,' replied the jobber. 'That is entirely my own firm's business. It is not anything material to this enquiry.' A long discussion ensued between the select committee and Heybourn's legal representative, the leading Stock Exchange barrister Walter Schwabe, at the end of which the witness agreed to hand in the following day, for private consideration only, a list of persons with whom he had placed shares. Schwabe explained why Heybourn felt himself unable to go any further:

> The reason is this: I understand my client did place a considerable number of shares with members of the Stock Exchange who are in the habit of following him; that is to say if he has some shares of some company to place they have confidence in him and they take some, some take so many and some so many others. In this particular instance one knows that the price was about 1½ when a large number of those shares were placed. If it is stated in public by the witness how many he placed on that date, he will be conveying to every single one of the persons with whom he dealt what proportion they got of the whole that he had to dispose of, and that he objects very strongly to giving.

There soon followed some fairly friendly questioning from a Liberal MP, Handel Booth, in which Heybourn was asked whether he could defend all that he had done before the Stock Exchange Committee. 'Yes, I was most careful,' was the jobber's reply. Heybourn also explained to Booth that the Marconi boom of the previous spring had not been an artificial one but had sprung out of technical and business developments in wireless, allied to the impact of the *Titanic* disaster:

> It was like a snowball; as the shares rose so it went all over the country. My business was in thousands of small bargains. I should call it a public boom.
> And you being a stock-jobber, if you had kept outside it would have meant that you were neglecting your business? – I was not keeping outside. I had been waiting 14 years for it.
> You were there to do all the business that was going? – Yes.

That was a rare autobiographical glimpse. Heybourn by now was playing for stumps, but at the last had to surmount a Tory attempt to provoke him into disclosing whether he had had an understanding with Godfrey Isaacs over the marketing of the 150,000 shares that Isaacs retained out of his original 500,000, the provocation being that it would have been a dangerous tactic on Heybourn's part not to have had such an understanding. 'That is entirely my affair, I think,' Heybourn replied.[13]

'The Marconi inquiry drags on,' Natty Rothschild wrote to Paris after Heybourn had finished his evidence, 'but it has become very tedious and several members of the Committee know nothing about business and those who do go on asking endless questions which lead to no result.'[14] In fact, the scandal had a further twist left in it, when at the end of April a stockbroker called Charles Fenner was hammered in his absence and a few days later his firm, Montmorency & Co., was declared bankrupt.

From an examination of his books it transpired that the Master of Elibank, until recently the government chief whip, had in the spring of 1912 purchased 3,000 American Marconis for his party. In June the select committee published its reports: a majority one signed by all its Liberal members whitewashing the government; and a minority one, written by Lord Robert Cecil, damning the actions of the ministers. Neither Isaacs nor Lloyd George went to the back benches, as would surely have happened in a later political era; and that autumn Isaacs became Lord Chief Justice, prompting (at first for private circulation only) Kipling's infamous, fiercely anti-Semitic poem *Gehazi*.

Percy Heybourn's personal reckoning was to come. Along with his partners Alexander Croft and William Bagster, Jnr, he was summoned before the Stock Exchange Committee and, though acquitted of having made a false market in American Marconis, was then accused of a breach of trust towards the brokers who had sent orders to his firm before the fateful 19th. Heybourn strongly denied that, in the context of a sharply rising market by the 19th, he had retained an undue proportion of shares for himself and failed to supply the brokers with as many as he had pledged. 'He did not consider that he was in a fiduciary position with regard to the orders he had received. When he bought the two lots of 50,000 he did not know what firm orders he had received, and these orders did not influence him to buy the further amount. At about eight o'clock on the evening of the 18th they started making out a list of orders and were surprised at the number received.' And: 'There appears to be some misapprehension in the minds of the Committee as to orders. We in no instance asked brokers to apply to us for shares but in response to brokers who made enquiries of us all we said was "If you like to send in we will see what we can do."' And again: 'The position in which we were placed was one of extreme difficulty. It was not easy to determine what was the best thing to do in all the circumstances. We gave it very careful consideration and decided upon the course which in our judgement was the right one. I would ask you, gentlemen, what course we should have adopted than this and what you would have done under similar circumstances.' And finally: 'We had every reason to believe that the brokers appreciated and accepted the course we adopted.'

The Committee voted by nineteen to three against accepting Heybourn's explanation and then eighteen to three that Heybourn, Croft and Bagster, trading as Heybourn & Croft, had brought themselves under the dreaded rule 16 about dishonourable conduct. There followed the inevitable letter from Heybourn with the inevitable phrases – 'profoundest astonishment . . . deepest regret . . . honourable association with the Stock Exchange and the members thereof for the past 18 years . . . never a single word or complaint regarding my honesty, integrity, and fair dealings' – but the resolution was confirmed by fifteen votes to four. Punishment awaited, but first the Committee got Heybourn & Croft to hand in a list of the forty-seven broking firms – including five in which members of the Committee were partners – to whom it had sold American Marconis at 1½. On 10 November 1913 the Committee formally announced that Heybourn, Croft and Bagster had each been suspended for five years, the maximum sentence less than expulsion; but that the brokers who had bought shares at such a spectacularly lower price than that available to the public when dealings formally began on the 19th would not be punished, on the tenuous grounds that the shares offered to them personally were for delivery, while those for their clients were for special settlement and they had no authority to buy for their clients for delivery, especially as those clients could have repudiated the bargains. 'The question immediately arises', *The Economist* observed in a justifiably sardonic tone, 'whether, had the clients been given the option of buying at 1½ for delivery, or at 3¼ for special settlement, they would have been likely to have hesitated a minute in their choice.'[15] As for Heybourn, he had brought off his long-nurtured market coup but lost his livelihood: yet another occasion when a Stock Exchange man cursed the existence of politicians.

The Marconi Scandal was *the* City story of 1912–13, but life in Capel Court continued to follow its predictably unpredictable rhythm. 'Stock Exchange's First Derby Throws Business in the Shade' was the *FN*'s headline on 6 June 1912, after Walter Raphael's Tagalie had come home by several lengths, heavily backed by the owner's fellow members. Four months later the House's predictive powers were put to a more significant test. Natty Rothschild on 2 October referred to 'the numerous on dits and canards which have been circulated in the Stock Exchange all day', on the 3rd to how 'in the Stock Exchange as usual endless rumours have been in circulation'. The cause was yet another Balkan crisis. According to *The Economist*, on Saturday the 5th, members had shown commendable calmness and done much to steady public nerves:

> The House declined to be ruffled. Prices went flat, and the markets, instead of giving way to fear, remained quite cheerful. The papers spoke of panic on the Bourses; the Stock Exchange went in its scores to see an impromptu fountain in Broad street . . . Somebody in the House started the grave report that Servia had ordered 2,000 lbs of powder, but this was not taken seriously. The Stock Exchange never does believe in war until war breaks out, but it takes time by the forelock in a liberal lowering of prices in advance . . . Doubtless the House has earned a sort of surprised respect for refusing to lose its head, and if part of the credit for this comes as the natural result of incurable, traditional optimism, by far the greater share is due to sober common-sense of members as a whole.

But the members got it wrong, and within days Turkey was at war with Montenegro, Bulgaria, Greece and Serbia. Prices crashed, though to general surprise there were only three failures. By February 1913 there was still a Balkan cloud hanging over the markets, as business one day ground almost to a halt. 'The brokers moving round the House merely stopped to chat with the jobbers standing idly from 11 o'clock to 4 o'clock', noted *The Economist*. 'That they "have never seen anything like it before" is the old cry of Stock Exchange men; that they "don't know what things are coming to" is its necessary corollary.'

A fastidious jobber called Duncan Scott had weightier matters on his mind. 'I shall be much obliged if you can see your way', he wrote to the managers the following month, 'to point out officially to Mr Norman Herbert that the towels placed in the members' lavatory are not intended to be used as handkerchiefs. It is with great regret that I should have to bring this disgusting practice to your notice, but do so in the interests of fellow members who use the washing room.' Herbert had been a member since 1879 (twenty-two years before Scott's admission) and the Committee, to whom the letter was passed on, declined to take action. Peace eventually broke out in the Balkans, but 1913 as a whole was not a good year for Stock Exchange business. Even the annual pre-Christmas japes had something forced about them, 'like drinking a sparkling wine without the sparkle' thought *The Economist*. However, 'huge hilarity was caused by a quite novel game introduced into the markets through the agency of the balloons such as are loved by even smaller children. Water was artfully poured into some of these toys, which were then thrown into one of the popular markets always ready for a game. When the inevitable burst came those underneath received unexpected showers, and this sort of thing went on for quite a long time.'[16]

The Stock Exchange, approaching the end of an era, was still fundamentally overmanned. In October, Teddy Grenfell of Morgans in London (by now called Morgan Grenfell) observed to a New York partner that 'most of the smaller Brokers find it hard to get a square meal and are in a very sad way'.[17] Still, at least the partners of Helbert Wagg had done their bit for their fellow brokers – by deciding to leave the Stock Exchange altogether. Their reason was threefold. The firm since the turn of the century had increasingly lost out to Panmure Gordon as 'pet brokers' to Rothschilds, especially in the lucrative area of placing underwriting; its gifted recent recruit from Japhets, Adolph Schwelm, was pushing hard for the firm's business to assume a larger, more financial character; and thirdly, perhaps the decisive factor, the firm had been in the vanguard of unsuccessfully opposing the introduction of a fixed scale of commissions, culminating in March 1912 when Arthur Wagg, a member of the Stock Exchange Committee for some forty years, was unceremoniously turfed out. 'Great City Sensation' announced the *Globe* on 6 December 1912, as the firm's decision became known. A day or two earlier Alfred Wagg had paid a courtesy visit to Rothschilds to tell them what was afoot. The grace note was conspicuous by its absence:

> On arriving at New Court, I asked to see Lord Rothschild privately and he came to see me in a little room at the back of the building. I gave him the letter, the terms of which couldn't have been nicer. He sat down and read it attentively. He then got up saying 'Well, you know your own business best', and walked out of the room. Not one word of good wishes or of regret that the hundred year old intimate connection between the two firms was to cease.[18]

*

Probably little of all this engaged the thoughts of Montagu Norman.[19] 'We much regret', Brown Shipley wrote just before Christmas 1912 to Brown Brothers in New York, 'to have to inform you that Mr Norman's health has lately been giving us considerable anxiety. He has worked at the Office consistently and steadily since his return last April . . . The last few days he has been suffering a great deal, and it has now been decided that he must take a trip of some weeks' duration in order to give his health a chance of recovery.' It had been decided therefore to send Norman, with another partner as a companion for him, on a swing through Trinidad and the West Indies, thence up to the West Coast of the USA, and eventually reaching Vancouver in March, 'when we think it is quite possible that some important business with regard to a new loan for the City will have to be decided'. It was only because there was this eventual working purpose involved, the letter added, that 'we were able to persuade Mr Norman to take such a long absence from this Office'. February found Norman in Panama, where he met a sympathetic bank manager who recommended the treatment of certain Swiss physicians, among them Carl Jung. With this hope in mind, Norman soon afterwards came straight back home from Costa Rica, not continuing with the proposed trip to Vancouver. His firm remained admirably sympathetic. 'Mr Norman, we much regret to say, is still very poorly,' it wrote to New York on 4 April, 'and is shortly leaving for Switzerland to see if he cannot obtain some opinion which will at any rate get at the bottom of the trouble from which he is suffering, and put him in the right line to recovery.' Norman had three sessions with Jung, but they failed to do the trick, and by May he was in Lausanne seeing a new doctor. This was a specialist in nervous diseases and he was sufficiently effective that Norman was back – if not necessarily back in harness – at Founders' Court by September. A snatch of Brown Shipley correspondence two months later catches him negotiating with the general manager of the

Stockholm Handelsbank a possible loan for the City of Stockholm that in the event went to Hambros.

What, though, had really happened in April 1913 between him and Jung, an encounter of two twentieth-century icons? It seems that Jung tested Norman's blood and spinal fluid and, though the results were negative, reckoned that Norman's general condition was such that he was unlikely to survive the summer. Norman had, Jung believed, the symptoms of syphilis, causing general paralysis of the insane. If so, it was not a judgement he openly shared with his patient. Norman himself at the time paraphrased Jung's stated opinion:

> Perfectly sound throughout, including blood serum etc., but head entirely exhausted and therefore unresponsive. Consequently unable to undergo his or any other cure. After a complete rest, lasting a 'lot of months', may come back to him and if sufficiently recovered, shall go thro' his treatment . . . Meanwhile lead quiet, easy, selfish life: no work at all: plenty of rest and amusement: travelling (and tropics): bed: massage and medicine useless: grub and air good . . . Cannot predict time needed for recovery nor ultimate result.

'That verdict was the finishing touch', he wrote later, 'having been going slowly downhill ever since January; I collapsed and nursed a raging head'.[20]

Norman retained his position as a director of the Bank of England, but had nothing to do with the gold reserves question that so dominated pre-war banking debate. In February 1913, at the by now well-established quarterly meeting between the Bank and the leading joint-stock bankers, Governor Cole took the chair for the last time and decided to move the thorny issue into a new phase. He pointed out that whereas at the end of 1892 the total liabilities (in deposit and current accounts) of the clearers was £256m to the Bank's £42m, twenty years later it was £616m to £67m. He argued that the government had done its bit: 'It has of recent years increased its balances at the Bank of England and thereby does assist in maintaining Gold against those deposits.' He also argued that the Bank itself was in the clear: 'You will find by its published figures that its average proportion [i.e. of cash to liabilities] which in 1892 was 44.2 per cent increased in 1902 to 46.4 per cent and in 1912 to 47.8 per cent. The Bank of England has to earn a dividend for its shareholders like any other bank, and if it keeps a proportion of cash approximately towards 50 per cent I, personally, do not think it can be asked to do more.' Cole then looked the joint-stock men straight in the eye: 'The question I want to put to the Clearing Bankers is – Has their reserve of cash to liabilities increased during late years in the same ratio as the figures I have given you for the Bank of England?'[21] The implication was clearly – and correctly – that they had not. Faced by this challenge, the decision was taken soon afterwards to set up a new Clearing Bankers' Gold Reserves Committee, this time to be chaired by Lord St Aldwyn, the former Hicks Beach. Its formation was publicly revealed early in April, just before the end of Cole's governorship, and the first meeting was set for 7 May.

Holden, to no one's surprise, spoke first. 'Bankers should not allow themselves to be subject to the criticism, from practically all over the world, that they did not assist the Bank of England in holding a sufficient amount of gold. He thought they held a large amount, but the public did not know it.' He therefore put forward his familiar suggestion involving compulsory publication of balance sheets showing the amount of gold held. Tritton of Barclays was unwilling to go so far. Rather, 'the first step was to ascertain as far as possible the amount of gold held by the bankers'; and he reckoned that, since 1900, the banks had increased their gold holdings from £25m to £50m.[22] Tritton's resolution, that confidential returns be requested concerning gold holdings on 28 May next, was unanimously adopted.

The secret census was duly taken, and on 11 June the CBGRC was informed that the quantity of gold held in British banks was just under £45m, compared with just under £38m at the Bank of England. St Aldwyn asked if £45m was a satisfactory figure, to which both Schuster and Holden 'dissented'. Holden still demanded compulsory publication and Schuster as usual disagreed. St Aldwyn for his part wanted the recently compiled figures communicated to the Bank, to see whether it 'had any observations to make concerning them'. Tritton demurred, saying that they should first report to the clearing banks themselves the result of the inquiry – for 'he had found a good deal of suspicion in the minds of the banking fraternity that something might be sprung upon them'. The discussion was adjourned for a week, whereupon Holden said that although he himself still wanted legislation to ensure compulsory publication, he accepted that most round the table did not; and so he called on his fellow bankers to decide upon a policy and adopt it voluntarily. It was eventually decided to send a deputation, including Schuster and Holden, to discuss the return with the Bank's new governor, Walter Cunliffe.[23]

There was, meanwhile, another aspect to the whole question. Holden maintained an animosity towards the India Office, derived in part from his recent campaign to establish a gold currency in India, thereby he believed reducing the drain of gold from London. Holden's intervention was part of a complex background, also involving the Montagu silver scandal, that led to the establishment in 1913 of a Royal Commission, chaired by Austen Chamberlain, on Indian finance and currency.[24] Cole, explicitly representing the Bank, gave evidence on 27 June, and

Chamberlain asked him whether he regarded the existing system – highly developed since the turn of the century, by which the India Office lent out India's substantial balances to the London money market – as 'open to objection in principle'. Cole replied in the affirmative, stating that it weakened the Bank's control over the money market. 'That control is the only buttress for the gold reserve of England?' Chamberlain asked. 'Quite correct', the former governor confirmed. Nevertheless, as Cole conceded later in his evidence, the lending out of India's balances was, in a sense, of benefit to the London market, in that it lowered the rates of discount – even if it did not help the Bank of England in terms of maintaining the gold reserve.

It was a tension that the young, super-confident John Maynard Keynes, a member of the Commission and author of *Indian Currency and Finance* (published a fortnight earlier), explored in his questioning of Cole:

> *The view of the Bank of England is that any increase in the extent to which London is an international money market makes their time a more anxious one?* – Any increase in the volume of transactions which pass through London for which the London money market is responsible, makes the maintenance of an adequate gold reserve here all the more important.
>
> *. . . You would not wish London to be less an international money market, would you?* – No; I want to see England maintained as the international money market, and that it should have the position it holds today.
>
> *Then you would be sorry rather than glad if India was to give up holding its balances here?* – From the point of view of the Bank of England I would rather they were what I call kept within more moderate limits; that is all.
>
> *From the point of view of the position of the money market, you would be sorry?* – I should not be sorry; it is merely a question of size.[25]

It was the first of Keynes' run-ins against the Old Lady, though on the larger question they were agreed, as against Holden, that India should retain a gold-exchange rather than a gold standard as such.

The CBGRC met again on 30 July, and it was agreed to communicate the results only to the clearing banks, not to the wider world. It was with some justice that the *Bankers' Magazine*, in its September editorial, took the line that the whole question was being shrouded in needless secrecy and that 'the public may perhaps be fairly excused in imagining either that the problem of higher gold reserves is incapable of solution or that action is chronically crippled by disagreement among the eminent banking experts'.[26]

Apparently unmoved, the Committee did not meet again until 12 November. Schuster now made his old suggestion of an independent secondary reserve, but kept physically at the Bank of England. In response Holden laid into Schuster before deliberately upping the ante:

> Sir Felix Schuster had not told the Committee if the total of gold, under his scheme, would be published, and the conditions under which each banker could withdraw it . . . Further, Sir Felix had not told the Committee what would be the effect of any withdrawal of such gold, and how it would reflect on the whole and not any particular bank . . . If the Committee could not come to any agreement in the matter, he personally would most strongly recommend his directors to publish their gold: he felt that if one bank published its gold, that bank would have a tremendous advantage over the others.

Having fired his big gun, Holden stayed silent for the rest of the meeting. St Aldwyn tried to mediate. 'It would be a pity', he observed, 'if, the meeting having expressed its opinion, there was any independent action such as Sir Edward had outlined'; and 'he could not see why some arrangement should not be made whereby the banks would keep a certain amount of gold ready to assist the Bank of England if required'. It was then unanimously passed that the Committee should be supplied twice a year with a return of gold coin and bullion held by the joint-stock banks. Just before the meeting broke up, Tritton (a supporter of Schuster) 'insisted' that 'the City of London must be spared the ignominy of going to the Bank of France for gold', a lame end to another largely fruitless session.[27]

The situation was not helped by the fact that the governor at this time was Cunliffe, one of the City's more rebarbative figures.[28] 'A little of Mr Cunliffe's society fills me up for the year', Teddy Grenfell had remarked to Jack Morgan a few years earlier, and the opinion seems to have been general. Even so, that rude and arrogant, not unaccomplished operator was only part – however vivid, even extreme a part – of a larger duality already located at the heart of the City for arguably a quarter of a century or more. In a crucial if ill-documented area, key testimony comes from a former governor, W. M. Campbell, discussing privately in 1917 whether the Bank should at last allow professional, joint-stock bankers to become Bank directors:

> I am strongly convinced that it would be of great value if some scheme could be devised, whereby the responsibility of national Banking could be shared with the Directors of our great Joint Stock Banks.
>
> This was aimed at some years ago, in Cole's governorship, & meetings took place – & they were I know appreciated – but unfortunately they have been wrecked by the present governor [Cunliffe] – and the bitter feeling which now exists, not with all but with most, will prevent any foregathering for some time.
>
> There is somehow an innate antagonism against the Bank of England, very largely due to the 'Superior' manners of some past governors.[29]

Campbell's account applied partly to events after the outbreak of war, but by no means wholly. On the eve of 1914 itself, Tritton and Schuster were genuinely seeking to bridge the gap, but found themselves outflanked by Holden on the one hand, Cunliffe on the other. It was not a happy prospect.

CHAPTER TWENTY
August Guns

On 29 June 1914, Natty Rothschild had much on his mind. Earlier in the month he had finally reached an agreement with the French and German groups over the terms for an unavoidable £20m Brazilian loan. According to Teddy Grenfell, who had attended some of the meetings, Natty had 'made strenuous efforts to get better terms for Brazil than were acceptable to other Bankers'. Now, however, the Brazilian government was unable to make up its mind whether to accept the terms, including as they did the hypothecation of the customs duties for the service of all the country's loans, as well as weekly remittances to London; and Natty informed his cousins that the issue of a loan would have to be deferred until the autumn at the earliest. He added, almost as an after-thought:

> The fate of the late Archduke Franz Ferdinand and of his wife is an awful tragedy. It is a sad example both of Servian brutality, the hatred of the Greek church for those of the Catholic Faith and last but not least of the morals and doctrines of the anarchical party.

Morals were one thing, markets another, and next day the *FT* breathed reassurance. 'The tragic death of the heir to the Austrian throne and his wife was taken calmly by the Foreign market', it noted, before moving on to other matters.[1] The City as a whole went about its normal business. For those paid to peek their heads over the parapet, Natty's view on 14 July that 'there is a considerable amount of anxiety in some circles about Austro-Servian relations, but . . . the chief source of anxiety here is always Ulster' would have found general consent. 'Lockwood's London Letter' to investors in the *FT* on Saturday the 18th was as cheery as ever: 'There has certainly been no definite happening in the week which gives ground for alarm. The friction between Austria and Servia is of long-standing, and there is no more reason to suppose that peace is threatened more seriously at this time than at any other'.[2]

The mood on Monday morning was altogether darker. 'Everything seems to be going wrong everywhere at present, but I hope the sun will shine again one day', Teddy Grenfell wrote to New York; and in the Foreign market 'a heavy tone' prevailed, the *FT* reported, 'owing to the weakness of the Continental Bourses, where fears were entertained regarding Austrian-Servian relations'. The next day it was still unclear how Vienna would respond to the assassination, let alone what would be the outcome of the Buckingham Palace conference that was beginning on Ulster, and markets continued 'in a nervous and depressed condition'. Farrer was just back from a long stay in America, and he wrote to Kidder Peabody in Boston: 'I find everyone here in very good spirits and many of them soon to disperse for their holidays. Business unfortunately at a low ebb and political affairs both at home and in the Near East in too disturbed a state to make anyone even wish for greater activity.' There was no change on Wednesday the 22nd, 'A Dismal Tone' being the *FT*'s markets headline. Natty Rothschild, however, was inclined to a cautious optimism: 'Nothing definite is known about an Austrian Ultimatum, but I rather fancy the well founded belief in influential quarters that unless Russia backed up Servia the latter will eat humble pie and that the inclination in Russia is to remain quiet, circumstances there not favouring a forward movement.'[3] Even the man of all City men supposed to be on the inside track could only whistle in the wind.

And all the time the machine whirred on. 'At certain points where the mass of humanity is more than usually congested – for example, at Liverpool Street Station between 8.30 a.m. and 10 a.m. or on London Bridge about 6 p.m. – the spectacle is really startling, alike in the magnitude of the aggregate, and in the hurried, serious, preoccupied aspect of the human units who compose it.' So Ellis Powell in 1910 introduced his readers to *The Mechanism of the City*, a Darwinian treatise in which the author (a leading financial journalist) claimed that 'the life of the City generates in those who live it an intellectual alertness, a rapidity of apprehension, an up-to-dateness which is quite a unique psychological phenomenon'. The census taken in 1911 showed that on one day in April between seven in the morning and seven in the evening, just over a million people and almost 100,000 vehicles (the majority horse-drawn) entered the City; while in terms of those who worked full-time, the 1911 total was 364,000 (compared with 301,000 twenty years earlier), of whom only 20,000 were residents.[4]

Yet neither on Lloyd's nor on the Stock Exchange, nor indeed in the City as a whole, was there likely to be the infusion of a more dynamic approach as long as the dominant unit remained the small or smallish family-run firm. Costs were low, business usually adequately plentiful, the way of life pleasant enough and generally undemanding – what incentive was there to turn a club into a meritocracy? The City was, in short, still a very personal world full of 'people' businesses.

Connection remained paramount; but crucially, the lifeblood of foreign talent – the tradition of Rothschild and Hambro, of Peabody, Kleinwort and Cassel – showed no sign of drying up. How did the City, grown increasingly jingoistic, even xenophobic over the past quarter of a century, view the continuing stream of newcomers from abroad? '"Another half-commissioned officer in the 64th Highlanders," said a grim old member of the Committee, when an evidently Semitic applicant for membership presented himself with a name that had been distinguished in the charge of the clansmen at Prestonpans.' Hartley Withers, in his 1910 guide to the Stock Exchange, then explained the allusion: 'This jibe riddled in one sentence the readiness of a certain class of foreign immigrant to deal for half the usual commissions, their introduction of the sixty-fourth of a pound as a fraction in Stock Exchange business, whereas the thirty-second had hitherto been the smallest division known, and their passion for disguising their origin.' Withers, sanest of City commentators and the nearest to Bagehot's heir, went on: 'English members sometimes growl at the manner in which their brethren of alien extraction cut the terms on which business is done, but it is probable that the Stock Exchange, like many other English industries, has learnt a great deal from foreign influence, and has been saved by it from the "take it or leave it" attitude which is one of the vices of our national character, except when we are spurred by the example of a keener and more hardworking race.' One of those alien brethren was a jobber called George Merzbach, a member of the House since 1904. In the words of his partner Conrad Russell, son of Lord Arthur Russell: 'His person is not handsome, his birthplace Frankfort a/m. His religion unreformed Jew. He is the best and kindest man in the world.'[5] Not all the locals, aristocrats by neither birth nor nature, were as liberal-minded.

Despite New York, despite Paris, despite Berlin – each of them on the rise – London in 1914 was still the leading international financial and commercial centre.[6] As the world's only free gold market, it offered a unique attraction to overseas depositors; it was the centre of international banking; bills of exchange drawn on London financed most of the world's trade; its capital market raised almost half the world's total exported capital; it remained the main market for insurance, many commodities, and such specialist activities as the chartering of ships. The City was as much as ever the indispensable place. Only one thing could spoil the party.

*

Thursday 23 July was reasonably steady in the markets, but the next day the City was hit by a double blow: the failure of the Buckingham Palace conference and the news that Austria had presented an ultimatum.[7] 'It is to be hoped that Servia will give every satisfaction', Natty Rothschild wrote to Paris. Teddy Grenfell described this Friday as 'one of the most depressing days in the Markets here, Berlin and Paris that I can remember'; the Smith St Aubyn journal noted 'pessimism everywhere', with 'Bourses very nearly in panic'. Lockwoods on Saturday morning did his usual uplift job – 'it is probable that the difficulties between Austria and Servia have been exaggerated' – but the Stock Exchange proceeded to have its worst day of price falls since 1870 and the discount market, according to Smith St Aubyn, 'stopped working'. Farrer by chance was in the City, unusually for him on a Saturday, and (he would recall) 'learned that some of the foreign bill brokers were offering large lines of the finest bank acceptances at 3⅛ without finding buyers; obviously someone had taken alarm'. Sunday was spent thinking about Monday. 'I have an appointment in the City at 12 o'c I cannot miss,' the stockbroker Ranald Laurie wrote to his client Francis Whitmore, 'and tomorrow is Settling day, and a beastly anxious one at that! with all these wars & rumours of wars about, & there is a lot of financial trouble all over the City.'[8]

'The Slump in Missouris' was the *FT*'s main leader on Monday the 27th, but the breaks were now everywhere. 'The end-July Settlement commenced under disastrous conditions,' the paper's market report written that evening began. 'The gravity of the war menace in Eastern Europe was such as to dwarf all other considerations.' With 'conditions in discount market chaotic', Smith St Aubyn drew some temporary comfort from the fact that 'on the whole the Joint Stock Banks behaved well' and did not call in too many loans. Serbia by now had rejected the Austrian ultimatum; and Brien Cokayne, a Bank of England director and partner in Antony Gibbs, informed a correspondent that 'the general feeling seems to be that there will not be war on the Continent, but it is by no means certain'.[9]

Next day, Tuesday, the discount market started to come under pressure from the joint-stock banks, which (following the example of foreign banks based in London) were also calling in loans from Stock Exchange firms, as well as starting to withdraw gold in significant quantities from the Bank of England itself. 'A Day of Forced Sales' was the *FT*'s market headline: 'From start to finish, with scarcely one rallying interlude, the Stock Exchange today has been plunged in gloom . . . While on Saturday and yesterday much of the selling came from holders who were scared into throwing stocks overboard, the heaviest liquidation of stock today consisted of stock that simply had to be sold, because the facilities for carrying it had been summarily removed.' Foreign bonds fell particularly sharply – 'hardly surprising', the *FT* commented, 'having regard to the way in which the Bourses have allowed London to be the dumping-ground for Europe', with the main continental stock exchanges being more or less closed by this stage in the crisis. In which light, 'London has risen to the occasion as the world's financial centre.'[10] Shortly after the House closed, news came through that Austria had formally declared war.

On Wednesday the 29th, the *FT* opened its evening market report with the bald sentence: 'This has been one of the worst days in the history of the Stock Exchange.' Seven firms were hammered, jobbers practically refused to make prices, and 'a further severe fall' took place in all markets, Consols at one point reaching 69½. Brown Shipley explained to its New York partners that 'the oldest Members of the Stock Exchange do not remember any time when London has been so near a panic'. As for the money market, where business continued very restricted, Smith St Aubyn recorded that 'the Joint Stock Banks began calling today in earnest and a very bad feeling was evident'.[11]

Natty Rothschild, meanwhile, gave an interview to the *Pall Mall Gazette* in which he claimed that 'there is more chance of the war being localised'; but Revelstoke, after much indecision, decided this day not to travel to Aix-les-Bains for his usual summer holiday. There were also two significant meetings. Bradbury of the Treasury paid a visit to the City, where Cunliffe, Cole, Revelstoke and Hambro all assured him that the Bank of England had the situation well under control; and at four thirty, St Aldwyn and the bankers convened at the Bankers' Clearing House. There the Gold Reserves Committee basically agreed the scheme that had been put to them a week earlier by Holden and Tritton, a scheme at last involving a coherent, united, independent approach to the gold reserves question by the joint-stock banks. It would now go before the Clearing House Committee and then, apparently, to the Bank of England. 'Before rising, Sir Felix Schuster expressed the thanks of the Committee to the Chairman for his conduct in the Chair and referred to the fact that this was the first Committee he had known which had reached the present stage.' The next meeting was arranged for Thursday 13 August – but would never be held.[12]

'Prices Again Heavily Down' was the familiar story in Capel Court on Thursday the 30th. There were few dealings, 'the virtual cessation of the usual practice of price-making', and 'prices fell in very limp fashion, closing at the bottom'. The day's failures included Derenburg & Co., brokers doing a large business with Germany. By this stage the atmosphere inside the House was reasonably calm, and it seems that many members drifted outside, with the City's bars and restaurants doing a roaring trade. 'Cheerful Stoicism' the *FT* called it:

> In face of the declaration and practice of war between Austria and Servia, with all its possibilities of a general European conflagration, Throgmorton Street indulges in high spirits. Edition after edition of the evening papers comes out, with staring announcements of panic. It is doubtful if their sensations sell a copy. The Prince of Wales' Stakes [at Goodwood] have a

keener interest. Your City man likes something that is moving. The Stock Exchange is not moving. It hasn't been moving for a long time . . . A horse-race is an event with immediate possibilities of gain or loss. You know the best or you know the worst.

'They talk in rather a loose way of closing the House', Natty mentioned to Paris; and indeed Panmure Gordon's Willie Koch, a leading stockbroker, proposed that day to the Stock Exchange Committee that it be closed on the morrow 'in view of the exceptional circumstances existing', but it was agreed to delay the decision until Friday morning itself. The real alarm on Thursday, however, resided more in the parlours of the accepting houses, becoming increasingly aware that remittances due to London from the Continent were drying up, and in the money market. Bank rate that day went up from 3 to 4 – modest enough, given that the Bank had shelled out £14m to the discount market in the past three days and almost as much again to the banking system.[13]

On Friday the Stock Exchange Committee closed the House until further notice, and Bank rate was doubled. Smith St Aubyn's diary entry was all the more expressive for its brevity: 'A bad day. Looks like panic. All business ceased.' With the clearing banks now starting to refuse or semi-refuse to pay out sovereigns, a queue formed outside the Bank of England, people going there to exchange notes for gold. On the steps of the Royal Exchange a crowd gathered to watch, no doubt including some homeless members of the Stock Exchange, others of whom found relief playing dominoes in the long room at Lyons. At one point a red-cloaked Bank of England official shouted ironically to the queue, 'Silver! Anybody want silver? Plenty of silver going cheap.' But he was greeted only with silent, sardonic smiles.[14]

In the distant, unimaginable world outside, Austria was mobilising against Russia. 'The situation looks very black', Cokayne wrote to his correspondent. 'Credit has already virtually broken down & the Bank Act will be suspended shortly.' Hope had not yet gone of the European conflict being localised – 'there are persistent rumours in the City', Natty told Paris, 'that the German Emperor is using all his influence at both St Petersburg & Vienna to find a solution which would not be distasteful either to Austria or to Russia' – but the main focus was the financial crisis itself. In particular, as Natty also related, there was that day 'a great deal of talk among a great many of the large Houses in favour of a "Moratorium"', talk that was particularly urgent on the part of houses like Kleinworts and Schröders who did a large German and Central European acceptance business. 'There is a great deal to be said for & against this policy,' Natty thought, 'but on the whole after very mature consideration, under the circumstances, it would be more than justified.'[15]

Saturday 1 August opened with the money market on the rack. The discount market was further handicapped by the Bank of England's reflex action, one that in the particular situation was wholly counter-productive, of raising Bank rate by a further two points, so that it attained the traditional 'crisis rate' of 10 per cent. With the clearing banks still more or less refusing to pay out sovereigns, an even longer queue than the previous day's straggled from inside the Bank into its courtyard. With the necessity looming of a large-scale issue of notes in order to protect the remaining gold reserves, Cunliffe managed by the end of the morning to obtain that familiar prop of any full-blown financial crisis since 1847 – namely, a 'Chancellor's letter' permitting suspension, if need be, of the Bank Charter Act.

No one this Saturday imagined that would be enough. 'The joint stock banks have made absolute fools of themselves and behaved very badly': so Basil Blackett at the Treasury wrote to Keynes in Cambridge, imploring him to come to London as soon as possible. Or as Patrick Shaw-Stewart of Barings correctly appraised the bigger picture, if perhaps overestimating the City's sangfroid: 'The simple fact is that, while there is no panic in London and no one is "talked about" or in a weak position, yet the entire existing machinery of credit is unequal to the international situation, and something new has got to be devised to carry us along.'[16]

On Sunday the 2nd, war was formally declared between Russia and Germany, a divided Cabinet discussed British policy long and fruitlessly, and the City's leading figures began to spend much of their time at the Treasury engaged in high-level consultations. By the end of the day it was clear that a month-long moratorium would, against Cunliffe's wishes, be granted for bills of exchange, thereby saving the skins of several accepting houses. Meanwhile, the leading joint-stock bankers, joined for the purpose by the managers of Union Discount and National Discount, devoted most of the afternoon and evening to lengthy meetings that eventually produced a coherent plan of action on the non-accepting side of the crisis. Writing to Lloyd George at 2 a.m. that night, Robert Martin-Holland (hon. secretary of the Clearing Bankers) outlined its main points: a subvention by the bankers to the Bank of up to £15m in gold; the issue as soon as possible of up to £45m of notes; suspension of the Bank Charter Act, including suspension of cash (i.e. gold) payments as soon as £1 notes were issued; and the application of a general moratorium. Such a package would, Martin-Holland asserted on behalf of Holden and the rest, 'allow of the business of this country being carried on under the present financial conditions which seem likely to become more onerous at every moment'.[17]

Monday, fortunately, was a bank holiday anyway. At a meeting that Cunliffe convened at the Bank that morning, all the leading bankers and others insisted that three more days of holiday were needed if adequate measures were to be taken. Cunliffe passed the request on to Lloyd George, who readily agreed. 'Saved for the time being' was Smith St Aubyn's graphic diary entry. Lloyd George himself was by this time shifting decisively towards the interventionist camp; and on Monday afternoon, against a background of the German ultimatum to Belgium and its rejection, Grey made his historic statement in the Commons that in effect committed Britain to military action. 'War seems to be an absolute certainty', Teddy Grenfell wrote to a former Morgans partner.[18]

Keynes by now was ensconced at the Treasury – having ridden down from Cambridge in the sidecar of his brother-in-law's motorcycle – and in the course of Monday the 3rd he wrote for Lloyd George a memorandum that, in the words of an appended note, argued 'if the foreign drain is not likely to be very large [which all the indications so far were that it would not be], and the internal drain can be obviated by other means [he had in mind mainly the issue of notes], it is difficult to see how such an extreme and disastrous measure as the suspension of cash payments can be justified'. Suspension, Keynes insisted, would 'damage our prestige as a free gold market'. And, in the memorandum itself, he took the forceful line that, 'if we suspend now, a marked tendency will set in for the secondary countries to keep a far larger proportion of their free resources in gold at home'. Nor was that all:

> Other important classes of business, as is well known, depend also, though much more indirectly, upon a continuance of this confidence. The existence of this confidence in the past has been one of the most important *differentiations* between London and Paris or Berlin. It ought not to be endangered except for the very gravest cause.[19]

Still a full believer in economic liberalism – the creed of free-trading internationalism with the City of London and all-powerful gold standard at the very centre – Keynes saw no reason why the golden age should end simply because of the panic-struck reaction of a bunch of joint-stock bankers seemingly incapable of distinguishing the suspension of specie payments from the suspension of the Bank Charter Act.

'More meetings at the Union Disc. Much talk & little done.' Smith St Aubyn's experience was no doubt mirrored elsewhere in the City on Tuesday the 4th, a day of shut banks, closed markets and little visible excitement. The leading accepting houses each received an invitation from Huth Jackson to gather at Huths at noon the following day to discuss the position. There was still a lot of talking to be done – above all at the House of Commons, where in late afternoon there began what would turn into a three-day conference between Lloyd George, various other politicians, and what the minutes described as 'representative bankers and traders'. After Yorkshire industrialists had stressed the need to be able to pay wages to their workforces on Friday, Holden endorsed their remarks from a banking point of view. The 'traders' then withdrew, while the bankers stayed behind. After some sparring about how many notes would be ready by Friday morning, Lloyd George – who had almost certainly read Keynes' memorandum earlier in the day – asserted that 'we are not ready for a suspension of specie', a policy that hitherto it had been assumed that he endorsed. To which Holden, still seeing the suspension of gold as inextricably linked to the emergency issuing of notes, replied: 'We are all against it, but it is a matter of life and death to us.' A little later, with the traders back in the room, there occurred a charged exchange between an unnamed colleague of Holden's and Cunliffe:

> *A Banker:* I understand one of the difficulties today is that the Bank of England cannot help us because they are afraid of a run on the gold supply. It is really a question for the governor of the Bank of England whether he wants people to come and ask for specie and not get it.
>
> *The governor of the Bank of England:* It is not true that if the Bank is open today I could not pay my way in gold.
>
> *A Banker:* I am very glad to hear it.
>
> *The governor of the Bank of England:* And if you could see the accounts of the Bank, which the Chancellor of the Exchequer has seen, you would be surprised that there is so much fuss.[20]

The question of abandoning the gold standard had become the new symbol of an old power struggle; and fortified by the support of Lloyd George and the Treasury, Cunliffe was not the man to underplay his hand. At about eight o'clock the conference broke up. Three hours later the British ultimatum to Germany expired.

*

Later in 1914, no longer at the centre of events, Keynes recalled the crisis. 'Schuster and Holden were the spokesmen of the bankers . . . The one was cowardly and the other selfish. They unquestionably behaved badly . . . By no means all of the other bankers trusted Schuster or Holden or agreed with their immediate proposals; but they were timid, voiceless and leaderless and in the hurry of the times did not make themselves heard.' Specifically, he levelled four charges against the bankers: that they had failed to stand by the Stock Exchange and thus prevent its closure; that by precipitately calling in loans from the discount houses, and thereby forcing those houses to borrow at punitive rates from the Bank, they had brought the money market 'near to demoralisation'; that the internal drain of gold had been caused 'not by the public running on the banks, but by the banks running on the Bank of England'; and that they had been needlessly ready 'to force suspension of specie payment on the Bank of England, while its resources were still intact, without one blow struck for the honour of our old traditions or future good name'.[21] Historians since have sought to defend or at least to explain the bankers' actions – on the grounds of most of their assets having become illiquid (as Holden stressed several times on the 4th), of their fear of gold hoarding by the public, of their wish for self-aggrandising reasons to maximise their own contributions to the emergency pool of gold once the government had accepted their gold-for-notes plan – but whatever the validity of these interpretations, Keynes' larger claim is surely justified: this was not the joint-stock men's finest hour.[22]

Was it anyone's? 'In these troublesome times everyone is very selfish and has no brain either and only thinks of strengthening his own position', Natty Rothschild wrote to his cousins on 30 July. Lloyd George, in his first close experience of financial men, was fascinated by the sight of the City in action. His somewhat egocentric account of 'How We Saved the City' in his *War Memoirs* includes a tactful but telling passage: 'Many of its leaders were too overwhelmed by the great dangers to which they saw themselves exposed to be able to think with their accustomed composure and to preserve unshaken their wonted touch. Financiers in a fright do not make an heroic picture. One must make allowances, however, for men who were millionaires with an assured credit which seemed as firm as the globe it girdled, and who suddenly found their fortunes scattered by a bomb hurled at random from a reckless hand.' Significantly, though, he added that 'the strongest and sturdiest figure amongst them was Sir Edward Holden, with the brogue and stout heart of Lancashire in all his utterances', a man who 'stood out amongst all these money barons'.[23]

Whatever the rights and wrongs of the financial crisis itself, the larger question remains: why did the City offer such negligible resistance to British intervention in a conflict so profoundly damaging to the City's interests? 'Whatever otherwise may be thought of the Government of Great Britain,' the *FT* wrote with misplaced confidence on Wednesday the 29th, 'it may at least be trusted to keep this country out of the area of conflict unless forced by some extreme and improbable contingency.' Two days later *The Times*' day editor reported to his colleagues that the Rothschilds, convinced that the paper's leading articles were 'hounding the country into war', had urged him to do what he could to reverse the aggressive tone. 'We dare not stand aside', *The Times* declared on Saturday, its forceful response to New Court. On that Saturday, Lloyd George received a visit from Cunliffe, 'to inform me on behalf of the City that the financial and trading interests in the City of London were totally opposed to our intervening in the War'. It was an opposition wholly endorsed by *The Economist*, which in its issue that day enjoined 'strict neutrality' and argued that the 'quarrel' on the Continent was 'no more our concern than would be a quarrel between Argentina and Brazil or between China and Japan'.[24]

Over the next forty-eight hours the picture fundamentally altered. In Lloyd George's own words: 'By Monday there was a complete change. The threatened invasion of Belgium had set the nation on fire from sea to sea.' There is no record of any attempt by the City, between the 2nd and 4th, to prevent British intervention. When on the 4th the *FT* re-appeared after its three-day break, it made no mention *at all* of whether Britain should go to war. Natty Rothschild himself, however, wrote to Paris later that Tuesday that 'there is no doubt that the Germans have invaded Belgian territory, and as that is an act which England could never tolerate the English government will no doubt inform the German government to that effect either tonight or tomorrow'.[25] Most City men over the long weekend seem to have fallen into patriotic line with little or no questioning. Such was patriotism's emotional charge in the late-Victorian and Edwardian City, who would have expected otherwise?

'The war came like a bolt from the blue and no one was prepared', Farrer admitted frankly on 7 August. Withers agreed. 'It came upon us like a thunderbolt from a clear sky', he began *War and Lombard Street*, written that autumn. Even Cassel, most astute of financiers, was caught somewhat humiliatingly on the hop: as late as Saturday the 1st he was still at the Villa Cassel in Switzerland and only with the greatest difficulty managed to struggle back to London. Another financier who knew all the angles, Émile d'Erlanger, would recall being 'incredulous that such an incredible thing as a European War should be allowed to break out'. Nineteen fourteen showed with a cruel clarity that the City had no special purchase on events – vaguely fearing them, yes, but neither shaping nor understanding them.

The guns of August were a particularly bitter blow to one man. Ellis Powell, editor of the *Financial News* and propagandist of an ever more elaborate and perfect financial machinery, had expressed two years earlier his most profound belief:

We have, up to now, been accustomed to think that the destinies of the world were, in the main, entrusted to the hands of politicians . . . But within the last few years it has dawned upon the most competent observers that this progress and contentment depend very much more upon financial than upon political factors . . . The financial and economic forces have become the predominant factors in our twentieth-century life, while the political elements have receded into the second place . . . This is a distinct gain for humanity as a whole, since political forces are capable of being distorted, minimised, and outwitted, while economic power is the absolute and inexorable auxiliary of every effort to advance the prosperity of the world.[26]

Surrounded by frightened monarchies and restless masses, *that* was the great illusion of the age on the part of the commercial middle classes, an illusion shared by merchants in Lübeck and stock jobbers in Capel Court as well as humble scribes in Queen Victoria Street.

PART TWO

1914–2000

Unreal City,
Under the brown fog of a winter dawn,
A crowd flowed over London Bridge, so many,
I had not thought death had undone so many.
Sighs, short and infrequent, were exhaled,
And each man fixed his eyes before his feet.
Flowed up the hill and down King William Street,
To where Saint Mary Woolnoth kept the hours
With a dead sound on the final stroke of nine.

T. S. Eliot, *The Waste Land* (1922)

CHAPTER TWENTY-ONE

Firing She££s

The crisis was recalled in January 1915 by S. F. Mendl, deputy chairman of National Discount Co., at the annual meeting at Cannon Street Hotel:

> Towards the end of July the increasing political tension, the large with-drawals of gold, and the continued heavy fall on the Stock Exchange, indicated the approach of a storm, and, as we all know, a financial tornado burst on the 31st July, when the Bank of England rate was raised to 8 per cent, followed next day by a further rise to 10 per cent, and when the Stock Exchange was closed – an incident unparalleled in the history of this country. The situation, however, was at once taken in hand by the government, assisted by the Bank of England, and the leading banking, financial and commercial authorities; and it was a fortunate circumstance that the Bank Holiday coming on the next Monday enabled the prolonged week-end to be made good use of. Before general business was resumed, an issue of paper currency had been arranged, the proclamation of a partial moratorium affecting bills of exchange had been declared, and the Bank Holiday was extended to the end of that week, by which time a general moratorium was in force. These unprecedented measures were, I think I may safely say, the salvation of the financial situation – (*hear, hear*) – and were absolutely necessary to maintain confidence, and to save the national credit from disaster. It is difficult to exaggerate the debt of gratitude owed by the financial and commercial interests, and by the nation generally, to the government, to the Bank of England, and to those men of banking and mercantile experience and capacity who assisted, by their advice and co-operation, in evolving and bringing into effect the emergency measures referred to. (*Hear, hear*).[1]

Mendl might have added that it was not only the various measures taken immediately before and after the declaration of war that saved the City's bacon, but also certain key decisions in the weeks and months following – above all, an extended moratorium and direct government assistance to the bill market, the accepting houses and the Stock Exchange, the last of which stayed closed until the beginning of 1915.[2] Mendl's account was entirely authentic, however, in reproducing the City's self-congratulatory tone. It had apparently been a miracle on Lombard Street. 'While our Fleet keeps the trade routes clear,' the *Financial Times* applauded ten days into the war, 'the London Money Market, thanks to wise statesmanship, has been enabled to resume its accustomed function of granting credits, which is as indispensable as a safe sea passage to the smooth carrying on of our commerce.' Once again, the pink paper asserted, 'the government and the leaders of the English banking world' had 'demonstrated their capacity for tackling boldly and effectively a national emergency'.[3]

Yet all was not really so smooth, Whiggish and morally uplifting, to judge by the verdict of the prime minister, Asquith, on the City's leaders during the early weeks of the war: 'the greatest ninnies I ever had to tackle', in 'a state of funk like old women chattering over tea-cups in a Cathedral town'. Or, as Asquith's Chancellor of the Exchequer, Lloyd George, put it more mildly, 'financiers in a fright do not make an heroic picture'.[4]

Nor was the story of loss and redemption necessarily such a national triumph. 'I wish we could have got a more substantial *quid pro quo* from the bankers than the mere assurance of co-operation,' Bradbury of the Treasury wrote to the former Chancellor Austen Chamberlain on 13 August, implicitly criticising Lloyd George.[5] Moreover, already looming on the horizon was the question of whether the general moratorium, due to expire on 4 September and by which payments arising out of contracts made before 4 August could be postponed, should be renewed.[6] Questionnaires were sent out on the 19th to the nation's men of commerce and within a week 8,256 returns had been received – 3,603 pronounced in favour of an extension, 4,653 against. Behind this vote lay a stark City/industry divide: whereas 78 out of 81 London bankers were in favour of continuing the moratorium, and 157 out of 227 London export merchants likewise, only 973 out of 2,897 provincial manufacturers felt the same. Lloyd George chose to side with the minority, explaining that 'the opinion, and an emphatic opinion, was expressed, that to bring the moratorium abruptly to an end might produce disaster, and we came to the conclusion that we would prolong it for at least another month'. As Natty Rothschild was honest enough to concede, in a memorandum written on 25 August for government consumption, 'the continuance of the moratorium in its present shape is for the moment very convenient for a good many people'.[7] A good many people, but few of them outside the Square Mile.

Significantly, many of those voting against the extension of the moratorium gave as a reason that it had been abused by the banks. One way and another it was the joint-stock clearing bankers – still for the most part regarded as outsiders by the City, and indeed by the wider Establishment – who took most of the flak during the crisis as a whole. On 5 August, at one of the high-level conferences held at the Treasury, the question arose of establishing a small plenary committee to arbitrate over the working of Treasury notes, which were about to be issued. The concern was that no bank should issue an excessive amount of these notes in order to make profits out of advances at a high rate of interest. The proposal was put forward that this committee should include two bankers chosen from among themselves. With the bankers temporarily out of the room, the governor of the Bank of England, Walter Cunliffe, was asked how many clearing banks there were: 'sixteen or eighteen', he replied, 'but there is such jealousy amongst them that they would not tolerate that'. The following morning he accused the bankers of hoarding gold, a charge hotly denied.

Over the ensuing weeks the joint-stock men were attacked from within and without the City, mainly on the grounds of their unwillingness to help traders and manufacturers in what was, all agreed, an intensely difficult situation. 'They do not seem to me to be playing the game on the evidence that we have got', Edwin Montagu, financial secretary to the Treasury, told Lloyd George on the 15th. 'They had been treated with great liberality. They will probably make large profits during the war, and I think we have a right to expect more from them than they seem willing to do.' Morgan Grenfell's Teddy Grenfell, filling out his questionnaire soon afterwards, agreed: 'In my opinion the Banks which have been given protection as regards their portfolios, by the government, have not, in certain cases, given proper facilities as before the war, to merchants to encourage imports and finance exports, by which alone the food supply, foreign exchanges and general trade can be restored.' And on 26 August, in the Commons, Lloyd George himself declared flatly that 'some banks had not behaved well, and I think that it is better that that should be said'.[8]

*

'Yes, we had to fight. But what a hateful necessity. I suppose Germany, our best customer, will be beaten. And what then?' Sir Charles Addis of the Hongkong and Shanghai Bank, a thinking City man, asked the question on 9 August 1914 and found no comfort. Almost all the City men who stayed behind, for one reason or another, shared a heaviness of heart as events unfolded. Like everyone else they wanted it to end; like everyone else they had no idea when it would. But as Gaspard Farrer of Barings put it in the conflict's early days, 'how trivial our little City worries are compared to our anxieties about the war and all those immediately engaged in it'.[9]

Looked at in a more detached light, the First World War was the worst thing that ever happened to the City of London. 'We cannot yet reckon up losses', wrote Maynard Keynes in the immediate aftermath of the August 1914 financial crisis. 'I do not believe that anything has yet occurred to derogate from the international position of London. Many things will be done differently in the future, but no seeds of grass have yet been sown in the City's streets.' He was wrong, for over the following four years not only did Britain have to liquidate some 15 per cent of its overseas investments in order to finance the war, but London's position as the world's leading international financial centre was decisively eroded. The de facto suspension of the pound's convertibility, amidst an array of wartime regulations, in effect meant that Britain was no longer on the gold standard and sterling no longer globally pre-eminent; this in turn weakened sterling as the currency, and the City as the provider, of international trade finance; while as an international capital market, after a century of largesse, London was badly hit by a mixture of government restrictions and severe practical difficulties concerning transfers and remittances. Instead the baton, which London had once assumed from Amsterdam, now passed to New York. The international clout of that financial centre had been markedly on the increase since the turn of the century, but almost three years of American neutrality gave it a huge push, further enhanced by the dependence of the Allies on the United States for much of their wartime finance and supplies. The conditions were apparently ripe for the US to become, in the words of one American politician, 'the dominant financial power of the world and to extend our trade to every part of the world'.[10]

Four years of often fraught war finance began in a serious way in November 1914 with the first War Loan, for £350m at 3½ per cent.[11] The loan was undersubscribed, and the Bank of England felt impelled to step in and underwrite a further £113m in addition to its original £40m, a decision taken by Cunliffe without troubling to consult his colleagues. For the City's merchant banks, involvement in high-level wartime finance was the prerogative of only a few. In particular the 'German' houses – above all Schröders, Kleinworts and Huths – were not only intrinsically suspect, but in such a parlous state that they were simply regarded as being out of the frame.[12] 'Houses trading with the Continent', noted Teddy Grenfell as early as 7 August 1914, 'are in an awful position as remittances cannot come during the war', and those firms with a large accepting exposure to German and Austrian clients found that it was all they could do to repay the interest on their large, life-saving loans from the Bank of England. Rothschilds had no such problems – either ethnic or financial – but was equally out of the frame. Natty died in 1915 and his brothers Leo and Alfred in 1917 and 1918 respectively. 'A nice old boy' who 'required time to think, but in due course usually came forward with some sagacious proposal' was how Lloyd George described his old adversary, after attending Natty's funeral on Good Friday 1915. Natty's younger son Charles now became senior partner, against the wishes of his uncles, but the following year his own health gave way and he spent most of the rest of the war recovering in Switzerland. And, as

Grenfell later noted, albeit with some exaggeration, the firm on Natty's death 'became of no a/c'.[13]

It was, however, a quite different story for Morgan Grenfell and Barings, both of which undertook a large amount of profitable as well as prestigious work on behalf of the Allied governments. In January 1915 the British government signed the Commercial Agency Agreement with J. P. Morgan & Co., by which Morgans in New York acted as purchasing agent in the US for Britain and her allies. The inevitable go-between, mediating between the British government and J. P. Morgan, was Morgan Grenfell in London, a role that greatly enhanced its already high standing.[14] Over at 8 Bishopsgate, Barings continued, as it had done for so long, to service the needs of the Russian government. In the first year of the war it organised no fewer than four loans or credits, totalling £75m, and in the autumn of 1915 was involved in thrashing out a £300m, twelve-month facility somewhat reluctantly given by the British government. In fact the Treasury tried to squeeze Lord Revelstoke (senior partner of Barings) out of the transaction, but with Russian help he was able to claw his way back in. 'The Treasury is inevitably unfamiliar with the details of banking arrangements', Bradbury admitted to Revelstoke following a Treasury blunder over the details. Revelstoke's reply was graciousness itself: 'I am fully cognizant of the difficulties which attach to your desire to secure a closer control over advances, and I trust that in future the Treasury will not hesitate to let us know if at any time we may be so fortunate as to be able to be of any service to them.'[15]

By then much had happened in the home sphere of *haute finance*, although in the early months of 1915 Cunliffe (recently made a peer) continued to forge an effective axis with Lloyd George. 'His natural tendency to silence has been a good foil to the verbosity of the Chancellor', Grenfell observed in January. 'They not only work well together but like each other.' And he added, following a recent conversation with Asquith, that the prime minister 'rightly put Walter Cunliffe very high'. Cunliffe and Lloyd George spent much of the first week of February together in Paris, at a major conference on Allied finance, and their relationship was further cemented. On his return Lloyd George 'spoke highly' of the governor to a crony: 'His manner is unfortunate, but his advice good. When any proposal was made which L.G. thought doubtful, he turned to Cunliffe and asked his opinion. If he replied, "I don't like it", L.G. knew that it could not be accepted and acted accordingly.' Or, as Lloyd George himself recalled in his *War Memoirs*, 'when a question arose as to a transhipment of gold the governor of the Bank of France expressed himself with great fluency. I then said: "The governor of the Bank of England will state the British view on the subject". He rose slowly, and after a few preliminary puffs ['grunts', according to another account] he said: "We do not mean to part with our gold", and then subsided into his seat.'[16]

Soon afterwards Cunliffe got rid of his own deputy, the port-wine merchant R. L. Newman, on the justifiable grounds of incompetence, and replaced him with the unexciting but efficient Brien Cokayne of the merchant bank Antony Gibbs. But by May, unfortunately for Cunliffe, the plates began to shift under his feet, with the war going increasingly badly and a major government reshuffle becoming inevitable. Lloyd George was interrupted in his shaving on the 20th by his maid, who told him that the governor was downstairs wanting to see him. 'I went down. The old boy blundered out, "I hear they want you to leave the Treasury. We cannot let you go!" and then he quite broke down, and the tears trickled down his cheeks.' Lloyd George gently explained that Cunliffe must go to see the prime minister about the matter, and Asquith subsequently related the outcome. 'I couldn't get anything out of him, except "We don't want to lose our man! Don't take our man away from us!"' [17] It was to no avail, for a week later Reginald McKenna replaced Lloyd George as Chancellor.

The new man was in his early fifties and, before the war, had won the City's respect by carrying through the Dreadnought programme while at the Admiralty. 'It is said that McKenna owes his present position to the fact that he is an illegitimate son of Sir C. Dilke', noted a Tory backwoodsman in 1910. 'Probably a mere fable, but it is difficult to explain advancement of such a very third rate man.' Margot Asquith found him 'cocky and cocksure to an irritating degree', but her daughter-in-law Cynthia liked him on the grounds that 'he is such a "Sunny Jim" and ripples on so easily'. Balfour would privately dismiss him as 'an able accountant', but Beaverbrook gave a rather more measured assessment: 'What is McKenna's character and nature? His abilities are brilliant and his logic remorseless. He is angular, emphatic, and positive. He likes to assert his view, and if you run against some projecting hump in his opinions you must merely nurse a bruise.'[18]

Unsurprisingly, McKenna proved reluctant to accept the disciplines of a learning curve. 'As regards Finance,' Grenfell wrote to Jack Morgan in August, 'undoubtedly McKenna is a very ignorant man and at first was inclined to try to appear wise.' By then Chancellor and governor were at loggerheads. In late July Asquith sought to mediate, telling McKenna that Cunliffe had 'rendered us invaluable service during the past year' and that, though 'he has (like most people) limitations of outlook and faults of temper', his 'deliberate judgement' was 'always well worth taking into account' and that he was 'perfectly straight'. Asquith added that Cunliffe had expressed to him his wish to resign, on the basis that McKenna 'had lost confidence in him and in his judgement, and found

co-operation with him difficult'. Things deteriorated still further during
the rest of the year. On the one hand, McKenna was not really on top
of his job ('he has a lot to learn, and we none of us can afford the time
to teach him', Grenfell observed); on the other, Cunliffe was 'thoroughly
overdone' and at one point went down with jaundice (diagnosed by
Grenfell as 'the result of the strain of the last two years and partly I think
the neglect of his teeth which have poisoned his system through inability
to spare a few hours in time with the Dentist'). McKenna would, according
to Beaverbrook's account, 'frequently urge Cunliffe the necessity of
providing more bank balances for the government in the United States',
to which Cunliffe 'would reply invariably, "Mr Chancellor, this is a matter
of exchange, and the responsibility here lies with me."'[19] Treasury/Bank
relations had not been so strained since the days of Harcourt, another
acerbic Liberal Chancellor.

The reference to the US and exchange was significant, for in the context
of massive exports from America to Britain, the financial authorities in
London faced an increasingly strenuous battle to maintain New York's
confidence in sterling and thereby keep up the rate of exchange. The role
of Morgans, on both sides of the Atlantic, was obviously crucial, but the
London partners found it a frustrating experience. Certainly Grenfell and
his colleagues suffered from a growing dislike of undue American
influence.

By November 1915 it was clear to everyone that a new, more systematic
approach to the financing of supplies from America was required.
Accordingly, on the 18th McKenna appointed what soon became known
as the London Exchange Committee, whose purpose was to ensure as
favourable an exchange as possible, and which was empowered to take
under its control all available gold as well as foreign currency and the
proceeds of securities liquidated on foreign markets.[20] Its four members
were Cunliffe, Cokayne, Holden and Schuster, and it was to be aided by
a subcommittee of four foreign-exchange men, one each from London
County & Westminster, Brown Shipley, Lloyds and London City &
Midland. The main committee met at the Bank of England, but on the
29th the question was discussed of an office outside the Bank for the
subcommittee's use, with its books, letters and so on to be kept at that
office. However, this was 'a point which Lord Cunliffe stated that he was
unable to concede as the business was government business and the books
should therefore be kept at the Bank'. Next day he added that he saw
the subcommittee 'merely acting as an expert advisory Committee', to
which Holden countered that, 'conducted in this manner, the business
would be a fiasco and that Gold would continue to go out'. Having
apparently been responsible for ensuring that the new body be given
unprecedentedly wide powers, Holden now found himself in the

frustrating position of not being able to use them, and on 3 December he wrote to Cunliffe that 'I cannot myself believe, as the Bank of England is the free Market for Gold, that it is wise for it to begin dealing in Foreign Exchange'. But, 'as you appear to have decided otherwise, which course in my opinion will result in failure and in losing our Gold, I am at a loss what to do'. Within a few weeks Holden had more or less stopped attending the London Exchange Committee's meetings, as it became clear that Cunliffe was determined to run the show, for all his protestations that 'as the Bankers' money was being used they had a right to know the method by which it was being used'.[21]

Cunliffe, recovering from jaundice, was not at the Bank on 1 January 1916 when one of his directors, Montagu Norman, spent his first day there since terminating his partnership with the merchant bank Brown Shipley. 'Free man today', his diary recorded. Subsequently the firm's senior partner, writing to Brown Brothers in New York, put this departure in context:

> The functions of the London Office have been mainly in connection with credits, exchange and banking operations generally, as distinct from securities business. You will recall the many discussions which have taken place from time to time upon this subject, particularly those of the Spring of 1914 . . . The principal point then before the House was whether the acceptance business should be entirely abandoned or to a great extent curtailed in favour of a security business on this side. We shall be within your recollection by remarking that Mr Norman urged a virtual adoption of the former course, but the consensus of opinion was against him.

The outbreak of war merely delayed Norman's decision to leave Brown Shipley, and for most of the time before he finally did so he was working at the War Office, not in Founders' Court. On the sixth day of his freedom he received a welcome letter from Cunliffe's deputy, Cokayne, asking if Norman would 'be so kind as to come, regularly, and "devil" for me'. Cokayne added helpfully that 'it appears to be quite understood in the City that you have left your firm to devote yourself to public work, and if you come and help me here your action will be more "intelligible" still'. Norman replied gratefully – 'I shall try to be, or to become, your willing and cheerful fag' – and soon, having hitherto been only an irregular attender at Threadneedle Street, had his feet under his desk at the Bank. It was just a shame about the governor. 'There goes that queer-looking fish with the ginger beard again', Cunliffe once said loudly on passing Norman in a corridor. 'Do you know who he is? I keep seeing him creeping about this place like a lost soul with nothing better to do.'[22] Now at long last, in his mid-forties, Norman did have something in which to immerse himself.

Soon afterwards Benjamin Strong, governor of the recently established

Federal Reserve Bank of New York, paid a longish visit to London with
a view to establishing closer Anglo-American financial relations. Apparently
the initiative was his, not the Bank of England's, but inevitably he would
have to meet Cunliffe. Grenfell made an appointment, as well as preparing
the ground. 'He tells me that Lord Cunliffe is very reserved, diffident,
but nevertheless quite positive in his views', Strong noted in his diary on
13 March. The following afternoon the two men met. 'Lord Cunliffe
impressed me most favourably, relishes a joke, and likes to make one. He
joshed me when I came in and . . . wanted to know why I had not let
him know in advance of my coming over.' Strong then explained his
scheme for more intimate co-operation in exchange matters, especially
over gold shipments. Cunliffe asked for a little time to think about it.
That evening Strong dined with Holden and a select group of City editors
whom he had invited. 'On Sir Edward's invitation the meeting developed
into a general "quiz" party – everybody asking questions. The last speaker,
Mr Reeve [of the *Daily Telegraph*], made the astonishing suggestion (and
I believe it was in all seriousness) that he believed it was a great mistake
to have English speaking people separated into two political and financial
organisations – that we ought to get under one roof again. That the
Reserve Bank System was really the Bank of England'. And: 'This caused
some amusement, but was roundly cheered. I did not find the gentlemen
present at the dinner particularly well posted in regard to the American
financial system.' A few evenings later Strong dined alone with Norman
and then on the 21st took lunch with Cunliffe, who agreed to Strong's
suggested arrangement. Towards the end, 'he emphasised again the fact
that he was most anxious to conclude his term as Governor of the Bank'.

On the 24th the American was again at the Bank, consulting Padgett,
'Chief of the Bill Division', about the Bank's bill business. 'I asked him
how they discriminated in the matter of finance bills. He said, that if he
were to address that question to Lord Cunliffe he would say they could
tell by the "smell".' Later that day, following a long session with Kitchener
at the War Office, Strong dined with Huth Jackson and various prominent
guests. Afterwards, in the library, his host 'told me a good many interesting
incidents connected with the crisis here in 1914', causing Strong to reflect:
'There is no doubt but that these Englishmen are great fellows for criticising each other, but I constantly gain the impression that this is simply
talk and when it comes to real business they generally get it done.' The
26th, a Sunday, he spent mostly with Norman, and the following morning
he was at Barings, where he had 'a nice chat' with Revelstoke: 'Repeated
my invariable story on the subject of American public opinion, with
which he was polite enough to agree but subsequent discussion rather
indicated that he, like the others, are rather skeptical of our good faith
and protestations of good faith.'

Strong later called on Holden – 'Found him quite miserable. He is full of complaint about the Government' – and then in the evening attended a Reform Club dinner full of City bigwigs. He heard there 'a good deal of criticism of the lack of flexibility in the English banking situation and apparently a growing desire to modify it so that the Bank of England would command a larger gold reserve', while 'after dinner a number of those present asked if some of the features of our new banking system were not applicable to the Bank of England'. On the 30th he was back at the Bank to make his farewells. He found Cunliffe 'just returned recently from a trip to Paris which he had made without anybody knowing it, and was in a frame of mind to criticise anything and everything the Banque de France did', accusing it of being 'distrustful' and generally unco-operative. Strong for his part was 'greatly amused at his humorous but expressive remarks about "the old bank". He admitted that the Bank of England was a museum, but that after all they could change when necessity required, whereas the Banque de France was much more a museum than the Bank of England and apparently did not have the capacity or courage to change.'[23]

Personal impressions aside, Strong's visit marked a turning point in international central banking.[24] Prior to 1914 it had existed, and then only patchily, at times of crisis. Neither Cunliffe nor his predecessors would ever have dreamed of going abroad on Bank of England business. Now it was Strong who, in the circumstances of war, began to shape a dialogue; he and his new friend, Norman, were already implicitly looking ahead to a partnership in peacetime.

*

'Keep your eye on the prospects of the opening of the Dardanelles, for it will be an important point in connection with your Wheat, Barley and Oats operations', Sir Archibald Williamson of Balfour Williamson instructed his man in Valparaiso in February 1915. For four years war was the ubiquitous fact of business life, benefiting some in the City and severely disadvantaging others. Sugar brokers, for example, virtually disappeared, as the government took early control of that particular commodity; but those dealing in timber enjoyed a three-year hiatus before the government moved in, and amidst high demand and sharply increasing prices there was plenty of profitable work.[25]

Yet, especially with minimum prices operating for much of the period on the Stock Exchange, the day-to-day mood of the wartime City was generally depressed. 'Conditions both as regards commercial business and the money market are entirely artificial', Farrer observed in February 1915. And in September 1917: 'Business very quiet and getting quieter all the time. The City looks empty even in the streets and is deserted by three o'clock.' Of course, some of the low spirits were caused by the semi-permanent absence on war business of many of the City's leading figures. The energetic financier Jimmie Dunn announced as early as September 1914 that 'as financial business in London is for the time being at an end I must try and turn myself to the only business that can be done' – in his case making a more or less honest penny by supplying the British Army with horses from Canada. Or take the accountants Price, Waterhouse & Co., whose partners devoted so much time to government work that as many as five were knighted. Though they combined their work in various ministries with keeping the firm going at 3 Frederick's Place, they knew better than most that for the time being the City was no longer at the hub of the Western world.[26]

Back in the 1890s the Bank of England had pioneered the City's employment of female clerks, and during the war their number rose to well over 1,000, as the men went to the Front. Cunliffe was so unnerved by some of the colourful dresses he encountered that a rule was introduced confining permissible colours to navy, black and very dark grey. Elsewhere in the City the trend towards female labour similarly intensified – 'something over half our men staff have gone and we have now more young women than men in the office,' Farrer at Barings remarked in June 1915. Mainly employed by banks as typists and coupon clerks, the women earned significantly less than their male counterparts: at the Hongkong and Shanghai Bank, for example, an average of 28s 9d per week, which was 6s less than the male average. It was a differential that Addis there justified on the grounds that ladies were only two-thirds as efficient as men, taking 'due account of the inability of the female sex to stand a prolonged strain, their more frequent absence from work, and their liability to nervous breakdown in face of sudden emergency'. Williamson was at first semi-inclined to agree. 'Don't blame us if mistakes or delay occur', he warned Valparaiso in May 1916. 'Most of the invoices you get are now made up and written by women clerks. Look at them. They are quite well done. Surprisingly so.' But by April 1918 he had become a complete convert: 'We here find we can do a wonderful amount of good work with the assistance of women. Both in our book-keeping and clerical departments they have come to the front . . . Up to the war we used them only as stenographers and secretaries, but there has been a great development, and they have come up to scratch and done well.'[27] Even so, he – like everyone else – assumed that the great majority would return to home and hearth once the war was over.

Male or female, one shared experience was the occasional, not unterrifying air raid. The City's first big one occurred on the evening of Wednesday 8 September 1915, when the German naval airship *L13* started to come over the City just before eleven o'clock. In quick succession bombs fell on Bartholomew Close, Little Britain, Aldermanbury, Basinghall Street, Coleman Street, Moorgate, Salisbury House (Finsbury Circus), London Wall Buildings, Liverpool Street (leaving a crater there) and Liverpool Street Station. Altogether thirty bombs were dropped, six people killed, thirty-eight injured and over £500,000 worth of damage done. In 1917 the Germans began aeroplane raids directly targeted at the City. The most successful was on Wednesday 13 June, coming late one morning out of a clear blue sky. Fifteen planes dropped bombs that killed over a hundred people and, as Grenfell wrote to Jack Morgan, 'in this crowded district, the bombs made a terrific noise as of course the sound reverberates amongst the high buildings and narrow streets'. He added that 'the nearest bomb to us failed to go off as it landed in a Churchyard, but the next one, just behind the Office, appropriately spoilt the Austrian Bank and missed Barings narrowly'.[28] One of the war's finest chroniclers was in the City that day. Siegfried Sassoon, on his way to Cambridge, needed to draw cash from his bank in Old Broad Street:

> When my taxi stopped in that narrow thoroughfare, the people on the pavement were standing still, staring up at the hot white sky. Loud bangings had begun in the near neighbourhood, and it was obvious that an air-raid was in full swing. This event could not be ignored; but I needed money and wished to catch my train, so I decided to disregard it. The crashings continued, and while I was handing my cheque to the cashier a crowd of women clerks came wildly down a winding stairway with vociferations of not unnatural alarm. Despite this commotion the cashier handed me five one-pound notes with the stoical politeness of a man who had made up his mind to go down with the ship . . . At Liverpool Street there had occurred what, under normal conditions, would be described as an appalling catastrophe. Bombs had been dropped on the station and one of them had hit the front carriage of the noon express to Cambridge. Horrified travellers were hurrying away . . . In a trench one was acclimatised to the notion of being exterminated and there was a sense of organised retaliation. But here one was helpless; an invisible enemy sent destruction spinning down from a fine weather sky; poor old men bought a railway ticket and were trundled away again dead on a barrow; wounded women lay about in the station groaning. And one's train didn't start.[29]

It was less than a month before the next round of unfriendly bombs. 'Great air raid on the City,' the Smith St Aubyn diary noted on Saturday 7 July, '22 enemy machines come and return to the Coast before one is brought down! 37 killed. 141 wounded.' Addis recorded the event − 'It was an awful sight. There was no panic' − while Grenfell was typically laconic: 'The planes were quite low and just missed St Paul's and Northcliffe's Office. They got the GPO and the Swiss Bank and broke Speyer's best stained glass . . . All the women clerks stand the shocks extraordinarily well. They deserve several votes.' Serious preparations were soon under way in the expectation of further raids: 'I have not yet been told where my own funkhole is, but I intend to get there – at the double – when the time arrives', Farrer admitted; but in the event the worst was over.[30] The largely intact City would stay thoroughly Victorian in appearance for a while yet.

Grenfell's Speyer reference was one among many, many manifestations of anti-German feeling that pervaded the City. Farrer at the outset took the civilised approach – 'it is right to draw a distinction between the German government and the German nation, and I reserve my bitterness of feeling for the former,' he wrote to a colleague three days after war began – but if, which was doubtful, many other non-Germans were inclined to follow, that possibility vanished with the sinking of the *Lusitania* on 7 May 1915. Both the *Financial Times* and the *Financial News* declared that it was the 'crowning infamy' of what the *FN* called 'a series of cowardly crimes against humanity'. A few days later a mass meeting was held on Tower Hill, 'when in drenching rain thousands of City men assembled to support a resolution calling upon the government to intern all alien enemies now in our midst, whether naturalised or not'. The anti-German mood did not abate. At Rothschilds, the German-speaking clerks continued for some time to talk German among themselves at the luncheon table, usually muttering '*Mahlzeit*' as they left it. Eventually in 1917, the story went, a thoroughly English clerk called Henfrey, 'able to stand it no longer, bore into the dining-room a *Daily Mail* poster bearing the words "Intern Them All", a message which he reinforced by shouting the words in the hoarse voice of a street-corner news-boy as he marched up and down the room'.[31]

The more eminent one was, the worse it was being of German origin, as Sir Carl Meyer and Baron Bruno Schröder both found. 'Poor Carl Meyer! he looks a broken man', Addis observed in February 1915 of the Hongkong and Shanghai's director, a well-known City figure since the 1880s and with a son serving at the Front on the British side. In September 1916 he was asked to resign. Addis noted: 'I was sorry for him but advised him not to resist – the feeling against Germans, even naturalised Germans, is too strong.' Schröder's plight was equally unenviable. Within days of the war beginning he had been naturalised, his partner Frank Tiarks working closely in harness with Cunliffe to avert the threat of sequestration (as enemy property) of such an important firm. The move was widely criticised, including in Parliament, with sentiment not improved by Schröder's elder son being conscripted into the German Army. Then came the sinking of the *Lusitania*, prompting Tiarks to write to his brother that 'no institution with a German name ought to be tolerated in London' – that indeed this was the last straw and he had 'decided not to go on with JHS & Co. after the war and to insist on a gradual liquidation' and would 'tell Bruno so tomorrow'. Soon afterwards, however, Tiarks was informed by Cunliffe that such a policy would be against the national interest, and Tiarks agreed to follow the governor's advice and 'peg away in the direction he wants'. Even so, Tiarks told Grenfell in November 1915 that (in Grenfell's words) 'he felt Bruno S could never work here again nor did T himself think he could work with Bruno S'. Schröder himself avoided the City throughout the war, though at one point he was challenged to say whether he wanted Britain or Germany to emerge as victor. He replied, 'I feel as if my father and mother have quarrelled.'[32]

Sad, embittering times too for Sir Ernest Cassel. Although in formal retirement after 1910, he kept in close touch with financial affairs, reassuring at least one person soon after the outbreak of war that he entertained 'no doubt of this country's solvency, whatever the pressure to which we might be subjected'. Yet even Cassel, in the prevailing febrile atmosphere, came under attack, and a fortnight after the sinking of the *Lusitania* he sent a letter to the press declaring that 'nearly half a century of my life has been spent in England, and all my interests – family, business and social – are centred here', adding that 'my unfailing loyalty and devotion to this country have never varied'. Nor had they, for over the years he had performed all sorts of important services, not least as Edward VII's trusted financial adviser. Later in 1915 there was an attempt to deprive him of his membership of the Privy Council. It failed, but hurt him deeply. And the following summer, after the Battle of Jutland, it was widely believed – entirely baselessly – that Cassel had actively conspired to maximise the adverse implications of that encounter in order to profit from a fall in the stock market.[33] He may not have been a lovable man, but he deserved better. And, taking the rabid anti-Germanism as a whole, the City was in danger of rejecting the cosmopolitanism that had been its single greatest strength.

*

The conduct of financial policy remained as sorry a spectacle after Benjamin Strong's visit as it had been before, though it was a spectacle hidden from public scrutiny. Norman, having quickly played himself in as a member of the Bank of England's inner circle, spent much of the early summer of 1916 at the Treasury, usually with the Chancellor (still McKenna) present. 'They neither grasp nor seem able to realise the true position', he wrote in his diary on 30 May. A week later, after another visit: 'All muddle & getting worse & worse.' And the next day: 'C. of Ex seems utterly blind to Exchange position & inevitable dangers ahead, being filled with immediate politics . . . For some unknown reason he is sanguine of turning up a trump & refuses to face the position.' Finally, on 27 June: 'It's a thankless job going to Treasury. I shall do it no more, for tho' knowing jeopardy threatens us in N.Y. one might as well talk to an airball as to them.'[34]

Nor, as the year unfolded, did Norman derive much comfort from the Bank itself. An entry on 24 October was laden with meaning:

Most of Treas Com [i.e. the Bank of England's Committee of Treasury, of which Norman was a member, but mainly comprising present and former governors] having agreed to G. [i.e. Governor Cunliffe] for another year: he sh[d] make a point of regular full disclosure of Bk affairs & of his advice qua Gov. This is due to them as Treas Com (by long custom) & essential now to begin preparation of *united* front, as Enquiry after war is certain – & it will be engineered with main object of substituting State Bank. Such a Bank seems to be in minds of C [i.e. Chancellor McKenna] & whole Treasury as well as grumblers in City & busy bodies in Parl'ment.

Over the next fortnight Norman's hoped-for united front failed to materialise, as Cunliffe and his predecessor A. C. Cole quarrelled openly, the latter denying Cunliffe's accusations about breaches of secrecy. On 8 November, Norman recorded, Cunliffe 'accepted job for another year – but unconditionally'. Soon afterwards, however, Norman spent a weekend in Bath (staying at the Spa Hotel) and, in the course of 'long talks' with a for once 'entirely reasonable' governor, managed to thrash out some sort of concordat. Cunliffe agreed that a female shorthand writer would attend Committee of Treasury meetings and provide a full precis; that those meetings would be more frequent; that all current business would be considered; that there would be a 'gradual bringing in of younger directors' into the Committee; and that in due course there would 'perhaps' be, on the Bank's Court as a whole, 'new directors drawn from Bankers &c'. The peacemaker's immediate reward came two days after his return from Bath: 'T. Com . . . Hatchet formally buried by G & ACC'.[35]

Meanwhile, Bank/Treasury relations continued to be deeply uneasy. Cokayne, deputy governor, said as much in his diary on 10 November: 'In evening saw [the Treasury's] Sir R. Chalmers (coming in with Grenfell, which was a mistake as it evidently gave the impression that I came to help him to get his way with the Treasury).' Bad faith remained the order of the day, the exchange position deteriorated still further, and on 29 November, noted Norman, 'finance in U.S. now becomes a Cabinet question'. Over the next three weeks Britain lost gold at the daily rate of over $5m, as the Federal Reserve Board (in the absence of the ailing Strong) deliberately undermined Anglo-French credit in an attempt to get the Allies to end the war. By the time the worst was over, though gold continued to drain away over the next few months, there was a new government in London. Lloyd George replaced Asquith in December, to the pleasure of the *FT*, which anticipated a government 'to be run on business as distinguished from party lines'. The new Chancellor was the

Conservative leader, and Norman noted in January 1917 that 'friction between Bk & Treasury has wonderfully lessened since Bonar Law became C'. The new year also saw the issue by Bonar Law of a major war stock – the Chancellor successfully exploiting patriotic feeling in his decision, backed by the Bank but not by the Treasury, to go for a long-term loan at 5 per cent rather than the more customary short-term one at 6 per cent. The *FT* called on the City to supply 'all the silver bullets it can turn out', while the *FN* greeted the War Loan launch as only it knew how: 'Every Cheque Is A She££ Fired At The German Trenches'. The exhortations worked, as Austen Chamberlain wrote to his sister in late February: 'The Loan is an even more marvellous success than I thought. You will see the figures in the papers. They exceed Bonar Law's wildest dreams.'[36] Almost £2bn had come in, though the problem of how to service that mammoth debt now began to exercise more thoughtful minds.

The two global events that dominated 1917 were the Russian Revolution and America's entry into the war. Since 1914 Barings had been undeniably resourceful agents for the Russian government, but arguably could have done more to save Russian capitalism. 'I wish some upright Commercial House here could play the strong hand in Petrograd', commented Grenfell in June 1916. 'Everything would point to Barings doing so, but they seem unwilling to jeopardise what they have got by pushing ahead and yet are inclined to crab anyone who does try to push.' On 19 January 1917 Revelstoke left London as number two to Milner on an Allied mission to investigate Russia's claim to a new loan of at least £400m. In effect Revelstoke was representing the interests of both the Treasury and the Russian government, a position that seems to have caused him few ethical qualms. After the best part of a month, during which some determined bargaining was combined with a strenuous social programme, the delegation departed on 21 February with the outcome still inconclusive. Soon after Revelstoke's return the tsarist regime fell. 'He thinks the army generally is sound for the continuance of the war', noted Addis on 29 March after a conversation with the Barings chief.

Wishful thinking, but then a week later America at last declared war on Germany. The governor was quickly across the herring pond. 'Cunliffe is for cash that fights' ran an American headline, and by early May he had helped to secure loans worth £300m.[37] Already hugely in hock to the United States, Britain was now in a state of dependency plain for all to see. The old country had become a debtor nation.

'We are expecting Cunliffe back any day now', Farrer told an American correspondent at the end of May. 'He has been badly missed here; he is by nature so silent that until he disappears temporarily from the scene one hardly realises how good a man and how strong he is.'[38] Shortly afterwards, duly back from his acclaimed trip, Cunliffe was embroiled in an extraordinary episode of high-level rancour.[39] Beginning as a fierce campaign on his part against the Treasury (in particular against Chalmers and Keynes) over what he complained was interference in questions of exchange, it took the form by early July – at a critical stage of the war – of an almost mad attempt to block the government's access to the Bank's gold in Canada. Cunliffe did this entirely off his own bat. Bonar Law, writing to Lloyd George on the 9th, was incandescent. He described Cunliffe's telegram to the Canadian government as 'an act of extraordinary disrespect towards the British government and a direct insult to me'. Next day Lloyd George summoned Cunliffe to Downing Street, reprimanded him severely and threatened (or so Cunliffe reported on the 11th to the Committee of Treasury) to 'take over the Bank'. He also gave Cunliffe a statement to sign, including the solemn words that 'during the War the Bank must in all things act on the directions of the Chancellor of the Exchequer'. Cunliffe, having consulted his colleagues the following day, refused to sign it. Lloyd George, after talking to Bonar Law, sent Cunliffe on the 13th a suggested letter of apology for him to send the Chancellor, 'the sooner the better'. It contained the offer of resignation in the absence of 'complete and harmonious co-operation' between the two men. Cunliffe's response – extolling the importance of a harmonious relationship between Bank and Treasury but declining to offer his resignation in the absence of such a relationship – failed to give satisfaction.

At this point, the 17th, the governor went off to Scotland on a fishing holiday, leaving Cokayne and Norman to try and mollify the Chancellor. Bonar Law reluctantly ceded to Cokayne's request that the deputy governor try again to get a fuller apology out of Cunliffe, with Bonar Law clearly wanting an offer of resignation. Over the next three weeks Cokayne wrote along these lines to the absent governor no fewer than four times. He warned that unless Cunliffe pocketed his pride, 'the position will become absolutely intolerable and there is bound to be a sort of public scandal'. Cunliffe for a time was adamant – 'let the Chancellor protest as he may, such a letter places my resignation in his hands and I simply become a government Official under his orders' – but eventually, on 12 August, he sent Bonar Law the letter that Cokayne had most recently drafted. In it he made an 'unreserved apology for anything I have done to offend you', but did not as such offer to resign.[40]

Cunliffe's days as governor, however, were numbered. By September, with his behaviour becoming increasingly erratic, Cecil Lubbock (a Bank director) was telling Norman that Cunliffe was 'no longer sane – if ever he was'. Briefly he seemed willing to go quietly, but on 10 October told Norman that (in Norman's words) 'it was in interest of Bk & Nation that he sh^d continue, that he could not continue once anyone else was selected, that he wished to go on until end of war & that he w^d be to me either a G. or an enemy'. Soon afterwards, at a meeting of the Bank's Court, he accused a former governor, W. M. Campbell, of being against him because he had been denied facilities to borrow. This time Cunliffe's bullying failed to work, and on 8 November the Court elected Cokayne and Norman as governor and deputy governor respectively from the following spring. Most men would have given up, but not Cunliffe. He now (in Grenfell's accurate words) 'changed his attitude to everyone outside the Bank. He toadied the press, the Bankers, the Treasury & the Gov^t. He tried to get the Bankers to move the Chancellor to ask that he Cunliffe should be retained at the Bank. He vilified Norman & the other directors.' So successful was Cunliffe in persuading his old enemies, the joint-stock bankers, to come to his aid that on 20 November they handed Bonar Law a resolution against the proposed change of governor. Cunliffe professed that the resolution came as a 'great surprise' to him, but under questioning from Norman admitted that 'he had known about & seen resolution last week'. Somewhat super-fluously, Norman added that 'he can't be trusted now'. The resolution failed to achieve its purpose, but by mid-December Norman was still noting that 'it seems more clear than ever that G. is consulting, if not intriguing with the Bankers – & esp Schuster'.[41]

Cunliffe was away in Spain for the whole of January 1918, but returned for a final acrimonious round. 'Clear case of megalomania', Norman reckoned on 27 February, following a 'violent display' by Cunliffe at the Committee of Treasury, 'behaving like a spoilt child'. And on 22 March, at a meeting of the Bank's shareholders, he 'read a longish speech – of wh D Gov & Directors knew nothing – i. eulogising the Bankers, ii. bum-sucking the Press . . . feeling very hot, & even DG much disgusted with such an unfriendly finale. A dangerous & insane colleague.' It was a speech that made the worst possible impression on Grenfell, who found himself 'reluctantly compelled to agree that able & strong as Lord C is, yet he is selfish, disloyal to colleagues & the Bank. He also has a bad yellow streak & is in no sense a white man.' The 'only excuse', Grenfell added, was that 'nearly all the members of the C family are slightly cracked & are not on speaking terms with each other'.[42]

On the Continent, by mid-July the military danger was easing, but when would that blessed period of 'after the War' come? 'The war has had a wonderful turning just lately,' the highly intelligent Robert Brand of Lazards wrote on 3 October to a New York correspondent, 'but we are still having a terrific struggle in France and it may be many months before the end comes.' Archibald Williamson, an MP as well as a leading City figure, agreed, telling Lima two days later that he was not expecting peace 'until some time next year', for 'the German forces are still formidable'.[43] The outbreak of war four years earlier had come as an almost complete surprise to the City; now its abrupt ending did likewise.

CHAPTER TWENTY-TWO

No New Blood

It was not just in the obvious sense – the dislocation of the pre-1914 international economy, with its free movement of people, capital and services – that the First World War represented a difficult time for the City. For the first time in anyone's memory it started to come under significant pressure from an alternative socio-economic approach: one that stressed the interests of the provinces as against the metropolis, and of industry as against finance.[1] 'Business as usual' quickly lost its viability as a slogan, huge swathes of the economy came under temporary government control, and the establishment of the Federation of British Industries in 1916 was a key straw in the corporatist wind. Free trade, the gold standard, the balanced budget – all three were crucial props to City influence and, for the time being, all three were *hors de combat*. Briefly, and tantalisingly, the producer held the aces.

Inevitably, the war saw renewed criticism of the City's provision of industrial finance, sharply intensifying a debate that had begun in the Edwardian period. Tellingly, some of this criticism was internal, including an important survey published in December 1916 by Robert Brand of Lazards on 'Industry and Finance'. Although acknowledging that the British banking system was 'safer and more liquid' than the German, he emphasised how 'a reflective mind is constantly struck by the peculiar lack of contact between the chief financial centre of the world and the industry of its own country'. He went on: 'There are no first-class financial institutions in London which act as organisers or reorganisers of companies, or which issue on their own responsibility industrial securities . . . In a word, there are no financial institutions in London whose aim it is, as it is the aim of the German banks, to act as a kind of general staff to industry.' Accordingly, 'industrial issues, and particularly new schemes, are left too much to the company promoter', who inevitably looks 'to make as large an immediate profit as possible regardless of the future welfare of the business'.

In a well-publicised lecture in April 1917 on 'The Financing of Industry and Trade', the economist H. S. Foxwell was highly critical of what he saw as an over-specialised City: on the one hand, 'the regular banks', though 'always ready to accommodate industry with temporary loans on excellent terms', refused to 'make a special study of industrial technique, or industrial problems generally, except so far as they affect short-loan business'; on the other hand, the issuing houses (i.e. mainly the merchant banks) 'fight shy of ordinary home industrial propositions' and 'prefer those put forward by foreign governments, municipalities, or the very largest transport companies', for 'as a rule our English industries are too small in scale to attract the issue houses'. In short, he concluded, 'we are involved in a vicious circle which it will want some courage to break'.[2] The crux, as both Brand and Foxwell recognised, was institutional conservatism.

With the City at large under attack, even the Bank of England accepted the need for a modicum of internal reform. In October 1917 – a few weeks after being attacked by *The Economist* on the grounds of excessive secrecy and inadequate use of industrialists and bankers – the Bank set up a committee under Revelstoke's chairmanship to consider 'the Direction and general working of the Bank'.[3] The others on it were Huth Jackson, Norman, Lubbock and Sir Robert Kindersley of Lazards, and many years later Norman recalled that whereas Revelstoke 'took a great deal of trouble and used carefully to prepare his "case" before every meeting', Huth Jackson 'took little interest and seemed unable to distinguish gems from paste in the meetings'. Each director was asked to make a submission, with the question of whether the Bank's 'direction' should be broadened to include joint-stock bankers being of paramount concern. 'I do not think it would answer to have Members of other Banks, as it would create jealousies', argued the merchant and former governor W. M. Campbell. 'Their presence would give the Banks represented a preferential advantage.' Grenfell had no problem with the idea (wanting only bill brokers to be debarred from consideration), but according to Cokayne, 'so long as none of the banks are directly represented on our Court, our advice (e.g. to the Treasury) on matters concerning their interests will carry greater weight'. R. L. Newman, befitting 'the port-wine man', went further and said that he would 'deprecate' the election of any director who did not 'belong to a definite mercantile firm'. The committee itself was split. Whereas Huth Jackson 'considered that it was essential for the Bank to secure the best available men' and that it was therefore wrong to exclude the clearers, and Norman (for all his later criticism) argued likewise, Lubbock was essentially hostile to the idea, on the basis that the functions of the Bank of England and of the joint-stock banks were 'essentially different' and that 'no advantage would be gained by a quasi-fusion of the two'. Kindersley agreed: 'He considered that these Banks had too much power already and he viewed with alarm the growth of huge deposits under one control. It was his opinion that a man with such responsibility would naturally consider first the needs of his own Bank and that it would be impossible for him to give a fair and unbiased opinion on the situation as a whole.'[4]

As for the rejected infusion of new blood, perhaps it would not have had such a rejuvenating effect on the Bank itself. 'They are too largely staffed, apart from the directors, on what in the Civil Service is called a second division basis', Keynes wrote in October 1914 to Alfred Marshall about the clearing banks. 'Half of their directors, on the other hand, are appointed on hereditary grounds and two-fifths, not on grounds of banking capacity, but because they are able, through their business connections, to bring to the bank a certain class of business.'[5] Keynes was perhaps an unduly harsh critic of the men at the very top – notably Holden and Schuster – but his general point held.

Since the late 1880s the banks had been engaged in an almost continuous amalgamation movement, and in 1918 it reached its denouement. 'Time to Stop!' declared the *Daily Express* on 4 February, in response to newly announced mergers: between National Provincial and the Union of London & Smiths; and between the London County & Westminster and Parr's. 'What does all this portend?' the paper asked. 'It is obvious that we shall see perfected in England a financial system equal to and even more powerful than that which the people of the United States found so tyrannous and irksome that in the end it had to be swept by the board.'[6]

Over the summer, to the surprise of some, Bonar Law waved through three amalgamations that were already in the pipeline – between the London City and Midland and the London Joint Stock Bank; between Barclays and the London, Provincial & South Western Bank; and between Lloyds and the Capital and Counties Bank – on the grounds of fair treatment between these banks and the ones that had already merged earlier in the year. In July, *The Times* noted that 'outside what may be described as the amalgamating or would-be amalgamating circles themselves, the dislike of the City as a whole for this latest type of fusion among the already reduced number of large joint stock banks is made manifest whenever this question is under discussion'.[7] Moreover, Bonar Law himself also made it clear that enough was enough. The 'Big Five' had been created, henceforth to be set in concrete; Barclays, Lloyds, Midland, Westminster and National Provincial had half a century of semi-oligopoly ahead.

'No doubt the motives before amalgamation, like most human motives, are mixed', Addis wrote in the *Edinburgh Review* in July 1918. He warned that 'the bigger the bank the greater the danger that with the lapse of time it will become entrenched in a bed of vested interests, inimical to change, discountenancing the introduction of new ideas and discouraging the more efficient methods of young and vigorous competitors'. In short:

'The latent power of the amalgamated banks in sapping competition will be very great.'[8] An all too plausible forecast, but Addis himself had just become a director of the Old Lady. Now that they were *so* big, would the joint-stock men at last pierce the City's inner shield and achieve ungrudging acceptance?

Committees of inquiry proliferated during the war, mainly with a view to post-war 'reconstruction', and from a City – and indeed national – standpoint none was more important than the Committee on the Currency and Foreign Exchanges after the war.[9] It was jointly appointed in the autumn of 1917 by the Treasury and the Ministry of Reconstruction, after Cunliffe had made it clear that the City did not want to come under the sole sway of the latter authority. It was Cunliffe who suggested most of the names for the committee, mainly bankers; and, with Austen Chamberlain unavailable, it was Cunliffe who was asked by Bonar Law to assume the chairmanship.

The committee met regularly from February 1918, and their report became public in late October, stating that 'in our opinion it is imperative that after the war the conditions necessary to have maintenance of an effective gold standard should be restored without delay', for 'unless the machinery which long experience has shown to be the only effective remedy for an adverse balance of trade and an undue growth of credit is once more brought into play, there will be grave danger of a progressive credit expansion which will result in a foreign drain of gold menacing the convertibility of our note issue and so jeopardising the international trade position of the country'. By contrast, the Federation of British Industries had insisted in its submission that the trade balance 'must ultimately depend on production in this country'. Elsewhere, the report had no suggestions to make about reforming the Bank of England and advocated the maintenance of the Bank Charter Act of 1844, including its fixed fiduciary issue and the rigid separation of the issue and banking departments. It added that gold should be concentrated in the Bank of England for use as a reserve, with a minimum of £150m.[10]

City reaction was broadly favourable. 'It seems pretty clear already', *The Times* reported on 31 October, 'that general financial opinion will firmly approve what is taken to be the governing principle of the report, namely, its making all its conclusions dependent on the main object of getting back, after the war, to an unimpeachable gold basis for our currency.'[11]

Implicit in the Cunliffe Report's conclusions was the belief that a speedy return to the gold standard would in turn help to ensure that London recovered her pre-1914 position as the world's leading financial and commercial centre. Earlier in 1918, replying to a letter from the venerable former *Economist* editor Sir Robert Inglis Palgrave, which included a communication from the governor of the Bank of the Netherlands, Revelstoke surveyed the situation:

> Mr Vissering takes a pessimistic view of the future of the accepting business in London, and I allow that the considerations he advances are true in the main . . . We cannot expect that London will soon resume 'its old importance as financial centre of the world's commerce': but with all modesty I cannot but retain a perhaps optimistic conviction that the supremacy of British credit, with London as the clearing house of the world, may not necessarily be considered as a dream of the past.

It was a fair retrospective point, for London's acceptance business had declined gently rather than startlingly during the war, with even the more 'German' houses like Kleinworts and Schröders still ticking over. But of course the New York challenge loomed large. Was it a threat or was it perhaps an opportunity? Shortly before the war ended, the *Economic Journal* asked Robert Wyse, London manager of the Guaranty Trust Co. of New York and soon to replace his counterpart at the Union Discount, to give his views on 'The Future of London as the World's Money Market'. They were broadly sanguine, as he asserted that New York 'may perhaps take financial precedence of London, but that is not just yet'. And he went on: 'It is beyond question that Great Britain and the United States can co-operate in many financial ways at home and abroad to the advantage of both. The estrangements of old times are at an end.' Perhaps, but he might have been interested in the private view of the American banker Willard Straight (much involved in China finance) two years earlier, that the British idea of co-operation was that 'the other fellow does what the Britisher wants him to do, takes as much of the profit as he can get and for this, in the Englishman's mind, he ought to be thankful'. Above all, Wyse insisted, what London needed was a return to pre-1914 cosmopolitan finance: 'The League of Nations is only a fiction if all the great nations are not involved therein, and the world's money market does not answer its own description unless the motives of all its participants are free from suspicion and confidence is complete.'[12] It was, after the past four years, asking a lot.

*

Peace came at eleven o'clock on Monday 11 November 1918. Arthur Wrightson (in the absence of the indisposed Charlie Clarke) stood on an improvised platform and, holding a gold baton presented by his fellow members, led the Stock Exchange in singing the National Anthem; Addis noted that 'the City was stunned and even awed' and that 'apart from hooligan lads & drunken lasses the restraint of the crowd was admirable'; and Sir John Ellerman, shipowner, financier and Britain's richest man, told his daughter that 'the man who holds a similar position to myself in Germany has just committed suicide. I want you always to remember the War has been a very close thing'.[13]

C. H. Rolph, son of a City of London policeman, was seventeen years old and had been working for the past two years in 'the rag-trade warehouse' of Spreckley White & Lewis at 13–15 Cannon Street. There, in the counting house, he sat at a high desk fitted with a foot-rail and 'wrote letters to customers and manufacturers in the "copperplate" script, downstrokes-thick-upstrokes-thin, which I suppose had really begun to die out with the dissolution of the monasteries but was taking a long time about it'. As he recalled sixty years later, on Armistice Day he and his colleagues 'all went mad':

> We had been told that the great news would be announced by the firing of maroons, which we had so long accepted as air raid warnings. It was ten past eleven when they went off in the City . . . Two or three people ran down the short flight of steps from the swing doors into the street, and then everybody followed, the building emptied as if someone had shouted 'Fire!' Work was over for the day, by informal mass resolution.
>
> In Cannon Street a man on a bicycle was broken-windedly blowing the All Clear with a bugle he could hardly control as his cycle wobbled through the growing crowds. For some reason we all moved towards the Royal Exchange and the Mansion House, the very centre of the City. At the Royal Exchange someone had run up the Union Jack, and a stiff breeze filled it out. The Royal Exchange steps were black with people. Queen Victoria's statue was covered with clingers-on. Buses were accumulating in all the streets converging on the Royal Exchange, because the dense crowds had slowed them to the pace of the general movement, and eventually they all had to stop. They were all empty inside. Everyone was on top, far too many for safety. People were standing and sitting on the canopy over the driver's seat. One bus, a No. 11, was marked in chalk FREE TO BERLIN and was cheered madly by everyone. Men and women had taken off their boots and shoes so that they could bang them against the metal advertisement sheets on the buses' sides: anything, everything that could make a noise . . . Then down came the rain, and no one cared a damn. Pianoorgans appeared and people danced in the roads – the one adequate way, it seemed, in which to express excited joy and otherwise inexpressible relief. Those who couldn't dance rang handbells, banged trays, adding to the din of the Klaxons, the screaming whistles, anything and everything that could bellow, echo, vibrate, or shrill.
>
> At last I reached Mappin and Webb's Corner, to find that a crowd later estimated at 100,000, crammed into the converging thoroughfares from every direction, had gradually stopped making a noise as the Lord Mayor, on the steps of his Mansion House, seemed anxious to say something to them. Inaudibly from where I stood, he said a few words that brought fresh cheers and tears, and then led three thunderous cheers for the King, followed by three more each for the Army and the Navy. And when he

(or someone) began singing the Old Hundredth, it was gradually taken up by the thousands of rain-soaked revellers in the mightiest quasi-musical roar I have ever heard; and I was astounded that everyone near me seemed to know the words:

> Praise God from whom all blessings flow,
> Praise him all creatures here below;
> Praise him above, ye heavenly host,
> Praise Father, Son, and Holy Ghost.

It was a colossal sound, frightening, isolating; it was as though the God of Thunder himself had taken possession of that mysterious entity by which any crowd exceeds the sum of its constituent members. The very road and buildings seemed to shake with it. It's a hymn with only one verse, but what comparable crowd could sing it today?[14]

CHAPTER TWENTY-THREE

Facing Facts

For war heroes and others, 1919 as a whole was a strange, disillusioning year of rapidly rising prices, Stock Exchange speculation, industrial strife and fear of Bolshevism. 'Every kind of industrial share is being hoisted up and numbers of companies are making fresh issues', Farrer noted in April. As the domestic boom gathered momentum, the leading banks increased the level of their advances by well over half. 'We ladled out money', Robert Brand of Lloyds (as well as Lazards) would recall. 'We did it because everybody said they were making and were going to make large profits, and while you had an uneasy feeling yet you thought that while they were making large profits there could be nothing said about ladling out the money.'[1] As for more creative finance, inevitably the company promoter was back in the thick of things. None more so than Clarence Hatry, born in 1888 the son of a prosperous silk merchant and educated at St Paul's. Before the war he had been an increasingly high-powered insurance broker, but this was merely a prelude to the heady days of 1919, when he used the Commercial Bank of London (situated in due course in handsome premises on the corner of King William Street and Gracechurch Street, with a fine view over London Bridge) as his personal vehicle for virtuoso wheeler-dealing. Amalgamated Industrials was typical: Hatry floated it for £1.6m in June, as a ship-building, pig iron, coal and cotton-spinning combine with precious little industrial logic, and within four months sold the controlling interest for £5m. At this time Hatry also did very well for himself through major speculations in oil shares, such as Shell and Mexican Eagle. By the start of 1920 he was a very rich man, but in February had to leave business in order to undergo a serious abdominal operation, to be followed by several months of convalescence in South America. In the centre drawer of his desk he left instructions to (in his subsequent words) 'sell all speculative holdings and to keep the bank's resources liquid'.[2] He knew that no boom went on for ever.

It was not a boom that inspired universal joy, dominated as it was by inflation unparalleled in anyone's peacetime memory, but seen by the government for much of 1919 as preferable to the apparent alternative of mass unemployment. Organised labour flexed its muscles, and in August a group of bankers (including Addis) was summoned to Downing Street, given a statement on the industrial unrest, and asked for its co-operation against Bolshevism. The following month the railway strike brought the City almost to a halt, though when one day a few trains did run, this was (the Smith St Aubyn diary noted) 'to the great content of the Engine drivers who were showered with silver'. Hitherto unionisation had been almost non-existent in the City, but this was now starting to change, albeit slowly and tentatively. The nationwide Bank Officers' Guild had already been established in 1918, attracting many recruits in the joint-stock banks. 'A serpent has raised its head in banking' was Holden's temperate reaction, adding, 'I'll smash the B.O.G. or die in the attempt.' Salaries were raised and share participation schemes introduced, but the banks obstinately refused to negotiate with the Guild. So too did the Stock Exchange with officers of the Stock Exchange Clerks' Guild, founded in 1919 and soon representing well over 2,000 clerks.[3]

As for the peace settlement generally, the City seems to have been merely relieved that the war was over. 'I only trust that this definite signature of Peace may foreshadow the dawn of a happier era of prosperity', Revelstoke wrote to a Paris banker in January 1920. Keynes' coruscating analysis of *The Economic Consequences of the Peace* had just been published, but Norman was probably correct when he described *Punch's* reaction as 'a summing up of many people's attitude towards Keynes' diatribe', as he enclosed the relevant verses in a letter to Benjamin Strong. 'There was a superior young person named Keynes,' they began, and ended:

> Still we feel, as he zealously damns the Allies
> For grudging the Germans the means to arise,
> That possibly some of the Ultimate Things
> May even be hidden from fellows of King's.[4]

Cunliffe himself was already encountering some of those ultimate things, having succumbed to septicaemia less than a week into the new decade.

We have a final glimpse. In April 1919, after the New York investment bank Kuhn Loeb had suggested an international issue for Belgium, Anthony de Rothschild called on Cokayne at the Bank of England to ascertain his views. 'The Governor', he reported to Rothschilds in Paris:

> repeated very much the same opinion as he gave us last month about the general situation and said that he did not think the London market was capable of handling any such operation, for the present at any rate. So long as we had to borrow money from the United States ourselves – and there was considerable uncertainty as to when we should have to meet our obligations in that country – it was most unsafe for us to lend money to other countries.

Following which, while Anthony discussed the matter with his cousin Charles, Cunliffe came in:

> He particularly emphasised the fact that it would be most unwise to surrender our international financial position more readily than was absolutely necessary and pointed out that if an international issue was made Paris could subscribe nothing, London might make a pretence of subscribing a little and New York would have to find practically the whole of the money, but that it would be worth while for London to appear as a participant.

De Rothschild went to see the Treasury's Bradbury, who entirely backed Cokayne, not his predecessor, and 'stated definitively that at the moment the Treasury would not be likely to give permission for such an issue in London'.[5]

The fundamentals, it was painfully clear, had altered.[6] 'I have been making enquiries in the City and elsewhere with regard to the view held on the general financial situation to the extent to which assistance can be given by London to other European countries', Brand a few weeks later informed Lord Robert Cecil, in Paris as chairman of the Supreme Economic Council of the Allies. 'I find the general view is that if the problem is as big as it appears to be . . . it is far beyond the capacity of the British Banks and Accepting Houses.' Next day Brand wrote to a Lazards partner in New York, reflecting on his own recent stint as Cecil's financial adviser: 'The longer I stayed in Paris, the more I was impressed with the enormous size of the financial and economic problem of Europe. Everything in reality depends on America's attitude and her willingness to lend freely and for long terms to Europe. Unless she does so the future is certainly very black and more than one country may be unable to escape a collapse.' The London market remained for the time being virtually closed to foreign loans, even for the best causes, and when in January 1920 Hambros approached Norman on the subject of a possible Danish issue, the deputy governor 'refused to hear the Danes or see them' and 'said the Danes sh^d go to N.Y.' Being a man of pre-1914 sensibilities, when London was the unrivalled capital market of the world, Norman added in his diary that 'this position' was 'generally unpleasing'.[7]

With the United States thus supplanting Britain as the world's creditor, how could the Americans be persuaded to deploy their abundant surplus capital on a co-operative as opposed to a competitive basis?[8] Writing from Paris (where he was an American delegate) in June, Thomas Lamont of Morgans in New York had ambitious co-operation in mind when he called on Brand to endorse 'a working partnership in business betwixt Great Britain and America':

America has ample credit resources, Great Britain has wonderful credit machinery all over the world. Why not make a combination of the two? Your people have splendid banks established in the Far East and all through South America. Now, we in America are right on the verge of duplicating every bit of that banking machinery by establishing banks of our own there and entering into very active competition with you. The result will be, you will make smaller profits, and so shall we, and we shall be very keen rivals. Why don't we avoid all that by our buying a half interest, no more, in a lot of your banks, and thus make a combination of your machinery and our credit resources? I suppose the very idea sounds fantastic to you. It did to Keynes when I sprang it on him the other night at dinner. His ready answer was, that your banks wanted to run their own business and didn't want any interference from outside. It was a very complete answer, because it showed the spirit of the whole thing.

As so often Keynes was on the money, for it would need more than a sudden change in the global pecking order to upset the assumptions of a lifetime. 'Senator Owen (Oklahoma) at Bk of E. Lunch', noted Addis late in 1918. 'A typical Yankee politician; not attractive.' Or as Farrer, writing to a sympathetic Dutch banker, characterised Wall Street some years later: 'Everyone there is more or less out for everyone else's throat, and it is a case of devil take the hindmost.'[9]

Undeniably, irrespective of prejudice, these were difficult, challenging times. Austen Chamberlain was chosen by Lloyd George early in 1919 to be his peacetime Chancellor, not least because the City regarded him as reassuringly sound; yet within weeks he was compelled to observe that 'when "the City" is acting by instinct and rule of thumb it is amazingly clever and sure, but when it is asked to advise on large new issues, it has no theory or policy to work upon, and is indeed a broken reed'.[10] The context was the debate about whether or not to continue to allow gold exports, and thus a theoretical gold standard, in the wake of the American decision no longer to support sterling. Cokayne and Norman saw the anti-inflationary advantages of maintaining a pegged dollar-sterling exchange rate at 4.76; the politicians feared the social and political consequences of deflation; and they received valuable backing from leading joint-stock bankers.[11]

As for the domestic situation, Cokayne expressed his keenness to check the post-war credit expansion, 'which has inevitably led, or at least contributed largely, to a great increase in the currency and to extravagant living'. And in general, Cokayne warned Chamberlain, 'the Court regard the restoration of the gold standard and the resumption of free gold exports at the earliest possible moment as of vital importance to the Country as a whole and consider that it is well worth a temporary sacrifice to secure that end'.[12] The counter-revolution had begun.

In early November, to the City's surprise, Cokayne managed to secure an increase in Bank rate from 5 to 6 per cent – though Norman observed to Strong that, pleased though he was, 'at the same time I cannot regard the certainty of sound money as definitely settled'. In particular he was worried about 'the advocates of expansion and the printing press, which to a considerable extent is the view held by many political leaders'. Debate over monetary policy intensified during the winter, and Chamberlain found himself caught invidiously between the Bank and the banks. There was by now an important new player. Holden had died suddenly in July while recuperating in Scotland. Typically he had travelled there by car, not train, in order to inspect some branches on the way. 'His one hobby in life was banking and all that appertains thereto', the *FT* justly obituarised. In his final year he had carefully trained the former Chancellor, Reginald McKenna, as his nominated successor, and McKenna was quickly into his stride, stoutly calling for national economy and an eventual return to the gold standard, but explicitly challenging the Bank's dear-money policy. 'Take my advice, don't run for the position of C. of E. when you enter Parl', Chamberlain wrote to one of his sisters in January 1920 after a wearying round of discussions. The clearing bankers have been accused of talking up their own books during this protracted tussle, on the grounds that higher rates would have led directly to 'damaging depreciation of their own and their customers' gilt-edged portfolios'; even if there is some truth in this, the fact remains that the joint-stock banks generally *did* have a somewhat wider grasp of the social consequences of dear money than that possessed by either the Bank of England or the Treasury.[13]

Praising dear money, and advocating still dearer, Cokayne in February commended the previous autumn's Bank rate rise to Chamberlain as having 'shown the intention of this country to face facts' – an early example in the modern era of the Bank's ability to apply a sharp twist of emotional pressure in order to raise the stakes.

Chamberlain himself was now privately backing Cokayne and believed the bankers to be 'biassed by their interest, timid & collectively selfish'; but several key Cabinet colleagues were still hostile to dearer money, and so he decided to 'disappoint the governor & put the Bankers on their honour to behave better than they have been doing'. The promise of credit rationing failed, however, to do the trick. There still appeared to be an inflationary boom that needed dampening down; the pound was still making a poor fist of it, as international confidence in Britain's post-war economic prospects waned; and on 15 April, a fortnight after Norman had succeeded Cokayne as governor, the rate was increased from 6 to 7 per cent.[14] Bank and Treasury (especially Bradbury) had proved a formidable coalition.

A revealing postscript to the rise was played out over the next few months. In fact the boom was already past its peak, and the depression setting in, but because of the poor quality of economic intelligence this was not generally recognised until the end of the summer. By July not only was Norman pushing for a rise to 8 per cent, for what was becoming the familiar mixture of domestic and exchange reasons, but Keynes was taking a stridently dear-money line, telling the Tuesday Club on the 8th that continuing inflation and fiscal extravagance demanded a tougher monetary stance. A week later Norman made his debut at the Lord Mayor's annual Mansion House dinner for bankers and merchants. 'They [i.e. the Bank] had been for months past pursuing a steady and consistent policy, which he believed to be the one and only policy which would ultimately place this country again on that eminence which it occupied before the war', he told those present (in his reported words). 'The object they had set themselves was, with as little delay as possible, to attempt to regain the gold standard, and to that end every movement had been directed.' But next morning there appeared in the *FT* what was from Norman's point of view an ominous editorial, highly critical of the desire in some quarters for a further rise in Bank rate. After a reference to the 'dear money fanatics', it went on:

> Still the desire to shoot has not been abandoned. The old-time reputation of the Bank Rate as an arm of precision makes them anxious to load it up and let it off. Suppose they had their way and, aiming across the broad Atlantic, fired their 8 per cent shell. It would explode ineffectually in the air, but the recoil would react with incalculable injury on home trade and industry.

Norman may on the 17th have told Hawtrey at the Treasury that 'the City fears higher rates simply and solely because of the consequent depreciation in their securities', adding that 'this reason is never mentioned', but in reality there was a broader agenda at work. Chamberlain simply informed the governor that another rise was politically impossible.[15] In the changed conditions of the post-war world – no 'automatic' monetary standard, volatile exchange rates, national and international financial considerations meshing far more closely than they had ever done before 1914 – it would become increasingly difficult for the high priests of the City to remain value-free technicians beyond criticism or even scrutiny.

*

'Dined with Norman at his house Thorpe Lodge on Campden Hill', jotted Addis in November 1919. 'Magnificently filled house for a lone bachelor.' And the following April, after Norman had become governor: 'I like him. A clever fellow. I only hope his health will stand the strain.' Though occasionally critical, Addis remained enamoured. In September 1922: 'That dear man Norman called . . . He is a friendly chap and singularly gifted with charm.'[16] It was at about this time that Anthony Blanche was telling Charles Ryder that charm was the English vice; in the hands of Montagu Norman, governor from 1920 to 1944, charm was perhaps his most powerful weapon, and certainly his most insidious.

A trio of set-piece descriptions and reminiscences enable one to start to see the man in the round. Émile Moreau, a governor of the Bank of France, first met Norman in Paris in 1926:

> He appears to have stepped out of a Van Dyck painting; elongated figure, pointed beard, a big hat; he has the bearing of a companion of the Stuarts. It is said that Israelite blood flows in his veins. I know nothing of this, but Mr Norman seemed, perhaps because of it, full of contempt for the Jews about whom he spoke in very bad terms . . . He told me: 'The Bank of England is my only mistress. I think only of her and I have given her my life' . . . Very mysterious, extremely complicated, one never knows the depth of his thoughts. Even so, he is very amiable, charming when he wants to be. That is the case when he tries to flatter me by telling me that the Bank of England was founded by French Huguenots.

Five years later Raymond Streat was one of a six-man deputation from the Manchester Chamber of Commerce who saw Norman at the Bank:

> I doubt if this man has an equal, never mind a superior, at controlling situations and putting the men who come to meet him where he wants them firmly and kindly but ever so effectively. Towards the end of the interview this remarkable man spoke with intense and burning feeling about the obligations of the City of London to set such standards of integrity, not merely in action but even in thought, as would leave her reputation as untarnished in the future as it had been in the past. This note of high moral sentiment took me by surprise but it was in excellent taste and on the whole impressive.

All who knew Norman at all well were aware of the many contradictions in his character, and writing in the 1960s, the veteran economist Sir Theodore Gregory made a fair stab at encapsulating them:

> He was both artistic and musical in his tastes and could be extremely kind. Yet, one of his oldest American *confidantes*, to whom he was obviously sincerely attached, could describe him as 'the most vindictive man I have ever known'. He could enlist warm friendships and elicit the most devoted service, yet he could seriously upset the nerves of some of his most faithful collaborators. He disliked politicians as such, but found a congenial soul in Baldwin . . . He could never have been a success on television. He would have despised it.'[17]

For all his personal qualities, one needs to explain how it was that Norman became the Pope of the City – a place that previously had tended to regard the Bank of England with at least as much scepticism as reverence. Nor on the face of it was Norman the City's type. According to Addis, his Mansion House speech of July 1920 had a 'strange' and 'mystical' quality to it – 'fine in its way but unsuited to his audience'. Clearly his length of tenure, conclusively ending the peacetime tradition of two-year gubernatorial stints, was crucial to achieving his ascendancy. Addis, writing in 1926 about the early part of the decade, gave a typically clear-sighted explanation:

> The orientation of our banking policy had been profoundly disturbed. The predominant industrial and financial position of England had been challenged and it was no longer possible for the central bank unaided to control the exchanges and prevent, as formerly, undue fluctuations in the value of gold by the accustomed use of the Bank rate. The only possible means of solving that question was to arrive, if that was practicable, at a common understanding with the central banks of the old world and the new in order to secure the adoption of a common monetary policy in which all could co-operate. The problem had become international. The Bank of England had ceased to be an insular institution. The suspension of the biennial rotation was justified by the necessity of securing continuity in the delicate negotiations required to adjust the administration of the Bank to the novel relations with the other central banks. This was not a matter of choice. It was a condition imposed by the war.[18]

So, inevitably with some acrimony involved, it was.

'At the beginning of next month, contrary to custom, I am beginning my third year', Norman wrote to Strong in March 1922, following a forceful appeal from Strong that he stay on. 'What will happen after that I have not the least idea, but I must confess that there is no understudy at the present time ready and qualified to step into the gap.' Certainly his deputy since 1920, H. A. Trotter, was not the man to grasp the new nettle of international central banking. Anyway, the next in line for the chair, Cecil Lubbock, had made it clear that he would not serve as deputy under Trotter. In October 1922 Trotter agreed to stand down ('he wishes to attend to his private business which is not doing well', Norman informed Strong) and Lubbock in effect became deputy governor, formally from the following spring. Norman also told Strong: 'I continue as governor (& my so doing may raise some criticism, as it will be my fourth Year & people prefer the Rotation: But how swap horses just now?).' A year later, in November 1923, the question of a successor to Norman was seriously considered. 'Grenfell says No! to Lubbock', noted Addis, who had already ruled himself out in a confidential discussion with Revelstoke. Lubbock was a capable man, but it would have been strange to have had a brewer (in his case Whitbreads) as governor in the complex world financial order that was taking shape. 'I am engaged here for 1924/5', Norman entered in his diary in February 1924. 'I am willing to be similarly engaged for 1925/6 and 1926/7.'[19]

Beyond the fact that the world had changed, beyond the City's seeming need for a single authority to help it make sense of that change, beyond that lodestar's longevity, there were Norman's considerable personal qualities, charm included. He made it his business to know what was going on in all the City's main sectors; his door was always open to the leading figures in those sectors; and by dint of 'moral suasion' – the dignified term for the raising of the governor's eyebrows – he exercised greater authority over the City than any of his predecessors or successors. 'His requests were taken as commands, and complied with to the letter, often at a real sacrifice', Lawrence Jones of Helbert Wagg recalled. 'A summons would come to Alfred Wagg, who must put on a top-hat in which to obey it, for the wide-brimmed soft hat that hung outside Mr Governor's room would tolerate no rival.'[20]

CHAPTER TWENTY-FOUR

Quite Impossible

Montagu Norman was, perhaps more than anything else, an internationalist – albeit one with certain strong prejudices about individual nations. During these post-war years, the governing tenet of his internationalism was that what the world needed was to return to the pre-1914 order of economic liberalism, with the global economy regulated by the benign dictates of free trade and free capital flows. London, he further assumed, would naturally revert to its position at the hub of that reconstituted financial and trading system. Accordingly, when Strong, visiting England in 1919, was told by Kindersley that the Americans had a moral obligation to forgive the huge war debt (almost £900m) owed to them by Britain – on the grounds that it had been a sacrifice for a shared cause – Norman unequivocally assured him: 'Pay no attention to Kindersley. His heart rules his head.'[1] In other words, Britain could not expect to be taken seriously as a commercial power if it reneged on its debts.

Eventually, in January 1923, Norman found himself in Washington advising the Chancellor, Stanley Baldwin, during the negotiations to settle the debt. Baldwin 'caught on from the very beginning', Norman was pleased to find, and was much influenced by the governor's advice. The terms they returned with – a settlement spread over sixty-one years, interest of 3½ per cent for most of that time – horrified the prime minister, Bonar Law, but received sufficient political and City support to ensure their acceptance. Addis demurred at the Bank, while McKenna briefly growled, before coming on board. Keynes was bitterly opposed, contending that whatever the international arguments in favour of the settlement (the prospect of American co-operation in future European reconstruction as well as the question of British financial honour), there were overriding national arguments against such onerous terms. Hitherto Norman had broadly respected Keynes, even on occasion picking his brains, but his attitude now changed. A 'clever dilettante' was about the best he could say for the man from King's.[2] In reality, as Keynes had feared, a future beckoned of at least as much American rivalry as co-operation.[3] The dollar was strong, US vaults were flooded with gold, key markets (particularly in Latin America) had been captured from Britain – Norman knew all that, yet trusted to force of habit and personal charm to keep the new world in tow to the old. But at least he did not have to watch his back. 'I think it is extremely unfortunate that the City has failed as yet to formulate its view and express it', the cerebral stockbroker Oswald Falk wrote at the start of 1923 to a concurring Brand about the debt question. 'I am afraid the City does not think sufficiently about these things.'[4]

For their part, Norman and Strong as early as 1921 were consciously formulating the principles of central banking, and the Englishman was comforting the American that 'if ever you should feel downhearted just you remember that, economically speaking, there is only hope through a community of interest & co-operation between all the Central Banks'. At the core of their shared conception was that central banks should maintain operational independence, free from government control, and should 'recognise the importance of international as well as national interests in the re-establishment of the world's economic and trade stability'.[5]

Though the international conference at Genoa in 1922 explicitly endorsed the value of central banking co-operation and looked ahead to a full-blown conference of central banks later in the year, Norman was unable to convene such an assembly that would have sealed his very personal vision. The Americans in particular would not play ball, and Strong subsequently explained that the prospect of a conference where he would 'represent the only lending market, while the others would all be borrowers', had had little appeal.[6] Norman was disappointed but not deterred, continued to propagate his belief in the freemasonry of disinterested central bankers as a necessary counterweight to grubby, vote-catching politicians, and in Washington in January 1923 fully endorsed Strong's views as to unacceptable debt settlement, whatever the potential political consequences at home. He had a larger – and longer – game to play.

Norman appreciated how important Central Europe had been in the pre-1914 economic scheme of things, and during the first half of the 1920s he managed to push through several major reconstruction loans for that part of the world, often with only muted City support: Czechoslovakia in 1922, followed by a large-scale Austrian loan in June 1923. The following year, a loan for Hungary seems to have happened only after Norman strong-armed Rothschilds and Schröders into undertaking it; though again, despite problems with the underwriting, it was a success, no doubt because its sponsors ('the Trinity' of Schröders, Rothschilds and Barings) managed to insist on a yield double that of Consols.[7]

Germany, of course, lay at the heart of the challenging process of reconstructing Europe.[8] The crux was the seemingly intractable problem of reparations. 'This question plays the devil with us all and hangs like a sinister cloud over the world', Edward Peacock (a Bank director who not long afterwards would join Barings) wrote to Norman in May 1922. He went on to argue that both the main parties were at fault – the French attitude 'technical & unyielding & exasperating', the Germans 'morally wrong', having 'not begun to do the possible' – and, Peacock concluded, '*we* pay the piper for the sins of both'. Norman, however, perceived only one villain, especially after the French occupation of the Ruhr. 'Here you have *all* the conditions of war except that one side is unarmed', he told Strong in April 1923. 'How long can Germany continue thus?' On New Year's Eve the newly appointed president of the Reichsbank, Hjalmar Schacht, visited London – being met by Norman at Victoria Station at 10 p.m. – and spent the first four days of 1924 in meetings with Norman and leading clearing and merchant bankers. 'Financially a man of sound and up-to-date views' was Norman's verdict.[9] Schacht was pressing for a large German loan, and Norman was fully prepared to back him.

On a visit to Paris in March he found the French 'still vindictive and unpeaceful', and that same month organised a credit by central banks to enable the establishment of the German Gold Discount Bank.[10] By the end of the summer there was international agreement behind the Dawes Plan, seeking to settle the reparations question – agreement that Norman much welcomed, though against his wishes the new German currency was to be put on a gold (in effect dollar) basis, as opposed to a sterling one.[11] 'It is the question of whether the dollar shall permanently retain a predominant position, or whether we are willing to surrender financial mastery to the Pound Sterling for good and all!' Paul Warburg of Kuhn Loeb in New York had written during the negotiations to an American member of the Dawes Committee. It is difficult to know how serious Norman was about seeking to establish a potential sterling bloc in Central Europe, especially granted the imminent likelihood of the world at large returning to a dollar-denominated gold basis. Even so, when at the end of May the New York banks at the last minute ducked out of the Hungarian reconstruction loan, Norman was palpably satisfied that Europe was able to go it alone and told Schacht that 'it would be ridiculous for Europe to be tied to the tail of America'.[12] Tied to that tail, however, Europe now was.

Integral to the Dawes Plan was the reconstruction loan for Germany. Farrer in July condemned 'the folly of people in this country lending money to Germany to put her on her legs', maintaining to a correspondent that 'it was the German State that was responsible for all the trouble, the German State that over and over again during the war showed the most cynical bad faith and dishonesty, and since the war repeated her conduct by wilfully depreciating the mark'. He added that 'it is quite certain that Germany as a State will never get a penny of my money, but I greatly fear that there are plenty in the City of London who do not share these views of mine'. In the event, though American investors took the lion's share of the huge 'Dawes Loan' issued in October 1924, London was responsible for some £10m. Norman struggled to bring the City into line, managing to persuade Rothschilds to participate secretly up to £1m, but noting in his diary on the 7th that the big joint-stock banks 'decline any official goodwill or support, unless all deposit Banks are named in prospectus'. However, on the 1st Addis had already correctly predicted that the loan would 'be a great success despite the adverse press – Daily Mail is gone mad in fermenting racial prejudices'. Addis had presumably read his *FT*, where the market report of the previous evening noted that 'the view that the loan would give a fillip to German competition has largely evaporated, giving place to a conviction that it may well act as a stimulus to world trade as a whole'. The underwriting was done easily enough on the 13th, though again, according to the *FT*, 'some few men there are who will have nothing to do with a German loan' on the grounds that 'the Germans, they say, have hoodwinked, cheated, damaged us in lives and pocket to an irreparable extent'. Farrer next day confessed himself 'rather surprised to find how easily the average Englishman has put senti-ment aside in this case' and could only offer the explanation that 'one's experience is that investors are rather like a flock of sheep'.

That was on Tuesday the 14th, and the loan was about to be so enor-mously oversubscribed that, according to the *FT* on Thursday, 'many firms of brokers slept members of their staffs in City hotels on Tuesday night, and stories were current during the day that senior partners who had never before been seen in the City earlier than half-past ten or eleven caused something like consternation in outer offices by putting in an appearance yesterday morning in the neighbourhood of eight o'clock'. Without the loan the Dawes Plan was a dead duck, and the City as a whole – encouraged by the attractive 7 per cent coupon – was prepared to play its part, welcoming a concrete step in the long, difficult road back to 'normality'.[13]

Soviet Russia remained beyond the pale. Predictably it was demonised, Norman for example confiding to Strong in 1921 his suspicion that that summer's coal strike was 'much more closely connected with Soviet activ-ities than most of us have any idea of'. The following year, having attended the Genoa conference, at which Russia was refused its request for a big loan, Brand told General Smuts in South Africa that he was 'of opinion that the chasm between the Bolshevik economic system and the system in force in Western Europe is too great at present to be bridged, and the Bolsheviks have to go much further in their return to such ideas as the sanctity of contract and the rights of private property before any trade worth speaking of is possible between Russia and the rest of the world'.

He added that if it did receive a loan, 'the Russian government would squander the money that it got'. In 1924, with a Labour government briefly in office, there was a semi-serious possibility of a British loan, but only if Russia was prepared to recognise the claims of pre-Revolution bondholders. The energetic stockbroker and financier Charles Birch Crisp, much involved in Russian affairs for almost twenty years, talked to Stock Exchange authorities and jobbers about a possible debt arrangement; 'not likely to be successful' was Norman's shrewd private assessment in July.[14] The City would have little to do with that part of the world for another sixty years.

*

All was not quite back to normal at the Stock Exchange. Although its old noisiness returned from July 1919, following the removal of the wartime injunction against open bidding and offering, the House remained closed on Saturdays throughout the 1920s, initially at the request of the joint-stock banks, their staffs much depleted by the war. Moreover, the jobbing system (411 firms in 1920, down from some 600 on the eve of war) was now starting its long-run decline, though this was as yet masked by its sheer numbers.[15]

By 1920 over one-third of the nominal value of London's quoted securities comprised British government debt, a ratio that rose still further during the interwar period. Norman naturally kept a close eye on the gilt-edged market. In April 1925 he was privately informed by W. H. Askew, of the dissolving firm of jobbers Gordon, Askew & Biddulph, that he intended to join Akroyds as senior partner: 'I say I have no objection . . . *He* must decide on personal question with other Jobbers.' The government broker was responsible for selling Consols and other gilt-edged stock to that market. Since time immemorial this business had been in the hands of Mullens, Marshall & Co., but back in February 1920 its senior partner, the rather dour J. A. Mullens, had returned from ten days' absence to be summoned by Cokayne and told that the Bank was unwilling to be left solely in the hands of Mullens' existing partners. 'Either M.M. & Co. at once add a new & competent partner to assist & replace at times J.A.M.,' recorded Norman, 'or we employ another firm of Brokers concurrently with M.M. & Co.' Mullens took the hint and the next year merged his firm with the brokers Steer, Lawford & Co., the new firm being called Mullens, Marshall, Steer Lawford & Co., in due course finding its next senior partner not from the Mullens side.[16]

Mullens himself was at the top of an ill-appreciated profession. 'Why is a stockbroker less beautiful than a Homeric warrior or an Egyptian priest?' asked Christopher Dawson in a lecture to the Sociological Society in July 1923 on 'Progress and Decay in Ancient and Modern Civilisation'.

The answer, according to Dawson, was self-evident: 'Because he is less Incorporated with life, he is not inevitable, but accidental, almost parasitic.' Nicholas Davenport, a young graduate who went to Rowe & Pitman in 1925 'to write the "economic stuff"', would probably have agreed: 'What struck me at first sight was the jolly vitality of stockbrokers. They were like healthy schoolboys, telling each other dirty stories, ragging around when the markets were dull, and occasionally de-bagging an outsider who intruded into the "House" . . . They were exceptionally quick-witted; their reactions to the ticker-tape were like lightning; they saw the future just a day ahead. Their intellectual level was about form four in the schools they had never really left.' It was true, Davenport went on, that 'to call their attention to the need for social change at that time would have been an unpardonable *faux pas*'. However, he added, 'what distinguished them from some of those who scoffed at and derided them' was that 'they were really prepared to fight and die for their Establishment'.[17]

Stagnation in the Stock Exchange contrasted sharply with the rapid, turbulent post-war growth of the London foreign exchange market. Indeed, Farrer in a November 1922 critique of the Stock Exchange contrasted the stock market's 'too high' scale of brokerage to the low charges imposed by what he called 'by far the biggest and free-est exchange market in the world'. H. W. Phillips, in his authoritative survey a few years later of that market, recalled what had happened:

> With the unpegging of the world's exchanges in March 1919, there started one of the largest businesses the world has seen. A veritable orgy of dealing took place, and every centre seemed to be besieging London on long-distance calls. From early till late at night (6 p.m.) foreign centres called London and immense business was transacted. Brokers increased, and by 1920 there were about 40 different broking firms in the business of the banks and financial houses. There was business for all . . . The amounts turned over on the London exchange market were huge. Day after day the staffs of the brokers fed at their switchboards and went home exhausted.

Among the banks that took the plunge was the Société Générale, one of whose London dealers was a young man called George Bolton, son of a Baltic Exchange trader. 'Confusion reigned supreme as the brokers' direct telephones were massed together on a table,' he wrote many years later, 'and the only means of identifying any call was by altering the ringing tone of each telephone by stuffing paper, cardboard, metal clips, etc. between the clapper and the bell. Contract notes were delivered by hand, very often to the wrong bank, and it seemed miraculous that any business could be satisfactorily settled. Techniques were invented as we went along.' There had been a certain amount of foreign exchange dealing in London before 1914, but in the new world of volatile currencies and seemingly permanent political instability this was something different. 'Foreign exchanges and currency problems which in the old days were relegated to experts have lately become a topic of popular discussion', the *FT* put it in January 1920, with perhaps a little exaggeration. Or as Winston Churchill wrote three years later to his stockbroker brother, Jack: 'What about selling a bear in marks? How can they keep this up long? It is a pure manoeuvre. France has got them by the balls.'[18]

By the early 1920s the foreign exchange market had settled down and no longer relied on improvising with metal clips. Noting that meetings in the Royal Exchange (anyway long superseded by the telephone) to deal in bills of exchange denominated in foreign currencies had finally expired in January 1921, Phillips described the market – a telephone market, with no physical meeting-place – in action:

> It is an extremely large and an astonishingly active market, swifter than stocks and shares and faster than cotton or wool. By a network of underground wires to the provinces; by sea-bed cables to Holland, Paris, America, etc.; by wireless to almost anywhere; by private wires to brokers and clients; the foreign exchange dealer finds himself a principal in a highly developed business. He is a telephone slave . . . He listens to the brokers making him prices, but his other ear takes in the requests and queries of his assistants. His voice is questioning the broker while his eyes and head are answering his colleagues. A spare hand is writing the cable to a foreign dealer, and his plug goes into the private line to a cable company, dictating as he writes. He is reasonably certain that his message has reached the cable company's New York office within 30 seconds, and the dealer to whom it is directed will soon after be at work on his order.

Not surprisingly, Phillips added, 'quotations are short and snappy' and 'conversations one or two words'.[19]

By the time he was writing (1925), some 120 banks were significant players in the market, serviced by thirty to forty broking firms (led by Harlow & Jones), which throughout the day quoted rates on all the main currencies. The banks included several leading merchant banks, such as Kleinworts, Schröders and Brown Shipley. It could be a tense business. Brown Brothers in New York cabled to Norman's old firm in April 1921 that 'a true friend of ours and yours tells us that your Exchange operations are creating comment in London even to the extent of the thought that you finance yourselves through them'. Edward Clifton-Brown replied indignantly, insisting that 'although figures are large', and that 'on occasions it has been advisable in order to bridge the gap in the "here and there" cash position to sell considerable lines of "cheque"', there was 'no warrant that we can discover for the suggestion made in your cable, the more so as our Operator absolutely assures us that our "cheque" has never been sold at any but the very finest rate' and 'has never been forced upon the market'. Even so, Clifton-Brown conceded, 'while we have been most particular about ensuring that no speculation was taking place in the rates of exchange, we have to a certain extent insufficiently appreciated the difficulties which might arise if actual dates of commitments are not closely matched'. In August the following year Brown Brothers reiterated anxieties about unmatched future positions, prompting Clifton-Brown to 'put on record our belief that our Operator has loyally adhered to the restrictions put upon him' and that 'every day and all day he has his exact position in front of him, and his figures are always ready for our inspection at any time of the day, and are brought into the Parlour for investigation at frequent intervals'.[20]

Almost certainly a less inhibited approach obtained at Helbert Wagg, following its acquisition in May 1921 of a foreign exchange capacity in the form of Bonn & Co. Two gifted young men dominated the firm's foreign exchange dealing in the 1920s: one was Lionel Fraser, the son of Gordon Selfridge's butler and in the process of starting to turn himself into a major City figure; the other, with an equally glittering future, was his deputy, George Bolton, who had moved to Helbert Wagg in 1920. 'Altogether, it was killing and frenzied work,' Fraser would recall, 'and except that the department was able to make a substantial contribution to the profits of the firm, I find it difficult to persuade myself that we were doing anything particularly constructive or helpful in those very disturbed times.' Perhaps so – but 'this unrestricted jungle warfare of the foreign exchange market' (Fraser's phrase) did offer a certain hum and buzz by now lacking in some other parts of the Square Mile.[21]

Not least in the City's traditional mercantile core. 'These are difficult times to live in – incendiary riots by Sinn Feiners in Liverpool, bombs thrown in the City today, Downing Street barricaded', reflected Harry Williamson of Balfour Williamson in November 1920. 'Meantime there is a steady decline in the price of every commodity. This eventually will be all to the good; at present it is a sore trial to merchants!'[22] The historically crucial Anglo-German connection, in terms of people as well as trade, had been seriously eroded; war had also given American rivals the chance to replace London, not only in securing supplies but also in marketing finished goods; and between the wars, though British commodity trade generally waxed with the Dominions (though not India), it waned with Western Europe, the United States, Latin America and China. Moreover, there took place a 'drastic slump in Britain's invisible income' – in other words from overseas investments, shipping, the provision of trade credit, and issuing.[23] One of many City merchants under pressure was Cecil Beaton's father, Ernest, who dealt in timber. By 1924 the family lived at 3 Hyde Park Street, and at dinner on Christmas Eve the usually good-humoured Ernest was in a thoroughly bad mood before he left to go to his City office. Cecil's diary entry offers a timeless vignette of commercial life:

> Mother sat in a chair and talked. 'We can't afford this house. We'll have to sell it and live in some cheaper place. Business has been bad. Ever since that brute of a Fox left, things have been getting slacker and slacker. Now you know Daddy has lost the American business. That brute Bowers has taken it away and given it to a man in Manchester. It'll make an awful difference: half of our income gone. No wonder your father's worried and edgy tonight. There's a cargo of stuff from Finland which may mean a dead loss of six thousand pounds. That's why he's gone to the office to see if any telegrams have come in.'[24]

Of consuming importance to Norman was the long, difficult route march that was the British return to the gold standard.[25] Early in his governorship he began to appreciate the way in which monetary policy in general, and Bank rate in particular, was becoming politicised. Interest rates, he observed to Pierre Jay of the Fed in September 1920, 'are now a political as well as a financial question', while two months later he reproachfully told the Chancellor, Austen Chamberlain, that 'when I call to mind your remark to my predecessor (that an independent Rise in the Bank Rate would be an unfriendly act); when I remember our continuing desire for higher rates ever since last July and indeed long before it, and your continuing unwillingness to consent, owing to political reasons . . . I wonder what (in the spirit as well as in the letter) is the meaning of "political pressure".' But in the long run, however much Norman may have wished otherwise, there was no avoiding this politicisation, with the price of money now being seen as impinging directly on levels of unemployment, housing policy and economic policy in general. The clearing banks, with their traditionally greater domestic orientation, remained at odds with Norman, whose fundamental belief was that domestic problems required international remedies. It was not only McKenna who pushed in the winter of 1920–1 for lower rates, but also the far more conservative Henry Bell, general manager of Lloyds. Norman told the latter in December that 'tho rate reduction might affect mentality at home it w^d not help sales abroad'. In addition, Frederick Goodenough (chairman of Barclays) was reported by Schuster to Norman in November 1921 as being largely responsible for stirring up opposition to official policy.[26] Eventually Bank rate did come down (to 3 per cent by July 1922), but all too slowly and timidly, granted the dreadful industrial situation.

As for the putative return to gold, the prospects of which would inevitably be hampered by an unduly cheap money policy that in turn undermined sterling, this was explicitly considered by Addis in late 1921 in his presidential inaugural to the Institute of Bankers. He accepted the need for further deflation in order to achieve it, seeing 'no hope of the restoration of the old standard of living and of comfort for the great middle class of this country until prices are further reduced'; called on the country to 'take a long pull, a strong pull, and to pull all together'; repudiated 'the ingenious and insubstantial nostrums of claustral economics'; and, calling for a return to gold as soon as possible, beseeched, 'Let us have done with short cuts and by-paths and, *ohne hast ohne rast*, bend our energies to return to the old standard.' Schuster, seconding the vote of thanks, was conscious of the City's critics, declaring that 'when we, as I believe most of us do, advocate a return to the pre-war standard, a return to a lower level of prices, we have in mind more than any other matter the well-being of our working classes'. Yet undeniably there was another, albeit rarely articulated agenda involved. Brand, clearly writing from the heart, touched on it in a letter to a French correspondent in August 1922:

> It seems to me that modern international industrial civilisation is becoming too complicated for the democracies of the world to run. They do not understand its mechanism, and the popular press understands it as little, and merely inflames their prejudices. Popular politicians were all right as long as they were compelled to work, without their knowing it, within the gold standard, but now that the delicate mechanism no longer works automatically, but must be kept at a pitch of reasonable efficiency by the politicians themselves, they are completely at a loss.[27]

Norman, with his profound aversion to the popular will and those who claimed to represent it, would have entirely agreed.

By late January 1924 the Chancellor was Philip Snowden, an instant victim of Norman's charm. 'I had seen caricatures in the Socialist Press of the typical financier – the hard-faced, close-fisted, high-nosed individual', he would recall. Instead, he found in the governor someone herculean in his efforts, of international cast of mind and with 'one of the kindliest natures and most sympathetic hearts it has been my privilege to know'. Norman himself told Strong on the 30th that after 'the bark' of Labour 'had frightened all our respectable friends nearly to death, the bite does not seem to be as bad as was expected'. However, he went on: 'We here in the City have suffered fearfully from forebodings of Labour or Socialism or whatever you would wish to call it. I confess to you that the mere idea of a Capital Levy, for instance, has lost to London a deal of international business which has belonged here for a generation or two'. If there was a honeymoon on the City's part, it did not last long. Teddy Grenfell, writing in early April to a sympathetic coal-owner and describing Labour as 'determined to wreck every industry in England', looked wistfully abroad:

I hear from all sides most extraordinary satisfactory accounts of the restoration of law and order and of the progress made in industry in Italy in the past three years . . . The middle class and the people with anything to lose have rallied under Mussolini in a most remarkable manner. The trains run punctually, the factories are prosperous and unemployment has been reduced from a million or more down to about 140,000 most of whom are wasters and unemployable . . . Unless the employers and the middle class, upper and lower begin to make a firm stand against Mr Bevin and Mr Maxten [*sic*] we shall deserve all we get or rather all we lose. In the bus strike last week the weather was bitterly cold though fortunately not wet and the clerks and employees in the warehouses and shops apparently showed no sort of resentment against the sympathetic bus strikers.[28]

Norman meanwhile, with both Snowden and the prime minister, Ramsay MacDonald, effectively in his pocket as far as monetary matters were concerned, could at last see the realistic prospect of a return to gold. Inasmuch as there was a debate in the public domain, the clearing bankers were soon all falling into line. In early 1925, during the annual round of bank chairmen's speeches, Goodenough viewed the return to gold as certain, following the recent appreciation of sterling, with only the date in question, and emphasised that 'it was of the greatest importance that there should be an early return to a free gold market for London'. Walter Leaf of the Westminster and Sir Harry Goschen of National Provincial broadly agreed, the latter asserting his belief, in line with 'the majority of people in this country', that 'the return to the gold standard and to a free gold market is most desirable in the best interests of all concerned'. And J. Beaumont Pease of Lloyds concurred: 'There is in fact no controversy. The whole world, though guilty of infidelity in varying degrees and in divers places and in spite of some coquettings in other directions, is returning to its old love. There is no effective rival of any standing or consequence. Gold is almost universally recognised as the only practical international measure of values.'

Inevitably the keynote speech was McKenna's, delivered to Midland's shareholders at the Cannon Street Hotel on 27 January. After some moderately positive words about the attractions of a managed currency, he turned to the gold standard's 'great and striking advantages', none greater or more striking than 'its moral effect':

A nation will think better of itself, will almost regard itself as more honest, if its currency is convertible into gold. The fear of being forced off the gold standard acts as a salutary check in the extravagance of governments . . . It is a real advantage to a nation to have a currency founded upon a value which is universally recognised: it inspires confidence and facilitates international transactions . . . So long as nine people out of ten in every country think the gold standard the best, it is the best.

Yet what did McKenna really think? Soon afterwards Goodenough told the new Chancellor, Winston Churchill, that he had had (as Churchill subsequently reported to Otto Niemeyer, the strongest person at the Treasury) 'private confirmation' that McKenna was 'personally opposed to the Gold policy and regards it as unnecessary and unwise'.[29] Presumably McKenna's reservations were genuine, but perhaps he felt that the situation had reached a point where the Midland could no longer afford to be out on a limb.

If McKenna could not quite make up his mind, the same was true in spades of Churchill himself. Monetary developments did not lighten his mood. In the face of an impending rise in the New York rate, Addis on 23 February 'urged' Norman 'to raise Bank rate at once', but noted that 'he hesitates', presumably due to his awareness of how sensitive Churchill was becoming about the unemployment situation. However, on the 26th at the Committee of Treasury, Norman consented, with the Court to take the formal decision on 5 March. Niemeyer, fearful of the reaction at No. 11, sent Churchill a minute on the 4th outlining in thoroughly pre-1914 terms the Bank–government relationship in monetary matters:

> It is not either necessary nor the practice for the Bank to consult the government of the day, though the Bank is naturally well aware of the political reactions of its decisions. The governor has on occasion mentioned to Chancellors that probably Bank rate ought to go up. I don't recollect that he has ever come and said that he is going to put it up tomorrow; and if he did, it would certainly not be with a view to seeking our approval. Our [i.e. the Treasury's] strong disapproval would no doubt have weight: but it would not be decisive. We have neither claim to be consulted nor power to enforce our views: and I think it would be generally recognised that in order to avoid political influence on these matters it is not desirable that we should have any such claim.

Bank rate duly went up next day, from 4 to 5 per cent.[30] On the 12th, however, the *Daily Express* launched a savage attack. 'What 1% More Means: Dearer Food, Fewer Houses, Less Work' ran the headline, with the article concluding: 'Mr Churchill could have kept the Bank rate down had he wished. He did not do so, and he is responsible for the consequences.' Niemeyer at once sent Churchill a note repudiating the attack – 'the great industrial complaint against high Bank rate is precisely that it *prevents a rise* in prices, on which they expect to make profits' – and Churchill that afternoon in the Commons opted for discretion. Asked 'whether the Bank of England raised the Bank rate without conferring with him', he replied, 'Entirely independent action is taken in these matters by the Bank of England.' In private, however, he had been seething. 'W. will never realise that he is not governor of the Bank', Niemeyer at one point informed a colleague. 'He would be very foolish to dissociate himself from sound finance by denouncing the Bank. The effect on national credit *abroad* would be exceedingly bad.'[31] So Churchill bit his tongue, but his distrust of 'sound finance' merely deepened.

On 6 March the financial section of the London Chamber of Commerce reiterated its long-standing preference for a return to a free gold market as soon as possible, and at about the same time Brand published an unequivocally pro-return article in the *Round Table*. 'A stable sterling exchange is of first-rate importance for the maintenance of London's pre-eminent position as the financial centre of the world', he declared, arguing: 'that she could permanently maintain her supremacy with a fluctuating exchange, when there were other centres such as New York with a stable exchange, is more than doubtful'. In sum: 'We have stable governments both here and in the United States. If we really believe that the gold standard is worth some sacrifices, we should not hesitate too long. The whole world believes we intend to return to par. If we wait too long, psychological influences will turn against us, we may miss the moment and it may be many months before it returns.'[32]

Churchill could avoid a decision no longer. He invited to dinner on 17 March a formidable quartet, comprising Niemeyer, Bradbury (formerly of the Treasury), Keynes and McKenna. Norman was away, recuperating in the south of France. On this occasion – for most of the evening anyway – Midland's chairman was on the side of the doubters, to judge by the only eyewitness account we have, written some twenty years later by Churchill's private secretary, James Grigg:

> The symposium lasted till midnight or after. I thought at the time that the ayes had it. Keynes's thesis, which was supported in every particular by McKenna, was that the discrepancy between American and British prices was not 2½ per cent as the exchanges indicated, but 10 per cent. If we went back to gold at the old parity we should therefore have to deflate domestic prices by something of that order. This meant unemployment and downward adjustments of wages and prolonged strikes in some of the heavy industries, at the end of which it would be found that these industries had undergone a permanent contraction . . .
>
> Having listened to the gloomy prognostications of Keynes and McKenna, Winston turned to the latter and said: 'But this isn't entirely an economic matter; it is a political decision . . . You have been a politician; indeed you have been Chancellor of the Exchequer. Given the situation as it is, what decision would you take?' McKenna's reply – and I am prepared to swear to the sense of it – was: 'There is no escape; you have got to go back; but it will be hell.'

McKenna, as Keynes would remark, 'always lets one down in the end'. Two days later, back in harness, Norman recorded in his diary: '12.45. Chancellor for Lunch in Downing St. Gold return to be announced Apl 6 or 8.' And on the 20th: '2.30. PM, Chancellor, Austen C, Bradbury,

OEN [Niemeyer]. Free gold statement to be in Budget about Apl 28.' Norman then returned to Threadneedle Street for tea and, Addis noted, 'much talk'.[33]

Five days before his Budget speech on the 28th, an apparently convinced Churchill – who two months earlier had memorably told Niemeyer that 'I would rather see Finance less proud and Industry more content' – wrote to King George V putting the move into its imperial context:

> The importance of a uniform standard of value to which all transactions can be referred throughout the British Empire and through a very large part of the world cannot be over estimated. It benefits all countries, but it benefits no country more than our crowded island with its vast world trade and finance by which it lives.[34]

'That our bank chairmen should have nothing better to cry than "back to 1914"', Keynes had commented earlier in the year, 'is not satisfactory . . . The "Big Five" have vast responsibilities towards the public. But they are so huge, and in some ways so vulnerable, that there is a great temptation to them to cling to maxims, conventions, and routine; and when their chairmen debate fundamental economic problems, they are most of them on ground with which they are unfamiliar.'[35]

Keynes' exasperation was understandable, yet on the part of the few more thoughtful City men there was an acceptance, even sometimes a public articulation, that simply to assume that the City's interests coincided completely with the nation at large was no longer intellectually sustainable – that, in short, there was a trade-off involved. Addis, so close to Norman and at one stage even more bullish about an early return, perhaps expressed it best. Speaking in April 1924 at the annual meeting of the Royal Economic Society, he conceded that the return to gold would, in the short term, lead to somewhat lower prices, with a knock-on deflationary effect on trade. But he asked: 'Is the comparatively small further drop, which is all that is required to bring us back to parity with gold, too great a sacrifice to ask of our people in order to restore the currency position on which the supremacy of this country in international trade and finance was formerly established? I do not believe it.'[36] Events after April 1925 soon showed the extent of the sacrifice that 'our people' – most of whom lived a long way from the Square Mile – would have to make.

*

London revived in the 1920s as a significant international capital market, while by 1928 its volume of acceptances (reaching a peak of some £170m outstanding) represented about four-fifths of the 1913 level.[37] Yet in a sense these were years of frustration and disappointment, especially once it became apparent that the return to gold had not automatically restored

London to its pre-1914 place at the centre of the financial universe. There was no doubt where the object of Norman's resentment lay. Early in 1926 he wrote to his mother: 'England is part of Europe: Europe has quarrelled: Europe has thus reached poverty . . . America is detached and has thus become rich: so Europe is the "promised land" to America: to be possessed without even competition!' Brand, discussing with Kindersley in October that year the future strategy of their firm, did not disagree: 'New York is going to be in my opinion incomparably the most powerful financial centre in the world. Can Lazards maintain a first-rate position in Paris and London without being really strong in New York?' Over a century of experience could not, of course, be wiped out overnight – 'It is a great mercy for us that America has not got the knowledge and tradition as well as the money,' Norman a few days earlier sought to console Schacht of the Reichsbank, 'or there would be no place and no business left for you and me!' – but that alone was not enough. Or as Norman candidly noted not long afterwards, following a discussion with Edward Hilton Young, editor of the *Financial News*: 'We agree the subservience of London to N.Y. market is better left alone in Papers.'[38] Yet, despite this failure to reverse the shift in the balance of financial power that had manifested itself during the war, the City of London – and indeed the British Empire at large – *did* stage something of a mini-comeback during the 1920s. 'The repute of the Sterling Bill, throughout Europe and perhaps the world,' Norman informed a correspondent in February 1927, 'has been wonderfully re-established since the return to the gold standard'; and if he somewhat exaggerated, that was surely pardonable considering the strenuous efforts he had made to achieve that return.[39]

It was Europe that now comprised much of the City's international orientation. Partly this was because there was so much to be done in relation to the post-war financial and economic reconstruction there; partly because, with various other parts of the world succumbing to the Yankee dollar, Europe was seen as a place where London could build up its financial strength relative to that of New York. Between 1926 and 1928, accordingly, Hambros made thirteen issues for continental governments, Barings twelve and Morgan Grenfell six.[40]

Germany remained at the heart of European reconstruction, and Schröders led the way in a series of loans from December 1925: for the German Potash Syndicate, for the City of Hamburg, for the City of Berlin and for the Hamburg Waterworks Co. The Hamburg loan of September 1926, also involving Barings and Rothschilds, brought home how the larger world had changed. On the 13th, with Baron Schröder away in Hamburg negotiating terms, Peacock optimistically reported to Revelstoke (also away, in his case at Balmoral) that Tiarks had been telling him 'that a 6% loan at 94–95 would go here'; that Tiarks had been 'assured' by Walter Whigham of Flemings 'that the Trust Companies would take a large amount of it on those terms and he thought the Insurance Companies would also'; and that since 'New York cannot issue on such terms', the Baron was 'therefore hopeful of doing the whole loan'. Five days later the 8 Bishopsgate update to Revelstoke, this time from Arthur Villiers, reflected the underlying realities: 'The Baron's endeavour to oust New York has not succeeded and there are certain advantages in London sharing the business with New York. For one thing, £5,000,000 is a large amount for London, and competition between New York and London would result in the lender getting worse terms.' In the event, Schacht insisted on reducing the total amount and London finished by being responsible for only £1m.[41]

There was also in these years a strong City commitment to Germany on the accepting side – for example, German commission earned by Kleinworts increased from £15,000 in 1921 to £117,380 in 1928. With demand for credit apparently inexhaustible, interest rates high and reparation payments being scaled down by the Dawes Plan of 1924, the logic was irresistible as Germany rebuilt her economy. Kleinworts obviously had a particularly strong German connection, but the same did not apply to Barings, where in 1925 almost half of the total income deriving from acceptance credits was earned on German account. The joint-stock banks also got keen, so much so that in the case of the Westminster, for instance, the bank's German commitments on acceptance credits were standing at about £4m by February 1929. At which point it was agreed by the board to make 'every endeavour' not to increase that figure.[42]

Norman's paramount concern was with the prerogatives of central bankers as a breed apart.[43] Back in September 1925 he had outlined to the Bank of England's Harry Siepmann his most cherished dream:

> I rather hope that next summer we may be able to inaugurate private and eclectic Central Banks' 'Club', small at first, large in the future, with the following familiar sort of qualifications for membership – subscriptions in the shape of exclusive relations; appropriate balances with other Central Banks; proper ratio of free balances and earning assets in each market; no undue regard for profit; political freedom by right or by custom; credits when there is bad weather in any particular place; and so on.

By 1927, indeed, that dream came somewhere close to fruition, with currency stabilisation proceeding apace (well over twenty countries returning to the gold standard) and central bank co-operation starting to take on an institutional character. In July there assembled the so-called Long Island 'Club', a gathering of Strong, Norman, Schacht and the Bank of France's Charles Rist, the latter deputising for Émile Moreau, governor from June 1926. 'World's Most Exclusive Club Meets Here for the First Time' was the headline in the *New York Herald Tribune*. In fact, the conference achieved little, if only because the four participants were seldom around the same table at the same time. And although Norman himself remained as attached as ever to his Olympian dream of central banking co-operation ('I want to make an umbrella, so that we can all get under it when it rains', he would remark in December 1928), the fullest, most productive phase of that co-operation had passed.[44]

Partly this was because of the shift in American attitudes, especially with the long illness of Strong before his eventual death in October 1928; but undoubtedly the crux was France, which correctly identified a very strong bond between Norman and Schacht. Norman himself made no bones about it, telling Addis in 1927 that 'whatever complaints may be made against Schacht, and admitting that he is at times impetuous and may have been rattled, you will agree that when rock bottom is reached he is a MAN!' In the eyes of the Bank of France, Schacht was less a man than a monster, and inevitably this greatly coloured its attitude towards Norman. During his two years in office, Moreau became an increasingly formidable figure as a result of the de facto stabilisation of the franc and the Bank of France's accumulation of large sterling balances.[45] The two financial powers represented by Moreau and Norman were set on a collision course. Should a hard rain fall on Europe as a whole, there was unlikely to be an umbrella in working order.

Even an intuitive, dedicated, but ultimately out-of-his-depth central banker like Norman could not avoid a pervasive feeling by the late 1920s that the world's monetary system specifically, and behind it the world economy at large, was heading for disaster. It was against this darkening backdrop that discussions began, in 1928, for what would eventually become the Young Plan on reparations and the creation of the Bank for International Settlements as an international clearing bank to facilitate further the reparations mechanism. No one imagined that these measures alone would suffice, and European eyes turned increasingly – and increasingly anxiously – to Wall Street and the extraordinary credit boom there. 'I had a long talk with M.N. this afternoon,' Peacock reported to Revelstoke on 18 February 1929, 'who tells me that on this occasion he had the hardest time in America that he has ever had. He is thoroughly unhappy about the situation there, as there is no leader and the F.R. Board are at odds with one another, drifting and not knowing what to do.' Perhaps earlier in the decade Norman could have knocked American heads together; now that was impossible. 'I do not know what to expect but the outlook is obscure and disagreeable', Norman himself wrote to Kindersley on 7 March about the American situation and its implications.

Altogether it was not a happy prospect. Or, as Revelstoke had characteristically expressed it the previous May, taking the big view, the worry was that the ever-greater speculative fever in the US would lead to a raising of American interest rates; this in turn would be 'a serious matter for us in Europe, where the "reaction", to use a horrible American phrase, may have a damaging effect upon our money market prospects'.[46]

A committee on reparations assembled in Paris in February 1929. The British expert was Sir Josiah Stamp, the statistician who had largely written the Dawes Report on reparations and had recently become a director of the Bank of England; he was seconded by Revelstoke. The latter, his temper not improved by a severe bout of flu, kept a diary that recorded his impressions of the others at the conference. Moreau, heading the French delegation, was intransigence personified and 'shuts his mouth like a steel trap when Schacht pleads poverty and inability to pay'. Schacht himself, 'with his hatchet, Teuton face and burly neck and badly fitting collar', reminded the diarist 'of a sealion at the Zoo, which is half out of the water on a rock, and is waiting to catch a fish thrown to him by his keeper'. Jack Morgan, on behalf of the Americans, was 'like a wild bison in a shop that sells Dresden china'. And the representatives of the British Treasury had a 'supercilious manner and sneering attitude for the whole of the rest of mankind'.[47]

The *real* problem, however, was Schacht, of whom Revelstoke declined to share Norman's good opinion. 'I do trust all these people will not be too lenient to that undoubtedly able and obstinate individual', he wrote to Peacock at the end of February. He returned to the theme on 8 March:

> Quite between ourselves, I sometimes wonder whether a knowledge of men and of the world would not rather lead one to an inner conviction that these Germans can really pay and continue to pay a larger sum than they seem disposed to offer.

The attritional discussions continued over the next few weeks (though Revelstoke was able to pay a brief visit to London), and on 13 April he wrote plaintively to Alfred Mildmay of Barings from 27 rue Faubourg Saint-Honoré: 'I have no sort of idea what is going to happen here . . . Best love to all at No. 8. How glad I shall be to see you all again.' On the 18th, the committee kept going until early evening, at which point the Germans stormed out, threatening to abort the conference. Revelstoke – still only in his mid-sixties, but seemingly around for ever, having as a young man righted Barings after the catastrophe of 1890 – summed it all up in his diary: 'Schacht was quite impossible today.'[48] The words were redolent of another, more congenial age.

CHAPTER TWENTY-FIVE

The Steady Drip

The return to the gold standard an acknowledged disappointment, public discontent increasing about the Bank of England's apparent sovereignty over monetary policy, a Labour government in the offing, Wall Street potentially on the verge of imploding – the City in spring 1929 was a troubled place. Revelstoke timed his exit well, dying in Paris in the early hours of 19 April. 'It is just too sad and terrible, and that is all one can say', A. W. Kiddy of the *Morning Post* wrote at once to Norman when the news reached London. 'A friend gone' agreed Addis, himself in Paris. A few weeks later Alec Baring confided from 8 Bishopsgate to an American correspondent: 'One is positively bewildered at the thought that this terrible thing has really and actually happened. It will take a long time to realise that we have just got to carry on without him.'[1] Nobody had anything original to say about a man who, whatever his virtues and faults, never uttered an original thought in his life.

On 3 October, Snowden, Chancellor again following Labour's return to office in June, announced to the Labour Party conference at Brighton that he would shortly be appointing a committee (eventually chaired by the Scottish lawyer Lord Macmillan) to inquire into the relations between finance and industry. It was an announcement that had a specific history to it.[2] The burden imposed on industry by the return to the gold standard, the contrast between the continuing travails of the older industries and the relative ease with which overseas borrowers could come to the London capital market, the disreputable character of the 1928 domestic new-issue boom (taking its cue from the over-ambitious company promoter Clarence Hatry), recurrent controversies over Bank rate: these had all contributed to an increasing general scepticism about the blessings conferred by the City of London. Or, in the words of the *Financial News* immediately after Snowden's announcement, 'noticeable in recent years' had been 'the growth of the belief that in some rather mysterious way "finance" is not organised for the general social advantage, but for the furtherance of the special interests of an inner world of financiers'.[3]

The very fact of the inquiry was momentous, potentially putting the City under the microscope – and compelling it to justify itself – in a way that had not happened since at least the 1870s. Moreover, however much Snowden and the Treasury might seek to emasculate or ring-fence the inquiry, there could be no guarantee that they would succeed. There was also, approaching the tenth anniversary of Norman's rule, the personal element. 'Is there not some danger', the Chancellor was asked by his private secretary, Grigg, 'of giving the impression that the Governor is being put in the dock?'[4] For someone who dreaded the public glare, and was far from his best under it, this was an appalling prospect.

Even before the inquiry began, however, an era of capitalist history had ended. Throughout the summer of 1929 the bull market on Wall Street had continued to roar away, as the American financial authorities reacted sluggishly to damp down the credit boom. It seemed a permanent state of grace, and in late July the very reputable stockbrokers Bourke, Schiff & Co. of 10/11 Austin Friars sent out to valued clients such as Barings a four-page letter extolling 'the attractive investment opportunities which we believe are now afforded by the leading American Railroad Shares'. In addition, as a further come-on: 'We give you attached hereto a selection of some of the standard and most attractive issues, which we can recommend for substantial future appreciation in market value, and hope that the same may prove of interest and service to you.' Even some of those who had had doubts now stilled them – most famously Oswald Falk, who from June, following a further visit to the States, became what has been described as 'evangelically committed to the future of American securities'.[5]

The crash – one of the seminal events of the twentieth century – came in late October, with the immediate flavour caught by four *Financial News* front-page headlines between the 24th and the 30th: 'Wild Day in Wall St', 'Black Day on Wall Street', 'New Wall Street Debacle', 'New Big Break on Wall Street'.[6] The overall atmosphere in the City itself was relatively calm, with no sightings of financiers throwing themselves off any of the few tall buildings, but for those intimately involved with American securities this was a dramatic enough time.

'It was, to begin with, a purely financial phenomenon,' the economic historian Sidney Pollard has written, 'but soon transmitted itself to the productive sectors, and as production and incomes contracted in the USA, the supply of dollars to the rest of the world fell drastically, and depression spread quickly to the rest of the world.' The profound consequences of the crash gradually sank in during the winter of 1929–30, with those having a large exposure taking the first hit. Falk paid for his folly in bulling New York by having to sell his country house, as well as falling out with Keynes over the running of their investment trust; while Kleinworts found its 'position' being 'discussed', in Grenfell's ominous words, on account of its close connection with Goldman Sachs of New

York. The general mood in the City soon became distinctly downbeat, as a bear market set in and commercial activity as a whole declined. 'As far as one can see,' Barings told Kidder Peabody in December 1929, 'prospects are rather dreary', and a few weeks later Brown Shipley informed Brown Brothers that, according to the 'reports' it heard, 'most other businesses' had had to sustain 'considerable losses'.

For at least a quarter of a million people working in the City the pervasive fear now became unemployment, and even for those born above the salt these were somewhat anxious times, even as the generally untroubled tenor of day-to-day life continued. Writing from 28 Austin Friars on a Tuesday in February 1930, a young stockbroker, Frank Holt, reassured his father-in-law:

> As I know you are interested in Yvonne & my affairs, I will explain the position to you.
>
> They are making me Junior Partner with a guaranteed minimum of £1,000 a year, and then a rising percentage of the profits, on a three year partnership contract, the reason being (all this is of course very private) that one of the older partners wishes, at the end of 3 years, to retire. On the lowest profit figures that there have been for many years, I should get £2,000 my 1st year, £3,000 the 2nd, & £4,000 the 3rd. At the present moment business is dead all over the City so this year which is just finishing will be bad for all Brokers, but my interest does not start till 1st April and we will hope business in general will improve. At the end of 3 years we would make a new contract, which should be still more beneficial to me.

Holt's father was Follett Holt, an important force in the South American railways world and a friend of Lord Faringdon, senior partner of the firm Greenwoods, which was now offering up such an attractive vista. Moreover, as was only reasonable to assume, business would soon be picking up. Indeed, the same month that Holt secured his berth at Greenwoods, another stockbroking firm, Cazenove's, felt confident enough to hold its first dinner party at the Savoy Hotel for partners and staff – a lavish six-course affair, complete with a cabaret of a comic man on a bike.[7]

Part of the City's malaise, funny turns on bicycles notwithstanding, was the reimposition of the informal embargo on foreign loans. The reason was the usual one – defence of the pound – and Snowden had made plain his wishes at the Mansion House in July 1929. Norman complied somewhat reluctantly. '"Embargo" may be a convenient but is not technically a correct expression', he explained to Mildmay of Barings in January 1930. 'I am sure you know this well enough. But I do not wish the idea to get abroad that we in the City are as yet dominated by Westminster or Whitehall: we all prefer to accommodate ourselves to their views and so avoid such domination for the present.' But whatever the semantics, the reality was made clear to one merchant banker when he went to see Norman later that month: 'Wagg. No foreign Issues except by agreement with me.'[8]

Ineluctably, as the larger economic and financial situation deteriorated, the weight of influence shifted from the private financier towards the central banker, however circumscribed the latter was by the political process. The establishment of the Bank for International Settlements was an important symptom of this shift.[9] During their heart-to-heart in September 1929, Norman told Snowden that such an organisation 'seemed to be the only way for Europe out of financial chaos'. And: 'What was needed was a real understanding among the Central Banks, not for operations and cleverness in the early years of the Bank but from the Governors mixing on neutral soil at a B.I.S. Club. The Chancellor agreed to all this.' Negotiations and preparations continued during the winter, not always smoothly. 'The setting up of this B.I.S. seems to be continuous, controversial and troublesome and it certainly takes me *all* my time', Norman wrote early in March; while a week later he conceded to another correspondent that 'there is no disguising the fact that, in some ways, the atmosphere in which the B.I.S. comes into existence is not what one might wish', in particular the fact that 'in Germany and in France the associations of the Bank with the Young Plan has led to its being mixed up, in the minds of the public, with politics and with Reparations'.[10] However, in April 1930 BIS did at last begin operations in Basle, and gradually developed into precisely that congenial, supra-political, European club of central bankers as originally envisaged by Norman: a club in which he himself was dominant.

Meanwhile, his efforts given a renewed urgency by the economic downturn, Norman was increasingly treading in industrial finance where no governor had trod before. A significant innovation was the backing that he gave from January 1930 to hire-purchase finance, through a major injection of capital into the City-based finance house United Dominions Trust, run along consciously American lines by J. Gibson Jarvie. Norman's motive was partly to improve the national credit machinery, partly to keep government out of the money market.

Rationalisation had become *the* Norman tune in the course of 1929.[11] In November the Bank of England had established Securities Management Trust (SMT), essentially a group of experts to advise Norman and see through rationalisation schemes. Norman himself was chairman and, even though the problems of industry had nominally left his room, was temperamentally incapable of not being closely involved on a day-to-day level. The strain was considerable. 'The process of rationalisation – if indeed it is a process – is turning our hairs grey', he wrote only half in jest to an adviser on 8 January 1930, 'and will surely take mine in sorrow and disappointment to the grave.' The stakes could not have been higher.

Two days later the Labour minister J. H. Thomas, who had been charged to deal with unemployment, gave an important speech in Manchester to local businessmen. A key passage had been drafted by the Bank:

> As a result of consultations which I have had, I am now in a position to state that the City is deeply interested in placing industry upon a broad and sound basis and ready to support any plans that in its opinion lead to this end. Those in the City who have been studying this matter are convinced that a number of our important industries must be fundamentally reorganised and modernised in order to be able to produce at prices which will enable them to compete with the world. Industries which propose schemes that, in the opinion of those advising the City, conform to this requirement will receive the most sympathetic consideration and the co-operation of the City in working out plans and finding the necessary finance.

In a sense it was not just the Bank of England, or even just the City, but capitalism itself that was on trial. The credibility problem, not only on the left, was encapsulated by the thoughts of the 27th Earl of Crawford. In the context of his family firm, the Wigan Iron and Coal Co., being about to be 'rationalised' and become part of the Lancashire Steel Corporation, he visited Threadneedle Street in January 1930 (on the 7th, perhaps contributing to Norman's grey hairs) and was distinctly underwhelmed by the governor and his colleagues: 'In their own affairs they have never given more employment than that vouchsafed to gardener, chauffeur, and valet. They are too much detached from the realities of production with its tremendous problems; they are usurers and nothing else . . . The banks sail serenely above the tempests of industrial trouble.'[12]

Not long afterwards, on 22 February, Norman outlined to Fisher at the Treasury his plans for a new organisation to complement SMT:

> It looks as if, within a couple of weeks, we should be setting up a new private Company to finance rationalised industry. This is a brief and particular object which should be accomplished within 5 years or never: therefore at the end of 5 years the Company will be liquidated. Moreover this object requires large credit but little money, so the Company will have a nominal capital of £4,000,000, £5,000,000 or £6,000,000 and a small paid-up capital. Thus it may come to be the outward and visible sign of what Mr Thomas describes as 'the City'.

The immediate process took rather longer, but over the next few weeks a name emerged – the Bankers' Industrial Development Company – and a board was chosen; it included Norman as chairman, Sir Guy Granet of the merchant bank Higginson & Co., Baron Bruno Schröder, Alfred Wagg and Edward Peacock, with Granet and two other merchant bankers as alternates to Norman, Schröder and Wagg respectively. 'It is the governor's intention', noted Norman's private secretary Ernest Skinner in early

March, 'that the Directors of the new concern should work mainly by means of their alternates.'[13]

Norman's other, more traditional response to the onset of economic depression was of course through monetary policy.[14] At first the Bank reacted with commendable promptness, getting Bank rate down to 5 per cent by the middle of December 1929. Historically speaking, however, this was still a steep rate; and over the next two and a half months, despite palpable evidence of rapidly deepening depression, Norman's inherent mistrust of cheap money, his nervousness about jeopardising Britain's position in relation to the gold standard, and his largely unavailing wish to co-ordinate monetary policy with other central bankers all combined to create what was undoubtedly a damaging monetary stance. Although the rate was at last reduced to 4½ per cent on 6 February, there was then another wasted month as Norman put back the lights to red. A fortnight later a further half-point was clipped off, but again it was too little too late. 'The Bank's policy seems to me quite inexplicable except by an unreasoning terror of cheap money', Grigg had complained to the Treasury's Hopkins at the end of February, and it was a plausible assessment, applicable not only to the peculiarly fraught circumstances of 1930.[15]

*

All such discussion was rather thrown into relief in the context of the world outside during the autumn of 1930. Germany's 'position has been worsened by the results of the Election and her need for money, almost before the new government has been formed', Norman told the leading British overseas banker Sir Bertram Hornsby on 1 October. And, 'in general, feeling everywhere is not less pessimistic than it was, nor is there any light at the end of the tunnel'. Evelyn Baring, writing to New York a week later, was still gloomier. After referring to how 'all over the world, conditions seem to be as bad as they possibly can be from an industrial and commercial point of view', he added that 'now, to increase our troubles, Brazil seems to have caught the revolution complaint, and just when we thought that matters were settling down in that country the news comes of battles and insurrections to depress the price of all Brazilian securities'. So inconsiderate of the foreigners, but the position was little better at home: 'The number of unemployed shows no sign of decreasing and I believe that our government is entirely at a loss to know what action to take. We hear rumours on all sides of a possible National government . . . One thing is certain, and that is that no party is anxious to introduce the next Budget.'[16]

The sense of an impending crisis was gathering momentum, and the form it would take was presaged in mid-November when, as reported by

Skinner, Norman told SMT of an exchange of views he had recently had with American bankers with whom he was on friendly terms:

> It had been said [i.e. by Norman] to them that if France and America did certain things it was certain to lead to trouble. They had replied that it was very likely that England would have to part with gold either to France or to the United States and if she did she would only have herself to blame. She had failed to rationalise; she had heavier taxation than anyone, to support social services and a dole on a basis that no country would pretend to sustain and which she also could probably not bear; there were likely to be three unbalanced Budgets running; wages also were too high and did not produce value for the amount paid. So long as this state of affairs continued it was useless for England to complain and no help would be forthcoming from across the way.

With the Labour government seemingly incapable of firm action, City eyes occasionally looked longingly elsewhere. 'It certainly reads to me to be good sound stuff', Michael Herbert of Morgan Grenfell wrote shortly after Christmas to the bank's correspondent in Mussolini's Rome. 'Your prime minister seems to be endeavouring to meet the crisis with that courage and determination which I am sure are part of his character.' By the end of the year the registered unemployed in Britain totalled 2,660,000, compared with barely a million when Labour had returned to office in the middle of 1929.[17] A vast and dreadful human tragedy was being enacted, but what primarily concerned the City and the short-term holders of sterling was whether MacDonald's hapless ministry was capable of balancing the budget.

The last days of January 1931 saw a perceptible heightening of the stakes. Norman's diary recorded an ominous visit from Granet (in close touch with Wall Street bankers) on the 26th: 'Dangerous prospect for stg [i.e. sterling]: complaints on all sides.' Next day Norman himself wrote to Snowden's private secretary:

> I only pass on to you a tithe of what I get, but when I see in a personal letter from one eminent banker abroad to his counterpart in this country a phrase like this – 'the people on the Continent are quite apprehensive about England and feel that she must either make a very large loan in America or a general capital levy and that there is a distinct possibility of a revision of the value of the pound during 1931' – I think you ought to share it. And as a type of the steady drip and of the unseen pressure on us, you may care to whisper it to the Chancellor.

Even the level-headed Brand was seriously perturbed by the prospect of a flight of capital from London. 'It doesn't seem to me that our political leaders have any idea of it', he told Keynes on the 30th. 'The trouble is that democracies seem unable constitutionally to make budgets balance.'[18] Over the next eight months or so, as the crisis of 1931 was played out, the

City had no alternative but to operate within the confines of the existing political process; but such was the instinctive deference towards the City of most politicians – especially Labour politicians – when it came to financial matters that it was not too difficult for the City to apply the frighteners.

During February the gold position was particularly parlous, following large outflows since November, although Norman was able to tighten the market rate and thus avoid what would have been an explosive rise in Bank rate. The 'steady drip' of international opinion, meanwhile, continued. It was, to a significant if unquantifiable extent, City-fed – a reflection of the City's belief that, unless the politicians could be persuaded to change their ways, then the game was up. A prime example of the drip-feed at work was the private cable that Teddy Grenfell sent on 2 February to Jack Morgan in New York:

> I wish you personally to realise that this country is passing through a period of increasing financial difficulties and perhaps dangers.
>
> The general causes are of course well known to you and affect the whole world.
>
> The particular causes on the other hand are apt to be ignored but they are our responsibility and are deep and continuing. They are due, I think, to our fiscal and economic and industrial conditions such as extreme taxation and socialistic policies – the dole and a high standard of living – a bad spirit and obsolete plants and lost trade.

'Fundamentally,' concluded Grenfell, 'it's a long tunnel we are in.'[19]

Nine days later some possible light appeared at the end of the tunnel, when Snowden agreed to establish an Economy Committee that would search for places to make spending cuts. This committee, he emphasised to the Commons, would be bipartisan (in the event, chaired by Sir George May, a distinguished actuary who had recently retired from the Prudential), and in the ensuing debate almost the only note of dissent was sounded by Lloyd George. Bringing back memories of his epic rhetorical battle against Natty Rothschild almost a quarter of a century earlier, he launched into a fierce attack on the City, declaring that it had Snowden in its pocket and that its deflationary obsession would ruin the country. Invariably reactionary, invariably out of touch with industry, the City had been found to be 'wrong every time' in its advice to government. And he remembered how, when before the war he had put forward his 'People's Budget', he had been 'received by City magnates with frigid and flopping silence, as if they were a row of penguins in the Arctic Ocean'.[20]

*

These were of course dismal times, for domestic as well as foreign issues, yet remarkably the City was about to produce a genuine innovation – the fixed unit trust.[21] Largely the brainchild of the merchant, entrepreneur and Bank of England director George Booth (*A Man of Push and Go* would be the just title of his biography) and of the stockbroker Walter Burton-Baldry, the First British Fixed Trust was issued on 23 April at 31s 9d per unit. It had Norman's informal blessing, and Lloyds Bank agreed to act as trustees, but it fared poorly, crucially hindered by the decision of the Stock Exchange Committee not to grant permission to deal in its shares. 'We would respectfully submit', protested one firm, J. Silverston & Co., 'that the creation of this Fixed Trust is bringing business to the London Stock Exchange, in a manner that can only be of benefit to both Brokers and Jobbers.'[22] But at least the principle of the fixed unit trust had been established – in explicit contrast to the pyramided investment trusts that had crashed in New York in 1929 – and the initial trust's parent company, Municipal and General Securities (the latter-day M&G), would within a few years be reaping a rich harvest, fair reward for seeds bravely sown.

There was not much else to cheer about in the spring of 1931, even if the sense of imminent crisis had receded somewhat. Snowden's Budget on 27 April did little more than provide a breathing space, pending the findings of Sir George May's Economy Committee. Soon afterwards Norman was invited to a small meeting at the House of Commons to discuss monetary issues with about a dozen MPs. 'With your permission,' ran his reply of acceptance, 'I propose to bring with me to the meeting Dr Sprague, an eminent banking economist from Harvard who has been helping us here for nearly a year now: I am only a banker.' So he was, and a deeply puzzled one, unable either through international co-operation or orthodox monetary measures to see a way out. A cable on 5 May to his counterpart in New York, George Harrison of the Fed, captured his mood of despair, of not knowing which way to turn: 'The general economic outlook appears in every way so discouraging that for my part I should like now to try the effect of reductions of ½% in your and our discount rates.'[23] Neither man was even remotely in control of the larger situation.

CHAPTER TWENTY-SIX

Going Off

'The leading bank in Austria and most important bank in Central Europe, perfectly good for its engagements', was the confident verdict of a report prepared by Lazards on 7 January 1931 for Westminster Bank. The bank in question was Credit Anstalt, which was indeed Austria's largest commercial bank and was controlled by the local Rothschild house, S. M. Rothschild und Söhne of Vienna. Its size was such that a host of other banks in London and elsewhere had some involvement in it, but a notable exception was Barings. Revelstoke had refused towards the end of his life to give it a credit, according to one colleague 'saying very firmly that we should not as he did not like the management of it and was sure that it would get into trouble sometime'.[1]

On 11 May, barely four months after the sanguine assessment by Lazards, it became known that Credit Anstalt was indeed in serious trouble.[2] Over the next few weeks Norman acted as decisively as he could – taking the lead in organising a 100m schilling credit from BIS to the Austrian National Bank, helping to establish a creditors' committee in order to try to prevent precipitate withdrawals, and in June advancing direct a 150m schilling (£4.3m) credit to the Austrian central bank. Norman's grave warning on 25 May – 'a monetary breakdown in Austria might quickly produce a similar result in several countries' – accurately reflected his overriding motive behind these steps.[3]

But the fact was that the City's claims in Vienna were now frozen, thereby intensifying the fundamental problem of London's illiquidity – in essence, the accumulation of a mass of short-term liabilities that had resulted from the City's post-1925 policy of courting 'hot money' from abroad in order to keep the pound on the gold standard. With simultaneously a return to semi-normality as an international capital market, disbursing foreign loans, the City had in practice been lending long while it borrowed short. International mistrust of a Labour government might alone not be enough to have the world's creditors knocking at London's door, but the freezing of a high proportion of London's European credits surely would.

So in a sense it proved, as financial instability in Austria spread rapidly to Hungary and Germany. The latter, owing to London's particularly high exposure there, was crucial.[4] 'I think probably we are the only prominent merchant banking firm who are doing nothing direct with Germany', Vivian Hugh Smith had remarked to Grenfell back in May 1926, but thereafter even Morgan Grenfell had entered the fray in offering commercial credits to German business. In 1931 itself, runs on German banks began in late May, soon exacerbated by the insistence of many American banks on repatriating short-term loans; but Norman – heavily committed to the international economy – applied strong pressure on London banks to keep credits running.

He would later be criticised for not having done more during June to protect the City's interests; but in the authoritative judgement of the financial historian R. S. Sayers, 'it was simply that implications for the financial structure of the City appeared, in the early summer of 1931, to be secondary to the maintenance of international trading relations'; therefore, in the mind of Norman, 'if only an international trading collapse could be averted, London creditors could in general be left to look after themselves'. Moreover, by late June the German situation seemed to have stabilised somewhat, in the wake of not only President Hoover's proposal of a one-year moratorium on intergovernmental debts, but the provision to the Reichsbank of a three-week $100m credit from the Bank of England and other central banks.[5]

The first day of July, however, saw the beginning of a new run of foreign withdrawals from German banks, and by the 8th the news from the Reichsbank was of the German financial system in a state of crisis. The City was by now extremely worried, and on 10 July the clearing banks and accepting houses established a Joint Committee to represent their German interests. It was in for a very long haul.

Ramsay MacDonald's position was certainly unenviable. 'You will readily understand that to the practical political and to the practical business man alike this is a policy almost of despair', he wrote in a long, worried letter to Norman on 18 June, in the wake of recent gloomy speeches by the Bank's Professor Sprague. Wondering if the central banks could not do more, co-operatively, to stabilise prices, he went on: 'I hope you will not resent my intruding in these technical fields. I scarcely dare to contemplate, however, what it will mean for the world, and for this country in particular, if all prices and wages have to be forced down to meet the fall in commodity prices.' Norman in his reply a week later saw the prospect of central banking co-operation raising commodity prices as a chimerical solution. The task was getting politicians, that regrettable necessity, to face facts; and Norman was determined that there must be no relaxation in the softening-up process.[6]

All through this early summer, May's Economy Committee was

beavering away, likely – as Norman well knew – to produce the ultimate facts that the politicians would have to be compelled to face.

The other report that was pending, and came out first, was the Report of the Macmillan Committee on Finance and Industry.[7] Having been told by Macmillan on 23 June that the committee had signed the Report and handed it to Snowden, Norman in reply three days later had speculated somewhat self-pityingly on its contents:

> Can it be that the Committee have designed for me an easy road by which to withdraw from a position which from year to year becomes increasingly difficult and exacting and has already been occupied far too long by
> Yours sincerely,
> M. Norman

The Report was published on 13 July, and it turned out that he need not have worried. The main criticism concerned the inadequacy of the information publicly provided by the Bank; and, far from seeking to truncate the Bank's powers, the conclusion reached was that it was the central bank's function 'to keep the financial structure upon an even keel', using whatever means were at hand. These primarily comprised altering Bank rate, conducting open-market operations, managing debt, dealing in the foreign exchange market, and exercising moral suasion over the rest of the monetary system – the last weapon specifically endorsed when the Report referred approvingly to 'the use of the Bank's personal influence over, or advice to, prominent elements in the money market'.[8]

The Report as a whole – which had been largely written by Keynes (one of the committee members), though he had by no means been given entirely his own way – was to a great extent taken up by a detailed analysis of the workings of the gold standard, monetary control and international trade. It is mostly remembered, however, for its closing pages, which lamented the relative absence of sound issuing houses for domestic industrial issues:

> There are, it is true, one or two first-class houses in the City which perform for certain first-class companies the same functions as the older issuing houses perform for foreign borrowers. In addition these latter are to a limited extent entering the domestic field . . . Again, the advice of stockbrokers, when asked for, may be a safeguard but it is scarcely sufficient to take the place of the responsibility of a first-class issuing house. With these exceptions the public is usually not guided by any institution whose name and reputation it knows.

While making it clear that 'we have no sympathy with the idea that the banks should in any way manage industry', there was nevertheless no denying that 'in some respects the City is more highly organised to provide capital to foreign capitals than to British industry'.

Who, then, should do the job of providing that capital and financial advice? The joint-stock banks, the Report assumed, were unsuitable, though no reasons were given; while as for the merchant banks, they were too bound up with acceptances, for 'it has always been recognised that acceptance business necessitates the maintenance of a high degree of liquidity and is not consistent with serious liabilities in respect of industrial financing'. Instead, the Report pinned its hopes on the Bankers' Industrial Development Company, which 'might form a nucleus for that closer co-operation between finance and industry which we think is required'.

Reaction to the Report from the City at large was distinctly muted. 'Preliminary perusal appears to have left a feeling of disappointment', noted the *FT*'s money-market column. 'From the practical standpoint it takes us no farther forward than we were before the Committee began its deliberations.'[9] It would of course take some time for the Report to be digested. At this particular moment, the City – never partial to such reports at the best of times – had rather a lot else on its plate.

*

The 13th was a Monday, the start of a traumatic week that July. On the same day that the Macmillan Report was published, news came through that one of Germany's largest banks, the Darmstadter, had suspended payments. The Reichsbank's warnings had been vindicated. 'Germany and Europe in Suspense' was the title of the *FT*'s leader on Wednesday the 15th, and 'Autolycus', the stockbroker-journalist Walter Landells, described the effect on the Stock Exchange that day of the German situation: 'Nebulous, vague and obscure apprehensions overhung the markets, preventing clarity of thought and trailing all kinds of side issues across the broad aspects of the case.'[10] By this time the Joint Committee of clearing banks and accepting houses was asking Norman, in some desperation, to allow them in effect to call in their credits; his response was that, quite apart from the fact that to do so might not actually be possible, even to attempt to do so would almost certainly make the German situation far worse. The plight of the British banks with a large German exposure was sealed when short-term credits were frozen by the German government, which also forbade the repatriation of foreign deposits.

The accepting houses most affected were Schröders, Kleinworts, Huths, Japhets, Goschen & Cunliffe, and Arbuthnot Latham. Norman, to the dismay of Kleinworts for one, declined to bale them out, though he did ask their own banks to look sympathetically upon requests for assistance. Accordingly, gladly or otherwise, Westminster lent £3.5m to Kleinworts and also gave substantial assistance to Schröders. For both these hitherto flourishing houses, their entire capital was now locked up – an unappetising prospect. Yet no one in the City had greater 'bounce' than Frank Tiarks of Schröders, and between late July and early September he masterminded the first Standstill Agreement, which guaranteed the interest on London's frozen credits to Germany. Unquestionably it was a major achievement on the part of Tiarks, who received important support from William Mortimer of the solicitors Slaughter and May, once the negotiations moved from Berlin to Basle.[11] Schröders and Kleinworts were down as a result of the German financial crisis, but not quite out.

Even before Tiarks began his work, however, the focus of the City as a whole had turned away from the German situation and towards what was developing into the long-expected, full-blown British financial crisis.[12] 'We are concerned and surprised at sudden drop of sterling today', Harrison wired Norman on Wednesday 15 July. 'Can you throw any light on this?' The immediate cause, not wholly clear to an even more concerned and surprised London, was twofold: worries about German exposure; and the publication two days earlier in the Macmillan Report of figures showing, with unprecedented starkness, that London was a net short-term debtor of £254m. For some, as gold flowed out over the next few days, it was confirmation that the perils of economic and financial internationalism were starting to be exposed. The Tory politician Leo Amery declared at a dinner on the 19th that 'We have preferred to be moneylenders to being manufacturers.' By the 22nd the Bank had lost £22m of gold in the course of a week.[13] Next day Bank rate, which had gone down to 2½ per cent on 14 May, was increased by one full point, but this most conventional of moves barely checked the outflow of gold.

By the following weekend it was time to look elsewhere for support. The French authorities were starting to worry that it would be their turn next, and on Saturday the 25th Kindersley was despatched to Paris to discuss a possible French loan to the Bank of England. Aid from America was instinctively more acceptable, and the following day Norman met Jack Morgan, who had just arrived in Britain. When he duly popped the question about a possible American credit, Morgan replied (as he reported back to New York):

> I said it seemed to me that before they could safely borrow in the USA, the government would have to show at least some plan of restoration of financial stability and should at least have expressed the intention to reduce the expenditures to come within their means. This he [Norman] agreed was quite right and told me he had Snowden's permission to discuss the subject with me and report to me on the result.[14]

Norman's agreement that Britain could hardly expect American support without first making it clear that it would get its own financial house in order was entirely sincere. He had recently seen, ahead of publication, the May Report, indicating that the budget deficit was likely to be £120m – an alarmingly large figure in the era before deficit financing.

Norman's own mental condition was starting to cause increasing concern to those around him, and indeed elsewhere. 'Can't he be persuaded to quit his panicky talk?' Russell Leffingwell of Morgans in New York implored Jack Morgan on Tuesday the 28th.[15] The next day Norman buckled. '12.30 about – left C. Treas^y & went home about 3 o'clock. Queer.' So noted his diary, and thereafter Norman was only a bit-player as the crisis unfolded. His capable deputy, Sir Ernest Harvey, stepped into the breach, and on the 30th Bank rate rose from 3½ to 4½ per cent. That same day the Joint Committee of the British Bankers' Association and the Accepting Houses Committee (i.e. of clearing bankers and merchant bankers) sent a strongly worded appeal to MacDonald and Snowden. In the eyes of the nine signatories, who included Goschen, Brand, Olaf Hambro, Anthony de Rothschild and Tiarks, the solution was as clear as the problem:

> London has for many years, and, indeed, until quite recently, been regarded as the most stable monetary centre in the world, and is the repository, therefore, of huge sums of short foreign money, which are placed here in order to obtain the unparalleled advantage of the freedom and liquidity of the London Money Market. In the Macmillan Committee's Report these foreign deposits were there estimated at about £400 million. They can be withdrawn at short notice, and, if the foreign investor once loses confidence in the stability of our exchange, they will be withdrawn, just as similar deposits have recently been withdrawn from Germany . . . If we were to pursue a sound budgetary policy and show reasonable elasticity in adjusting ourselves to world economic changes, we should be able to maintain our exchanges without any difficulty . . What we have urged other nations to do, we must now do ourselves, namely, restrict our expenditure, balance our budget, and improve our balance of trade.[16]

The publication on Friday the 31st of the May Report, with its disturbing budgetary projection and accompanying recommendation that government achieve a cut in unemployment benefit of £67m, served to fortify the bankers' argument.

Even Sayers, most sober of financial historians, has argued that the Report 'presented the government's deficit in grossly exaggerated fashion'; but what mattered was contemporary perception, which broadly speaking took May's findings as gospel. Not least MacDonald and Snowden, especially after the former had been told by Harvey on the Friday afternoon that the Bank's reserves had fallen by £55m since the middle of the month. By the Saturday it seemed that the point had been carried, as MacDonald announced the appointment of a Cabinet economy committee, which would meet for the first time on 25 August in order to make a detailed policy response to the May Report. Moreover, also on Saturday the 1st, the Bank announced that it had had made available to it for three months two major foreign credits, in the form of £25m each from the American and French central banks. It seemed that the crisis had been postponed, pending a reasonable examination of the budgetary situation. For the City, the underlying objective remained unchanged. 'Whether we returned to the gold standard too early or not is debatable,' Peacock of Barings wrote to a correspondent that day, 'but is no longer a matter of more than academic interest. To go off the gold standard for a nation that depends so much upon its credit as we do would be a major disaster.'[7]

With such its fundamental and, for the time being, unwavering priority, the City naturally viewed the May Report as a welcome stick with which to beat the government. Not surprisingly, some in the Labour Party viewed matters rather differently. Beatrice Webb, in her diary note of 4 August on the Report, anticipated the eventual political outcome: 'Luxury hotels and luxury flats, Bond Street shopping, racing and high living in all its forms is to go unchecked; but the babies are not to have milk and the very poor are not to have homes. The private luxury of the rich is apparently not *wasteful expenditure*.'

On Wednesday 5 August, the second business day after the Bank Holiday weekend, Norman struggled back to the Bank for the regular weekly meeting of the Committee of Treasury, ten days before he sailed for Canada and convalescence. 'Governor suffering from nervous dyspepsia', Addis noted. 'Better but not well.' Keynes, writing to MacDonald, touched on what he saw as the 'lack of clear guidance' coming from the City: 'The Accepting Houses, who constitute the major part of the Court of the Bank of England, are many of them more or less insolvent. The governor is probably near the end of his nervous resources. It is now a problem for the government rather than for the City.'[18] In a sense he was right, in that ultimately it was a government problem; but in fact, over the next fortnight, the City – and in particular the Bank – would give increasingly clear advice to the beleaguered politicians.

Even as Keynes was writing, sterling was coming under a renewed bout of severe pressure. This new and, as usual, international run on the currency seems to have been prompted partly by alarm at the grim findings of the May Report; partly by abiding doubts about the willingness – or even ability – of the Labour government to take tough remedial action; and partly by a tactical error on the part of the Bank itself, which failed to use its new credits to defend the pound when it came under attack in the foreign exchange markets of Paris and London. This failure, in the subsequent words of one Bank official, 'completely confused the market, created chaos in the continental exchanges, and administered an irreparable blow to confidence in the pound'. On this fateful day, Wednesday the 5th, the Bank lost no less than £4.5m of gold and foreign exchange. Next day Harvey sent a major letter to Snowden, one that took the crisis into a new, still more serious phase:

> We are doing all that we can but our power to act is rapidly diminishing. As I tried to explain to you last week, the reports which reach us all show that the sign which foreigners expect from this country is the readjustment of the budgetary position, and this attitude on their part has again been forcibly expressed today in messages from both Paris and New York. I am most anxious not to step beyond my province but I feel I should be failing in my duty if I did not say that with the prospects as they present themselves today the time available for the government to reach decisions on this subject (as a means of safeguarding the value of sterling) may be much shorter than recently seemed likely.[19]

When did financial advice turn into political interference? Harvey, who in many ways had the character of a top-class civil servant, was determined not to overstep the mark, invisible and shifting though it was. Villiers, writing on 11 August to Barings' man in Berlin, had some sympathy with the government's position: 'It knows the justice of what is written in the May Report and yet it knows that its followers will not support the carrying out of the recommendations.' However, he went on, 'an increasing number of people are beginning to realise that we must restore the confidence of the foreigner in the pound, and this cannot be done unless genuine attempts are made to make the Budget balance'.[20]

Wednesday the 12th saw much activity: the Cabinet's economy committee starting work earlier than had originally been envisaged; the Stock Exchange 'thick with rumour', according to 'Autolycus', including the rumour of an ultimatum from the bankers to the government 'threatening that, if something drastic were not done in the way of retrenchment and reform, the banks would refuse to accept Treasury bills'; Harvey making to the Committee of Treasury what Addis, who had been recalled from his holiday in the Scottish borders, termed 'a grave & disturbing statement'; and the deputy governor also keeping up the pressure on MacDonald, telling him that if losses continued on their present scale, 'the £36 millions left to us in our Credits will not last us very much more than a week'. That letter ended with a classic injunction from banker to politician: 'I cannot express too strongly my feeling that any apparent hesitation to supplement your encouraging words to the Press by definite action might speedily undo the good which you have already achieved.' And writing to Bradbury on the 17th: 'We are having a desperate struggle in the hope that the government, on whom we are keeping a strong pressure, will adopt and announce this week a programme of financial reform which will sufficiently restore confidence abroad . . . At the present moment it looks like being a neck and neck race.'[21] Would MacDonald and his colleagues do the decent thing?

By Thursday the 20th, the prime minister was starting to be squeezed hard from both sides. The TUC announced its opposition to most of the envisaged cuts, which in turn significantly hardened the resistance of at least several members of the Cabinet, especially towards a reduction in unemployment benefit. The City as a whole was becoming increasingly exasperated. 'Nothing transpired', noted 'Autolycus' at the end of another day's depressed trading on the Stock Exchange, 'to remove the unpleasant impression of the government's reluctance to grasp, with any degree of courage, the necessity for putting retrenchment before taxation.'

Harvey, however, sensed victory. 'I have no information yet as to how matters are likely to swing in the West End,' he wrote to Bradbury that day, 'but from one or two indications which have reached me today I am hopeful that they might go in the right direction.' At the same time, he now sanctioned a cable that Grenfell sent in the late afternoon to Morgans in New York. It canvassed whether the British government might be able to place there a $250m loan – *if* it first made a 'satisfactory announcement as regards balancing Budget', an announcement 'which appeared to you and us indicative of real reform in finance and one permitting you to paint a satisfactory picture'.[22]

By Friday, with £33m of the £50m credits having been used up, the Bank was increasingly looking to the possibility of a private American loan to get it out of its immediate hole, after Morgans had told Grenfell how problematic it would be to place a long-term, public loan. MacDonald and Snowden, however, had only managed to persuade the Cabinet to accept cuts totalling £56m, over £20m less than had been provisionally agreed two days earlier; and on being told this, Harvey and Peacock informed MacDonald and Snowden that not only would such cuts be insufficient to enable further credits to be secured from abroad, but also that such was the current flight from sterling, and such the desperation of the exchange-support operation, that the Bank's reserves were likely to be exhausted in only four days. The coming weekend, it was apparent, would pay for all, and at Cabinet on Saturday the recalcitrant colleagues of MacDonald and Snowden were confronted with a proposed programme of cuts now totalling £68.5m, including a 10 per cent reduction in the dole. That evening Grenfell wired his New York partners, in effect asking whether the proposed economy plan would be sufficient to persuade them to grant a large and immediate short-term credit. Addis, meanwhile, was completing his first full day back in harness: 'At Bank till 9. Dined at Basque restaurant with Peacock, Grenfell. Lafite 1917!'[23]

'It is the financiers, British and American, who will settle the personnel and the policy of the British government,' Beatrice Webb noted in her diary on Sunday the 23rd, following the previous day's manoeuvrings. And she added: 'It certainly is a tragically comic situation that the financiers who have landed the British people in this gigantic muddle should decide who should bear the burden. The dictatorship of the capitalist with a vengeance!'

That Sunday proved to be a momentous day. By early evening Harvey and Grenfell were waiting at the Bank for the response from the Morgans partners, deliberating on Long Island. Eventually it came, saying that an answer to a firm request for a short-term credit could be given within twenty-four hours and asking for confirmation 'that the programme under consideration will have the sincere approval and support of the Bank of England and the City generally and thus go a long way towards restoring internal confidence in Great Britain'.[24]

It was almost nine o'clock by the time the cable confirming the telephone message had been received. Thereupon, according to Grenfell's subsequent account: 'The Deputy Governor, who had been rung up three times by the P.M., took the message down to him at the Cabinet meeting. The P.M. seemed very flustered, came out, looked at it and rushed back and read the whole thing to the Cabinet . . . The Cabinet continued to sit and it was clear that there were very violent discussions.' There were indeed, as virtually half the Cabinet refused to support the proposed cut in unemployment benefit, by far the most important single item in the package before them. By quarter-past ten, intending to resign, MacDonald (accompanied by Harvey) was at the Palace, where King George V was dining with his financial adviser, Peacock.[25] MacDonald was induced to defer his decision until the morrow, and Harvey and Peacock accompanied him back to Downing Street. There they tried to persuade him that he could still serve the country by taking his place at the head of a National Government – a government, of course, fully committed to the enhanced programme of cuts.

At ten o'clock on Monday morning MacDonald was asked by the King to form a National Government. For the City it was a day of mixed emotions. 'Meetings, meetings, all day', noted Addis at its eventual end. 'Leader in "Times" stating credits all exhausted has had a bad effect on the Continent. We lost over £10 millions today. At this rate we can only go on for two or three days more.' On the other hand, once the news was out by the afternoon of an imminent coalition government, it undoubtedly served as a significant fillip to the City's rather battered morale, lifting (recorded 'Autolycus') an 'invisible weight from the Stock Exchange mind'.[26] That night, as the *Daily Herald* was being put to bed, the City editor Francis Williams announced to the night editor, 'It's nothing but a ramp'; and the following morning Williams' story on the crisis appeared with the headline 'Bankers' Ramp', and thus a deeply emotive catchphrase was born.[27]

MacDonald did not consider whether the City's doubts about the Labour government had accentuated the international crisis of confidence, nor whether the undue deference of himself and Snowden towards the bankers had allowed the latter to set the larger agenda, but in broad terms he was surely correct to deny that it was a ramp.[28] First and foremost, throughout the weeks leading up to his government's fall, the bankers' unwavering priority was to save the pound; and they saw no way of doing this other than by major cuts in government expenditure. It was not their aim to force the Labour government from office; indeed they believed that such cuts as were necessary were more likely to be generally accepted if they were implemented by a Labour government. Sincerely convinced that there was no alternative but to strain every sinew in order to stay on the gold standard, and deploying to masterly effect that 'odour of sanctity'[29] so beloved of bankers, especially central bankers, they gave the politicians precious little room in which to manoeuvre. If politicians fail to challenge the assumptions of bankers, that ultimately – then as later – is their responsibility.

*

By late August 1931, the City's mood was at best distinctly edgy. Everyone was waiting for Snowden's emergency Budget on 10 September. It more or less followed the lines of the package that the Labour government had failed to agree upon and received a predictably enthusiastic response from the *FT*, which claimed that the 'resurgence of confidence in sterling is now well on the way to re-establishment, thanks to adhesion to an open and honest policy'.

By this time Keynes was advocating devaluation, and next morning the *Financial News* turned on him savagely. To do so, it claimed, would mean losing 'the sheet-anchor upon which our place as an international monetary centre depends', and it asked: 'Is this country to plunge the nations of the world into a new chaos because we have not the force of character or the common sense to free ourselves from the tyranny of trade union opposition to a revision of nominal wages?'[30]

On Tuesday the 15th came news that there had been 'unrest' among the naval ratings at Invergordon – protests about pay cuts, which press headlines quickly turned into the appearance of a full-scale mutiny. Almost six and a half years on, the final act of the ill-fated return to gold was about to be played out.

'It is now realised that this country is determined to do its utmost to avoid a depreciation of sterling', Paul Einzig's 'Lombard Street' column in the *Financial News* declared on Wednesday the 16th; that afternoon,

Mafeking relieved, Saturday 19 May 1900 at 11 a.m.:
Charlie Clarke, *centre*, prepares to lead the Stock Exchange's singing of the National Anthem.

Waiting for lifts at Bank ticket office on
the recently built Central Line, 1901.

Watching the gold:
the Court of Directors of the
Bank of England, 2 July 1903.

Sir Ernest Cassel:
international financier and private banker.

High jinks in the City, October 1908.

Barings, 8 Bishopsgate, autumn 1921.

French Correspondence Department

Postal Department

Netball Team

Montagu Norman outside Claridge's, 1931.

The flattened City, looking east from St Paul's Cathedral, *c.*1942.

Queen Victoria Street, 1945: rose-bay willowherb, ragwort and groundsel.

challenged by the reports from Invergordon, ministers made a poor show in the Commons of toughing it out over the announced cuts in government expenditure. The Bank's reserves, which had been gradually ebbing away during the month, lost £3.5m in the course of the day. Anxieties about a precipitate general election further drained away the last vestiges of international confidence in sterling, and on Thursday the Bank lost no less than £10m. Although some in the City thought that an early election would have a stabilising effect on the situation, the Bank itself decidedly did not and was pushing hard for that election to be delayed. However, during the course of the 17th it became clear that the dominant Conservative element in the coalition was – for fairly blatant party political reasons – committed to as early an election as possible.

'It is believed that withdrawals owing to distrust in the future of sterling have largely come to an end', stated Einzig's column on the morning of Friday the 18th, in one of the more off-the-beam remarks in the history of financial journalism. In the course of the day the Bank lost £18.75m. It was an enormous sum, partly explained by the fact that at some point in the morning the Bank, apparently without consulting ministers, gave up on the gold standard and let sterling go.[31] Invergordon, the probable imminence of an election and a new, serious Dutch banking crisis all contributed to the decision – essentially a reluctant conviction that the game was no longer worth the candle.

At 9.45 that evening, at what MacDonald privately called the most solemn conference ever to have been held at 10 Downing Street, the prime minister met Harvey and Peacock. Harvey explained that the day's losses 'had exhausted the dollar credit', but that 'there was £15,000,000 available from France'. He added that he 'did not himself think that we could raise enough to save the situation'; that 'if the situation could not be saved it was merely waste of more money'; and that 'he did not see that it was worthwhile raising £100,000,000 if people were only going to draw it out'. To which statements MacDonald 'agreed that if one could not see one's way through it was better to acknowledge it now'.

The discussion then turned to practicalities:

> The Deputy Governor stated that it was better to stop on Monday morning as that would give time to warn the press, and the public could be stopped from rushing the banks. It might be necessary to stop the Stock Exchange tomorrow – by an unhappy chance they were meeting on Saturday for the first time [i.e. since the war] . . .
>
> The Prime Minister asked what would the effect be on things in general, particularly on the internal situation, of this upset? Mr Peacock replied that it would be an awful blow to everyone, but that the banks would loyally support one another in trying to keep working, and if the press played up, appearances at home might not be too bad. (The Deputy

Governor interpolated that the shock would be felt most keenly by wealthy financiers: there were lots of people who had in fact said that this was the one cure for our ills.) Mr Peacock went on to explain the shock to our people all over the world in Ireland, Egypt, India and so on: in every village a bill on London was looked upon as cash – and it would be cash no longer.

At the end of the meeting, Peacock remarked that 'no one could accuse this country of not having made every effort before letting the pound go'; and 'it was pointed out' – by Harvey? by Peacock? by MacDonald? – 'that by having balanced the Budget, whatever happened, this country had at least demonstrated her will to play the game at all costs'.[32] It was, no one added, a game that had wreaked enormous damage.

A formal announcement was made on the Sunday, and next day the press sought to bolster the City's confidence. The patriotic *FN* contrasted the 'panic-stricken scramble for gold' that had occurred abroad with the stoicism at home, 'where the development of the crisis has been faced with our characteristic coolness and good humour'. *The Times* anticipated that once the trade account had been balanced in the same way that the budget had been, 'this country will return to the gold standard'.[33]

During that Monday, with the Stock Exchange closed, the atmosphere was far less troubled than some had feared, but for Grenfell it was a sad, even dreadful day. 'You will see by this morning's papers that after all our struggles we are driven off the gold standard', he lamented to Vice-Admiral Sir Aubrey Smith at Iden near Rye. 'It has been rather a losing fight for some time – one rung a day – until the Navy business knocked us clean off the ladder. England was represented to the foreigner by the Navy and the Bank of England. It is all very bewildering and distressing.' Keynes, by complete contrast, was in jubilant mood, described as 'chuckling like a boy who has just exploded a firework under someone he doesn't like'. Yet Virginia Woolf perhaps had the right of it. 'We're off,' she scribbled in her diary on the 21st, '& I write about Donne. Yes; & what could I do better, if we are ruined, & if everybody had spent their time writing about Donne we should not have gone off the Gold Standard – thats my version of the greatest crisis &c &c &c – gabble gabble go the geese, who cant lay golden eggs.'[34]

For Eric Blair, the future George Orwell, it was all an even more massive irrelevance. On Saturday the 19th, after two and a half weeks hop-picking in Kent, he and his new friend Ginger returned to London, going to a 'kip in Tooley Street', just south of the river. They stayed there for about a fortnight, and several mornings, while it was still dark, they walked across London Bridge and found some work in the fish market at Billingsgate. An integral part of the City – close to the Monument and barely quarter of a mile from the Bank of England – it was a world apart from the hereditary grandees:

You go there at about five and stand at the corner of one of the streets which lead up from Billingsgate into Eastcheap. When a porter is having trouble to get his barrow up, he shouts 'Up the 'ill!' and you spring forward (there is fierce competition for the jobs, of course) and shove the barrow behind. The payment is 'twopence an up'. They take on about one shover-up for four hundredweight, and the work knocks it out of your thighs and elbows, but you don't get enough jobs to tire you out. Standing there from five till nearly midday, I never made more than 1s 6d.[35]

CHAPTER TWENTY-SEVEN

Credits and Debits

Confirmation of the City's unwillingness to brave the shock of the new lay in the fact that between 1905 and 1939 only about one-fifth of its fabric was rebuilt. The 'old' City was almost everywhere: down towards the river from St Paul's, secluded courts and alleys like Pope's Head Alley, Honey Lane, Russia Row and Turnagain Lane; north of Paternoster Row, a labyrinth so impenetrable that Mrs Dalloway's daughter lacked the courage to 'wander off into queer alleys, tempting bye-streets, any more than in a strange house'; in obscure courts buried behind Cornhill, seemingly timeless chop-houses like the George and Vulture (a favourite of Mr Pickwick) and the Jamaica Wine House (London's first coffee-house); near Eastcheap, the Georgian and early Victorian offices and warehouses of Love Lane; and nearby, in Great Tower Street, an almost unbroken mass of mainly undistinguished Victorian shops, offices and warehouses.[1] The list was almost endless.

In a 1934 supplement marking the golden jubilee of the *Financial News*, there appeared an article entitled 'What Would Wren Have Built Today?'. After diagnosing the Square Mile as increasingly overcrowded, badly lit and generally impossible to work in efficiently and pleasantly, the answer was confident and uncompromising:

> We must give up the building rule which restricts the height of buildings, and we must not only do that, but we must build office blocks twice as high as St Paul's, and have green spaces and wide roads in between the blocks . . . Two dozen skyscrapers, though they would obviously dwarf St Paul's, would not take away from its beauty if they were beautiful themselves. They would alter the sky-line, certainly, yet we should not sacrifice health, time, and comfort to one skyline because we have not the courage to create another.[2]

The author of this clarion call to modernise the City was a young architectural writer called John Betjeman.

A personal gloss on this type of attitude – one that was soon to be immensely powerful – was provided in the 1970s by the architectural historian Sir John Summerson, in his concluding remarks to a survey of the Victorian rebuilding of the City, as he sought to recall from memory the still essentially Victorian interwar City:

As a student I was conscious only of its sombre intricacies, its multiplication of sad and sooty ornament and, more than anything, its nauseating excess . . . The eye of the 1930s saw the City as dead: a petrified theatre of bad architectural rhetoric. Today, half demolished and overwhelmed by a harsh and shimmering modernity, it begins to live again and to move.[3]

The later Betjeman, that doughty City conservationist living in Cloth Fair, would no doubt have nodded his head sadly.

What was life actually like *inside* these mainly dark, ill-lit buildings? In the early 1930s, Phillips & Drew was a typical small stockbroking firm almost entirely dependent on private client business. Dougie Phin, half a century after being recruited as an office boy at 12s 6d a week, would recall life at Palmerston House in Old Broad Street:

It was a real Victorian pile – great echoing halls, scrappy old offices – it was a real Dickensian office. You went up in a great hydraulic lift where you had to pull the rope, and a young chap there in a scruffy old uniform, and then you went in the office, and it was a great old coal fire at one end – sixpence a bucket was the coal, and the office boy had to go down and get it from the dungeons . . . It was very dark – dark paint and dark mahogany desk – and the usual slit in it where the boys put their stock in, and then they scribed on it, 'Died waiting, 1934', and then the office manager would see you and come round and clip your ear. Our desks were the old-fashioned sloping desks with the big brass rails across the middle. You sat on a very high stool, and believe it or not they were very comfortable because you had a foot-rest and a flap . . . The first duty of an office boy was to fill up the ink-wells – blue, red and copper [i.e. black] ink, because all the contracts were written by hand.

Though fully recognising the 'charm' of the ruling family, Phin was not inclined to be unduly sentimental: 'On the whole, a damned happy old office, although the Drews were bloody mean and you were expected to work your guts out.'[4]

At the time, it was easier for some than for others to express disenchantment. Reay Geddes, ambitious youngest son of the businessman and politician Sir Eric Geddes, and educated at Rugby and Cambridge, managed via Sir Guy Granet to get a berth at the Bank of England, starting in March 1933. 'Wants to come because he thinks there must be a great opening on the foreign side', stated the initial report on him. 'Does not think of coming into the Bank in the ordinary way nor of going through the mill at the ordinary pace.' Over the next eighteen months he spent time in various parts of the Bank and achieved good reports for his aptitude and attitude. By December 1934, however, Geddes had decided to leave, and he took the opportunity to send to the chief of establishments his observations.

He noted at the outset that 'the boys who the Bank enlist have a good general standard of education, no experience other than that of school and holidays, and no definite bent', and that 'the vast majority do not come at their own express request, but on the choice of their Fathers, who are glad to find a gilt-edged investment for the capital represented by a son who is "developing rather late"'. He went on to explain how, because of the policy of deliberate over-manning (in order to be able to cope with the occasional brief rush), the new recruit found himself not only quickly bored but also corrupted:

It is quite inevitable that the recruit should start work in one of the outer offices. There he meets and works beside 'Disappointed men' who are always willing to tell what dreadful luck they have had at the hands of God, disease, the war and the Bank's complete disregard for merit. These gentlemen have one curious loyalty: if their superior winks at the custom of coffee or tea being taken during office hours, it is quite understood that each clerk enjoys these pleasures entirely at his own risk, if there are complaints from the 'case'. The recruit then learns that the foremen allow rules to be disregarded, but deny any knowledge of such transgressions. This cannot increase the recruit's respect for his superior. Apart from this loyalty, the disappointed ones have none. With their mocking of keenness, their obstruction of questions and their eyes on the clock, they are a strong and undesirable influence on boys fresh from school, during the latter's almost inevitable periods of doubt and apprehension.

Inevitably, disillusion set in – exacerbated, according to Geddes, by older clerks often saying to the recent recruit, 'Does it ever strike you that you will be like me one day?' As a result, Geddes calculated, some 2,000 men, roughly half the Bank's total workforce, were condemned 'to work at which their education only serves to make them uncomfortable – either openly discontented or passively awaiting a pension'. In his view, it would be altogether more desirable if the work was done by those better suited to it:

The objections to a cheaper grade of labour than the Bank employ at present are behaviour, appearance and intonation. A visit to the Clearing House would show how difficult it is to pick out Bank men. This is not to suggest that the Bank's standard is lower than in years gone by, but that mass-produced clothing and general knowledge have spread a certain 'savoir faire' which used only to be obtainable in conjunction with expensive education.[5]

Geddes himself had a notable business career ahead, while his report was carefully filed away, to gather dust.

The Bank merely led by example, for almost everywhere in the City was run along rigid, hierarchical lines. 'I shall have failed to convey the feudal atmosphere of the place', Ronald Palin memorably remarked in his memoir of interwar New Court, 'if I leave the impression that the partners were regarded simply as ordinary human beings whom an accident of birth had placed in control of a great business and thus also of the lives of a number of other human beings.' Rather, 'they were a higher order of creation', so that 'it was in the nature of things that a young male Rothschild should inherit a partnership in the family business when he attained a suitable age in the same way as he inherited material possessions and it did not enter anybody's head that any other qualification could ever achieve the same result'. In 1931, when Rothschilds decided to recruit a Cambridge graduate called Michael Bonavia, he was unequivocally told by the staff manager that however well he did, there was absolutely no prospect of becoming a partner.[6]

Paternalism ran deep, a relationship typified in many firms by that unquestioned boon, the annual staff outing. Quite often this took the form of a day trip to the senior partner's country house. And implicit in paternalism was job security – there is no doubt that the prevailing City culture remained that of one berth lasting a lifetime. Michael Verey would recall the sixty or so clerks whom he got to know during his early days at Helbert Wagg in the 1930s:

> They were the most splendid people for integrity and hard work and devotion to duty. Not probably madly ambitious, as I was, they were content to have a good steady job with a patron like Alfred Wagg. They were better paid and looked after than their equivalent in any merchant bank. One or two of the clerks were literally found on doorsteps in the East End. The firm never had to advertise for staff. If somebody retired or died – they practically never resigned – the head of department already had a list of people who had applied for jobs.

Nevertheless, in practice it all depended. At Kleinworts, for instance, the extremely difficult situation in the early 1930s meant that staff numbers were more or less halved, through a systematic programme of dismissals each Friday. The commissionaire's dreaded words, 'The staff manager would like to see you', became the stuff of nightmares, especially as the chances of a clerk who had been made redundant finding another job were at best slim. At Bensons, by contrast, there were no redundancies. 'In all the partners' discussions about economising,' that firm's historian notes, 'it was the one option never once considered. The attitude was that Bensons was a family firm that stuck together through thick and thin, and everyone counted.'[7] This was indeed the acceptable face of family capitalism, fortified by the knowledge born of long experience that financial markets tend to be cyclical.

The regular working day was not, by modern standards, all that long. At Barings, the rule from March 1929 was that new clerks would henceforth have to start work by 9.30, clerks of less than ten years' service had to be at the office by 9.45, those with more than ten years' service by ten, and clerks over sixty years old 'do not sign the Attendance Book'.[8] Even so, in the City as a whole, there was not only the compulsory Saturday morning, but most contracts stated that an employee could not leave the office until the day's work had been completed – which might not be until well into the evening.

Pay was adequate, rather than wonderful. At James Capel, for example, a new clerk would start at about £70 a year, receive annual increments of £5 or £10, and eventually break through the £175 barrier, at which point he was permitted to marry. At another stockbroking firm, Phillips & Drew, there was a striking comparison in the share-out for the year ending March 1936: whereas the five partners received an average of £1,530, even the relatively well-paid Tommy Tomkinson, sole telephone operator as well as responsible for the post and the jobbers' books, took home a screw of only £4 5s a week. Moreover, although many firms did in this period start to introduce profit-sharing schemes and thereby put bonus arrangements on a more orderly and equitable basis, there was still plenty of scope for individual capriciousness, as the unfortunate Henri Jacquier of Kleinworts found to his cost – a run-in with his manager over some South American accounts resulted in no salary increase for fourteen years. Also in Fenchurch Street, at Austin Reed's flagship branch, the young Philip Horton, who went there in 1923 from Watford Grammar School, made the mistake of asking the authoritarian manager, Percy Osborn, for a salary rise on the grounds that he thought he was doing his job well. 'Of course you do your job well,' replied Osborn. 'You wouldn't be here if you didn't. We don't give salary increases for doing your job. We give salary increases for doing more than your job!'[9]

There was also, of course, the whole question of pension arrangements, traditionally a case of grace and favour. H. B. Reynolds had retired from Barings in 1912, and on the last day of 1924 he humbly petitioned that bank's directors for an increase to his pension, in the context of the post-war increase in the cost of living. 'I am nearly 77,' he observed, 'and am not likely to trouble you much longer.' The request was granted (his pension being increased to £540 a year), and Revelstoke was suitably paternalistic: 'Any such representation from so old and so valued a member of our staff is entitled to our very particular sympathy.' Reynolds, from his home in Woodford Green, replied gratefully: 'I ought now to be able to get along comfortably, and can only hope that the ease of mind this gives me will not so lengthen my life that I may be looked upon as a nuisance by Baring Brothers & Co.'[10] By the mid-1930s most of the merchant banks had introduced pension schemes (usually contributory), but many other firms, including stockbrokers, had not. Thousands of clerks still worked until they literally dropped, or became physically incapable, and it was not uncommon to have a working span in a single firm of sixty years or even, in some cases, seventy. It was not yet, in fine, the era of the 'bobo' – burnt out but opulent.

As for the work itself, if there had been a hint of mechanisation prior to 1914, between the wars it became more than just a hint. Stephen Graham, in his quickfire *Twice Round the London Clock* of 1933, was particularly struck:

> As I stand waiting to see the manager at a big bank in Bishopsgate, my ears are assailed by a sort of jazz, a rapid tapping and screwing, as of flat kettle-drums and toneless saxophones, the chorus of adding machines.
>
> No longer do innumerable pens waiver over the desks. The City is no longer full of penpushers, but of handle-pullers, tap-tap-tap screw, tap-tap-tap screw. It seems even more mechanical than pen-work, but the clerks are proud of their machines.[11]

Whatever the clerks may have told Graham, there was in general considerable suspicion, and even hostility, towards the whole process of mechanisation, not least (especially from a male point of view) because of its employment implications. Union Discount was a graphic – perhaps extreme – case in point. The first accounting machines arrived at 39 Cornhill in the 1930s, and the staff at once made a dead set against them. 'They took jolly good care they didn't work', Robert Wyse's 'boy' at Union Discount, H. F. Goodson, would recall. 'They didn't put sand in the machines, they just didn't press the right buttons.' One of those compelled to operate the new machines and finding the experience memorable, during their disastrous trial period, was Howard Planterose. Once:

> We had to work all night because we couldn't strike a balance. We had a bottle of whisky and bars of chocolate, and at five o'clock in the morning we went down to the Unsecured Deposit office and found a basket of slips that had been left and not collected. Finally we balanced and pushed off to the Charing Cross Hotel, where we had baths and shaved and had breakfast. We got back to the office at half-past ten and were ticked off for being late.

The pay-off came at the end of the three-month trial period: 'The message came out from the Managers' Room, "how long will it take you to get back to hand-posting?" We said "we'll do it tonight!" and we did too.'[12]

*

In 1934, the grandson of a former governor of the Bank of England turned up at 20 King William Street for his first day at the family coffee business (E. Johnston & Co.) and, despite his pedigree, proved unsuited. 'I was not cut out for the City life,' Brian Johnston would recall of life on the third floor of Stafford House, 'and never understood its argot – draft at ninety days sight, cash against documents less 2½%, etc.' A brief ray of sunshine was an exchange with the office manager. 'Mr Johnston, you should have been here at 9.30.' 'Why, what happened?' A year in the City office was followed by spells in Hamburg, Brazil and back in London, and during the five years before the war he grew to detest everything about the business of coffee. *It's Been a Lot of Fun*, Johnston would characteristically call his memoirs, but it had not all been cakes and japes.[13]

Of those who failed to last the course, however, the definitive City experience was that of T. S. Eliot.[14] In his late twenties, and as a seemingly more attractive alternative to school-teaching, he joined Lloyds Bank in March 1917, entering the colonial and foreign department at 17 Cornhill. 'Perhaps it will surprise you to hear that I enjoy the work', he wrote early on to his mother, elaborating soon afterwards to another correspondent:

> I sit in a small office with a mahogany desk and a tall filing cabinet, and feel much more important than my salary warrants, as I have charge of all the balance sheets of their foreign correspondents, filing and tabulating and reporting on them. Not that I know anything about banking, but the business is so huge that I don't suppose more than half a dozen men in the bank know more than their own little corner of it. I share an office with Mr McKnight [the original of Eggerson in *The Confidential Clerk*], who lives in a suburb, polishes his silk hat with great care when he goes out, and talks about his eldest boy.

By 1920 Eliot had moved to the information department at head office, dealing on his own with knotty points – usually legal and international – arising out of the Versailles Treaty. The City itself, however, he now saw as spiritually null, redeemed only by the lunchtime haven of its churches; as he had graphically written to Lytton Strachey as early as 1919, 'I am sojourning among the termites.' Eliot had a breakdown in the autumn of 1921, and that winter he wrote much of *The Waste Land* while convalescing in Lausanne.

He was back in the City by early 1922, and over the next few months often met the American writer Conrad Aiken for lunch, usually a rump steak in a Cannon Street pub. Aiken would recall how Eliot invariably had with him his pocket edition of Dante's *Inferno*. That October his poem appeared in the *Criterion*, whose publisher was R. Cobden-Sanderson of 17 Thavies Inn, EC1. The immediate acclaim for *The Waste Land* probably only intensified Eliot's despair. 'Of course I want to leave the Bank,' he told Ezra Pound in November 1922, 'and of course the prospect of staying there for the rest of my life is abominable to me.' The following July he returned to the colonial and foreign department, which by this time had moved to 20 King William Street. 'A little room under the street' was how a colleague would describe Eliot's new office. 'Within a foot of our heads when we stood were the thick, green glass squares of the pavement on which hammered all but incessantly the heels of the passers-by.'[15] Over the next two years Eliot wrote a regular, anonymous article on foreign exchange for *Lloyds Bank Monthly*, until at last, in November 1925, he left the bank and took up a position with the publishers Faber and Gwyer. He had been in the City for just over eight and a half years.

Those nine lines in *The Waste Land* – 'Unreal City . . .' – remain the most haunting lines about the City in the whole of twentieth-century literature; they echo, consciously or otherwise, Herman Melville's description in the 1850s of 'that hereditary crowd – gulf-stream of humanity – which, for continuous centuries, has never ceased pouring, like an endless shoal of herring, over London Bridge'. Eliot too saw the crowd flowing over London Bridge and 'had not thought death had undone so many'. His extraordinarily grim lines, however, tell only one truth about the City. J. B. Priestley, some years later, told another, in the person of the middle-aged cashier, Smeeth, as with pipe lit he walks down 'the chilled and smoky length of Angel Pavement'. There, 'everywhere would be a bustle and a jostling, with the roadway a bedlam of hooting and clanging and grinding gears, but he had his place in it all, his work to do, his position to occupy, and so he did not mind but turned on it a friendly eye and indulgent ear'.[16] Eliot's vision or Priestley's? The City experience embraced both, and so, in a Forsterian connection, must we.

Yet at the time that remarkable politician-cum-writer Charles Masterman was not so sure. His study of *England after War* appeared in 1922, the same year as *The Waste Land*; in it he described, almost equally hauntingly, the inhabitants of an imaginary London suburb called Richford:

> Every morning that terrific progeny of Free Trade, the City of London, sucks in from all the Richfords overcrowded trainloads, hurrying rapidly one after the other, of respectably and dingily garbed human beings. They spread themselves in that labyrinth from attic to underground cellar, with nimbleness and apparently without repugnance, to spend the best of their days in copying other men's letters, adding up other men's accounts, or distributing, in vast numbers, in written or printed instructions, the requests and demands of other men for the alteration of universes which they have never known. Every evening they trample their way back to Richford. And the evening and morning are one day. They are all either clerks in banks or shipping companies, or accountants, or insurance officials. And they are all rearing children to be insurance officials, or accountants, or clerks in banks or shipping companies.
>
> There are fifty or a hundred churches in that same City of London, most of them built by Christopher Wren on the sites of former churches consumed in the Great Fire. Their spires and domes flash upwards, pointing to the planets or the fixed stars: with the legend which Paul found at Athens, marked as if graven upon them: 'To an Unknown God'.[17]

*

The ninefold increase in the national debt caused by the First World War meant that British government securities – gilts – retained throughout the interwar period a far more dominant position in relation to the stock market as a whole than they had done during, say, the thirty or forty years prior to 1914.[18] It is true that of the 5,629 securities officially quoted in March 1938, over a quarter were industrial and commercial; but in terms of market value, the Funds comprised almost 40 per cent, industrial and commercial securities only 14 per cent. In a non-inflationary age, gilts continued to be seen as fundamentally more sound investments than equities, and few institutions included substantial holdings of ordinary shares in their portfolios. These institutions – above all insurance companies, but also investment trusts and (from the 1930s) unit trusts – were becoming an increasingly significant force. In 1933 the *Financial News* calculated that institutional investors had total holdings of about £1.7bn and generated around one-fifth of Stock Exchange turnover. Even so, the private investor was still king and, in the words of the *FN*, 'investors, on the whole, seem to prefer to have the fun of managing their investment themselves through their own stockbrokers rather than to entrust their savings to an insurance company, an investment trust or a building society'.[19] These individual investors tended to be much more willing to take a punt on ordinary shares and were less deterred by the general absence of reliable financial information about companies, especially the true value of their assets. The Stock Exchange itself hardly encouraged popular capitalism. As early as 1923, a year after it began, the BBC asked for permission to broadcast prices – a request granted, with the utmost reluctance, only three years later, a concession rendered almost useless by the stipulation that no prices were to be broadcast prior to 7 p.m., long after the end of trading.

Overall, whether in government or industrial securities, the market was becoming increasingly domestic in its orientation – in marked contrast to its essentially global character during the golden years prior to 1914. No longer, especially in the 1930s, did capital flow unfettered around the world; while in various ways the Stock Exchange did not help its cause, for example by its attitude to international arbitrage, which was at best indifferent and at worst hostile. Inevitably the result was that much of London's international business between the wars bypassed the Stock Exchange. 'When it is remembered that there must be taken into account exchange rates, commission charges, interest, cables, insurance, fluctuations in money, settlement days, and the possibility that a commitment entered into in one centre may not be successfully undone or closed in another,' F. E. Armstrong symptomatically noted in 1934 in his semi-official *The Book of the Stock Exchange*, 'it will be seen that arbitrage is a highly skilled and technical business.'[20] These were hardly words to enthuse the troops.

In 1938 the Stock Exchange's total membership was 4,132, of whom 2,491 members were brokers, 1,433 were jobbers and 208 were inactive. The 2,491 brokers belonged to 465 firms, working out at an average of 5.4 members per firm.[21] What qualities did these brokers bring to bear? 'I found new faces but little advancement in stockbroking as a financial science', George Aylwen would recall of his return to J. & A. Scrimgeour at the end of 1918. 'Most members were merely passers on of information and gossip, there was little or no attempt to sift information, to analyse prospects of equities, or indeed to justify the recommendation of the many and various tips toddled out by the market and the many outsiders who frequented clubs and other convivial places where people with more money than sense assemble.' Donald Cobbett, who as a young man in the 1930s combined financial journalism with working on the floor of the House, was no more flattering: 'The average stockbroker merely conjured a few current ideas out of his topper and trusted to the excellent fino sherry at Short's or the Jamaica to impart an impression of high promise. The compliant clients were then plied with the current inspirations . . . Few stockbrokers in those pre-war days boasted what could be dignified a statistical department; few even had a competent statistician.' Admittedly the shortage of reliable information on the equity side was a powerful discouragement to the development of investment analysis. When Foster & Braithwaite decided in 1934 to create a statistical department, the partners disarmingly noted that this was 'with a view to improving the publicity side of the business' – as opposed, in other words, to altering the approach to investment itself.[22]

Nevertheless, the Stock Exchange in this period seems to have made little or no effort to improve the general calibre of its members, one of whom, William H. Tapp, justifiably complained to the Committee in 1938. His particular beef concerned 'the so-called "three decker Members"'. These were the gentlemen who achieved membership of the Stock Exchange, as of other desirable London clubs, through a mixture of personal connections and money. Personal connections were needed in order to find a nomination (by which a new member replaced a retiring member) and three sureties, each by the mid-1930s putting up £500 in case of default. Money was needed to buy the nomination (about £300 at this time); to buy three shares in the ownership of the Stock Exchange (about £210 each); and for the entrance fee of 600 guineas. There would also be an annual subscription of 100 guineas. Tapp, almost certainly a broker himself, was indignant:

> There can be no doubt that an enormous amount of harm is done to the prestige of the Stock Exchange by people who are allowed to join as full Members even although they are under Sureties, without any training whatsoever for their profession . . . We could do a vast amount of good

if under some statute the Stock Exchange could be reformed so that every Member had to have at least three years' training either with a Stock Exchange firm, or a Chartered Accountant, before he could become a Member at all.

'The majority of stockbrokers are decidedly an ignorant class who know very little more beyond 8ths, 16ths, and 32nds', one witness had complained some sixty years previously to the Royal Commission on the Stock Exchange, and in the eyes of Aylwen, Cobbett and Tapp not much had changed.[23]

In a nutshell, whom one knew still mattered more than what one knew. Most stockbroking firms did not rely just on their partners to achieve the crucial introductions to prosperous clients, for they also employed a wide range of half-commission men, who in return for bringing business from the West End and elsewhere would retain half the commission thus generated. One such was Gubby Allen. After Eton and Cambridge, he started in the City in 1923 with Royal Exchange Assurance, but over the next ten years his main preoccupation was playing as much first-class and club cricket as he could. He toured Australia in 1932–3 and, as a fast bowler, refused to adopt the controversial, ungentlemanly 'bodyline' tactic. On his return he joined the stockbrokers David A. Bevan & Co. on a half-commission basis, becoming a member of the Stock Exchange later in 1933. From the firm's point of view, he brought with him not only his sporting reputation but also a host of friends and acquaintances whom he had made on and off the cricket field; and in 1936–7 he captained the next English tour to Australia, almost but not quite managing to wrest back the Ashes from another stockbroker, Don Bradman.[24]

During the voyage out Allen probably did not read Keynes' recently published *The General Theory of Employment, Interest, and Money*, with its celebrated Chapter 12 on the psychology of investment. 'The social object of skilled investment', Keynes declared, 'should be to defeat the dark forces of time and ignorance which envelop our future.' In practice, however, 'the actual, private object of the most skilled investment today is to "beat the gun"'. And, in a particularly memorable passage, he went on:

Professional investment may be likened to those newspaper competitions in which the competitors have to pick out the six prettiest faces from a hundred photographs, the prize being awarded to the competitor whose choice most nearly corresponds to the average preference of the competitors as a whole; so that each competitor has to pick, not those faces which he himself finds prettiest, but those which he thinks likeliest to catch the fancy of the other competitors, all of whom are looking at the problem from the same point of view. It is not a case of choosing those which, to the best of one's judgement, are really the prettiest, nor even those which average opinion generally thinks the prettiest. We have reached the third degree where we devote our intelligences to anticipating what average opinion expects the average opinion to be.

A powerful indictment, and entirely compatible with the make-up of the average stockbroker of the period; but arguably there was another, even stronger reason why the Stock Exchange of these years, and indeed for a long time afterwards, was so poor at analysing economic fundamentals and distributing financial resources accordingly.

This was the prevalence – barely recorded in the contemporary literature – of what would eventually be termed 'insider dealing'. It was, as Michael Verey of Helbert Wagg would recall, a process in which the stockbroker tended to be the crucial lubricant or middle-man:

> Kit Hoare would have dinner with the investment manager of the Pru, and the investment manager of the Pru after dinner probably let a few secrets go that he, the Pru, had been told about this, that and the other. So Kit Hoare went round to his friends the next day and said, 'I think probably ICI or whatever it might be is a jolly good buy at this price'. A great deal of word of mouthing . . . And there was a good deal of directors in clubs with their friends, stockbrokers and, 'we're doing jolly well at so and so' – there was a good deal of that. So that this all percolated through stockbrokers to Helbert Wagg.[25]

Insider dealing began to be outlawed in the United States in the 1930s, but in Britain it was not until the 1960s that it started to be generally recognised as a form of theft, let alone made illegal. Instead, the reputation of many brokers stood or fell by their ability, on the basis of inside information, to provide their chosen clients with profitable tips. From a broker's point of view, moreover, there seemed little point in spending money on analysing the form – even if one had the ability or inclination to do so – when instead it was possible, for the most favoured brokers anyway, to go straight to the horse's mouth.

Did, for example, the partners of the government brokers, Mullens, indulge in insider dealing, either for themselves or for their clients? The very thought was unthinkable – after all, as the car of the sartorially impeccable Sir John Mullens turned each day past Mansion House, at the end of its journey from Belgrave Square, he would be saluted by the policeman on duty. Inevitably we have no evidence either way. Mullens himself, on retiring at the end of 1928, was succeeded as senior partner by the more congenial Edward ('Eddie') Gosling, who had joined Mullens as a result of its merger with Steer Lawford in 1921. His successor in turn, in 1937, was Edward ('Ted') Cripps, recruited some years previously from his family firm of Simpson & Cripps and, unusually for Mullens, not an Old Etonian. Cripps would not have joined Mullens had it not been for the premature death of Hugh Priestley, successor-designate to Gosling and whose move from Wedd Jefferson had been very much on the urgings of Montagu Norman. Priestley was immensely tall, a lover of games, never went abroad and sent his son James to Winchester, from where he went to his father's old firm, Wedd Jefferson. 'What would the boys have thought about someone going into the Stock Exchange for a career?' Jimmy Priestley was asked many years later. 'I don't think the boys ever really discussed that very much,' he replied. 'Certainly the City hadn't got a very high name. I think most people thought the people who went there were rather like me who had very little brain but hoped to make some money.'[26]

Many sons were happy enough to take their due place among the City elite, their lives virtually pre-ordained at birth. Ernest and Cyril Kleinwort, the sons of Alexander, were two such who, following careful if rather oppressive training, became competent merchant bankers. 'Never become emotionally involved in any business problem', Alexander taught his boys, having had that dictum drummed into him by his own father; and on Alexander's death in 1935, Norman was able to receive reassurance from Herman Andreae of Kleinworts: 'Ernest & Cyril K are sound & safe & reliable. Most of Sir Alex[a] fortune is already theirs . . . His death in no way affects standing of Firm.'[27]

It was not a turning that the young Victor Rothschild, on coming down from Cambridge, was prepared to take:

> It came as rather a shock at the age of twenty-one to learn that I was expected at least to try the life of a banker in the City of London. This I did, but the moment was unfortunate. In 1931 there was a world recession; the City seemed moribund, boring, rather painful. I did not like banking which consists essentially of facilitating the movement of money from Point A, where it is, to Point B, where it is needed.

So a man of much brilliance, the future 3rd Lord Rothschild, was lost to New Court. Three moribund decades would ensue, as control continued to be vested entirely in the hands of other Rothschilds willing to put in the hardly strenuous hours.[28]

Ultimately, what really counted in the day-to-day conduct of City business was trust and reputation – qualities that both, in large measure, derived from mutually shared values as well as background. The French writer Paul Morand, on the basis of a visit to London in 1933, tellingly described the money market in action:

> After two o'clock in the afternoon it is difficult to find day money, but until then nothing is easier. Money abounds in London. It is a real country market in which the eggs and chickens are millions. You can get a million pounds in a moment, without any contract or immediate proof. But to

do that you must be well known, well dressed, and well educated – at Eton, Harrow, Winchester or Rugby. Here the public school spirit comes in again. The money which these gentlemen go on foot to find, sometimes chewing a Canadian apple, does not circulate materially: it is merely a matter of accepted credits, merely the matter of a signature; but one only gives it to someone who is well shaved, with agreeable manners, who is quick on the ball or rides hard to hounds, whom one calls by his Christian name and with whom one has played cricket for fifteen years . . .

'Manners' have an importance in the City, undreamed of by the foreigner.

'And if a young man has bad manners?'

'Well, then he never gets a good rate of discount, and it is all up with him.'[29]

Was the interwar City a more 'closed' world than it had been prior to 1914? There are some obvious grounds for believing that it probably was. In November 1930, some six months after it had become clear that the Stock Exchange remained generally unwilling to re-admit ex-members of German origin, and would continue to uphold its 1918 rule that anyone born in Germany, Austria, Hungary, Bulgaria or Turkey was ineligible for membership, the chairman of the Baltic Exchange, John Parry, decided – probably somewhat nervously – to test the waters in his market. In a letter to members, he argued that the existing policy, which was similar to that of the Stock Exchange, 'is prejudicial to the interests of the Members inasmuch as it limits scope and volume of business that can be transacted on the Exchange'; he suggested that, twelve years after the end of the war, the time had come to open up membership to nationals of all countries, reflecting the fact of 'the business of the Exchange being international in character'. Ahead of an extraordinary general meeting called for 12 December, there ensued the predictable storm of protest, and the meeting was first postponed, then adjourned and finally abandoned. The following year a watered-down reform was introduced, with naturalised British subjects being permitted to become clerks, but this hardly made it a market open to all the talents.[30]

Many of these excluded foreigners were, of course, Jews. That did not stop fevered fantasies (though mainly outside the City) about the Jewish conspiracy in international finance, fantasies that Paul Einzig implicitly addressed in an authoritative overview in the *Banker* in 1933:

> Those who talk about the predominant Jewish influence in British banking ought to be reminded that there is not a single Jew among the directors of the Bank of England, and hardly any among the directors of the 'Big Five'. Even among the banking firms the Jewish element does not by any means predominate. In fact, Jewish banking houses of international standing could be enumerated on the fingers of one hand; they are N. M. Rothschild & Sons, Samuel Montagu & Co., M. Samuel & Co., Seligman Brothers, and S. Japhet & Co. Most other leading banking houses are

essentially non-Jewish. In the various sections of the London financial market, it is only the bullion market in which Jews predominate. Their relative influence in the foreign exchange market has declined to a fraction of what it used to be, as a result of the extension of foreign business by the joint stock banks. Though there are many prominent Jewish Stock Exchange firms, in the aggregate, they form a small minority. As for the money market, it is essentially non-Jewish.[31]

Would there have been greater Jewish representation – for example, on the Court of the Bank of England or on the boards of the major clearing banks – if there had not been widespread anti-Semitic prejudice in the City? Presumably there would, for undeniably there was such prejudice. 'They are very well known here, Jews but quite nice people to do business with', was how Vivian Hugh Smith described M. Samuel & Co. in 1925 to Morgans in Paris; while over the years it was plausibly believed at Sebags that the reason that stockbroking firm never got any business from Morgan Grenfell was an unwillingness to deal through Jews. The Pope of the City shared the prejudice. 'I refuse to see Baldry – who is a Broker & Jew', Norman recorded in his diary in 1932; and although, inevitably, he accepted that there were some Jews in the City who were too important to be shunned, he rarely if ever seems to have established warm relations with them. Lionel de Rothschild, for instance, was always addressed by him in correspondence as 'Dear Mr de Rothschild', unlike the pet names Norman accorded to many other leading figures. Lawrence Jones, a humane as well as perceptive observer of those around him, saw the City's anti-Semitism as 'endemic' but 'mild':

> There were no fears of conspiracy: there were no accusations of corruption. There was an Anglo-Saxon suspicion of cleverness, a school-boyish contempt for people who cared little for fresh air and field-sports, and a Philistine mistrust of taking the arts seriously enough to spend money upon them. But above all I believe most Anglo-Saxons are subconsciously shocked by the Jew's devastating commonsense and objectivity. We Britons like to wrap up both our aims and our means of achieving them in a comfortable vagueness. We hope to attain something, somehow. The Jew knows precisely what he wants, and exactly how to get it. And when he comes out with it, sharply, we are apt to shudder, as if the bedclothes had been whipped off as we lie in bed.[32]

The metaphor is apt, for over the centuries a series of remarkable Jews have come to the City, found it slumbering, given it a rude awakening, ignored the often emotive protests and bequeathed a wholly beneficial legacy.

Some firms, of whatever ethnic character, were more open than others to the advance of merit. At Rothschilds there was no chance of a partnership unless one was born a Rothschild; at Cazenove's it was still unknown to come in at the bottom and rise to the partners' room; while at James Capel, out of the interwar intake of ten partners, only one, the dealer George Rushton, was essentially self-made, and he had to content himself with becoming a salaried partner, unlike such full partners as Pleydell Keppel Stephenson, the Hon. D. G. Fortescue and George Sholto-Douglas Pape. Elsewhere, however, there were signs of a less restrictive approach. At Glyns, under General Sir Herbert Lawrence, the partnership began to be less dominated by the Glyn, Mills and Currie families; at Wallace Brothers, whereas during the sixty-three years from its establishment as East India merchants in 1862 only three out of fifteen partners and directors had not had a family connection, from the mid-1920s the pattern changed completely, so that over the next forty years only two out of eleven directors *did* have such a connection; and at Samuel Montagu, what that firm's historian describes as 'a narrow, conservative family business' was transformed in the 1930s by two key appointments to the partnership – one definitely a City insider, David Keswick, the other an outsider, a gifted Belgian called Louis Franck.[33]

Clearly there is a balance to be struck in the historical judgement, a balance perhaps embodied in the four-man partnership of the very successful finance house Cull & Co. Gilbert Russell was a cousin of the Duke of Bedford; Hugh Micklem (a brother of Charles Micklem of Cazenove's) and Eric Cull were former oil jobbers; and fourthly, offering the financial creativity, there was Hermann Marx, described in 1929 by one Morgan Grenfell partner as 'a Jew' with 'a reputation of being a pretty shrewd man'.[34]

That same year, after Revelstoke died in Paris, the new Lord Revelstoke sought to reassure King George V. 'You will see', Cecil Baring wrote to the private secretary Lord Stamfordham, 'that the concern remains, as a whole, a family affair, although it has always been laid down here, and we of the family constantly recognise, that there can be no place for one of our members unless he shews the requisite character and brains.' The last three words begged a fundamental question, but certainly no one was keener than Peacock to ensure that blood alone no longer provided an automatic entrée. In July 1937, a Barings memo recorded, he received a visit from 'Lady Lovat with her younger son, the Hon Hugh Fraser, with reference to an understanding she had had with the late Lord Revelstoke (Cecil) that Mr Fraser should come to No. 8 for a period as soon as he had finished his education'. Fraser was at Oxford, with two years still to go there. However, 'it was made quite clear [i.e. by Peacock] to Lady Lovat that anyone coming here came on six months' probation, and that the extension of such a period, in the case of people like her son, depended entirely on whether we considered them sufficiently promising to go through all the departments of the Office or not'. Moreover, 'Sir Edward made it clear that, unless a man could produce something quite out of the way in qualifications, he could not expect to spend his life at No. 8'.[35] This was, of course, only an ideal, but it was significant that it was articulated. Peacock himself was a Canadian, one of many foreigners – though not as many as before 1914 – for whom the City still provided a profitable if not always entirely welcoming home. Already the power behind the throne in the 1920s, he in effect led the bank after Revelstoke's death, being particularly prominent in the areas of international finance and corporate finance. Cecil Baring may have privately called him 'The Paycock', but neither he nor the other active members of the family imagined they could do without him.[36]

Of course, most of the City's immigrants still came from the Continent, and here the story of that dynamic outfit Singer & Friedlander was particularly instructive. Before the war it had been a stockbroking firm, with origins that were manifestly not Anglo-Saxon, and as a result of the Stock Exchange's policy during the war it turned itself into a banking business, with arbitrage, foreign stocks and bonds, and bill discounting as its main specialities. New partners from 1920 were Julius Stern, formerly with Japhets, and Max Ullmann, who would subsequently found his own merchant bank; while by the mid-1920s the driving force was increasingly the very young, very talented arbitrageur Marcel Pougatch, of Russian birth but educated in Paris. There were also the Hock brothers. The founder at the turn of the century of a Vienna banking house, Richard Hock in 1923 decided to take an interest in Singer & Friedlander and accordingly sent his son Francis to join it. Five years later Francis became a partner, and in 1932 he was joined as a partner by his elder brother, Dr Hans Hock, who had already been a partner in the family bank in Vienna, had trained as an economist as well as a banker and specialised in foreign bonds. A rapidly growing concern (incorporated in 1933, with a paid-up capital of £200,000), Singer & Friedlander would for a long time be positioned at some considerable distance from the City Establishment – reflected in the joke that, in a cricket team of merchant banks, Singers would keep wicket because 'it never misses anything'. In that same team, it was always assumed, Barings would bowl uphill into the wind, loyal and uncomplaining.[37]

Siegmund Warburg was presumably the all-rounder, as cultured as he was dedicated, as intellectual as he was ruthless.[38] The bare facts of his early life are that he was born in 1902; after university, took his place in M. M. Warburg & Co., the family bank that was based in Hamburg; spent time as a trainee in Boston and New York, as well as in London, where he was with Rothschilds; in 1930 became the bank's resident partner in Berlin; and, as a Jew, left Germany not long after Hitler came to power, taking up permanent residence in England in 1934. That October he was closely involved in the formation (or re-launching) of the New Trading Company, operating out of three small offices in King William Street. There are various, somewhat conflicting accounts of how this came about, but according to Denzil Sebag-Montefiore, a reasonably inside source, Warburg on his arrival in England 'was befriended by the Rothschilds', who already owned the New Trading Co. as a subsidiary that they 'used for transactions they did not wish to be directly associated with, usually because the transactions were too small for them'; accordingly, as an act of friendship, the Rothschilds 'sold him or, perhaps, gave him' the company. The problem with this version of events, and others in biographies of Warburg, is an entry in Norman's diary for 15 October: 'Sir A. Stern. "The New Trading Co." for Barter, anywhere except Germany. Majority held by Paris & Ldn Sterns in Engl & French Cos. Minority held by Dutch Cos of German connections. I say there is no objection.' Norman's visitor was 'Bertie' Stern, by now helping to preside over the long, inexorable decline of Stern Bros, which in the middle of the nineteenth century had been one of the great Jewish merchant banks. This brief interview with Norman – in effect, enabling the governor to give his blessing to the venture – may well have been Stern's single largest contribution to the City.[39]

What we indubitably know is that NTC's chairman from October 1934 was Sir Andrew McFadyean, who had had a distinguished career at the Treasury, and that the joint managing directors were Siegmund Warburg and Harry Lucas. The latter, several years younger than Warburg, had made rapid progress after university to become assistant manager of National Discount, until tuberculosis enforced his departure and a year of convalescence in Switzerland. Almost certainly he was a match for Warburg, a tribute by the *FT* after his death reckoning that 'few men had a more acute analytical mind, which grasped fundamentals so rapidly and seized upon the most important points so eagerly'. Over the next few years NTC became an established rather than a major force, as Warburg got his measure of the City and spent much of his time enabling Jewish families to get themselves and their money out of Germany. Indeed, he took directly under his wing in King William Street three immigrants – one Austrian, Eric Korner, and two Germans, Ernest Thalmann and Henry Grunveld. In the long run the most important of the trio was Grunfeld (as he would soon become), who after a gruesome encounter with the Gestapo in 1934 had already established himself in the City before being recruited by Warburg in 1937 and becoming his utterly trusted right-hand man. Two things struck Grunfeld most forcibly, he would reflect half a century later, about the City of the 1930s: on the one hand, its prevailing ethos of trust, the reality of the word being the bond, a reality that enormously facilitated the execution of business and thereby enhanced its volume; on the other hand, a hostility – especially on the part of the traditional merchant banks – to innovation or any new ideas, a hostility that Grunfeld could only attribute to a deeply entrenched complacency, even arrogance.[40] It was a duality that, more for good than ill, he and Warburg would do much to destroy.

The world of joint-stock banking was, however, where the balance between old City and new City – or closed City and open City – was most nicely adjusted. Throughout the interwar period the 'Big Five' comprised Midland, Lloyds, Barclays, National Provincial and Westminster, of which Midland was the biggest. Its chairman, McKenna, explained matters to Morand in 1933: 'None of these banks, except the Westminster, is of London origin. Thirty years ago they all came in from the provinces and now they have succeeded in eliminating the old system of private banks with six or seven partners.'[41] Spoken like a triumphant outsider, yet taking the Big Five as a whole, it is clear that in both the portentousness of their new City head offices and in the composition of their boards, there was a craving for respectability and acceptance rather than an instinctive assumption of natural superiority over old, outmoded City dynasticism. It is pretty clear that the City Establishment, for its part, continued to view the five banks as something of a necessary evil: the Court of the Bank of England remained obstinately closed to its representatives, while for a long time Norman's personal relations with McKenna and Goodenough (chairman of Barclays) were notoriously difficult. In the larger relationship, the concessions were mainly one way. In the old days, Holden may have half-seriously imagined rivalling or even supplanting the Bank of England as the main source of monetary power and influence, but none of his successors amongst the joint-stock men seem to have scouted the possibility. Rather, the process under way was much more that of absorption into the existing City Establishment, a process strengthened by the semi-oligopolistic character of commercial banking in the wake of the great amalgamation movement between 1890 and the end of the war. Once Goodenough had gone (he died in 1934), and McKenna and Norman had developed a working relationship, there would be nothing to stop full-blown absorption, a far cry from the competitive iconoclasm of an earlier era.

Inevitably, however, it was not an Etonian who undertook the unremitting, day-to-day graft of running a big clearing bank like the Westminster. Charles Lidbury, joint general manager from 1927 and chief general manager from 1930, was the son of a Cheshire schoolteacher and himself left school at the age of thirteen. Thereafter, by dint of intense effort, he had worked his way up from the very bottom of the banking ladder. His personality was forceful, occasionally domineering, and his monetary thinking was impeccably orthodox. By 1932, when Raymond Streat of the Manchester Chamber of Commerce was invited to lunch at the bank's head office, Lidbury was at the height of his powers. Streat found his host 'forthright to a degree', before he 'dashed off in great haste – I imagine that to be the style he affects – and left his calmer colleagues to see me off the premises'. Overall, Lidbury's efforts were appreciated, and in 1936, while still chief general manager, he was elected to Westminster's board – a sign that the gulf between the players and the gentlemen was starting to close, albeit very slowly.[42]

CHAPTER TWENTY-EIGHT

Two Fingers

'Somehow I feel resigned – almost stunned by recent events', the jobber Roy Sambourne recorded on Tuesday 22 September 1931. 'It has been a terrible strain & shock – & I shall have to economise rigorously. The Athenaeum & Garrick will have to go.'[1] The following morning Norman docked at Liverpool, to be told formally that Britain had, in his absence, been compelled to leave the gold standard. In London, on Thursday, he saw Baldwin and Snowden, but then retreated to the country for a long weekend to prepare himself for the ordeal of returning to his humbled fortress.

Of wider consequence to the City was the reshaping of British economic and monetary policy in the wake of the 1931 crisis. 'There are few Englishmen who do not rejoice at the breaking of our gold fetters', Keynes optimistically declared a week after that event. 'We feel that we have at last a free hand to do what is sensible. The romantic phase is over, and we can begin to discuss realistically what policy is for the best.' A few weeks later, in the preface to his *Essays in Persuasion*, Keynes still more memorably summed up the state of play:

> There is a lull in our affairs. We are, in the autumn of 1931, resting ourselves in a quiet pool between two waterfalls. Scarcely anyone in England now believes in the Treaty of Versailles or in the pre-war gold standard or in the policy of deflation. These battles have been won – mainly by the irresistible pressure of events and only secondarily by the slow undermining of old prejudices. But most of us have, as yet, only a vague idea of what we are going to do next, of how we are going to use our regained freedom of choice.[2]

Moreover, quite apart from the question of what the new policy should be, there was also the matter of *how* that policy should be arrived at. In the eyes of Ramsay MacDonald, it was high time that the Cabinet acquired a much greater degree of control in monetary areas, and accordingly, soon after the election, he set up a Cabinet committee on currency questions. But in practice he was thwarted: partly because the Treasury and the Bank were equally determined that between them they would keep control over these areas, and partly because three of MacDonald's most important colleagues – Baldwin, Snowden and Neville Chamberlain, the last having succeeded Snowden as Chancellor after the landslide election victory of the National Government on 27 October – successfully persuaded the rest of the Cabinet not only that 'liaison' with Norman 'could hardly be more close', but also that 'government control' of Bank policy was 'undesirable'.[3] Even so, as the first half of 1932 would show, the Treasury and the Bank could only maintain an omnipotent monetary axis provided they charted a new course that was satisfactory to their political masters.

Protection was the first pillar of the 1932 settlement.[4] Broadly protectionist since 1930, the City had not been inclined in the interim to return to its traditional free-trade allegiance, as the economic crisis deepened. The historic announcement – of a 10 per cent general tariff, although with temporary exemption for Empire goods – came from Chamberlain on the late afternoon of 4 February. 'The government's tariff proposals were very favourably received in the City', the *FT* reported of the response next day, and for its part asserted that 'British capital will be encouraged, foreign investment in our industries quickened and an enduring fillip given to confidence and economic recovery.' Significantly, it was not so much the intended reduction of imports, but rather 'the revenue-producing aspect that was accorded the best reception in the City'. Additional revenue, the City clearly believed, would help to achieve a balanced budget, keep up the value of sterling and keep down personal tax rates; whereas the reduction of imports was of little obvious benefit outside the manufacturing sector.[5] Economic internationalism temporarily ended in the early 1930s, globally speaking, to be replaced by autarchism; but the City as a whole – thoroughly rattled, or perhaps merely defeatist – had little compunction about selling the pass.

What about sterling itself?[6] There was little support in the Treasury for a return to gold even in the mid term; instead what now pervaded Treasury thinking on the subject was how to manage the sterling exchange in such a way as to foster the recovery of British industry – a nationalist orientation, in other words, quite unlike the internationalist assumptions that back in 1925 had underpinned the return to gold. By early March 1932 the Treasury had devised what it believed would be the appropriate mechanism for the management of sterling, and on 19 April the creation was announced of the Exchange Equalisation Account. Endowed with the authority to borrow up to £150m, and with the avowed aim of guarding against undue fluctuations in the value of the currency (in either direction, from a target of around $3.50 to the pound), it received what the *FT* described as a 'cordial' reception in the City. The paper itself hoped that eventually there *would* be a return to the gold standard, but accepted that 'that will be at some time in the future which cannot be specified until the world has settled down'.[7] Many in the City may have shared that wish, but in terms of policy in the here and now – and indeed in the foreseeable future – there was no alternative to managed money.

There was also an imperial theme.[8] It became increasingly clear that some sort of de facto sterling bloc was in existence, comprising most of the British Empire as well as the Baltic States, Egypt, Iraq and Argentina. The Treasury as well as the City at large generally welcomed this development – essentially the result of the continuing hegemony in large parts of the world of British trade and/or credit – but Norman was initially reluctant to accept the concept of the sterling area, presumably seeing it as a rival to the gold standard, and somewhat slow to grasp its potential for helping to restore the City's international position. Keynes, as so often, subsequently called it right, if perhaps a little generously. 'The sterling area', he remarked in 1944, 'was a brave attempt on our part to maintain the advantages of multilateral clearing to the utmost possible extent.'[9] It may not have been the world that Norman had known as a young man, or sought to recreate in middle age, but sterling's new lease of life as an international currency was in practice a crucial counterweight to the danger (as he would have seen it) of the City turning wholly in upon itself.

The last part of the new dispensation, and strictly for domestic consumption, was cheap money.[10] The departure from gold had pushed Bank rate to 6 per cent, where it stayed until February 1932, well into the period when sterling had started to stabilise or even improve. On the 11th of that month, as Norman adamantly insisted that no change be made, he came under strong attack from three of his directors – Sir Josiah Stamp (the eminent statistician-cum-businessman), Sir Robert Kindersley (of Lazards) and Sir Basil Blackett (formerly of the Treasury). 'I am afraid', Blackett said, 'that if the 6% Rate is maintained much longer there will be a concentrated and formidable attack upon the Bank and also upon you personally.'[11] A week later Norman at last abandoned his insistence that the rate must remain at 6 per cent until a further £80m of foreign currency credits had been repaid by the Bank, and the rate came down to 5 per cent. Over the next two months the Treasury was increasingly insistent that the rate must get down to at least 3 per cent, and by 21 April that had been achieved, with a further reduction (to 2½ per cent) following on 12 May. The sources do not record the degree of reluctance with which Norman implemented these changes, but what is reasonably clear is that cheap money was a policy driven by the Treasury.

The final move downwards, witnessed by 'Autolycus', came on Thursday 30 June, when the government broker went to the Stock Exchange to declare the new Bank rate; he held up 'two fingers to indicate the new Rate, which immediately flashed out, without a tremor, from the electric indicators'.[12] So 2 per cent it was, for the first time since September 1897.

Then, such a rate had been compatible – just – with adherence to the gold standard; now, it seemed wholly incompatible.

An obvious concomitant of low Bank rate was lower long-term interest rates, which was something that the Labour government had wanted to bring about before being overwhelmed by the 1931 financial crisis. In practice this meant a 'Conversion' of the 5 per cent War Loan, the giant stock created in 1917.[13] On 6 June Norman noted that 3½ per cent was the rate he would be advising the government to convert the stock to. Just over a fortnight later he reached another important decision – that the converted stock would be, in effect, irredeemable. On Tuesday 28 June it was announced that the Stock Exchange would open on the following Saturday: no reason was given, and the general assumption was that a conversion operation must be in the offing, especially as the competing attractions of Henley and Wimbledon meant that there must surely be a very good reason for throwing open the doors of Capel Court on a Saturday at the beginning of July.

Thursday the 30th duly ended the rumours. Within hours of Bank rate having come down to 2 per cent, Chamberlain stood up in the Commons and announced the terms of the conversion operation. 'Holders of the Five per Cent War Loan will gasp this morning', the *FT* declared on 1 July. 'Hardly one of them can have anticipated so deep a cut into the return, or so drastic an alternative.' That alternative was repayment in cash, and was available only to holders who specifically stated that they did not wish to convert by the end of September, whereas in previous operations the convention had been that holders of stock would receive cash unless they specifically opted to buy the new converted stock. From the start the patriotic drum was beaten loudly and insistently. Chamberlain's announcement, asserted the pink paper, 'represents the most magnificent gesture of confidence in the credit of Britain ever witnessed', and 'the operation is of the highest importance to national economy'. It would only work, however, if the big holders of War Loan showed the way. A couple of exasperated entries in Norman's diary showed one notable institution declining to do so, on the grounds of a higher responsibility to the interests of its depositors and shareholders. On 7 July: 'McKenna. I appeal to him to convert (along with all other bks). He refuses.' An acrimonious discussion followed, culminating in Norman – in a dramatic as well as important gesture – saying that he would buy £25m of Midland's £30m holding of the stock, with McKenna handsomely agreeing to convert the remaining £5m. That same day Norman also saw, at less expense to the Bank, leading figures from the discount houses.[14] Overall, the tactics worked. From 12 July the government-run War Loan Conversion Publicity Bureau published each day a list of 'principal organisations', including leading City institutions, that had agreed to convert. The great majority of small holders did likewise over the next few weeks, and eventually £1,920m was converted out of the £2,085m total stock. The actual task of processing all these conversions represented a huge, if stressful, achievement by the Bank of England, one that was important in helping it recover its collective morale after the public humiliation of the previous year.

Keynes, already gratified by the move to cheap money, praised the complementary conversion as 'a constructive measure of the very first importance'.[15] Why had such a large proportion of holders agreed to convert? Clearly there was some element of passivity, some element of patriotism, and some element of self-interest – and different commentators have given different weightings.[16] In the City itself, the role of Norman was undoubtedly crucial, with the conversion operation offering as it did the opportunity for a classic exercise in moral suasion. The stock may have become irredeemable, but a mixture of gubernatorial and national approval offered, in an essentially conformist milieu, an alternative means of redemption.

Protection, Exchange Equalisation Account, sterling area, cheap money: within a year of going off gold, the economic and monetary environment in which the City functioned had changed fundamentally. Looking through a glass darkly at this changed world, and indeed essentially out of sympathy with it, Norman refused to abandon his belief that economic internationalism remained the last best hope – and that it would have worked in the 1920s if central bankers had not been let down by politicians and their democracies.

The symbol, and to a significant degree the substance, of that economic internationalism was Germany, the country whose fortunes Norman had done so much to try to rebuild during his early years as governor. Nor was it only the world, he believed, that needed a strong German economy, but also the City itself, granted the sheer extent of its financial and trading links with that country. Not surprisingly, then, Norman had supported Tiarks of Schröders in the engineering of the Standstill Agreement, eventually reached in September 1931, which had saved the skins of the City's leading Anglo-German accepting houses. Equally unsurprisingly, in the winter of 1931–2, he backed Tiarks in the successful renewal of that agreement, having pointed out to him that 'it seems quite impossible that the £75 million due to this country from Germany should be repaid when it falls due', with the implication that there was therefore little alternative to renewal. Germany's creditors in the City included the clearing banks as well as the accepting houses, although only for the latter was it a matter of life and death that the German credit agreement be renewed, and thus interest on the debts continue to be paid, with the ultimate hope of the debts themselves being repaid. It was not a situation that best pleased Lidbury – 'Why should we add, by sacrifice of interest which in fact we

may take as a reduction of principal debt, to the fund of exchange available for the Accepting Houses to rob us by?' he asked in June 1932 of
one particular proposal – but by the second half of that year there was
a widespread feeling that Germany might be about to come right again.[17]
The international agreement at Lausanne in July virtually ended the
reparations saga, the economy was showing signs of picking up, and as
for politics, the prevailing note of reports from Berlin tended to the
sanguine.

'I feel quite certain that Hitler has missed his chance and the best he
can hope for in the future is to become a party leader, but he will never
become a German Mussolini', argued a generally optimistic memorandum
on the German position sent to Barings early in September. Two months
later Sir Edward Reid of Barings was in Berlin himself (staying at the
inevitable Hotel Esplanade, where English bankers always put up), from
where he wrote to a colleague about the Chancellor, Franz von Papen:
'It is impossible for him and Hitler to come together. Von Papen is a
"gentleman" in every sense of the word, wears collars that you would
approve of, and so on, while Hitler has all the bad qualities of the so
called lowest classes.' As for the possibility of the Austrian house-painter
becoming Chancellor: 'It should have no very untoward results, as Hitler
is more reasonable in action than in speech, and the Chancellor by himself
does not have a very great amount of power.'[18] Yet again, the City grandee
knew no more than the man on the Clapham omnibus about how the
dice would tumble.

*

For Norman himself, life in the City was never quite the same again after
1931 – symbolised by his abandonment of the top hat, unless it was strictly
necessary – but he still had an appetite for the work, an appetite fortified
by his happy marriage in January 1933 to a much younger woman, cause
among other things of some predictable Stock Exchange jokes about Bank
rate going up (and down). He wanted, despite occasional protestations
to the contrary, to continue as governor; he alone knew where all the
bodies were buried; and no plausible successor was yet in sight. At one
point there was talk of Niemeyer (who had moved from the Treasury to
the Bank), but on lunching at the Bank in November 1937, Addis found
that Kindersley 'is strongly against on account of his German origin'.[19]
That was becoming, in some quarters anyway, an increasingly damning
indictment.

Whatever the loss of prestige suffered as a result of the events of 1931,
Norman's Bank continued to exercise a large, even growing, degree of
influence over most parts of the City. The major exception was the insurance sector, whether inside or outside Lloyd's. Traditionally the Stock

Exchange and its member firms had comprised virtually as independent a community as that of Lloyd's, but by the 1930s this was no longer the case, especially as the long-term consequences of a vastly enlarged national debt began to be institutionalised. In February 1932, for instance, it was inconceivable that Mullens could decide who should fill the shoes of Hugh Priestley without submitting its candidate to the governor's scrutiny. Ted Cripps was duly summoned: 'Long talk: satisfactory in all ways, eg manner, ideas, Natl Service capacity – but ?health'.[20]

As in the 1920s, however, perhaps the prime example of Norman's moral sway over the City was in the area of the flotation of new issues of foreign loans, not wholly ruled out of court but in general much discouraged by the authorities. Baron Émile d'Erlanger came to see him in July 1932: 'Wishes to arrange advance to Holland 1 year. I most strongly protest. He will at once withdraw proposal & do nothing.' The following March it was the turn of a supremely well-connected stockbroker, Lord Charles Montagu: 'I say he cannot in any way sell or place French T Bills in London: contrary to Embargo.' Even Charles Hambro, a Bank of England director, received a fairly curt negative in March 1934: 'As regards your Turkish proposal, I think from your angle it is little less than silly. There is nothing to be said in favour of the Turks; they have nothing to do with you; and if they need financing for orders they place here it is up to the government and not to the City.'[21]

Elsewhere, the foreign exchange market, so active during the first half of the 1920s, picked up again after Britain's departure from gold. By 1939 it comprised over 140 banks and other large financial institutions, brought together each day by some thirty brokers who in effect acted as telephonic intermediaries. One of those brokers was Godsells of 1 Great Winchester Street, the creation of Wally Godsell, an East Ender who before the war had been a docker. The dealing table was the centre of each broking firm's activity – a large, rectangular table around which half a dozen or so dealers sat, each with his own telephone and dealing board – but Godsell was probably not alone in concluding many foreign exchange deals over a drink or two with bank dealers in Coates Wine Bar on London Wall.[22] It was, as recalled by George Bolton, by now running the Bank's foreign exchange department, a market with a less than salubrious reputation:

> There was widespread corruption, including the sharing of commissions between dealers in the banks and foreign exchange brokers, and the practice among brokers and dealers of taking foreign exchange positions on their own accounts; if a loss was made the original exchange contracts were then passed in the name of the bank which employed the dealer. At Christmastime in London it was impossible to hire a 'District Messenger' as they

were employed in trundling around the City cases of champagne, enormous hampers, turkeys, whisky and port, gramophones, etc – but these were for the clerks; the seniors received cheques and motor cars . . .

I cannot stress too strongly the complete ignorance of the banks of the consequences of the collapse of the gold standard and the emergence of a new breed of operators, undisciplined, remarkable in their capacity to take a short view, and without any long-term objectives. Many of these operators were European, mainly Central European, and the magnitude of their transactions completely overwhelmed the embryonic accountancy and control capacity of the banks they served.

Bolton himself did much from the mid-1930s to clean up this market, in particular exercising a direct form of quality control by giving the Bank's own business – which was very substantial – only to firms that he considered honest. The Bank was also instrumental in promoting the establishment of the Foreign Exchange Brokers Association, which oversaw a Bank-endorsed code of conduct. The central bank, furthermore, required London banks to do their foreign exchange business solely through Association members.[23]

The banks and other leading users of the market also had their own body, originally called the Committee of London Foreign Exchange Managers, but reconstituted in 1936 on a more formal, regular basis as the London Foreign Exchange Committee. 'Hitherto it has been simply a self-constituted body of technicians,' the Bank's Harry Siepmann noted in October that year, 'without authority to impose its will or its rulings, and often unable even to take a decision.' Accordingly:

> We want to make it really representative of the market as a whole and we want its rulings to have binding force. What has been done so far has been done not merely with our approval but on our initiative. On the other hand, we do not intend ourselves to do the job of remodelling the Committee nor do we mean to be represented on it. We are in the market but not of it . . . What needs to be improved is its status as a body, and its relationship to the big institutions with their (sometimes) self-important General Managers and their (generally) suspicious and competitive outlook towards one another.[24]

'In the market but not of it': it was a classic Bank position.

In both the foreign exchange and gold markets, Norman resisted as far as possible the spread of forward dealings, which he regarded as inherently speculative and destabilising.[25] It was an uphill, largely unavailing battle, for the general economic turbulence of the 1930s inevitably meant that in both markets there was considerable speculative activity. Indeed, the decade arguably represented the heyday of the London gold market, it being estimated that up to two-thirds of Europe's private gold hoards were physically located in the vaults of London's gold merchants.[26] A letter to Phillips of the Treasury in April 1935 was symptomatic of the problems faced by Norman:

> I want to try and avoid any attack on the pound, and at the same time I must try and avoid attacks on the European currencies: the two go together: and I include, of course, gold. To achieve anything I must start with the Clearing Bankers. If I can get agreement with them I can take the Houses next, then the foreign banks, and so forth. I am trying, you see, to leave the Exchange Market free but to keep dealings within the bounds of decency and honour.

A month later Norman had won the informal assurance of the clearing banks that they would assist the Bank's efforts to curtail speculation in both gold and foreign exchange, while by June the American banks in London were being persuaded to sign up along the same lines. In the temporarily more austere climate that ensued, London's bullion brokers reduced their forward commitments, including those in silver, which was fortunate because later that year a sudden change of American purchasing policy in relation to that metal led to a crisis in the London silver market that might have had very serious consequences. Even so, there had been 'overtrading' (to use Norman's term), particularly on the part of one London broker, Sharps & Wilkins.[27]

The forward march of bullion and foreign exchange business was irresistible, whatever the governor's sensitivities, and over the next eighteen months the Bank itself not only plunged for a time into the forward dollar market but even actively co-operated with the Bank of France in the execution of that central bank's forward transactions.[28] After all, as Norman sometimes tacitly acknowledged, the Bank could hardly hope to influence the markets unless it too operated in the real, changing world.

Norman himself continued during the 1930s to keep the closest possible tabs on the discount market, especially through his Thursday afternoon tea-parties for the market's representatives; and he was determined that it should not go to the wall, against his instincts even accepting that it should start dealing in short-dated government bonds (in competition with jobbers in the gilt-edged market) in order to scratch a living. He also, between September 1933 and February 1935, brokered three gentleman's agreements between the discount houses and the clearing banks, to ensure that the market was running at least at a modest profit. The final agreement was especially significant, for this saw the clearers consenting to stay out of the weekly Treasury bill auction, leaving the field clear for generally very cosy arrangements between the discount houses and the Bank, a cosiness fortified by the houses themselves devising and implementing a firm 'syndicate' agreement 'to cover the tender' on a quota basis. Rather less palatable to some of the houses was Norman's determination to 'rationalise' the market, with £300,000 explicitly set as the minimum capital for each firm. By the end of 1938 the number of houses was down to eighteen, compared to twenty-four at the start of the decade.

The willingness of the clearing bankers to do Norman's bidding in relation to the discount market reflected a relationship between themselves and the Bank that had been transformed since the more abrasive era of Holden and Schuster. Norman saw the chairmen regularly, conveyed his own and/or the government's views and/or requests to them, and in a tacit reciprocal arrangement was increasingly regarded by them as the sole channel for conveying their own wishes and problems to government.[29] Occasionally his requests were refused – as over the question of the banks providing greater and more accurate detail in their monthly statements of assets and liabilities – but mainly Norman got his way. Various factors contributed to this relative ease of moral suasion: Norman's personal mix of charm and forcefulness; the death of Goodenough and the taming of McKenna; the absence of outstanding figures among other chairmen of the Big Five; the significant decline in banking profits during the 1930s, which probably had the effect of making the banks less assertive; and the sense in which, following their relatively untroubled survival of the world as well as national slump between 1929 and 1932, they had indisputably and permanently 'arrived' on the financial scene, whatever their provincial origins.[30]

Norman, characteristically, did not confine his attentions to the Big Five. In October 1932, for instance, he saw the chairman of Martins, in order to 'suggest Nigel Campbell or Max Bonn or Gordon Munro and Gordon Leith (tho' a disagreeable fellow) as future Directors'; while the following year, when Edward (Ruby) Holland-Martin, of that same family bank, became an executive director of the Bank of England, it was the first time that a clearing banker had penetrated to the Court. Such a step would have been almost inconceivable twenty years earlier, but no one seems to have complained. Undoubtedly, however, the clearing bank that most concerned Norman in the 1930s was Glyn Mills, with its increasingly threadbare capital resources. From the mid-1930s he and the bank's Sir Herbert Lawrence considered, explored and ultimately rejected various merger possibilities, until by autumn 1938 the two were agreed that the best option was to take refuge under the Royal Bank of Scotland's umbrella. Martins made a late bid, but in the final summer of peace the partners of Glyns, the 'last private bank in Lombard Street', sold their capital to the Royal Bank.[31] The name lived on, but in terms of deposit banking in the City it was the end of a proud, defining tradition.

Henceforth, the onus of carrying on that 'private' tradition would in effect rest with the merchant banks. They themselves were hardly in great shape during the 1930s – the two main arms of their business were the issuing of foreign loans and accepting, neither of them flourishing activities during these largely difficult years.[32] As the floating of overseas loans almost dried up, and by 1938 'practically reached the vanishing point' according to one observer, there was an even more obvious incentive than in the 1920s for the merchant banks to move into the field of domestic new issues.[33] Morgan Grenfell, Helbert Wagg, Barings and Bensons had already to an extent made that move, and they were now joined by Hambros; even so, for most of them and a few others it was still a somewhat hesitant, provisional step, as they continued to hope and trust that the world would eventually return to its pre-1914 senses. On the accepting side, as world trade only stutteringly recovered from the slump and national governments became increasingly autarchic, there was much less money to be made than in the 1920s. Whereas in 1925 Kleinworts had led the way with acceptances outstanding of £17.6m, followed by Schröders on £13.9m, Hambros on £10.1m and Barings on £10m, by 1932 Kleinworts was still ahead, but only on £10.3m, followed by Hambros on £7.8m and Schröders on £5.5m; while six years later, at year-end 1938, it was Hambros that had forged ahead (£11.4m), followed by Kleinworts (£7.8m), Erlangers (£4.4m) and Schröders (£4.2m). Unlike Kleinworts and Schröders, the balance sheet of Hambros was not full of frozen German credits, and the opportunity was there at least to look for new accepting business, especially in relation to the finance of domestic trade. It was a switch of emphasis specifically endorsed by Norman, who in 1936 told the senior partner of the merchant bank Guinness Mahon that 'he was most anxious to keep the accepting houses going'.[34]

In general, with so much less business to go round, there tended to be a sharper edge to getting whatever business there was. Even Barings was not immune. 'We have the feeling that if it were perfectly agreeable to you we would rather like to have a first glimpse of any business suitable to the London market which you may obtain', Evelyn Baring requested Kidder Peabody in New York in October 1936, after that bank had taken a recent 'share deal' to Cazenove's first. Nevertheless, *among* the leading merchant banks, the old courtesies did not disappear. When Francis Rodd of Morgan Grenfell was approached the following year by Dresdner Bank to see whether Morgans would be interested in financing the Iraq government on the security of oil royalties, the decisive information was, he noted, that it 'appeared that two substantial London banks had been interested in the business'. Accordingly, Rodd 'explained that if substantial London banks of the standing of M. G. & Co. were already interested in the business, M. G. & Co. would not wish to compete, since it was a tradition with such Houses that although they might participate in each other's business, they did not compete with one another to secure what appeared to be other people's business'.[35] Barings, as was fit and proper, duly did this rare foreign issue, of £1m for the Iraq government.

The City in the 1930s, at both an institutional and a personal level, was far more embroiled in the often intractable difficulties of British industry than it ever had been before. Among the clearers, Midland was especially concerned with trying to restore the fortunes of the Lancashire textile industry; the two main industrial areas that preoccupied Lloyds were coal in the north-east and steel in South Wales; while for National Provincial, concerns about iron and steel were supplemented by the problems of the Yorkshire woollen trade.[36] For all three banks, these may not have been a wholly welcome set of preoccupations, arising as they did out of imprudent lending soon after the war, but (as in the 1920s) their involvement could not be gainsaid. For the merchant banks, the main orientation was towards the iron and steel industry – for instance, Rothschilds and Dorman Long, Morgan Grenfell and United Steel, and Hambros and Consett Iron Co.[37] Or take a handful of individuals whose involvement went far beyond passive advice and/or execution. The Ostrer brothers (Isidore, Maurice and Mark) were financiers who effectively ran Gaumont-British – making films, distributing them and owning cinemas – before selling out to J. Arthur Rank in 1936.[38] Leo d'Erlanger joined the family bank after the war, developed what his biographer calls 'a passionate interest in the aviation industry', and during the 1930s was not only largely responsible for the formation of British Airways, but also did an enormous amount to ensure that such manufacturing concerns as de Havilland and Short Brothers were adequately financed.[39]

The supreme case in this period, however, was that of a youngish stockbroker, Edward Lewis.[40] During the 1928 new issue boom his small, recently established firm, E. R. Lewis & Co., had acted as brokers to the Decca Record Co., which manufactured and sold many gramophones, but only a few gramophone records. This struck Lewis as poor strategy, and when the newly floated company – hitherto a rather staid family business – ran into problems the following year, he found the money to enable Decca to take over the Duophone Record Co. At this point he joined the board, and by the early 1930s was effectively in charge of a business that was hit, like so many others, by the slump. In 1933 Decca's bank was about to pull the plug, but agreed to give Lewis three weeks to find at least £120,000. With only two days to go there was still a significant shortfall, with few in the City showing much inclination to back Decca, before the situation was saved by the financier Harley Drayton deciding to take a £40,000 punt. Lewis needed the money in order to buy an American record company, Brunswick, whose star turn was Bing Crosby; and the following year, with that purchase made, Lewis was able to form the American Decca Co. For almost another half-century Lewis remained the commanding figure at Decca in Britain; and, as a good City man, his approach was essentially personal. 'He would do business with you if he liked you, but not otherwise', an associate recalled. Until the early 1960s things went swimmingly, but the turning point in Decca's fortunes was the fateful decision not to sign up the Beatles – a decision that perhaps would have been different, had Lewis himself been exposed to Brian Epstein's charm.

Turning back to pre-Cavern days, the 1930s, it is the clearing banks that have been subjected to most criticism in relation to the City's alleged failure during those years to help – or to help sufficiently – British industry. Three main charges have been made against them: that their approach rarely went beyond disciplining and reconstructing management, when it should have embraced large-scale reorganisation and rationalisa- tion; second, that their lending policies were unduly conservative, with a paramount emphasis on short-term loans and an undue obsession about liquidity; and third, that those lending policies were deliberately skewed against small and medium-sized firms. The considerable, inevitably some- times conflicting literature on the subject makes it clear enough, overall, that while each charge has some substance, there is not only a body of evidence suggesting that the banks in practice often went beyond their traditional cautious precepts, but also a danger of overlooking the difficult economic environment in which the banking system – admittedly, a cartelised banking system – was operating.

'At a time of bad trade, and in an atmosphere charged with impatience and irritability, quite insufficient recognition has been given to what has been done and is still being done by the Joint Stock Banks', an unre- pentant Lidbury stated in February 1933 to a meeting of industrial managers. 'I am particularly impressed by the fact', he went on, 'that apparently neither the compilers of the Macmillan Report nor the govern- ment, nor the industrialists, nor the Press, desires the Joint Stock Bank to live and make a profit.' And he insisted that 'the ultimate risk should be borne by the owner of the equity, who is the owner of the fruit which should flow from the exploitation of the business', whereas 'the function of the Joint Stock Banks is to assist in the direction of the utilisation of credit, and I do not think that they fall short of their duty in this respect, but rather believe that through an exaggerated regard for the public duty they land themselves constantly into losses which a more commercial regard for themselves would lead them to avoid'.[41] Such rhetorical flour- ishes apart, Lidbury well knew that nothing mattered, in the end, so much as the profit-and-loss figures; and though it may have been an approach that lacked commercial imagination as well as national vision, there was and is much to be said for stability in a banking system.

CHAPTER TWENTY-NINE

Jitter Bugs

The City did not, on the whole, have an insuperable problem with the idea of authoritarian government. At the end of January 1933, the front page of the *Financial News* had two main headlines: in the top left-hand corner: 'Kaffirs Higher Still'; in the top right-hand corner: 'Herr Hitler – Chancellor of Germany'. The main editorial was entitled 'Heil Hitler!' and began: 'If ever man had a right to chuckle, the little Austrian pocket-Mussolini has justification for chuckling today.' The paper then argued, however, that Hitler would be the prisoner of the non-Nazi majority in the Cabinet, indeed that 'it is, to say the least of it, highly unlikely that the Nazis would attempt to base their power on armed force'. The *FN*'s pink rival was almost equally comforting: 'Finance is left in the capable hands of Count Schwerin von Krosigk'.[1]

On 21 March 1933, some seven weeks after Hitler's elevation, Reid in Berlin sent Alec Baring a letter: 'Hitler himself now holds very sensible views, and he and most of his colleagues are doing their best to control the situation.' Two days later, on 23 March, Hitler successfully demanded the passing of the Enabling Act, effectively creating the Nazi dictatorship. In his report next day, Reid (by now in Frankfurt am Main) noted that Hitler's speech had made 'an excellent impression' and that 'he is well advised, and listens to his advisers, and his responsibilities have made a real man of him'. As for those obstinate stories in the foreign press about anti-Semitic atrocities, they were 'gross exaggerations', and Reid added that 'the removal of Jews from their public posts, which has occurred on quite a large scale, is largely justified'.[2]

It is easy, of course, to job backwards, and it is only fair to remember that Reid's concerns (like those of almost any City man) were primarily financial, not social or political. 'Over here most people feel that, in the long run, Germany may settle down and overcome its troubles success-fully', Alec Baring at 8 Bishopsgate wrote at the end of March to an American correspondent, and most would have concurred with what was a wish as much as an opinion. Nor, anyway, were the larger, international politics of the situation as clear-cut as they would ultimately become. 'His attack on the Versailles Treaty will nowhere in the City be resented', the *FT* asserted after a major speech by Hitler in May, and the City's view was widely shared. So too, at this stage, was its admiration for the senior dictator. 'The Renaissance of Italy: Fascism's Gift of Order and Progress' was the title of an *FT* special supplement the following month, which came complete with a signed photograph of a studious-looking Mussolini.[3] Over the next six years – as hope gave way to fear and then eventually to a slightly unsteady resolve – the City was rarely out of step with the national mood.

*

Within months of Hitler's rise to power the City had achieved a financial modus vivendi with the new, rather unsettling German regime. The first, and indispensable, step was the renewal for the second time of the 1931 Standstill Agreement, whereby the German banks agreed to continue to pay interest in return for the huge credits that had been made to them staying frozen. In the City there was some resistance from Midland, which felt that the two British delegates in Berlin – Tiarks and Brand – were trying to 'bounce' the London bankers as a whole into the renewed agreement. 'I have good hope', Brand sought to reassure Frederick Hyde at the end of February 1933, 'that unless political disasters intervene, the Standstill creditors may be able in a year or two to dispense with the Standstill.' And he added, about the concessions over interest and discount rates that he and Tiarks had felt compelled to make, that 'very powerful interests in the new German government have opinions about interest rates and foreign debts decidedly different from those of bankers, and there seemed a considerable risk for the future in our adopting a completely uncompromising attitude'. Midland agreed to stay in the Standstill arrangements, and on 16 May all the City's bankers were shocked when the Reichsbank warned the Bank of England that Germany would henceforth be unable to pay in foreign currency the interest on all outstanding loans. Tiarks and Brand at once travelled to Berlin, lobbied extremely hard and were rewarded on 8 June when Standstill credits were excluded from the interest transfer moratorium on Germany's external obligations that was declared that day.[4]

For accepting houses like Kleinworts and Schröders, the continuing existence of the Standstill Agreement, broadly in the form as established in 1931, was integral to their very survival. There was also, from the point of view of these Anglo-German houses, a strong *emotional* commitment to the revival of the Germany economy – a revival that would, of course, enable the credits to be unfrozen and a welcome return to commercial and financial normality to be achieved. It was a viewpoint which, as applied to the international banking stage, was wholly shared by Norman. 'I believe the interests of the B.I.S. [Bank for International Settlements], the Reichsbank and the Bank of England to be identical', he informed a fellow central banker that September. 'I do not think any of them should act without the others.'[5]

So it largely continued in 1934, as Hitler suppressed all opposition at home and engaged in a thorough policy of what has been aptly described as 'bloodcurdling warnings interspersed with conciliatory gestures'. Early in the year Norman defined 'a Hitlerite' in a positive way, being someone who 'accepts private initiative subject to public advantage'; while in early July he offered Grigg a revealing commentary about the very recent Night of the Long Knives:

> We [i.e. in London] are engrossed in the purging process by which Hitler is dealing with the Nazi Party: late as many think, and therefore more bloody; but maybe not too late to save and maintain a moderate situation. My friends declare that the lateness of Hitler has been due to his affection for the buccaneers and burglars who stood with him throughout the hard years, of whom he was loath to believe extreme intentions and still less disloyalty.

The sense is of reportage, but Norman did not distance himself from the interpretation. Later that month he was in New York, where a partner of Morgans summarised his latest thoughts: 'Monty says that Hitler and Schacht are the bulwarks of civilisation in Germany and the only friends we have. They are fighting the war of our system of society against communism. If they fail, communism will follow in Germany, and anything may follow in Europe.' Norman pinned quite unrealistic hopes on Schacht, who by August 1934 was minister of economics as well as president of the Reichsbank. Norman's congratulatory letter to him sounded a regretful note – 'financially as well as economically our affairs have come to be more and more dominated by politics' – but expressed the hope that 'in your double role you may somehow be able to surmount the difficulties ahead of you without abandoning those sound principles with which all through these years your name and policy has been associated'.[6]

Again, it is important to get the right historical perspective. The Labour politician Hugh Dalton a few months later would publicly note that Norman was 'rumoured' to be pursuing 'pro-Nazi polities'; but even as early as 1934 it would be true to say that Norman's stance was pro-German rather than pro-Nazi, even though he was still prepared, for the time being, to give Hitler himself the benefit of the doubt. In this stance, he broadly reflected as well as influenced City opinion as a whole. Certainly, there was little inclination yet in the Square Mile to ride the Russian horse as an alternative to the German. In April 1934, after H. G. Wells had mentioned to Brendan Bracken (chairman of the *Financial News*) that Ivan Maisky, the Russian ambassador in London, was complaining that he never met any bankers, Bracken sent on Wells' letter to Lidbury, and added: 'If you have no strong objection to Russians as such, it might be desirable to get Maisky to lunch – more especially if you still retain your view that we may go Bolshie after the next general election.' To which Lidbury replied: 'I am not sure that I ought to meet "M" at the office, but it might be that one evening next week I could perhaps arrange a little dinner at my Club.'[7]

Hitler's unopposed reoccupation of the Rhineland on 7 March 1936 – months after Mussolini's invasion of Abyssinia – confirmed that the dictators had an almost free hand. 'Herr Hitler has acted with his customary precipitancy', the *FT* declared on the Monday morning after this Saturday jolt, before arguing that from the event 'may well emerge in the end a clearer prospect of European peace than has existed for a generation past'. On the Stock Exchange itself, the mood on the Monday was similarly calm, according to 'Autolycus':

> Strange as it may appear, the majority opinion seems to be rather pleased than otherwise at the abrupt turn which the politics of Europe have taken under the direction of Herr Hitler. That some step of this kind was bound to occur, it is generally agreed: that it would come quite so soon is the more matter for surprise.
>
> In no part of the House did I hear any suggestion of a European conflagration. Provided that people keep calm at the present time, it is considered that the action of Herr Hitler is likely to prove in the interests of peace rather than of war.

By Tuesday the 10th, Landells noted, Stock Exchange markets had 'all but regained their accustomed attitude of financial philosophy that was somewhat rudely shaken by the unexpectedness of Herr Hitler's action last Saturday'. Or, expressed more musically, 'the rattle of the sword in its scabbard died away to a quiet piano'.[8]

If, however, the City as a whole wanted peace above everything, and could not get very steamed up when what most saw as a legitimate griev-ance was redressed, that did not mean that the positively pro-German lobby (which from 1935 took institutional form in the Anglo-German Fellowship, of which Tiarks and Kindersley were both individual members) could operate without constraints. Early in 1936, during the run-up to the annual Standstill renewal, the opposition of Anthony Eden as the new Foreign Secretary prevented Norman from pushing hard for Germany to become a member of the sterling bloc;[9] in May that year allegations in the House of Commons concerning credits and advances made to German borrowers outside the Standstill Agreement forced a formal denial from the clearing banks and accepting houses;[10] and later in the summer Norman conceded, following that parliamentary 'hullabaloo' (as he typically called it), that 'whatever the intrinsic attractions of the scheme, political conditions make impossible today any large German refunding operation', given that 'the subject of German loans is so prickly that you could not be sure of a rational consideration'.[11] Nevertheless, the City was by this time sufficiently well disposed towards existing German loans. 'Personally I do not think Germany will default on these Bonds', the stockbroker Vernon Laurie wrote in August 1936 to a client, Colonel Francis Whitmore, recommending German government 5½ per cent Young Bonds. Laurie's reasoning was that such a default by Germany 'would be entirely contrary to her present desire to become a respectable first-class power once more'.[12]

From July 1936 there was another theatre of attention. 'A survey of the situation in Europe is not encouraging', Dallas Bernard of Mathesons observed two months later. 'In Spain we have a fight between Communism and Stability, say Fascism.' The City's attitude to the Spanish Civil War generally mirrored that of the British government: formally neutral, implicitly sympathetic to the nationalist side. In the case of Kleinworts that sympathy took a very tangible, if secretive form, with the bank's José Mayorga actively involved on behalf of one of Franco's leading supporters, Juan March, in hoarding and disbursing bullion in order to pay for Italian help. But in one country where there was little trouble about republicanism, the diary of the jobber Roy Sambourne near the end of 1936 had a terse tone:

> *7 December* (*Monday*). I dread the markets. I pray God all may go well & the King decide rightly. Markets weak – uncertainty – what will the King do?

> *9 December*. Rumours of the King's abdication from Paris.

> *10 December*. A late street – when the King's decision became known – by a broadcast at 4 pm in the House.

The market's reaction to the news was instantly bullish, and when Robert Bruce Lockhart had lunch next day at Anthony de Rothschild's, he found the City 'relieved that Edward has gone'. His host quoted his brother, Lionel, who had apparently remarked, 'If anyone had said years ago that a King of England had abdicated and on the same afternoon there had been a boom on the Stock Exchange he would have been qualified for a lunatic asylum.' That same day, writing to New York, Villiers of Barings agreed that it had all turned out surprisingly well: 'Naturally the abdication of the King has been a very great disappointment, but we are very fortunate in having a successor who has an extremely nice wife and everybody is confident that they will be a success.'[13]

*

For all his desire for peace, and contrary to what is sometimes assumed, Norman was not *wholly* the prisoner of wishful thinking. A significant, very hush-hush development was under way from autumn 1936, for which the inside account comes from George Bolton:

> The governor, for reasons never revealed, let it be known to Siepmann, Catterns, Cobbold and Edward (Ruby) Holland-Martin that a war book might be prepared but that he was not to be officially informed or consulted. There was a very precise understanding that this was to be an entirely normal Bank precaution against an emergency never likely to happen: moreover, the circle in the know was to be the smallest possible, no secretaries were to be used and we must make doubly sure that nothing leaked to the Press, to Whitehall and especially not to Ministers. Siepmann and I had a series of discussions on strategy and tactics but conclusions were hampered by his conviction that no one could cater for chaos . . .
>
> In consequence, Cyril Hawker and I talked about the possibilities and, despite his personal revulsion against any idea that his hockey-playing friends in Bonn University would support or even welcome a Second World War, we began to hammer out a series of ideas to deal with the problems of financing our imports of basic necessities in time of war . . .
>
> After weeks of laboured consideration, Hawker and I decided to recommend a total mobilisation of resources, without any consideration of the rights of the individual, and comprehensive exchange control with the aim of conserving for as long as possible our exiguous foreign exchange purchasing power. The consequential interference with private business and financial life raised problems of great magnitude; although our self-imposed terms of reference appeared superficially to concern, say, the foreign exchange market, overseas finance, commodity markets, gold, portfolio investment etc., the execution of our projected measures would require official interference with practically every aspect of personal and institutional activity. But we plunged ahead undeterred.

By June 1937 a lengthy memorandum on 'War Measures' had been prepared, followed towards the end of the year by the rough draft of an Exchange Control Act.[14]

The Bank of England's willingness to countenance the possibility of war, and to think the unthinkable when it came to planning the financial execution of that war, owed much to Bolton personally and contrasted sharply with the Treasury's very conservative approach at this time to much the same set of problems that the Bank was addressing.[15] 'I was continuously driven on by gloomy forecasts in the reports of those whom I knew and trusted in foreign banking', Bolton would recall about his growing conviction that war was inevitable, on the basis of 'the information and warnings that I daily received from those deeply involved in European affairs', from men such as Albert Palache of Helbert Wagg, Louis Franck and David Keswick of Samuel Montagu, and Siegmund Warburg, as well as 'the many contacts I had through the foreign exchange market'. It was a tribute to the Bank that it largely gave Bolton his head and that its preparations for foreign exchange control in the event of war were therefore so advanced. What these preparations did *not* mean, however, was that Norman and those close to him, let alone the City as a whole, either saw war as a foregone conclusion or were psychologically unready to go the extra mile to avoid it. Some of Norman's illusions may have gone – in October 1937 he described Germany and Italy as 'powers, whose international gospel professes to be the repelling of Communism, adopting in world affairs an attitude essentially similar to that of the Communist in domestic matters' – but he remained resolutely attached to that most understandable, not entirely ignoble of causes, appeasement.[16]

Schacht lost his position as economics minister in late 1937, but remained president of the Reichsbank, and Tiarks and Norman continued to invest unrealistic hopes in him. In February 1938, Eden resigned as Foreign Secretary in protest at Chamberlain's conduct of foreign policy. 'Those who stand on the wrong side of 50 are generally for the prime minister', was how the Bank's Siepmann gauged City reaction to this apparent demand for a stronger approach, whereas 'those who are younger are generally with Mr Eden'. One of Siepmann's colleagues, the up-and-coming Cameron ('Kim') Cobbold, disagreed. He argued that though the 'vast majority' had 'a great regard for Eden' and that all their 'sentiments are in favour of its policy and of telling the dictators to go to the devil', nevertheless 'at the bottom of its heart' this majority feels that 'the best chance of recovering lost ground is to put sentiment aside and follow unattractive but solid, determined, common-sense Birmingham'. Addis for one concurred: 'My sympathies are with Neville Chamberlain. By all means enter to conversations with Mussolini: and Hitler too. Even if they fail as they well may they may help to clear the air.'[17]

Irrespective of opinion, after the Anschluss of 13 March everyone knew that Hitler's next move would be in the direction of Czechoslovakia. Over the next six months the pace of rumours flying around the City rarely abated – a typical one was that if only Chamberlain would back Czechoslovakia, then high-ranking officers in the German Army were prepared to bump Hitler off – but Norman, suffering from shingles, was seldom at his desk to hear them. On one occasion during the summer when he was in London, he mentioned to Chamberlain the desire of Schacht (as recently expressed to him in Basle) that British foreign policy should take more account of the attempt that he – Schacht – was making to moderate the Nazis. Chamberlain's response to Norman was brusque: 'Who is Schacht? I have to deal with Hitler.' Norman and Schacht had formed their alliance in the 1920s, the age of the central banker, but that age had gone. Norman, and other bankers who thought like him, could do little more than give their full support to Chamberlain, whom in a letter to General Smuts on the last day of August 1938 he described as 'not being deluded like an ostrich but rather in his wisdom has been facing facts and, in spite of what may be thought of the autarchic rulers, trying bravely to reach a solution with them on all outstanding questions'.[18] Over the years, 'facing facts' had always been the highest City wisdom; and the new, rapidly looming fact was Hitler's designs upon Czech territorial integrity, at a time when Britain was unprepared – in almost every sense of the word – for war.

'The Stock Exchange and the great majority of its clients refuse to believe that there will be war in Europe', asserted 'Autolycus' on 9 September. Three days later came Hitler's intensely aggressive anti-Czech speech at Nuremberg, and shortly afterwards it was announced that Chamberlain was to fly to see him at Berchtesgaden. Markets rallied on the first day of their meeting, Thursday the 15th, and 'in the Stock Exchange', according to 'Autolycus', 'nothing but satisfaction and pleasure were expressed at what is recognised as a brave grasp of a situation which evidently held an even greater measure of gravity than most of us had realised'. Over much of the next week, following Chamberlain's return, the skies seemed reasonably blue, as the Czechs reluctantly submitted to Anglo-French demands that major territorial concessions be made to Hitler. The closest reading of the City during these days came from 'Dives' in the *New Statesman*:

> Although the City as a whole supports Mr Chamberlain's policy of scuttle, it must not be assumed that anybody welcomes the prospect of temporary peace with dishonour. As far as I have been able to check up City opinion, I find that even reactionary and Die-hard Conservatives feel humiliated by the abject submission of a British prime minister to the German Dictator . . . A few, who see the ruin of Stock Exchange business if Herr Hitler maintains this tension for another twelve months, are even regretting that the 'show-down' has been postponed. However, if there is to be peace with dishonour it is generally assumed that there will be no disarmament.

By the time these words appeared, however, Chamberlain was about to begin another round of talks with Hitler. 'A day of acute tension & weakening prices', Sambourne recorded on Friday the 23rd, as 'grave news' started to come through from Godesberg. 'No hope of a settlement – but it is almost desperate', he added feelingly.[19] Hitler had ratcheted up his demands, and by the weekend war seemed inevitable.

With London in a state of high tension, and trenches being dug in Hyde Park, representatives of the Committee of London Clearing Bankers spent Wednesday the 28th in Staffordshire, inspecting the buildings of the Trentham Park Amusement Hall as a possible site for an emergency central clearing house in the event of war. Meanwhile, the Accepting Houses Committee met at four o'clock at 16 Bishopsgate, home of H. S. Lefevre & Co. Early on it was stated that the discount market was not functioning properly and that the clearing banks were not buying bills, but most of the meeting comprised a general discussion about what to do if war broke out. But then, at about a quarter to five, just as the merchant bankers were breaking up, a telephone call came from Kleinworts to Cyril Kleinwort, who was able to announce to the others that news had been received from the House of Commons that Chamberlain would shortly be flying to Munich. The news had already led to stirring after-hours scenes outside the Stock Exchange, according to 'The Diarist' in the next day's *FT*:

> Within a minute or two of Mr Chamberlain's surprise announcement in Parliament brokers and their clerks came rushing into Throgmorton-street from every entrance.
> An outburst of vociferous bidding spread like a tidal wave from Shorter's Court round the corner eastwards into the Oil, Industrial and Kaffir markets, spending its force among the few remaining Rhodesian and West African jobbers. Telephones were overwhelmed. You had to wait two or three minutes before the 'dialling tone' could be got on the automatic instruments. Trunk calls were virtually unobtainable.[20]

'A Chance for Reason' was the *FT*'s leader headline on Thursday the 29th, with the paper describing Chamberlain's 'efforts to preserve the peace' as having 'assumed heroic proportions'. According to 'Autolycus', the Stock Exchange's slogan for the day was 'The war is over!' Sambourne however, and no doubt many others, underwent a private agony – 'I am still very anxious. How will it end?' – but the following morning's *FT* had the headline that almost everyone in the City wanted: 'Midnight Pact at Munich'. The accompanying editorial stated that 'dismemberment is a painful thing for a proud country to contemplate', but 'it possesses the one virtue, that it will have spared countless millions the horrors of a war more intense and destructive even than that of 1914–18'. That Friday a mood of massive relief pervaded the City. On the Stock Exchange, according to 'The Diarist', there was 'heartfelt thankfulness and a paean of praise for the Prime Minister'; in the Lloyd's building in Leadenhall Street, shortly after noon, the chairman Stanley Aubrey mounted the Rostrum and, after two strokes on the Lutine Bell, announced to prolonged applause that the Committee was sending a congratulatory message to Chamberlain; while Sambourne, having thanked God 'a million times', returned home to Kensington and gave his servants 'a Pint of champagne to celebrate'. One wily City bird had called it right. 'Chamberlain returned from Munich bringing "Peace with honour"', Addis noted at the end of this historic day. 'The Consols I bought two days [ago] at 66 are today quoted 75!'[21]

Over the following week there was a chance for reflection. The only minister to resign was Duff Cooper, and according to 'The Diarist' on

Tuesday 3 October, his protest 'reflects a point of view which has had a good many exponents in the City'. Almost certainly, however, 'Autolycus' that same day, in his almost euphoric post-Munich assessment, was closer to the City pulse: 'Many ups and downs, many hopes and disappointments are inevitable, but the optimist will look forward to such peace in Europe as shall make this continent a more secure and abiding resting place for industry, capital and enterprise than it has been within the memory of most of us.' The Stock Exchange as a body sent an official congratulatory message to Chamberlain, while the financier Philip Hill gave 550 guineas to the Westminster Hospital in thanksgiving for the preservation of peace – the sum denoting fifty guineas for each company of which he was chairman. Yet perhaps the last City word on what would become one of the most myth-laden episodes of modern British history should go to Morgan Grenfell's Lord Bicester, the former Vivian Hugh Smith. Neither an Anglo-German intimate of Norman nor a friend of the appeasers, he wrote to New York on the 6th, warning that Hitler was a 'fanatic' and that Goering and Goebbels were 'gangsters'.[22] He would not have played it differently from Chamberlain; but unlike some, he did not imagine that Munich was more than a stay of execution.

*

A letter to Schacht, in early November 1938, encapsulated what would be Norman's attitude almost until the sirens sounded:

> You and I are no doubt in agreement that European prospects have improved since Godesberg and München where our Prime Minister, alongside the helpful attitude of your Führer, showed a courage and initiative which is not usual or easy in a highly democratic country. We may well be thankful to have escaped war, certainly for a short and, I hope, for a long period. It is in the early future that the habit of reason and reasonableness and give-and-take should surely replace alarm and threats as the international method.

In mid-December Schacht paid what was theoretically a private visit to London (seeking support for a scheme to assist the emigration of German Jews), but Norman arranged for him to see ministers and others unofficially. Some of those others included leading City figures, such as M. Samuel & Co.'s Lord Bearsted, whom Siegmund Warburg warned not to have any truck with someone who was seeking only to 'improve his own personal position with the Nazi government'. Not surprisingly, assessments by Paul Einzig and Norman differed as to the success or otherwise of Schacht's visit. 'The hope that he might be able to rally the pro-Nazi and pro-German influences in the City failed to materialise', the tireless anti-appeasement journalist wrote some months later, adding that 'most of the bankers who in the past had agitated in favour of humouring Germany by granting her new credits had either changed their views or considered it expedient not to express those views in public'. Norman, however, writing to Schacht's daughter the day after he had put her father on to the boat train at Liverpool Street Station, declared that Schacht had 'found here a real welcome from everyone he saw and no one made a disagreeable remark'.[23]

Even before Schacht's visit, Norman had cleared it with Chamberlain that he himself would be paying a reciprocal 'private' visit to Berlin, in order to attend – as a godparent – the christening of Schacht's grandson. The Foreign Office was not told. 'We heard tonight that that mountebank Montague [*sic*] Norman is off to Berlin,' Halifax's private secretary, Harvey, exploded on 2 January 1939. 'Such a visit can only do harm – by encouraging the pro-German proclivities of the City, by making American and foreign opinion think we are doing another deal with Germany behind their backs – another example of the P.M.'s pro-Nazi tendencies – and finally in Germany itself where it will be regarded as proof of our anxiety to run after Hitler.' By Tuesday the 3rd, news of Norman's impending trip had leaked to the press and was on the front pages, being given a City reception that, admittedly according to Einzig, 'could not, with the best will imaginable, be described as favourable'. Early on Wednesday, the day of intended departure, Norman received a letter from the Foreign Office seeking to deter him. He steamed round at eleven, 'in a rage' according to Harvey, and said that the visit had been 'agreed long since with PM – Ch Ex – N. Henderson – H. J. Wilson'.[24] At 1.45 p.m. he caught the Dover train from Cannon Street Station, thereby neatly sidestepping the pressmen gathered at Victoria for the two o'clock train.[25] By the time he reached Berlin on Thursday morning, the trade union leader Ernest Bevin was publicly warning about the harm that his visit might be doing 'to the cause of Democracy and Freedom' and declaring that 'we shall never get peace whilst we allow this financial underworld to operate against the interest of the public'.

Norman himself, presumably oblivious, at once called in on the British Embassy and, according to the official account, 'said that apart from a visit of courtesy to Dr Schacht he was of opinion that, private visits from personalities such as himself who warmly supported the prime minister's policy of appeasement, did nothing but good and were like straws thrown into a stream in order to test which way the current was running'. The christening took place that Thursday afternoon in the Reichsbank building – the little boy's first name was Norman – and the godfather was back in the Reichsbank for most of Friday, before dropping in on the embassy prior to catching the night train to Basle. He told Pinsent at the embassy that he had spent most of his time with Schacht and Reichsbank officials, that at lunch he had met a few German bankers and industrialists, and that he had not seen any members of the German government. None of the conversations, Pinsent reported back to London, 'was concerned with any concrete proposals, nor has the governor "done any business", as he put it'. And, 'the governor said that he had always been in favour of establishing and extending contacts with the more moderate elements in Germany and doing anything which might serve to strengthen their hand'.

Back in London the following week, Norman reported to the Foreign Office. 'He considers S.E. Europe to be a natural field for the development of German trade,' an official noted. 'He was not optimistic about the possibility of finding a solution to the European question; but he does not believe in the likelihood of war this year.'[26] As usual, Norman also reiterated how he was pinning his hopes on Schacht to be a restraining influence – but unfortunately, on the 20th, the president of the Reichsbank received the order of the boot from his Nazi masters. Some weeks later Norman penned a tribute to his long-standing friend, describing him as 'full of courage and resource', 'a true internationalist', someone who sought 'to support London as the essential money market of Europe', and 'the sane man among a party of dangerous totalitarians'.[27] Whatever the validity of the judgements, they were the words of one almost impotent central banker about another.

Generally, putting aside individual interests and prejudices (even beliefs), it was the City's usual lack of imagination that made it so difficult for it to grasp what Hitler was about. Finance and ideology tend to mix badly, and during these anxious, febrile times the City constantly found itself coming up against the limits of rationality and not knowing where to turn next. Typical – including in its sense of being at the mercy of events – was the assessment that Sydney Parkes, joint chief general manager of Lloyds Bank, offered at the end of January 1939 to a business friend abroad. After noting that 'everyone in the City' had recently had 'a very bad dose of what the Home Secretary calls the "jitter bug"', so much so that 'the topic of conversation at every table, in business and out of business, seems to be war, the preparation for war and the defence against war', Parkes took comfort in what he saw as the underlying logic of the situation: 'My own impression is that the internal position of Germany is exceedingly bad and that Hitler and company at the present time have got all that they can do to look after that position, to provide their people with the necessaries of life and to keep them reasonably quiet'.[28]

On 15 March, however, Hitler annexed what remained of Czechoslovakia. Initially, when the news came through, the Stock Exchange tried to shrug it off – 'Autolycus' referring to 'the prevailing impression among members that nothing serious will come of the Czecho development' – but later that day, after the House had closed, Chamberlain took a tough line in Parliament. Prices fell next day, and 'Autolycus' began his column memorably on Friday the 17th: 'Herr Hitler, had he ever been a member of the Stock Exchange, London, might have better understood what he obviously failed to appreciate at the present time: to whit, that a bargain is a bargain.' That evening Chamberlain made a much-applauded speech in Birmingham in which he denounced what Germany had done. 'There can be no doubt now that Mr Chamberlain's sweeping condemnation of Herr Hitler involves a major reorientation in British foreign policy', the *FT* declared on Monday. 'It could not have been otherwise.'[29]

Less than a fortnight later, on the 31st, there was announced the Anglo-French guarantee to Poland, the pivotal point of the year's diplomacy. For most of that day the markets were dull, waiting for Chamberlain's afternoon statement. When it came, it (according to that evening's stock market report) 'met with general approval and imparted firmness to prices at the close'. 'The Diarist' agreed, noting that 'the Prime Minister's statement put new heart into the Stock Exchange'.[30]

The City – and the national – temper had changed, and during the spring and early summer of 1939 this gave a rather different context to Anglo-German financial relations. Schröders and Kleinworts in particular remained in a thoroughly uncomfortable position, as the discount market increasingly cold-shouldered Standstill bills, and indeed Kleinworts had to go to the Westminster Bank in April for a £1m loan. In the end an agreed British position was reached – Standstill to be renewed, though under the threat of being terminated after six months unless the Germans made a substantial cash payment – but as late as mid-May, while final negotiations were going on in Berlin, Lidbury was compelled to cable to Tiarks there that all the clearing banks had 'the gravest objections to the institution of any three year lines of any sort or kind', with the clear implication that Tiarks needed further stiffening.[31]

That the Anglo-German houses still wanted to continue as much as possible, and as late as possible, with a business-as-usual approach was graphically shown during the summer when Kleinworts entered into a £330,000 credit agreement with Krupps. Equally instructive in its way was the controversial case of the 'Czech gold'. This was the work of Einzig, who from mid-May was engaged in a brilliant, relentlessly sustained exposure of how the Bank for International Settlements had successfully instructed the Bank of England to hand over to the Reichsbank a gold deposit of some £6m belonging to the Czechoslovak National Bank. Einzig's campaign caused considerable embarrassment not only to the British government but also to the Bank of England, which of course was represented on the BIS. Had the British directors known in advance about the decision? If so, had they agreed to it? There were other questions involved as well, and the Bank of England emerged from the episode with its reputation somewhat damaged – partly the result, Einzig himself subsequently reckoned, of its unwillingness to depart from its time-honoured policy of 'never explain, never apologise'.[32]

The City at large, and the Stock Exchange in particular, was prey to many mood swings during this last summer of peace. 'Autolycus' on 5 June noted that 'fear of possible shocks still lurks in men's minds', while on the last day of July 'The Diarist' wrote buoyantly of how 'confidence appears to be gradually returning to the Stock Exchange'. A striking paragraph followed:

> The democratic circle is in the ascendant and the autocratic Axis in semi-eclipse. Mars, which recently approached us closer than for a generation, is now in forced retreat. According to one of the best-known of Stock Exchange philosophers: 'Almost before this year is out we shall be more concerned with what we can do to save Germany from economic disaster than with worrying about the prospect of war'.[33]

None of which prevented the City from achieving an impressive degree of readiness in case of war breaking out.[34] Basil Catterns (deputy governor), Cobbold, Bolton and Cyril Hawker were all key figures at the Bank of England in this respect, as was the chief cashier Kenneth Peppiatt. A major physical concern was gold, and in April 1939 Peacock asked the Bank whether it would be willing to store gold to the value of £2.5m currently held by Barings on behalf of that bank's customers. The vaults at Barings, he said, were old, security was not first class, and anyway there were plans to evacuate London in the event of an emergency. Ruby Holland-Martin, however, turned down the request, on the grounds that not only was the Bank of England already at full stretch dealing with gold, but also that other banks and accepting houses would demand the same facilities as Barings, if its request was accepted. The Old Lady was indeed at full stretch, and during the summer it shipped to Canada a huge amount of both its own gold and that belonging to customer central banks. 'We took enormous risks,' according to Bolton, 'and when the war actually began we had about £500,000,000 of gold afloat in ships of 5,000 tons upwards'; happily, 'we did not lose one bar of gold throughout this period'.[35]

In general, Bolton also recalled, 'during the last few months of "peace" we were busily engaged in organising the banking system and the City to meet the strains of war' – and inevitably this brought the chief general managers of the clearing banks very prominently into the fray. Bolton, not the easiest of men to impress, was struck by these managers' 'complete co-operation and single-minded devotion to the objectives of ensuring the survival of the country irrespective of their own banking interests', and he paid particular tribute to Lidbury as 'a tireless and dedicated man who was more than willing to do everyone's work and, indeed, even to think for them'. Cobbold, also in retrospect, agreed: 'Lidbury was an awkward chap, but when he got moving he could shift mountains. [Cecil] Ellerton [of Barclays] was his charming expert self, but without Lidbury's gun-fire I do not think we should easily have got the banks lined up before the outbreak of war.'[36] This involved establishing the appropriate machinery for exchange control; ensuring that the clearing system (to be transferred to Trentham Park) would work smoothly; and a thousand and one other matters, often very tricky in relation to the many bank customers with substantial overseas business interests. Overall, the contrast was stark compared with that summer exactly a quarter of a century earlier, when the City had stumbled into war in an almost wholly unprepared way. Then there had been another 'awkward chap' among the clearing bankers, but Holden had been given less of a chance to 'shift mountains' and thereby earn the City's gratitude.

The final weeks were played out in an atmosphere of depressed markets, stagnant business and many City men being at the seaside rather than behind their desks. 'When I got back last Friday,' Parkes noted on Tuesday 8 August, 'I found a certain feeling of nervousness in the City putting war on a 50/50 basis, but, personally, I still feel reasonably optimistic.' The following week saw the Stock Exchange at a virtual standstill. According to 'Autolycus', 'the Little Mining Market introduced a darts board by way of diversion', and 'the Sea Scouts benefitted to the extent of five or six pounds from the sale and distribution of fragrant lavender sachets'.[37]

By Tuesday the 22nd the betting, according to 'Autolycus', remained open: 'One body of Stock Exchange opinion holds stoutly to the view that there will be no war; another maintains that conditions have so closely approached the precipice that, short of another miracle or a similar happening, nothing can prevent a clash of arms. A third party frankly admits that it is impossible to tell what may happen.' On that day, however, the Stock Exchange – like the rest of the City – had to take on the chin the news of the just-announced Nazi–Soviet Pact. Parliament was recalled, and Norman cut short his holiday on the Isle of Man. On Thursday the 24th the *FT*'s leader ('Resolute and Calm') warmly described the City's endorsement of the Cabinet's communiqué about defending Poland, minimum prices were introduced for gilt-edged stock, and Bank rate was doubled to 4 per cent.

By the following week there was little that most in the City could do other than watch and wait. 'Days pass with no relief from the tension,' the bill broker Ronald Gillett wrote to his mother, 'but that is better than having war. The City looks very depressing with every other building lined with sandbags, and many buildings empty through the evacuation of businesses and staffs to the country.' According to 'Autolycus', the

Stock Exchange on Tuesday the 29th was calm enough: 'People refused to sell. In spite of the appearance of the City streets, holders decline to be sandbagged out of their shares.' Wednesday was another phlegmatic day on the Stock Exchange – 'Autolycus' attributing the market's 'cool confidence' to 'a growing conviction that whatever happens now will be the prelude to a firm and lasting settlement in the future' – but Thursday the 31st was rather different. Roy Sambourne, as usual, eschewed understatement:

> Alas after a good start – & the usual St Ex optimism – we get a bombshell.
> Evacuation of Children – Calling-up of Navy – practically complete mobil-
> isation. Prices begin to fall & intense gloom prevails. The Stock Exchange
> to be closed tomorrow. Still one or two optimists still are to be found.
> I have practically – God help me – given up all hope.

The closure of the Stock Exchange was intended to be only temporary, in the context of the evacuation of children, but Lex of the *Financial News* did not exaggerate when he observed on Friday morning that 'a grim Tchekovian gloom hangs over Throgmorton Street'.[38]

Germany invaded Poland that day, 1 September. On Saturday, while the British government eventually made up its mind to send an ultimatum to Germany, Norman replied to someone called H. Lipschutz, who had asked him how he could hasten the process of naturalisation. 'I have to admit', Norman's letter ended, 'that there is nothing I can now do towards giving effect to your suggestions. And, while I have been searching, the sands of peace have been running out . . . so that there is no more for me to say . . . except to wish you well.' The ultimatum expired at 11 a.m. on Sunday the 3rd, and a quarter of an hour later Chamberlain was speaking on the wireless. 'From now on,' a mordant Norman announced to his secretary during that lovely sunlit day, 'we shall be simply rubber stamps.'[39]

CHAPTER THIRTY

All Blasted

'None could wish more than I for a speedy outcome,' Norman wrote to a Japanese banker during the first week of war, 'when it may be hoped that men of goodwill and principle in all nations will be able again to co-operate constructively and effectively.'[1] Norman, however, knew as well as anyone that the terms of trade with Hitler had fundamentally changed; and, with its deeply conformist streak, the City as a whole was most unlikely to break ranks with the albeit somewhat queasy consensus that this was a war that had to be fought.

How to pay for it?[2] An important letter in October 1939 from the Bank of England director Sir Alan Anderson to the deputy governor reflected an appreciation that the social and political climate would not permit a repeat of the rentier-friendly policy of the First World War:

> Some City friends of mine have been talking to me about a hope and a fear that possess them. In this time of stress when rich and poor have gladly offered themselves and have been forced to offer themselves as soldiers they hope that the City will not ask the State to pay 4% or 5% for the money it needs. They fear 90% of the Stock Exchange would say that money today is worth 4% or 5% and would stop at that and as a sequel the non-monied man in the street would be confirmed in his impression that conscription applies to him and not to the rich.

Norman broadly agreed with Anderson and his friends that this time round it must be a 'cheap money' war – but was naturally uncomfortable with the high-tax implications of such a policy. On 2 November, shortly after Bank rate had returned to 2 per cent, he told Wilson at the Treasury that in his view 'taxation has been pushed very near if not quite to the limit'.[3] The larger argument, however, prevailed, and in the closing weeks of 1939 Norman was instrumental in persuading the City about the virtues of what *The Economist* would shortly dub the 'Three Per Cent War'. So it was, with issues done mainly on a 'tap' basis via the government brokers, Mullens & Co.

The war was also paid for through individual savings, as well as large institutional funds, and here the key initial role was played by Kindersley, long-standing chairman (later president) of the National Savings Committee.

Kindersley was deeply wedded to the voluntary approach to savings, but Keynes published two articles in *The Times* in mid-November in which he argued that reliance on voluntary savings would not only fail to reduce consumption but also be inflationary. Accordingly, he argued for compulsory savings, in the form of deferred pay. The City's reaction was largely hostile, but when Keynes towards the end of February 1940 published his pamphlet *How to Pay for the War* – elaborating his ideas and seeking 'an advance towards economic equality greater than any which we have made in recent times' – he found support from a surprising quarter. One of the pamphlet's recipients was Norman, who invited his old antagonist to the Bank on 8 March. The conversation went well, and soon afterwards Keynes privately noted that, 'after long estrangement', his scheme had achieved the welcome by-product of 'a personal reconciliation' with Norman. Kindersley remained resolutely opposed to the compulsory approach, but the fiscal arguments were moving inexorably the other way.[4]

Exchange control was, from the City's standpoint, the other fundamental aspect of financial policy during the war – an aspect that included the consolidation and institutionalisation of the sterling area, eventually including a still reluctant Canada.[5] 'Major holdings of sterling (those who held reserves in sterling and could maintain exchange control) were invited into a novel imperial nexus where all internal transactions were free, all external ones tightly controlled, and capital outflow virtually forbidden in the interests of the whole', is how the historian Keith Middlemas describes what he rightly terms 'a flexible and remarkably unbureaucratic system', which was essentially the achievement of the Commonwealth's central banks under the Bank of England's 'consultation and tutelage'.[6] British implementation of exchange control was, of course, the responsibility of the Bank itself, which as before the war continued to set the pace – in terms of making exchange control effective – while the Treasury dragged its heels.

'Suddenly everyone was on our doorstep with questions of bewildering complexity', one of the Bank's young men, Leslie O'Brien, would recall:

> We made up rules as we went along and we made them fast under the pressure of insistent enquiry and the threat of unjustified loss for the enquirer. To those in the Bank who liked the challenge, and that was most of us, the exchange control was highly stimulating. Many of us excelled ourselves, even over-reached ourselves, as never before. Long hours meant nothing in such a vibrant community which for some years worked and slept in Threadneedle Street. As the machine necessarily expanded with new offices being created, promotions and appointments came thick and fast and they caused some uneasiness, if not jealousy.

Elsewhere in the Bank, O'Brien added, 'there was little of our excitement to be found', with 'numerous women' having 'taken over jobs formerly the male preserve as men were released for war service'.[7] Exchange control now represented an important rationale for the Bank's existence – and over the ensuing years, an important element of its authority in the City.

In many ways, exchange control mirrored the larger triangular relationship between government, central bank and City. In the fourth week of war, the Chancellor, Sir John Simon, wrote to Norman asking him to ensure that the clearing banks restricted their advances to such winning-the-war purposes as the needs of the armaments industry and the export trade. Norman duly passed on Simon's letter to Colin Campbell, chairman of the Committee of London Clearing Bankers; and thus was established what would become the firm unwritten rule that all communications between the Treasury and the clearing banks were, in either direction, mediated by the Bank of England.

More generally, according to Hugh Dalton, 'as between the Treasury and the Bank of England in particular the relationship has been completely revolutionised', in that 'the governor of the Bank of England is to a much greater extent than is openly admitted or legally recognised, today the agent and servant of the Treasury rather than an independent financial dictator as has been the case in the past'. Typically, Dalton overstated his case – there had already been a significant shift in the disposition of power between Bank and Treasury during the interwar period – but war did make a difference. Nor, in the course of the first winter, was it only the Treasury to which Norman found himself having to be subservient. In late February for example, shortly before an issue of War Loan, he saw someone from the dreaded Ministry of Information. 'He is settling details for next week,' Norman noted wryly, '& I promise to obey his orders!'[8]

As the war went on, most of the City's leading clearing bankers settled comfortably enough into the role they had been assigned as de facto civil servants. 'One thing which is impressing all of us', Parkes of Lloyds informed his bank's New York representative in March 1940, 'is the clever way in which the Treasury is handling the financial situation; by having a closed economy they have control of the situation which is being handled very skilfully.'[9]

Norman was not entirely dismayed, for if war undoubtedly reduced the Bank's power vis-à-vis the Treasury, it equally strengthened it in relation to the rest of the City. Norman's diary entry for 1 March, when he and Catterns saw R. P. Wilkinson, deputy chairman of the Stock Exchange, could not have been terser: 'No fortnightly settlements'. The question was closed. In war, as in peace, he remained the indispensable source of guidance as to appropriate or inappropriate behaviour. Early in May 1940 he received a call from Helmut Schröder, only surviving son of Baron Bruno. 'Sh[d] he serve, without waiting to be called up – or sh[d] he mind the Schröder concerns & claim exemptions', was how Norman noted his visitor's dilemma. He may not initially have expressed a view, but three weeks later – after a parliamentary question had been asked about the allegiance of the no-longer-umlauted Schroder – he most certainly did, when Helmut came again. 'He swears to be neither seen nor heard in any way by anybody anywhere', Norman recorded.[10] A lengthy exile from the City beckoned, just as it had for Helmut's father a quarter of a century earlier.

Helmut did not miss much business – or fun – at 145 Leadenhall Street. Richard Roberts, the historian of Schroders, summarises succinctly why few of the City's sectors suffered as much from the war as did its merchant banks:

> Foreign-drawn bill business disappeared because of the problems of inter-national transfers, while the securing of supplies by government bulk purchasing from the Dominions and through Lend Lease [from 1941] all but eliminated the need for acceptance finance for British trade. Foreign exchange dealing, a significant source of revenue for some merchant banks in the 1930s, disappeared as an activity at the beginning of the war because the accepting houses were omitted from the official list of authorised dealers, but even when they secured recognition there was little business to be done. Issues for private borrowers became rare events as the capital market was reserved for funding the wartime requirements of the state.[11]

In almost all the merchant banks, accordingly, it was 'care and mainten-ance' that preoccupied the partners, at least for the first two years of the war, and not the getting of business. Most of the firms in the discount market were similarly gloomy during the early stages of the war, as its traditional commercial bill business almost vanished. 'What hope for reasonable profits for small discount Houses?' one bill broker asked Norman after less than two months. 'Very little during the war' was the discouraging reply.[12]

None of these difficulties mattered much in comparison to the need to get the financial mechanism right for the conduct of the war, and in two key areas – savings and exchange control – Keynes intensified his efforts. In fact, both questions were starting to go his way, and he could afford to be generous. 'The real trouble is, of course, that in thinking his movement can be adequate he has got the order of magnitude quite wrong', he wrote to Brand on 3 May about Kindersley's voluntary savings campaign, adding that Brand's distinguished partner 'never had much of a head for figures!' Five days later, having submitted a lengthy memo-randum on exchange control, Keynes went to the Bank of England to discuss the subject with Henry Clay, Siepmann and Bolton. The ensuing conversation, he told Clay next day, 'was one of the most heartening I have enjoyed for a long time', for 'it was extraordinarily agreeable to discover for once people in executive positions who were in a drastic state of mind, seemed completely competent and equal to their job and were *not* enjoying living in a perpetual twilight, dim and incomplete'. On a copy of Keynes' letter, Norman scribbled some words that would once have seemed unimaginable: 'He must come again: his support of Exch policy will be most important under new Cabinet. Treas^y have neither time nor knowledge to help – but feel bound to interfere!'[13] Politically, the old guard – dominant since Lloyd George's fall in 1922 – was on the way out; and by the time Norman scribbled his words, Churchill had, on the evening of Friday 10 May, become prime minister. What is striking, however, is that Keynes by this time did *not* see Norman's Bank of England as part of that old guard. Again, this was unimaginable from an earlier, return-to-gold perspective – and, among other things, a reflection of how much the Bank had changed since the trauma of 1931.

Not that Norman himself, for understandable reasons, was wholly ecstatic about the change of national leadership. 'Now I know that I shall never cross the threshold of No. 10 again', he accurately predicted on hearing the news. It was news that came within hours of Hitler's invasion of the Low Countries, prompting a predictable tumble of Stock Exchange prices. The war was getting serious, and on Monday the 13th the one o'clock radio news was, for the first time, broadcast live in the Stock Exchange – an innovation that was greeted enthusiastically. That same day 'Autolycus' took the pulse about the coalition government – including Labour figures – that the new prime minister had shaped over the weekend: 'Sympathy is generally expressed with Mr Chamberlain. The driving power of Mr Winston Churchill is not questioned, and it is driving power, according to the general view, that the country requires at this crisis.' Yet, away from the public prints, many members perhaps shared Roy Sambourne's forebodings. 'Prices fall all round', he noted the following evening in a far from Churchillian frame of mind. 'The news gets worse & worse. Italy practically certainly to fight against us – America will do nothing – Germany's might is overwhelming – & I do not see how the French and English can stop them . . . So with a heavy heart I go home on a No 9 bus.'

The series of catastrophic military reverses could only deepen this jobber's gloom:

28 May. The ghastly news reaches me in the City that the King of the Belgians has capitulated . . . It is all so fearful that one can scarcely realise it. Prices naturally fall.

18 June. Churchill's speech [in the Commons, invoking the 'finest hour']. Heartening in a way – but what a change of tone – 5 short weeks has seen a debacle.

20 June. One of our worst days in City. Prices fall heavily everywhere except gilt edged . . . I should like to chuck it.[14]

Soon, all financial considerations seemed petty. 'Life is going on in a normal way here,' Reid of Barings wrote to New York on 28 August, 'except that air raid alarms make us lose a little sleep at nights.' Six days later, on the first anniversary of the war beginning, Sambourne recorded the latest from the floor of the House: 'Air raid warnings 10.20–11.30 & 3–4 pm. No business.'[15] The old grimy, historic City – Herman Melville's 'Cindery City of Dis' – was about to disappear for ever.

*

The first bomb on the City had already fallen: on 24 August, landing on St Giles' Churchyard in the Barbican. A few days later bombs landed in Old Change and Paternoster Row, but it was the massive bombardment of the Docks and East End on Saturday 7 September that made Londoners generally realise that the Blitz had truly begun.[16] The following night there were more bombs, and in the words of the Dean of St Paul's, Walter Matthews, 'once more we could see from the roof a great conflagration in the east, which spread for many miles along the horizon, while nearer at hand there were smaller fires all round the Cathedral'. St Augustine's in Watling Street took a direct hit, with those on the roof of St Paul's seeing its spire first bend and then collapse into the nave below. Nor was Mammon immune, as the Bank of England discovered on the Monday night. Norman ruefully described 'our so-called barrage' to John Martin, a Bank director who spent the war in South Africa ensuring regular gold supplies from there:

> A No. 1 bomb fell in Threadneedle Street a few yards from our outside wall and made a hole about 15' x 20'. It really did little damage except to glass, gas mains, etc. Another bomb fell on our roof, happily at a very strong point close to the corner of Lothbury and Tokenhouse Yard, which smashed the telephone exchange, kitchens and a bit of the two top storeys on that side. And a shell which was fired at Ealing – or some such friendly spot – but never exploded, came through the roof near the corner of Princes Street and Lothbury and smashed the ceiling and the water pipes and made a mess but did no other harm.[17]

Over the next two months, until the Luftwaffe temporarily concentrated on the provinces, few parts of the City were entirely unaffected. The raid on the night of 10 October was particularly destructive, with St Paul's taking its first direct hit and many bombs falling on Cornhill. A month later, on the night of 12 November, 32 Lombard Street, the London home of Guaranty Trust, took a direct hit, and with much of the building reduced to rubble the firm was given hospitality by Glyn Mills.

During that autumn each firm and institution worked out its own way of coping. At the Cornhill head office of Lloyds, at any one time several hundred staff were staying round the clock, while fire squads did fortnightly turns of duty. At Kleinworts, turns were taken at firewatching, and the men played poker long into the night. At Bensons one morning, after bombs during the night had destroyed nearby buildings, the staff looked at the surrounding rubble and unanimously decided that they had been mistaken in appointing each other as executors.[18]

For all concerned, the daily inconvenience was considerable, as Norman described to Martin towards the end of October:

> You may not realise it, but for us one of the great troubles now is travel. The stations in London are for ever being bombed and closed for some days or else the tracks and perhaps bridges are busted – or again the bus roads in and out of London become unusable. Instead of an hour morning and evening from door to door many of our folk take two or three hours and may have to walk a good step . . .
>
> Our higher floors are hardly used and most work is done below ground, where mercifully there are several floors of huge desolate vaults. And soon perhaps as many as 1,000 men and women will be working two or three days running and sleeping here for one or two nights and then going off and staying at home for a couple of days. In this way travel should be ever so much reduced and, along with it, weariness and wet skins and all the ills and miseries of winter.

Norman himself was now sleeping at the Bank two or three nights each week – and occasionally a lowly member of staff would sight that still alert and vital figure wearing a dressing-gown emblazoned with a dragon.[19]

'On Sunday night,' Virginia Woolf recorded on the first day of 1941, 'as I was reading about the great fire, in a very accurate detailed book, London was burning. Eight of my city churches destroyed, & the Guildhall.' It was not only Guildhall that was badly damaged and eight of Wren's churches that were razed to the ground on the dreadful night of 29 December; the destruction also included much of the area around St Paul's (including the book trade centred on Paternoster Row), the textile warehouses there and in the Wood Street area off Cheapside, and most of the buildings in Cannon Street. R. C. M. Fitzhugh, a firewatcher on the roof of Guildhall, would never forget what he saw:

> The block bounded by Brassishaw Hall, Fore Street, Aldermanbury, and Basinghall Street appeared to be one solid mass of flame. St Stephen's, Coleman Street, was soon enveloped in flames, and we could see the steeple and weather-cock fall. Fires were everywhere in the City area. From time to time, heavy high explosive bombs or land mines were dropped . . . There would be the sound of something rushing through the air – then a brilliant flash would light up the entire sky and horizon and be followed within two or three seconds by the most resounding explosion.

Overall, the night *could* have been worse – 'St Paul's Cathedral, built by Sir Christopher Wren, her great dome towering above the capital of the Empire, is burning to the ground as I talk to you now', Ed Murrow misleadingly informed his American listeners – but even so, it *should* not have been as catastrophic as it was. Many of the firms whose premises were destroyed had failed to employ firewatchers; most of those buildings could perhaps have been saved, had firemen been able to effect an entrance; while, even more frustratingly, the water supply failed early in the night.[20]

'Gigantic German Attempt to Set the City of London Ablaze' was the headline of the *Evening News* on Monday the 30th. Another witness recalled the bewilderment that still prevailed on the Tuesday morning. 'Numbers of City workers walked about with dazed and stunned looks', Charles Graves observed. 'They were the people who had arrived the previous morning and found that their place of employment was gutted and were coming back on the following day simply because they had nothing better to do.' On 10 January it was reported that the thirty or so pillarboxes that had disappeared under the City rubble had at last been dug out.[21] Next day a bomb landed on Bank station, killing 117 people who had been taking shelter down on the platform. It also caused, almost directly in front of the Royal Exchange, a vast crater, which for virtually a year could be traversed only by a hastily erected Bailey bridge. Among those tending the wounded at Bank station was a Hungarian doctor. He paid his tribute: 'You English cannot appreciate the discipline of your people. I have not found one hysterical, shouting patient.'

Early in the New Year a visiting American politician, Wendell Wilkie, was also struck by the country's cohesion. 'He is amazed', Harold Nicolson noted, 'that Big Business are as determined on victory as anybody. They know that it means their ruin, but even Montagu Norman had said to him, "Ruin? Go to hell. We must win."'[22]

What was, however, starting to dismay Norman was a growing awareness that one of the major costs of war would be a huge shift in international financial relations. As he wrote to Brand after a year and a half of the conflict: 'I have never realised so strongly as now how entirely we are in the hands of American "friends" over direct investments, and how much it looks as if, with kind words and feelings, they were going to extract them one after another!' Away, however, from *haute finance* – where surely the dominant attitude was that, at almost whatever cost, the war was something that had to be seen through – the pervasive atmosphere was one of sheer, unheroic tedium, as the clock seemingly went backwards. Over thirty years later, one of Norman's minions would remember without any misplaced nostalgia 'those airless vaults it was part of our fate to endure, on one of those nights which were a mixture of extended hours of work, interrupted by meals, with an occasional spice of danger but mostly made up of hours and hours of empty boredom'.[23]

It was during the autumn of 1940 that George Orwell wrote his marvellous extended essay, *The Lion and the Unicorn*, published in February 1941. 'If we can survive this war,' he argued, 'the defeat in Flanders will turn out to have been one of the great turning-points in English history':

> After the French collapse there came something that could not be laughed away, something that neither cheque-books nor policemen were any use against – the bombing. Zweee – boom! What's that? Oh, only a bomb on the Stock Exchange. Zweee – boom! Another acre of somebody's valuable slum-property gone west. Hitler will at any rate go down in history as the man who made the City of London laugh on the wrong side of its face.[24]

On 16 April 1941 there occurred what became known as 'The Wednesday', when a thousand tons of incendiaries and high explosives rained down on the City during one night. St Paul's was the particular target – the architectural writer J. M. Richards, who was also a firewatcher at the cathedral, would call it 'the roughest night of all' – but Wren's masterpiece survived. Three days later Sambourne was less than happy about the British retaliation: 'I am terrified over what the consequences to London will be after our raid on Berlin. We are fools & fools we shall remain . . . God only knows how we can win this war. Germany so far has been triumphant everywhere.'[25] His fears about what would happen to London were justified, for the City's very worst night still lay ahead. It came on 10 May, when almost all the surviving buildings near St Paul's succumbed, there was huge devastation in several other parts of the City, and the London Commercial Sale Rooms, for so long the epicentre of the Mincing Lane commodity trades, were razed. Up to that night the City had been at least as much a commercial as a financial centre; subsequently it would be predominantly financial in character. It was one of the less obvious ways in which Hitler's bombs ripped the heart out of the old City.

*

Following Sir Josiah Stamp's death in April after a bomb had landed on his house in Kent, there was a vacancy on the Court at the Bank. On George Booth's initiative, the bold decision was taken to approach Keynes. After the Chancellor, Sir Kingsley Wood, had given his consent to the idea, Norman went to the Treasury to pop the question on Friday 5 September (the day before his own seventieth birthday, the normal retirement age for Bank directors, although the rule had been waived for Norman). After thinking over the matter during the weekend (and remarking to his mother that if he was not careful he would become a bishop next), Keynes told Norman on Monday afternoon, when the latter returned to the Treasury to get his answer, that he would be delighted to accept.[26]

On the 18th the public announcement was made. 'At last orthodoxy has caught up with me', said Keynes of this richly symbolic moment. And: 'I do not know if it is I or the Old Lady who has been made an honest woman of.' Keynes himself went to the Bank most Thursdays, for a Court meeting followed by lunch. After one visitation he left with Booth, slumped back in the car they were sharing, and declared: 'I do enjoy these lunches at the Bank: Montagu Norman, always absolutely charming, always absolutely wrong!'[27]

On the same day that Keynes made his debut at Court, the Bank prepared a memorandum on its relations with government – a memorandum written very much with a view to use in future controversy, especially the question of whether the Bank should be nationalised. Essentially it was a prepared defence, arguing that the relationship was in fundamentals the same in war as it had been prior to war, in that on the one hand 'the government, through the Treasury, seeks continuously the advice of the Bank, both on technical and wider questions, but retains undivided responsibility for major questions of policy', while on the other hand 'the Bank remains the confidential adviser and the administrative agent'. The defence ended with a classically empirical statement: 'Like many of the institutions that form the mainstay of this country, the Bank has reached its position by a process of growth and whilst, in theory, it may seem to be open to criticism on this ground or that, in practice – like the Common Law of England – it works.' Anxiety levels about the Bank's future were clearly rising, and Norman reiterated to Martin at the end of October that the election of Keynes as a director was not in itself enough in terms of broadening the Court, and that 'what we have now need to find is another candidate or two (of a Leftish tinge) for next spring'. By December the name of the leading pottery manufacturer Josiah Wedgwood, from a traditionally 'leftish' family and author of *The Economics of Inheritance*, was in the frame, and Wood promised to find out on Norman's behalf whether he was a member of the Labour Party. Presumably the enquiries were satisfactory, for Wood agreed in January 1942 that Norman could approach Wedgwood.[28] That spring he duly became a director, replacing the over-age Cecil Lubbock.

Norman himself, however, was increasingly pessimistic that such changes of personnel would be enough to prevent the Bank from having to undergo a fundamental change in its status. Indeed, in March 1942 he frankly told the Committee of Treasury that 'in his view it had seemed for a long time past increasingly likely that some form of nationalisation would be applied to the Bank, not long after or even during the war, whatever the political party in power'. Furthermore, he believed that 'the interests of the Country and Empire and the maintenance of the credit structure and of a valuable tradition would be best served by the conversion of the Bank into a public utility corporation; and perhaps the sooner the better'. But as he added, 'no action could be taken for the time being, owing mainly to the personality of the present Chancellor, without whose determined support no such conversion was possible'. Although he did not spell it out, presumably Norman's thinking was that if nationalisation was going to happen anyway, it was better for the Bank that it was done before rather than after a Labour government was elected. Predictably, however, his mood fluctuated on the nationalisation question. Towards the end of that year, while similarly addressing some of his close colleagues in the Bank, he noted with a degree of resignation how 'all decisions on policy were in fact taken in Whitehall' and, in terms of the Court, referred to 'the presence, in Lord Keynes [ennobled earlier in 1942], virtually of a Treasury representative'. Yet in September 1943, speaking at *The Economist*'s centenary lunch, his attitude was more robust. 'Norman was very short', Raymond Streat observed. 'He traced the community of interest over the 100 years between *The Economist* and the Bank of England – both privately owned but both, he thought, rather the better able on that account to serve the public interest.'[29] His heart, in short, was not obeying his head – a not unusual Norman occurrence.

As for the Stock Exchange, that was an institution more on the defensive than it had been at any time since being subjected to a Royal Commission in the 1870s. Its role in a planned post-war economy was uncertain, while in terms of stockbroking's perceived contribution to the current war economy it must have been disconcerting that the profession was ranked only forty-sixth in the order of reserved occupations – with the fact that stockbrokers came just after flower-sellers an additional humiliation.

In all sorts of ways the world was changing. The floor of the Stock Exchange remained an all-male preserve, but in March 1942 the Committee considered a request from two firms, Haley & Co. and A. Sherriff & Co.: each, being short of staff, wished to introduce a lady (Mrs Miller and Mrs Judd respectively) as settling-room clerks. A month of deliberation ensued, and on 20 April there took place a historic 12–11 vote 'in favour of women clerks being admitted to the Settling Room only as a war measure'. If that was a minor chink in one wall of prejudice, another wall was wholly intact. 'Here comes another fucking Jew!' A. R. Barton exclaimed just over a fortnight later, at 12.15 on Thursday 7 May, when he looked up and saw another member, John Michael, while he was answering a call in the telephone room. Michael at once lodged a complaint, on the grounds that Barton, whom he described as having been 'so drunk he should not be allowed in the Stock Exchange', had sworn in front of the female telephone attendants. 'I had a severe attack in the morning of Kidney Trouble owing to having stones, and took Gin to relieve the pain', was Barton's rather lame defence, and he was warned as to his future conduct.

Nor was any action taken later that year, in December 1942, when another Jewish member, the elderly Leopold A. Abrahams, made his complaint: 'I wish to most strongly protest against the practice of Horse Play in the Oil Market, of which today I have been the victim, being forcibly thrown to the floor, receiving cuts on my nose and head injuries; apart from the dangers of these practices, I feel that it lacks decorum and lowers the prestige of the Institution.'[30]

If few cared about such incidents, quite the reverse was the case with the City's merchant banks. Naturally, circumstances varied from bank to bank, but some were in trouble. In the context of war, it was a significant help to a merchant bank's situation if there was already a strong tradition of doing investment business on behalf of well-off – or reputedly well-off – individual clients. Kleinworts, for example, had no such tradition and suffered accordingly, whereas Barings, with its connections deep into British society, prospered in this area. 'We are in financial straits', Lady Diana Cooper wrote to 8 Bishopsgate from the Dorchester in 1942. 'Can you help us out by selling our worst shares? If I don't get £2,000 soon they will put me in jug.' Hambros was another house faring not too poorly – with Olaf successfully cultivating inland acceptances – whereas by contrast, and presumably unbeknown to Kindersley and Brand, Peacock visited Norman in October 1943 to ask why Lazards had 'a bad smell & reputation'. There were also problems at Brown Shipley. E. Clifton Brown, the governor's former partner, called on Norman in December 1942. 'Firm's position: I say lack of Cap . . . He is angry & hurt and inclined to threaten.' At this time Norman was also worried about Morgan Grenfell's inadequate capital (down to £1.5m), and over the next few weeks he seems to have devised the idea of a merger between it and Brown Shipley. However, although Bicester proved amenable, Brown did not, and the idea was abandoned. Instead, Morgan Grenfell fortified its position by acquiring (despite Norman's initial opposition and against competition from Hambros) Cull & Co., whose elderly partners were keen to sell out.[31]

There is no doubt what was *the* great might-have-been of these difficult years. It began when Norman saw Anthony de Rothschild in December 1941: 'Seems overwrought & worried: Lionel seriously ill & future uncertain'. Lionel, an inveterate cigar-smoker, died the following month, and it was left to Anthony to carry on alone. The precise financial position of Rothschilds at this time remains a mystery, but in April 1942 Norman told Cobbold 'in all secrecy of R's dependance on Bk – wh is a bar to more freedom to Acc Hses'. Later in 1942 there were three of the most pregnant entries in all of Norman's diaries:

8 September. Pam [Albert Pam of Schroders]. Why sh^d not Schroders, Rs & Barings amalgamate? Or why sh^d not Barings take over the other 2?

10 September. ERP [Peacock of Barings]. ?BB & Co. + JHS & Co. + NMR & S: he will consider.

2 October. ERP. BB & Co. not willing, after consideration, to join with JHS & Co., whose methods are impossible & unpopularity great – nor with NMR & S who are entirely a *Jewish* family concern.

Of course, even if Peacock had been willing to transform 'the Trinity' into a single deity, it is far from certain that it would have been a runner. It is, nonetheless, a supremely tantalising moment in City history. Over the next few months Norman continued to note regular visits from Anthony de Rothschild. 'He shows an improving position but has a long way to go.' And: 'They must go very slow.' Pam, meanwhile, would call again in August 1943, when there was another tantalising Norman entry: 'Future of Schroders: I mention Roth^s, Brandts, Browns, wh he will consider.' Nothing came of it, nor of Pam's own idea later in the year of a merger with Guinness Mahon.[32] For better or worse, most of the hallowed names would still be in place when the war ended, even if some of their businesses were in distinctly poor shape.

As for that post-war future, in December 1942 the Beveridge Report was published, laying the foundations of the Welfare State. Over the next year and a half, the City tried hard to have a restraining influence on post-war welfare and employment commitments, but generally found itself in an uncomfortably isolated position as the 'reconstruction' process gathered momentum.[33] It was difficult for the City not to feel under threat. Even a Tory radical like Robert Boothby, in his prognosis of *The New Economy* that lay ahead after the war, anticipated not only a nationalised Bank of England, but also 'the transformation of the banking system from a private profit-making concern into a public service'. In February 1943 Norman invited to lunch the Home Secretary, Labour's Herbert Morrison, and presumably hoped to exercise his feline charm. Their topic of conversation, presumably not chosen by the guest, was the unhappy one of the 1931 financial crisis. 'He charges Bk with plot against Labour and dole', Norman recorded without comment.[34] Integral to the domestic side of the reconstruction process was that old chestnut, the relationship between finance and industry. Bevin in particular, a former member of the Macmillan Committee and now a member of the War Cabinet, helped to propagate the view that the City in the past had let down industry and that it was time for a fresh start in that vexed relationship. Above all, that meant at last doing something satisfactory about the 'Macmillan gap' – the provision of capital to medium-sized firms. Much would turn on how it was filled.

Back in December 1941, almost two years after the Bankers' Industrial Development Company had in effect been wound up, the Bank's Henry Clay was starting to look ahead to the question of long-term finance for British industry after the war. He argued that the London capital market was unsatisfactory in its present form: its costs were too high, it was geared almost entirely towards providing a market for existing concerns, and 'there is no industrial financing concern on which borrowers can fall back'. Accordingly, he suggested the establishment of such a concern – an institution that, he presciently noted, 'would have to take an equity interest so that profits might offset losses'. Almost certainly it was helpful that Clay became a member in July 1943 of a committee on post-war domestic finance, which the Bank had set up four months earlier under Niemeyer's chairmanship. The committee was not entirely convinced of the economic value of what it was doing: Niemeyer defined 'the misfits' of industry as 'too small for issues, too disorganised, ill-advised' and argued that in post-war Britain 'these misfits will have a political importance disproportionate to their real importance'. That autumn, however, his committee proposed the establishment of an institution, capitalised at £50m, that would provide, in Niemeyer's words, 'temporary finance for some who later go to the market' and 'permanent finance for others (mainly small) who cannot get to the market'. The capital would have to come from the clearing banks, but as Niemeyer observed, 'if such a scheme is to keep Whitehall from more governmental forms of industrial finance, it has got to be substantial and demonstrably so'.[35]

If Norman was sceptical, as he may well have been, that scepticism disappeared once he became aware, as he did by early December, of apparently competing Board of Trade schemes that, according to his faithful Ernest Skinner, were a 'bureaucratic monster'. Over the Christmas period Norman was in tacit alliance with the Treasury's Sir Wilfrid Eady about formulating a proposal that would be acceptable to government, and on 7 January 1944 he explained his thinking: 'My purpose', Norman stated frankly, 'is to satisfy Whitehall: to keep them out of the Banking Business and free of malevolence towards the Bankers – which at this moment are stakes worth playing for.' Appended to Norman's letter was a draft prospectus. Two new institutions were now envisaged. One, aimed at larger firms, was to have capital of about £30m (supplied by the insurance companies and investment trusts) and in many ways was to be a retread of BIDC, with industrial restructuring its aim. The other, with capital of some £20m mainly to come from the clearing banks, was to be directed at the provision of finance for rather smaller businesses. The latter was far the more contentious proposal.[36] Above all, would the banks wear it?

In persuading them to do so, the Bank received valuable softening-up support from Eady, who on 10 February lunched at National Provincial with that bank's chairman, Colin Campbell, who was also chairman of the Committee of London Clearing Bankers, and its chief general manager, Ernest Cornwall. 'Campbell thought it would have to be done but Cornwall nearly had a fit', Niemeyer recorded afterwards on the basis of what he had been told by Eady. 'It is quite plain that Eady more or less indicated unpleasant alternatives propounded by Whitehall, if the Banks did not play.' Over the next few weeks the clearers suggested a compromise solution – of individual subsidiaries to do business with small firms – but received no encouragement from the Bank. By mid-March Lidbury was complaining bitterly to his Chairman about the consequences for the clearing banks of what he called 'the present political ferments', in particular the 'indirect levy on the resources of the commercial banks for the subsidising of commercial and industrial "adventures" in the interests of the "full employment" campaign'. Although Anthony Tuke of Barclays was more pragmatic – arguing that the banks had no alternative but to find the 'least objectionable' way to proceed, given that the Bank of England was seemingly 'more nearly allied to the government than to the clearing banks' – it was Lidbury who, at the end of March, had his way in formulating a strongly worded response to the Bank from the clearers as a whole. After a stout denial that the 'Macmillan gap' even existed, and an assertion that after the war the banks would be competing 'far more fiercely' for lending business than before the war, there followed a paragraph that only he could have penned:

> It is obviously undesirable to countenance the raising of hopes and expect-ations of people whose request for financial assistance will not, and cannot, satisfy the scrutiny and examination dictated by common business prudence. It may be feared that this class may constitute the unsatisfied demand.

Even so, the clearing banks did concede that 'notwithstanding the reasons which support their belief that existing credit facilities do, in actual practice, cover all requirements which are able to provide economic justification, there may be considerations of a public nature of sufficient psychological importance to render it expedient that a further organisa-tion should be formed'. That did not mean, however, that they could 'look with equanimity on a project which may saddle them with substantial losses made outside their own control'.[37] Put another way, though there was no derailing the reconstruction train, Lidbury wanted to make sure that he was in the signal box keeping the lights set on red.

The other key aspect of reconstruction, from the City's point of view, was the nature of the international financial order that would emerge from the war.[38] There may at a personal level have been a rapproche-ment between Keynes and Norman, but within a few months of Keynes becoming a director of the Bank in September 1941, it was clear that in a larger sense there remained a gulf between the two men. Believing that 'the post-war world must not be content with patchwork', Keynes that autumn pushed hard the concept of a Clearing Union, essentially as a means of achieving multi-lateralism by means of international agreement rather than traditional laissez-faire. The Bank's instinctive response was to view this approach as not only unrealistically Utopian, but also a threat to the future of the sterling area. Early in December 1941, looking ahead to the post-war world, Norman asserted to Martin in South Africa that 'nothing is more important in my view than that the Commonwealth should hang together as closely as, if not more closely than, they are now doing and should maintain the Sterling Area, to which with advantage might be added some more adherents when the time comes'. Soon afterwards, Keynes tried personally to persuade Norman of the merits of his plan, describing it as 'a bold bid to combine the great historical advantages of the XIX Century Gold Standard with modern ideas and the requirements of the post-war world'. Norman declined to be seduced, but in practice the Bank could do little other than (in Cobbold's words at the end of December) 'allow J.M.K.'s stuff to percolate where it will'.[39]

The Bank may have feared Keynes' inclination to accept without ques-tion the fact of post-war American economic and financial dominance – Leo Amery discovered in January 1942 that Norman 'shares my anxieties as to American ambitions to make the British empire a lebensraum for their exports' – but during the rest of the war it was Keynes, not the Bank, who made the running on the British side. By February 1944, with the Bank continuing to uphold the claims of the sterling area as against the plans for an international monetary fund that Keynes and the Americans were developing – and anyway naturally resentful of any new organisation apparently designed to go above existing structures of central banking co-operation – Keynes exploded. 'The Bank is not facing any of the realities', he told the Chancellor (Sir John Anderson), explaining that it was failing to allow either 'for the fact that post-war domestic policies are impossible without American assistance' or 'for the fact that vast debts and exiguous reserves are not, by themselves, the best qualifica-tion for renewing old-time international banking'. Early in March, writing to Beaverbrook, he almost went over the top:

Twice in my life I have seen the Bank blindly advocating policies which I expected to lead to the greatest misfortunes and a frightful smash. Twice I have predicted it; twice I have been disbelieved; twice it has happened . . . My conviction is that here is a third occasion. The Bank is engaged in a desperate gamble in the interests of old arrangements and old-fashioned ideas, which there is no possibility of sustaining. Their plan, or rather their lack of plan, would, in my firm belief, lead us into yet another smash.[40]

Third time round, however, Keynes' fears were exaggerated, for nothing – not even Bank of England obstruction – could stop the International Monetary Fund from being established.

Even as Keynes remonstrated, his old adversary was no longer in the game. Over the previous year Norman's health had palpably started to deteriorate, sharpening the question of the succession.[41] One possibility was again Niemeyer, but Churchill (who would never forget the return to gold) ruled him out. Another was Cobbold, who was very much Norman's protégé and, like Niemeyer, had become an executive director shortly before the war, but he was not yet forty – in City terms, almost a babe. The front-runner emerged as Lord Catto, whom Norman trusted and whom he believed would, with his range of contacts in government as well as in the City, best protect the interests of the Bank. Catto himself, based in the Treasury, was agreeable, but Norman recorded on 7 January 1944 that Anderson at No 11 was 'undecided & may be going to sound Colleagues'.[42]

Barely a week later Norman's health at last decisively gave way, and the situation suddenly became urgent. He was diagnosed as having pneumococcal meningitis, his doctors determined that he must not continue as governor, and towards the end of March he accepted their verdict with infinite reluctance. 'It's not going back that will kill me', he told Peacock. The new governor, formally elected at the meeting of the Bank of England's stockholders on 15 April, was Catto, with Anderson having been given little time to canvas other possibilities, though there is no reason for thinking that he was not happy enough with the choice. 'It seems that everything is falling about my ears', Norman wrote, the day before the stockholders met, to the Bank's chief accountant. 'I am as good as gone, and have to find some way of avoiding the qualities of a vegetable.' Nor was his mother, still going strong at ninety-six, inclined to look on the bright side: 'They should have let him finish his twenty-five years.' And, reputedly, she added: 'I do wish I could find him a job.'[43]

*

Thomas Catto, sixty-five when he became governor, had had a remarkable life: his father was a shipwright; he left school at fifteen; and before the First World War he became a successful merchant, mainly in the Near and Middle East. During the war he was chairman of the British Food Mission, before spending most of the 1920s in Calcutta as head of the Calcutta-based merchanting firm Andrew Yule & Co., in which Morgan Grenfell had a large interest. In 1929 he returned to London to head Yule, Catto & Co. and also become a partner in Morgan Grenfell. He was created a baron in 1936. In all, he was (as the Bank of England's Humphrey Mynors would put it) 'a leading example of the Scottish boy of comparatively humble origin who rose to the top rank in the City of London through a combination of innate qualities and of grasping opportunities wherever they offered'. Catto had a memorable physique, which Streat encountered in 1945: 'One of the smallest men I have met. Dapper, alert, sharp-eyed, Scots accent.' Or, as Mynors nicely as well as shrewdly described him: 'In appearance he was very short of stature, with a fresh complexion and clear blue eyes. His open countenance and quiet manner perhaps tended to conceal his shrewdness and skill as a negotiator.'[44]

Leslie O'Brien was the new governor's private secretary for a year, and noted that it was hard for the Bank's permanent officials, like himself, not to feel that Catto had 'a rather exaggerated respect for Treasury opinion and quality'. Few, however, could deny the sheer depth of Catto's commercial experience, the soundness of his judgement, or the appropriateness of the fact – at this particular juncture in the Bank's history – that he was neither a government stooge nor a deeply entrenched member of the City Establishment. In January 1945, six months after the Bank had celebrated its 250th anniversary and Catto had taken the opportunity to reaffirm publicly that its purpose in relation to government was 'to give independent and candid advice based upon experience', Keynes assured Brand in Washington that 'Catto is very decidedly getting his hand on the helm, much quicker and more firmly than I felt confident of, and is a great success.'[45]

Shortly after he became governor, the long-running discussions about the post-war monetary and trading order culminated in the international conference at Bretton Woods in July 1944, when the basic principles were established of an International Monetary Fund designed to stabilise exchange rates and a Bank for Reconstruction and Development (the future World Bank) designed to provide long-term loans. Catto and the Bank of England, however, remained only bit-players in the process, with Keynes from his Treasury base continuing to be the dominant figure on the British side. All that could be done was to attempt to exercise a restraining influence. 'I am anxious that it should be made clear from the very beginning that the proposed institution is not intended for relief purposes', Catto wrote to the Treasury a month before Bretton Woods, about the proposed Bank for Reconstruction and Development. 'Unless the institution is run on a strictly commercial basis, its resources will gradually be frittered away and the high ideals of its intentions will end in disaster and recrimination.' He added that he 'should like to make another plea that the institution should be called something other than a bank'. That particular plea fell on deaf ears, but the governor did manage to secure at Bretton Woods what became known as 'the Catto clause' – in effect, a reluctant acceptance by the United States that, even in a world run by the almighty dollar, other nations had the right, as a last resort and in consultation with the IMF, to vary their exchange rates. 'Bolton will have told you all about Bretton Woods', Brand in Washington wrote to Catto after it was over. 'I did what I could in the case of the Bank, generally aiming at getting the conference to be sufficiently conservative. Some people on the American side and in other quarters had, to my mind, many inflated ideas as to the immense sums of money that ought to be available at once for international lending.' Brand added that Bolton, representing the Bank of England, 'was not in a very easy position, but he acquitted himself admirably'.[46]

Overall, the City's response to Bretton Woods was polite rather than enthusiastic. The *FT* expressed anxiety about whether the Bank for Reconstruction and Development would make its loans selectively, pointing out that 'the creditworthiness of the borrower as well as the nature of the work helps to determine the ultimate fate of the loan and of the lenders' money', while the *Financial News* strongly criticised the system of IMF quotas, on the grounds that they gave the United States 'such a figure as will make her attitude, at any future moment, decisive to all intents and purposes'. Parkes of Lloyds, however, reflected privately that 'on the whole I think a very good job has been done and I think it augurs well for the future that the powerful countries amongst the Allies are honestly endeavouring to restore economic sanity to the world'. He did not deny, nevertheless, 'the leaning there is over here in certain quarters in the direction of bilateral trade treaties instead of multilateral'. It was a leaning with which Catto sympathised to only a limited extent. 'It is sheer madness', he declared the following spring in a note on commercial policy, 'to think the Empire can create a cave where we take in one another's washing and ignore the rest of the world! . . . The countries we sell to are not necessarily the countries from which we buy, and if we begin unilateral trading we return to *barter, the survival of the fittest* and *more war!*'[47] The implications of the choice were financial as well as commercial. Put another way, was the whole world to be the City's oyster, as it had been before 1914 and even up to 1931? Or, with the dollar now conclusively paramount in global terms, was it more sensible, if less glorious, to rely almost solely on the sterling area?

On the domestic side of post-war reconstruction, the new governor had by now successfully brought the clearing banks into line. The nub was the proposed Industrial and Commercial Finance Corporation (the future 3i). 'Such a company, concerned only with industrial matters and independently managed,' ran Skinner's briefing for Catto ahead of the latter's crucial first meeting with the clearers on 11 May 1944, 'would not only make a good public appeal but would be a wise step for the Banks to take and go a long way towards allowing them to get on with their legitimate business in peace.' At the meeting itself, Catto emphasised that 'a new organisation for each Bank would be quite impracticable' and that what was needed was a larger organisation showing to the public 'that the banking entity are anxious to play their part in the finance of small businesses'. Edwin Fisher of Barclays reluctantly agreed:

> We all feel that we can do this ourselves – rightly or wrongly – Banks would be able to advise if they had applications which they could not deal with. I think there may be political reasons but if unorthodox banking must be done I think there is much to be said for the formation of a separate institution with the help of the Bank of England. If you have a separate company it does preserve the reputation of British Banking from the imputation that they are getting into a system of continental banking.

To which Catto remarked that 'there is no suggestion that this should not be run on a strictly commercial basis'. The outcome of the meeting was a committee to draft specific proposals for government approval – a committee in which the most powerful figures were Niemeyer on behalf of the Bank, determined that the ICFC should happen, and Lidbury, whose private view remained that 'the damn thing isn't wanted'.[48]

Niemeyer had his way, not least in the context of that summer's landmark White Paper on full employment, which to the City's relief did not include the establishment of a National Investment Board. Necessarily, the implicit price of that exemption was a more whole-hearted commitment to industry on the part of the banks, a logic that even Lidbury was unable to evade. Detailed proposals went to government, via Catto, in October; and in January 1945 Anderson announced in Parliament the intended formation of the Finance Corporation for Industry (FCI), aimed at large businesses, alongside the much more politically charged ICFC, which would specialise in supplying medium- and long-term capital for small- and medium-sized businesses, in amounts ranging from £5,000 to £200,000. The Big Five would be the ICFC's main shareholders (contributing £11m out of £15m), and Anderson emphasised that neither new institution would be subject to government direction. 'Even if it can be regarded as little more than a gesture,' the *Financial News* asserted about the ICFC after the announcement, 'the gesture is a sympathetic one and indicative of the best intentions.'[49]

Few imagined that the impending post-war world would not be more heavily regulated than had previously been the case in peacetime. A touchstone was the Cohen Committee on Company Law, which was set up by the Board of Trade and began to take evidence in 1943. One witness that year was the reform-minded financial journalist Hargreaves Parkinson, a strong advocate of the compulsory disclosure of any transfers to secret or inner reserves. 'Would you in that respect draw any distinction between trading or commercial companies on the one hand, and banking, insurance and investment companies on the other?' he was asked. 'That is a very delicate question. Personally I should not draw such a distinction, but I am afraid that would bring the wrath of the banks and insurance companies down upon me.' On another area of disclosure, Captain Nutcombe Hume, managing director of the various Charterhouse organisations (mainly involving industrial finance), disdained ambivalence:

> I think if the remuneration of the chairman of banks and of some of the other great national enterprises in this country were made available to the public at large – because you cannot confine such information to the shareholders only – in the annual reports of those companies, it would create a quite wrong impression in the minds of a very large number of people that they were being paid more than they should get. I do not think the average member of the public can properly assess what is the right rate of remuneration for the leading executives, particularly of the big companies.

In the course of 1944 it remained a moot point whether the Cohen Committee would advocate a fundamental overhaul of company law. Harold Brown, a former senior partner of the solicitors Linklaters & Paines and according to that firm's historian 'a recognised expert on company law', strongly hoped not. 'There are black sheep in the flock', he conceded to the committee, but during his forty years in the City he had been 'impressed mainly by the honesty and high standard of conduct generally displayed by those controlling and carrying on business in this country', which he added made for 'a pleasant contrast to the standards which seem to prevail in some foreign countries'.[50]

In the event, the Cohen Report of June 1945 did lead to far-reaching changes – in particular, the compulsory consolidation of accounts – while accepting that it remained for the Stock Exchange alone to decide which issues should or should not come to the market. It was, from the Stock Exchange's standpoint, a vital endorsement, at a time when the popular mood was running all the other way. 'Some people, it was declared, think of the House as a gambling casino', reported 'Autolycus' regretfully, in the wake of a meeting of the Stock Exchange's shareholders near the end of the war. 'Others regard it as a place where the public, if they deal, are bound to lose money. Such impressions, it was claimed, might be met by the appointment of a well-paid Public Relations Officer who would instruct the public in the service, and the value, of the Stock Exchange.'[51]

The final year of war was not, in general, a happy time in the City. The flying bombs began to hit London in June 1944, and over the next few months there was considerable destruction in the City. For instance, 31 Old Jewry took a direct hit on 6 October, and Freshfields turned to the Bank of England for temporary sanctuary. As late as March 1945 the diarist James Lees-Milne was recording that 'three hundred people' had been killed by a rocket attack 'in the City'. Nor, despite the 30-Share Index continuing to rise (up to 116 by the end of the year, representing a remarkable recovery in real as well as nominal terms from under 50 in June 1940), was there a lot to occupy the days. When Lionel Fraser returned to Helbert Wagg early in 1945, he found that 'life seemed crushingly dull' and that 'the City had not got back into rhythm'. Moreover, the sense of gloom was compounded by a widespread pessimism about the City's future. 'At the beginning of this year we had a little business to do and managed to sell two issues', Evelyn Baring rather mournfully informed New York in March 1945. 'They were both very successful, but the profit from our point of view was insignificant. However, I suppose we have got to expect that in this new world.' Still, even in this dreaded new world, high-level contacts would presumably continue to matter. 'Lunched at New Court with Tony Rothschild', Churchill's private secretary, 'Jock' Colville, noted on 4 May. 'Lord Bennett [former prime minister of Canada], Sir Basil Brooke [prime minister of Northern Ireland] and Colonel Vickers were the other guests.'

Three days later the European War at last ended. Tuesday the 8th was VE Day, and 'Autolycus' recorded that 'not a few members' came to town to make sure for themselves that the Stock Exchange really was closed for business. 'Other people who came to the City', he went on, 'were a fair number of country cousins, who wandered round the Bank of England and the Mansion House, listened to the blaring of the canned music and sympathised with the bank staffs.' He added that 'the visitors could hardly fail to have been impressed by the City's decorations'.[52]

The general election was in July. Evelyn Baring wrote to New York on the 28th, summarising reaction at 8 Bishopsgate to the Labour landslide: 'I need hardly say that the result came as a complete surprise to all of us . . . Anyway, we are in for an interesting time. A new era has started which may be less comfortable than that to which we have been accustomed in the past.' There was a different response from one prosperous underwriter at Lloyd's. 'To my astonishment,' recalled the journalist John Gale, 'I found that my father welcomed the Labour victory. "There might have been trouble if they hadn't got in," he said. I never asked how he voted.'[53]

Less than a fortnight later, on 6 August, came Hiroshima. Nagasaki followed, and the Second World War was finally over. Thirty-one years after the guns of August had signalled the abrupt end of the City's golden age – an age that Montagu Norman had tried in vain between the wars to recreate – the Square Mile found itself at its lowest peacetime ebb in living memory.

CHAPTER THIRTY-ONE

Moving Among Ghosts

At the end of the war the City of London was devastated, and not just physically. In practically every respect the outlook seemed dark: internationally the dollar reigned supreme; almost one-third of overseas investments had been liquidated; export trade was in shreds; the domestic industrial base was ravaged; and debts, largely to the United States, the Dominions and the colonies, were enormous. In sum, it is generally reckoned that Britain had lost about a quarter of its pre-war national wealth.

Not surprisingly, given that daunting legacy, it took a long time for anything like a vibrant atmosphere to return to the post-war City. The sense of lassitude prevailing at 20 Fenchurch Street, home of Kleinworts, was typical of many other overmanned offices. With each department having formed its own coffee syndicates, the nearby Lyons and ABC coffee houses were full of idle clerks and typists, 'all drinking coffee at 4d a cup and smoking like chimneys'; while one assistant manager recalled this as a period dominated by the chore of 'locking the safes'. What work there was on hand tended to be hamstrung by a panoply of wartime controls that had not yet been relaxed. 'Business today', a manager of Hambros lamented in 1949, 'does not only mean selling or buying – that may often be the easiest part – nor financing, but the most intricate and time-wasting labour is in complying with all the various regulations here and abroad'. Capital market restrictions (under the auspices of the Capital Issues Committee), continuing exchange controls, world trade still in a battered state – it was hardly a propitious environment in which to operate. Moreover, perhaps because of the Labour government's instinctive dislike of futures trading, with its unpalatable speculative connotations, it took an extraordinarily long time for most of the City's commodity markets to reopen. Rubber in 1946 and tin in 1949 were exceptions, but others remained firmly shut until the new decade. Also in mothballs until the 1950s were the gold and foreign exchange markets; and two principals in the market, Geoffrey Astley and Vi Pearce of Astley & Pearce, went so far as to leave the City entirely for six years, forming a Surrey-based company specialising in industrial clothing.

Very slowly, however, the City began to revive. Some of this revival took an international form – marine insurance at Lloyd's, for example, or ship chartering at the Baltic Exchange – but mainly it related to the British economy. The interwar shift in the Stock Exchange, away from the international and towards the domestic, now became even more palpable (in terms of both government and industrial securities), while the trend in the money market was similar. The inexorably increasing British component of the London Trust Co.'s investments, measured by book cost, was symptomatic: 45 per cent in 1933, 54 per cent in 1939, 64 per cent in 1945 and 76 per cent by 1951.[1] For better or worse, the City was now locked – for the time being, at least – into the fortunes of the British economy.

The international role would eventually return, but the sharp decline of the commercial City was irreversible.[2] On the eve of war, 26 per cent of the City's floor-space had been occupied by warehouses; ten years later, in 1949, the comparable figure was only 18 per cent. This was largely the result of bombing, but London did not help its cause when it failed to prevent the National Dock Labour Scheme in 1947, which over time would mean that the Port of London virtually priced itself out of existence.[3] Yet among these and other factors, most important was the loss of human capital entailed by the war, above all the amalgam of specialist knowledge and an intricate international network of connections. By the 1950s, when some semblance of normality had returned, almost all of that human capital (much of it foreign in character) had been eroded, and a more insular City had painful lessons to relearn. Some it was able to, but many had gone beyond recall. It was an appealing but misleading fact that the original adventures of Thomas the Tank Engine and friends were published in the City from 1945 by Edmund Ward of Bishopsgate; for the post-war City would become predominantly financial, not commercial, in composition, purpose and outlook – the reality at last corresponding to the popular image.

This narrowing of the City's base was perhaps regretted, but the prevailing post-war assumption was that as long as sterling could somehow be enabled to survive as a world currency, albeit subordinate to the dollar, then the City would not be entirely reduced to a parochial financial centre. Over twenty and more years the strength of sterling – and, behind it, the sterling area – was equated, automatically and unquestioningly, with the strength of the City. It was an understandable assumption, but in the event an almost wholly fallacious one.[4] Instead, as the final third of the century would conclusively demonstrate, what really mattered to the City's well-being were two other, quite different matters: the degree to which it would escape from state control; and the extent to which it would be open to talent from outside. Of course, any such outsiders would inevitably have to wrestle with the entrenched City culture – a culture appreciably more conservative, inward-looking and 'clubby' than forty or fifty years earlier. Nowhere epitomised that culture more than the merchant banking sector. Yet within months of the war ending, two merchant bankers were poised to shake up the City.

One, Kenneth Keith, brought to bear ruthless, aggressive determination rather than financial creativity or cerebral qualities. His vehicle was the issuing house Philip Hill (not yet a member of the Accepting Houses Committee and, in that sense, not yet a pukka merchant bank), whose eponymous founder – a bête noire of Montagu Norman – had died in 1944. The reassuring figure of Hubert Meredith was left in charge, and Keith joined the firm in April 1946. Before the war, as an ambitious young accountant at Peat Marwick, he had done some work for it; and during the war, as a POW, he had struck up a close friendship with Brian Mountain, the heir apparent at the insurance company Eagle Star, which had a signifi-cant stake in Philip Hill.[5] During the early post-war years, while Keith won his spurs in corporate finance, Philip Hill was still based in the West End, but was even more active in promoting new issues than it had been in the 1930s. Keith had gentlemanly attributes – educated at Rugby, an imposing physical presence, a good war record with the Welsh Guards – but felt no excessive veneration for playing by the gentlemanly rules.

The other merchant banker – just as resolute, but not so obviously a bruiser – was Siegmund Warburg.[6] In 1980, thirty-four years after estab-lishing S. G. Warburg & Co. as the successor to the New Trading Co., he gave his first full-length interview, to the American magazine *Institutional Investor*:

> *What qualities do you look for in someone you hire?*
>
> I think the most important thing is the courage and the common sense of a fellow. Experience is for me completely secondary. As a rule, those with whom I am close in my firm are people with whom I can also talk about books, about music, about human beings, human problems.
>
> *What about someone who says he has been so involved in business that he hasn't had time for these other things?*
>
> I wouldn't be too favourably impressed. And if a fellow would come to me and say his only interest is athletics, I wouldn't think he would stand a chance.
>
> *One of your stranger hiring procedures is that everyone considered for responsible positions must go through handwriting analysis. Why do you insist on that?*
>
> I was always very interested in graphology. I read lots of books about it and I knew some very important graphologists. I believe that graphology is a very important element in psychological analysis.

Does everyone you hire for a responsible position have to submit to this?

I think the word 'submit' is not the proper term. Nobody has ever refused me.

Another Warburgs practice that people have gossiped about over the years is your custom of having two sittings at lunch in order to squeeze more clients in. Do you encourage your colleagues to schedule two different luncheons for the same day?

Isn't this question of yours rather irrelevant?

No, it isn't. So many people have taken interest in this that I feel you should answer it.

Well, since you insist, I will say that I don't approve of this idea of someone having two luncheons in one day. This all started when my wonderful colleague and friend, Eric Korner, was very active – and there were so many people he wanted to have lunch with in a week that he had Mr X at 12.30 and Mr Y at 1.30. That happened perhaps five times a year.

It was an act of enormous audacity to start a new merchant bank in London, as you did, from scratch. Did people say you were crazy, that you wouldn't make it?

Every one of my personal friends thought it was right, even people who were not close personal friends but who were close acquaintances. Only some members of my more distant family thought it was wrong.

Did you always think you could mould the firm into an important merchant bank?

I didn't think in terms of an important merchant bank. It may sound a little bit conceited, but I thought it could be something good sui generis. I felt that I brought something to England which was a little bit different because I was a damn foreigner, a German Jew. I like to be a nonconformist, and I thought I could contribute something quite different from the others.

Didn't it help that many other merchant banks were a bit sleepy in the post-war period?

Absolutely. I don't have such a terribly high opinion of myself, but wasn't it Lloyd George who said that the last war was won because the enemy made so many mistakes?[7]

At 82 King William Street, where S. G. Warburg & Co. opened for business in January 1946, Warburg drew much support during the early months and years from the 'Uncles', the firm's other three founding fathers: the ultra-realist Henry Grunfeld (largely responsible for persuading Warburg to change the bank's name), the more dynamic Eric Korner and the meticulous Ernest Thalmann. From the start the pace of work was intense, the frequency of double-lunches greater than Warburg would later concede and, in the field of industrial finance, the firm found itself pushing at an almost open door. Warburg had some friends in high places – including at Rothschilds – but he had little or no instinctive affinity with the City Establishment as a whole. 'Most of the important people in the City', he privately reflected, 'are so anxious to avoid any unpleasantness that they will knowingly make blunders, with the sole aim of sparing themselves any conflict.' Was the prevailing, somewhat malevolent atmosphere of gossip and rumours, he speculated, 'a way of compensating for some sexual deficiency in those people'? Warburg, working incredibly long hours (by the standards of the day), travelling all over the world in order to forge contacts and always trying to take the long, disinterested view on behalf of his clients, was not inclined to be charitable either outside or inside his office. 'He knew neither pity nor even compassion', a French colleague recalled:

> One lapse and one immediately saw his face close. If the fault was judged serious, it closed for ever. Average transgressions entailed a period of penitence lasting from three days to three months. For others, he was pitiless, an attitude of permanent suspicion on his part would drive the wrongdoer to resignation within a few weeks or a few months.[8]

Life at Warburgs was not, in short, the world of gentlemanly capitalism to which the City had become accustomed.

*

'We hardly know what the future of Houses like ours will be under the present administration', Evelyn Baring confided to an American banker in November 1945. 'Nationalisation is the order of the day . . . Perhaps our turn will come. Anyway there seems little incentive to private enterprise.' And he added, more in hope than in expectation, 'I think we all feel that what is wanted today is a National Government under the leadership of a man such as Churchill.' In the City at large, certainly among those at a senior level, precious few during these perturbing months after the landslide election dared to come out as Labour supporters.[9]

Of course, there were perfectly rational grounds for being opposed to the Labour government – not only higher personal taxation, but the nationalisation programme that at a stroke wiped out significant areas of popular investment – but in many cases the City's attitude went beyond reason (typified by the stockbroker who insisted on referring to the prime minister as 'A. T. Lee' because he looked Chinese) and the paranoia was, as ever, overdone. 'The City in the middle of a socialist state is as anomalous as would be the Pope in Moscow' may have been Clement Attlee's purported view, but in practice the City escaped remarkably unscathed from its first experience of Labour in office with an overall majority. Why? To a variety of impersonal explanations – including an obstinate adherence to physical controls as the best way of planning the economy, a

Keynesian belief that the state did not need to command all the commanding heights, and a view of industry that favoured industrial rather than financial solutions – one should surely add the personal element. Chancellor of the Exchequer for almost the first two and half years of the Attlee administration was Hugh Dalton, a robust and in some ways attractive figure whose approach to the City was fatally undermined by a mixture of ignorance and emotional immaturity. Typically he relished Lloyd George's term for the City Establishment, the 'flapping penguins', but despite being the author of an often-reprinted textbook on *Principles of Public Finance*, his grasp of the City was sketchy. 'Stop talking details, Nicholas! Stick to principles', he would boom whenever his City friend Nicholas Davenport tried to explain its workings; and by the time he became Chancellor he still did not understand the functions of the government broker, let alone the difference between brokers and jobbers.[10] Moreover, in a larger sense, neither Dalton nor his colleagues seriously questioned the national desirability of a strong sterling area, an assumption that inevitably demanded that sterling be a powerful (or anyway, as powerful as possible) world currency, whatever the domestic deflationary consequences.[11] Bevin, that old critic of the City going back to Macmillan Committee days and earlier, was now Foreign Secretary; and he would have been the last to countenance a policy that might jeopardise Britain's assured place at the top table. One way and another, the City was safe in their hands.

Nevertheless, these were not easy years for either party in the relationship: politicians were at the mercy of economic forces beyond their control, while the City had to adjust to an unprecedentedly marginalised peacetime existence. The negotiations in the autumn of 1945 leading to a huge American loan – the defining economic event of the Labour government – revealed a shared powerlessness.[12] Keynes led the British delegation in Washington, and the basic deal that he reluctantly accepted was a $3.75bn loan in return for multilateral trading arrangements, early convertibility of sterling and an interpretation of the Bretton Woods agreement that gave the whip hand to the Americans.

London – above all the Cabinet – could do little more than agree. 'The consequences of present refusal of American aid would be more grievous than the possibility of subsequent failure to live up to its conditions,' the *Financial Times* (which had recently merged with the *Financial News*) conceded in December, explicitly supporting Dalton's similar line in the Commons. Most Conservatives abstained in the key vote, and the general mood in both the City and Westminster was troubled. Some weeks later Keynes privately explained these misgivings: 'England is sticky with self-pity and not prepared to accept peacefully and wisely the fact that her position and her resources are not what they once were.' As unreconciled as anyone was Montagu Norman (by now Lord Norman). 'He is entirely opposed to Bretton Woods and the whole of the Washington Loan ramp', Leo Amery recorded after a conversation with him in March 1946. 'In his curiously ingenious way he said that he did not understand the economics of the matter but that he had a strong hunch that we were being done down and resented it.'[13] A month later Keynes, with whom Norman had had such charged dealings and non-dealings over the years, was dead.

Norman was even unhappier about what had been happening, almost simultaneously, to the love of his life: the Bank of England.[14] The commitment to nationalise the Bank was an integral part of Labour's election manifesto, and within days of the change of government Catto emphasised to Dalton his hope that 'the method giving the least possible disturbance to the existing set-up would be chosen'.[15]

The process unfolded with remarkably little trouble. The bill to nationalise the Bank (praised by Dalton as 'a streamlined socialist statute, containing the minimum of legal rigmarole') worked its passage through Parliament during the winter, amidst only muted discussion and public controversy; and on 1 March 1946 the Old Lady, now almost 252 years old, passed into public ownership. Two days earlier, on 27 February, the 'Last Supper' took place there: native oysters, clear turtle soup, lamb cutlets and fruit salad with ice cream were washed down by 'Old Trinity House' Madeira, Steinberg 1935 hock, and Cognac 1884 brandy. Catto coupled the toast – 'Long live the Bank of England' – with the name of his predecessor, who 'has given all the best years of his life in living up to that Toast'.[16]

Inevitably nationalisation made a difference. 'The prestige of the Bank is not what it was', Villiers of Barings informed an American correspondent in January 1947. 'Various Directors have been appointed for their political views. Some of the Directors are excellent and others just average. To be a Director of the Bank in former times was a considerable honour; today that is not the case.' The larger point, however, is that nationalisation failed to make enough of a difference: there was no vision of how a central bank should function in the new era of a more planned economy; no convincing model of the ideal triangular relationship between government, central bank and commercial banks; and no insistence that the Bank shed its highly damaging culture of secrecy and the deliberate cultivation of mystique. There was an obligation on the Bank to start publishing an annual report, but when the first one appeared in 1947, the *Banker* was scathing: 'On the finances of the Bank itself, nothing whatever is revealed . . . On the Bank's internal activities, the only glimpses behind the curtain reveal facts which are mainly of formal significance.' This instinctive unwillingness on the Bank's part to accept the burdens of public accountability, to complement public responsibility, both reflected and exacerbated its reluctance to stake the intellectual high ground.[17]

In the markets themselves, the Stock Exchange for a time actually benefited – to its surprise – from Dalton's chancellorship, in particular his passionate espousal of cheap money.[18] Declaring that the occupant of his office 'must be on the side of the active producer as against the passive rentier', and quoting with approval Keynes' famous phrase about how ever-falling interest rates would lead to 'the euthanasia of the rentier', Dalton sought strenuously to place credit on a 2½ per cent footing. April 1946 saw a new 'tap' issue in the form of 2½ per cent savings bonds: this went reasonably well, though Dalton later claimed that he could have got better terms, but for flawed advice from Kim Cobbold, deputy governor at the Bank. At this point investor sentiment to the further cheapening of money, following the economic successes of cheap money policy since the early 1930s, was by and large favourable. 'We are in the middle of a Stock Exchange boom', Villiers noted fairly soon after the new issue was announced. 'One Member of Parliament even suggested in the House that a statue should be put up to Dalton in Throgmorton Street as he has been the principal factor in bringing it about.'[19]

With plaudits, sincere or otherwise, ringing in his ears from all sides, Dalton decided by the autumn of 1946 to go for broke and convert 3 per cent Local Loans into a 2½ irredeemable Treasury stock. Within hours of the announcement, on 16 October, Dalton was addressing the City's assembled bankers at the Mansion House. It was a speech that lacked nothing in bounce, as the Chancellor repudiated recent suggestions that his cheap money policy had been made possible only by large-scale intervention in the market, compared explicitly his newly announced move to Goschen's historic conversion operation in 1888, and generally called on the City to continue to show all its time-honoured 'skill and experience' on behalf of the national economic cause.[20] There was, the market rapidly decided, only one possible name for the new 2½ stock: 'Daltons'.

Immediate City response was mixed, but the financial press made an almost unanimous dead set. According to *The Economist*, it was asking investors 'to give a complete hostage to the policy of ultra-cheap money for a generation', while the *FT* even started to quarrel with the cheap money policy as a whole, calling it 'a powerful discouragement to thrift'. However, the most compelling attack came from Wilfred King in the *Banker*, as he appraised 'The Modern Goschen'. Amidst much technical refutation, he argued that this latter-day statesman was asking investors to assume not only 'that Governments for a generation and more to come will always rely, and rely successfully, upon physical control to maintain equilibrium whenever demand for capital outruns supply', but also 'that the Governments of the future will never return to the classical policies that were abandoned in 1932, but, through good times and bad, will ever eschew the interest rate as an instrument of economic control'. The strong instinct of Dalton and his colleagues, King implicitly maintained, might be to consign traditional monetary policy to the dark ages of Norman, but there was no guarantee how long that instinct would continue to prevail. In short, 'The fate of gilt-edged investors now turns absolutely on the whim of the Chancellor, on the scale and direction of his operations.'[21] The attack hit home, and by the end of the year it was clear that, despite heavy government propaganda, 'Daltons' would be at best only a very qualified success.

The new stock, following the end of the tap, was floated in January 1947 – just as a memorable winter was about to take grip, leading to the fuel crisis and an annus horribilis for the Labour government, culminating in August in the unavoidable crisis caused by the short-lived, US-enforced convertibility of sterling. Even 8 Bishopsgate suffered. 'Life here is quite impossible', Evelyn Baring reported to Al Gordon of Kidder Peabody in mid-February. 'From 9 to 12 and 2 to 4 we work in the dim glow of candlelight or nightlight.' A colleague, Villiers, looked at the broader aspect of the fuel crisis: 'The immediate effect is to put thousands of fellows out on the street at a peculiarly unpleasant time for them, because the weather is very cold and most of their homes are very badly off for fuel. To some extent, it is their own fault for having deserted Churchill even before the war ended – a most ungrateful thing to have done. Even in this wicked world, ingratitude seldom pays.' By early March the big freeze had still not relented, and at about that time Oscar Hobson ran into Norman (three years before his death) on the steps of the Athenaeum. The financial journalist made some remark about the difficulties of the economic situation and the possibility of stricter rationing of food. 'Yes,' Norman replied, 'I think grub will be short.'[22]

By the summer, confidence was rapidly waning in Dalton's policy – in the Treasury and in the Bank, as well as in the City at large – and it was clear that 3 per cent, not 2½ per cent, represented a realistic floor for cheap money. Dalton would later blame the City (and its helpmate the financial press) for having sabotaged his policy, while at the Bank of England the effect was merely to intensify already well-entrenched suspicions about academics and intellectuals getting involved in the practical niceties of market matters.[23] So much turned, in retrospect, on October 1946 and the creation of 'Daltons': the product of a finance minister in the throes of hubris and an uncertain, newly nationalised central bank unable to restrain him.

In relation to the City, he lost the important battles, and somehow it was a suitably bathetic end. Going into the Commons on 12 November 1947 to deliver his Budget, he absent-mindedly leaked a secret to the

Star's lobby correspondent and the following day was compelled to resign. During the speech itself he had turned to his proposed fiscal changes with the remark that 'it is past four o'clock and the Stock Exchange will soon be shut'. To which a Tory MP gleefully cried out: 'It closes at three o'clock.' City reaction to the resignation was summed up by Villiers a week later: 'He was an unpopular figure and there were not many regrets, although I think he got a little sympathy because he made a clean breast of his stupidity and no one made a penny through his indiscretion.'[24]

The new Chancellor was Stafford Cripps, whom the City instinctively found preferable to his hectoring predecessor. Indeed, by this time the City as a whole was probably feeling less threatened by Attlee's government than at any time since its formation. Physical controls over the economy were easing, the Marshall Plan was about to swing into action and 'the carrot-crunching Cripps' (as Brendan Bracken liked to call him) was a not wholly unpopular figure. He tacitly accepted that 3 per cent rather than 2½ per cent constituted 'cheap money', had a perceptibly more relaxed attitude than Dalton's towards the gilt-edged and discount markets and in April 1948 produced a Budget that won broad praise from the *Banker*, above all for its deflationary implications.

Inflation would be a great post-war fact of life, invariably raising the question of how to control it, and it could be argued that the original modern monetarist was the Labour minister Douglas Jay.[25] As Economic Secretary, he argued forcibly from late 1947 in favour of reducing the money supply, partly through keeping a tight rein on the advances made by clearing banks. During the first half of 1948 the Bank made little more than non-committal noises, while the volume of bank advances and deposits steadily grew. Robert Hall, who since the previous year had been running the government's Economic Section (and keeping an invaluable diary), was in a scathing mood by September:

> There is quite a hunt going on against the Bank over the increase in deposits . . . The Bank tends to the early 19th century heresy that because prices are rising therefore more money is needed. It is astonishing to find this view held in 1948. But the whole relationship is astonishing, especially after the nationalisation of the Bank by Dalton. If ever there was anything done for show, not for effect, this is it.[26]

The political temper was starting to rise, and in late November the first meeting was held, under Jay's chairmanship and involving Bank as well as Treasury representatives, of a Working Party on Bank Deposits and Advances. Its recommendation, pushed strongly by Hall, was for a ceiling on bank advances – a recommendation far from the taste of the Bank. 'The more I think about it,' Cobbold wrote to the ailing Catto on 8 December, 'the less do I like any idea of trying to limit advances by asking the banks to keep down to certain figures. If it is necessary from the angle of credit policy to try to keep advances down, I still believe that the only satisfactory way is the old-fashioned one of making borrowing more expensive.' That 'old-fashioned' approach was of course, in Labour's eyes, fatally tarnished by its association with Norman and interwar monetary policy; but Catto on his sickbed was not deterred from writing to Cripps in the strongest terms shortly afterwards. It was with 'the utmost alarm' that he viewed the suggestion for 'a ceiling for deposits and advances', being 'not practical' and likely to 'land us in a mess of violent deflation'. And, in distinctly intemperate language, he declared that 'it is an entire fallacy to suppose that pressure from the Bank of England on the banks could rectify inflationary pressure which comes from overgearing the country's economy'.[27] No doubt Catto genuinely believed the macroeconomic truth of that argument, but almost certainly what he and Cobbold were at least as concerned about was the threat posed by the quantitative 'ceiling' approach, not only to the workings of the banking system, but also to the Bank's own powers of moral suasion over that system – powers that relied heavily on discretion and judgement rather than directives and figures.

By Christmas a compromise had been reached, and it largely ceded to Catto's standpoint. During 1949 the growth in the money supply was checked, not really thanks to the Bank, and the controversy over credit policy temporarily abated. But as Jay's working party faded into obscurity, unmourned by the Bank, the reality was that there had been no fundamental tightening up of the mechanism of bank credit, and in somewhat bitter retrospective mood Hall noted in September 1949 that 'we have been defeated by the direct cowardice or else disingenuousness of Cobbold, whose people have on several occasions agreed to do something and then gone back on it'.[28] Government, the Bank and the banks: a triangular saga was only just beginning.

Cobbold himself, after four years as a particularly strong deputy governor, had succeeded Catto in March 1949. There had been other possibilities (including Bolton), but it was hardly a shock appointment. His office had been next to Norman's, with a connecting door, and from the time Cobbold became an executive director in 1938 he was generally seen as Norman's anointed. An empiricist to his fingertips, Cobbold's ultimate strength was that he had a sense of proportion and slept well at night. Few in the post-war City – still a profoundly non-intellectual place – would have wished for a different sort of governor. Altogether more resonant, in City terms, was the appointment of Michael Babington Smith, deputy chairman of Glyn Mills, to the Court in March 1949. He thereby became the first clearing banker, albeit not from one of the Big Five, to be a Bank director at the same time.[29] Little fuss, however, was made – itself a reflection of how, since far-reaching internal changes initi-ated between the wars, power in the Bank rested almost wholly with the full-timers.

*

Following devaluation in September 1949 – a belated recognition of ser-iously weakened British economic and financial power – the vexed matter of sterling and its future was never far from thoughtful minds. Significantly, the European Payments Union eventually came to fruition in 1950, with little thanks to the Bank of England, whose attitude during the protracted negotiations was almost uniformly suspicious and negative.[30] 'The special position of sterling has virtually disappeared', Bolton complained in June 1950 about the emerging European dispensation; while in the apt words of John Fforde, looking back on the late 1940s when the negotiations began, 'it no doubt required a considerable effort of mental adjustment in London, the centre of the sterling world, to accept that the tune should at this time be called by a minor power like Belgium'. In the City, as in British politics at large, there was an almost automatic assumption during these post-war years that questions of Empire and sterling area had a higher importance and priority than those of Europe. Typically, one of the few who questioned that assumption was Warburg. 'After the Second World War,' he recalled some thirty years later, 'I said to everyone – I even put it in writing – that we have become a debtor nation instead of a creditor nation, and a reserve currency status doesn't make sense for a debtor country. It's a very expensive luxury for us to have.' Had the Bank of England appreciated that viewpoint? 'No, the Governor of the Bank of England at the time didn't like this statement at all, it was against the general view.'[31]

Such was the background – the assumption that sterling and the sterling area represented Britain's financial ticket to the world's top table – as the City met the outbreak of the Korean War in summer 1950. The Labour government's response until January 1951 was hugely to increase the country's rearmament programme, a policy whose economic wisdom the City never seems to have challenged, to judge by the compliant tone of the *FT*. In fact, not only were there very adverse effects on domestic investment and consumption, but international confidence in sterling began yet again to erode. During the first nine months of 1951 various ideas flew around the Bank and elsewhere – of further revaluing the sterling–dollar exchange rate, of floating the pound – but for the moment the general preference, on the whole shared by a politically enfeebled government, was to avoid drastic action.[32]

Hugh Gaitskell had become Chancellor in October 1950, and during his year in that office, under the economic shadow of the Korean War, he came under considerable pressure from the Bank to strengthen sterling and check inflation by sanctioning an increase – albeit modest – in Bank rate.[33] He gave no ground, and instead pushed – as Cripps had done in the late 1940s – for a greater degree of co-operation within the banking system in restricting the increase in advances. The arch-Wykehamist among post-war politicians, Gaitskell had been ever less impressed by the men from the east. 'I must say', he wrote about Cobbold in his diary on 10 January, 'that I have a very poor opinion not only of him – he is simply not a very intelligent man – but of also most of the people in the Bank. Whether they are right or not in matters of judgment, they are singularly bad at putting their case, and judging by experience they are usually wrong in their conclusions.'[34]

Lack of harmony in the policymaking sphere reflected the continuing gulf between Labour and the City. The latter rightly suspected that the sands of time were running out for the people's party. A general election was called for 25 October 1951. 'The market reaction', noted the stockbrokers Read, Hurst-Brown & Co., 'was one of immediate relief at the prospect of the end of the Socialist discrimination against the investor and the still-birth of dividend limitation.' Three days before polling day, while the Stock Exchange Council was failing to come to a decision over the momentous question of whether the waiters should revert to the pre-war practice of wearing top hats, the Bank's Kenneth Peppiatt wrote to 'Gus' Ellen, formerly of Union Discount, asking him to call on the 24th. 'Perhaps I should add that I do not wish the fact you are coming to see me to be known to your old friends at the UD!' With the imminent prospect of a Conservative government, Cobbold had every hope of something like a return to what he regarded as proper monetary policy, and Ellen's guidance was required in relation to the very rusty mechanism for Bank-rate changes. On the night of the 25th and the day after, the *FT* sponsored a large election results board near the Royal Exchange, and crowds of City workers thronged the streets to cheer Churchill home.[35] The six-year nightmare was over.

CHAPTER THIRTY-TWO

Sterling Assumptions

The stockbrokers S. C. Maguire & Son, despatching their regular *Monthly Financial Report* shortly after the Tories returned to power, took an unashamedly global perspective. 'Considerable importance should be attached to the psychological result of the Socialist defeat,' they proclaimed, 'to the substantial recovery of confidence in Britain which will spread all over the world, and to the lifting of frustration and defeatism at home. We shall regain confidence in ourselves and we shall be welcomed back to play what part we can in world leadership.' Nevertheless, it would not all be plain sailing, for 'ever since 1940 we have been out on a spending spree' and consequently 'seldom has any new administration inherited so appalling a legacy'. The new Chancellor was 'Rab' Butler – to the disappointment of the City, which had hoped for its own man, the more right-wing Oliver Lyttelton.[1]

In the day-to-day world, away from high policy, the City gradually returned to something approximating normality. Even under Labour, early in 1951, the cocoa and tea markets had reopened, while that December the new Conservative government reopened the foreign exchange market. By the end of 1953 most of the remaining commodity markets had reopened, followed in March 1954 by the gold market. On the Stock Exchange the mood of confidence became such that, despite continuing restrictions on new issues, the FT 30-Share Index rose from 103 in June 1952 to 224 by July 1955. Overall, the City's contribution to Britain's invisible earnings almost tripled between 1946 and 1956, up from £49m to £145m.[2] A success story, of a phoenix rising from the ashes, was in the making.

Nevertheless, the City was only starting to recover as an international financial centre.[3] Exchange control was still in place; sterling was less than robust and prone to sudden collapses of international confidence; and London's historical role as an exporter of capital barely functioned. There were other troubling trends. The City's post-war recovery as a trading centre was at best patchy and temporary; the futures markets in commodities were starting to be outstripped by international rivals, especially the markets in New York and Chicago; foreign exchange dealing, pending the full convertibility of sterling, stagnated for most of the decade; and insurance, always a key sector in terms of the City's earnings, was in relative decline internationally.[4] Nor was the City of the 1950s, if looked at more anthropologically, permeated by that 'independent, competitive spirit' that Lionel Fraser fondly imagined as he sought to defend its reputation before the bar of public opinion. 'One of the dominant attitudes in the City is tolerance towards mediocrity', Siegmund Warburg noted bitterly in 1956, and he was right. Or as another outsider, an American banker who in the 1950s served a London apprenticeship at Morgan Grenfell, remembered wryly rather than affectionately: 'By Thursday afternoon at four, one of the senior partners would come across to the juniors and say, "Why are we all still here? It's almost the weekend."'[5] The work ethic was more pronounced at the clearing banks, but there was little excitement in the air.[6] 'It was like driving a powerful car at twenty miles an hour', Sir Oliver Franks recalled about his eight years as chairman of Lloyds Bank. 'The banks were anaesthetised – it was a kind of dream life.'[7]

Overall, the relationship between bankers and the Bank may not have been one of equals – Anthony Tuke, chairman of Barclays, would compare it to 'the type of co-operation which exists between a headmaster and his prefects', namely 'a bit one-sided' – but there is no doubt that both parties were essentially content.[8] At one level it was underpinned by the hierarchical, even public-school code of that era; at another, it allowed the banks access to government via the Bank with an ease and speed denied to most interest groups; and for the nationalised Bank, its combined role of sole spokesman for, and de facto regulator of, the City did much to fortify its potentially endangered authority. All in all, then, it was a snug set-up: insular, personalised and deeply resistant to change.

For Cobbold, as for the City at large, an important aspect of the Conservative Party's return to power was its commitment to denationalise the recently nationalised steel industry.[9] Mindful, however, that there would be nothing to stop a future Labour government renationalising steel, the task of selling off the industry to British investors was not the City's dream ticket. 'Barings and Morgans feel that this is all difficult and intensely political', Cobbold noted in November 1951, following a visit from Peacock exactly a week after the election.[10]

During 1952 the Bank obdurately resisted the idea of sponsoring the issues, until at last in April 1953, with the bill denationalising steel about to receive the Royal Assent, the City was compelled to get its act together, under Cobbold's firm, not entirely unsympathetic leadership. The next six months were taken up with the all-important preliminaries, with the attitude of the institutions (above all the insurance companies and investment trusts) throughout seen as critical to the chances of the operation's success. The price for the first of the steel sell-offs, United Steel, was set at 25s a share (politically too low, thought the Treasury; dangerously high, thought the bankers, but in fact more than adequately discounted); the institutions played the game, subscribing in strength ahead of the public flotation; and the issue as a whole was oversubscribed three times.

Unfortunately, especially for the many small investors, United Steel shares soon went to a discount, largely through a shortage of buying orders from the institutions, still nervous about possible renationalisation. Moreover, 'the Pru', Cobbold was told on 20 November, 'are talking about cutting their participation in future steel underwriting arrangements'. Early in 1954, although the Bank of England acted as a longstop in the underwriting, the Lancashire Steel Corporation's offer engendered a disappointing response. A pause for reflection ensued. 'We spoke about Steel,' Cobbold noted in late February after seeing Butler, 'and agreed that it should be left to simmer for a bit and that there was nothing to be gained by rushing any fences.' Two months later, in discussion with Sir George Erskine of Morgans, Cobbold agreed to 'have a word with the Chairman of the Pru'; and in June, helped by a bull market, the successful issue of Stewarts & Lloyds marked the turning point in the steel denationalisation programme. When an offer was made early in 1955 of ten million ordinary shares of Colville's, as many as 150,000 applications were received for a total of 130 million shares.[11] This completed the sale of six of the biggest newly privatised steel companies; in all, although Erskine's invention of a system of irrevocable applications by underwriters had been immensely helpful, it had been a triumph for the old-style City, dominated by the elite merchant banks and led from the front by a Bank of England governor possessing considerable force of personality.

Almost concurrent with the selling of steel was the rise of the 'takeover' (the term itself coming into general usage in 1953) and the City's rather muddled response to this disturbing phenomenon.[12] The disclosure aspects of the 1948 Companies Act, enabling would-be corporate predators to make more accurate financial estimates, reduced dividend pay-outs to shareholders as a result of increased company taxation since the war, and the natural appeal to shareholders of tax-free capital gains – these, among other factors, fuelled the coming of the takeover bid. Its most proficient exponent during the 1950s was that pragmatic, hard-bitten outsider Charles Clore. A biographer's phrases are striking. He possessed an 'utterly ruthless honesty'; his will had 'the force of granite'; a pair of 'cobalt eyes made people cringe'; and 'he expected the worst of people and was rarely surprised'. An entirely self-made man (the son of Russian Jewish immigrants), he was in his late forties by 1953 and had made most of his money in property. At this stage he had relatively few friends in the City, apart from Philip Hill and the stockbrokers Sebags. The City, however, was compelled to take notice of him that January and February, as he made a contested bid for J. Sears & Co., parent company of Freeman, Hardy & Willis. Investment Registry (based in the West End) acted for him; and amidst much press attention and the despatch of rival circulars to shareholders, Clore's offer proved too good to refuse. The valedictory words of the departing Sears chairman were eloquent: 'We never thought anything like this would happen to us.'[13]

*

'Market Boom Goes On' was the *Banker*'s headline in May 1954, with the magazine warning that 'the optimists in the markets would do well to remember that, at these speeds and these altitudes, the stresses are apt to be both severe and unforeseen'. Four months later Cobbold had 'a gossip' with Sir John Braithwaite, chairman of the Stock Exchange. 'I asked whether he was concerned about speculative positions. He agrees that there are signs of rather more speculation than he would like but he cannot put his finger on any danger spots and is keeping his fingers crossed.' The forces were gathering for a pre-election boom, and some weeks later Cobbold told Butler that he was 'a little bothered' about the 'atmosphere of complacency which showed signs of developing'. He went on, 'I was all for an optimistic view but was nervous about ideas which seemed to be gaining ground that increasing prosperity is certain and that there is no reason why anybody should work too hard or be content with their present reward.' The less moralistic *FT*, however, was sanguine, declaring on New Year's Day that 'with the monetary weapon available to check inflation', Butler in his Budget (due as usual in the spring) would be able to concentrate on reductions in taxation, in the long run 'the best incentives to higher production and increased productivity'.[14] Expansion without tears, boom without bust, go without stop: the tantalising chimera of post-war British economic life was making the first of what would become regular appearances. With monetary policy charged at the start of 1955 with turning that chimera into reality, Cobbold found himself in an unenviable position.[15]

A couple of Bank rate rises took some of the immediate heat out of the situation, but on the same day as the second rise, 24 February, the governor warned Butler that other, non-monetary measures were needed – in order, it did not need to be spelled out, to protect sterling, keep control over inflation and avert a balance-of-payments crisis. Yet could more be done on Cobbold's own patch? Hall certainly thought so, arguing forcibly in early March that credit policy needed to be tightened and, pregnantly, that 'if a central bank has not got adequate powers to control the other banks, it undoubtedly ought to have such powers'. Hall's memo was for the Chancellor, and Butler informed Cobbold at the start of April that 'some of his Treasury advisers were critical of the Clearing Banks and doubtful whether credit policy was working through quickly enough'. The two met again soon afterwards, when Butler 'again referred to the Treasury's anxieties about credit policy but added that he was not bothered himself'.[16] Bank advances might have been rising twice as fast as in 1954, but Butler had no desire to trespass in Cobbold's domain.

He had, anyway, a politically very sensitive Budget on his mind. On 15 April the new prime minister, Eden, announced the date of the general election (26 May), and four days later Butler proceeded to cut the standard rate of income tax by sixpence, while publicly pinning his faith on 'the resources of a flexible monetary policy' in order to counterbalance this fiscal generosity. Cobbold's unease can only have deepened, especially in the light of his conversation the previous day with Lord Aldenham and David Robarts of the clearing bankers. The banks, they complained to him, were 'finding great difficulty in practice in selecting what sort of advance they ought to restrict', to which Cobbold responded by saying that although he 'recognised the difficulties', he had 'heard a good deal of gossip round the place that there was little or no change in the attitude of the banks towards lending', and he 'thought this ought to be put right'. Next day Peppiatt glossed Cobbold's note of that exchange: 'If they want HMG (present and future) to run their business, this is the way to go about it. The banks should read the signals themselves and act accordingly.' Hall laid the blame elsewhere. 'The Bank of England haven't been as co-operative on monetary policy as they might have been', he wrote in his diary on Budget day. 'They have never been too keen on being tough with the banks. Now the Governor tells the Chancellor that he is being tough with them, but Oliver Franks tells me that this is not so.' Hall added ominously that 'altogether we are working up to some sort of *éclaircissement* with the Governor, but whether the Chancellor will support us I don't know – he has always felt that the Governor is in the saddle and that it is a very serious thing to disagree with him.'[17]

Conscious of the imminent election and anxious not to see a change of government, the City's response to Butler's giveaway Budget was broadly to cross its fingers and hope. 'The Chancellor was right to take his risks on the side of expansion', the *FT* stated categorically; and while it did not deny Gaitskell's charge that it had been an inflationary Budget, it argued that 'as Mr Butler has been prepared to use the Bank Rate, there was no need for him to rely on the budget as the sole disinflationary influence he can exert'. At the election itself, with the stockbrokers Read, Hurst-Brown & Co. warning that in the event of a Labour victory 'the rentier could safely expect treatment which would make Dr Dalton's efforts look like those of a clumsy amateur', the Conservatives – to the City's general relief – increased their majority.[18] Butler's Budget had achieved its political task.

The City's post-election reckoning came soon, in the face of renewed inflationary and balance-of-payments pressures during the summer. In August the practice began of the Bank providing each week a report on the general money-market position, especially the Bank's own operations in it, with the chief cashier (O'Brien) coming to the Treasury each Monday to discuss it. Nonetheless, as the Treasury's Sir Herbert Brittain noted, the purpose of these weekly discussions was 'for our education only', and 'we should not appear to question or criticise the Bank's management of the market'.[19]

By the autumn, the inadequacy of Butler's reliance on monetary policy alone had been exposed by the emergency Budget that, following severe pressure on sterling, he delivered in late October. Cuts in government expenditure did not, however, take the spotlight off the monetary aspect, and on being told by the Treasury in early November that ministers were 'critical' of the way in which the credit squeeze was being implemented by the clearing banks, Cobbold responded strongly that 'in the last few months they had done much more than anybody else to fight inflation'. Nor did he believe that the emergency package was enough, telling Butler on 10 November that he 'continued to feel doubts whether it was possible to run a defence programme and a social programme of the present size at the same time, without keeping the economy overloaded'.[20] Increasingly, East End was telling West End how to run its affairs, and vice versa: an unhappy situation. The Treasury more or less believed that it and Butler had been the victims of a tacit conspiracy between the Bank and the banks not to implement credit policy with sufficient stringency, while the City despaired about what it saw as government profligacy.

Harold Macmillan, who succeeded Butler as Chancellor shortly before Christmas, had watched with interest as the events of 1955 unfolded – in particular, the tax-cutting Budget of April and the ensuing widely believed accusation that it had been designed solely for electoral purposes. 'I do not think it really was that', Macmillan reflected after becoming Chancellor. Rather, 'it was due to ignorance, lack of proper statistical information, bad Treasury advice, a weak Governor of the Bank, & resistance of the Clearing Bankers'.[21]

*

'Besought him not to make a lot of speeches or talks to journalists & to drop veiled threats of "tightening the credit squeeze"', Cobbold recorded on 6 January 1956 after one of his first talks with the new Chancellor. 'Can he not invent a new catchword & stop talking about "inflation" which nobody understands?' The suspicion between these two Old Etonians was mutual. 'I find the Governor of the Bank rather hard to pin down to any definite decisions', Macmillan noted some days later. 'It is essential that the "credit squeeze" sh^d be operated with ever increasing effect during the next few weeks.'[22]

The new Chancellor, with his expansionary instincts, must have been feeling distinctly boxed in, and relations between the two men continued to be strained. 'The Governor is putting a fast one over me, I fear', Macmillan noted in early May after a further discussion on the vexed issue of liquidity ratios. 'Anyway, I want to know more before I commit myself.' That question was temporarily settled by late June, when a joint Treasury/Bank working party ruled out the concept, unless in an emergency, of a prescribed liquidity ratio. Instead, it would be business (since July 1955) as usual, with the banks being asked to go on with the squeeze. Macmillan accepted this verdict, but informed Cobbold on 4 July of the price for his assent. 'I want to see & talk to the Clearing Bankers myself', Macmillan wrote in his diary later that day. 'Mr Governor does not like this, as he regards himself as the right person to deal with the Clearing Banks. We compromised. He will see them, & tell them my wishes this week. I will see them later on in the month.' The encounter duly took place on the 24th. 'At 4 p.m. 17 Bankers came to the Treasury', Macmillan recorded. 'This is without precedent, I am told. I made them a speech & then there was quite a good discussion. Some of them asked some good questions; others were puerile. It took just over an hour & the communiqué was agreed.'[23]

Within days of that meeting, however, all such matters were put into a state of suspended animation by President Nasser's nationalisation of the Suez Canal Company.[24] 'The Prime Minister has defined his policy as one of firmness,' the *FT* observed with approval on the 28th, and over the succeeding weeks and months the broad consensus in the City seems to have been that if necessary the West would have to use force against Nasser.

In the Stock Exchange the intense volatility in the oil market was more than made up for by the huge turnover. 'I remember never looking up from my book booking bargains from ten o'clock through till two o'clock', Brian Peppiatt recalled about his time as a blue button with Akroyd & Smithers, which had recently merged with the major oil jobbers Blackwell. 'There was no question of going to the loo or having a cigarette or anything, you were just absolutely glued there, but it was an immensely exciting time.'

Military action began on 31 October but ended after only a week, as a result of intense financial as well as political pressure on Britain from the United States. As early as 1 November the discount market was told by Cobbold that 'the pressure on Sterling was considerable and that he didn't wish it to continue in this way for 365 days in the year'.[25]

Suez marked, with brutal clarity, the end of Britain as a world power.

It also cost Britain, between 30 October and 8 December, $450m of reserves. A week later, on the 15th, the *FT* asked two crucial long-term questions about sterling and its role: 'The first is whether the extent of Britain's banking commitments through sterling is not excessive in comparison to the country's real economic power and resources. The second is whether British economic policy is not now too much influenced by attempts to calculate the reactions of foreign exchange dealers to British policy.' Yet in Cobbold's eyes – as in the City's generally – there could be no thought of answering either question in the affirmative. 'The feeling of the markets both here and abroad is quite clear', he unequivocally told Macmillan five days later:

> They do not anticipate early devaluation. But they have been shocked by the weakness exposed by recent developments and they have their eyes firmly fixed on what they regard as three question marks; our willingness to live within our means, our overseas commitments and our productive capacity (or will to work). Unless these questions are answered to their satisfaction, the underlying pressures will remain against us and will become stronger.

And, having identified the holding of the currency with the maintenance of 'our way of life', Cobbold ended his letter by asserting that 'we are, I believe, at a cross-road, where the whole future of sterling, and everything which that implies, depends on the decisions of the next few months'.[26]

Macmillan, as requested, showed the letter to Eden, who responded shortly after Christmas. After acknowledging that during the crisis Britain had been at the mercy of an international loss of confidence in sterling, and conceding the problems of going any further with either the credit squeeze or public expenditure cuts, Eden threw out an idea perhaps more in hope than in expectation:

> We should ask the Governor whether there is any means of reducing our vulnerability to the 'confidence factor'. This inevitably springs from our position as bankers for the sterling area. As such we no doubt derive benefits. But do these offset the damage our reserves suffer when sterling is under pressure? The gains we painfully win from improved trading returns vanish almost overnight. Is there any way of meeting this?
> Why must sterling continue always to bear all of these burdens?

Macmillan's reply on New Year's Eve was wonderfully laconic:

> There is no way of avoiding the dangers to sterling which come from being bankers to the sterling area. We have inherited an old family business which used to be very profitable and sound. The trouble is that the liabilities are four times the assets. In the old days a business of this kind, like Coutt's or Cox's Bank, would have been sold to one of the big five. The trouble is I do not know who is to buy the sterling area banking system . . . So we must either carry on the business with all its risks, or wind it up and pay 5s in the £.[27]

Macmillan may have seen the sterling area as an inescapable deadweight – but at least, unlike almost everyone in the City, he did see it as a deadweight. There, one of the few notable exceptions was, typically, Sir George Bolton, who by the end of the Suez crisis was starting to believe that sterling's days as a major international currency were numbered and that the City of London would have to reinvent itself for a post-sterling future.[28] Early in 1957 he left the Bank of England, after a quarter of a century, and became chairman of the Bank of London and South America (BOLSA). Bolton's perception was probably shared by Siegmund Warburg, but in almost all other minds the City's fortunes remained inextricably entwined with those of sterling and the sterling area.

*

To the City's satisfaction (according to Cobbold), it was Macmillan, not Butler, who succeeded Eden as prime minister on 10 January 1957. The move had a significant City repercussion, for one of Macmillan's Cabinet appointments was the Earl of Perth (formerly Lord Strathallan) of Schroders. It proved a crystallising moment for that bank, which had been having problems at the highest level.[29] Almost certainly Perth had done more than either Henry Tiarks or Helmut Schroder to rebuild the business since the war – and there is no doubt that his surprise call to the political colours left the partnership (as it still was, though the firm was about to be incorporated) in something of a hole.

The saviour was a man without a drop of City blood in his veins. Born in Nottingham in 1915, the son of a well-off local provision merchant, Gordon Richardson read law at Cambridge before becoming a successful London counsel specialising in company law. In 1955 he decided to try his luck in the City, going to the Industrial and Commercial Finance Corporation chaired by William Piercy. Such was his immediate impact there that by the following year Piercy, in conversation with Cobbold, was identifying Richardson as a possible successor. That, however, did not materialise – partly because of Piercy's unwillingness to step down, and partly for reasons recorded later in 1956 by Humphrey Mynors after a conversation with 'Ruby' Holland-Martin. Richardson, it had transpired, 'is not happy to end his days with ICFC', apparently on the grounds that 'it is not the kind of business nor does he in general meet the sort of people which he hoped for when he left the Bar'. Accordingly, 'E.H.-M. asked me to bear in mind that he would be on the transfer list'. It was much to Helmut Schroder's credit that, at this difficult and important moment in his family firm's history, he decided to recruit at a very senior level someone of Richardson's background. 'There was something very agreeable about Schroders', Richardson himself recalled. 'I talked to the people and they were very nice, and of course it was after the German debt settlement so the agonies, so to speak, were over. The situation offered a tremendous challenge.'[30] In other words, a berth at Schroders offered a potential passport to the innermost circles of the City in a way that even being the chairman of ICFC never could.

The contrast between Schroders and Rothschilds, which had been going through a not dissimilar crisis, was illuminating. Rothschilds' troubles began in June 1955, when the senior partner, Anthony de Rothschild, had a severe stroke. 'I took the opportunity of saying to Lord Ashburton', Cobbold recorded some weeks later, 'that I hoped Barings (who are their oldest friends) would hold Rothschilds' hand a bit during this awkward time. He said they were conscious of the difficulty and would certainly do their best.' During the autumn it became clear that Anthony would never return to work. The problem was that the only other partner, his nephew Edmund, had plenty of energy but was not regarded in the City as a heavyweight. Over the past few years he had been much involved with the British Newfoundland Corporation (Brinco), which would ultimately lead to a massive hydroelectric project at the Churchill Falls; but reports filtering back to the Bank of England were less than complimentary about his role, not least when Sir John Woods of English Electric described him to Mynors in October 1956 as 'a headache' and 'a pain in the neck to the local management'. Edmund de Rothschild himself recognised some of his limitations, but it was still an awkward position in which the bank found itself, as ever refusing to bring in partners from outside the family. Granted that deep-seated obstinacy, Cobbold and Peacock agreed in November 1956 that 'there was for the moment nothing to be done', though fortunately 'it seemed that the younger Rothschilds were shaping gratifyingly well'.[31] No doubt they were, but Schroders had the right of it in their respective attitudes to new blood.

Nine months after Macmillan took office, September 1957 saw not only the imposition by Chancellor Peter Thorneycroft of a 7 per cent Bank rate (leading to a high-profile inquiry into the reputed 'leak' of the news), but also the temporary forbidding of London banks to use sterling to finance third-party trade. Dollar deposits had already been mounting up in Paris and London – in part reflecting the Cold War reluctance of Soviet and East European banks to trust their dollars to New York – and it was these dollars that some of London's banks, with the encouragement of the Bank of England, now sought to use in order to keep intact their trade finance business. Such, in a nutshell, were the 1957–8 origins of what would become known as the Eurodollar market.[32]

One of its pioneers was Bolton, who early on spotted the potential of Eurodollars: partly to enable him to transform BOLSA from a regional (South American) bank to an international bank, as he would later put it; and partly because he believed, or at least was starting to believe, that

Eurodollars might give the City an international future in a world after sterling. It was not an inevitable outcome. In terms of the financing of trade between foreign countries, 'the natural solution' – the evergreen Paul Einzig, one of the earliest chroniclers of the Eurodollar market, commented in 1964 – 'would have been for New York banks to seize upon the opportunity to take London's place'. However, 'generally speaking, American banks were kept too fully occupied with expanding domestic credit requirements to be too keen on increasing their foreign commitments suddenly and substantially'; 'nor were any of the continental financial centres', including most notably Paris, 'ready or able to step into the breach to anything like the full extent required'. In short, 'There was a distinct gap in the international financial machinery. In the circumstances the appearance of the Euro-dollar system was well-timed and providential.' One should not exaggerate the immediate impact. The Eurodollar system in 1957–8 was still in its infancy, operating essentially as an inter-bank deposit market; while in the apt subsequent words of one merchant banker, 'You would have drawn a fair number of glazed looks in the City if you mentioned Eurodollars in those days.'[33] Even so, what was happening was a crucial pointer – arguably, *the* crucial pointer – to the City's future.

In a more familiar market, the Stock Exchange, things were booming during most of 1958. The Thorneycroft clampdown may have taken its toll (the FT 30-Share Index lost almost nine points on 19 September 1957), but from March it was one-way traffic, with the Index bursting through its 1955 high of 223.9 by the end of the year. Cheaper money helped, as did a better-than-expected American economic backdrop, prevailing financial liberalisation and an increasing belief that Macmillan was, against the earlier odds, on course for re-election.[34]

This sustained bull market set the seal on the so-called 'cult of the equity' that had been developing during the 1950s.[35] The single figure most commonly associated with implementing it was George Ross Goobey, who became the first investment manager of Imperial Tobacco's pension fund in 1947. Soon afterwards he put his Bristol-based fund into the shares of a long string of smaller companies, attracting much publicity, which in turn helped to make the cult self-fulfilling. By 1955 some two-thirds of British company securities were being issued in the form of ordinary shares, not debt; and as the price of Consols headed ever south-wards, traditional principles of investment, based on the assumption that money would hold its value, were stood on their head. Not that the rush into equities was by any means impetuous. Even a notably progressive stockbroking firm like Phillips & Drew was distinctly cautious as, in successive editions of its brochure on *Pension Fund Investment*, it advised what percentage of a fund might legitimately be devoted to equities: 10 per cent by 1949, 20 per cent by 1952 and 35 per cent by the end of 1956.

The City's conservatism was hardly out of character. Take the experience of the young Edward du Cann, as he toured the Square Mile in search of backers for a new unit trust management company, based on the idea of – in an increasingly affluent society – popularising share ownership:

> All without exception gave the same discouraging two-part response. The first part was a flat statement that the idea was very unlikely to succeed. No one I spoke to had the least confidence in it. The second part of the response was in effect the coup de grâce: 'If this is such a good idea, Mr du Cann, pray tell us, why has no one else thought of it before?' All those I saw, merchant bankers, investment trust managers, entrepreneurs, the representatives of the UK's leading financial institutions, thirty or so in all, were plain sceptical; some were disdainful; a few were rude; all told me that my optimism was misplaced, if not foolish . . . My carefully typed prospectus grew increasingly dog-eared with repeated handling.

Unicorn Unit Trust, involving a life-assurance element, was nevertheless launched in October 1957; and despite strong criticism from actuaries it became a huge success, begetting many imitators, not least the very merchant and clearing banks that had poured scorn on the idea.[36]

Another Tory MP trying hard to convert the idea of a share-owning democracy from rhetoric into reality was Sir Alec Spearman, senior partner of the stockbrokers Grieveson Grant. Specifically he wanted the high-street clearing banks to sell share units over the counter; but in October 1957 the CEOs of the clearers voiced their opposition to this. A year later Midland's chairman, Lord Monckton, considered an internal memo on 'Trust Units':

> A degree of pressure is undoubtedly mounting to persuade Banks to undertake to sell Trust Units over their counters.
> In common with the other Banks, we have given much thought to the matter. There is sympathy with the idea of extending the investment habit over a wide field but it is felt that there are both points of principle and practical difficulties which warrant the Banks adopting a very cautious attitude to the whole subject.

One of the problems was the implied approval of the trust units being sold; another was that the sale of such units was 'not in the direct line of a Bank's business'.[37] In practice, over the next twenty years, the decline of the individual investor would be as steep as the rise of the institutional investor was irresistible. The trend would mean, among other things, that the City seemed an irrelevance in the day-to-day lives of most people.

In 1958 the financial liberalisation that was helping to fuel the bull market took various forms. One was the return of option dealing on the Stock Exchange, banned since 1939. It was an outcome that, hitherto, Braithwaite had managed to prevent – for example, in May 1953 telling the Council (as the Committee was now called) that a return to options would fortify 'the "casino" legend' surrounding the Stock Exchange, and inflict damage on 'the major policy of defending the Stock Exchange against the attempt that is sure to be made sooner or later to bring it under Government control'. In May 1958, shortly before a mass meeting of members, he told the governor that (in Cobbold's words) 'the agitation stems from only two or three people, and that any more general support is merely due to vague sentimental feelings that this is something the Stock Exchange used to be free to do, and they ought to get rid of any shackles on their freedom'. Cobbold himself reiterated to Braithwaite the Bank's opposition: 'Just at a time when the Stock Exchange are engaged in telling the public that they are not a gambling den but an essential service to British industry and public authorities, they would be most unwise to hand this particular weapon to their critics.' But later that month, the day after the meeting, Braithwaite was compelled to inform Cobbold that the Council would not be able to resist 'the overwhelming vote' in favour of restoring option-dealing facilities. 'He had considered resignation as he still takes a strong view against', noted Cobbold. 'He has, however, decided it would serve no useful purpose.' However, when option dealings did restart in October, a new rule meant that a member could deal in options only with another member – a rule that, according to a letter of complaint within days from Leon Bros and five other firms, represented a 'crippling restriction'.[38] Braithwaite had, in his final year as chairman, salvaged something.

The options story mirrored the larger problem for the authorities in 1958: how to maintain an adequate measure of control while permitting financial liberalisation. By the spring it was clear that the days were numbered for the credit restrictions that had been put in place in July 1955, in effect a self-denying ordinance on the part of the banks. With memories of that year still fresh, as well as of the subsequent sterling crisis of 1957 that had led to the dramatic rate hike, the Bank of England pinned its hopes on a scheme known as 'special deposits', a form of ratio control by which it could seek to dampen demand for credit by calling for cash deposits from the banks.[39] In late June, with the new Chancellor, Derick Heathcoat Amory, intending shortly to announce the easing of credit restrictions, Cobbold made his pitch to the clearing bankers at an informal meeting held at the Bank. Cobbold argued that if the banking system took the initiative over special deposits (something that he knew Macmillan was keenly in favour of), this would help to pre-empt future legislation 'putting banks under more direct control and some "hand in the till" machinery'.[40] The bankers reluctantly agreed to play ball and the following week, on 3 July, the Chancellor lifted the restrictions on bank lending.

An immediate aspect of the new, more liberal dispensation was Cobbold's decision to allow the clearing banks to buy into hire-purchase concerns, a very profitable, barely regulated part of the financial services sector. By the end of July, following some hectic activity, four major clearing banks had acquired stakes in hire-purchase companies. 'I was away on holiday in Wales at the time,' a prominent clearer recalled, 'and came back to find the whole bloody lot in hire purchase. They went into it like the herd of Gadarene swine.' Yet despite the buying panic – prompting the Bank's deputy governor, Mynors, to complain that the press was indulging in 'much too much ballyhoo' on the subject – it was all done with a certain air of holding a handkerchief over the nose. 'It is not ourselves engaged in the selling of hire purchase any more than we sell groceries', Tuke of Barclays announced after his bank had taken a 25 per cent stake in United Dominions Trust, apparently disreputable a quarter of a century after being blessed by Norman. Still, as Tuke himself had deathlessly observed earlier in the year: 'It is extraordinary what you can get on hire purchase these days.'[41]

Midland (jointly with its subsidiary the Clydesdale Bank) acquired a Birmingham-based hire-purchase business, Forward Trust. For Midland watchers, it was a sign that the somnolent giant (the biggest bank in the world in the 1930s) was at last starting to flex its competitive muscles, helped from July 1957 by its new chairman, the barrister-turned-politician Walter Monckton.[42] In September 1958, just two months after Heathcoat Amory's announcement, the revitalised Midland showed an impressive turn of speed, as it pioneered (in terms of high-street banks) what it called 'personal loans'. And a few days later this was followed by the introduction of a 'personal cheque account' service. With a full-time PR man appointed for the first time, Midland was leading the way in looking outwards.

'You certainly put the cat among the banking pigeons', Macmillan wrote to Monckton after the introduction of personal loans. He did not exaggerate. On 16 October, ahead of his Mansion House speech that evening, Cobbold informed Franks of Lloyds that he would be publicly welcoming the resumption by the banks of more competitive services, but added that he did not intend to suggest 'an indiscriminate "free for all"'. The next day Franks replied, 'I agree that competition between the Banks cannot be unrestricted. At the same time Banks have lost a great deal of ground over the last 25 or 30 years by not adapting themselves to changing social patterns. Also I think some response must be made to the engaging initiatives of the Midland.' The cat was indeed among the pigeons, as the other banks hastily rediscovered the joys of competition. 'There is a good deal of soreness around', Cobbold updated Heathcoat Amory later in October concerning recent banking developments, explaining that 'some people think the Midland bounced the others a bit quick and there was a major row inside Barclays about whether or not to do personal loans'. Broad-mindedly, Cobbold added his own view about the banks (which traditionally had ignored the working class) that 'the more they can attract the new highly paid classes to open bank accounts the better'.[43]

There was another part to the liberalising jigsaw: the full convertibility of sterling.[44] This was achieved, simultaneously with the French and West German currencies, on 29 December 1958. Congratulations poured in to Threadneedle Street at this hugely important moment, both symbolically and substantively, in the City's determination to reassert itself as an international financial centre. There were few notes of public dissent. Even so, earlier in 1958 a 'Penguin Special' had been published that would become very influential in starting to reshape left-of-centre economic thinking. This was *British Economic Policy Since the War*, written by Andrew Shonfield, formerly of the *FT* and now economics editor of the *Observer*. An astringent intellectual, with a Central European background, Shonfield argued strongly that – especially in the light of the financial crisis of September 1957 – the policymaking priority given to the strength of sterling and the sterling area imposed an unacceptable burden on British industry and economic growth generally. Lucidly outlining the strain on the balance of payments caused by Britain's obligations to the rest of the sterling area, and noting that 'the suggestion that the strain is worth bearing, because the sterling system somehow brings us "a great deal in the way of wealth", is a standard traditional view', Shonfield argued that in fact at least two-thirds of the City's total estimated £125m of foreign exchange earnings would remain intact, even if sterling was not a major international reserve currency. He did not deny, however, that 'what would inevitably suffer is the City's banking and acceptance business'.

In all, it was not an analysis calculated to endear Shonfield (who during the war had served in the British Army as a gunner and intelligence officer) to the authorities. In May 1958 an internal note by Mynors, shortly after the book's publication, referred caustically to 'the output associated with names like Kaldor, A. C. L. Day and Andrew Shönfeld'.[45] Either one played the game or one did not, and in that crucial respect Shonfield was found wanting.

CHAPTER THIRTY-THREE

Monkey Business

For Siegmund Warburg and his bank there remained, even as a member of the Accepting Houses Committee, no primrose path into the City's inner circle. Now, however, his historic moment was at hand.[1]

With a bull market, easier money and the clearing banks showing the way in their acquisition of hire-purchase houses, the conditions were right for a sustained wave of takeover bids. One company ripe for the plucking was British Aluminium (BA). It had never properly recovered from the war and was badly short of financial and smelting capacity. Its management in 1958 could hardly have been in more traditional hands: managing director was Geoffrey Cunliffe, son of a former governor of the Bank of England, and chairman was Lord Portal of Hungerford, Chief of Air Staff during the war and now president of MCC. The BA board realised it needed outside help, and from early summer was in negotiation with the giant Aluminium Company of America (Alcoa) about some form of partnership. These discussions were soon given added urgency as it became clear that the aggressive, expansionist Reynolds Metals of Virginia wanted to acquire BA and in particular the plant in Quebec that it had recently started to build. Reynolds' financial advisers were Warburgs, which insisted that if the bid was to succeed it would have to be made in conjunction with a British firm. The ally chosen was a Midlands-based engineering group, Tube Investments (TI), in large part the creation of the self-made Sir Ivan Stedeford. TI in turn took advice from Helbert Wagg (headed by the equally self-made Lionel Fraser) and Schroders. Together, Reynolds and TI quietly built up a 10 per cent stake in BA by the early autumn.

On 25 November, shortly before skirmishings turned to open warfare, Stedeford came at short notice to see Mynors at the Bank. 'I think his main purpose', Mynors told Sir Roger Makins at the Treasury, 'was to ensure that the Bank had his side of the story correctly, as the only direct contact on his behalf had been through Mr Grunfeld of Warburgs, who might have been misunderstood.'[2] Three days later, flanked by his advisers (the pre-eminently respectable 'inner' City houses Lazards and Hambros), Portal announced that BA had signed a contract by which Alcoa would subscribe to one-third (as yet unissued) of the company's capital at a price of 60s per share. The recently made Reynolds–TI offer, equivalent to 78s per share, was therefore deemed irrelevant. The price differential was such that it was a palpably unconvincing standpoint. Nor did it help BA's cause that Alcoa, unlike Reynolds, had as yet no clear international strategy, and that whereas Reynolds was prepared to supply the firepower (floating a new stock issue in the States in order to raise the cash), Alcoa was not.

'A great row is developing about the future of the British Aluminium Company', Macmillan noted in his diary on 2 December, adding that his Chancellor, Heathcoat Amory, owned shares in the company and accordingly was going to leave it to him to take the lead for the government. By this time it was also known that the largest single British shareholder in both BA and TI was the Church Commissioners, a fact described by Mynors as 'the only comic relief' in the situation. As the Treasury became involved – in due course deciding that BA shareholders must be allowed to consider the Reynolds–TI offer, which was open until 9 January – an impatient Warburg attempted to short-circuit the process. On 2 December he telephoned the Bank 'with a suggestion that the head of an independent City House like Barings should be consulted to express a view on the ethics of the present position as he would not expect officials in Whitehall to be able to judge on these aspects'. He was, however, politely told that 'the Bank would be able to reflect City opinion on this matter'. Next day Mynors (in the continuing absence of Cobbold) reported to the Treasury that 'City opinion dislikes the Alcoa proposal which they think has been very badly handled by the BA Board.' Over the next week or two Warburg – who had been advised by his friend Bolton to 'either fight or get out' – continued to force the pace. He telephoned the Bank again on 9 December. 'They have decided', the Bank's note of the conversation ran, 'against requisitioning a meeting of shareholders as being an unnecessary complication. They are aiming at getting a straight 51 per cent of the shares by means of the offer and Mr Warburg seems confident that he will get at least this majority because he reckons that he will get the support of the Institutional investors.'[3]

The BA board was by now very much on the back foot, so much so that on the 16th there appeared in the press the first-ever major 'defensive' advertisement against a hostile bid, a tactic that would in time become an art form. A photograph of aluminium ingots at the company's Falkirk Rolling Mills accompanied the text, which emphasised Alcoa's resources and the nationalist theme: 'British Aluminium is not "selling out to the Americans". It is going into partnership with them.' Even when Portal tried to attack, it served him ill. Thus when he rashly accused Reynolds–TI of seeking to acquire 'a powerful empire for the price of a small kingdom', many were baffled as to why in that case Alcoa should have been let in (as *The Economist* later put it) 'for the price of a minor principality'. And when he suddenly announced that, if the Alcoa deal went through, the BA board would increase its 1958 dividend from 12 to 17½ per cent, *The Times* wondered about the economic logic and remarked that such a move 'invites the criticism that the increase is solely the result of Tube Investments' intervention'.[4] What were BA's City advisers doing to help the beleaguered company? Ten days before Christmas, Mynors was put in the picture by the government broker about one aspect of the emerging line-up of forces:

> Mr Arthur Anderson (Rowe & Pitman) and Mr Antony Hornby (Cazenove's) would like it to be known here that they are Brokers to both BA and TI. They are therefore taking a neutral position and are not even sounding out institutions on what they intend to do . . .
>
> I guess that behind this lies the fact that the names of various Merchant Bankers appear on one side or another in the contest but that the Brokers appear to have been left somewhat in the cold.

Soon afterwards Anderson and Hornby called on Mynors, to whom they confirmed that 'they were not consulted by either side in the formative stages of the dispute' and that 'in the circumstances they decided that their only course was to remain completely neutral'. They added, however, that 'they were resisting some pressure that they should now appear to commend one side or the other'.[5]

They were indeed being put under 'some pressure' during what were highly charged pre-Christmas days, as Hornby subsequently related to an absent partner:

> Arthur and I were summoned to a meeting by Lazards and Hambros, at which practically all their partners were present, and we were told that in their view 'he that was not for them was against them', that they could not accept neutrality and that they must have brokers working for them, and naturally very badly wanted us. We reiterated at this meeting that they had done their best to lose us by not consulting us, because I didn't see why we should be put in the position of being 'naughty boys'. We said that we must have a little time to make up our minds, but we very soon found that our sympathies were, and had been all along, with British Aluminium, whose citadel was being stormed, and decided that we must go and tell Lionel [Fraser] that we must resign from being brokers to Tubes. This naturally was a sad thing to have to do.

Hornby added that although both Fraser of Helbert Wagg and Jock Backhouse of Schroders felt 'sore' that Cazenove's and Rowe & Pitman had not made up their minds earlier, 'this was a situation without precedent and what I have learned from it is that neutrality is untenable in this sort of affair, and Englishmen are not neutral by nature, and one simply cannot sit on a fence'.[6]

Nor were Hambros and Lazards bent merely on coercing the brokers into line. On the 22nd, Cobbold received a visit from Sir Charles Hambro and Lord (Hugh) Kindersley, who had succeeded his father as the dominant figure at Lazards:

> They went over the history of developments whilst I was away, stressing their view that HMG's attitude, whatever its intention, was having the practical effect of favouring Tube Investments at the expense of British Aluminium Board. They also stressed that Warburgs had behaved extremely badly, although they had no complaint against Helbert Wagg and Schroders who had only come at a late stage as Tube Investments' bankers and advisers.
>
> They also told me that they and others are now organising a powerful City group, which will come out shortly with a firm recommendation in favour of the Board's proposals, and with a syndicate ready to acquire a sufficient number of shares which, together with shares they know to be firmly held, would block the Tube Investments' proposal.

Cobbold himself, whatever his instinctive affinity for Hambros and Lazards and his equally instinctive distaste for Warburgs, was determined that the Bank should remain scrupulously neutral and above the fray. There matters rested over Christmas, though on the 27th Macmillan found himself shooting at Arundel in the company of, among others, Portal. BA's chairman said 'a few discreet words' to the prime minister, but according to Macmillan he understood that the government could not publicly show its hand until the shareholders had made up their minds.[7]

With rumours and counter-rumours flying around the City and the press paying considerable attention to the story, the Aluminium War (as it would become known) entered its decisive phase on New Year's Eve, a Wednesday. 'BAC/Reynolds/Tube Drama crescendo' ran Bolton's diary entry. 'S.W. continually on telephone.' Cobbold spent much of the day speaking to Kindersley and Hambro, who had duly formed a City consortium to defend BA from the unwanted attentions of Reynolds and TI. Describing it as 'a ridiculous situation, damaging to the City as a whole and to everybody concerned', Cobbold told the two merchant bankers that it was his intention to arrange a truce between the parties. In principle they were not unwilling; and on being prompted by Cobbold to talk to Stedeford, they found that he too was apparently amenable. For his part, he noted afterwards, Cobbold promised that 'whilst I could not prevent Reynolds or anybody else giving orders to Warburgs to buy shares, if TI could stop Reynolds I was prepared to see Warburgs and discourage them from any monkey business'. The word from the Treasury was also encouraging, with Makins phoning Cobbold to say that ministers 'would be pleased to see a truce'. All the governor's efforts, however, came to nought, for 'Lord Kindersley and Sir Charles Hambro telephoned at 5.30

to say that it had not proved possible to persuade the lawyers [presumably for TI] that the TI offer could be withdrawn' and that 'they therefore felt it necessary to go ahead with the banking group's offer', which 'will therefore appear in the Press tomorrow morning'.[8] It was a guarantee, Cobbold perhaps wearily reflected, that 1959 would start with a bang.

On the Thursday morning, in a circular published in all the leading papers, the great City consortium at last came out. Fourteen august houses, headed by Hambros and Lazards but also including Morgan Grenfell, Brown Shipley, Samuel Montagu and Robert Fleming (though excluding Barings and Rothschilds), publicly affirmed to BA's shareholders their support for the Alcoa solution and made a partial bid, worth up to £7m, for BA shares at 82s each, four shillings more than the Reynolds–TI offer. Why did these famous names put themselves out on such a limb? Almost certainly it was not the result of dispassionate analysis of the industrial problems facing BA, though in fact there was a perfectly good industrial case to be made for that board's preference. Nor probably was it on nationalist grounds – despite some propaganda points in the circular – for most good judges realised that, whatever the outcome, BA would effectively find itself under American control. Nor did it simply come down to a snobbish dislike of the outsiders or parvenus on the other side, above all Warburg. Hostile takeover bids were still a relative rarity, and undoubtedly there was a strong natural disposition to support the party being attacked. Hornby's dislike of BA's 'citadel' being 'stormed' was wholly genuine, and for all the widespread criticism of BA's clumsy handling of the situation, many others would have fully shared that feeling. Ultimately, on the part of the City Establishment, it was an emotional reaction in an unfamiliar, disturbing situation, reflecting an entrenched belief that, within its citadel, the board knew best. Not only Warburg, however, begged to differ; also on New Year's Day an interview appeared in the *Evening Standard* with Lionel Fraser, who condemned the consortium's action as 'unprogressive' and declared that 'the whole thing smacks of fear'.[9] So it did, and it was already apparent that the battle for BA was shaping up to be a hugely symbolic, epochal episode.

On 1 January itself the key document – indicating conclusively the destiny of the battle – was written by Makins, after Cobbold had called at the Treasury at 2.30 p.m. to give the latest news:

> Talks between TI and Hambros and Lazards went on until late yesterday evening. As a result Sir Ivan Stedeford on behalf of TI agreed not to buy any more shares. But the American Reynolds Group are buying like fury and Sir Ivan Stedeford cannot control them. Nor does the Governor feel that he can intervene to prevent the share buying activities of an American company. Meanwhile the British Consortium of Merchant Banks are holding off. They do not want to bid the shares up.

Put another way, one team and half of the other team were playing the game, but the remaining half-team was not. 'Counselled full show of compromise but no weakness' was Bolton's note of his advice that day to Warburg – presumably with the emphasis on 'show'. Cobbold may have promised to warn off Warburgs from any 'monkey business', but for whatever reason he had seemingly failed to do so. To Makins, the governor 'added that he did not quite know what the next move was'. A baffled Cobbold returned to the Bank, twice ringing the Treasury in the late afternoon to report that 'the City Group' and TI were in 'very friendly discussions', but that the problem was how to stop Reynolds buying. At the end of another difficult day he sent an identical note to Portal, Stedeford and Kindersley, as well as to the Treasury:

> The City group and TI have continued friendly discussions but cannot see a basis of solution, because of the Alcoa–Reynolds situation.
>   There seems no prospect of bringing both Alcoa and Reynolds in on terms acceptable to all parties. BA would not and probably could not drop Alcoa out of the picture. TI are not prepared to drop Reynolds out of the picture.

Accordingly, Cobbold's note ended, the City group and TI had agreed that there was no further point in continuing talks.[10]

Friday the 2nd was another hectic day, with much of the inside story revealed by Cobbold's carefully written note for the record:

> The Prime Minister proposes to take no decision before Monday. It is realised that by this time the TI/Reynolds group will have acquired a large holding by market purchases, which would make any pro Alcoa action by HMG (if they should decide in that direction) more difficult. They had seen both Stedeford and the bankers' group this morning and had cross-questioned them about assurances on British control. The more convincing assurances seemed to be forthcoming from the TI group . . .
>   Mr Warburg came in. He said that he understood I had seen Sir Ivan Stedeford and he did not therefore wish to develop their side of the case. He wanted, however, to say that if at any time I wished to hear his side of the story, he would be glad to give it to me, as he understood there was a lot of criticism of him in the City. I said that this was undoubtedly the case, but I did not wish to get into the details.

Undoubtedly the government's tacit support of the hostile bid was crucial. Its prime concern, understandably, was the future of the British aluminium industry, and on 3 January the Economic Secretary to the Treasury sent a memo to Macmillan stating that, by this criterion, the Reynolds/TI bid was preferable 'on grounds of national interest . . . mainly because legal control would remain in British hands'. A month earlier BA's managing director had expostulated to Heathcoat Amory that TI 'knew nothing about the aluminium business and the decisions would all lie with the

Reynolds Company', but clearly Geoffrey Cunliffe lacked the bullying persuasiveness of his father.[11]

Warburg's tactics were now relatively simple: not only to ensure that Reynolds–TI increased their offer (which they did, to 85s, on the 4th), but also to continue to orchestrate massive buying on the open market of BA shares, thus ensuring that their price became and stayed well above the consortium's offer. It was a strategy that depended on the willingness of the shareholders to sell and the reluctance of the consortium to mount a counter-operation in the market. Both these assumptions proved correct. Importantly, Warburg had the press on his side, especially the Beaverbrook papers. Some of the smaller sellers may have had a misguided patriotic motive, and some of the institutional sellers may have been antagonised by the consortium's rather overbearing tone, but in essence the spur was the same time-honoured one for all concerned: an eye to the main chance. Making an estimated £500,000 from selling at this propitious moment were the Church Commissioners, though the *Church Times* was unable to persuade their spokesman to divulge details.[12] What is less explicable is why – after peace discussions under Cobbold's auspices had broken down by the end of the 1st – the consortium, with its considerable resources, did not mount a serious buying operation on its own account. Perhaps Hambros, Lazards and their allies were unduly influenced by the government's refusal to back the Alcoa solution; perhaps Alcoa's own semi-reluctance in comparison to Reynolds was a further factor; and perhaps the informal steer from Cobbold was that a pitched battle in the market could only further damage the City's reputation.

'It would be a grave political error to interfere now', Macmillan privately reiterated on the 5th. 'Let the rival forces fight it out . . . It's the only safe course. But it is not a pleasant one, for I fear that a great deal of ill-feeling has resulted from the Tube Investment/Reynolds methods & a lot of our friends in the City are upset.' Next day the war was over, as Reynolds/TI achieved majority control of BA even before the postal response to its formal offer was completed. Lunching at Vickers on the 7th, Macmillan chatted to Morgan Grenfell's Lord Bicester and was 'relieved to find' that Bicester 'thought we had done quite right in letting the contestants for British Aluminium fight it out between themselves'.[13]

This presumably was a source of comfort when on the 12th *The Times* published an extraordinary letter by Olaf Hambro, declaring that the wishes of the City had been violated and roundly criticising the financial editors. This view received little sympathy from Harold Wincott in his *FT* column. He expressed astonishment at the initial remoteness shown by the BA board towards 'the man-in-the-street shareholder', who, 'given half a chance, would express his displeasure with his directors as surely as passengers on London Transport express theirs when they similarly feel they are being pushed around without being told the reason why'. Warburg considered making a public reply to Hambro, before being dissuaded by Cobbold, but the leading jobber Esmond Durlacher did enter the lists, referring in *The Times* to 'a body of men who also work in the City, men of good common sense, of good standing and probity', for whom the consortium, however impressive, had not spoken. A rising Labour politician, Anthony Crosland, argued in the same paper that during the episode the City had failed to attach enough importance to the larger economic consequences. As for the houses that had formed the unsuccessful consortium, 'Their outlook appears about as contemporary as the architectural style in which the City is now being rebuilt; both make one shudder.'[14]

Almost twenty years later Cobbold would wryly refer to the Aluminium War as 'a troublesome little trouble'. Indeed, it had, among other things, delineated as never before the limits of the governor's papal power. It would have needed a Norman to keep Warburg in check – and perhaps not even Norman could have done so. In the immediate aftermath, feelings against the German outsider continued to run high. 'I will never speak to that fellow again,' Kindersley was heard to say, and over the years it would become part of City folklore how, in a chance encounter in the street between the two men, probably on New Year's Day, he had put the question directly to Warburg, 'Are you buying shares?' and had been given the economical answer, 'No.' There was, however, one notable reconciliation. Warburg himself, in his 1980 interview, told the story:

> About three months after the British Aluminium war, a mutual friend came to see me and said, 'Olaf feels so sad that this old friendship between him and you doesn't exist any more.' I said this is nonsense. His people had behaved strangely but I have nothing against him. And this friend said, 'Oh, then would you be prepared to see him again?' I said, 'I would be delighted. In fact, I'm perfectly prepared to ring up Olaf Hambro and go to see him in his office.' So I went around to see the great Mr Olaf Hambro in his office.

> *What happened when you got there?*

> Have you ever been in Hambros? To get to his room you had to go through the big partners' room. So I came in from one side, and he came in from the other. And when we finally met in the middle of the room, he took his big arm around my shoulders – he was very tall, about three heads taller than I – and he said, 'Siegmund, haven't we been awful fools?'

> *So that was the turning point in your acceptance in the City?*

> Yes. From about that time onward, we started gradually to be recognised as members of the British establishment.[15]

Whether the recommendation to Reynolds that it acquire BA was ultimately such good advice was another matter, but unquestionably the Aluminium War established Warburg's reputation as a master financier.

It also came to be regarded as a watershed in the history of the City. Not only was it a severe blow to the prestige of the City Establishment that the consortium symbolised, but it was as if the whole atmosphere now changed, becoming altogether more competitive. 'A decisive blow had been dealt to the unhurried, "gentlemanly" style of business', was the retrospective view of Edmund de Rothschild, adding that 'for better or worse, the City never seemed to me to be quite the same again'.[16]

*

The finance of trade may have been a profitable activity, but the commercial City as a whole continued, broadly speaking, to decline during the post-war years.[17] As usual, the floor-space figures tell the story: by 1968 warehouses occupied only 13 per cent of the City's utilised space, half of the area they had occupied on the eve of war, whereas in the same period the space occupied by offices had increased from 45 to 62 per cent. The human figures are even more striking: whereas in 1911 more than 95,000 of those working in the City owed their employment directly or indirectly to the commodity markets, by the mid-1960s the comparable total was less than 44,000. An outsize shell was still proudly displayed outside the Bishopsgate offices of M. Samuel & Co., but the larger reality was that the City's character was becoming ever more financial.[18]

The two last commodity markets to be reopened were the futures markets in sugar and coffee, in January 1957 and July 1958 respectively. Both were based in Plantation House in Mincing Lane and both, as it happened, bucked the generally gloomy trend. Yet so often in the commercial sector it was an uphill struggle. The correspondence of Tribble, Pearson & Co., East India merchants since 1896, sheds some revealing light on these larger difficulties. Based at Leadenhall House, 101 Leadenhall Street, and with the portentous Geo W. Church firmly in charge, the firm plugged away through the 1950s with diminishing rewards. In February 1953 Church half-opened his heart to Messrs J. K. Doss & Group Industries of 211 Old China Bazaar Street, Calcutta:

> As you are doubtless aware, the format of business with India has considerably changed during the past 13 years, and many lines previously shipped in large quantities have ceased due to the growth of industrialisation in your Country, or curtailed on account of existing economic conditions, or restricted under present Import Licensing regulations and quotas. We have therefore been compelled to exploit many other avenues, both as regards imports to and exports from India, and although this has entailed a great deal more work which has not yet been rewarded, on the whole we are not dis-satisfied with the results to date.

Perhaps; but what Church almost invariably saw as the forces of ignorance on the subcontinent made his life no easier. 'Import Licences [i.e. in India] seem to be more plentiful,' he grudgingly conceded in March 1954 to the son of a Calcutta merchant with whom he was on good terms, 'but values constantly dwindle, and new Firms continue to come into existence with increasing regularity. Generally speaking the majority have little idea of business or of the goods for which they have been granted Licences!' Church seems to have been a well-meaning man, but often, as in a dismissive letter in October 1955 to the Madras branch of Messrs Capco Limited, his tone could descend to one of bullying paternalism:

> You will, of course, appreciate that in these days of keen competition there is not any margin left from which we can afford to grant you any return commission, let alone 3% or 5% as suggested by you, and we can only suggest that you place your orders with any of our competitors who are quoting £9. 12. 6. per ton and can also give you 3% or 5% return commission, but at this point we may state without fear of contradiction that your efforts will be unsuccessful.

The product in question was Gibbs' Brand English Powdered Whiting, a speciality of Tribble's.

In May 1958, when a complaint reached Tribble's from the merchant Sudhangshu Bimal Chowdhury, of Chittagong in East Pakistan – 'I painfully inform you that in my last consignment of 88 Cwt of Lump Chalk imported from you . . . I received less than half the quantity due to my bad luck' – Church was predictably adamant in his denial of any blame:

> Any damage sustained occurred either in transit (which is unlikely) or on discharge at Chittagong where the stevedores and dock labourers are prone to use hooks in dealing with cargo packed in sacks and paper bags . . . We can assure you that every care is taken at this end to ensure that all our shipments in such packings are delivered to the Docks and stowed on board in perfect sound condition.[19]

Yet for all his pride in the City's mercantile traditions and standards, and for all his stern words of admonition to those elsewhere, Church himself was about to sound the retreat. Shortly before the end of 1959, Tribble, Pearson & Co. left its offices in Leadenhall House and began to operate, on a reduced scale, from Church's own home at Dragonstail, 114 Creighton Avenue, East Finchley. The winds of change were blowing, the British Empire was being wound down, and London was no longer the world's commercial centre.

*

Church left behind an environment that was also starting to change fundamentally. 'After the Great Fire, Charles II called for "a much more beautiful City than is at this time consumed". After 280 years the City has a magnificent new opportunity for comprehensive rebuilding.'[20] This clarion call by *The Times*, made in August 1945 as one-third of the City lay in ruins, would have found few dissenters either then or over the next two decades. The problem, however, was how best to execute such a noble vision.

During the immediate post-war period the City Corporation's consultants for the rebuilding programme were the architect Charles Holden and the town planner William Holford. Their first report, published in 1946, fully accepted the need for a road system capable of carrying twice the existing traffic, but sought to balance the criteria of utility and beauty: 'What is now picturesque should be retained, wherever possible, no matter to what period it may belong nor how various its component elements may be; it should be swept away only to make room for a redevelopment which has equal architectural value as well as being more convenient. The City cannot afford mediocre architecture.' Indeed, if one now reads that report, together with the following year's final report and the consultants' subsequent accompanying commentary in their historically well-informed *The City of London: A Record of Destruction and Survival* (1951), one is struck by the moderation of both the tone and the proposals. 'It would not be wise', Holden and Holford declared, 'to adopt a new aesthetic and a new scale for building for the City of London until the old one has been definitely lost or outmoded; and at the present time the opinion of the authors of the plan is that the seventeenth-century scale should be preserved and that St Paul's Cathedral – the noblest in the City – should remain architecturally, as in other ways, its chief building.' Nevertheless, the latent prescription for wholesale, high-rise change was there, couched though it was in those high-minded terms so typical of the prevailing post-war climate of planning and reconstruction. Thus:

> It is not the directors, or chief officials, on the first or on the top floors of large buildings who have to be thought of, so much as the bulk of City workers – clerks, typists, warehousemen and others – who require daylight for as long as it is obtainable every day . . . The effects of planning for adequate daylight will call for an architectural revolution in the City. It will mean the abandonment of small internal courts and their replacement by buildings which have the bulk of their accommodation towards the centre of the site and then step down in stages to street level.

Developers must therefore be encouraged 'to place the mass of floors in a building in the centre of the site rather than along its frontage to a street'; this meant that 'offices will be quieter and better lighted and streets will not be such canyons of noise and petrol fumes'. In general, for all their warnings, Holden and Holford were sanguine enough about the prospect of change and the new: 'The City is tremendously absorptive.'[21]

Given the government's understandable preference to accord a higher priority to public housing and factory regeneration than to offices, when it came to allocating building licences in the era of rationing, the reconstruction of the City remained largely on hold until the mid-1950s. As the volume of business steadily picked up, especially with the first post-war bull market under the Tories, there were inevitably some problems. Explaining that its present lease in Throgmorton Street was shortly to expire, and that it was having difficulty in finding alternative office accommodation within reasonable distance of the Stock Exchange, the stockbrokers Vickers da Costa managed to persuade the Stock Exchange Council in 1955 to let the firm move as far away from the market as the first floor of Regis House in King William Street. 'The shortage of suitable accommodation is so acute that we really have no alternative,' stated its irrefutable plea. One young newcomer to the City at about this time was the future novelist Leslie Thomas, working as a sub-editor at the Cannon Street offices of the Exchange Telegraph Co., the rather moribund international news agency:

> I used to spend my lunch hours walking around the City of London, much of which was still scarred with wartime bomb-sites, looking for stories. I found a family of wild cats living among the shut-off ruins and then realised that there were whole tribes of the fierce and skinny animals hunting the wide spaces in the centre of London . . .
>
> The fencing-off of large areas of the City, which had been cleared of rubble but still remained void, resulted in colonies of wild flowers appearing, foxgloves, dog roses and honeysuckle . . . Countryside birds appeared; there were rumours of foxes. Owls nested . . .[22]

By the mid-1950s the first wave of post-war office buildings was starting to go up. A key moment in the triumph of the modernists came in 1957, when Dr Nikolaus Pevsner published, as part of his series *The Buildings of England*, his survey of the City of London. His individual judgements lacked nothing in certainty. The 'vast pile' being erected in New Change for the Bank of England was 'shockingly lifeless and reactionary'; the new head office being perpetrated by the same unfortunate architect, Victor Heal, at the corner of Queen Street and Queen Victoria Street for BOLSA was merely 'lifeless and reactionary'. More generally, Pevsner complained that 'to this very day the City has hardly a major building which is in the style of the C20' and warned that 'the lack of architectural enterprise which is so alarming makes one doubt if sufficient enterprise will be shown by the City'. Pevsner's test case was the not-yet-begun Barbican development, where the City Corporation hoped to reverse a century-and-a-half trend by encouraging those who worked in the City also to live there.[23]

The pivotal year, in retrospect, was 1959. Among other things, it saw the passing of the Rights of Light Act (1959), immediately introducing what one historian has described as 'an orgy of new building . . . to prevent rights of light arising twenty years after the destruction of the original buildings in 1940'. Indeed, as early as January the City's own weekly paper, the *City Press*, looked ahead optimistically to progress on several key fronts: final permission from Common Council for both the Barbican scheme and the development of the Paternoster precinct to the north of St Paul's; just to the south of the Barbican, 'another big occasion soon will be the opening of the first section of the 62 feet wide carriageways of Route 11 between Aldersgate and the London Wall–Moorgate junction'; Common Council's imminent decision 'on the scheme to build overhead footpaths around and across this part of Route 11'; and the widening of Cheapside that would be necessitated by large new blocks there.

On 7 July the intrepid Duchess of Kent opened the first section of the new route, to be called London Wall. 'Route 11 Puts Accent on Beauty' was how the *City Press* billed the event. Four months later, on 11 November, Common Council approved both the Barbican scheme and the principle of high-level walkways over and alongside Route 11. The village paper gave the story perhaps its best headline yet: 'City Prepares for the 21st Century'.[24]

The signs of change – from 'old' City to 'new' City – were soon apparent in other areas. In autumn 1963, for delivery in early 1965, Phillips & Drew ordered an IBM 1440, employing a system specially designed for a stockbroker's office. The eventual cost was about £100,000. By March 1966 it was running for an average of more than twelve hours each day, sometimes deep into the night, and the firm's comptroller was authorised 'to make suitable arrangements over amenities, with particular regard to refreshments and a music programme, whether by radio or Muzak'. Even so, not everyone was happy, and a year later a partner noted after taking soundings that the computer 'had not been properly sold to the staff, as they see many people in the General Office still working overtime and the broad difficulties of a computer are not properly appreciated'.[25] For so long essentially Luddite in its working practice, it was hardly likely that the City was going to give an enthusiastic welcome to the dawning of the age of HAL.

A lot else changed in the 1960s. Partly through natural growth, partly through taking over smaller companies, the size of most leading firms significantly increased. James Capel, for instance, had a staff of about 180 by 1964, more than twice that of seven years earlier. The result, inevitably, was a greater sense of anonymity in office life, a loosening of the old personal ties. 'It was no longer practicable for new entrants to be conducted round the office and introduced to everybody', Ronald Palin noted regretfully in the 1970s about his latter years at Rothschilds. 'Increasingly one saw faces about to which one could not put a name.' Equally inevitably, the employee's traditional sense of loyalty to his firm – that indispensable, reciprocal part of the paternalist package – began to be eroded. Peter Swan of Phillips & Drew, from his vantage-point as head of selling equities to the investment institutions, reflected illuminatingly in November 1963 on the new culture, and in particular on what he and some of his partners saw as 'the lack of enthusiasm of many of the staff':

> The causes of this, I think, arise from our recent expansion both in income and staff [almost 200, and rising rapidly]. In the old days a man's efforts were more noticeable than today. An order then worth £50 is now more like £5 or £10 percentage-wise in the total day's take. In the old days we all knew if we dealt for A. R. D. Thomson, did a large gilt-edged switch, or did a large equity order. We all knew who did the security analysis. With our size, we seem to be moving towards a civil service approach . . .
>
> With one or two exceptions, they do not seem concerned at how the rest of the firm works and, although reasonably good at arriving, go promptly at 5.30 p.m. Apart from reading the usual papers, I should not think they do any homework.

Fuelling this more instrumental approach towards work, and job mobility, was the increasing competition for capable staff. By 1968 (when the annual New Earnings Survey began) the average gross salary, excluding bonuses, for a full-time non-manual male in the City was £1,966 a year, significantly above the £1,648 for Britain as a whole.[26]

One way in which the post-war City *did* mirror British society was in the continuing virtual absence of women from positions of any seniority. The male secretary may have vanished, and many of the punch-card and computer operators may have been women, but the notion of a female partner in a merchant bank, a female bill broker, a female member of the Stock Exchange or a female director of the Bank of England remained inconceivable.

Half a million or so men and women worked in the City at one time or another during the twenty years after the war; yet we know dismayingly little about what it really felt like to be one of that sea of faces emerging each morning from Bank station. The perspective of Michael Burns may have been recognisable to many. A grammar-school boy from the suburbs, he went in 1956 to the stockbrokers Ross-Munro, Duff & Co. and was there for a few eye-opening years:

> RMD's most flamboyant partner was Henry Duff. A slim, slightly round-shouldered man with a generous, Jimmy Edwards style moustache who was always dressed in the formal City wear of black jacket and waistcoat and striped trousers. He lived in Winchester and never arrived in the office before 10 a.m. and left soon after 3.30 p.m. He was at his most entertaining

in the afternoons when he was recovering from his frequent alcoholic lunches. During this recuperation period before he left for his unsteady walk to 'The Drain', he never needed much encouragement to start reminiscing about his days as a prisoner-of-war.

The long-running boom [in the stock market] meant that after I finished in the dealing room each afternoon I was required to go into the general office to help with the enormous amount of clerical work that was generated. No extra money was paid for these overtime hours. Instead there was a promise of a golden handout in the form of a Christmas bonus. During these interminable evenings it was my task to enter the day's bargains into the enormous red, leather-bound loose-leaf 'Bought' and 'Sold' ledgers. At the time of the fortnightly balance we all had to add and check long lines of figures, and not until both ledgers were balanced to the last farthing, was anybody allowed home. On some occasions it was past ten o'clock before I made my weary way down a deserted Moorgate.

As a reward for our loyal service, the partners laid on a lunchtime Christmas party for the staff. Glasses and bottles were collected from the Red Lion next door and on the last lunchtime before the holiday, the office staff and the partners came together to uncomfortably sip our light ales, nibble ham sandwiches and stare out at the frost-covered girders that had been growing up on the building-site opposite. This structure, which was normally populated by sure-footed Irish navvies, was deserted, that is until we saw Henry Duff, a gin and tonic in one hand, tightrope walking across a six-inch girder, fifty feet above the ground. One of the inebriated Guinness-drinking navvies was persuaded out of the pub to climb up and lead our swaying partner down to earth. Duff then invited all the building workers, whose skills he had been admiring over the months, to join us at the office party.

Christmas was also the time when RMD's staff were informed as to what their annual bonus was to be. I was staggered to be told that, after months of relentless overtime and at a time when the firm had been making record profits, I was to be awarded the princely sum of £50. £50 in crisp, white, five-pound notes was what, every Friday afternoon, the office manager handed Henry Duff for his weekend's expenses.

Firsthand experiences of such inequalities gained the Labour Party a supporter.[27]

CHAPTER THIRTY-FOUR

Euro-vision

'The big firms have become regarded as intelligence service for the City, at the centre of the telephone network of mmms and wells and meaningful grunts', Anthony Sampson noted in 1962 in his *Anatomy of Britain*. '"Better ask Cazenove's", a banker will mumble, and the answer will come back with the authority of the market-place.'[1]

This stockbroking firm had become a major force between the wars, and during the post-war period it consolidated its position, partly through the continuing excellence of its connections, but perhaps even more through its sheer Anglo-Saxon reliability – the fact that, if it said it would do something, it did it. Certainly it was far from a thrusting meritocracy. Cedric Barnett and Geoffrey Akroyd were both the sons of former partners. Barnett, an austere, dignified figure in charge of gilts, had technical ability but lacked force. 'I suppose he's taken his top hat for a walk round the market', another partner remarked one afternoon when his absence from the office was noted. When not perambulating, Barnett was responsible for coining the three aphorisms that between them were emblematic of the whole, post-war gentlemanly City: namely, 'shoes have laces', 'motor cars are black' and, most tellingly of all, 'jelly is not officer food'. As for the red-faced, good-natured Akroyd (almost a complete nonentity in business terms), his most celebrated bon mot was the avuncular advice he gave to one newcomer to the firm, 'You'll find the Savoy a jolly nice little place for lunch, and nice and handy because you can get there on a number 11 bus.'

Of course, there was another, quite different side to Cazenove's. For one thing, it became from the 1950s the unwritten rule that a partner could bring in only one son, and that that son had to run 110 yards to everyone else's 100 in order to prove himself; for another, it was becoming possible in this period for the occasional self-made person to emerge as a major figure in the firm, perhaps epitomised by the unassuming Ernest Bedford, a supremely persuasive as well as conscientious placer of shares with the institutions. Beneath the gentlemanly facade lay a toughness and professional edge – an edge that owed much to Peter Kemp-Welch, whose progress had been blocked at Foster & Braithwaite before coming to

Cazenove's immediately after the war. Convivial, and with a quick, humorous mind, he took stock of the situation and in August 1948, while nominally on holiday in Scotland, prescribed what he saw as the necessary medicine. His memo noted various current failings on the part of the firm, including the fact that 'we don't produce many "ideas" or up to date offers, other than our own issues'; remarked that 'we have always rather prided ourselves on being enthusiastic amateurs'; and concluded bluntly enough that 'one doesn't want to take business too seriously but there is bound to be a grave risk of losing efficiency by not taking it seriously enough: the trouble is that if we don't take it seriously enough someone else will!'

Kemp-Welch's memo was for the eyes of Antony Hornby, the firm's commanding presence for a quarter of a century after the war. That autumn, on the basis of Kemp-Welch's analysis, Hornby persuaded the partnership as a whole of the need to adopt a more systematic, serious-minded approach. Hornby himself, born in 1904, was a Wykehamist, an increasingly renowned art collector, arrogant but unstuffy, occasionally hot-tempered, a convinced non-egalitarian, and the embodiment of his own, oft-quoted dictum that 'merchant bankers don't want long faces'. In 1960, with the firm doing especially well, he listed with typical self-confidence what he perceived to be some of the reasons:

> Reliability. Secrets are safe. We do not make use of confidential information for our own ends.
> We all work hard and full time. We know our job and most of the answers!
> We are known not to be gamblers in private or business life.
> We are not unduly mercenary. Obviously one wants to make money, but we are not greedy. The amount of money to be made out of a business is not the reason for doing it.
> We are a happy firm at all levels and enjoy our business life and show it. We are serious but not too desperately serious.
> The firm is run as a benevolent autocracy, but is at the same time essentially democratic.

And, undeterred by that apparent contradiction, Hornby added that in the future 'we must be careful to have in the partnership people who fit and who think the same way as us, and whom we are really fond of'.[2]

In 1961, in another of his inimitable memos, Hornby put down on paper his investment philosophy. While not denying that 'the analyst's role is necessary and important', he contended not only that most of their reports were 'too lengthy for us to have time to read them', but that even a concise piece of analysis was inadequate without being 'cross-fertilised by the sea of experience' and having added to it 'a good pinch of flair or hunch'. There was, he insisted, 'more to it than figures, past profits, and projection of future profits', and 'it is an enormous help to know the personalities involved, to become intimate with the flavour of a business'. How well did this method – essentially a cast of mind – work on behalf of the partners and their clients? Pretty well presumably, although one client had rueful memories of being allowed to walk up the main staircase at 12 Tokenhouse Yard:

> I was taken – as if I was being anointed with class and quality – to Cazenove's in 1964. They looked at me as if I was an idiot and they were geniuses, and proceeded to buy for me a lot of shares that were a disaster. I lost about £40,000, which was a lot of money in 1964. I was about twenty-eight at the time and so, when I first met Cazenove people I was tremendously impressed – here were these very posh people in suits. I'd been recommended to see them by a peer of the realm and I felt as though I was being let in Valhalla.

The young wannabe was the film director Michael Winner, who may or may not have been consoled by Hornby's timeless investment apophthegms: 'Don't worry; don't be impatient; don't press; don't panic; don't fidget. Enjoy the whole fascinating affair.'[3]

While some firms such as Phillips & Drew became proficient in investment analysis, the crux of the matter was that the City was not yet ready for new-style, cerebral stockbroking. The official line was that the coming of investment analysis later in the course of the 1950s, fuelled by the investing institutions' demand for greater professionalism, dramatically changed practices such as insider dealing. 'The days of the third-hand "tip", offered over a glass of sherry, are happily long past', the member-journalist Donald Cobbett optimistically declared in 1957. The truth was surely different. The jobber Geoffrey Green recalled insider trading as 'a fact of life' in the Stock Exchange of the 1960s; and when the young Christopher Heath joined the stockbroking firm of George Henderson & Co. near the end of the decade, he encountered a world in which PA (personal account) trading was still the norm. Perhaps Peter Spira of Warburgs put it best. 'Insider dealing was a regular occurrence', he observed. 'The reason why people had their investment affairs managed by merchant bankers and stockbrokers was precisely because they had better information.'[4]

Partly because of the increasing importance of institutional clients, partly because of the growing use of the telephone, 'a fundamental change in the transaction of Stock Exchange business has taken place due to the considerable number of deals which are negotiated by Brokers between non-members and which only reach the Jobber on put-through terms'. Such was the Stock Exchange's own admission in November 1958, strictly for private consumption. The big jobbers had the resources to deal direct with these non-members; the small ones did not. Was the answer, in order to keep the jobbing system within the Stock Exchange family, perhaps for the brokers to buy into many of these jobbers? Early in the 1960s an ad hoc committee set up by the Council recommended that before any outside capital be brought into the jobbing system, broking firms should be given first refusal at providing it. This recommendation, however, was rejected: the concept of single capacity remained, as it would for the next two decades, the great sacred cow. Meanwhile, the jobbing system itself was contracting ever more rapidly – from 100 firms in June 1960 to a mere fifty-nine five years later. 'In my mind,' the jobber Douglas Eton wrote to the Council in July 1962, 'there is absolutely no doubt that, in ten years at the current rate, there will be about twenty Jobbing Firms left'; and he urged that henceforth any proposed merger between firms dealing in the same stocks should require the Council's approval. Another member, P. F. S. Moore, writing a year later to the Council, was even more apocalyptic. After comparing the existing jobbing system to 'a 1926 vintage Rolls-Royce, supreme in outward appearance, with no wheels', he went on:

> With all due respects to the planners of the new Stock Exchange, it does appear as if the floor trading area is a little on the huge side for the number of men who will be available to stand on it within the next decade . . . I visualise the new Stock Exchange in ten to twenty years' time as a small cathedral of city life, with a galaxy of bishops, few in number, surrounded by an admiring group of archdeacons, a little more in number, and a few deacons; but no congregation, and they all sing harmonious hymns in praise of each other.[5]

Few of those who actually spent any time on the floor of the old House, before its demolition began in 1966, ever forgot the experience. A clutch of reminiscences, from a quarter of a century later, evoke something of its uniqueness – attractive or rebarbative according to taste:

> I didn't think that I could possibly stand it, because the noise and the people, as a Guards officer at Dunkirk so wittily said, appalled me. It was like being at a cocktail party without any drinks. But within a week I discovered the people were delightful and the noise I didn't even notice. It was like a rugger club, it was all boys together . . .
>
> You still had that wonderful atmosphere where you had a laugh and a joke; a situation where they played the fool when there wasn't much business; the old idea of buying a box of chocolates outside, eating the chocolates, then placing the box on the market floor with water in it, until some idiot came along and kicked it, which always happened. And the idiot would of course get a soaked foot . . .
>
> I think it was the way of letting off steam. There was always the throwing of paper balls and that sort of thing, particularly at guys that were wearing top hats; and another joke was putting torn-up newspaper – little bits of

newspaper – in a chap's umbrella, put down his umbrella and then as he started to walk out, up went the umbrella, so of course the shower of paper came down . . .

There was a chap called Lightfoot, and he had a habit when he was called of waving his handkerchief from his top pocket. The waiter would repeat 'Lightfoot', and then all of a sudden four or five hundred people would take their handkerchiefs out and they would all be waving them . . . I remember when the King died there was a junior there, who wasn't wearing a black tie, and he got really told off over this. 'How dare you come into the market, don't you realise?' The Queen's birthday, the King's birthday, the Stock Exchange Choir always formed up in the gilt market and always sang the National Anthem and the whole market joined in . . .

The particular thing that impressed me more than anything was this old man who would occasionally come into the gilt market and the whole House would sing 'Jerusalem'. It was a most magnificent sound. I mean it brought tears to your eyes. It was unbelievable, and I don't think I've ever been impressed with anything more than that.[6]

Some markets were more boisterous than others, while the introduction of the visitors' gallery in 1953 occasionally made members think twice about doing something outrageous; but under the world's third-biggest dome there remained a real continuity between the Stock Exchange during its Victorian heyday and that now inhabited by the not-so-New Elizabethans.

*

Gradually and grudgingly, some of the oldest houses began to open their doors, the classic cases being Rothschilds and Morgan Grenfell. David Colville had been an 'assistant' to the partners at New Court since 1946, after being recruited from Lloyds Bank, and was renowned for his investment expertise. On 30 June 1960, the same day that the retirement of Anthony de Rothschild was announced (five years after his stroke had removed him from action and created a serious hole at the centre of the bank), Colville was made a partner – the first person outside the family to receive that honour. He was followed in October 1961 by Michael Bucks, thirty-seven years after coming to New Court. 'There's not enough talent to go round', Colville openly admitted on the occasion of this second break with precedent. 'To attract the right people, it's useful to point out that it's possible for partners to come from outside the Rothschild family.' Even so, the family itself remained firmly in control, and everyone knew that the bank's fortunes would depend heavily on how the new generation of Rothschilds (specifically, Evelyn and Jacob) shaped up. If Rothschilds was hardly a byword for dynamism, neither was Morgan Grenfell, where Vivian Hugh Smith's

son, 'Rufie', succeeded to his father's chairmanship in 1956, as well as
to his title of Lord Bicester of Tusmore. 'Rufie is not very bright, but
everyone likes to do business with him' was the line uniformly given
to Diana Mallory as she prepared an article in 1961 for *Queen* on 'The
Merchant Bankers'. It was under his genial chairmanship that at last in
1961, with the promotion to the board of the very capable Kenneth
Barrington of the new issue department, 'a player became a gentleman'.[7]
In Morgan Grenfell as in Rothschilds, this represented a tacit recognition that even the most comfortable houses could no longer afford
wholly to ignore how the world outside was changing.

'Before the Second World War,' the historian Hugh Thomas noted in
1959, 'the City was probably more powerful than industry, but the relationship has now been altered in industry's favour, due to the decline of
British worldwide commercial eminence.' Moreover, whatever their
comparative standings, both City and industry shared an inability to
attract young talent. Instead, 'the really bright people all went into the
Foreign Office or the Treasury', as the future Stock Exchange chairman
Sir Nicholas Goodison self-deprecatingly noted in the context of the late
1950s, when he joined his family stockbroking firm, H. E. Goodison &
Co. More bluntly (but perhaps less typically), a non-City man, the
educationalist Harry Rée, recalled being told at his public school,
Shrewsbury, that 'only shits go into the City'.[8] Either way, the underlying
fact was that those with something positive to offer were not, on the
whole, making a beeline for the Square Mile.

Undoubtedly, there was by the late 1950s a growing perception that
the City had become remote from the British mainstream. Victor
Sandelson – an intelligent stockbroker, former journalist and a rare critical
voice from within – put it best:

> The City establishment, if not fanatically and openly Conservative, is certainly
> conservative by instinct and training to an extent that cuts it off from the
> life of the nation in a much more deep-rooted way than political bias alone
> could ensure. Its public school standards of conduct; its upper-class standard
> of life, its sports and its formality; even its assumption that the City is of
> vital importance to the economic well-being of the country and that free
> markets are inevitably the best markets, mean that it lives in a world, physi-
> cally and mentally, apart from the world of the vast majority of the popula-
> tion. This, when the City is undoubtedly economically very powerful indeed,
> is certainly dangerous. There is nothing to parallel the situation (with the
> possible exception of Russia) in any other advanced industrial country.[9]

Would the City reconnect with the rest of the country? And, if it did so,
would it be on the City's terms? The next forty years would see these
two questions resolved – in both cases, eventually, in the affirmative, but
only through the creation of a very different City itself.

Of more immediate concern was the question of whether 1959 would bring, as the City strongly hoped, a hat-trick of Conservative election wins? Macmillan saw a familiar obstacle to his hopes. 'Just as Montagu Norman was obsessed by the gold standard,' he privately reflected in February, 'so Cobbold is obsessed by "funding". So he is selling securities when he ought to be buying – at least that is what I feel.' To Midland's Monckton, a bank chairman with especially keen political antennae, Macmillan held out the beguiling scenario that if only ministers were allowed to pursue a Keynesian stimulus to consumption, then 'the Conservative party will be re-elected, prosperity will be secured, the Bank of England will be preserved, and funding in 1960 will be easier than ever before.'[10]

On 29 July, the Chancellor, Heathcoat Amory, went with Cobbold to see Macmillan. They reiterated their apparently shared view about taking no action yet to check expansion, while in terms of when such action might be taken, this might be 'autumn'. Cobbold added that 'in the event of an autumn Election and a Conservative victory some boom conditions might develop rather quickly'.[11] Cobbold perhaps guessed that at this particular juncture it was not a warning likely to cause Macmillan or even Heathcoat Amory to lose much sleep.

There was another aspect to this memorably hot summer, as several controversial contested takeovers occurred, fuelled by easy credit and the stock market boom.[12] The most publicity was given to a £20m bid (in the event unsuccessful) by Charles Clore's Sears Holdings for the brewer Watney's on 25 May, barely four months after the government had changed for ever the market in corporate control by siding with the aggressor during the Aluminium War. 'We had a talk about takeover bids', Cobbold noted as early as the 29th, after calling on the Chancellor that day. 'He feels, as I do, that it may not be a bad thing in some instances, but that it is damaging to the general idea of prudent and conservative management of companies and might, in a few cases, be excessively embarrassing.'[13] The general election had not yet been called, but Cobbold had been around long enough to spot a hot potato.

This summer, however, was above all about the Radcliffe Report into the workings of the monetary system. Publicly available from 19 August but released a fortnight or so earlier to key figures, it had, from a specifically City-cum-Bank standpoint, perhaps six main aspects: a broadly clean bill of health for both the clearing banks and the discount market, with no great objection being raised to their anti-competitive elements; the recommendation, in the light of the 'leak' of 1957, that the Bank's part-time directors be excluded from Bank rate discussions; the further recommendation that Bank rate changes be made at the explicit directive of the Chancellor of the day; the assertions that economic policy needed to be integrated, that monetary policy alone was not enough and should not be allowed to pursue autonomous objectives, and that within monetary policy, interest rate changes were a more effective weapon than attempts to control the money supply; a call to the Bank to provide more statistics and information generally; and, finally, the recommendation that a Standing Committee on monetary policy be set up, to include representatives from the Bank, the Treasury and the Board of Trade, with the chair to be taken by the Economic Secretary to the Treasury.[14]

Cobbold's institution did not entirely escape censure as soon as the report was published, with *The Economist* for example noting that 'the Bank comes in for a fair dose of criticism . . . and most of it is well deserved'. As for Cobbold's willingness or otherwise to accept the report's recommendations, he did not have any great problems with either the part-time directors or the statistical/PR aspect, but he did unequivocally tell the Treasury's Makins on 17 August that he was unhappy 'that the full responsibility for Bank Rate decisions should be transferred to the Chancellor' and that 'a Standing Committee should be appointed in Whitehall to which all decisions on monetary policy should be referred by the Chancellor for advice'. He insisted that 'Bank Rate is an integral part of the Central Bank's own business' and, while not disputing the fact of the Chancellor's 'over-riding decision', maintained that 'to place on the Chancellor direct responsibility for what is essentially a market and operational decision would blur the real responsibilities'.[15]

Yet, in at least three significant ways, the report and the way it was implemented meant that the City was leaving the 1950s in a weaker state than need have been the case.[16] First, it was a chance missed – just at the time of financial liberalisation and the emergence of new money markets – to shake up the domestic banking system, after some forty years of cartelised ossification. Some specific improvements resulted (for instance, in the areas of servicing agriculture and small businesses), but the larger structure stayed in place. Second, Radcliffe's conclusions that 'money' was not measurable, that interest rates alone were not sufficient to control the domestic economy and that monetary policy objectives were ultimately political had the total effect, within the domestic sphere, of confirming and indeed underpinning the Bank's subordination to the Treasury. And third, more broadly, the Bank's passionate, entirely understandable wish that its day-to-day independence be upheld would mean that in practice it continued to be marginal to the ever-growing Whitehall machine, with the result that whatever influence it did wield depended to an unhealthy degree on the political clout (or otherwise) of the governor of the day. The age of corporatism was about to dawn, with the Bank of England – and thus the City – largely missing from its ranks.

*

If there was a truly visionary figure in the City in the early 1960s it was surely Sir George Bolton, once of the Bank of England, now chairman of the Bank of London and South America (BOLSA).[17] In December 1960 – fourteen months after an historic Conservative electoral triumph achieved almost wholly on the back of a boom economy and rising material prosperity – he sent, without Cobbold's knowledge, a bold paper to Macmillan in which he inveighed against exchange controls, not just in Britain but in Western Europe as a whole:

> The existence for twenty years of such a policy has produced a political and national feeling in Europe that capital should be used primarily in the country of origin, and that it should be jealously hoarded and not made available to the foreigner. While this was a wartime and an immediate post-war necessity, it now makes no sense whatever, and conflicts with the interests of the United Kingdom.

Accordingly, Bolton called – in typically sweeping terms – for the comprehensive mobilisation of Western European finance. Or, as he put it a few weeks later to a City audience, at the annual banquet of the Overseas Bankers' Club, 'the real cause' of 'the world-wide hunger for capital' was 'the persistence of exchange controls, the restriction over the movements of people and the consequent granulation of Europe's capital and human resources into isolated jealous particles'.[18] Capital had not flowed freely round the world since 1914; but Bolton well knew that if it once more began to do so, then London – with its entrepôt expertise and traditions – would be the spectacular beneficiary.

Before the Eurobond market, however, there was the Eurodollar market, and Bolton's BOLSA was, at the end of the 1950s, one of the London banks already pushing hard for dollar deposits.[19] It was purely a telephone market, and over the years old-timers in Fleet Street would enjoy instructing novice photographers to call at the Bank of England and obtain a picture of a Eurodollar. An early public sighting of the term itself occurred in *The Times* on 24 October 1960. In a piece entitled 'London – Centre of the Euro-Dollar Market', 'the so-called Euro-dollar market' was described by the City editor William Clarke as 'a market where dollar deposits earned and owned by foreigners can be left and still earn a higher rate of interest than is available in New York'; and he emphasised recent German and Swiss moves to restrict such deposits entering their own financial centres. According to the financial journalist Gordon Tether in June 1961, it was a market deploying 'considerably more than the $1,000 millions that is a fairly generally accepted estimate of its size', and he tried to show how this huge pool of international credit centred upon London was utilised for many purposes, but above all for the financing of trade.[20]

Why London rather than, say, Paris or Frankfurt or Zurich? It was not just because of the more liberal attitude of the London authorities, important though that was; there were also, in the admiring words earlier in 1961 of a leading French financial commentator, Paul Turot, London's 'excellent technical organisation' and its 'abundance of specialised personnel'. In terms of who was making the running in this rapidly expanding market, Tether thought that 'top names' included 'such widely differing types of institution as the Bank of London and South America, Schroders, the Société Générale, the Australia and New Zealand Bank, Kleinwort Benson, and Brown Shipley – the last two institutions claiming to be the originators of the market in its present form'. Back in the mid-to-late 1950s the British clearing banks had been to the fore, but the requirement that 8 per cent of all their deposits, in any currency, had to be held at the Bank of England blunted their competitive capacity in bidding for funds. Accordingly, by 1960 their Eurodollar market share (that is, of dollar and foreign currency deposits held by non-residents with UK banks) was down to less than 10 per cent, whereas American banks, British overseas banks and accepting houses were running respectively at about 35, 20 and 16 per cent.[21] There were still not many American banks in London, but the trend was clear.

Bolton had two key allies in his ambition to make London the unrivalled international financial capital of Europe. One was Warburg; the other was a Baring, Lord Cromer, governor of the Bank from 1961 and largely responsible for temporarily relaxing its attitude towards exchange control.

Unbeknown to most in the City and virtually ignored by policymakers outside, 1963 would be the most important year since 1914 in the history of London as an international financial centre.[22] The origins of what would come to be known as the Eurobond market lay partly in the existence of the huge floating pool of stateless Eurodollars, with much of that pool residing in London, but arguably even more in the peculiarities of the New York foreign dollar bond market.[23] Between 1945 and the early 1960s – the era of the almighty dollar – that market raised some $6.5bn, largely for governments and state-owned bodies in different parts of the world. Yet such was the insularity of the American investment community that increasingly the secondary market for these issues resided not in the US, but in Europe. It was, from a European perspective, an illogical, even exasperating situation. In the immortal, retrospective words of Julius Strauss, whose stockbroking firm Strauss Turnbull specialised in placing foreign dollar bond issues, 'the American houses got all the cream but did none of the work'. Strauss himself was later credited with coining the term 'Eurobond', but if there was one figure who appreciated more than anyone that the 'cream' lay in arranging the underwriting, and that there was no reason why European syndicates should not sell foreign dollar bond issues to what was anyway largely a European clientele, that figure was surely Siegmund Warburg. Through his close connection with the New York investment bank Kuhn Loeb, and in particular that firm's Gert Whitman, he had learned much about the European marketing of foreign dollar bond issues; by the early 1960s he was conscious that the freedom of the New York foreign dollar bond market was under threat from the worsening US balance-of-payments position; and by early 1962 he was busy negotiating a London-based dollar loan for the European Coal and Steel Community (ECSC), which had previously looked to New York to arrange its issues.[24] In the event that ECSC issue failed to get much beyond square one (possibly because Warburg decided against treading on the toes of Kuhn Loeb and company, possibly because ECSC decided it did not need the money), but what it did do was point Warburg, his firm and the City of London in the most fruitful of future directions.

Warburg and Bolton were pretty close over the years, and that summer it was Bolton who made significant progress on a rather broader front. 'I spoke to you last week', he reminded Cromer on 6 June, 'about a certain exchange of ideas that is currently taking place regarding the opening of the London market to a wide variety of borrowers for loans denominated in foreign currencies.' He added that 'conversations, so far, have been kept within the very small group of representatives of Barings, Samuel Montagu, Warburgs and ourselves [i.e. BOLSA], but we would not wish to proceed more actively unless the ideas have the general blessing of the authorities'. An enclosed note put forward the arguments in favour of the proposals; some weeks later, on 11 July, Bolton updated Cromer, telling him that 'Charles Hambro has been brought into the group', having 'expressed a wish that Hambros Bank should be associated with this kind of transaction if they are permitted'. As for the plans themselves 'for helping to restore London's function as a capital market and for finding some alternative to the greatly weakened New York market', Bolton mentioned various possibilities. These included Belgium looking for a $50m loan, a group of Austrian public utilities seeking to raise $50m, and Hambros and Warburgs examining the possibility of placing 'in Europe' a $15–20m loan for the kingdom of Norway, which Kuhn Loeb had been forced to back out of because of deteriorating conditions in the New York market. Almost a fortnight later Cromer at last replied, noting various practical difficulties (such as those relating to bearer and stamp duty) that would need to be overcome, but emphasising that 'we are sympathetic to this proposal and will give it what practical support we can'.[25] It was, for Bolton, Warburg and a few others, enough.

That autumn both Warburg and Bolton were in the States, where they each learned important things – Warburg from friends at the World Bank that around $3bn was in circulation outside the US and thus potentially available for the purpose of long-term loans; Bolton from contacts on Wall Street that American banks were under pressure 'to cease giving financial loans to foreign customers', in the context of continuing pressure on the US balance of payments and the dollar. 'The Administration have no legal powers to prevent non-residents borrowing dollars, either short or long-term, and if methods of persuasion fail I would not exclude legislation', Bolton added in his memo on his return. 'In any event, I now regard the restoration and revival of the London Market machinery to enable issues of foreign loans to be made as a matter of immediate importance to the Western World . . . The only centre that can help New York is London, as we are all uncomfortably aware of the isolation and inefficiency of the European capital markets.'[26]

By the end of 1962 it was neck and neck as to who would arrange London's first foreign currency loan. One of Warburg's many European banking friends was Guido Carli, governor of the Banca d'Italia, and it emerged that Finsider, the steel-making subsidiary of IRI (the Italian state industrial holding company), urgently needed funds. However, the word from Whitman (whom Kuhn Loeb had generously seconded to Warburgs in order to lend his considerable expertise in the foreign dollar bond market) was that an issue explicitly in the name of Finsider would be critically hobbled by the fact that its statute did not allow it to pay interest on bond coupons without deducting Italian coupon tax. Consequently Finsider arranged, at a price, that the apparent beneficiaries should be Autostrade, the Italian toll-motorway company whose statute did allow it to pay coupons gross. Autostrade was also an IRI subsidiary, and on 14 January 1963 an agreement was formally reached between IRI and Warburgs.[27]

Then, in mid-May, Samuel Montagu managed to arrange a placing for the Belgian government of $20m in 5 per cent bonds. *The Times* saw the importance of this development: 'As the first non-sterling foreign loan to be organised by the City since the war, it signals the resurgence of London as an international capital market.' And the paper added that 'the use of "Euro-dollars" for subscriptions to this placing marks a major step forward towards the use of non-resident dollar deposits for medium-term financing'. The *Banker* agreed that it was 'the City's first foreign currency loan since the war', with the issue being purchased at par by a consortium of banks (including Schroders and Kleinwort Benson) 'out of their substantial holdings of Euro-dollars'. It also noted that 'no market will be created' in these bonds; and that is why over the years this Belgian loan has not generally been regarded as representing the start of the Eurobond market.[28] There was, in other words, no retail element. That, however, was about to come.

'UK Shares in $ Loan to Finance Italian Motorways' was the *FT*'s not entirely accurate headline on 2 July 1963, the day after Warburgs and the rest of the underwriting syndicate had gathered in London to sign the underwriting agreement with Autostrade. It was to be a $15m loan, with a 5½ per cent coupon for the fifteen-year bonds.[29] On the 18th, the Eurobond market's defining moment occurred, as President Kennedy sought to protect the US balance of payments by announcing the Interest Equalisation Tax (IET), which crucially involved a 15 per cent tax on the purchase by Americans of foreign securities from foreigners. The story goes that, as the news came through, the Chairman of Morgan Guaranty in New York, Henry Alexander, at once gathered together some senior colleagues and uttered a trenchant forecast – 'This is a day that you will remember forever. It will change the face of American banking and force all the business off to London. It will take years to get rid of this legislation.' However, to read the *Wall Street Journal* of the days immediately after the 18th is to be struck by the sheer absence of discussion about the possible damage that the IET was liable to inflict on New York as an international financial centre. Indeed, the New York bond markets reacted almost bullishly, with one dealer declaring that 'if enacted, this tax would keep more money in this country and some of it would find its way into US Treasury and other bonds'.[30]

As far as the new London market itself was concerned, the key fact was that the Bank of England remained firmly, if a tad unenthusiastically, onside. Maurice Parsons, on the international side at the Bank, wrote on 23 August that:

> We do not put any obstacle in the way of such issues on the basis that London is thereby conducting a brokerage business, which on the whole we are inclined to favour. Admittedly, we in the Bank would much prefer to see this kind of business done in sterling but unfortunately that is only possible in the case of a limited number of countries.

A month later Jacob Rothschild rang the Bank to check that it had no problem over Rothschilds floating dollar-denominated foreign bond issues in London. The Bank, he was told soon afterwards, had no problem. Almost a century and a half after Nathan Rothschild's drive to centre the international capital market on London, possibilities were afoot in what Mynors by November 1963 was tentatively calling 'the Euro-Capital Market'.[31] The City, in truth, was poised to become at least as much a dollar as a sterling City.

By the mid-1960s, in the context of the growth of the Eurodollar market and the coming of its younger alter ego the Eurobond market, it was a rather different place from what it had been even in the late 1950s – though large pockets of it, such as Lloyd's and the Stock Exchange, remained fundamentally unchanged. In particular, although the great rush would come in the second half of the decade, American banks were starting to arrive in numbers.[32] The main lure, naturally, was the Euromarkets, although there was also a 'push' factor in the form of stifling US banking legislation, which made the more ambitious banks look hard for opportunities abroad. There was, moreover, by now a Japanese dimension, as the four big Tokyo securities houses (Daiwa, Nomura, Yamaichi and Nikko) all became established presences on the back of no fewer than eleven Eurobond issues for Japanese concerns between December 1963 and April 1964. It was the American challenge, however, that loomed far larger in the collective mind of British banks – not surprisingly, granted the ever more dominant position of American banks in the Eurodollar market – and among the clearers the most innovative response came from Midland. In 1963 it came together with three continental banks to set up the European Advisory Committee, a venture designed to provide large-scale international financing for specific projects. The following year, in alliance with Toronto Dominion Bank, Standard Bank and Commercial Bank of Australia, it set up Midland and International Banks, based at 36 Throgmorton Street and the first of what became known as the consortium banks, whose main purpose was to use the Eurodollar market for medium-term lending.[33]

This process of internationalising the City was something that the Bank of England under Cromer's governorship thoroughly welcomed, and it was keen that the relatively flexible legal and tax framework for foreign banks in London should in no way be jeopardised. What was potentially a rather different matter was the question of sizeable foreign stakes in British firms. The Bank did not object to First National City Bank of New York acquiring a one-sixth stake in M. Samuel, publicly announced in February 1963; but when, a few weeks later, Continental Illinois told Parsons that it was thinking of likewise taking a stake in a London merchant bank, he intimated that it was 'a slightly delicate question' and that, while there was 'no formal barrier', nevertheless 'if a foreign bank were to attempt to acquire a majority holding it would confront us with some difficult problems'. If that was one sighter of the City's future, namely the whole question of ownership, so too was Jack Spall's experience in 1961 when, after fourteen years with the old-established East India merchants Wallace Brothers, he joined the ranks of the 'thundering herd' – the American brokerage house Merrill Lynch:

> It was a complete culture shock. Its offices were just by Fenchurch Station and it was a whole new ball game to me. People earned a lot of money, there was a sudden display of wealth, which I was unused to. I wanted some of it, in the normal way. The offices were grotty. Rain used to come through the roof, they tried to tart it up a bit but it was unsatisfactory.

Most of the dealers were Americans and because it was the early days of Merrill Lynch in London, there was a good spirit of camaraderie . . . It wasn't paternalistic in the way that Wallace Brothers was, but we actually got paid money and that was the difference. One of my colleagues was a woman, who was absolutely spot-on and one thought, 'God, I'll never be as good as she is'. I probably thought, 'My God, if I can't do better than a woman, then . . .'[34]

Americans *and* women: the harbingers of the late twentieth-century City were already present.

*

In his April 1963 Budget speech, the Chancellor Reginald Maudling made an unequivocal declaration: 'I absolutely reject the proposition that a vigorous economy and a strong position for sterling are incompatible.'[35] Perhaps by this time, he may have reflected, a Conservative administration had shed enough of the burdens of Empire; as for the City, certainly outside the Eurodollar market, it remained axiomatic (and virtually undebated) that sterling's strength and its own strength were umbilically connected.

The Maudling boom was in full swing. 'The car was now going downhill fairly rapidly' was how Mynors characteristically expressed it at the end of October to the discount market, adding that 'before long the brakes may be rather difficult to apply'. Maudling himself, arguably to his credit, acknowledged as much. 'He was rather amused', Alec Cairncross (the government's economic adviser) recorded three weeks later after a conversation with him, 'at way everything shaping for a splendid bit of expansion next spring followed by election and then efforts by Callaghan and Co. to cope with exchange crisis. Said nobody would believe we hadn't planned it.'[36]

Maudling's private view that Labour would win was widely shared, and the City during the winter of 1963–4 made its dispositions and looked gloomily ahead. The Stock Exchange, particularly anxious not to be vulnerable in what was expected to be a bitter election, spent £35,000 on what its Public Relations Committee described as 'an extensive campaign [mainly corporate advertising in the popular press] to emphasise that the Stock Exchange is essential to the running of the nation and that it provides a good service both to the direct and indirect investor'. At the Bank, Cromer recruited a young, Labour-sympathising economist, Christopher (Kit) McMahon. 'As to his political views,' the governor told a correspondent in January 1964, 'he mentioned them to me and I feel in no way perturbed. He has such a good objective mind and this is what counts most.' At 8 Bishopsgate, Nicholas Baring told a Wall Street banker that, with a Labour government expected by the end of the year, 'it seems a fair assumption that Wilson himself will prove to be, if anything, rather more left-wing than he has appeared in the initial stages of his campaign'.[37]

Harold Wilson's relations with the City had been mutually bad since the Bank rate leak of 1957; and now in February 1964, in the context of poor trade figures for February, he convinced himself that dirty work was afoot at the crossroads concerning the country's true external situation, in particular the state of the sterling reserves. Accompanied by his Shadow Chancellor, James Callaghan, he had a top-secret meeting on the 26th with Maudling and the new prime minister, Sir Alec Douglas-Home. 'H.W. made allegations that Bank of England was "cooking the books"', Cairncross recorded. 'Offered to keep quiet but only if Tories didn't publicly accuse Labour of endangering sterling.' A deal was done along those lines, though the ministers also insisted that the allegations were 'unfounded' and that Wilson 'must not attack the rise in Bank Rate and rock the boat'. During spring and into the summer the Tories began gradually to whittle away Labour's opinion-poll lead, but the expectation remained of a Labour victory in what was now certain to be an autumn election. What would be the attitude of a Labour government to sterling? Responding in July to a Treasury paper on 'The Next Five Years', Cromer insisted that, whichever party won, the Bank of England's fundamental priority would remain unchanged: 'Let us be quite clear that the international standing and use of sterling is an inherent and essential part of our external economic relationships, and not merely some out-dated slogan exclusive to "The City".'[38]

'The stock market was more volatile in the course of this election campaign than in any other since the war', John Littlewood (then an analyst with a stockbroking firm) has aptly recalled of the feverish month leading up to polling day on 15 October 1964. 'Fear and greed exchanged places from day to day'. Was this fear irrational? Littlewood, reflecting on the fact that memories of the Attlee government were 'still fresh in the minds of many people,' argues not: 'There were genuine reasons to fear that a Labour government could easily erect barriers to contain and control financial assets within a highly effective ringed fence.'[39]

The City fully shared the anxieties of investors at large, but for just over the first fortnight of the campaign there was some market optimism that the Tories might yet snatch a famous victory. The mood had been fuelled by a series of opinion polls showing little to choose between the parties, but then on Sunday the 4th a Gallup Poll gave a 4.5 per cent lead to Labour. Over the following week the Index lost 20.7 points, equivalent to a 5.5 per cent fall, and thereafter market confidence never really recovered.

For Cromer the most unsettling moment came on the 1st, after the *FT* had reported Wilson declaring in a speech at Norwich that the latest gold and currency reserve figures, due to be issued on the afternoon of the 2nd, were going to 'dominate this Election'. This prompted Cromer to telephone the prime minister's office and let it be known that he was 'worried at the possibility of the adjustment of the September figures to take account of Central Bank support becoming a factor in the political situation', in that (the office further noted) 'the extent to which the September figures had been cooked would be clear in due course from the Bank of England Bulletin and the Federal Reserve Bank Review and he might be accused of conniving at a political manoeuvre'. Cromer accepted that 'it was out of the question to think of publishing the true figure but said that the compromise that he had in mind was disclosing it privately to the Leader of the Opposition'. The matter was left to Maudling, who told Cromer later that day that he must not even think of volunteering 'the true figure' to Wilson, and Cromer reluctantly complied.[40] The next day the published figures showed a politically containable fall of £16m.

A week later the discount market's representatives saw Cromer, who naturally did not allude to the matter. Instead, 'a lot was said, very little of it of any importance', they noted. 'The Governor said he thought the outlook was very difficult to assess and not very convincing.' Cromer spent election night itself at a series of parties – at *The Times*, the *Telegraph* and, hedging his bets, the *Daily Mirror* – as it gradually became clear that Labour was going to win, but not by much. 'If Labour wins, there will be no question of industry or the City of London refusing to co-operate', the City's conscience, Harold Wincott, had written in the *FT* the previous week. 'A Labour Prime Minister will be welcomed and applauded at Guildhall, and Mr Callaghan at the bankers' dinner at the Mansion House.'[41]

CHAPTER THIRTY-FIVE

The Facts of Life

'The stock exchange was seesawing but no profound losses were reported so far,' ran the Fed's report on a phone conversation with the Bank of England on Friday 16 October 1964. Next day the new government's three top ministers – Harold Wilson as prime minister, James Callaghan as Chancellor of the Exchequer and George Brown in charge of the newly created Department of Economic Affairs – made the cardinal decision that, despite the grave balance-of-payments situation (with the deficit being estimated at around £800m), there should be no question of even considering devaluation as a serious possibility.

'This decision was to put the government in a straitjacket for the next three years', Barbara Castle justly observed two decades later, yet more in sorrow than in anger, for it would have been a huge surprise if Wilson had jumped the other way. He had, after all, been a member of the government that had devalued in 1949; he had no wish for Labour to be known as the party of devaluation; and, as he had told the House of Commons in July 1961, a second post-war British devaluation 'would be regarded all over the world as an acknowledgement of defeat, a recognition that we were not on a springboard but on a slide'. It was a view with which the Bank of England, imbued with a deep sense of responsibility to the holders of sterling, fully concurred. Nor was rational discussion of the subject encouraged, to put it mildly. 'It was rather an emotional place then,' McMahon drily recalled of his recent arrival at the Bank, 'and merely to mention devaluation was like saying a four-letter word in church.' Indeed, so potent was the identification of the strength of sterling with the strength of Britain that much the same applied in the wider, opinion-forming world – to the extent that among financial journalists there increasingly applied what was known as 'the self-denying ordinance': a tacit agreement not to discuss the potential merits of devaluation as a policy option. Devaluation may or may not have been the right thing to do in October 1964 (though from July 1966 it surely was); either way, it was hardly a propitious atmosphere in which to formulate policy.[1]

No doubt encouraged by the non-devaluation, the City for a few weeks did not give Labour the bumpy ride that many had anticipated.

On 11 November, Callaghan presented an emergency Budget to try to tackle the deteriorating economic situation. Taken as a whole it was deflationary, and indeed the initial stock market response was positive.

By Friday the 13th, however, that relief had been replaced in the equity market by a mood that Kenneth Fleet in the *Sunday Telegraph* described as 'something approaching despair', as brokers and institutional investors began to contemplate the corporation tax and amplified capital gains tax that Callaghan was pledged to introduce the following spring. In his Budget statement he had not divulged either the rates or the mechanics of these new taxes, and over the next few weeks it was largely fear of the unknown that ate into the soul of the investing class. As for the foreign exchanges, they took against the Budget more or less from the start. Sterling had a bad day on the 12th, and Tether explained in the *FT* that, in the eyes of international opinion, 'the toughness Mr Callaghan has shown is not generally considered there to be of the type that the situation demands'. The pound fared even worse on the 13th, and that day Cromer wrote to Callaghan asking him to raise Bank rate from 5 to 6 per cent. Such a rise, Cromer believed, would 'mitigate the danger of a further serious fall in confidence'.[2] Still less than a month into the lifetime of the new, growth-minded government, it was the traditional banker's red-light panacea.

In a meeting at Downing Street with Cromer on the 24th, Wilson observed that 'he was coming to the conclusion that an acceptable alternative to devaluation, in both political and economic terms, might be to let the rate float', but this elicited no response from Cromer. In due course:

> It was agreed that no firm decision should be taken until the following day but it might then be desirable to operate on forward sterling and to approach the Germans and other Europeans as well as the United States and Canada for short-term assistance. The *Prime Minister* said that if these measures failed there would be no alternative but to consider seeking a mandate for devaluation. *Mr Governor* replied that to go to the country on that issue would mean putting Party before country.

Faced by the threat (serious or otherwise) of a 'bankers' ramp' election, Cromer had blinked first. It would be his task – duly performed in the next few days – to send round the begging bowl to the world's central bankers without a binding promise from the British government to adopt the policies that he believed to be necessary. According to Wilson's own, retrospective account, Cromer did say that he was 'doubtful whether this could be done unless he was able to convey to them news of major changes of policy'; but Wilson was adamant that he would not 'sacrifice the constitutional rights of a newly-elected Government'.[3] With the ghosts of 1931 almost palpably in the air, it was a significant moment in British political history.

The run-up to Christmas again saw the City's nerves thoroughly taut, and on Monday the 21st Cromer despatched a formal warning to Wilson: 'This last week has evidenced in business and financial circles at home the most serious lack of confidence that I recall. Rumours and exaggerations have been rife at home and abroad, creating a most dangerous atmosphere . . . It would take very little to trigger off a movement against sterling beyond our power to arrest. We are close to the brink of the abyss.' Cromer then called for action, along the usual belt-tightening lines, and ended, 'I am, Mr Prime Minister, at your disposal to wait upon you at all times.' Next day, while Downing Street pondered, Cromer spoke on the telephone to Al Hayes at the Fed. The American asked (according to the Fed's account) 'why the Bank of England had not seen fit to give the government a public "pat on the back" in connection with some of their recent actions to defend the pound'. To which Cromer replied that there was 'a high degree of solidarity between the Bank and the government' and that 'the Bank habitually is loath to make statements of any kind'. On Wednesday afternoon Cromer was at No. 10, but this time he and Wilson tacitly agreed to forgo the fireworks of four weeks earlier. He 'was not a deflationist at heart or in desire,' the governor insisted, 'but was driven to the conclusion that something more had to be done'. For his part Wilson refused to be defeatist, and Cromer agreed that on the foreign exchanges 'there was every hope that there would be a somewhat different atmosphere in January'. They also agreed, as a fairly inconsequential discussion approached its end, that the end-of-month reserves figures should be adjusted to show a loss of only £8m, whereas the real loss was £115m.[4]

There may have been more than seasonal goodwill behind this thaw, for both men were probably conscious of the intensifying public criticism of the City/government relationship. That had reached a public nadir when Wincott on 15 December devoted his weekly *FT* column to an 'Open Letter to the Chancellor', in which he asserted that the proposed capital gains tax and corporation tax represented a 'fiscal putsch' on the part of one of the government's main economic advisers, Nicholas Kaldor, and that 'there really hasn't been anything like it since Hitler wrote "Mein Kampf"'. Callaghan protested strongly, but a flood of letters to the paper, including ones from the well-known City figures Esmond Durlacher and Walter Salomon, backed Wincott. The episode was the cue for two normally Conservative-supporting financial journalists to give the City a dressing-down. Urging both sides to call a halt in their war, the *Sunday Telegraph*'s Fleet described the City as succumbing to a state of 'hysterical semi-paralysis' and liable soon to find itself accused of being 'incapable of operating unless conditions are tailored to its own liking as they were for a decade under Conservative Governments'. Across at the *Sunday*

Times, William Rees-Mogg argued that the City had 'already allowed itself to drift too far away from the rest of national life', as a result of which 'the great majority of Englishmen underrate the City's value as a national asset . . . and suspect it far too much'. He also took the line that after a week of 'mostly ill-informed' rumours and 'mostly ill-conceived' fears, it was time for the City to grow up and take a more realistic view of what he believed to be an essentially conservative administration. 'As for devaluation,' he added with typical confidence, 'that will not happen.'[5]

*

By March, the build-up to Callaghan's first regular, full-scale Budget was intense. On the 10th, Cromer wrote to Callaghan himself. 'If confidence were not to be restored by the Budget,' he warned, 'I must make it quite clear that I could see little prospect of a further international rescue operation to support sterling. I fear that foreign opinion would regretfully conclude that it was no use any further trying to save us from the consequences of our own policies.' The crux, he insisted, was reducing public expenditure, though he also counselled 'against any measures either in the Exchange Control field or in the nature of discriminatory taxation, which could be interpreted as moving in the direction of a siege economy'.[6]

On 6 April there were duly significant public expenditure cuts, and two days later the discount men found the governor 'cheerful and relaxed', saying that he 'considered the Budget was good for the pound and by and large he thought many of the measures to be aimed in the right direction'. But if Cromer was relatively relaxed, that was far from the case with the stock market, which was dismayed by the details of the new capital gains and corporation taxes. The Budget was, one City gentleman standing in Throgmorton Street told the television cameras soon after Callaghan had sat down, 'a most disgusting attack on anyone who wants to make his way in the world. It's Marxism: they want a communist state. Personally, I shall fight like hell on the beaches, and on the streets and in the farms we will fight them.'[7]

There then followed several weeks of the most serious pressure on sterling so far in 1965. The problems involved in holding the $2.80 rate once again loomed large. On 5 August there was 'a gloomy session at the Bank', noted Cecil King, the newspaper magnate and now non-executive director of the Bank. 'There has been a run on gold and a run on sterling, and the reserves are in sight of exhaustion. It is not thought that any further deflationary gestures would produce any effect. The Governor thinks the only card left to play is a wage and price freeze. This might impress foreign opinion; nothing else would.'[8] For someone like Cromer whose larger economic instincts were wholly free-market, this remedy was a measure of how the defence of the sterling parity transcended everything in his psyche.

Next month, George Brown at the Department of Economic Affairs produced its long-awaited, much-vaunted National Plan. Britain's annual growth target was to be an ambitious 3.8 per cent, amounting over the six years 1964–70 to total growth of some 25 per cent. 'George Brown's presence ensured that the plan would be launched with the maximum of bravura and panache,' Callaghan's biographer, Kenneth Morgan, has justly observed. 'Sterling would be rescued by socialism. But most economists viewed it with considerable doubts.' The *Banker*'s view was fairly typical of the City's jaundiced reaction. 'The fundamental flaw of the Brown "Plan" is that it confuses what ought (however arguably) to be done with what can be done and what will be done', it asserted in October, before making an unexpected reference to television satire. 'To join a topical idiom with a Victorian one, we have here not so much a programme, more a pipedream or reverie. In short, a brown study.'[9]

During the winter of 1965–6, sterling was relatively stable, the mood of the stock market was neither bullish nor bearish, and the City was starting to get used to a Labour government. By early 1966 there was a growing City suspicion that Labour would soon look to another election to increase its slender majority. Writing in February to a correspondent in Buenos Aires, John Phillimore of Barings caught the mood: 'Here, it rains every day, the economy of the country continues to deteriorate and it looks as if we may shortly have another Socialist Government with a larger majority. In fact Argentina looks quite attractive by comparison.'[10]

On election night itself, 31 March, with Labour heading for just short of a three-figure overall majority, Wilson told a television interviewer that the Tories might understand finance, but Labour understood industry. It seemed at the time the more fruitful, as well as more attractive, priority. One of the re-elected government's first jobs was to decide who should succeed Cromer. In the end it was the deputy governor and former chief cashier, Leslie O'Brien, who in Callaghan's admiring retrospective words 'had entered the Bank of England on the bottom rung without the advantage of family or school' and was 'modest, quiet, considerate of the views of others but firm in his own beliefs', as well as 'technically proficient'. O'Brien was surely correct in judging that his meritocratic background appealed to Callaghan and Wilson, as did the fact that he was not part of the City Establishment in the same way as Cromer.

O'Brien would be the first governor to have come up through the ranks, but he was manifestly such a competent, straightforward central banker that the prospect did not alarm the City grandees. 'Good plain cook: won't argue about the menu' was reputedly the reaction of Morgan Grenfell's Lord Harcourt. There was an expectation that the new governor would shift the Bank's centre of gravity westwards, especially given his long-standing friendship with Armstrong at the Treasury. Yet any assumption that O'Brien would be the government's 'yes man' underestimated both the man himself and the reliance that the City still placed on the Bank as its principal means of leverage with the government.[11]

Cromer's last day in the office was Thursday 30 May, and Cecil King after the weekly Court had 'a long talk' with the Bank's chief economist:

> [Maurice] Allen says (1) the latest [trade] figures coming up are worse than ever and (2) that our reserve figures are faked, thanks to the co-operation of the Americans – a very powerful weapon they hold over our heads. I asked what should be done. He said in default of some large increase of productivity, of which there is no sign or likelihood, the Government should (1) run down its overseas commitments much faster than it is doing, (2) enforce a wage freeze, (3) introduce control of imports. A wage freeze by itself just now would not be enough, as it would not operate quickly enough, and we have, at most, eighteen months. I said I saw no chance of this Government eating its words to the required degree.

That evening the Bank held a farewell reception for Cromer, which Wilson attended. To King's wife the prime minister 'looked a broken man – bigger, warmer and nicer, but he now knows he can't do it'.[12] The retiring governor, though, was far from broken, as he looked forward to returning to Barings and the more congenial world of private banking.

July 1966 proved a memorable debut for his successor.[13] On the 8th, shortly before leaving for Basle, O'Brien called on Wilson to tell him that continuing attacks on sterling and exchange losses were once more threatening the parity of the pound. The situation had not improved by Tuesday the 12th, when O'Brien sent a six-page letter to Callaghan on 'our general situation'. Although his tone was less hectoring and censorious than Cromer's, he argued strongly that unless the right measures were taken quickly, 'a collapse of the sterling parity – which is increasingly widely and cynically being forecast on all sides – will be inevitable'. The right measures, he believed, included major cuts in overseas expenditure and the reducing of domestic demand, even if this raised the level of unemployment. However, as he opportunistically noted, 'a long period of very low unemployment has not produced the hoped-for breakthrough on productivity and restrictive work practices'. O'Brien also suggested a total wages freeze for a year or eighteen months in order to help bring about those 'major changes in attitude' without which, according to him, it would be impossible for the UK to 'secure a reasonable and sustained external balance'. In sum: 'Certainly exhortation is now a debased currency. But a total temporary wage freeze (it would have to be total – harsh, crude and unfair though that would be) represents a way – somewhat dangerous perhaps – in which real leadership might arouse the country.'

O'Brien had already suggested a Bank rate increase, and on Thursday the 14th this duly took place (up from 6 to 7 per cent); at the same time it was announced by Callaghan that there would soon be further measures to restore overseas confidence in sterling. 'This is the last chance', declared the *FT* next morning, insisting that the government 'either takes steps itself to avoid devaluation, or the rest of the world will make up its mind for it'.[14]

The sustained attacks on sterling on Friday the 15th accelerated Labour's agonised decision-making process about whether the avoidance of devaluation should remain the supreme goal, if its inevitable consequence was drastic deflation so soon after an election won on the premise of planned economic growth. Stressing practicalities rather than morality, O'Brien wrote Callaghan a strong anti-devaluation letter, prior to an early evening meeting with him and Wilson at No. 10. Wilson was indeed determined not to devalue, still convinced that to do so would leave Labour fatally holed in terms of its reputation for economic management, and he and Callaghan explained to O'Brien their plans for a deflationary, confidence-inspiring package. 'It would be quite wrong to produce a package which was regarded overseas as being half-baked', the governor insisted after listening to them. Finally Wilson (presumably with a view to securing ammunition for the Cabinet battle that lay ahead) asked O'Brien for his view on devaluation. The official minute suggests that the governor reiterated his opposition in surprisingly eloquent terms:

> If the British Government were to devalue, it would be regarded by overseas countries as a device by a Socialist Government to avoid having to face the real decisions which were essential if our payments were to be brought into balance. This view he restated on three occasions, and he used a graphic phrase, namely that devaluation would be regarded as the Socialist Government's 'recipe' for dealing with a situation which in fact demanded unpleasant internal measures. On the other hand, if a Socialist Government could maintain the parity of the £ in spite of the present pressures by introducing tough measures, it would once and for all demonstrate worldwide its determination to solve the problems without recourse to devaluation. From this he believed the Government would gain enormous benefit.

Wilson would later pay tribute to how, during the July 1966 crisis, O'Brien's 'calm and reasoned advice made a deep impression on my colleagues and myself'; and at this critical moment in the Labour Party's history, three and a half months after it had won a commanding majority for the first time since 1945, O'Brien's apparently not unsympathetic stance may have been decisive in stiffening ministerial resolve to place the needs of sterling above those of economic expansion.[15]

Some twenty-four hours later, returning from the governor's annual cricket match at the Bank's sports ground at Roehampton, O'Brien called, at George Brown's request, at Brown's official flat in Carlton House Terrace. By now the minister knew that only devaluation could save his cherished National Plan, and O'Brien remembered how 'after being harangued for some long time by George pacing round the room in his shirt sleeves we were joined by William Armstrong'. However, 'neither of us would budge and George eventually gave up'. Following Wilson's return from an unfortunately timed visit to Moscow, there was a five-hour Cabinet meeting on Tuesday the 19th, at which the six in favour of devaluation were outvoted by the seventeen against. Next day Wilson announced a heavily deflationary package. It went down well enough in the City, and the sterling crisis eased, though at their weekly meeting that Thursday the discount market's representatives expressed some disappointment to O'Brien. 'It was difficult to think what more could have been done except perhaps a bigger cut in Government expenditure', O'Brien replied, and he went on: 'Although, in his position, he could not express political views, the action taken was the result of nearly two years of boss shots and now that they have hit the target, nobody believes it. Labour have a built-in disadvantage. This is not fair but is one of the facts of life.'[16] So indeed it was.

*

The Eurobond market was now predominantly located in London, but irrespective of nationality, its community in these early years had a distinct and very attractive character: intimate but cosmopolitan, co-operative as much as competitive, intellectually creative and thoroughly can-do in spirit. 'Withholding tax, exchange control, the difficulty of getting judgements and foreign currencies, sovereign immunity, the stock exchange regulations and problems about negotiability were all major problems', Nicholas Wilson of the solicitors Slaughter and May recalled of this pioneering phase. 'They all seemed insuperable at times, but nevertheless the driving force of people at Warburgs, White Weld and other issuing houses was such that solutions had to be found, and they were found.' English law, moreover, was trusted, London and New York had a common language, and the issues had a fixed commission structure (unbreachable for many years) that appealed greatly to the Swiss banks.[17] All in all, it was a new and hugely stimulating market that caught the imagination of bankers.

In the City of the mid to late 1960s, however, nothing was quite so alluring as a juicy takeover battle, with its attendant glamour and prospective fat fees. Rules tended to be bent, and the City's guidelines (admittedly somewhat more forthright after a revised version of the Notes on Amalgamations appeared in 1963) still left a lot of room for manoeuvre.[18] An improving stock market from late 1966 stimulated takeover and merger activity, leading to three episodes that, as the financial journalist Richard Spiegelberg nicely put it, 'finally damaged the delicate fabric of the Queensberry Rules beyond repair'. These were the controversial Philips/ Thorn struggle for Pye; a stock market 'slogging match' involving Courtaulds, with the wholesaling business of Wilkinson & Riddell as the prize; and the battle for Metal Industries fought between Thorn Electrical Industries and Aberdare Holdings. It was the third episode that earned the most publicity, with Kleinwort Benson (acting for Metal Industries) being much criticised for its apparent disregard of shareholders' rights. Almost immediately afterwards, at a City dinner on 18 July 1967, Wilson called on the City to promulgate 'formal and clear ground rules' about takeover battles and to see that those rules were carried out. O'Brien read the runes, at once getting the Issuing Houses Association (IHA) to recon- vene its working party on the subject, as well as telling its chairman, Michael Bucks, that the Bank was now in favour of 'a standing advisory committee' in order to implement the takeover code and, if necessary, 'hold the ring'. When Bucks demurred, O'Brien told him frankly that 'if the City were not capable of putting their own house in order it would be open to me to advise HMG that there was no alternative but to introduce a securities and exchange commission on the American model'.[19] Bucks and his colleagues took the point, and soon the regulation (or, rather, non-regulation) of takeover battles would never be quite the same again.

Meanwhile, a large quantity of mediocre dross was still attached to the Stock Exchange and its immediate environs. When Jonathan Aitken in 1967 went in search of *The Young Meteors* of thrusting, meritocratic New Britain, he found few anywhere near Capel Court. One of his interviewees, a twenty-six-year-old Old Etonian now ensconced in the family stock- broking firm, was definitely a non-meteor:

> Do I work hard? Well, frankly no. I get down to the office after the rush hour – about 10.15 – and I leave just before it, about 4 o'clock. Some keen chaps arrive before it and leave after it, but it doesn't really do them much good. Occasionally, if I've been out at a thrash and got harry pissers I don't get in till about half eleven. That is a bit idle, but you know it's astonishing the business you can do indirectly by being seen at the right places, like deb dances and so on. I once sat next to a man I'd never seen before in my life at a dinner party before a dance, and we got talking when the girls had gone out, and to cut a long story short, we're now managing his whole portfolio.

Aitken, though, also talked to a grammar-school educated twenty-eight- year-old stockbroker with an economics degree. 'I'm frustrated all the time because I could get far more business if only the City wasn't hide- bound by these elaborate family connections, which give the family firms all the contacts', he confessed. 'I've got no chips on my shoulder about it, yet I'm quite certain that if I had gone to Eton, which seems to provide about half the people in the City, I'd do far more business through social contacts.'

However, though appalled by the overall quality of the people working in the City ('The investment managers for insurance firms are often ludicrously bad, and as a result they can't see through bad stockbrokers who work by virtual guesswork'), he did see hope for the future in the fact that 'while the old firms continue with their private clients and their new issue business, the more go-ahead firms like ours [perhaps Phillips & Drew?] are concentrating on investment analysis', which 'brings in work from fund managers of unit trusts who are young professional people like ourselves, and who above all respect efficiency'. In sum, this broker concluded, 'that's the way the City ought to be moving, but today the old school tie still reigns triumphant'. It did indeed, but the inexorable rise of the institutional investor, hastened in the mid-1960s by the existence of a Labour government that seriously undermined private client confidence, at last meant that that undisputed sway was under threat.[20]

If there was a race of financial supermen in the City of the mid-1960s, most observers felt that it resided at Warburgs at 30 Gresham Street, the so-called 'Night Club in the City', where desks were occupied by nine in the morning and often after seven in the evening.[21] In the traditional City, these were unheard-of hours. 'When I came out of the office in the evening,' Martin Gordon (who joined Warburgs in 1963) recalls, 'the only other people I would ever see would be Japanese bankers.' At that time the firm numbered about 150 people; and for the rest of his life Warburg would set his face, not entirely successfully, against size for its own sake.

Lunches were famously abstemious (for many years beer, cider or mineral water was the only choice of drink with the meal), while a pronounced work ethic pervaded the whole atmosphere. Ascot, the Lord's Test and Wimbledon were still important points in the City calendar, but 'it was frowned upon in Warburgs if we took the day off for such occasions', Peter Stormonth Darling has written in a memoir of the firm. The cult of the all-round, preferably sporting amateur, still a potent force elsewhere in the City, was entirely absent; and one of Stormonth Darling's more iconoclastic colleagues, Andrew Smithers, would enjoy smuggling in cricketing metaphors at meetings where Warburg was present, though the great man never let on until afterwards that he did not understand what a googly was. Otherwise, internal communication was of the essence, with Warburg and the other founding 'Uncles' deliberately encouraging an open-door, partnership approach.[22]

Was it, overall, a happy place? Certainly, for most of the younger generation, working at Warburgs in the 1960s was memorable and usually formative, but not everyone relished the ultra-competitive atmosphere. At any one time one was either 'in' or 'out', and for those who dropped out of favour (not always for purely explicable reasons) there was sometimes no way back. For others it was a hugely enriching experience, combining hard and purposeful work, intellectual stimulation and a sense of being in an elite team getting new business and trying to do it in new, high-quality ways. 'Warburgs was indeed an acquired taste', Stormonth Darling remarks, but it is easy to see why some very able people acquired it.[23]

The business itself, for all the firm's steeply climbing reputation, was far from the biggest among the City's merchant banks: Warburg had no wish to build up the banking side and challenge firms like Hambros or Kleinworts on their own terrain. Instead, he wanted Warburgs to stand or fall by its deeds in company finance and in the world's capital markets, especially those of London and the rest of Europe. Indeed, one of his fundamental principles was never to let corporate financiers get their hands on capital – on the grounds that it would make them lazy, using money instead of their brains. In practice, it proved quite a struggle for the firm's corporate finance arm to land big British companies. Significantly, two were Grand Metropolitan Hotels and Thomson Newspapers, both run by outsiders; but eventually by the end of the 1960s the achievements of Warburgs in the Eurobond market began to translate into a string of major UK corporate clients, the most prestigious being ICI. Revealingly, however, Warburg had limited enthusiasm for the activities of the investment department. 'When he telephoned me, he would ritually ask, "How's the market?",' Stormonth Darling recalls, 'but he paid not the slightest attention to my answer other than to see whether I knew. If I told him it was up when it was down, he was in no position to correct me, nor did he care.'

Warburg had always taken a dim view of the intelligence of stock exchanges, not least the London Stock Exchange, and in their herd-like tendencies he could find none of the subtlety that rendered business life vital. By contrast, he worked ceaselessly to foster his firm's international connections. 'In putting deals together,' an obituary would perceptively note about his thinking, 'the handicap of small size could be overcome by using banking syndicates, the growth of which in London Warburgs was to pioneer.' Yet it was not all plain sailing, and at the end of 1964 he ended his firm's formal connection with Kuhn Loeb, largely as a result of personality disagreements.[24] Warburg may have tried instead to form an alliance with Lehman Brothers, far more go-ahead anyway than Kuhn Loeb, but it came to nothing. Back in the nineteenth century the Achilles heel of Rothschilds had been the absence of an effective American bridgehead; but for the moment such a deficiency would not matter to Warburgs, so long as capability and ambition remained in alignment.

Of Warburg himself, Stormonth Darling observes that 'He was the boss, and you didn't easily forget it.' The positive side to this was that during these years Warburg pursued a systematic search for young talent and was an unstinting mentor to those prepared to listen. 'Above all,' Stormonth Darling reflects, 'Siegmund liked to be thought of as a teacher.'

'A man of vision, courage, wisdom and boundless energy', Peter Spira wrote after Warburg's death. 'He was innovative and cultured, yet ruthless and vicious, a wonderful friend to many and a dangerous enemy to a few. Siegmund was mercurial, highly emotional, often irrational, hypnotic and impulsive, provocative and conciliatory, prudish yet fascinated by the erotic. In sum, a character of multiple contrasts – and a German Jewish refugee to boot.'[25] It was no wonder that, in the rather grey post-war City of London, he was such a compelling, divisive and myth-laden figure.

*

One of the decade's emerging figures was the high-profile Jim Slater, whose very name still evokes a particular era.[26] His pre-City years showed that he already had something special about him. Slater was born in 1929 and brought up in Wembley; his father owned a small building-cum-decorating business; after going to the local grammar school, he qualified as a chartered accountant; and by 1963, seven years after going into the motor industry, he had become right-hand man to Donald Stokes at Leyland and seemed next in line to succeed him. For some time Slater had taken an active interest in the stock market, and he now persuaded Nigel Lawson, City editor of the *Sunday Telegraph*, that he should write a monthly share-tipping column. Making his debut on 3 March 1963, 'Capitalist' set out his stall: 'My object is not to try and crystal-gaze into the future, but rather to spot anomalies on the basis of existing information before the market does. For the market is not perfect: if it were there would be no point in buying one share rather than another.' His stated aim was capital gain rather than income, with no sentimental attachment to the shares that he selected: 'If by any chance there is any adverse trend, such as a poor interim dividend or statement, I would recommend selling immediately.' Within three months 'Capitalist' was boasting a 30 per cent profit, way above the market's overall rise, but he warned his readers, 'The important thing is not to chase the shares the Monday following my article. If you wait for two or three days you should normally be able to pick them up at no more than 5 p.c. above my own price.' Slater had promised Lawson that he would not exploit the column for personal gain; but according to his resourceful biographer, Charles Raw, he pulled in at least £25,000 in less than two years.[27]

Although they already knew each other, it was probably during the winter of 1963–4 that Slater became friendly with Peter Walker, who – having done well out of insurance, property and unit trusts – was now, as a Tory MP, focusing on his political career. Slater rang Walker, wanting to talk to him urgently. 'He had, by investing, built up some capital of his own, he told me, and probably had £100,000 of his own resources he could call upon', Walker recalled over a quarter of a century later of their seminal conversation. 'He felt there were opportunities in investing in badly managed businesses, pulling up their management and doing well in the process.' Should he therefore leave Leyland? 'I did say that if he decided to go off on his own, I would give him any help I could. I was ready to put in capital if he wanted more investment and to introduce him to the many friends I had in the City . . . A few days later he phoned to say he had decided to go it alone and would appreciate my help.' So was conceived and soon afterwards born Slater Walker. In summer 1964 they hatched plans for the Slater Walker Industrial Group (SWIG). According to Raw, this was intended to become 'the instrument through which Slater Walker implemented its new policy of using large shareholdings to influence the management of industrial companies to adopt Slater's gospel of efficiency', and 'the receptacle into which investors were to be invited to pour large amounts of cash'.[28]

On the last day of October, a fortnight after Labour had come to power in a positive frame of mind towards conglomerates and industrial restructuring, a small story in the *FT* revealed that Slater was intending 'to form an industrial group'.[29] Slater Walker's new group was announced on 3 February 1965, with a circular to shareholders declaring that SWIG would acquire 'substantial stakes' in companies that the directors deemed capable of 'considerable development'. *The Times* observed without comment that its formation meant that there were now six sides to Slater Walker's activities, 'ranging from property owning and investment management to industrial development'. The other three 'sides' were an investment trust, trading in securities and management services. 'With benefit of hindsight,' Raw wrote, 'it is easy to see just how open to abuse Slater's elegant structure was':

> The larger part of his company's profit was to be derived from investment advice to clients whose combined resources represented a significant sum of money in stock market terms, especially in relation to the size of many of the companies selected for investment. Simultaneously, another corporate limb was to find companies deemed to be in need of management help and to press that help upon them by acquiring effectively controlling shareholdings – yet, on its chairman's own admission, he was not interested in 'long term' investment. Add to this combination a plethora of share dealing companies and a stated interest in 'special situations', and it is not hard to see the danger that existed.

All in all, Raw concludes with some elegance himself, it was a 'combination of functions' that 'would have tried the most punctilious of men'.[30]

As yet, Slater stayed based in the West End, not the City, though his investment department did move there in 1966. Always there were many balls in the air, but Raw's version (by far the most detailed) is that during 1965–6 there were two defining strands to Slater Walker's multifarious activities. One was the systematic use of clients' money in order to acquire control of companies; the other, having acquired that control, was to make a quick buck by stripping each company of its supposedly under-utilised assets. 'By 1966 Slater's avowed policy of taking over sleepy companies, ripping out (and selling off) the loss-making sectors to build up a profitable core, had become received wisdom among Conservative radicals', the property developer Nigel Broackes recalled in his 1979 memoirs, before adding regretfully that 'somewhere along the line, indus-trial rationalisation turned into pass-the-parcel'. 'Alluring dance of the asset strippers' was the heading of an *Observer* article in January 1967 by the paper's City editor, John Davis. '"I have at least five situations on the boil," says Jim Slater, today's leading exponent of buying assets on the cheap and chairman of Slater, Walker Securities,' it started. 'Last year Slater cleared close on a cool £1 million profit on two deals alone.' Davis ended with another pearl from 'the man with the golden touch': 'The problem is not finding the asset situations, but being able to negotiate out of them on a reasonable profit.'[31]

It was during 1967, against the background of a bull market and the start of the merger boom, that Slater Walker really took off, together with Slater's own reputation as a self-made man uniquely in tune with the financial and industrial zeitgeist of big-is-best, industrial efficiency and general go-go. Most of Slater Walker's money was probably being made through opportunistic share dealings, but in the financial and business press he would soon be acquiring something akin to hero status. 'One per cent of £3 million is worth a day or two of Mr Slater's time' was the title of a *Sunday Times* piece in August 1967. With his group now valued by the stock market at around £10m, Slater was in expansive mood as he discussed the shortcomings of British management: 'A business should be run like an investment portfolio – cut your losses and let your profits run – in other words concentrate your efforts on the profit-makers rather than loss-makers. A lot of British boards seem to do the opposite . . .' Slater himself denied vigorously that Slater Walker was overstretching itself: 'We get assets first and then profits. We always have a solid base to work from.' As for accusations that Slater Walker was building up a ragbag of interests, he was adamant that 'the only thing that fits in the group as far as I'm concerned is one I can make money out of'. Inevitably, Slater was identified as one of the young meteors. 'We're rather a new breed of merchant bank', he told Aitken (who himself subsequently joined Slater Walker). 'We have no traditional business coming our way obviously, so we have to go out and get it, and we compete with new methods and perhaps a slightly more aggressive attitude than longer-established bankers.' As for the future, Slater remarked that he would only be happy when 'we've built up one of the leading merchant banks'.[32]

Such thrust, such ambition: it was a million miles away from the comfortable, entrenched world of Lloyd's, where according to Aitken such was the strength of 'the follow-my-leader unthinking tradition' that recently several underwriters had 'actually stamped, in all seriousness, an insurance form for "Baa Baa Black Sheep" because one of the leading syndicates had stamped the form as a joke to see who would follow them'. Yet by this time, unbeknown to Aitken and indeed almost all the underwriters and brokers at this City bastion, fundamental and fateful change was in the offing. The unwitting catalyst was Hurricane Betsy, which in September 1965 had done huge damage to the offshore oil industry in the Gulf of Mexico and was directly responsible for the two worst years at Lloyd's in anyone's peacetime memory. Names (whose numbers had grown from fewer than 2,000 before the war to more than 6,000 by 1966) had the disconcerting experience of writing out cheques rather than receiving them, and predictably some decided to put their money elsewhere.[33] Consequently by 1967 the 'capacity' of the market was starting to diminish, at the very time when, as in banking, the American insurance industry was looking to compete hard in London. Could the club still do the business? At Lloyd's, as elsewhere in the City, that was no longer an idle question.

*

In the autumn of 1967, as Labour entered its fourth year in government with the pound still hanging on at $2.80, London's almost wholly domestic-oriented equity market was buoyant, partly because of the expectation that devaluation would come sooner rather than later and thereby stimulate the economy in a relatively painfree way. Things naturally looked rather different from O'Brien's vantage-point. 'People must be punch-drunk', he sardonically remarked to the discount market on 14 September, after the exchanges had reacted surprisingly calmly to the latest bad trade figures, but over the next few weeks a series of blows put sterling on an irreversible one-way ride towards devaluation. On 18 September a dock strike began in London, Liverpool and other ports; then in mid-October the EEC published a report questioning sterling's long-term future as a reserve currency, the monthly trade figures were even worse than expected, and a Bank-rate rise of half a per cent was less than the foreign exchange markets had anticipated. Armstrong at the Treasury told Cairncross on the 13th that the question of devaluation now 'rested with Leslie, whose tactics were to exhaust all possible lines of assistance before throwing in his hand'.[34]

By late October, with a £500m deficit being forecast for both 1967 and 1968, sterling was being sold so heavily that O'Brien seems to have conceded to Armstrong that at last he saw devaluation as inevitable. However, when he saw Wilson on 1 November, he said that he was still unable to recommend devaluation. Instead, the decisive intervention came from Cairncross, who next day sent Callaghan a memo arguing that realistically there was no alternative. The Chancellor saw Cairncross on the morning of the 3rd and reluctantly agreed. Shortly before seeing Wilson (who did not demur) on Saturday the 4th, Callaghan met O'Brien:

> After three years of incessant borrowing and ever-rising debt Jim Callaghan felt he had come to the end of the road and I agreed with him. He said that unless we could mobilise support for sterling of a medium-term character, say three to five years as a minimum, we must accept the inevitable conclusions. I had to advise that I saw no hope of such medium-term support, although I was prepared to put the question to my central banking colleagues. Meanwhile we must prepare for devaluation. A move so large that it provoked many other countries to follow would clearly serve little useful purpose. My soundings suggested that we could devalue by 15% without being followed.[35]

It would be a smoothly organised move, in that for a couple of years a highly secret Bank/Treasury group had been preparing the detailed, complicated mechanics that would be required in a devaluation. The group's code-name of FU accurately reflected official feelings about the contingency.

Public life's rituals, meanwhile, continued as Parliament debated the Queen's Speech. Cromer, speaking in the House of Lords, took the opportunity to declare that 'during the last three years the business world has become progressively more confused and disillusioned', adding that the latest crop of policies was 'inadequate and largely irrelevant to the needs of the nation at present'. Over the following weekend O'Brien was at Basle, where his fellow central bankers accepted the principle of a 15 per cent devaluation by Britain without any retaliatory devaluation by themselves.

On the morning of Monday the 13th, before returning, he rang Callaghan to ask if the government would accept as an alternative to devaluation (in Callaghan's subsequent account) 'a smaller loan of say $2 billions from the IMF, with milder conditions than those initially proposed by the United States'. This, O'Brien said, would 'stop the rot', at least temporarily; but Callaghan now preferred to keep his room for manoeuvre, including if need be devaluation, and anyway reckoned that $2bn was not enough. Early that evening, having returned from Basle, O'Brien went with Callaghan to see Wilson, who did not dissent from the Chancellor's course of action. The trio then went off to the Lord

Mayor's Banquet at Guildhall, where according to Callaghan 'no one could have told from the Prime Minister's demeanour that anything was amiss', before the two politicians returned to Downing Street. There, at 11.15 p.m., they (as Callaghan put it in his note for the record) *'decided finally'*.[36] The pound was to be devalued to $2.40, probably over the coming weekend.

The October trade figures on Tuesday the 14th were startlingly bad (at £107m, comfortably the largest monthly deficit yet recorded), and Callaghan was left in no doubt by the Treasury that there must be a significant package of measures if the proposed new rate was going to stick. That evening, at what his biographer calls 'a ferocious Cabinet meeting', Callaghan told his colleagues that sterling would be devalued on Saturday the 18th and insisted that there must also be major expenditure cuts. Wednesday was quiet, but Thursday and Friday were both days to remember. Thursday began with the Cabinet formally deciding in favour of devaluation, while almost at the same time O'Brien was, according to King, being 'more forthcoming than is usually the case' as he put the Court broadly in the picture:

> We could make one last borrowing from the IMF, but if that went, we should be quite helpless. O'Brien plainly implied that we should have to devalue on Saturday and use these final resources for controlling the situation post-devaluation . . . He thought the sterling area countries would follow us and they hoped the non-sterling ones would not . . . When this exposition was over, Alf Robens [Lord Robens, in charge of the National Coal Board and, like King, a recently elected, Labour-sympathising, very non-executive director of the Bank] passed me a paper: 'Glad to see you can still smile, 1931'.

Later that day, in the Commons, Callaghan found himself put horribly on the spot. In what would swiftly earn the reputation of being the most expensive parliamentary question ever posed, a Labour backbencher, Robert Sheldon, asked him whether press reports about a possible $1bn loan from abroad were true. Faced by an impossible situation – in which the answer 'yes' would have been a lie, but any other answer a tacit admission of imminent devaluation – Callaghan said that he had nothing to add to previous statements.[37]

The implications of Sheldon's question were played out in the foreign exchange market, where the almost certain knowledge of imminent devaluation gave the speculators an irresistibly easy killing. Next day, Friday the 17th, the Bank spent well over a billion dollars defending the rate, for the last time. 'The pound was under siege in the world's foreign exchange markets yesterday', the patriotic front-page report in *The Times* began next day. 'In London, the Bank of England battled courageously, non-stop, in an attempt to beat off the biggest selling wave ever seen.'[38]

Devaluation was announced by the Treasury at 9.30 p.m. that Saturday, the 18th. At six o'clock the following evening Wilson made his ill-fated 'pound in your pocket' broadcast. On Monday afternoon, addressing a packed Commons, a suitably sombre Callaghan expressed the hope that devaluation would confer 'a lasting and substantial improvement' in Britain's balance of payments and gave details of the accompanying package of measures. That day, however, eyes were also on the City, even though all the main markets were closed. Throgmorton Street, the man from *The Times* found, 'had the atmosphere of a black carnival, with market men – jobbers, brokers and clerks – crowding the pavements and formed in clusters alive with conversation'. Even though there was no possibility of business, few City men felt able to stay away, not even Sir Robert Adeane, the 'entrepreneurial investor with an aristocratic style' (in Stormonth Darling's phrase) now running the Drayton group. 'Bloody devaluation,' he complained afterwards, 'I had to miss a whole day's shooting.'[39]

Nevertheless, even for those who believed it was overdue, the actual event of devaluation was a traumatic moment in the City psyche. The sense of humiliation was compounded by the knowledge that neither Australia nor South Africa had decided to devalue, which in effect signalled the end of the sterling area. The tendency, inevitably, was to put all the blame on the government. Devaluation, Cromer told the House of Lords on the Tuesday afterwards, 'need never have occurred if determination to put the integrity of the country, surely the first responsibility of Government, had been given credence by appropriate policies as well as fine words'. He cited, as examples of 'party political dogma', the corporation tax, the selective employment tax and the capital gains tax 'with its all-embracing stranglehold'. Like many in the City, he did not question that devaluation would be a seriously damaging blow to London's position as an international financial centre.

It was just over eighteen years since, on a Sunday evening in September 1949, Cobbold had told the Court that 'devaluation can be done once but can and must not even be in question a second time unless there have been major events such as a world war in the intervening period'.[40]

CHAPTER THIRTY-SIX

Go-go

'He had met the new Chancellor and was quite impressed by him', the discount market was told by O'Brien in mid-December 1967. 'He did not think that he would put politics before the necessary measures but he did not expect any announcement to be made before Christmas. He could only hope that before the end of January some of the Sacred Cows might have contracted Foot and Mouth.' The new, post-devaluation occupant at No. 11 was Roy Jenkins, who was already uncomfortably aware that the markets regarded the measures that had accompanied devaluation as far from adequate. But sterling spent the closing weeks of the year under renewed pressure; and four days before Christmas, King learned from O'Brien and Maurice Allen at the Bank that 'they do not think another devaluation in 1968 is inevitable, but they think it is odds on'. By the New Year the prevailing tone there was positively apocalyptic, with Parsons telling King on the 4th that 'the present crisis is as grave as that of 1940 – with no Winston Churchill waiting to take over'. A fortnight later Jenkins announced an additional £700m of spending cuts, but soon O'Brien confessed to the discount market that the measures had 'disappointed' him. The governor, his listeners thought, 'appeared very depressed'.

In the City, as elsewhere, the expectation quickly developed that Jenkins' first Budget, due on 19 March, would (as Allen told King) 'either break the pound or give us a breathing space'. With less than two weeks to go, O'Brien confidently predicted to the discount market that 'there would be no flabby Budget' and that 'the Chancellor's intentions were good and an incomes policy was expected'. The reserves, though, continued to haemorrhage (having lost over £1bn since the previous October), and on Wednesday the 13th King found both O'Brien and his deputy extremely pessimistic. 'They say they are living from day to day – last Friday was disastrously bad and, as the Governor said, pushed us even nearer the brink . . . O'Brien and Parsons both say we may get by if the Budget is tough enough.'¹

Next day the Queen Mother paid an official visit to the Bank. She may have spotted a certain tension in the air. 'Everyone at the Bank gloomier than they were even yesterday', King noted. 'It appears that the rush for gold is quite out of hand.' During that week the London gold pool that the Bank of England had been operating since 1961 on behalf of most Western governments came under intolerable strain from speculators convinced that the dollar was no longer strong enough to hold gold's price at $35 an ounce. The once almighty dollar had long been vulnerable because of the worsening US balance of payments, and now the Tet offensive in Vietnam made nonsense of the pledge given by Bill Martin of the Fed that the $35 price would be defended 'to the last ingot'. During this tumultuous week so much gold had to be flown from Fort Knox to London that the floor of the Bank of England's weighing room finally collapsed. Martin realised by the Thursday that the game was up, asked O'Brien to close the London gold market the next day, and summoned an emergency meeting of central bankers and others for the weekend. Late on Thursday evening O'Brien went to No. 10 to recommend the American request to Wilson and Jenkins. 'If we were to do as the Americans asked,' he told them, 'we would stem our own currency outflow except in the New York market. Our available funds might or might not suffice for that market, they would almost certainly not suffice to maintain the parity of the £ in London through Friday. The choice was between closure and letting the rate go . . .'[2] He got his way, and in the small hours Friday was proclaimed a bank holiday, with London's stock and foreign exchange markets to be shut, as well as the gold market.

That weekend in Washington, with O'Brien present, a two-tier system for gold was agreed, in effect creating an artificial distinction between official and private transactions. The Americans were adamant that the London gold market must remain closed for the time being, and in agreeing to this O'Brien seemingly overrode the advice of his expert colleague Roy Bridge, who was convinced that such a move would result in South Africa diverting its sales elsewhere. The London gold market eventually reopened on 1 April, and some months later Louis Franck of Samuel Montagu called on O'Brien to tell him that London had 'lost the gold market to Switzerland' and that the fortnight of closure had been directly responsible. Zurich, henceforth, would be the main centre for physical gold, and typically Franck added that he was 'proposing to develop the gold market activities of his Swiss subsidiary in order to keep his foot in the door'.[3] It was – seemingly – the end of almost three centuries of London dominance in the world of gold.

'I am certainly breathing a little more freely than I expected when I saw you last week', O'Brien, back from Washington, wrote on Tuesday 19 March to Cobbold (now Lord Chamberlain). It was Budget day, and Jenkins recalled how in the run-up he had had 'two or three talks' with the governor, who had been 'modestly reticent about advocating specific courses, although he expressed a general preference for a big Budget (that is, a lot of additional taxation) and for indirect as opposed to direct taxation'. Jenkins added that he had found O'Brien 'a useful sounding board for how badly any Special Charge (or non-recurring mini capital levy) would be received in the City'. The Budget itself was grimly austere (removing over £900m from the economy in a full financial year), made a virtue out of the battle to right the balance of payments and was warmly welcomed by the *FT* as 'designed to hold back consumer expenditure hard without weakening the incentive to earn more profit and income through greater efficiency'. O'Brien, who enjoyed a positive working relationship with Jenkins, agreed. 'The Budget was a good effort and better than he expected it to be,' he told the discount market, 'and he felt like showing his approval by lowering Bank Rate, although the public sector was still taking too much of our money.' Half a point was indeed clipped off Bank rate on the 21st, from 8 to 7½ per cent, and Cairncross noted with some amusement that 'the comic side' of this cut was that 'the Governor regarded it from the start as a vote of confidence *by the Bank* in the Budget as if – to quote Denis [Sir Denis Rickett of the Treasury] – the Bank was quite independent of HMG and itself decided what to do with Bank rate'.[4] On the face of it this was the old story of separate empires, as if the Radcliffe Report had never happened, but in truth the O'Brien governorship did involve a perceptible strengthening at all levels of the Bank/Treasury relationship, helping to diminish (if not banish) the Bank's relative marginalisation of the Cromer years.

For King, a frankly political appointment to the Court and whose presence first Cromer and then O'Brien had always resented, the end was approaching of his regular visits to Threadneedle Street. During April he started to become convinced that there was a conspiracy afoot to conceal the true gravity of the financial situation facing the country. 'He showed me some of the secret figures', he noted on the 14th after a recent conversation with Allen. 'They were clearly disastrous.' Yet, he added, the fact was that the 'spending spree' continued and 'the Stock Exchange index goes on up and up'. On the 24th he quoted O'Brien ('We are just holding on – afraid almost to breathe unless we bring something down on us'), and on 1 May he recorded without comment that 'we are to announce an increase in our reserves of £21 million in April', even though 'the real figure is a loss of £80 million'. Just over a week later, on the 9th, King tendered his resignation as a director and the following day an outspoken front-page article entitled 'Enough Is Enough' appeared under his name in the *Daily Mirror*. Claiming that the Wilson government had lost all credibility, he declared: 'We are now threatened with the greatest financial crisis in our history. It is not to be removed by lies about our reserves, but only by a fresh start under a fresh leader.' The clear implication was that the Bank of England was complicit in these lies, and no one there mourned his passing. 'He never took the trouble to find out or try to understand what the functions of a central bank were', O'Brien recalled. 'His scorn for everyone was lofty and unending . . . Not by a long chalk one of Winchester's most attractive products.'[5]

*

The year 1968 would come to mean different things to different people, but for many in the City the dominant image was of a raging bull market, peaking on 19 September when the FT 30-Share Index reached 521.9, but staying strong for the rest of the year. Fiscal policy may have been on the tough side, and interest rates uncomfortably high, but equities boomed on the back of devaluation (the inflationary aspect of which was still viewed as positively good for equities), large company profits and intense speculative activity, often taking the form of takeovers. 'This was the era of Mr Jim Slater and many like him who realised that the acceptability of highly rated paper (price–earnings ratios of 30 and 40 were common) made possible the takeover of asset-rich companies which had failed to join in the share price race', Barry Riley would explain to *FT* readers a generation later. The paper's then editor, Sir Gordon Newton (knighted in the same 1966 list as Warburg), recalled a rare moment, probably from 1968, when prime minister and Square Mile were at one:

> One evening I received a message asking me to call in at No. 10 on my way home, which I did. It had been a good day on the Stock Exchange and our 30-share index had reached a new high, so when Wilson asked me how the City was feeling, I mentioned this to him. He was delighted. He poured two small glasses of brandy and we drank a toast to the FT Index. He said that this was probably the first time that the prime minister and the editor of the *Financial Times* had drunk a toast to the FT Index in the Cabinet room at No. 10. I replied that it certainly had never happened before and would almost certainly never happen again. He agreed.[6]

On the back of the bull market and the merger boom, the merchant banks were cleaning up probably more than at any time since 1914. 'He and his like are making a great deal of money', King noted in early September after lunching with Kenneth Keith at Hill Samuel. 'He said his profits last year were 40 per cent up on the previous year and this year are 40 per cent up on last.' Two days later the diarist had a surprisingly 'hilarious' lunch with Richardson of Schroders. 'Gordon was perfectly clear that the last year had been a disastrous one for the country while large numbers of people had made a lot of money. He agreed that the Government had had a relatively easy time in spite of its failure, just because so many important people were making so much money.'[7]

Not everyone in the City was in buoyant mood. 'The lack of confidence arising from devaluation of the pound is bound to be detrimental to international trade as a whole and to London in particular as a centre for commodity trading and for international financing', the annual report of the credit department at Barings noted gloomily at the end of 1967. It was, in its own terms, a justified pessimism. The Basle Agreement of July 1968 confirmed that sterling's days as a reserve currency were numbered, while the following month John Cooper of Schroders told Cairncross that that merchant bank was now advising its clients to invoice in dollars. 'I well understand the concern felt by you and others in the City at the withdrawal of authority to extend sterling credit for third country trade', O'Brien wrote that autumn to Cromer, after his predecessor had apparently lodged a complaint; but the present governor was adamant that, in the context of 'our present reserve and balance of payments position', there was no alternative. 'I must admit to some surprise', O'Brien nevertheless added, 'that you consider that the London houses would not be competitive if the financing of this third country trade was switched to a Euro-dollar basis.' Crucially, O'Brien could afford to be sanguine, for that same year the Committee on Invisible Exports (of which the former journalist William Clarke was Director General) demonstrated not only that even before devaluation the City had been reducing its dependence on sterling and increasingly using Eurodollar financing, but that the shift had done nothing to impair the City's major contribution to Britain's invisible earnings. Put simply, the City's international functions – in insurance, in brokerage, in banking, in merchanting – did not depend fundamentally on the strength or otherwise of sterling. By 1970 only 20 per cent of international trade was denominated in sterling, compared to 50 per cent in the 1950s, yet as an international financial centre the City had almost immeasurably advanced.[8]

The late 1960s represented a time of increasingly chronic financial instability: added to British devaluation in November 1967 was the gold drama in March 1968, an acute Franco-German financial crisis in November 1968, French devaluation in August 1969, German revaluation in October 1969, and throughout it all the Bretton Woods system struggling to stay intact, as the dollar started to buckle under the strain of paying for the Vietnam War and the Great Society. The pervasive instability both increased the volume and accelerated the pace of short-term capital flows all round the world, mainly taking the form of Eurodollars, and in varying degrees national governments began to feel that their economic sovereignty was under threat.[9]

It was an unmistakable sign that London was moving towards a dollar standard when in May 1968 the Bank of England allowed most of the discount houses (except those with foreign exchange broking subsidiaries) to deal as principals in bills of exchange in currencies other than sterling.

As far as the Eurodollar market itself was concerned, growth continued to be phenomenal: having been around $1bn in 1960, $3bn in 1961 and $10bn in 1965, its estimated size in 1968 was $25bn and in 1970 no less than $46bn. London branches of US banks were by the late 1960s the utterly dominant force in the market, sending huge quantities of Eurodollars to their head offices (as much as $3bn in three weeks in June 1969), as well as relending to companies (mainly US subsidiaries) and relending inter-bank for liquidity purposes. Overall, the *Banker* estimated in August 1969, 'it would seem reasonable to assume that at present some 80 per cent of the Euro-dollar pool has been borrowed through London'.

The City's new, so-called parallel money markets in sterling also continued their irresistible rise, above all the inter-bank market in sterling deposits, attaining a size by the end of 1969 of around £2bn – well above the total assets of the traditional discount houses. Mainly used by non-clearing banks to adjust their liquidity from day to day, it remained a market for those with strong nerves, given the preponderance of very short-term deposits and the volatility of interest rates. The growth of the inter-bank market had a particular significance in City history because of the way in which it encouraged fringe (or so-called secondary) banks to use its resources in order to take on many profitable lending commitments that the clearing banks, because of the credit ceilings applied to them, were unable to do. By 1970 almost ninety of these largely non-deposit banks were competing aggressively for funds in the wholesale banking market with little supervision. The well-informed academic observer Jack Revell noted as early as September 1968 that 'any attempt to control the operations of these secondary banks by the imposition of liquidity controls or by requiring deposits with the Bank of England' would be 'very difficult'.[10]

By the end of the 1960s the City had once more become a truly cosmopolitan centre of finance, as it had been before the catastrophe of 1914. The figures said almost everything: in 1960 there were 77 foreign banks (14 of them American) with branches in London; by 1970 there were 159 (of which 37 were American). It was an emblematic moment when, in 1968, Bankers Trust moved the head office of its international department from New York to London. That year no fewer than eight US banks opened branches or representative offices in the City, followed in 1969 by another eight.[11] The most sizeable operation was that undertaken by Citicorp (in other words First National City Bank of New York, or Citibank), which by 1969 employed almost 700 people in London. Citicorp was also, to the consternation of British clearers, starting to compete hard in the UK corporate loan market. The next biggest US operation was that of Chase Manhattan (about 400 staff in London), followed by Morgan Guaranty (about 325), where the Eurodollar book was the responsibility of the very able Dennis Weatherstone, the son of a London Transport worker who would move to New York in 1971 and eventually become chairman of J. P. Morgan – a rise, it was often remarked, that would not have been possible in the more class-conscious City.[12]

Inevitably, there was some indigenous hostility towards the 'Avenue of the Americas', as Moorgate was becoming dubbed. In the *Banker* in 1969, 'a general manager of a leading clearing bank' itemised the objections to the American invasion: pushing up City rents, high enough even before; 'touting of business'; 'poaching of staff'; and 'syphoning away Euro-dollars', with the effect of artificially increasing Eurodollar rates. The anonymous British banker, however, was inclined to discount these grumbles. 'Over many years the market dominance of the Big Five clearing banks led to a complacency which has now been rudely shattered by this new development', he argued in relation to the hard-sell approach that apparently came as second nature to the American bankers. 'The days of waiting for customers or potential customers to come to the bank for help are over: increasingly the need is seen to approach the customer, telling him what services are now available.' More generally, he could not deny that the American banks in London had been 'the source of many new ideas later adopted by British banks', and he cited their pioneering of 'personal loans, negotiable certificates of deposit, special savings accounts, and the introduction of lending rates geared to the cost of money rather than to Bank rate, as well as the concept of the roll-over loan'. In sum, 'it ill becomes the City, with its reputation for financial flexibility, to complain about competition'.[13]

The following year, in the recently founded *Euromoney*, Daniel P. Davison (in charge of Morgan Guaranty's London office) put forward 'One American's View of the City'. What would happen if the US eventually mastered its balance-of-payments problems and lifted the financial controls of the 1960s? Davison was broadly sanguine:

> London's sole eminence may be somewhat diminished by renewed competition from Wall Street but the City will have a future. For one thing, success has made London a banking bazaar unrivalled in history. The Moscow Narodny Bank, whether it is appropriate Bolshevik doctrine or not, sits almost cheek by jowl with the Bank of China, and rubs elbows with the capitalist banking institutions of the West. There are about three times the number of American commercial banks in the City as there are in New York, our principal financial centre . . . The City of London beats Baghdad as a bazaar by a country mile.

In short, the American friend concluded presciently with almost British-style understatement, 'it is too convenient a place to do business to be ignored'.[14]

*

Throgmorton Street, 19 September 1949: the day after devaluation,
with the Stock Exchange closed.

Simon Elwes' painting of the partners' room at Cazenove's, 1957.

Brigitte Bardot in the City, 1955.

Sir Siegmund
Warburg.

Stock Exchange
Floor, 1958.

London Bridge in the
rush hour, 1950s.

The new City side by side with the
old: the corner of St Mary Axe
and Leadenhall Street, 1980.

One of the first women allowed on the Stock Exchange Floor, 10 March 1973.

The new Stock Exchange Floor, 1977.

'The Room' at Lloyd's, 1974.

Lloyd's building, designed by Richard Rogers, 1999.

'He thought there would be an election in September which Labour would lose,' Cecil King noted at the start of 1970 after dining with Warburg. 'He thought Heath would be a worse P.M. than Wilson and that after an interval – round about 1972–3 – there would be a coalition under Wilson. He thought [Enoch] Powell resembled the German party that in the 'thirties was to the right of the Nazis.' Over the next few months the conventional City wisdom remained that Wilson would wait until the autumn. In the event, encouraged by favourable opinion polls, he took the gamble of announcing on 18 May that the general election would be exactly one month later. During the campaign, in which Labour stayed steadily ahead in the opinion polls and the stock market was largely pessimistic in tone, there were two main 'City' moments. The first occurred in late May when a leading Labour backbencher, the left-wing Ian Mikardo, used the publication of the select committee's report on the Bank of England to displace Colonel Lancaster, a fellow MP, and chair a press conference. 'He proceeded to say some pretty rough things about the Bank,' O'Brien later regretfully noted, 'not at all in keeping with his courteous behaviour during our long examination. Once again the vulgar political animal had won the day.' Soon afterwards, on 1 June, an old friend of the Labour government's appeared on *Panorama* in order to dispute Jenkins' claim that Britain now had one of the world's strongest balance-of-payments positions. 'There's no question that any government that comes into power is going to find a much more difficult financial situation than the new government found in 1964', Lord Cromer controversially declared. 'The very large debts which are still outstanding – there seems to be some idea abroad that they have been completely paid off. This is very far from the case.' As for the specific question of the current £500m surplus on the balance of payments: 'When you take a closer look at it, as bankers do, the figures are not so glamorous as they appear on the surface.' Next day, responding to Cromer's comments, Wilson understandably compared the current surplus with the £800m deficit he had inherited in October 1964. '"I do not see," he said bitterly,' *The Times* reported, '"how the most committed politician could describe that as a worsening of the situation."'[15]

Right up to and including Thursday the 18th, almost all the opinion polls continued overwhelmingly to point to a Labour victory. In a rare display of prescience, however, the stock market scented a more congenial outcome, and each day during election week the Index rose. Heath's generally unexpected triumph produced a piquant coda for Jenkins, who after losing office put out feelers, but (in his own words) got a 'singularly unforthcoming' response from the City in terms of actual job offers. 'It could not fail to cross my mind that as an ex-Chancellor who had, maybe by luck, acquired some reputation for stringent management of the economy and for success in turning round the balance of payments, I was being treated utterly differently from the way that an analogous Conservative politician would have been.'[16] The rest of the decade would give the City the chance to show just how tribal its attitudes to Labour could be.

*

Everywhere by the early 1970s there were symbols of the 'new', forward-looking, cut-and-thrust City. The old London Bridge, built in the 1820s, was demolished in 1968 (subsequently re-erected at Lake Havasu City, Arizona) and replaced by an unmemorable effort; two years later Rothschilds, the last surviving major partnership in British banking, became a limited liability company; not long afterwards the market men of Union Discount started carrying walkie-talkies on their 'money walks' around the City so that they could be in constant touch with the state of the money book at 39 Cornhill; in 1973 the nightly watch on the nation's gold reserves by the picquet from the Brigade of Guards was replaced by more mundane electronic surveillance at the Bank of England; and that same year, most poignantly of all, road widening at Bishopsgate compelled the demolition of Barings' homely, elegant Victorian premises, replaced by a twenty-storey tower block.

Sartorial standards were also changing in these years – above all with the swift demise of the bowler hat, the stiff white collar and the compulsory white shirt – but what mattered more was the passing of old ways of doing business. Stockbrokers less often did the daily round of the merchant banking parlours, but instead relied much more on the telephone to take orders. Desk-bound in their offices, more seldom visiting the investing institutions or going down to the market floor to talk to the jobbers, many brokers (certainly in the larger firms) now relied on a mixture of in-house analytical reports and the market price display service that the Stock Exchange had introduced in February 1970.[17] All in all, these years saw, for good or ill, a perceptible decline in the old intimacy and the reliance on personal contact.

There was, moreover, a new Stock Exchange itself, another emblem of modernity, where trading began in June 1973, seven months after the formal opening by the Queen. One stockbroker, Nicholas Goodison, vividly recalled how it seemed at the time:

> The new Market was a large cavernous concrete building, public gallery again looking down through plate glass over one side of it. It runs up three storeys, so it's a tall building, with a pseudo-concrete dome over the top, a lot of acoustic tiling. Facing the Public Gallery, there's a concrete wall with a map of the world on it, with little lights showing the main centres of activity. On the floor, you've got something new, you've got

organised jobbers' pitches, instead of the old higgledy-piggledy jobbers' pitches round pillars and all over the place. You've got some hexagons, built specially for the purpose, and with room for jobbers to get to telephone terminals and computer terminals inside the hexagons, and there are seats around the outside of the hexagons, and their boards on white plastic behind them, which they can pull down and write on, so everyone can see them . . . There's very little public bidding and offering going on by the jobbers too, so those of us who have been brought up in the old Market slightly regret this rather clinical new floor, but it is very efficient and the communications are very efficient, and as long as you get your dealing done efficiently, and the client's getting the best deal, that's what the main aim is.

Efficient, yes, but the romance had gone. Once, at quarter past three, there had been the welcome sound of the waiter's rattle, allowing smoking for the last part of the trading day; now the Council decreed that there was to be no smoking, on the grounds that 'the floor of the new Market is of rubber tiles' and 'considerable damage and disfigurement would be caused to the floor if lighted cigarettes were allowed to fall on it'.[18] Many of the older members had hung on until the ceremonial royal opening (an occasion for full evening dress, including white tie and medals), and their departure soon afterwards conclusively confirmed the end of the old, larger-than-life House, for so many years a world within a world.

To many others, it seemed that a virtuous circle was already in place. Following the 1967 Companies Act, which had removed the legal maximum of twenty partners, firms were becoming ever larger; simultaneously there continued the inexorable rise of the institutional investor (owning almost half the equity market by 1975); and under pressure from these institutions (particularly the more aggressive fund managers), allied to the start of price-earnings ratios in the mid-1960s and the 'performance cult' that developed as a result of the 1967–8 bull market (together with the disclosure requirements in the 1967 Act), the major stockbroking firms inevitably found it much harder to get away with second-rate investment analysis and service. Even the most prestigious brokers felt the need to raise their game: when the energetic, business-getting Michael Richardson moved in 1969 from Panmure Gordon to Cazenove's, he caused some consternation with his habit of taking copious notes at meetings, but in time his example was followed elsewhere; while at Rowe & Pitman it was decreed in March 1970 that henceforth partners must be at their desks by 9.30 in the morning. The trend was similar in other sectors, such as law and accountancy. Slaughter and May took the pioneering step in the mid-1960s of appointing an administrative partner and then in 1968 moved out of Austin Friars to rather bleak and characterless, but functional, modern offices in Basinghall Street; Price Waterhouse adopted a more sophisticated management structure from 1966 and nine years later relocated to the new Southwark Towers by London Bridge Station, on the 'wrong' side of the river. Both firms were growing rapidly and felt few sentimental regrets about the price of progress, even if it meant leaving the City's historical core centred on the Bank of England.[19]

Amongst all the changes, however, some things remained. There was only one systematic sociological study of the City in the 1970s, by Richard Whitley of Manchester Business School, but its findings (largely based on 1971 data) revealed how little the characteristics of the City elite had altered. Over four-fifths of the directors in his sample had attended fee-paying schools, with Eton easily dominant; Oxbridge was by far the favoured place of higher education; and nearly half belonged to one or more of London's nine most prestigious West End clubs. The sample also produced plenty of overlapping directorships, perhaps inevitable granted that more than three-quarters of the 402 directors were also directors of other companies. There were also, of course, manifold kinship relationships, and in all Whitley felt able to conclude that 'by outlining and measuring degrees of connection and commonalities between members of the financial élite' he had 'indicated a certain homogeneity of background and closeness of connection which enables us to treat them as an élite'.[20]

On the question of the other sex, the veteran broker Graham Greenwell spoke for many in his celebrated (or infamous) June 1971 letter to *The Times*, asserting that the Stock Exchange was 'not an institution which exists to perform a public service'; instead it was essentially a 'private men's club' and, as such, was perfectly entitled to choose whom it did or did not elect to membership. Even after the citadel fell, the aliens were given a pretty rough ride. 'The girls all got given nicknames by the men', Jane Partington, who went on to the floor as a blue button in 1975 while still in her teens, remembered:

> I was the Night Nurse, there was Sweaty Betty, Super Bum, the Grimsby Trawler, the Road Runner, Stop Me And Pick One. They were very cruel. Stop Me And Pick One was because she had acne. You had to have broad shoulders and a good sense of humour because you would be the butt of a lot of jokes . . . You'd think carefully about what you wore. They'd sit ripping up newspapers and sticking it all together and then creep up and clip it on to your skirt so you'd walk off and have a thirty-yard tail behind you.

Eventually the presence of women became more or less accepted – 'I must admit some of the girl dealers, the female dealers were OK', one jobber, Geoffrey Green of Bisgoods, grudgingly conceded – but the floor stayed essentially a male domain for the rest of its life.[21]

Overall, in the City of the 1970s, there was a still a formidable culture of mutual favours, epitomised by the sub-underwriting process, in which corporate brokers doled out almost invariably lucrative chunks of sub-underwriting to investing institutions in implicit return for their business in the secondary market. There was also still an obdurate culture of secrecy and lack of accountability – a culture strongly deplored by the journalist Richard Spiegelberg in his well-informed, even-handed survey of the City published in 1973. 'Only to itself is the City in any real sense account-able', he argued. 'Values are established essentially by the City, for the City, in the City.' He did not, despite greatly increased financial coverage in the press, see the answer to this lack of accountability as lying with the fourth estate. Instead, he contended that several factors blurred the relationship between the City and financial journalism: the ownership question (he pointed to Pearsons owning the *FT*, the *Investors Chronicle* and a major stake in *The Economist* on the one hand, Lazards on the other); the presence of City men like Sir Kenneth Keith and Evelyn de Rothschild on the boards of large newspaper publishing companies; the dependence of the City pages of the national papers on financial adver-tising; the prevalence of share-pushing in some City pages; and the fact that 'good news in the City is easier to come by than bad news'. There was also, as a further source of non-accountability, the huge shift of investment power to the big institutions (insurance companies, unit trusts, pension funds and investment trusts). In all, it was a formidable case, and at the end of his book Spiegelberg asked: 'What safeguards are there that this mammoth power is not abused? As members of a democratic society, have the British public not assigned to the City the privilege of immunity – an immunity which no other power structure in the country of any comparable size enjoys?'[22]

*

Despite (or perhaps because of) having once worked for Brown Shipley, the new prime minister, Edward Heath, had no great regard for the wisdom of the City, which he believed to be badly in need of modernisa-tion. His view of the City was not improved by the Rolls-Royce debacle.[23]

By September 1970 that famous symbol of British industrial virility was privately warning that it faced severe financial problems; and over the next two months, through heated negotiations within the City and between government and City, arrangements were made to keep Rolls-Royce going. A syndicate of accepting houses (led by Lazards, which had long been Rolls-Royce's merchant bank) would continue to provide a revolving acceptance credit of £20m, while the immediate cash shortage of some £60m would be met by the company's bankers (Midland and Lloyds, £5m each, the Bank of England £8m) and the government (£42m). Heath himself, 'not unnaturally angry and impatient', in O'Brien's subsequent words, had via the governor leaned heavily on the bankers (both merchant and clearing) to obtain even those commitments, taking the line that 'all those who had advised or provided finance to the company hitherto have done well out of it, should have known in good time how its financial affairs were deteriorating and should now stand by it'. After one particularly 'acrimonious' meeting, O'Brien recalled, Heath, 'perhaps more than half seriously, offered me a peerage if I could rid him of one clearing banker who, in his opinion, was being particularly unhelpful'. O'Brien received even less thanks from the bankers themselves, particularly Oliver Poole of Lazards, and Bolton reported to King in November that 'what remained to O'Brien of his prestige had vanished with his clumsy attempts to raise money for Rolls-Royce'.

The collapse of Rolls-Royce, in early February 1971, was a profound shock to most of the City, with Anthony Sampson noting that even 'shortly before . . . many brokers were recommending the company to their clients'. The word from the Bank of England to the Fed was that the stock market had been 'stunned' by the news that a receiver had been appointed, though there was some satisfaction that the government, despite its avowed intent not to rescue 'lame ducks', would nationalise the company and thus prevent it from extinction. In due course a new chairman was appointed: none other than Hill Samuel's Kenneth Keith.

As the dust settled, the merchant banks were, to put it mildly, extremely angry to discover that government, Bank and clearing banks had not in the event coughed up the supposedly promised £60m the previous autumn, following an investigation by Cooper Brothers (under Henry Benson) that had thrown fundamental doubts on Rolls-Royce's financial viability, even with that injection. They contended, probably with some justice, that they had not known that government support for Rolls-Royce was contingent on a satisfactory report from the investigating accountants. Or, as Gerald Thompson of Kleinworts laconically put it, in a memo about the matter, 'Put not your trust in princes.'[24]

More generally, the real significance of the episode for the City was that it threw an uncomfortable spotlight on the quality of its advice to British industry. At the time there was much public criticism, and the *Banker* conceded that 'the serene claim that bankers need not "understand industry" except from a financial point of view now sounds a little hollow', and there was 'an urgent need for serious thought to be given to the right role of the banker in the affairs of industry'.[25]

In fact, from the late 1960s there had been a growing tendency towards City intervention in the affairs of British companies, most notably when Keith in the winter of 1969–70 successfully led a revolt of major institutional shareholders against the existing management of Vickers. Press response to that démarche was far from favourable ('the managerial expertise of the City is not the same as that of the industrial executive suite, and consequently the City's judgement of managers is fallible', *Management Today's* Robert Heller argued), but Rolls-Royce was clearly ammunition for the interventionists. Few in the City had such interventionist instincts as Charles Villiers, who after the unceremonious demise of the IRC (Industrial Re-organisation Corporation) early in the Heath government did not return to Schroders but went instead to Guinness Mahon as chairman. It was time, he told the *Investors Chronicle* in March 1971, that merchant banks concentrated less on raising capital for British industry and more on 'the reorganisation of existing businesses'.[26]

Since the mid-1960s the public image of merchant bankers had increasingly become one of dynamic, industry-moulding financial supermen. This image would have taken something of a battering if more people had known that one of the most prestigious merchant banks, Morgan Grenfell, had come close to catastrophe through its foolish involvement in the late 1960s and early 1970s in the financing of films. Probably most to blame was Lord Catto, son of the former governor, who seems to have succumbed to the tinsel glamour – even to the extent of dining with the stars (presumably including Brigitte Bardot) of *Shalako* on location. Almost thirty years after he had given a pessimistic prognosis for merchant banks after the war, Bolton in *Euromoney* in March 1971 still saw cause for gloom: fund management, he asserted, had become 'barely a profitable activity'; 'their role of financing British industry abroad has been progressively restricted by successive Governments and overseas investment has been reduced to a bare minimum'; there was 'the problem of foreign competition in the Eurocurrency markets, notably the activities of the New York investment houses'; and all in all, 'unless the private banks find it possible to spread their wings and actively engage in world-wide financial business with larger capital resources, their importance will tend to diminish'.[27]

'We see ourselves as somewhat between the go-go and the stuffy', Michael Verey of Schroders remarked in 1972, and there is no doubt that in the early 1970s the City's real go-go merchants were not the members of the Accepting Houses Committee. When in August 1971 *Management Today* published its annual City Growth League (for which Slater Walker, mistakenly judged to be still essentially an industrial concern, was not eligible), the major gains were for newcomers like Pat Matthews' First National Finance (top of the league), Tiny Rowland's Lonrho, Tom Whyte's Triumph Investment Trust and Nigel Broackes' Trafalgar House. 'The pickings', Heller reflected sanguinely, 'have gone to self-made, sharp-eyed men who have muscled in on institutional territory and have extended that terrain [for example, in property and insurance as well as lending] beyond the dreams of the life-time career employees in the City's marble halls. That is a thought which should give the senior inhabitants of those halls pause for considerable thought.'[28]

*

The early 1970s represented a time of fundamental monetary change almost everywhere. Above all, these were the years that saw the collapse of the post-war Bretton Woods system of fixed exchange rates, which had tied the whole world to the US dollar, redeemable at the rate of $35 to one ounce of gold. The break-up, after years of increasing strain intensified by the impact of the Vietnam War on the American economy, began in summer 1971: such was the flight of international funds out of the dollar that in May both the Deutschmark and the Dutch guilder were floated; and in August the US left the gold standard. The world's first financial futures market, enabling the hedging of currency fluctuation risk, began in Chicago in May 1972; just over a month later its founder, Leo Melamed of the Chicago Mercantile Exchange, was in London trying to encourage participation in it. During his visit to the Bank of England he suggested (probably to Jasper Hollom, the deputy governor) that if the Bank really wanted to help the new market it would kindly float the pound. A strained smile greeted the wisecrack – and next day, 23 June, the newspaper headlines announced that this was what the British authorities had indeed decided temporarily to do, though for different reasons. The trade balance had been deteriorating rapidly, and the probability of an imminent docks strike had led to such pressure on sterling that the government decided that floating was preferable to another ignominious forced devaluation. Some in the Bank saw it as the soft option, a political evasion of the financial discipline of a fixed exchange rate, but O'Brien was not among them.[29] In February 1973 the yen was floated, soon afterwards the dollar was further devalued, and on 19 March the major central banks formally abandoned their commitment to maintaining their exchange rates within a predetermined band in relation to the dollar. The era of flexible exchange rates had conclusively arrived.

Would the end of Bretton Woods give New York a chance to claw back some of the considerable ground that since the late 1950s it had de facto given to London? At the end of February 1973, with the near-certainty of the US going shortly to dismantle its capital controls, Midland's chairman, Sir Archibald Forbes, asked O'Brien how he saw London's future as an international financial centre: 'The Governor replied that to the extent that the Euro-dollar market had thrived on the artificiality induced by e.g. the Interest Equalisation Tax, London would inevitably lose some business, but the market was well established and in any case bankers did not come to London only for Euro-dollar business but also to service multi-national companies.' The terminology may have been somewhat confused (the IET had given birth to the Eurobond market), but O'Brien's point was well made. The offshore (or 'Euro') markets, largely based in London, were indeed now 'well established'; and he might justifiably have added that, despite some occasional doubts about destabilising aspects of those markets, the Bank in the early 1970s remained as keen as it had been in the 1960s to keep them based in London, along with as broad a range as possible of foreign bankers and others. Its supervision of newcomers, moreover, continued to rely almost wholly on an informal, personal touch. When Gottfried Bruder and his boss from Frankfurt were preparing the ground for the reopening in 1973 of Commerzbank's London branch (closed in 1914), they went to see James (Jim) Keogh, Principal of the Discount Office. What permissions were required? What regulations did they have to comply with? None, Keogh told them. What, then, was necessary in order to become an authorised bank in London? 'Keogh looked at us,' Bruder recalled, 'and he said: "In London a bank is a bank if I consider it to be one."' Once up and running there was also the occasional, indispensable afternoon ceremony. 'You had to go round and have a cup of tea at the Bank of England, from time to time, and explain what you were doing', Philippe Muûls of Banque Belge remembered from that era. 'It was very informal.'[30]

In at least two areas, the messy, rather chaotic end of fixed exchange rates did the City a favour. One was the gold market, where London managed to revitalise itself – and recover from the apparent knock-out blow of the March 1968 temporary closure – by making a virtue of no longer being that commodity's physical centre. Instead, London became the speculative centre for gold, the place where the keenest two-way price could always be found, much stimulated by the price volatility that ensued once gold was no longer pegged at $35. Younger traders, often with a background in foreign exchange dealing, were now attracted to the market, for in the frank words of one of them, 'the simple spot quotation for gold in the international sense means loco London and nowhere else'.[31] The other area that benefited, for obvious reasons, was foreign exchange dealing itself, particularly as one venerable London institution moved with impressive speed to exploit the implications of the end of fixed parities.[32] 'As a result,' a Reuters internal memo observed in February 1972, 'industrial and commercial entities are forced to devote far closer attention to foreign exchange and money market operations, and stand to gain or lose considerable sums of money on these transactions. Our proposed service should fill an information gap.'[33]

The foreign exchange market had up to now relied upon telephones and telex for the latest quotations, but when Reuters started its computerised 'Monitor' service in June 1973, *International Insider* noted that 'the system enables subscribers to receive the latest foreign exchange and deposit rates on television terminals' – a significantly quicker way, in a world where seconds counted, of transmitting market information. It was, at first, slow going to persuade the City to utilise the new service. When, soon after its launch, Russell Taylor of the Italian International Bank (one of the new consortium banks) asked Midland's foreign managers what they thought of it, he received a mouthful:

> It's bad enough having people like you around, queering our pitch, but Reuters is the end. What's the point of having decent dealers, if a television screen gives all the world the buying and selling prices from every Tom, Dick and Harry of a bank that thinks it ought to be a forex [i.e. foreign exchange] dealer? We used to take a good point out of any deal we did with a continental bank, even Deutsche Bank, for God's sake, and now we are lucky to get a fraction of that.

At the outset few of the established banks believed that Monitor would work, but in the course of the mid-1970s it became clear that they were wrong; and in 1977 even the London Foreign Exchange Brokers Association, which had mistakenly (if understandably) seen it as a threat to its business, ordered the service. That service's full name was Reuter Monitor Money Rates, for it included a full range of money as well as foreign exchange rates, and it was a development brilliantly in tune with the much more fluid, much more international post-Bretton Woods financial world.

Principally attracted by the various offshore markets, foreign banks were still arriving in the City, though at a slower rate than in the 1960s. American banks continued to make their presence felt most visibly, but there were also, in a distinct category of their own, the Japanese banks and large securities houses. 'The Japanese people', Emperor Hirohito told an audience at Guildhall in 1971, 'have always looked up to the City of London . . . as the depository of financial and commercial expertise and observed, with wonder and respect, its indomitable spirit of freedom, strict code of gentlemanly conduct, and courage to make a startling departure from old practices as occasion arises.' Not surprisingly he received a standing ovation for these warm words. However, when the following year the Ministry of Finance at last allowed Japanese banks to lend to non-Japanese entities, this led not only to a much-increased Japanese presence in the City, but also to a flooding of the syndicated loan market in the form of lower-spread, long-maturity loans arranged by Japanese banks. American and European bankers condemned these tactics as unnecessarily aggressive, accusing the Japanese of 'rate cutting' and, an even more heinous offence, 'dollar dumping'. Those discomfited by the phenomenon – essentially a reflection of the huge gold and dollar reserves that Japan had accumulated on the back of its new-found manufacturing and trading muscle – found consolation in their own apparently greater mental agility. 'I used to spend hours at Nomura', Peter Ogden, a Morgan Stanley director, recalled of the 1970s. 'They wanted to know how you innovated. "How do you innovate?" They had 20 to 30 PhD students working on it. They couldn't understand how we kept having ideas and they didn't have any.'[34]

For Britain's two largest banks, Barclays and National Westminster (following the merger in 1968 between Westminster and National Provincial), 'international' meant ambitious pursuit of big-league status. At Barclays the great apostle of international growth was Anthony Tuke, son of 'The Iron Tuke' who had chaired Barclays during the 1950s; he himself was chairman of Barclays International (formerly Barclays DCO) from 1971, before two years later becoming chairman of Barclays itself. 'Anthony and I had a vision', a close colleague, Julian Wathen, later remembered, 'that we should turn the bank into a proper international bank. We wanted to compete with Citibank and see them off. We didn't see why we should be buggered about by the Americans.' Unfortunately, Wathen felt compelled to add, this attractive vision had 'one weakness' – namely, 'we didn't have the right people'.[35] That arguably was also the fundamental flaw at NatWest, where the meritocratic recruitment, training and promotion of potential senior managers was similarly backward, quite unlike Citibank since the late 1950s. Some of those who worked at NatWest in the 1970s recalled the fundamental change of direction from early that decade:

> We had McKinsey consultants in here to advise us in 1970, and they said we were too small to survive in a global economy and that we could only maintain our leadership by creating a bigger, more viable bank. And that is what we did . . . In 1970, we were just a UK bank and we had only three people abroad, all in New York City. To make up for all those years [going back to the 1920s, when Barclays DCO began] when Barclays was a global bank before we were, we got involved in sovereign loans . . .
>
> The theory was that your large domestic deposit base would be the foundation for starting businesses overseas and above all in the USA.

At the time, perhaps understandably, the bank did not admit to having any qualms about its new strategy. 'We are delighted with the way international business is going – it is a major contributor to profits', Alex Dibbs, about to become chief executive and on his way to open an office in San Francisco, declared in September 1972. 'We are setting out to offer our services right across the world.' Asked in the same interview about the possibility of encountering 'world competition' in the process, Dibbs replied that he was 'not dismayed' by the prospect. 'The City of London', he added, 'has an unparalleled reputation. But we must beware of becoming smug.'[36]

*

The bull market peaked at 543.6 on 19 May 1972, nine days after Patrick Sergeant had observed to the many small investors who faithfully followed his *Daily Mail* column that 'cash is unfashionable but, before too long, you may be awfully glad you've got it'.[37]

For O'Brien and others at the Bank these were dog days. 'The Governor can get no answers from the Chancellor and finds it hard to meet Ted,' Morgan Grenfell's Sir John Stevens told King towards the end of May. 'The Bank cannot reduce the supply of money without causing a setback to the business recovery.' A month later the essentially political decision to float sterling – one that had already been foreshadowed in Anthony Barber's Budget speech assertion that henceforth growth would have a higher priority than maintaining parity – meant that a greater premium was placed on getting monetary policy right than at any time since the 1950s. In theory this was good news for the Bank, but in reality its control over monetary policy had rarely been so weak in peacetime.[38]

More generally, the Bank of England would later be much criticised for failing to apply adequate supervision during this period of headlong growth.[39] The standard defence was that, under the 1967 Companies Act, responsibility for that supervision fell at least as much on the DTI and the Treasury; but inevitably the retrospective spotlight was on Threadneedle Street, in particular the Discount Office, where since 1967 Hilton Clarke's successor as principal had been Jim Keogh, a mercurial Irishman who tended to divide opinion, both inside and outside the Bank.

The latter part of O'Brien's governorship must have been deeply frustrating, not least during autumn 1972, as the finance-and-property boom continued almost unchecked and, in Keith Middlemas' words, 'real interest rates fell to historically low levels': around 1.2 per cent by the end of the year. In accordance with the recent provisions of Competition and Credit Control (CCC), the government policy designed to loosen up the British banking system and make it more competitive, Bank rate had been replaced in October by the Minimum Lending Rate (MLR), which was intended to be more market-responsive, following rates rather than leading them; in practice it merely compounded the ineffectiveness of monetary policy. Towards the end of the year O'Brien even observed (in a much-quoted remark) that there was no such thing as a monetary policy that would simultaneously stimulate expansion and control inflation, despite Barber's claim that the government had managed to square that circle.

However, if there was a greater villain than government in the Bank's eyes, it was undoubtedly the trade unions. On 9 November, three days after Heath had executed his fateful U-turn by introducing a Statutory Prices and Pay Standstill, a Fed memo recorded the thoughts of the Bank's Norman Robson:

Sterling began to decline yesterday and declined earlier today as people considered the rejection by the TUC [of] talks on prices and wages during the period of freeze. In essence, the TUC has painted itself into an impossible situation by balking all overtures from the government and has to continue to make intransigent statements to satisfy union membership.

On the other hand, looking ahead to phase II of the prices and wages policy, there will be need of some co-operation from the unions, and as long as they continue to be unyielding there is little hope for long-term improvement in the wage situation.[40]

At this time there was also a clear sense of the City itself starting to come under fairly sustained attack. On 13 November the Stock Exchange's chairman, Sir Martin Wilkinson, sent a strong letter of complaint to Lord Hill, chairman of the BBC, following a recent *Money at Work* programme on BBC2 that had marked the Queen's opening of the new building. The treatment, he wrote, 'was biased in the extreme and much of the time was given to tendentious and abusive criticism, largely unsupported by evidence', including allegations of market malpractice. Less than a fortnight later there was a heated debate in the Commons about recent trends in takeovers, with both sides of the House singling out the asset-stripping activities of John Bentley for special criticism.[41]

Inevitably, a particular focus of external criticism was insider dealing – a practice that was widely believed, with some reason, to be endemic in the City.[42] Early in February 1973, Wilkinson and Lord Shawcross (chairman of the Takeover Panel, which since 1968 had administered the City Code on takeovers and mergers) urged Peter Walker, as Secretary of State for Trade and Industry, to consider including legal sanctions against insider dealing in the government's proposed new Companies Act. Walker responded positively, but the headline in the *Daily Telegraph*, 'Days of the Insider are Numbered', was on the optimistic side: for various reasons it took another seven years for legislation to be enacted. On this and other matters the prevailing City culture was still firmly in favour of self-regulation, though an exception was the stockbroker Victor Sandelson who, fourteen years after his critical essay on the City Establishment, argued in the *Sunday Times* that self-regulation was no longer able to cope with 'the growing difficulty of keeping an ebullient and inventive City within the confines of legality and general ethics'. Noting that 'it is by now widely accepted that the [Takeover] Panel is only limping sadly behind events', and calling for a British version of the US Securities and Exchange Commission (SEC), he deftly sketched the larger context:

When the City community was small and was drawn from a homogeneous social background a fairly effective discipline was imposed by the imperative need to remain 'reputable' in the eyes of one's equals and, especially, of the Governor of the Bank of England. This informal discipline still retains some force. But as the City has expanded and drawn heavily on a much wider social reservoir of talent, the 'gentlemanly' standards have lost much of their former force.[43]

No doubt there was some truth in this analysis, essentially a variant on the Cobbold-imposing-Etonian-standards line. Yet historically it was precisely those with the very best connections – whether school, club, sporting or family – who had been most enabled to benefit from insider dealing. On the basis of that compelling logic, the City would become more fundamentally honest only when it became more fundamentally meritocratic, and not before.

The markets, meanwhile, were increasingly convinced that the government could neither deliver real economic growth nor contain inflation. Prices started to crumble on Monday 22 January 1973, partly in fright at the dividend controls involved in the recently announced Phase Two plans; but arguably the real moment that the bear market set in came three days later, when the headline 'Jim Slater says shares are still too high' appeared above Sergeant's City column in the *Daily Mail*. The two men had lunched the previous day at Slater Walker's offices, and the result was one of those rare articles that truly made the financial weather. 'Mr Jim Slater thinks our shares are between too high and much too high. He will be surprised if the FT Index [currently 478.2] is better than 425 by June 30.' Sergeant also revealed that Slater Walker had been going liquid ever since the previous May, adding that 'as lunch went on, Jim and I concluded that the best investment was – cash', notwithstanding the risk of inflation.

Almost immediately there ensued a wave of selling, especially by small investors, and Slater – *the* central, bellwether City figure of the early 1970s – found himself widely criticised. Much of that criticism merely reflected the jittery mood, not helped by renewed turmoil on the industrial relations front, and in February the monthly circular that Cazenove's sent to its private clients was positively hysterical in tone, referring at one point to how 'the general lack of respect for important values (ignored murders in Ulster, indiscipline and public exhibitions of filth) have all helped to numb our minds'. In a more humorous, less apocalyptic vein, Phillips & Drew's Paul Bazalgette told his readers that he had recently been to Germany, where 'they do not actually retch at the mention of such things as the British economy, sterling or labour relations, but the disfavour on their finely chiselled features is plain for all to see.'[44]

On 8 February, O'Brien's sixty-fifth birthday, it was announced that he would retire as governor at the end of June, to be succeeded by Richardson of Schroders. Middlemas has argued that it was O'Brien's own initiative that he should go, reflecting his dissatisfaction with being unable to persuade the government to accept a substantial rise in MLR, but that was certainly not King's understanding at the time. 'Leslie O'Brien was sacked,' he noted on 9 March after lunch with John Stevens, 'under rather harsh circumstances, as he was not felt to fit in sufficiently quickly with Ted's financial and commercial ideas. Gordon Richardson was appointed to succeed him by the PM.' And on 3 April, after lunch with Bolton: 'George confirmed that Leslie O'Brien was sacked, and not allowed to suggest his successor.' A few weeks after the announcement, Bolton wrote a letter to Richardson that was more than just congratulatory:

> You have taken over the responsibilities of the Governor of the Bank at a time when few men would welcome the challenge and your position is all the more exposed because, in recent years, the Bank has lost a great deal of power and influence in the City – the reasons being many and varied. Leslie O'Brien did a most remarkable job in helping to restore some of the lost internal morale [i.e. as a result of Cromer's governorship] but he never had the experience or the imagination to build up around him a group of independent-minded men who could make an impact both on Whitehall and the outside world. The tendency has been to promote from within and import the ready-made academic mind.[45]

This may not have been a wholly fair analysis, but it was essentially true; and it was certainly timely, coming as it did just as the post-war corporatist-cum-Keynesian consensus – of which Richardson, like Heath, was very much a part – was about to face its most searching challenge.

Before then, much of the City's attention during May was focused on a larger-than-life figure: Tiny Rowland.[46] Almost two years previously, in September 1971, Warburgs had resigned as Lonrho's merchant bank in protest against Rowland overriding its advice, though by spring 1972 Rowland had managed to achieve a semi-rehabilitation in the City by accepting pressure from O'Brien that the Lonrho board be broadened to include the eminently respectable Sir Basil Smallpeice, a former managing director of BOAC and chairman of Cunard. Rowland did not mend his ways, and eventually Smallpeice and seven colleagues (the 'Straight Eight') sought through a High Court action to have him removed as chief executive. The trial, which lasted from 8 to 14 May, failed to achieve that, but by throwing up many damaging allegations about Rowland's running of Lonrho as a corrupt personal fiefdom it did inspire Heath, in the Commons on the 15th, to condemn the revelations as 'an unpleasant and unacceptable face of capitalism' – a phrase that almost instantly became associated not just with Lonrho, but with all the other buccaneers who had done so well out of the finance and property boom of the early 1970s. By this time Heath was frustrated and thoroughly disenchanted with the City, and the feeling was somewhat mutual. 'Recently Ted addressed a party of bankers at No. 10', King had noted in early April on the basis of information from Bolton. 'Tuke, chairman-designate of Barclays Bank, told him [i.e. Bolton] Ted had lambasted them for not investing more in British industry. This went down very badly.'[47] As for Rowland, the judge's decision that the management of Lonrho was ultimately a matter for the shareholders gave him his escape. On the last day of May the ranks of Lonrho's small shareholders gathered at the Central Hall in Westminster and, in defiance of the wishes of the City institutions and much of the financial press, backed Rowland amidst noisy, exultant scenes. It was as if, in the age of corporatism, Rowland was a latter-day Barney Barnato, a capitalist hero.

*

'It is almost platitudinous to say that there is movement afoot for the greater control of the City', Midland's Stuart Graham reflected in July 1973. 'This undoubtedly includes the domestic banking system, and I think this movement transcends the bounds of the party political dogma and is most probably the brain-child of Whitehall.' By 'Whitehall', Graham no doubt had in mind the Inter-Bank Research Organisation's report, 'The future of London as an international financial centre', commissioned by Lord Rothschild's think tank. As with all reports, only a few sentences were widely quoted:

> It is a fact that many people in the country doubt if the City is making a good enough contribution to the economy as a whole. The City is not generally well regarded by industry, by educated and professional people, or by the populace at large. Even in the City itself sober people say privately that some of our financial institutions are sluggish and complacent and in certain cases overpaid.

Accordingly, 'a conceptual framework is needed within which freely competitive financial institutions largely in the private sector will be seen to be capable of meeting the economic and social needs of modern society'.[48] As for 'the party political dogma', later that summer the Labour Party published a Green Paper formally proposing nationalisation of the banking and insurance sectors.

Of course by this time the City had a new headmaster in the person of Gordon Richardson. For several months he kept a low profile, and that autumn Bolton rather cruelly told King that the new governor 'had been angling for the job for ten years' and that 'he wants the prestige and the peerage, but knows nothing of central banking'. Whatever the truth of those charges, the fact remained that Richardson was undeniably a class act – and, in City terms, had been since the mid-1950s. Henry Benson, who after retiring from Coopers became an adviser to the governor, rightly described Richardson as both 'a man of scrupulous integrity' and 'a perfectionist'.[49] At a potentially critical moment in its fortunes, the City could not have done much better.

By the time that Richardson took office there were already rumblings about the secondary banks, whose share prices by now were a long way below their 1972 peaks. Did this mean that the secondaries, in the late summer and early autumn, were suddenly drawing in their horns? Almost certainly not, to judge by the striking testimony of Richard Langdon, a leading City accountant who was also on the board of First National:

> By 1973 the game seemed to be coming to an end. There were signs of developers over-extending themselves. The writing was on the wall. But you had created a high earnings capacity in the secondary banks and if you said you were going to put your balance sheet right by going for cash, it was withdrawing from the race, going into port . . . People who have known success don't believe in less success.

Nor did the more cautious clearing banks necessarily find it so easy to end the profitable lending binge, much of it to the secondaries, of the previous two years. Graham's July 1973 memo was suggestive:

> Given the market environment [i.e. CCC] in which we have to work, the Inter-Bank Market is essential. It is the only speedy and efficient market in which the large volume of volatile short-term funds with which we deal can be channelled into profitable use . . . There are inevitably the 'whiz-kids'. But, provided we deal only with first class names, pay due regard to volume in one hand, and watch market developments closely we should come to no harm.

At least, unlike Barclays and NatWest, Midland was trying to confine itself to 'first class names'.[50]

Heath's continuing deep reluctance to apply the monetary brakes did not help. Admittedly there were two sharp interest-rate rises late in July (largely because of pressure on sterling), and in September Richardson felt able to issue a reasonably tough new letter to the clearers about 'further restraint on lending for property development and financial transactions'; but the underlying economic policy reality was that Heath, Walker and a few other ministers still hoped against hope that, in the words of Heath's biographer John Campbell, 'the Government was on the brink of achieving its breakthrough, despite the commodity price explosion, the alarming trade balance and the sinking pound'. After all, as late as September *The Economist* still felt able to state, with its usual impervious confidence, that 'Britain is two-thirds of the way to an economic miracle'.[51] Moreover, even though turnover remained (as it had been for several months) depressingly low, the Stock Exchange that month mounted a mini-rally on its new floor, with the Index gaining almost

7½ per cent, up to 429.4 by the end. On 6 October, however, Egypt invaded Israel and, in the City of London as in the whole Western world, all bets were off.

Two leading figures at Lloyd's had something marginally more parochial on their minds during that crisp early October. That institution had one of its periodic golf outings on Thursday the 4th, and paired on the Walton Heath course were Ralph Rokeby-Johnson and Roger ('Orator') Bradley. Small talk dried up after three holes, as each wondered whether the other would broach the unmentionable subject. At last, as they waited on the fourth tee, Bradley popped the question: 'What can you tell me?' Rokeby-Johnson's reply, eventually to become much quoted, was given as a stage whisper: 'What I can tell you is that asbestos is going to change the wealth of nations. It will bankrupt Lloyd's of London and there is nothing we can do to stop it.'[52]

CHAPTER THIRTY-SEVEN

Stop

Despite a major dose of governor's gloom in Richardson's first Mansion House speech, the brakes remained off, as banking advances during October 1973 rose by £850m and MLR even came down by a quarter-point, to 11.25. Still, it did not take a genius to detect that, globally speaking, the balance of economic power was shifting; and at this stage the main talking-point in the City's parlours seems to have been Morgan Grenfell's rapid, controversial exploitation of that shift. As the news leaked out that Morgans was organising a huge $200m loan to the Emirate of Abu Dhabi, there was a storm of protest from the merchant banks with Israeli allegiances and a general disbelief in Morgans' protestations that the loan was for peaceful purposes. The loan had been secretly negotiated by Morgan Grenfell's chairman and chief executive, Sir John Stevens, and it may well have been the strain of the controversy that caused him to die suddenly on 27 October. He had been a dynamic influence, all the more notable given his central banking background, and his death effectively meant that Morgan Grenfell would put on hold until the 1980s any ambitions of rivalling Warburgs as the City's 'powerhouse' merchant bank.[1]

Wall Street was in a jittery state from the end of October, when the Arabs began talking about cutting oil supplies by 20 per cent or more, and on 9 November it had a particularly sharp fall. The impact of that, coupled with the miners' rejection of the Coal Board's latest offer, led to the London market losing almost 2 per cent on Monday the 12th. Next day it was hit by a veritable triple whammy: appalling trade figures for October, the start at long last of a serious credit squeeze (MLR being raised to 13 per cent) and the government's declaration, to counter the impact of the miners' already implemented overtime ban, of a national state of emergency. That day the Index lost 4 per cent, down to 405.5; and despite the fillip next day of a royal wedding, the slide continued almost unabated, with the Index down to 365 at the end of November.[2]

The notion of a City-led panic is rather confirmed by a snatch from James Lees-Milne's diary. 'Sachie [Sir Sacheverell Sitwell] full of gloomy forebodings', he noted on 12 December. 'Influential City friends warned him that "we" had only three months to clear out of England. Another told him to hoard his cartridges, for there would be shooting within that time.' The following evening, on television, Heath announced the start of the three-day week, and by the close of trading on Friday the 14th the Index languished at 305.9, representing a fall of 29 per cent since 9 November – five weeks of, in John Littlewood's apt words, a 'bear market within a bear market'.[3]

On Monday 17 December, Barber presented an emergency mini-Budget. In order to meet what he called 'our gravest situation since the end of the war', he made large public expenditure cuts, added 10 per cent on surtax, restored hire-purchase controls, announced that he would be introducing a development gains tax aimed at curbing property specula-tors, and – just over two years after the introduction of the liberalising CCC – introduced the so-called 'corset'. Later that week, Midland's Forbes explained to his board that last aspect:

> The Chairman reported on recent restrictive measures which had been introduced by the Bank of England, principally to counter the growth in the money supply and the use of arbitrage operations in the inter-bank market. He explained that the banks had been offered the alterna-tive of 'ceilings' on advances (similar to those imposed on previous occasions) or a limitation of the banks' ability to increase their deposits. The banks had chosen the latter method as giving them slightly more manoeuvrability.

For the secondary banks, the combination of immediate credit controls and the prospect of an early assault on the property sector – sending property shares into freefall, even as the stock market as a whole slightly recovered – was little short of lethal. 'The Government had set in motion the events which had led to the availability of credit on a huge scale; now it was reversing its policies at the very moment when the market which it had so casually fuelled (I will not say deliberately) had clearly over-reached itself', Edward du Cann later wrote with unmistakable bitterness. 'The emergency budget hit the banking and property worlds just at the very moment when signs of serious crisis in both were becoming apparent. That budget was an act of unimaginable folly.'[4]

On Wednesday the 19th, the Fringe Banks Standing Committee met. In Keogh's absence, it was chaired by his deputy, Rodney Galpin, who at an early stage mentioned 'the critical position of Cedar' (i.e. Cedar Holdings). After other specific cases such as Cornhill Consolidated ('an incurable case') and First National had been considered, and Barclays had mentioned 'one possible invalid' in the form of Western Trust and Savings, came the fateful moment:

Mr Wild [NatWest's Sidney Wild] suggested that a support fund should be set up as a means of providing the potentially large amounts of assistance which could be needed for joint rescue operations. He thought it might be no exaggeration to speak of a total of well over £1,000m. Mr Wild suggested a fund amounting initially to 1% of eligible liabilities with contributions coming from a wider grouping than just the clearing banks.

As far as one can tell from the record, initial discussion did not dissent from Wild's basic idea, the genesis of what would become known as the 'Lifeboat'; but it seems to have been agreed – perhaps with Bank of England prompting – that 'it would be difficult to widen the list of contributors beyond the London Clearing Banks without publicity, which should be avoided if possible as it might only exacerbate an already dangerous situation'.[5]

In all it was a £72m support package for Cedar, but the public announcement that Barclays and Cedar's institutional shareholders had, between them, made arrangements 'designed to ensure that the depositors and the account holders can be repaid as their monies become due' – an announcement made simultaneously with the suspension of Cedar's shares – had the very reverse of a calming effect. Suddenly, as it sank in that a substantial concern like Cedar had in effect been brought low by a flight of deposits, it seemed as if the whole of the secondary banking sector was in jeopardy. The City rumour mill got going with a vengeance, and the share price of many secondaries plummeted by as much as one-third.[6]

Richardson himself, some five years later, showed no misgivings when for the first time he publicly justified the Bank's decision to launch the Lifeboat:

> We had to support some institutions which did not themselves deserve support on their merits, and, indeed, institutions which fell outside the Bank's established range of supervisory responsibilities. But I felt, as I saw the tide coming in, that it was necessary to take the Bank beyond the banking system proper, for which it was responsible, into those deposit-taking institutions, because collapse there was capable of letting the wave come on to the institutions themselves; and the fact that very rapidly we had to extend our support to a wider circle, which included some reputable banking institutions, showed that our instinct that we were on very treacherous ground was sound.[7]

Crisis management had long been a Bank of England speciality, and if there was one benign ghost that hovered over the Old Lady during this gloomy Christmas, it was surely that of William Lidderdale, governor during the 1890 Barings crisis and architect of the original lifeboat. The 1973 version, under the calm, firm chairmanship of the deputy governor Jasper Hollom, held its first meeting on 28 December and for the next year was in almost continuous session.

Despite the news on Christmas Eve of another steep rise in the price of crude oil – up from $5 a barrel to $11.50, four times what it had been at the start of the Arab–Israeli War – there was a sneaking feeling in the City at the start of 1974 that, at least as far as Britain was concerned, perhaps the worst was almost over. For three weeks the Index stayed fairly stable at around 330, until it became clear that miners and government were on an irreconcilable collision course, and on 7 February Heath called a 'Who runs Britain?' election, to be held on the last day of the month.

The February issue of the *Banker* went to press as Heath was still pondering whether or not to make his gamble. 'The City is miserable', it declared in a notably eloquent editorial:

> Books go on being published which say that the City doesn't do its job properly – or not as well as the smart boys across the Channel, or the Atlantic. And then there is the Labour Party threatening to pull the dear old place apart . . .
>
> Who would guess from this that the City is probably Britain's biggest exporter? To people in the City itself, the Labour Party and many other critics appear strictly mad. What on earth can be the national interest in destroying or sniping at one of the few really efficient and competitive sectors of its economy? Is there a single manufacturing industry in Britain that can hold a candle to the City in terms of international respect, earning power and future prospects?

With that off its chest, the *Banker* acknowledged that 'by far the most common and influential class of criticism' was 'the pure emotional assertion that the City is no more than a band of robbers, who contribute little to the country whilst making fortunes for themselves'.[8] There was now an unprecedented sense of being under siege from alien forces in society at large.

*

'Almost all members of the Labour Party regard the City as their implacable enemy', the political journalist Nora Beloff had noted towards the end of 1973. She was right. In his autumn speech to the Labour Party conference, Wilson had made a three-pronged attack on the City: calling for investment to be directed to productive, non-speculative purposes, through the establishment of a 'state-owned merchant bank', somewhat along the lines of the old Industrial Reorganisation Corporation; arguing that there should be 'a high-level inquiry' into the Stock Exchange, which he called a 'casino' and accused of 'not channelling the tides of investment, so much as exaggerating the sloshing to and fro of the bilgewater of capitalism'; and castigating speculative futures dealings in the commodity markets. In the City, the ensconcement after Labour's return to power in March 1974 of Michael Foot at Employment and Tony Benn at Industry was, as Littlewood puts it, 'received with foreboding, as these areas straddled the boundaries between the public and private sectors'.[9]

What of Denis Healey, the new Chancellor? He would never attain Benn's bogey-like qualities, but he had reputedly promised to squeeze the wealthy until 'the pips squeak' and the City's initial attitude towards him was at best guarded. He himself later claimed that his relations with the City 'were always relatively good' and that he 'never had much problem with the markets except when the Bank of England encouraged the City to play silly buggers'. Certainly, there were strains in the Healey–Richardson relationship: Healey was unfavourably struck by how the Bank still tried to uphold 'the cabbalistic secrecy' of the Norman era, 'seeing itself as the guardian of mysteries which no ordinary mortal should be allowed to understand'; Richardson was, according to Healey (almost certainly correctly), 'upset' by the Chancellor's insistence on making his 'own personal contacts with the financial institutions in the City', thereby subverting the Bank's traditional prerogative as sole intermediary between City and Treasury. Even so, Healey recognised Richardson as 'a highly intelligent and cultured' man, while Richardson in due course came to respect Healey as a capable, ultimately pragmatic operator, and initially each perhaps recognised that the other was learning on the job.[10] Each may also have acknowledged that the other had his own unreconstructed backwoodsmen to contend with.

'The City is pleased and prices are up – as is the pound', King noted the day after Wilson had formed his new administration. 'It is presumably relief that we now have a Government, even if it is only a Labour one.'[11] One of the more stabilising influences that spring was the general City perception that, thanks to the Lifeboat operation, the worst of the secondary banking crisis was over. However, on 17 May – the last day for some time that the Index closed above 300 – it was reported that the large property company Stern Holdings, run by the Hungarian-born Willie Stern, was in cash difficulties. As well as loans going back to the palmy days, Stern owed banks and other lenders almost £160m. 'Something nasty is about to happen', the *FT*'s Lex could not help but fear on 25 May, eight days after the Stern revelation, and by this time rumours of financial institutions in trouble were rife all over the City.[12]

During the first half of July the mood of bankers almost everywhere was fragile in the extreme. 'Only now is the enormity of the international financial crisis becoming apparent, and as each week passes more banks are forced to disclose their difficulties', *International Insider* noted on the 15th. 'The next few weeks will prove crucial as to whether the banking system will survive or collapse on an unprecedented scale.' Nevertheless, the magazine also commented that the recent monthly Basle meeting of central bankers (with Richardson to the fore) had apparently confirmed that, if necessary, central banks would bale out commercial banks; and a week later it quoted a London banker: '10 days ago, I thought the whole structure would collapse. Now, I think the worst may be over.' Moreover, the particular nettle that Richardson had grasped at Basle, and would grasp again there in September with persuasive effect vis-à-vis his fellow central bankers, was the notion of what he called 'parental responsibility' – in other words, in the context of the increasing internationalisation of banking, the principle that 'the parent and therefore its central bank should have responsibility for the branches and subsidiaries'. As far as the City was concerned, this particularly affected the consortium banks, and the upshot that autumn was that the Bank of England required shareholder banks to provide written guarantees ('comfort letters') for these joint ventures. In several cases, merchant banks (with small balance sheets and natural concerns about liability) sold out their stakes in consortium banks, often to US regional banks wanting an international presence and entry into the Euromarkets. Moreover, the very fact of shareholders having to provide letters of support could not but raise fundamental questions about the value and rationale of consortium banks. Although 1976 would see the peak in terms of numbers of consortium banks, this was arguably the beginning of the end of a distinctive phenomenon.[13]

In 1974 itself, the second full week of August saw pessimism more rife than at any time so far in the year. Sterling was under pressure; the July trade deficit was £478m; perhaps most damagingly of all, Benn's White Paper, 'The Regeneration of British Industry', anticipated not only planning agreements with leading companies, but also the establishment of a National Enterprise Board. On Monday the 19th the Index dipped briefly below 200 – an event that, according to Littlewood, 'had a devastating psychological effect', as 'a paralysing pessimism took hold of a significant number of stock market practitioners, fund managers and company directors'.

These were strange days, and on 4 September, writing to a sympathetic spirit in the person of Enoch Powell, Bolton elaborated on how 'fear of a total collapse of the system is an all-pervading emotion'.[14] Two weeks later, Wilson announced (to no great surprise) that the second general election of the year would be held on 10 October.

On election day itself the Index closed at 195.4, but then lost 4½ points on the Friday as it became clear that Labour had won an overall majority, though of only three. The City, the *Investors Chronicle* commented in a cogent post-election editorial the following week, 'should ponder the fact of its political isolation and take steps to re-integrate itself into the community'.[15]

One of the City's earliest concerns, once Labour had been given its fresh mandate, was how to respond to an idea recently floated by Harold

Lever, the member of the government most closely attuned to financial matters.[16] Interviewed by the *Sunday Times* on 15 September, he spoke of establishing 'a medium-term credit bank' in order to supplement the efforts of the commercial banks and ensure that industry did not suffer from the near-collapse of the capital market:

> The medium-term credit bank should say to the commercial banks, and perhaps other investment institutions of unquestioned credit: 'Look, you can have this money provided we get the appropriate certificate that you have passed it on in the form we require [later in the interview he spoke of trying to produce "a certain regional bias"]. You have in return a reward for your responsibility and risk taking.'

Shortly afterwards Healey endorsed the idea, though there had been no mention of it in Labour's manifesto. From the outset the City was hostile to the notion of a new, state bank, however worthy its objectives; and soon, especially following a letter from Morgan Grenfell's Philip Chappell in *The Times*, a view emerged among bankers that the most suitable vehicle for meeting Labour's aspirations in this field was Finance for Industry (FFI), created the previous year through the merger of ICFC and FCI, those twin pillars of the 1945 Labour/City settlement.[17]

On 20 October, a week and a half after the election, Lever told Radio 4's *The World This Weekend* that the government was now seriously intending to establish a national investment bank in order to channel, through the commercial banking system, up to £1bn to industry. Three days later Richardson and the clearers discussed the whole question. As they always did in these situations, the clearers wondered whether the insurance companies and pension funds might make a contribution. On 8 November, Midland's board agreed to participate – on the grounds that 'this step was much in the interest of preserving the whole concept of private enterprise' – and Healey duly announced the £1bn fund in his Budget. The clearing banks would provide £300m, with most of the rest coming from the 'institutions', in other words insurance companies and pension funds. Not all that institutional support was enthusiastically given, and Standard Life may not have been alone in adamantly refusing the Bank of England's request to contribute.[18] Still, the larger point held: like Norman between the wars, Richardson had managed to keep the government out of the finance/industry relationship.

This achievement, though, was far from banishing the underlying question that haunted the City during the autumn of 1974: would free markets ever flourish again? 'The Stock Market is very sick and we must appeal for help', was the plaintive cry of the Stock Exchange's chairman George Loveday at the Lord Mayor's Banquet soon after Wilson's fourth election victory in ten years. Rowe & Pitman's circular for November upped the rhetoric: 'This bear market is the financial equivalent of the Great War. Lamps going out, end of an era, casualties numbered in millions, does the country know what's happening, will it ever end?'[19] Jim Slater was also in the news that autumn when a member of the Shadow Cabinet, 'outed' for having stockpiled a huge quantity of tinned goods, said that she had got the idea from him. Apparently what Margaret Thatcher had in mind were Slater's widely publicised remarks at a brokers' lunch earlier in the year: asked in a light-hearted way what one needed in order to cope with all contingencies in the present situation, his answer had been an ample supply of tins of baked beans, a bicycle, krugerrands and a shotgun.[20] It was, in retrospect, a tantalising moment of interaction between one era that was effectively over and another that was yet to start.

Nevertheless, it would perhaps be wrong to assume that the City of 1974 suddenly became the austerity City of 1947. At Pember & Boyle the worrying news came through that another broking firm, Grieveson Grant, had closed down its kitchen. 'There was a lengthy partners' debate about what they should do in order to cut back and save money', Jeremy Wormell recalled. 'In the end it was decided that they would go from having four vegetables to three vegetables.'[21]

*

The endgame of the second of the City's two great peacetime bear markets of the century began on Monday 16 December with a meeting at the Prudential that would acquire an almost mythic quality.[22] Apparently on his own initiative, without any pushing from the Bank of England, one of the Pru's joint investment managers, Edward Hatchett, decided it was time that the investment institutions stopped sitting on their piles of cash and instead put some money into the equity market with a view to encouraging a recovery in prices. Accordingly the investment managers of the other leading insurance companies were invited to a lunch at Holborn Bars. Some declined to participate in the plan, but the almost immediate outcome was that four companies (Prudential, Legal & General, Commercial Union and Sun Alliance) between them went on a £20m buying spree.

Despite this, however, the equity market remained for the time being in the doldrums, closing on Christmas Eve at 158.8, as the jobbers held on to their short, profitable bear positions. On the floor there was still a surprising amount of festive spirit: £120 was raised for charity through active trading in a thousand badges inscribed 'I am a weevil. Harold hates me.' And a particularly extrovert member, Eric 'Ginger' Baker, donned his Eighth Army khaki shorts and pith helmet and gave his annual rendition of 'Oh, for the wings of a dove', followed by some singing (mainly carols), before – as usual – a couple of men in white coats came to take him away. Meanwhile, it was rumoured that those firms that were offering their staff a choice of Christmas present – a partnership or a turkey – had run out of turkeys. Fortunately for what remained of the market's health, the more important news did not get out that the Bank of England was having to draw on its own reserves in order to avert the collapse of several major financial institutions. Details would remain sketchy, but presumably the Lifeboat's agreed £1.2bn had been used up. An appeal for help went out to the leading insurance companies, and though some toed the line, Standard Life again gave Richardson an uncompromising refusal.[23] Prudently run, never part of the City inner circle and with its head office still in Edinburgh, it saw no reason why its policyholders and pension clients should pay for an act of *noblesse oblige*.

On Monday 6 January 1975, against a background of rumours about liquidity problems at Bowater and the liquidation of Aston Martin the previous week, there was yet another downward movement in the Index, to 146.0, amounting to a 73 per cent fall in just over two and a half years. It was the lowest point since 3 May 1954, the week that Roger Bannister broke the four-minute mile. 'Is the UK turning into another Italy?' was *International Insider*'s headline on the 6th, about Britain's current inability, in either the private or public sector, to borrow on the international capital markets. And the magazine quoted a London-based foreign banker: 'Put crudely, the UK is now a second-rate credit and is fast turning into a borrower to be classed alongside an undeveloped country.'[24] It all seemed a long time since the optimistic exploits of the New Elizabethans.

*

'To have been involved in the London stock market of January 1975 is an experience none of us will forget', Rowe & Pitman's James D'Albiac wrote at the start of February. 'Few will remember it pleasurably . . . there was a consensus of pessimism that surely equalled anything in market history. But within days the market was roaring upwards in a crescendo of buying. Despite what they may now claim, most investors were wrong-footed by this sudden change and remained imprisoned by the seemingly irrefutable logic of their gloom.' The bare facts of this rally were that the FT 30-Share Index, having closed on the 6th at 146.0, reached 236.9 by the 31st.

Inevitably there was a strong streak of irrationality in the market's sensational bounce back, in that much of the economic news remained gloomy; nevertheless, there was truth in D'Albiac's argument, which he had been propounding since Healey's Budget in November, that 'this Labour government – duly moving to the right, the longer it stays in office – is in the process of coming to recognise the necessity for high profits and healthy share prices for the attainment of its humanitarian and social policies'. The bull market continued to roar away during February, with the Index reaching 301.8, more than double what it had been in early January. 'At the end of it all,' Littlewood writes of these eight weeks, 'feeling in the City was one of overwhelming relief. The patient had returned to good health after months in delirium. Portfolios had survived. The Stock Exchange did have a future after all. Commissions and fees were rolling in again. Normal service had been resumed.' The City's mood during 1975 was also helped by the gradual receding of the secondary banking crisis. Some of the fringe concerns were allowed to collapse, and the Lifeboat peaked at £1.285bn in March (the Bank of England having to meet the excess above the agreed £1.2bn limit), before slowly but surely that figure came down.[25]

That spring, the almost all-pervasive preoccupation was the spectre of Weimar-style 'hyper-inflation'. By April, when cash limits on public spending were adopted, the UK's consumer price index was increasing at an annual rate of 21.7 per cent, by far the highest rate of inflation among the industrial countries. Practically every week there was evidence that the much-vaunted Social Contract was in smithereens: on the 3rd the power workers accepted a 31 per cent pay deal, on the 14th civil servants accepted 32 per cent, four days later doctors accepted 35 per cent and on the 30th seamen declined 30 per cent. 'Awareness of the threat to their savings is spreading amongst all sorts of people, far away from the prudent money managers of the Square Mile or Charlotte Square [in Edinburgh]', Rowe & Pitman noted at the start of May; equally, outside as well as inside the City, everyone knew that it was politically impossible for the Wilson government to tackle wage inflation effectively until after the referendum on British membership of the EEC, due on 5 June.[26]

The City, as far as one can tell, was almost unanimously in favour of a 'Yes' vote. Two months ahead of voting the clearing banks had agreed to contribute £200,000 to the 'Britain in Europe' campaign; soon afterwards, after senior partners of Stock Exchange firms had been approached by the campaign for funds, the Council sent them an encouraging letter stating that in its view 'the withdrawal of the United Kingdom from the EEC would be disastrous both for the Nation and, in particular, the City of London', with an accompanying statement referring to 'the growing internationalisation of Stock Exchange business'.[27]

The referendum result has been plausibly identified as a key political moment of the mid-1970s, when the left wing of the Labour Party lost not only over the EEC issue, but also in terms of 'the right to claim that their political and economic wishes should dictate the political agenda, on the grounds that they alone spoke for the working class'. The symbolism was palpable as, within days, Wilson replaced Benn at Industry with the appreciably more moderate Eric Varley. The next day, the 10th, the monthly investment circular by the brokers Simon & Coates exuded a sense of relief, declaring that after the referendum 'at least the worst fears of a siege economy can be put at rest' and that 'the Chancellor has two or three months' grace in which to work out his counter-inflationary policy'.[28]

Far removed from macroeconomic policy, the *FT*'s main front-page headline on Saturday 25 October packed a punch: 'Jim Slater "retires from City"'. With little appetite for the long-haul prospect of rebuilding a slimmed-down Slater Walker in a largely hostile environment, Slater had spent much of 1975 trying to find a buyer, preferably for the whole company. Tiny Rowland was one possibility, Adnan Khashoggi another, and Slater's close friend (and substantial shareholder in Slater Walker) James Goldsmith a third. At 6.45 in the evening on 24 October, the news came through on the Extel tape. 'I find that my wish to retire from the City and the interests of Slater Walker Securities are now identical', Slater's statement declared, adding that 'I am pleased to be handing over the chairmanship of Slater Walker Securities to Mr James Goldsmith, as a man of proven ability with a long record of success in the companies in which he is interested.' It was, the *Daily Telegraph* next day said, 'the end of one of the most remarkable stories in the City's long history – the rise of builder's son Mr Jim Slater and his creation of possibly the most remarkable investment machine ever seen'.[29]

Slater Walker itself, propped up by the Bank of England, staggered on for two years under Goldsmith, before in 1977 a major reconstruction saw the Bank of England (at considerable, much-criticised expense) taking over the banking arm, while other parts of the business were reconstituted under the name of Britannia Arrow Holdings. As for Slater, after surviving various legal challenges, doing some well-timed property deals to help restore his personal finances and writing some children's books as well as his autobiography, he became during the 1980s an almost invisible man, before re-emerging in 1992 with a best-selling and characteristically incisive investment manual, *The Zulu Principle*. Like Clarence Hatry, the financier who hit the rocks in 1929, he was resilient in adversity; also like Hatry, Slater would never be forgiven by the City Establishment, for sins both real and imaginary.

A fortnight after Slater's departure Britain applied to the IMF for a $2bn loan. During the rest of the year the economic news was poor, but the stock market (ending the year with the Index on 374.8) went into 1976 in a surprisingly upbeat mood, encouraged partly by the IMF approving the loan. Optimism was also nourished by a significant event in the Eurobond market, with the first dollar-denominated issue by a

British nationalised industry for two years. Overcoming much initial scepticism, particularly on the part of continental investors, Warburgs succeeded in tapping the market for a $60m, five-year deal for British Gas. The Bank of England projected it as a 'showcase' issue, demonstrating that a major UK entity could borrow on the finest terms (the coupon was a respectable 9 per cent), but perhaps it was not such an achievement. 'In the argot of the drug-addict,' *International Insider* commented shortly afterwards, 'the international bond market is experiencing a "super-high": new issues keep pouring out of the pipeline but investor enthusiasm shows no sign of waning.' Consequently, 'in the market's current state of euphoria borrowers – even if they are British – can do little wrong'.[30]

*

The tumultuous events of 1976 began in March with a fraught episode in the long-running saga of sterling and the foreign exchange markets.[31] The Treasury had come to the view that, with cash limits and incomes policy both more or less satisfactorily in place, a carefully calibrated devaluation by stealth of sterling was now needed, from just over $2 to perhaps $1.90, in order to make British exports more competitive. An interest-rate cut was the Treasury's chosen means, and it was decided that MLR would be reduced on Friday the 5th by a quarter-point, to 9 per cent. At the Bank, according to Stephen Fay's account, Richardson 'disliked the whole concept of manipulating the currency', while Kit McMahon, as the Bank's overseas director, 'warned the Treasury that the market was unstable and might not behave as civil servants and ministers thought it ought to'.[32] Presumably backed by Healey, the Treasury insisted that its plan be executed.

Before this could occur, an entirely unscheduled drama on the afternoon of Thursday the 4th took place, as the pound fell sharply, at one point to a record low of $2.0125. There had been, *The Times* reported next morning, a 'sudden wave of selling . . . thought to have largely emanated from London', with currency dealers describing the sudden movement as 'inexplicable'. Before long, the precise circumstances of those few hours had become a matter of vexed, even bitter controversy. An early version was provided in a *Times* leader the following Tuesday:

> What appears to have happened is that the foreign exchange market misconstrued some heavy selling of pounds by the Bank of England – at the time the market did not know who was selling – as evidence either of hostile selling by another sterling area central bank or as a cunning attempt by the Treasury to drive the pound down in order to encourage export-led reflation. All the Bank of England, who may have been rather ham-fisted, were trying to do was to prevent a sharp rise in the price of a pound which, for some reason, it feared.

The *FT* was also critical, while according to *International Insider*, on the basis of its banker contacts, 'the Bank was supplying Sterling to the market as the Dollar was weak in order to top up the reserves'; unfortunately, 'it missed a turn in the market and was seen selling Sterling in a falling market', which 'was then followed by a dealer-inspired panic, and in currently thin markets Sterling's domino fell after the French Franc'.

In the event, the Bank took most of the stick, accused by the Treasury of having sold sterling in a falling market and thus of unnecessarily precipitating a sterling crisis. Such was also the view of Healey, who in his memoirs accused the Bank of having 'failed dismally' to 'outwit' the financial markets.[33] The Bank's defence was that it had started selling on the 4th as it became known that large buying orders from commercial banks were pushing the currency up, which it knew would displease the Treasury. Few, however, were prepared to listen.

The following days compounded the Bank's discomfort. On Friday the 5th, despite Richardson's fears and apparently on Healey's instructions (notwithstanding his subsequent blame-shifting), MLR was duly cut, and the pound ended the day below $2 for the first time in its history, at $1.98. 'Everything the authorities are doing seems designed to weaken the pound in the most dramatic way', an opposition spokesman, Norman Lamont, commented. 'Today there was a mystifying cut in the minimum lending rate which can only weaken the pound further.' From Monday to Wednesday came unavailing efforts to halt the slide, and the pound finished on the 10th at $1.91. The Treasury had got its devaluation, but certainly not by stealth, and certainly at the cost of international confidence in sterling – and, arguably, in the Bank of England.[34]

A few days later on the 16th, Wilson surprised the world, not least the City, by announcing his resignation. 'Early scenes on the London trading floor were described as pandemonium', *The Times* reported of the Stock Exchange, 'as dealers tried to assess the implications'; while in the City at large, there was widespread agreement that Wilson's decision was 'extraordinary', given the recent 'intense currency turmoil'. Looking ahead to the incomes policy's next stage, the paper's financial editor added that 'many people quite reasonably take the view that Mr Wilson is the only person capable of repeating something like the £6 a week agreement'. In the *FT* there was no warm tribute – 'we remarked many years ago that the Prime Minister's characteristic weakness is to mistake activity for action' – and few in the City would have been disappointed by its absence.[35] Yet one final phase lay ahead in Wilson's relationship with the Square Mile – a phase in which, by an ironic twist, he would do his least favourite place a surprising favour.

*

Despite the reassuring figure of James Callaghan at No. 10, the first nine months of the post-Wilson era proved a bumpy ride for politicians and markets alike.[36] Callaghan became prime minister on 5 April, the day before Healey delivered a Budget in which he made most of his tax cuts conditional on achieving a 3 per cent incomes policy with the unions and perturbed the markets by announcing a projected PSBR for 1976–7 of £12bn. Nevertheless, talking to the clearers on the 7th, Richardson drew comfort from the passage in the speech affirming Healey's determination not to allow the money supply to get out of hand. The following week Callaghan had his first official meeting with the Chancellor: 'I was astonished when I saw D.H. He said that Bank had spent $2bn in supporting sterling since 1 Jan 1976.'[37]

On the foreign exchange markets, sterling continued to fall during the last days of May. By 3 June, notwithstanding a 'don't panic' broadcast from Healey, sterling had plunged to a new low of barely $1.70, and on Friday the 4th the Dutch central banker Dr Jelle Zijlstra, also president of the Bank for International Settlements, proposed an international standby credit to support the pound. With the British government's blessing, this was duly arranged by the Bank of England, with a total of $5.3bn to come from the central banks of Germany, Japan, Canada, France and Switzerland, the BIS, the Federal Reserve and the US Treasury. There is some evidence that, even at this stage, Richardson was unhappy and would have preferred the government to go to the IMF, which from his point of view would have had the huge advantage of making the loan explicitly conditional on major public expenditure cuts. In any case, it seems to have been Richardson who played a key role in getting Edwin Yeo of the US Treasury to fly to London on Saturday the 5th and tell Healey to his face that there were no circumstances in which the standby credit would be extended beyond six months. In other words, the standby could be renewed once (after three months), but if it had not been repaid by early December, then the government would have no alternative but to go to the IMF if it wanted further assistance. On Monday the 7th, as Healey announced the standby credit (and the miners approved the new pay policy), sterling rose four cents, to just over $1.75. The pound was temporarily saved, but over the previous few feverish days both the Bank and the Treasury had told the Cabinet that it would not stay saved unless the PSBR was brought down from £12bn to £10bn.[38]

The crux was whether the government had the willingness and/or capacity to deliver cuts of a size that would persuade the markets to take the heat off sterling. Healey wanted cuts of £2bn, Richardson presumably wanted more, but in the end (after seven acrimonious Cabinet meetings) the package announced on 22 July comprised cuts of just under £1bn. As the stockbrokers Simon & Coates put it on the 27th (by which time the Index at just over 370 was almost fifty points off what it had been three months earlier), 'Markets have not been impressed by the Chancellor's package . . . The cuts continued the long British tradition of delaying necessary actions and then taking them in several half-hearted bites, ostensibly so as not to antagonise public opinion.'[39] Perhaps the markets would have been more impressed if they had had a greater sense of history. In February 2000, on the occasion of the Labour Party's centenary, the political historian Brian Brivati argued that the party had really 'passed away' on Wednesday 21 July 1976, when by accepting the £1bn package of cuts the Cabinet had 'abandoned Labour's historic mission to alter the nature of the capitalist economy' and, under pressure from the international financial markets, de facto 'conceded the argument that the market economy was a better way of allocating the economic cake than any form of state intervention or planning'.[40]

For their part, though, the markets merely scented weakness and wanted more blood. After sterling had held fairly steady at about $1.77 during August, it managed to stay at that rate in early September only because of heavy (some $400m) Bank of England support, but by the 24th it was down to $1.70. By this time Healey had told the Cabinet that another sterling crisis was on the way and that there was no alternative but to make an imminent application to the IMF. Sterling then dropped further, to $1.637, and Healy annnounced the IMF application – for $3.9bn, at the time the largest-ever application to that body – on Wednesday the 29th.

Sterling rallied three cents on the day, but share prices lost further ground, with the Index closing at 330.4, almost twenty points down on the week so far. Next day at Blackpool there were, in the eyes of the City – and of international financial opinion more generally – two signal events: the Labour Party conference's decision, despite Callaghan's warnings that he would never accept such a policy, to vote in favour of nationalising the banks and insurance companies; and the loud booing during Healey's five-minute speech, as he rejected all talk of a siege economy and spoke of the necessity of doing 'things we do not like as well as things we do like'.[41] By the end of a long week, sterling was at $1.66, while the Index closed at 317.5.

October proved a nervous, confusing month, pending the arrival in London of the IMF negotiating team (headed by a former Bank of England man, Alan Whittome) on 1 November. Over the next six weeks, the pound remained fairly stable, mainly between $1.62 and $1.67, nudging upwards as it became clear that a further package of cuts was going to be agreed. Eventually on 15 December Healey announced the cuts to the Commons. In essence, government spending was to be reduced by £1bn in 1977–8 and £1.5bn in 1978–9. Press comment was generally critical, but the markets responded just about enthusiastically enough, with the pound closing the year worth $1.70 and the Index on 354.7.

In the end, the key figure, on which everything had hinged, turned out to have been wrong. The true PSBR in 1976–7 was £8.5bn, not £10.5bn as forecast by the Treasury. Had all the trauma been unnecessary? The answer is surely not, in that whatever the validity or otherwise of the £10.5bn forecast, what had mattered was the perception of the markets – that the Labour government could only be relied upon to pursue sound economic policies if it made another sacrifice, to supplement the one in July that the markets had immediately viewed as inadequate. The cuts, in short, were symbolic sacrifices to market nostrums of 'good' economic behaviour.

For those attached to the economic sovereignty of the nation state there was now an uncomfortable awareness that, after the break-up of Bretton Woods, things had changed. For Britain's central bank, charged with the day-to-day running of Britain's currency, that was not necessarily good news; against that, the government was now committed to monetary targets, and in the dawning world of monetarism it would be perverse not to assume that the Bank of England would exercise an increasing influence over economic policymaking as a whole. Furthermore, despite the occasional grumbles of international bankers, there was no reason to think that the events of 1976 had damaged London as an international financial centre. The Eurobond market, above all, had flourished as never before, with huge issues including $300m for the EEC, $125m for Hydro Quebec and $100m apiece for Denmark and Norway. There was one particularly emblematic moment: Morgan Stanley had hitherto based its European operations in Paris, but when it came to starting a trading capability in the secondary Eurobond market, it decided to site it in London.[42] The domestic problems of a medium-sized economy were, in short, no longer of critical relevance to the quite different concerns of a by now well-established offshore financial centre.

*

The very act of the Labour government reluctantly swallowing the IMF medicine seemed to transform the British economy during 1977. The government now had credibility in the financial markets, as demonstrated by the $1.5bn UK loan successfully raised in the Euromarkets early in the year; the medium-term prospect of North Sea oil transforming the British balance of payments was widely touted; sterling was stable at around $1.70; and interest rates fell rapidly, down to 5 per cent by October. Equities responded enthusiastically, with the Index starting the year at 354.7 (already well up on the dog days of the previous autumn) and in mid-September hitting a new high of 549.2. Simultaneously, there were even more remarkable gains in gilts. Soon afterwards in his monthly Phillips & Drew column Paul Bazalgette pondered on 'the strange and sudden turn in Britain's fortunes':

> A year ago we were indeed in what Bunyon termed the Slough of Despond, or as another chap put it, the sedge was withered from the lake and no birds sang . . . What do we find a bare year later? The £ so strong against the $ that it has to be held down by sheer brute strength. Balance of payments well in surplus, the gold and dollar reserves so large that we are fast running out of vaults in which to store them. Hot money fighting its way into the country through every crack and crevice, and a gilt-edged market which makes the rubber booms of my youth appear tame and tepid by comparison.[43]

Things then on the whole quietened down, with the Index ending 1977 on 485.4, while at the start of September 1978 it stood at 498.5.

But if it was a broadly improving situation, that was far from meaning that the old antagonism towards Labour and its supporters had suddenly vanished. In the Stock Exchange's *Annual Report* for the year ending June 1978, after recognising that inflation had come down in the past two and a half years, the chairman Sir Nicholas Goodison wrote:

> We want Britain's economy to thrive. We want the Government to recognise the important place of business in the economy and of individual effort in bringing prosperity about. If businessmen are reduced to complaining about the lack of incentive and if the young go abroad because of our so-called 'progressive' system of taxation, where does the fault lie? Let the Government drop its anti-business prejudices and allow industry and individual effort to thrive.

Or, as Rowe & Pitman put it in September, after Callaghan had fatefully decided not to call an autumn election, 'the fact that markets (in money terms) are high and rising does not imply that the City approves of this Government, is pleased that it will be around for some months longer, or is unaware of bureaucratic waste, the squandering of North Sea revenues and the stifling of enterprise through excessive marginal taxation'.[44]

The conjunction of circumstances in 1977–8 was favourable to increasing the Bank of England's influence on policymaking, and Richardson did not let the opportunity slip. The battleground was the attempt of the Keynesians, led by Sir Douglas Wass, Permanent Secretary at the Treasury, to fight back against the monetarists. Early in 1977, Wass warned Callaghan that if over-precise monetary targets continued to be pursued, 'many of us believe that the transitional adverse effect on economic activity and employment would be both serious and prolonged'. However, as during the next six or eight months sterling recovered, inflation came down and unemployment only marginally increased, the monetarists found themselves with the higher cards to play. There was also a personal element.

Richardson saw himself (unlike O'Brien) not as the Permanent Secretary's opposite number, but as the Chancellor's; and his dealings with Wass tended to be condescending, even though they were both old boys of Nottingham High School. Moreover, when Callaghan during 1977 established 'The Seminar', a group that met roughly every other month to look at the big fiscal and monetary picture (under his chairmanship but Lever's leadership), Richardson – despite his membership – simply refused to allow it 'to issue him with instructions', in the words of Bernard Donoughue from the Policy Unit at No. 10. Donoughue also recalled the Callaghan/Richardson relationship: 'These two men always treated one another with considerable respect; after one particularly sharp discussion, when the Governor was being at his most impressively and courteously obstinate, Mr Callaghan said to me: "He has to do his job. I either back him or sack him, and I am certainly not going to sack him."'[45]

Another significant Labour/City subplot in the 1970s concerned the question of regulation. After the manifest regulatory failure that had led to the secondary banking crisis, any government would have started to draft new banking legislation; but from the Bank of England's standpoint it was crucial – certainly in Richardson's eyes – that the Bank henceforth take supervisory responsibility for all banks. With that in mind he successfully insisted that the new legislation embody a two-tier system, in effect distinguishing between 'proper banks' and licensed deposit takers. The Banking Act received the royal assent in April 1979 and came into operation six months later.[46]

More contentious politically was the familiar question of whether the policing of the financial markets as a whole should continue to rely on self-regulation, or whether something along the lines of the US Securities and Exchange Commission should be introduced.[47] For two years, from 1974 to 1976, the Department of Trade deliberated. Predictably, in its March 1975 submission, the Stock Exchange whole-heartedly endorsed the speed and effectiveness of self-regulation by practitioners. 'The effectiveness of the existing system of self-regulation within the financial community', it stated, 'rests largely on the good communications and close relationships between the various bodies concerned. Within the City, this is achieved through the Bank of England; but, between the financial community and the Government, communication is not so readily achieved.' Presumably there were few doubts, but just in case David LeRoy-Lewis and two other Council members visited Washington and New York later that year, mainly to look at the SEC in action. 'The legalistic approach would not be beneficial to the regulation of the securities market in the UK', LeRoy-Lewis reported. 'It is not sufficiently flexible and can be used at times to frustrate legitimate and desirable activities, especially in the takeover field. Certainly it gives rise to uncertainties and a level of legal activity which few in this country would wish to see emulated here.' Eventually, largely on the say-so of the minister Edmund Dell, the decision was taken to stick with self-regulation, but to attempt to make it more ambitious. This led to the launching in spring 1978 of the Council for the Securities Industry – an almost entirely tooth-less body stuffed with representatives of City institutions. Later that year this new self-regulatory watchdog made its first major public statement, on the hotly debated question of insider dealing, but symptomatically confined itself to a résumé of the problems involved.[48]

In the public mind, insider dealing was now becoming the test issue of City ethics. The precipitate February 1974 election had aborted Peter Walker's proposed legislation, but from 1976 there was a renewed move-ment (including from the City Company Law Committee) to revive the proposal that insider dealing should be made a criminal offence. Dissenters included the retired Cazenove senior partner, Sir Antony Hornby. 'Only those stockbrokers who buy shares for their clients in companies about which they know nothing or which are likely to go down will keep out of prison', he publicly complained in December 1977. 'Only the buyer of Premium Bonds – the pure gambler – will be safe and respectable. The rest of us must either use a pin or be condemned to uninspired uniformity.' The following July the government published a White Paper that sought to define what insider dealing was – essentially, dealing on the basis of information that was both privileged and significantly price-sensitive – but in the expectation of an autumn general election the City took little notice. All that changed once Callaghan had decided not to go to the country. First, in a speech in late September, Goodison announced that he and the Stock Exchange Council were having second thoughts about the desirability of a legal ban on insider dealing, arguing that a practitioner-based body like the Council for the Securities Industry would be better equipped to stamp out the practice, which anyway did not lend itself easily to legal definition; then, on 20 October, Dell announced that he did intend to legislate. Yet only weeks later, it was February 1974 revisited. This time what came to the City's rescue was not a snap general election, but Dell's decision to leave the government and take up a position at the merchant bank Guinness Peat.[49] Once again the issue found itself in the proverbial long grass.

*

Despite the presence of the international Euromarkets, the largely UK-oriented stock market was still the natural terrain of the City Establishment. In general, the traditional investment community remained suspicious of huge swathes of the developed world. 'In 1975 I raised £1.7m for an investment trust targeted at Japan', Christopher Heath remembered twenty years later about a key moment in his career when he was still at the stockbrokers Henderson Crosthwaite. 'There was a lot of resistance to the idea. "They're just a nation of copycats," people would say, or "They behaved badly in the war." It was quite a struggle.'[50] The fact was that by 1979 only about 8 per cent of the £97bn in invested assets of the four main groups of UK institutional investors – insurance companies, pension funds, investment trusts and unit trusts – were abroad.

For the merchant banking sector as a whole, it was a generally difficult period. Above all, the merchant banks were no longer major players on the international scene – exemplified by the fact that in the Eurobond market the only significant force was Warburgs, which despite its lack of distribution still had strong relationships with borrowers. Of course there were partial exceptions (Lazards, for example, in export finance, or Barings as joint adviser to the Saudi Arabian Monetary Agency), but the larger point held. Did these distinctive, if chameleon-like, City creatures have a future? 'If sterling weakens again in the 1980s, as so many merchant bankers expect,' *The Economist* concluded in March 1979, 'there will be a rather odd look once again about a financial system in which so much highly educated Oxbridge talent devotes its considerable brainpower to finding ways of remaining competitive in a business which foreigners are far better equipped to carry out anyway.'[51]

At New Court there was growing disharmony between the Rothschild cousins, Evelyn and Jacob. A personality clash masked genuine matters of substance: in particular, Jacob – the more cerebral of the two – reacted somewhat apocalyptically to the City's general mid-1970s crisis and pushed hard the strategy of a union-as-strength merger with Warburgs, but was unable to persuade Evelyn. Senior people were being almost forced into rival camps, prompting Rodney Leach, one of the most gifted bankers of his generation, to leave Rothschilds in 1976 and go to Edmond Safra's Trade Development Bank. The following year the cousins talked to *Euromoney*. 'Investment banking in New York is a murderous business today', Jacob declared. 'The whole business is demoralised, and it doesn't know where it's going.' Evelyn (who was by now chairman) countered, 'We don't want to give you the impression that we have no plans for the States. We take the view – would you not say so, Jacob? – that the States provide the best long-term opportunities for merchant banking.' Having already retreated from the Eurobond market, as well as having sold its stake in Rothschild Intercontinental Bank to American Express (which renamed it Amex Bank), Rothschilds was approaching the end of the 1970s in a divided, directionless state.[52]

'It's obvious that size is going to count in the end', Hill Samuel's Sir Robert Clark pessimistically observed in 1977. 'There's a great deal you can do with brains, but you can't stay out in front with them. And clearly, if they set about it the right way, all the big banks can get as much talent as the merchant banks have.' The belief that brawn (in the shape of capital) and brains could successfully complement each other was particularly strong at this time, for example prompting Lord Camoys (formerly Tom Stonor, and one of the more capitalist gentlemanly capitalists) to throw in his lot with Barclays Merchant Bank (BMB), formed in 1975. BMB was certainly not a member of the Accepting Houses Committee or even the Issuing Houses Association, but reputedly its name went through on the nod at the Bank of England because the governor was on holiday. There was little initial sign, though, that the merchant banks' dominant position in corporate finance was going to be seriously threatened by the clearers. 'Personalities matter,' a BMB man remarked in July 1977, 'and it will be years before people think of County Bank [NatWest's merchant banking subsidiary] or BMB before Schroders or Warburgs.'[53] The far bigger – and far more expensive – thrust of the clearers was in the international sphere. With Barclays and NatWest having led the way, Midland by 1975 was anxious to catch up.

As for Lloyd's, it was about to enter the stormiest, most troubled phase of its long history.[54] The troubles would come as a rude shock to many members of the British upper-middle class who, since the relaxations following Cromer's report of 1969, had flocked to become external members (or Names) there. In 1970 there had been fewer than 5,000 external members, but by 1979 there were almost 14,000. With the market enjoying some excellent years, in particularly stark contrast to the stock market in the mid-1970s, the attractions were obvious; and if they were not, members' agents – engaged in an increasingly systematic recruitment campaign – did not hesitate to point out the tax advantages of becoming a Name. It was subsequently claimed that, in the years immediately after the 1973 Walton Heath golf-course conversation, knowledge about the scale of looming asbestos claims became widespread among Lloyd's insiders and that there was a conscious policy of recruiting as many new Names as possible to help the market meet the threat.[55]

However, the unfavourable headlines that from the late 1970s started to undermine the reputation of Lloyd's were not about asbestos. Instead, there was first an embarrassing row in 1977 as two brokers disputed a claim following a fire on board an Italian ship, the *Savonita*. On one side was a small broking firm, Pearson Webb Springbett, whose chairman, Malcolm Pearson, awkwardly insisted that the claim was fraudulent; on the other was a much bigger broking outfit, Willis Faber, which warned that the London market would lose much Italian business if the claim was not settled. Questions were raised in the Commons (with Jonathan Aitken championing Pearson), but the eventual inquiry initiated by Lloyd's came down heavily on the side of Willis Faber. Its findings were not made public until December

1978, at which point the press gave Lloyd's a roasting. *The Economist* called the report 'a shoddy document that smacks heavily of kangaroo justice', while according to the *Sunday Telegraph*, 'Lloyd's has succeeded in making itself appear both incompetent and somewhat cowardly'.[56] To compound matters, following the *Savonita* affair, it emerged during the winter of 1978–9 that the 114 unfortunate members of the Sasse syndicate – run by Tim Sasse, a high-profile underwriter – faced losses of well over $20m on fire and computer leasing insurance in North America. Crucially, it was becoming clear that these losses owed much to negligent underwriting.

Nevertheless, it was the *Savonita* rather than the Sasse affair that led in early 1979 to the establishment of an inquiry (headed by Sir Henry Fisher, a former High Court judge) into self-regulation in the Lloyd's market. 'Hal' Fisher was very much Richardson's choice (one lawyer trusting another), and indeed the inquiry itself may have been imposed by Richardson upon a reluctant Lloyd's chairman, Ian Findlay, who apparently found it hard to accept that there had been an erosion of commercial morality. 'I cannot really believe', he was quoted as saying, 'the time has come when Lloyd's, as a society of underwriters and as an insurance market, needs a governing body equipped with, and ready to use, ever more draconian powers in the maintenance of law and order.' In short, 'if it really came to the point where one expected good faith, honesty and decency to be the exception rather than the rule, then one might well wonder whether it was worth carrying on at all'.[57]

*

On 17 January 1979, a veteran City figure, never shy of painting the big picture, spoke to the Institute of Bankers:

> The Welfare State was born and is now foundering. The result of the success of the Keynesian school has been continuous inflation which until quite recently has been regarded as an incurable disease to be restrained by controls and abnormally high rates of interest. The symptoms are unemployment, rising prices, social unrest and demands for higher wages . . .
>
> I can think of only one European country that has real possibilities of growth, and the name may surprise you. It is Great Britain. We are not a poor country but a very wealthy one, and in spite of being misgoverned for 30 years still command authority in all the international service industries. We are the only European industrialised country with surplus coal and oil resources. If we could throw away the stranglehold of the economists' demand management, substitute stable money and extinguish the disease of Socialism, we could become a proud people once more.[58]

Still going strong three years before his death, George Bolton had made his name as a man of the markets – and, unlike many in the City during the Keynesian heyday, had never lost faith in their curative qualities.

During March, as the feeling grew that Callaghan could not avoid a spring election, the stock market – confident of a Conservative victory – boomed. On the evening of the 28th the government lost a no-confidence vote, and by the end of the next day, when an election was called for 3 May, the Index stood at 540.8. The Tory manifesto, unveiled on 11 April, promised to switch the emphasis from direct to indirect taxation, cut back public expenditure, give an overarching priority to monetary policy and curb the power of the trade unions. 'The one hesitation in the City about the Tory manifesto', noted Leith McGrandle, City editor of the *Evening Standard*, 'is not that the City doesn't like what it reads or hears but still can't believe that it would be possible to carry it all out. But, as Mrs T. might say, faint hearts never won elections.' He added that the City had 'written off' Callaghan's chances, and for most of the campaign that remained the case. Nevertheless, on Tuesday 1 May there was a last-minute wobble. 'Anybody's Race? Jim Sniffs Hope' was the *Standard's* headline, with one new opinion poll giving Labour a 1 per cent lead. The Index closed more than 14 points down, at 537.0, and McGrandle remarked that 'many in the City are astonished at the way the Conservatives have let Labour cast serious doubts on their tax-cutting proposals'. But two days later, on polling day, the mood was once more bullish. 'Shares vote for Maggie!' was now the *Standard's* headline, as what it called 'a buying bonanza' saw the Index closing on 553.5, its all-time high.[59]

The Tories duly won, with an overall majority of forty-three, and on Friday the 4th the Index rose to a new high of 558.6. Bazalgette, by now senior partner of Phillips & Drew, was carefully apolitical in his post-election contribution to the firm's *Market Review*, although he did have an eye on the aesthetics of the situation: 'Perhaps it is only because I am an ageing connoisseur of mature blondes that I advance the opinion that Prime Minister Margaret is a distinct improvement in female haute couture on the mid-Oriental and far-Oriental ladies who have preceded her to the wicket.' He also hoped that Mrs Thatcher would take the lead in a related matter:

> Heaven knows that recent female fashions, particularly in length of hemline, have been decidedly unacceptable, and it is my hope that all this will now change for the better. Let me remind you that when hemlines rise, so traditionally does the Stock Market. It is not the prime function of this column to tender investment advice, but you may feel inclined on this to get in, or if already in, to stay in.[60]

CHAPTER THIRTY-EIGHT

Blue Skies

'Thank you so much for your resolute support for the Government's policies', Margaret Thatcher's PPS, Ian Gow, wrote in October 1980 to the Stock Exchange's Nicholas Goodison. He added that he was showing the text of Goodison's recent Mansion House speech to the prime minister, who had herself earlier in the month declared that the lady was not for turning. Shortly before Christmas, with recession deepening every day and the clamour growing for a 'U-turn', Siegmund Warburg wrote to Peter Spira (who was no longer at Warburgs):

> I have often felt in the course of this year a temptation to speak out publicly in favour of the courageous and positive elements in the policy of the Thatcher Government. Moreover I am shocked by the completely negative and destructive comments which emanate from various leading people in the City and in British industry who, instead of giving every possible help and backing to the Government, indulge in almost treacherous criticism rather than putting forward constructive suggestions . . .
> I am convinced that Mrs Thatcher has shown outstanding valour and fortitude in making it clear that after successive Conservative and Labour governments had encouraged the country to live far beyond its means this reckless course of self-indulgence is long overdue for a radical change. I think in starting this new chapter in Britain's post-war history that the Government has done great things in the fiscal and taxation field as well as in several other parts of the economic scene.[1]

Warburg's letter raises the larger question of whether City sentiment as a whole was supportive of Thatcherite economics during these early, highly controversial years of the Thatcher era. Broadly, as far as one can tell, it was – though no doubt at times for want of any plausible alternative. In retrospect, it was Sir Geoffrey Howe's obstinate, unrelenting Budget of March 1981 – raising the tax burden in the middle of a recession – that made it definitively clear that there would be no going back to the Keynesian economics of demand management.

Ten months later, in January 1982, unemployment reached three million, more than double what it had been when Thatcher came to power. In April 1982, however, inflation at last came down to single figures;

that summer there were some real signs of economic recovery, as well as feats of derring-do in distant islands; in August there began in Wall Street what would be the greatest bull market of the century; and two months later the Index (414.2 at the end of 1979, 474.5 at the end of 1980, 530.4 at the end of 1981) at last crossed 600, a long fourteen years after first reaching 500. Inflation, the all-pervasive phenomenon of those years, now seemed a monster slain (or at least sleeping), and in May 1983 the Index went through 700, partly on the back of justified confidence in a Tory election win the following month. In fact, the Index itself was so industry-based that it had become a somewhat blunt recorder of market mood, and a truer reflection of the new bullishness was the All Share Index, which on polling day, 9 June, stood at 442.8, up 58 per cent (compared with the ever less adequate 30-Share Index's 29.4 per cent) on 3 May 1979.[2]

Viewpoint, at this most polarised of moments in post-war British politics and society, was all. 'The bewilderment of the proverbial Birmingham manufacturer at the behaviour of the London stock market is a well-documented social phenomenon', observed Lex in April. James D'Albiac, in his first *Market Report* for Rowe & Pitman after Thatcher's landslide victory, almost admitted as much: 'It is a time when the "good news" that might appeal to headline writers in the popular press – "booming Britain! Surge in output brings hope to the unemployed" – would be bad news for our bull market.' It was a bull market, he believed, that still had a long way to run. 'Thatcherism, of one sort or another, appears', he declared, 'to be the dominant economic philosophy in the world today: the British people have just re-elected a Government which is likely to pursue with the greatest vigour the logic of that philosophy.'[3] For almost everyone in the City, it was a prospect that pleased.

*

Did Warburg have the governor of the Bank of England in mind as one of those 'treacherous' critics in December 1980? Certainly, government/Bank relations in the early 1980s were as bad as at any time since the days of Cromer, and this time round Labour was not even in power.[4] Howe subsequently wrote how he had come 'to rely a good deal' on Gordon Richardson's 'impressively measured wisdom', but there would be no such encomium in Thatcher's memoirs. Those privileged to watch the two of them in uncomfortable action together – the 'canine' politician, the 'feline' central banker – were struck by the hopelessness of the personal chemistry, at least after the initial, quasi-honeymoon phase. She found him patronising and vain, as well as frustratingly unwilling to take a strong, readily comprehensible line, quite apart from his being tainted as a survivor of the old corporatist order; he found her strident, impatient and almost wholly unwilling to accept that practicalities, not ideology, should determine the workings of monetary policy. Thatcher's instinctive prejudice against the received wisdom of Richardson and the Bank was fully shared by the financially very literate Nigel Lawson, Financial Secretary to the Treasury until September 1981. It was he who did much to create, by spring 1980, the Medium Term Financial Strategy as the centrepiece of macroeconomic policy, including by far the most specific targets yet for monetary growth; according to Lawson, he did so against the 'deep-seated' opposition of the Bank, which 'wanted to retain complete and unfettered discretion over monetary policy'.[5]

Curiously, it was a clearing banker who – for the first time – was chosen to succeed Richardson as governor after the expiry of his second term in June 1983.[6] Richardson himself, now in his mid-sixties, would have been happy to go on, but that was never a realistic possibility. The name finally announced just before Christmas 1982 came as a complete surprise to almost everyone, whether inside or outside the City. It was NatWest's chairman, Robin Leigh-Pemberton, as much a Kentish country gentleman as a professional banker. 'The failure to choose a successor with greater experience and standing both in international and domestic banking circles is a cause for concern', the *FT* observed in a typically understated way, and right from the start the governor-elect was widely viewed – fairly or unfairly – as little more than Thatcher's puppet.[7] As so often during this Manichaean decade, she was taking her revenge, this time on the Old Lady.

She may also have been irked by a perceived reluctance on the Bank's part to get fully behind the early, pioneering phase of privatisation – so important in defining her government's character.[8] The process began in February 1981 with the £150m offer for sale of British Aerospace, a flotation managed by Kleinwort Benson in conjunction with an apprehensive Bank of England. Nor were all Kleinworts' co-underwriters much more bullish, with Schroders and Morgan Grenfell, for example, being reluctant participants, with little or no faith in privatisation as such. The issue, however, was three and a half times oversubscribed, and that autumn Kleinworts was again to the fore in the £224m privatisation of Cable and Wireless. The government had recently had to postpone its plans to privatise British Airways and much hinged on this Cable and Wireless issue, then a record for the size of the offer of shares in a previously unlisted company. The equity market at the time was thin and jobbers generally nervous, but the outcome was wholly gratifying to those concerned. 'Rush for Cable & Wireless Shares' was the *FT*'s headline at the end of October, and it quoted a harassed official at NatWest (receiving bankers to the sale): 'Some people can't read instructions. We've got cheques here attached to forms with matches, hairpins and industrial staples. We asked for pins.'[9] Popular capitalism, it seemed, was starting to return to the City scene.

Some things never changed, however. Royal Insurance had developed an empty site at 1 Cornhill into a prestigious banking hall and was looking by 1980 to let it to a tenant. The only serious offer came from Bank of Credit and Commerce International (BCCI), a rapidly growing concern, mainly servicing Muslim and Third World clients, registered in Luxembourg but with London as its international operating headquarters. Just across the road, the Bank of England heard what was afoot and told Royal's chairman, Daniel Meinertzhagen, that the new tenants were unacceptable. Royal, accordingly, decided to convert the site into its own head office.[10]

Even so, BCCI was still free to pursue its nefarious activities; and as Peter Cooke, head of banking supervision at the Bank of England, frankly conceded, the explosion of international banking over the previous two decades conclusively meant that 'this is no longer a cozy club in a village called the City of London where everyone knows each other'. He was speaking in the light of the fundamental changes introduced in October 1979: the implementation of the Banking Act, which for the first time put the Bank's supervision within a statutory framework, and the abolition of exchange controls, which inevitably reduced its flexibility and informal authority. Cooke himself still hoped to get the best of both worlds. 'When we judge the reputation and standing of an institution relative to giving it our "seal of Good Housekeeping", we like to think we have the opportunity to get the views of those within the marketplace to help us make a decision', he told *Institutional Investor* in March 1980. 'And a banker who doesn't play according to the market's rules – which are essentially our own – will lose, because the market will reject him.' The magazine also quoted a London-based French banker, still apparently happy to play by the old rules: 'If the Governor invites you to tea and casually mentions that he thinks credits to the textile industry are rather high, you rush home and cut your credits to the textile industry.'[11]

In the wider field of investor protection, external faith in traditional methods of self-regulation was eroding quite rapidly, as the City was beset by a series of minor, but cumulatively important, scandals. In June 1980 – at long last – insider dealing became a criminal offence, though few were holding their breath that any such criminals would be put behind bars. There were also at this time various scandals in the lightly regulated field of commodity dealing (described by a judge as 'a jungle suitable for hunting for large and experienced animals but one in which a small animal is at very serious risk' – in short, 'a most perilous state of affairs which merits attention by Parliament'); while in July 1981 the Manchester stockbroking firm Halliday Simpson wound itself up, with its share deals being investigated by the Stock Exchange.[12]

It was in the same month as the Halliday Simpson scandal broke that the Trade Secretary, John Biffen, asked Professor Jim Gower, author of *The Principles of Modern Company Law*, to undertake an inquiry into investor protection. Nine months later Gower published a discussion document in which he castigated the shortcomings of the City's existing system of regulation in terms of 'complication, uncertainty, irrationality, failure to treat like alike, inflexibility, excessive control in some areas and too little (or none) in others, the creation of an elite and a fringe, lax enforcement, delays, overconcentration on honesty rather than competence, undue diversity of regulations and regulators, and failure to achieve a proper balance between Governmental regulation and self-regulation'.[13] It was quite a charge sheet. The eventual Gower Report was still some way off, but it was already clear that City regulation – or, more precisely, self-regulation – would never be the same again after this tough-minded one-man commission.

Few people were more committed to the tradition of self-regulation than the combative Peter Green, chairman of Lloyd's from January 1980. He conceded, though, that the old disciplines were no longer so easy to enforce. 'If something was going on, it used to be sufficient for the chairman to say, "Look here, this has got to stop," and the chap would stand, cap in hand, and do as he was told', he observed soon after taking office. 'Today if a headmaster tells a schoolboy to do something, he'll turn around and ask, "Why should I?" It's a little bit like that here.'[14] In May 1980 the Fisher Report was submitted, and in effect backed continuing self-regulation, calling for a new Lloyd's Act that would give enhanced disciplinary powers to a newly created governing Council, the majority of whose members would be internal. It also recommended that, on the grounds of inherent conflicts of interest, brokers should be compelled into divestment of their underwriting syndicates (also known as managing agencies). It was not a recommendation that enthused Green, but he publicly conceded that there was no alternative.

For anyone involved, wittingly or otherwise, in asbestos, in two distinct ways the early months of 1982 were the key. First, it is claimed, Green successfully persuaded his Committee not to divulge to anyone the findings of a recent, secret Bank of England inquiry into Lloyd's. According to someone who saw the relevant letter from the Bank to Green, summarising the inquiry's findings, it 'warned of enormous losses, resulting from asbestos claims which were about to engulf the Lloyd's market and of the disastrous effect they could have, not only on Lloyd's itself, but on those banks who had provided Lloyd's guarantees or lent money to Lloyd's syndicates'. Second, it is also claimed, Green equally successfully masterminded a cover-up of Lloyd's books in order to ensure that Parliament did not get wind of the rapidly gathering asbestos crisis before it passed the Lloyd's bill giving it immunity from civil suit. 'Why should a body that has been negligent be protected from its own negligence?' one Tory lawyer pertinently asked the Commons during a debate on the bill. Ironically, and perhaps influenced by the trade union analogy, the view from the opposition benches, as expressed by Michael Meacher, was that to withhold immunity 'would expose the Corporation of Lloyd's in a manner which would severely restrict the effectiveness of its supervisory and regulatory powers'.[15] Peter Green could not have put it better himself. Meacher had, to be fair, as chairman of the committee scrutinising the Lloyd's bill, waged a doughty fight to ensure that the eventual Act would include compulsory divestment (separating brokers and underwriters), overcoming Green's preference for a more voluntary approach. The bill received the Royal Assent in July 1982.

Richardson maintained an essential belief in the virtues of self-regulation, whether at Lloyd's or elsewhere; but generally at the Bank there was a growing feeling that not only was Lloyd's badly under-managed, but that it needed more independent input. Shortly before Christmas, he asked Ian Hay Davison, formerly with Arthur Andersen, to go to Lloyd's as its first chief executive. With some reluctance, Davison eventually agreed: 'Above all I admired Gordon Richardson and he asked me: I would not have accepted for anyone else.' He started in February 1983, with a brief to clean up the place (including the tax-evasion aspect) and initiate a new rule book. By the time he arrived there was an increasing realisation that the framers of the new Lloyd's Act had, following Fisher, placed too much reliance on divestment, while overlooking, in Davison's words, 'the much more serious abuses of conflicts of interest involved where agents put their own interests improperly ahead of their duties to their Names'. On television some thirteen years later Davison spelled out a particularly prevalent abuse:

> One of the things I discovered when I went to Lloyd's is that the under-writing agents all had their syndicates, and the Names were on the syndicates, but they all ran little syndicates on the side, called baby syndicates, to which only a few favoured friends belonged, and on the baby syndicate was put the most attractive business, and effectively they were diverting profits from the outside investors, the Names, to the pockets of the insiders, the members of the baby syndicate. This was quite clearly improper. I would have said that every single member of the Committee of Lloyd's was a member of a baby syndicate.[16]

For some twenty years there had been 'two Cities'– in Richard Roberts' words, 'the free-wheeling, unregulated, international City of the Eurocurrency markets, and the sterling-based, cartelised, domestic City, whose bastion was the Stock Exchange'.[17] After Geoffrey Howe's October 1979 abolition of exchange controls, however, and with transactions across the markets now possible in any currency, there was no longer any economic logic for that divide. The great question, though, was how well the natives would fare when the City once again became a seamless whole.

One prominent tribe did not enter the momentous decade with plaudits ringing in its ears. 'Something is seriously wrong with Britain's retail banking system', the *FT*'s Michael Lafferty declared in May 1980. 'It is dominated by a handful of institutions known as the clearing banks whose profitability is the envy of commercial banks all over the world, yet its UK management is wholly in-bred and often less than sparkling. It is a system badly in need of a shake-up.' Which was the best way forward for these large, slow-moving, much-criticised organisations? Crucially, there was still a prevailing obsession with size for its own sake, as measured by total assets. This obsession took a blow – unfortunately, for most of the Big Four, not a fatal one – with the Latin American debt crisis, which burst upon the international banking world in August 1982 when Mexico suspended debt payments. The central bankers soon got involved, with Richardson playing a leading role at the critical IMF meeting in Toronto in early September, and eventually more than thirty countries were covered by rescheduling agreements.[18] In the immediate wake of the crisis, 'securitisation' (by which multinationals converted bank loans into tradeable bonds) became the name of the game, thereby permanently reducing the profitability of wholesale banking. However, among the Big Four, only Lloyds – badly hit by the debt crisis – would have the sense and the absence of corporate grandiloquence to make a virtue out of grasping the retail nettle. Barclays was still the top clearer throughout the first half of the decade, increasingly threatened by the more aggressive NatWest. Chairman at Barclays from 1981 was Timothy Bevan, from one of the bank's founding families – an advantage denied to the other main candidate, the more dynamic Deryk Vander Weyer, thereafter always known as the best chairman Barclays never had: according to the subsequent verdict of a close colleague, the much-respected Sir Brian Pearse, 'they just didn't have the balls to make him chairman, and the whole bank resented it'. Unabashed, Bevan ran Barclays along distinctly Etonian lines (much swearing and loss of temper, occasional bursts of warmth), with scant regard for his board. 'Unbelievably Dickensian, and distinctly divided into aristocrats and peasants', was how one observer described it. 'Nobody ever challenged the aristocrats.'[19] Moreover, although there had been a Bevan in Lombard Street since 1767, there was little sign that this one possessed a coherent, let alone convincing, overall vision of where his bank was heading.

How different was it at 41 Lothbury and the NatWest Tower, formally opened by the Queen in June 1981? 'In London bankers' eyes,' noted

Euromoney the following month in a profile of NatWest, 'it's a bank that can afford to give loans the quaint name of advances, to have a promotional ladder and a salary scale system that appear to be modelled on the British civil service, and to have a tradition where senior staff are called "Sir".' The article, though, was entitled 'The Puzzling International Approach of NatWest', and its thrust was that as yet the bank had failed to devise a plausible strategy for its increasingly important international business. Most senior people in the international division were from a strictly domestic banking background; and 'to those who do not know the bank well, the structure of National Westminster's international operations makes the Roman Empire look like an easy management challenge'. There was one aspect that the profile did not touch upon. In April 1981 Robert Maxwell took over the near-bankrupt British Printing Corporation (BPC) and, through ruthless rationalisation, returned it to profit. BPC owed £17m to NatWest, money that the bank had not expected to get back; so when it did, it was not surprising that NatWest proved a loyal backer of Maxwell's subsequent ventures. Others also facilitated Maxwell's rehabilitation in the City – his biographer, Tom Bower, mentions for example Sir Robert Clark of Hill Samuel and the flamboyant stockbroker Jonny Bevan of Grieveson Grant – but nothing helped more than to have in his corner the utterly respectable, loan-friendly, morally neutral clearing bank.[20]

For the merchant banks, which tended to find the troubles of the clearers a source of amusement, the early 1980s were generally a difficult time. Antony Gibbs, once a great name, was completely taken over in 1980 by the Hongkong and Shanghai Bank, which had had a 40 per cent stake since 1974, compelling it reluctantly to give up its membership of the Accepting Houses Committee; that same year Keyser Ullmann was sold for £43m to Charterhouse Japhet, which according to du Cann 'got a bargain'; not long afterwards Arbuthnot Latham had the first of its four changes of ownership during the decade, being sold to Dow Financial Services; and at Guinness Mahon there was almost constant upheaval, eventually leading to Harry Kissin (ennobled in 1974) leading a management buyout of the commodities division and re-establishing it as Lewis and Peat Holdings.[21]

This was also a new era for Warburgs, after Siegmund Warburg died on 18 October 1982. His last months had been unhappy, presiding over the unravelling of Warburgs' latest attempt to achieve an effective American presence. 'He wants to reign, by sweetness and persuasion, but totally', reflected one of those involved. Nevertheless, the tributes paid at his death were unanimous in acclaiming that no man had done more to restore London's fortunes as an international financial centre. He was, like Nathan Rothschild and Ernest Cassel before him, an undisputed giant of City history. How would Warburgs fare without him? Peter Stormonth Darling remembered the founder's own sense of foreboding:

> Some while before he died, and on more than one occasion, Siegmund told me with conviction, and I am sure others too, that within five years of his death Warburgs would break several of his most cherished rules. We would, he said, change the name of the quoted company, Mercury Securities, to incorporate the Warburg name; we would produce glossy annual reports in place of the plain off-white ones we traditionally used (he actually used the word 'glazed'); we would have brochures with photographs of members of the firm, as all our competitors had; we would advertise; we would grow too big and have too many people; and worst of all, we would join the City establishment and inherit its complacency.[22]

*

Writing in the *Spectator* in January 1982, Tony Rudd addresssed the difficulties facing the money market:

> The problem arises when markets become very volatile. Then the delicate mechanism which allows the relatively modestly capitalised group of discount houses to balance the vast pyramid of short-term debt in the market can be thrown off its pivot. The operators who have been accustomed to dealing in a thirty-second or a sixty-fourth of a point suddenly find that they are having to cope with a move, up or down, of a whole point or more in a single afternoon. The strains are becoming enormous.
> Nothing is going to damp down this volatility short of a return to the orderly international markets the world was accustomed to before the Bretton Woods system broke down . . . The prospect for a return to that orderliness is remote at present. The only answer therefore in the markets is for the introduction of methods by which the growing risks can be effectively offset.[23]

Happily, Rudd saw comfort on the horizon, in the shape of the London International Financial Futures Exchange (LIFFE, pronounced 'life'), which opened nine months later on 30 September. During the year and a half of preparation, the single most important theme was that it was going to be a thoroughly eclectic market, transcending both nationality and traditional City divisions. By the eve of opening there were some 261 members in possession of the 373 available seats, with just under a hundred of the members being overseas-based. UK commodity brokers held 97 seats, followed by overseas banks (63), UK banks (55) and Stock Exchange firms (35). As yet, there was little systematic attempt to make the market attractive to individual, Chicago-style operators, the so-called 'locals'; notwithstanding their liquidity-providing potential, they were too associated with speculation, and at this stage the market's founder, John Barkshire, was much concerned to stress its more respectable 'hedging' characteristics. By a mixture of imagination and good fortune, the site for the new exchange was none other than the Royal Exchange – intensely historic and resonant in its associations, but for the past century hardly used for active trading. In 1979, with the roof unsafe, it had to be closed to the public; and almost the only activity left was the selling of charity Christmas cards, leaving the pigeons undisturbed for the rest of the year. The venue put LIFFE right at the heart of the City.

There was never any doubt that it would be an open outcry market, but it was a conscious decision to base it physically on the Chicago model of futures markets rather than on, say, the cocoa or coffee markets in London. This model had three prime characteristics: pits (not rings), with steep steps; open, low booths (not boxes that allowed private conversation); and a big display board. The Chicago model also dictated that the traders would wear coloured jackets, never before seen in the City. Each member chose something different, and almost the only one rejected by LIFFE was a Union Jack design, the worry being that it would be seen on television as selling the pound down the river.

How much business would the jackets be doing? 'It is no coincidence that Chicagoans invented these instruments and so far have been the only ones to make them work well', *The Economist* pessimistically observed. 'New Yorkers, by contrast, and possibly Londoners are temperamentally inclined to view the futures markets as an investment medium or a safety net, rather than a casino. If they all want to hedge and none to speculate, a financial futures market is on a one-way ticket to the mortuary.' The *FT*'s Lex was particularly worried about the lack of interest – even understanding – shown to date by the market's potential end-users. 'Hands up who knows what a fill or kill contract is?' it asked any corporate treasurer who might be reading. The most non-committal assessment came from Richardson. 'The design of successful futures markets is notoriously difficult,' he told the Court a fortnight before opening, 'and no one has any real idea whether LIFFE will be a roaring success or just fade quietly into the background.'

On the first morning Richardson himself cut the tape, a bell was rung that had been a doorbell of the Royal Exchange after its rebuilding in the 1840s, and the multicoloured throng got down to business with undisguised enthusiasm. Next day the *FT* described 'the gum-chewing lady trader with a voice like a klaxon making her presence felt in the currency pit among her vividly dressed colleagues', and the *Daily Express* quoted a 21-year-old dealer, Julian Rogers-Coltman (presumably not with a cockney inflection): 'I know it looks hectic but it works. It is certainly a young man's game. In fact, it is an ideal opportunity for a young man without commitments to make money provided he's ready to work hard.' Laudable sentiments no doubt, but the new market's overall progress during the first six months was steady rather than spectacular, with most days fewer than 5,000 contracts being traded.

Things picked up somewhat during the early summer of 1983, helped by the election campaign giving a stimulus to the long gilt contract, and by the end of the first year daily trading volumes were running at almost 7,000. Overall, in terms of commitment to the market matched by resources, the contribution of the American banks was critical. Gerrard & National's Brian Williamson, who had been on the preparatory working party for LIFFE, told *Euromoney* that 'it's difficult to imagine how different LIFFE might be if Salomon Brothers hadn't committed itself so much at the beginning'. Other fully engaged American members included Citifutures and Continental Illinois.[24]

Williamson's point about the American contribution had a larger resonance. Not all the seventy-eight American banks in London in 1983 were starting to flex their muscles, but some were certainly doing so, including Goldman Sachs. When Spira decided in 1982 to leave Sotheby's and return to the City, but not to his old firm Warburgs, he approached Goldmans among others. After a two-day grilling by the New York partnership he received and accepted a handsome offer – news that prompted an old friend who was chairman of a London merchant bank to write 'that I was out of my mind if I thought that Goldman Sachs would survive in London for more than an extremely short period'. Spira started at Goldmans (then based in Queen Victoria Street by Blackfriars Bridge) in January 1983; though far from finding it a sympathetic environment, he was immediately struck by the creative, business-getting zeal, reminding him of the formative, hungry years at Warburgs. Much of this competitive creativity was targeted at the British-cum-European corporate sector:

> One of the advantages that Goldman Sachs had over a lot of UK houses was that they had a whole raft of American products to offer European companies, ways of raising money in the States . . . Commercial paper in those days [i.e. the early 1980s] was very much an American product; that was a way of raising money short-term, and it could be cheaper than just raising from the bank, and Goldman Sachs were the leading house in commercial paper . . . We caused a tremendous amount of angst at the British merchant banks. They all hated us, because we actually produced brighter ideas, and were more dynamic.

By this time the American banks were making significant inroads in other areas, including energy finance, commodity finance and accepting. As for bank lending, by spring 1983 the Americans had by far the biggest share (44.2 per cent) of the foreign banks' lending to the UK market and accounted for 12.4 per cent of all bank lending in the UK.[25] In short, the American banks were like runners approaching the starting line before a race: creeping up, creeping up and just waiting for the gun to be fired.

*

At precisely the same time that the logic of the abolition of exchange controls in October 1979 compelled the London Stock Exchange to return to its pre-1914 roots and reorientate itself internationally, it found itself almost completely hobbled by having the well-intentioned but inappropriate Office of Fair Trading (OFT) on its back, with the eventual court case not expected to be heard before 1983 at the earliest.

In June 1980 there was support for the Stock Exchange from a no longer influential quarter. The report of the Wilson Committee (chaired by the former prime minister) generally gave the City a far cleaner bill of health than might have been anticipated in the mid-1970s; and although it accepted that the existing Stock Exchange system required 'substantial change', it argued for removing the Stock Exchange from the debilitating threat of the court case and instead asking the Council for the Securities Industry to undertake an inquiry. In the face of a mute government response, Wilson himself wrote to Thatcher in October asking her to lift the case against the Stock Exchange, on the grounds that 'almost everything they do as a financial institution has now got to be transacted under the eyes of solicitors and barristers'. In her uncompromising reply, Thatcher insisted that 'so far no arguments have been advanced to justify the substantial erosion of the principles of competition – supported by both main parties since the war – that the exemption of a body very much in the public eye would cause'. With no great instinctive warmth towards the City and troubled relations with the Bank of England, the government was happy enough to let the judicial procedure take its protracted course. It was probably at some point in 1980 that Goodison took tea with Gordon Borrie, recently reappointed as director general at the OFT, and tried to persuade him to drop the case. Quite apart from the way in which it was inhibiting long-term decision-making, Goodison and his colleagues felt real concern that court-enforced change could lead to chaos, granted that the government was planning to allow only nine months for that change to be implemented. Borrie, however, was immovable, taking the line that as an independent statutory official his overriding duty was to get on with what Parliament required him to do. That was also his line through the early 1980s when any minister raised the possibility with him of stopping the case. 'My greatest mistake lay in being reluctant to promote a deal with the Stock Exchange on abolishing the market's restrictive practices', he subsequently conceded with admirable honesty. 'I insisted on pursuing the matter through the courts.'[26]

Assuming that the case did eventually get to be heard by the Restrictive Practices Court, there seem to have been few who expected the Stock Exchange to win the day. One who did was Ian Fraser of Lazards, particularly after his friend Mr Justice Lincoln had ruled in September 1982 that it would not be sufficient for the OFT simply to attack the Stock Exchange rule book, but that it must also formulate a viable alternative constitution. On the whole, though, expectations ran the other way, especially once it emerged that the Prudential would, if required, give evidence for the OFT. One in three at best was how a senior official at the Stock Exchange rated its chances by autumn 1982, and he gloomily quoted Yeats about things falling apart and the centre no longer holding.[27]

It was against this background – the increasingly manifest need for change, but change being approached in the wrong way – that Richardson at last moved centre stage. Having since 1979 intermittently tried to persuade the government to find an alternative to the court case, he stepped up his campaign from 1982, as David Walker became an executive director at the Bank and assumed responsibility for the City's markets. '"He abhors a vacuum," says a colleague, who has watched Walker involve himself in virtually all the City's recent preoccupations', the journalist Stephen Fay noted some years later. 'He strides unstoppably through the corridors near his office like a ship under full sail . . . Richardson spotted him in the Treasury, where he was unlike most civil servants, and when he came [in 1977] to the Bank it was clear that he was unlike most central bankers. He lacks their patience and prudence, and they call him Walker the Talker.'[28] Increasingly concerned about the tardiness and impracticality of the judicial route, and about the damaging effects on London of Stock Exchange weakness, he commissioned the Bank's Andrew Treadgold to produce what became known in November 1982 as the 'Blue Skies' plan. Based to a significant extent on fact-finding visits to New York, this envisaged an open, deregulated Stock Exchange, including an automated market-making system along the lines of NASDAQ in the States. By early 1983 the Bank as a whole, including the gilts division under Eddie George, was fully behind a negotiated, out-of-court settlement.

Immediately after the Tory victory on 9 June and the obligatory Cabinet reshuffle, Goodison sent a handwritten letter to the new Trade Secretary, Cecil Parkinson. He asked him to lift the court case, warned that in the event of an adverse judgement he would not be able to guarantee the 'integrity' of the market and pointed out that in effect a decision had to be reached by the end of July, when Parliament was due to rise. Soon after receiving Goodison's letter Parkinson discussed the matter with the new Chancellor, Nigel Lawson, who as a former financial journalist understood the City far more intimately than Howe had. 'Cecil told me he favoured a deal in which the Stock Exchange would be exempted by law from the ambit of the Restrictive Practices Act in return for an undertaking that it would reform itself. I told him I agreed, provided the reform was genuine.' Lawson's own perception (again described retrospectively) was that largely as the result of 'woeful' undercapitalisation, 'while the City of London remained one of the world leaders – if not the world leader – across a whole range of financial markets, such as the foreign exchange market, in the securities market it was in danger of becoming a backwater'.[29]

Together they managed to persuade Thatcher that although the immediate party politics of letting the Stock Exchange off the OFT hook were undeniably awkward, the potential gains were unignorable. On Friday 1 July Parkinson put the notion of a deal to an entirely receptive Goodison, and there followed two to three weeks of detailed, secret negotiations between Goodison and the government, with few ministers in the know and Borrie sidelined. On Tuesday the 19th there was a leak in the *Guardian* that an out-of-court settlement was on the cards, requiring Thatcher to tell the Commons that afternoon that, although the case was still before the court, that 'does not preclude the Stock Exchange Council from making proposals to settle the matter'.[30] The leak also led to the hasty convening of an emergency Council meeting on 21 July, which continued into the next day.

Eventually there was a vote on the resolution to accept the package on offer. It had four elements: the Stock Exchange would dismantle the minimum commission system by the end of 1986; an appeal tribunal would be established, 'to review and if appropriate over-rule the Council's decision to reject an applicant for Membership'; the Stock Exchange's present Appeals Committee would henceforth have a majority of people who were not Stock Exchange members of the Council; and, in liaison with the Bank of England, lay members would be brought on to the Council. The resolution was passed unanimously.[31]

'Doing the City a favour' was the headline in *The Economist* about news of the accord, and on Tuesday the 26th *The Times* took much the same, critical line. It was an unpromising background for Parkinson's attempt to sell the deal to the Cabinet that morning. 'Willie [Whitelaw] suddenly tossed a spanner in the works saying, "Are we doing the right thing?",' he recalled, 'and we had quite a lot of rumbling.' But eventually, after the Cabinet had insisted on an ad hoc subcommittee redrafting the statement later that day, Parkinson was able to announce the deal to the Commons on the afternoon of the 27th, expressing the wish that single capacity would be 'preserved for the time being in its present form'.[32]

It is impossible to be sure to what extent the architects of this deal had been conscious of how fundamentally it would change the character of the traditional, sterling-oriented, 'domestic' City; but it was not long before everyone was aware that the Yanks – and the banks – were in town.

CHAPTER THIRTY-NINE

Top Dollar

Jacob Rothschild was the first, rather chilling prophet of the new world. 'The rules by which London has so successfully played the game are being rewritten by our international competitors', he declared at a London conference on 24 October 1983, before outlining 'a nightmarishly complicated scenario' in which financial conglomerates offering the widest possible range of services to the widest possible range of clients in the widest possible range of countries would become all-dominant. Barely two months before the start of 1984, his predictions sounded Orwellian: 'As the process of deregulation continues, the two broad types of giant institutions, the world-wide financial service company, and the international commercial bank with a global trading competence, may themselves converge to form the ultimate, all-powerful, many-headed financial conglomerate.' He declined, moreover, to make any sanguine noises about the City's ability to compete in this bracing environment. For too long, he argued, it had been inward-looking and risk-averse; its banks (even the clearers) were undercapitalised in comparison to its foreign competitors; as for its protected brokers and jobbers, Rothschild merely noted that Salomons, the American investment bank, had made more money in 1982 ($500m) than the member firms of the London Stock Exchange put together. The challenge, in short, was enormous, but it could not be ducked: 'We can expect the emergence of a number of financial conglomerates with interests straddling disciplines which have been traditionally distinct. I believe it is important that one or two concerns in the UK show themselves willing to jump in with both feet, and to play an active part in the redefinition of the financial sectors' competitive boundaries.'[1]

For all Rothschild's big-picture certainties, the prevailing mood in the City that autumn was one of confusion mingled with apprehension. Certainly there was no sense of either government or Bank of England magisterially unveiling a blueprint for the future. Parkinson fell to scandal in early October, Lawson was new as Chancellor (albeit supremely self-confident) and Leigh-Pemberton was not only new, but was viewed by the City and wider world as a weak governor with a somewhat semi-detached attitude. The Tory minister Alan Clark may have found him 'unexpectedly good, crisp and clear', but arguably the key word was the first one.[2] How exactly the Stock Exchange evolved in the wake of the July agreement would, in short, largely be down to the practitioners themselves.

Granted that there was a general expectation that the 29.9 per cent maximum on outside ownership of Stock Exchange firms would be only temporary, how much did the question of the nationality of the prospective new owners figure at this stage in the Bank's thinking? Had it already conceived the idea of 'national champions' to fight the almost inevitable foreign invasion? However, the Bank's 'immediate concern', the financial journalist Barry Riley speculated in November, 'is that there might be a sudden rush of mergers and link-ups, triggered by somebody's decision to make the first move . . . With the ending of the threat from the Restrictive Practices Court, there could now be a domino effect. There are a great many potential players, but there are not many aces in the pack for them to play with.' Of course, he added, 'all the potential bidders have the option of trying to poach analysts, dealers or salesmen – whether as individuals or teams – rather than paying large amounts of goodwill for whole firms'.[3] Granted that this was the 'chance of a lifetime', as the saying went, to break into London's hitherto ring-fenced securities industry, and that there were indeed appreciably more potential new entrants to this market than there were high-scoring existing broking and jobbing firms, it cannot have been easy to stand back and form a rational view as to whether it was wise to take the plunge, let alone at what price to take it. There would subsequently be much criticism of banks for having behaved in a herd-like, essentially irrational fashion. But arguably, even with the imminent disappearance of the old commissions cartel, it was not acquisition that was the faulty policy, but rather the way in which those acquisitions were managed, from the point of purchase onwards.

How would the jobbers and brokers play the unique situation that was unfolding? No one knew for sure, but Riley offered some predictions, one of which – that 'after a hugely profitable year in the London equity market the individuals and the firms no doubt have a highly inflated idea of what they are worth' – was spot on.[4]

'RIT and Northern in £400m merger with Charterhouse' was the *FT*'s headline on 4 November, heralding the creation of a new entity to be called Charterhouse J. Rothschild and chaired by Jacob Rothschild. 'There is no blood on the carpet', John Hyde, chief executive of Charterhouse (which included the merchant bank Charterhouse Japhet), confidently announced. 'It will be a super group at the end of the day.' Rothschild himself was now, according to Richard Lambert, 'going for the big time'; and more generally Lambert saw the move as what 'may turn out to be the first in a whole series of realignments among City firms'. Three days later it was announced that America's largest bank, Citicorp, was spending

£20m on a 29.9 per cent stake in the brokers Vickers da Costa.[5] Then, on Monday the 14th, came the big one. In Lex's words, 'after a couple of warm-up fixtures over the last fortnight, the first City deal between two domestic first division players has now been unveiled'. This was the news that Warburgs was to buy a 29.9 per cent stake in the jobbers Akroyd & Smithers, at an estimated £41m.[6] Another deal was announced in December, as Rothschilds paid £6.5m for a 29.9 per cent stake in another jobbing firm, Smith Brothers, which would become Smith New Court. 'Gold card for Smith Bros' was Lex's headline, the column emphasising the smooth fit between Rothschilds' 'historic position at the centre of the London bullion market' and Smiths' 'particular expertise in the market for gold mining shares'. The idea was to set up an international dealing company, with Smiths owning 51 per cent and Rothschilds 49 per cent. 'The international dealing side is the attractive bit of the deal', Michael Richardson (now at Rothschilds) commented. 'But until the Stock Exchange approves the international dealing rules we will not know whether we are playing cricket or baseball.'[7]

This was the last deal to be announced in 1983, but there was no let-up in the pace of secret meetings, amidst a swirl of rumours and counter-rumours. On 28 December a leader in the *FT* tried to apply some sober realism. Arguing strongly that 'there is a risk of going too far in the vogue for financial supermarkets', it made four major points: first, that 'in terms of style, structure and corporate culture, a clearing bank has very little in common with, say, a jobber'; second, that the appropriate price of entry into the Stock Exchange was very difficult to judge, not least given 'the maturity of the bull market and the fact that commission income is about to be slashed in some classes of business'; third, that the experience of Wall Street in recent years showed that 'the investment banking business is becoming increasingly "transactional" in nature', with company treasurers for example using different firms for different services, thereby rendering redundant the much-trumpeted idea of 'one-stop shopping'; and fourth, another lesson from Wall Street, 'the huge increase in the capital base of the US investment banks in recent years has not primarily been the result of mergers', but rather the key had been 'the large profits that they have made out of heavy trading activities in a bull market'. In sum, the *FT* contended, for 'the majority' of City firms 'organic growth is likely to be a more satisfactory course than indiscriminate merger activity'.[8]

The next month, a report was presented to the Stock Exchange's Markets Committee that surveyed how members saw the best way ahead in terms of dismantling commissions. 'Nearly all the major London firms that have replied,' it emerged, 'have come out strongly in favour of the Big Bang' – an early sighting of that celebrated tag. There were apparently several reasons for this preferred option: it would keep control in the matter of negotiating commissions in the hands of individual member firms; it was a solution that applied equally to all firms; and it would keep down computer costs. The survey also found that most City associations (including the Accepting Houses Committee, the Unit Trust Association and the Committee of London Clearing Bankers) were similarly minded. A fortnight later, on 7 February, there was a virtually unanimous vote by the Stock Exchange Council that the 'Big Bang' approach be adopted for the dismantling of the minimum commission structure, not earlier than autumn 1985. At the same meeting, Patrick Mitford-Slade of Cazenove's reported on the growing City conviction that retention of single capacity was no longer feasible. He explained why:

> First, there was the growing internationalisation of the securities markets and the inevitable competition from overseas houses; second and more important, both the Government and the Bank of England had adopted a 'laissez faire' attitude. Neither body had been of any help in attempting to preserve single capacity but seemed to be driving the City inexorably towards financial conglomeration, in order to balance the power of the foreigner, and consequently towards opening up the securities markets, which would inevitably lead to dual capacity trading.

No irrevocable decision was yet taken on this emotionally charged question, but the following week the Stock Exchange did announce that the new rules to liberalise dealing in overseas securities would take effect on 9 April, in effect permitting member firms to set up international dealing subsidiaries (IDs) to trade in overseas securities on a negotiated commission basis.[9]

There was one other change for market practitioners to digest. Monday 13 February 1984 saw the start of the Financial Times–Stock Exchange 100-Share Index, an index formed of the shares of the 100 companies with the largest capitalisation and providing a more serious measure of portfolio performance than the FT 30-Share Index. Next day Lex declared that 'the new FTSE Index – "footsy" to its friends – answers an obvious need for a market measurement which is both comprehensive and up-to-the-minute'. By the end of the week the spelling had changed; and though the older Index did not immediately disappear from the headlines, in due course the neatly named 'Footsie' became the dominant measure of market sentiment and indeed a household name.[10]

In March, the Restrictive Practices (Stock Exchange) Act 1984 became law: the Stock Exchange was officially off the hook. On the same day, as the FT 30-Share Index (which had been climbing almost continuously since the Tory election win the previous summer) hit a new high of 865.0, Lawson in his first Budget gave share prices a major stimulus by introducing radical tax reforms, halving stamp duty and abolishing the National Insurance surcharge. The mood in the City was buoyant, but it was not necessarily the most helpful background for making rational decisions about long-term involvement in the London securities market. Exactly a week later the Stock Exchange Council again discussed what structure that market should have once minimum commissions ended. On the 22nd another tie-up was announced – Hambros buying a stake in the medium-sized stockbrokers and Eurobond market specialists Strauss Turnbull, with the two setting up a joint international dealing business with Société Générale – and next day NatWest's chief executive, Philip Wilkinson, expressed his confidence that by the autumn the Stock Exchange would have lifted the 29.9 per cent maximum to 49.9 per cent, with 100 per cent outside ownership being permitted by 1985 or 1986.[11] 'Many people suppose that the last place in which revolutionary change was possible would be the City of London', Andreas Whittam Smith reflected in the *Daily Telegraph* on Saturday the 24th. 'Yet that is a fair description of what is happening to the structure of the stock market. Almost every day new alliances are announced which would have been inconceivable a few years ago.'[12]

By the end of the year, almost all the Stock Exchange marriages had been arranged. From earlier in 1984, these included the stockbrokers Rowe & Pitman joining Akroyds under the Warburgs umbrella; the rather battered Midland Bank (following an American misadventure) buying, through its Samuel Montagu subsidiary, the stockbroking firm Greenwells; and Hill Samuel, Kleinworts and the Hongkong and Shanghai Bank each buying other stockbrokers. Lazards and Lloyds both eschewed this rich man's lucky dip, but two of the clearers, Barclays and NatWest, bought ambitiously, with the former's acquisition of the stockbrokers de Zoete & Bevan and the jobbers Wedd Durlacher paving the way for the subsequent formation of the fully integrated BZW. Then in mid-October, having failed to clinch a deal with either Rowe & Pitman or Phillips & Drew, Morgan Grenfell settled for the much cheaper (£10m) Pember & Boyle – an eminently respectable if rather unexciting firm, which unfortunately specialised in gilts at a time when equities offered by far the better money-making prospect. Morgan Grenfell's Bill Mackworth-Young died a few days later, and that merchant bank's chances of making a real go of it in the securities business further receded. Soon afterwards, in early November, 'Swiss role for P&D' was Lex's witty way of greeting the news that Phillips & Drew had plighted itself to Union Bank of Switzerland (UBS). 'We weren't the highest bidders', UBS told the *Wall Street Journal*. 'It was a combination of price and concept that made the difference.'[13] Later in the month Chase Manhattan simultaneously got its hands on two brokers (Laurie Milbank and Simon & Coates), and just before Christmas tie-ups were announced between North Carolina National Bank and Panmure Gordon, and Banque Bruxelles Lambert and Williams de Broë Hill Chaplin. A few more unions would be announced in 1985, but the main wave was over.

'Some of the purchases were calmly calculated, some derived from instinctive opportunism, but many were little more than a panic move to avoid being left out', John Littlewood subsequently reflected. 'All too often, a rash temptation to buy a barely understood business was met by an equally rash temptation to sell out to a little-known buyer or an ill-defined future.' On the basis of known figures and some informed guesswork, he estimated that (once the initial stakes, mainly 29.9 per cent, had been raised in due course to 100 per cent, as almost invariably they were) a total of some £450m was paid for the nine leading brokers that sold out, another £400m for twenty-two broking firms that were more medium-sized and £300m for the five leading jobbers – coming to a grand total of some £1,150m for thirty-six firms. It was not a cheap exercise, and a notable feature was that a high proportion of the leading American banks and investment houses, including Bankers Trust, Crédit Suisse First Boston (CSFB), Drexel Burnham Lambert, Goldman Sachs, Morgan Guaranty, Morgan Stanley and Salomons, saw little advantage in buying at the top of the market and instead opted for organic growth. The same applied to Merrill Lynch, apart from its eventual acquisition in 1985 of a small gilts dealer; and it, like most of the others, already had a significant London presence. Moreover, some asked themselves, what exactly would they be buying? At one point Bank of America came close to acquiring Phillips & Drew – until, the story goes, a leading figure at the bank declared that he was damned if he was going to pay out a small fortune on 'assets that go up and down the elevator'. Admittedly there was usually a 'golden handcuffs' mechanism, but with money burning a hole in their pockets the natural desire of many of those assets was to be making the downwards ride. There were also the haunting words of Brian Pitman, as he crisply explained in December 1984 why Lloyds was not going into the international securities business: 'It's unrealistic to believe you can be the best in every financial market and in every financial product.'[14]

For those who were taking the gamble (whether for aggressive or defensive reasons), there was perhaps comfort in the two words 'British Telecom'.[15] The Conservative government's decision to privatise just over 50 per cent of British Telecommunications, originally announced in March 1982, had huge City implications, in that it involved an equity issue of almost £4bn – the biggest that any stock market, let alone the London capital market, had ever seen – and moved the privatisation process into an altogether higher gear. In due course the mandate went to Kleinwort Benson, where the key figure was Sir Martin Jacomb, abetted by James (Lord) Rockley and David Clementi. Initially, there was far from universal confidence or indeed enthusiasm in the City. At a dinner party attended by Lawson but mainly comprising 'captains of industry and pillars of leading City merchant banks', the Chancellor was struck by how, with the notable exception of Jacomb, 'each and every one of them roundly declared that the privatisation was impossible: the capital market simply was not large enough to absorb it'. The government too had its moments of doubt, wanting to do the sale in more than one tranche, before bowing to Jacomb's insistence on a single tranche.[16] Partly because it could not be assumed that the institutions alone would bite off such a large issue, and partly because of the political attraction of spreading the virtues of popular capitalism, the government was determined to reach out to private investors and – beyond them – the general, more or less City-ignorant, public as a whole.

Could it be done? In his *Spectator* column in August 1984 Christopher Fildes expressed scepticism that the City would be able to sell BT to the mass of potential individual shareholders, lacking as it did 'road show' techniques, appetite, and so on. That autumn, however, a massive and – in City terms – wholly unprecedented television advertising campaign, together with an equally systematic PR campaign to reach the tabloids, created a high degree of general awareness, helped no doubt by the generally bullish tendencies of the market, recovering strongly after a nasty dip in the summer. On 12 November, just over a fortnight after the release of the 'pathfinder' prospectus (itself an innovation), Arthur H. Poole was moved to write to the Stock Exchange. After outlining how, as 'an East End boy with nothing but an elementary school background', he had become an office boy with Bourke Schiff & Co. in 1922 before eventually building up quite a clientele of private investors, finally with Henry J. Garratt & Co., he went on:

> You will never have a better opportunity than you have at this moment to attract the small investor, than the forthcoming Brit Telecom issue. I have been approached by so many people who have never invested before, as to whether they should apply for shares, and how they go about it. With other de-nationalised offers in the pipeline, and with the advent of thousands of would-be Clients, you have a real chance to recapture the long lost small investor.[17]

The formal offer for sale, or 'Impact Day' as it was called, occurred four days later, on 16 November: 3,012 million shares were to be sold at 130p each, raising £3,916m; 47 per cent of the issue was to be allocated to the UK investing institutions, 39 per cent to the British public and 14 per cent to overseas investors.

It was soon clear that the issue was a palpable hit, being no fewer than five times oversubscribed. When dealings began in the Stock Exchange on 3 December the shares were at an almost 100 per cent premium, and not surprisingly there were some hectic scenes on the floor, which when Poole watched them on television may have reminded him of nothing so much as the frenzied rubber boom of July 1925. Everyone was a winner, it seemed, in this most visible of triumphs for 'the market'; it was also, in retrospect, the episode that signalled that the Thatcher era was moving towards its high tide. Yet for the City itself, although profiting hugely, there was a disquieting aspect, as over the next few weeks much of the market in BT shares shifted (under Morgan Stanley's auspices) to New York, where Americans were eager to sell to British institutions.[18] It was the clearest possible indication that the market in leading equities was becoming global – and that, within that market, there would be no room for London to hide.

*

In June 1985, the Bank of England published a list of the twenty-nine firms with which it would be prepared to deal in the new gilts market. The total capital commitment was estimated at over £600m (some four to five times bigger than the £100–150m currently being deployed in the market), and *The Economist*'s best guess was that there would be 'stabbing room only'. Those lined up for the widely expected bloodbath included major American banks like Bank of America, Bankers Trust, Chase Manhattan, Citicorp, Goldman Sachs and Merrill Lynch, as well as most of the main British merchant and clearing banks. The view of the stockbroker Gordon Pepper was typically brusque: 'Given the degree of competition, anyone who's assuming that money can be made from the market in the first two years is indulging in wishful thinking.' Over the next year that remained the conventional wisdom, prompting Bank of America in March 1986 to withdraw as a primary dealer and then Union Discount to do the same four months later, despite having spent £250,000 on computer equipment for its gilts operation.[19]

Union Discount's experience was a salutary reminder of the money that, ahead of Big Bang, was starting to be poured into the seemingly bottomless pit of new technology. 'Open markets mean more competition, more volume, more complexity, above all more risk; technology offers tools to help. But selecting the right tools takes time, money and a clear view of the future. All are in short supply. Can British firms – and British markets – wire up and plug in to meet foreign rivals on equal terms? Or will they lose a chance in a lifetime to leapfrog the competition.' This introduction to *The Economist*'s July 1985 survey of technology and the City caught the increasingly febrile mood, and its author, Merril Stevenson, raised a fundamental question: 'Many of the dealer-support and banking systems now on the market or being developed offer some help in risk control. They all seem to fall short of what is wanted. Are British bosses, risk-averse by tradition, in danger of expecting too much from their systems and too little from themselves?' And she quoted one of the City's American heavyweights, Jack Hennessy of CSFB: 'If you've never gone to the casino, you don't know how to manage risk. It's embedded experience, betting the bank every day. The technology makes it all possible, but it's the people who make it happen.'[20]

Over the next year it proved increasingly difficult to stand back objectively from the race to avoid technological obsolescence, but in November 1985 the Stock Exchange's George Hayter did warn member firms against 'spending such enormous sums of money in preparation for the change' without thinking hard about the fixed overheads that they were 'building up for themselves in the months and years to follow, overheads which may make it more difficult for them to adapt, as they may need to, in response to changing business conditions or to a revised perception of their most successful business strategy in the new City'. Of course, much of this spending was now being underwritten by their new owners, and over the next six or so months a series of huge, high-tech, almost space-age dealing rooms were proudly unveiled by the outfits, such as Kleinworts and BZW, which intended to be among the big players. But if these had an obvious if pricy allure (some £18m worth of technology in BZW's case alone), the same did not apply to the back office, where a survey conducted by Coopers & Lybrand about three months before Big Bang (set for 27 October 1986) found that, in the Banker's summarising words, 'much of settlement will be done manually for the foreseeable future, management control of dealing exposure is, with few exceptions, lacking and support systems have yet to catch up to the sophistication of what the dealer has at hand'.

The back office, though, had never been a favourite City subject, and what preoccupied decision-makers more was whether or not trading would continue on the Stock Exchange floor after Big Bang. In fact, partly under pressure from member firms anxious to be able to play it both ways, the Stock Exchange did spend a significant amount of money ensuring that jobbers who chose to stay on the floor would not be short of screens, terminals and all the rest. Although there was a general consensus that there would be an immediate, ultimately irresistible shift away from face-to-face trading, by September 1986 as many as twenty-eight prospective market makers (as jobbers would now be called) had signed up for a pitch, with Smith New Court making particularly trenchant noises about keeping at least four dozen dealers on the floor. Sentiment perhaps played a part, but there was also an understandable fear of telephone lines becoming completely jammed.[21]

Indeed for most practitioners, what really concerned them about Big Bang was whether the humdrum mechanics were going to work, come the great day. On Saturday 18 October – two days after Leigh-Pemberton in his Mansion House speech had called on 'all market participants to exercise a degree of restraint' in the post-Big Bang world – there was a full-scale dress rehearsal for the new screen-quoted prices system, SEAQ. It did not go brilliantly. '"Mickey Mouse" systems get blamed for Big Bang problems' was the *Guardian*'s headline, and though the Stock Exchange pronounced itself satisfied, there were many complaints from individual member firms. The gilts market dress rehearsal went rather better, though it was hindered by a fire at the Central Gilts Office in the Bank of England. Not surprisingly the sense of nervousness increased. 'I had American firms ringing me up saying, "We simply haven't got enough space on the trading floor. We must have it." All the market makers seemed to believe that the trading floor would survive', Goodison recollected.[22]

Partly because of its arresting tag, Big Bang attracted an enormous amount of media attention, even before it happened. Accompanying that attention was a tendency, perhaps inevitable, to assume that it was a truly momentous event. However, one of the City's most acute minds, Tim Congdon, chief economist at the stockbroking firm Messels, argued otherwise in a compelling piece in the *Spectator* a week before the off. 'The importance of the Big Bang has been exaggerated', he stated bluntly, and went on:

> It is a sideshow to, indeed almost a by-product of, a much Bigger Bang which has transformed international finance over the last 25 years. This Bigger Bang bears about the same relation to the Big Bang as the construction of Canary Wharf to the refurbishment of the Royal Exchange. One totally overshadows and dwarfs the other. Whereas the Bigger Bang is a new departure in the pattern of international financial activity, the Big Bang merely alters the way in which a long-established business is conducted; and whereas the Bigger Bang has affected the availability and form of finance to industries and governments around the world, the Big Bang's immediate relevance is mainly to the British corporate sector and the British Government. More fundamentally still, the Bigger Bang is – on all the relevant criteria – a multiple of the size of the Big Bang.

What did Congdon mean by 'the Bigger Bang'? In essence, 'the rapid growth of offshore (or Euro-) financial transactions and the tendency for the City of London to capture the lion's share of the associated business'. After noting that Eurocurrency deposits stood by March 1986 at almost $3,500bn, he made some intensely revealing comparisons:

> Last year the turnover in the Eurobond market was between $1,500bn and $2,000bn, while that on the Stock Exchange was, at $600bn, less than half as much . . . In 1985 the total amount of money raised on international markets was $256.5bn, according to figures prepared by the OECD. About 80 per cent of this was raised by the issue of securities, with the remainder accounted for by bank loans. So the flow of new securities coming on to the market was over $200bn a year, equivalent to about $800m each working day. By contrast, the London Stock Exchange raised just over $8bn in 1985, equivalent to a little more than $30m each working day.

Accordingly, 'an extraordinary situation has arisen where the Euromarket, which has no physical embodiment in an exchange building or even a widely recognised set of rules and regulations, is the largest source of capital in the world'. Even so, although 'in some senses the business belongs to no country, since it involves intercontinental flows of funds and cross-frontier communications', the fact was that 'most of the significant work is completed in large financial centres' – and 'of these, London is clearly dominant'. Therefore, 'in effect London has become host to the greatest and most rapidly growing capital market in the world'. That, according to Congdon, was 'the Bigger Bang', especially involving as it did major spin-off effects on London's foreign exchange dealing, money broking and fund management industry. He then turned to another conventional nostrum:

> The Big Bang is said to be necessary to improve the City's international competitiveness. The comment is extraordinary after a 25-year period in which London's world financial role has been transformed beyond all recognition. In 1960 its prime international function was to act as the clearing-house of the sterling area, which is now virtually defunct. Today it is the hub of a new and vast international capital market without rival anywhere. It is surely preposterous to describe the City as 'uncompetitive'. It would be more accurate to say that the London Stock Exchange has lost ground relative to the Eurobond market and that a change in rules is necessary to enable the Exchange to see business on more even terms. This is the sense in which the Big Bang is a by-product of the Bigger Bang.[23]

Congdon was surely right. The Stock Exchange in the mid-1980s was at last, after twenty semi-wasted years, seeking to reintegrate itself into the international market – a market that had now more or less returned to the seamless capital flows that had characterised the pre-1914 world. The real heroes of the story remained Bolton, Warburg and the other Euromarket pioneers of the late 1950s and early 1960s.

Still, if one had spent the best part of a working lifetime on the floor of the Stock Exchange, the end of minimum commissions and single capacity, together with the move to largely screen and telephone dealing, did undeniably represent *quite* a big bang . . . Friday the 24th was the last day of the old world. It came complete with japes: a grey (or green, according to another account) pantomime horse, with kickable rear-end supplied by a clerk; pinstriped traders being sprayed all over by aerosol cans of multi-coloured 'Silly String'; the appearance of a *Spitting Image* puppet of the Chancellor of the Exchequer; and at the end, as 3.30 approached, choruses of 'Auld Lang Syne' to a background of popping champagne corks. 'A little horseplay before the big race' was the headline next day in one paper, and that was about right.[24] It was time, at last, to get real.

*

The financial services revolution of the 1980s was accompanied, perhaps inevitably, by a revolution in the City's physical appearance and indeed whole way of life. Curiously, however, the single building that came to symbolise the new City had nothing at all to do with Big Bang and in fact had been conceived while Callaghan was still at No. 10. It was in 1978 that Richard Rogers, fresh from building the Pompidou Centre in Paris, won the commission to build a new home for Lloyd's. He did so not with a specific design, but with what he called 'a design strategy', one that he insisted would not only be sympathetic to the surrounding 'intricate mesh of narrow streets', but responsive to an unknown future:

> We propose a free and open-ended framework where the ever-changing performance is the dynamic expression of the architecture of the building . . . A place where ever-changing activities overlap in flexible well-serviced spaces, the café, the restaurant, the pub, the tailor, the bank, the meeting rooms, the underwriting Room, the food market, the sports room, the corner shop, the offices, each playing its role, growing or shrinking depending on demand.

The new Lloyd's was completed in 1986, and from the start its strikingly 'inside-out' design attracted enormous, mainly positive attention. 'The most consistently innovative building the City has seen since Soane's Bank of England, breaking absolutely with its usual preference for architectural safe investments', Simon Bradley hailed it in his 1997 update of Pevsner.

Rogers had, in sum, given the City 'its first twentieth-century building that can truly be called famous, in the way that St Paul's or the Tower are famous'. It was not of course to everyone's taste. 'Poor old Lloyd's', one underwriter observed in April 1986, gesturing at miscellaneous pipes and tubes. 'After three hundred years . . . We started off in a coffee-house and finished up in a coffee percolator.'[25]

The momentous changes of 1983–4 meant that the City Corporation was coming under pressure to produce something more sensitive to the probable future needs of key financial practitioners – above all, the perceived need for vast, open-plan, high-tech trading floors where all the different arms of the new securities conglomerates could be housed under one roof. Such trading floors were not compatible with narrow Victorian frontages. As early as January 1985 a poll by Savills of 251 City occupiers revealed that more than two-thirds of respondents expected to be looking for large, open-plan areas, with nearly half feeling that floor sizes of over 10,000 square feet were 'most suited to their needs'.[26] Citicorp was inevitably among those searching for such premises, even if they were not in the very centre of the City, and that summer its move to the northern edge of the Thames was effectively confirmed when the City Corporation gave its first consent to a new dealing floor – in the form of a conversion of the old Billingsgate fish market. For the moment, however, the

November 1984 draft plan – affecting two-thirds of the Square Mile – was still on the table.

The final nail in its coffin was the entirely unexpected emergence of a new, rival development. Some years later the *FT*'s Vanessa Houlder provided an authoritative account of the remarkable turn of events:

> In February 1985, Dr Michael von Clemm [the American chairman of CSFB in London] went to the Isle of Dogs, a watery wasteland two miles east of the Bank of England, to look for a packaging plant for the Roux Brothers' restaurant chain [of which he had been a long-time backer, for gastronomic as much as business motives]. An enterprise zone had been set up [in 1981] in the area to attract development. From the barge where he was eating lunch, von Clemm spotted a disused banana warehouse. Forgetting the Roux Brothers, von Clemm started to toy with the idea of converting the warehouse into a back office for Crédit Suisse First Boston.
>
> After several more visits he consulted Ware Travelstead, a US developer who advised First Boston on its real estate investments. Ware Travelstead turned von Clemm's idea on its head. He knew that the bank had wasted five years in trying, unsuccessfully, to obtain a new front office location in the City of London. The real question, he insisted, was: 'Can we consider Canary Wharf on the Isle of Dogs as a front office location?'
>
> The question was breathtaking in its audacity, suggesting a 180-degree reversal of London's pattern of development. For generations, any institution with wealth or influence has gravitated towards the west of London, while the east has been associated with poverty, dockyards and sweatshops.[27]

By that summer a financial consortium comprising CSFB, Morgan Stanley and First Boston Real Estate had been assembled, as had a development team under Travelstead, and soon afterwards the full plans were revealed. The Canary Wharf scheme would comprise 71 acres, feature Europe's three tallest towers and provide 8.5 million square feet of office and dealing space. It was intended to be operational by the end of the decade and would be the largest real-estate development in Western Europe. Opinion was sharply divided as to its chances of success, but there was no disputing that Canary Wharf represented a direct challenge to the City planners.

The man most closely identified with the rapid and ambitious redevelopment of much of the City was Michael Cassidy, chairman of the Corporation's Planning Committee for three years from 1986.[28] A finance-minded lawyer who had just completed an MBA thesis on the Big Bang, he was intensely aware of the potential threat to the City's critical mass – and international credibility – if it failed to meet the spatial demands of the large new international players, above all the Americans. Not everyone appreciated this drastic liberalisation, or Cassidy's penchant for the limelight, but the vision was both right and timely at a testing moment in City history.

One development above all encapsulated the new, aggressive, 'American' mood.[29] This was Broadgate, the brainchild of two genuinely visionary developers, albeit very different characters, Stuart Lipton and Godfrey Bradman. Although One Finsbury Avenue had already been built (one of the City's pioneer atrium blocks along American lines, and in due course occupied by Warburgs), the crucial breakthrough in terms of the development as a whole was the demolition in 1985 of Broad Street Station, to which generations of City men had travelled in the North London Line's pre-1914 heyday. In July 1986 the prime minister, dressed in blue but not disdaining a white hard hat, topped out the development's first two phases, amidst much talk of this being the City's largest building project since the Great Fire more than three centuries earlier. In addition to Warburgs, tenants already included Shearson Lehman/American Express, Security Pacific, Lloyds Merchant Bank and UBS. For lovers of the Victorian City, of which Broad Street Station was emblematic, there was an obvious sadness – though the considerable compensation was that the development (with its imaginative sculpture, circular amphitheatre and skating rink, as well as shops and restaurants) was of an altogether higher order than, say, the miserably unimaginative blocks that had gone up on London Wall in the 1960s. Broadgate quickly came to symbolise an international financial centre that was assuming an increasingly cosmopolitan character. It was merely a geographical coincidence that that centre happened to be situated on what was still in many ways a tight little, right little island.

*

During the two years before Big Bang the American influence did much to alter the City's way of life. 'I have to get in at 8.00 a.m. now – before the Americans arrived the working day started at 9.15', Neville Wood of Messels (in the process of being taken over by Shearson Lehman) told *Futures World* in January 1985. 'I arrive before the tea lady now.' It was not just a case of American-style hours for their own, virtuous sake – these extended hours reflecting, as Barry Riley observed in June 1986, both 'the globalisation of the investment industry, making it possible to transact business in other time zones' and 'the growing amount of professional trading in the markets', in the sense that 'because the professionals are at their desks all day watching screens, they are ready at any time to trade anything that moves' – but undoubtedly there was a cultural element in the shift. Time had become the new master. It was, as the secretary of the City Club in Old Broad Street eloquently complained to another American journalist, a sad day when his members no longer had the leisure to sit around over a drink or two.[30]

Did the material rewards make it all worthwhile? 'Top salaries in the

City fair make one gasp, they are so large', none other than Margaret Thatcher confessed to *Newsnight* just over a year before Big Bang. Back in year zero (1979) things had been rather different – at Morgan Grenfell, for example, a director's remuneration was about £40,000, which was tidy enough but hardly a source of stunned disbelief. However, the whole point of the Thatcher project was no longer to pursue egalitarian goals, while a further stimulus to City pay levels was the outlawing in 1980 of insider dealing, thereby cutting off (or certainly discouraging) what had traditionally been a lucrative source of revenue to those in the know. Over the years the whole question of how much those who were something in the City actually earned had received surprisingly little outside attention, but that began to change in 1982 following the headline-attracting news that the leading Lloyd's underwriter Ian Posgate had been paid over £320,000 in a single year. 'People in the City have a great deal of contact with markets and with money', Philip Burnford of Hay Management Consultants perhaps superfluously told the *Observer*, confirming that average earnings there were well above those in industry. 'They have to be very aware of market focus and they tend to apply the same principles to themselves.'[31]

Most of the figures, nonetheless, were still far from startling, with a survey by Lloyd Incomes Research that year into the merchant and international banking sectors finding that neither corporate finance executives nor chief foreign exchange dealers were likely to earn above £50,000. Nor did the situation significantly change over the next year or two. In his autumn 1983 survey of the wider situation, following the Parkinson/Goodison agreement, Jacob Rothschild found that, on the basis of published figures, top people in the City were far less well paid than on Wall Street; for instance, most directors at Rothschilds only got somewhere around £100,000, whereas their counterparts at Salomons or Morgan Stanley were likely to be receiving at least five times as much. It was the same further down the ranks. 'At the crunch point, you simply say to yourself, "One has been in business since eighteen hundred and something. There have been bad times and good times. If it means I must have leaner expectations, so be it"', a senior manager at an accepting house told Paul Ferris at about that time. 'Wall Street has much greater orientation to personal gain. London wants to be successful, too, but the rewards are more in respect. They don't necessarily come through the wallet.'[32] However, through a mixture of American influence and competitive gearing-up for Big Bang, together creating an aggressive, bonus-driven culture, such an attitude was about to become almost antediluvian.

An important moment was the highly publicised episode in July 1985 when Kleinworts poached eight people from the Wedd Durlacher arm of BZW, with the jobbers receiving between them £1m to defect, and upwards of £2m for their first year's salaries. Soon afterwards, on the basis of information from headhunters, *The Economist* revealed the latest salaries (probably including bonuses, share options and suchlike): £250,000 or more for top gilts dealers; up to £300,000 for Eurobond dealers; £200,000 for experts in American equities; £250,000 for currency dealers; and £150,000 for swaps specialists. 'All these figures', the magazine added to cheer up its readers outside the Square Mile, 'are still barely half what similar people command in New York.' As a point of further comparison, the governor of the Bank of England was currently on some £85,000 a year. A gold rush had begun, and the following month a financial recruitment specialist observed that 'an unprecedented number of accountants, lawyers and MBAs are coming to us looking for an opening in financial services, on the back of what they read about City salaries in the newspapers'.[33] New terms were also entering City vocabulary. Not just 'golden hello' (the opposite of a golden handshake) and 'golden handcuffs' (deferred payments in order to lock people in), but also the so-called 'Marzipan Set', usually comprising young high-fliers below the icing (partnership level or the equivalent) but above the cake (those unfortunates without serious prospects). When Chase Manhattan acquired two stock-broking firms, it was in order to keep the marzipan boys sweet that it reputedly went out and bought thirty-seven Porsches in a single day.

In March 1986, soon after Thatcher had again distanced herself from the phenomenon ('On salaries in the City, I am the first to say this does cause me great concern. I understand the resentment . . .'), Nicholas Coleridge sought to offer some numerical perspective:

> It is difficult to estimate the number of young investment bankers, stock-brokers, and commodity brokers earning £100,000 a year. Perhaps there are only a couple of thousand, but they are so mobile and noisy that they give the impression of being far more numerous. Most are aged between 26 and 34, and two years ago they were being paid £25,000, in some cases even less, until the opening up of the City markets precipitated an epidemic of headhunting and concomitant salaries.

The pre-Big Bang scramble, meanwhile, was continuing unabated, and that same month there were reports of Morgan Grenfell Securities picking up a four-man team of analysts from Grieveson Grant for a total package ('golden hellos' and promised first-year salaries) of somewhere in the region of £1.5m. Carl West-Meads, a personnel consultant, put it aptly during the summer: 'People have lost touch with what a salary market is. It's now a recruitment-premium salary market, and greed is exponential.' Of course, in addition to these mainly young dealers, analysts and others commanding such a remarkable premium, there were the former partners of stockbroking and jobbing firms – estimated to be 500 or more

– who had become millionaires overnight through selling their firms to outside owners. There were also the well-established City figures running the merchant banks, who saw no reason not to have a share of the honey, especially since in many cases their businesses had been booming anyway. For their work in 1986 the directors of Morgan Grenfell received an average of some £225,000 – a fivefold increase on 1979.[34] The City revolution had been good for them.

*

'*La "City", un îlot de prospérité dans un océan d'austérité*' was the evocative headline in a French paper in November 1982, as part of a series on the state of Britain as it started to come out of the deep recession of the early 1980s. That same year Anthony Sampson observed how, during the two decades since his first *Anatomy*, 'the contrast between the City and the rest of Britain has become more extreme', in that 'bankers and dealers have become more international while industrialists and others have been bogged down in the country's economic constraints, and politicians have pursued their own national policies'. In other words, 'the Square Mile of the City has become like an offshore island in the heart of the nation'. Emphatically this seasoned, perceptive commentator did not see this bifurcation as a good thing:

> The inhabitants of this extraordinary island – like those of other banking islands such as Hong Kong, Singapore or Manhattan – view the world very differently from those on the mainland. They can see across the whole globe, but they see it through money; they clearly perceive Britain's economic problems, but they see the British people in terms of balance sheets. They are constantly dealing with bits of British industry, restructuring companies, joining their boards, merging them or rationalising them. But they still remain aloof from the real industrial problems; and their business (as Jim Slater described it) is making money, not things.

British politics was at its most polarised since 1945, with Thatcher and Foot as the respective party leaders, and in 1983 the City found itself at the centre of a major, hostile protest for the first time since the Chartists in 1848. This was the 'Stop the City' movement, which held its first demonstration in September and another, bigger one the following March.[35]

It was just after a Stop the City demo (probably the first one) that Paul Ferris asked a merchant banker ('oiled hair, pink cheeks') about the notion of more money being put into a high-unemployment place like Liverpool. Shaking his head, he replied, 'Politicians hire buses and take businessmen around Merseyside. Well. Would you invest there? In a lot of bloody-minded Liverpudlians? People complain that the City doesn't invest in places like Liverpool. Why should I? It isn't efficient.' Sadly, this merchant banker preferred to stay anonymous, as did the ninety-eight

City people (mainly stockbrokers, jobbers and merchant bankers) interviewed by the sociologist David Lazar in 1985. His pioneering study brought out both the intrinsic satisfaction that many of his interviewees found in their work ('I do genuinely feel quite proud that I've got something right for somebody', one stockbroker told him) and the way in which they viewed financial markets as an exciting, demanding arena ('Every day is a new challenge, every day is different', one very senior jobber stressed). Of his interviewees, he felt able to give an ideological classification to ninety-one of them: 7 per cent were neo-liberals (that is, out-and-out supporters of the wholly free, unconstrained market); 46 per cent had an outlook somewhere between neo-liberalism and what he called 'Traditional Conservatism'; and 33 per cent were more or less traditional Conservatives.[36] The City, in short, was not for turning – and in retrospect, the ascendancy of the market had only just begun.

In October 1986, the arrival of Big Bang itself enabled, at least potentially, a moment of stocktaking. 'Ancient prejudices against finance are being stimulated by the growing belief that the City has become an unpatriotic casino which pays itself obscenely high salaries for dancing on the grave of British industry', David Goodhart and Charles Grant declared in the *New Statesman* on the Friday before the 27th. On that memorable Monday morning, however, and at this self-consciously historic moment, the most engaging – and in a way most perceptive – commentary came, surprisingly enough, from Jon Akass in the *Daily Express*:

> For most people, the City is an alien place. The humblest lift-operator in a Moscow department store will have some inkling of how Communism is supposed to work. They would have endured lessons at school. Hardly anyone in Britain knows how capitalism is supposed to work and we are especially befuddled when it comes to the City. The Big Bang might clear the air just slightly because there is a suspicion that the old City cherished its mysteries and the notion that it was some kind of secret society. It is harder to be mysterious in front of a computer screen. Everybody is beginning to understand computers . . .
>
> There will be winners and losers, which we can all understand. But we will still not understand why and how.[37]

CHAPTER FORTY

Hong Kong West

In the City's new dealing rooms most of the systems stood up well enough on the day of Big Bang, and there was a general mood of qualified relief. From the start the Stock Exchange floor was less populous, and over the next few weeks, as phone-and-screen trading became the norm, the numbers rapidly dwindled. By January 1987 even the trading floor's staunchest supporter, Smith New Court, reluctantly decided there was no point in retaining a presence. Soon afterwards it became the sole preserve of the Stock Exchange's traded options market. 'We've got a viewing gallery and nothing to see', Stephen Raven (of Warburg Securities) lamented.[1] That was true enough, though the melancholy sight of all the spanking new – but now abandoned – telecommunications technology on the floor served as a reminder of the City's abiding reluctance to embrace change until it was virtually a fait accompli.

Market sentiment was still mainly bullish in the closing months of 1986, with the FT 30-Share Index going into 1987 on 1313.9, representing a gain of 15.5 per cent on the year. The climate was therefore congenial in early December for the biggest privatisation so far, the £5.43bn 'Tell Sid' sell-off of British Gas, following what *The Economist* rightly called 'a persistent, numbing but nevertheless effective advertising campaign'. Unlike BT, the issue was not a roaring success (two times oversubscribed, as opposed to five), but it was a success. Was a culture of private share ownership being established? By September 1987 (following recent British Airways and Rolls-Royce privatisations) the *FT* was still sceptical, noting that 'the hard fact is that private investors' business is more costly for the brokers' and that 'as long as that is the case the City's response to calls for popular capitalism will be lukewarm'.[2]

Big Bang itself had hardly happened when the City – and especially Morgan Grenfell – found itself under a blacker cloud of scandal than anyone could remember. The curtain-raiser was on 10 November 1986, as Geoffrey Collier, joint head of securities trading at Morgan Grenfell, resigned because of insider dealing for which he was eventually given a suspended prison sentence. Yet this was nothing compared to the story that was about to break. In early December, following revelations by the

disgraced American arbitrageur Ivan Boesky, the DTI began an investigation into an alleged share-support operation during the weeks leading up
to the Guinness takeover of Distillers earlier that year, in which Morgan
Grenfell and Cazenove's had acted for Guinness.

It had been crucial to the Guinness takeover strategy that its share
price kept above the level at which Morgan Grenfell and Cazenove's had
underwritten the bid. In consort with the Guinness chief executive Ernest
Saunders, several parties had secretly acquired large numbers of Guinness
shares in order to keep the price artificially high, safe in the knowledge
that Guinness would compensate them for any loss. Amongst them were
Schenley Industries, run by 'Rik' Riklis, part of whose business was as
a US distributor for Distillers; the British businessmen Gerald Ronson
and Sir Jack Lyons, who had both been recruited into the operation by
their stockbroker Anthony Parnes; Bank Leu, a large Swiss bank whose
chairman, Dr Artur Furer, Saunders had once worked with at Nestlé;
and Henry Ansbacher clients, one of whose managing directors was Lord
Spens.

'Neither I nor anyone at Morgan Grenfell knew of, or had any contact
with, Schenley or with Boesky over any special arrangements or sweetheart/
support deals', Morgan Grenfell's Roger Seelig flatly insisted to the press.
'We were not party in any way to any improper deals with Boesky, Riklis
or Schenley.' Shortly after Christmas it emerged that Lord Spens had
given details to DTI inspectors about the informal indemnification
arrangements that had been made between Seelig and himself during the
closing stages of the takeover battle. Seelig's resignation from Morgan
Grenfell was announced on the 30th. 'I am extremely sad', commented
Spens. 'The man has been thrown to the wolves. I consider it inconceivable that he was acting on his own authority. Roger was always very
professional and very cautious.'[3] The pressure was still on Morgan Grenfell,
which on 13 January 1987 (the day before Saunders was dismissed) announced
an internal review. The press scented a whitewash, and within days the
government – anxious about public opinion, with a general election in
the offing – was telling the Bank of England to take some action. The
Bank (through the intermediary of the former governor Lord O'Brien of
Lothbury) obliged, and Morgan Grenfell's chief executive, Christopher
Reeves, and its head of corporate finance, Graham Walsh, resigned on
the 20th. It was a total humiliation.

The Bank also insisted that Spens must walk the plank, which he duly
did on the 22nd. By about the same time hints of the roles of Gerald
Ronson, Sir Jack Lyons and the City men Anthony Parnes and Ephraim
Margulies were starting to emerge. Inevitably, attention now turned to
Cazenove's (the only major stockbroking firm that had retained its inde-
pendence during the Big Bang process), and in particular David Mayhew.

'King Caz's deafening silence' was a *Standard* headline as early as the 21st, while four days later the *Observer* reported the government's determination that the firm 'should not escape censure for its role in the Guinness share support operation, even if there is no direct evidence that the firm was involved in any of the illegal activities'. The stakes were further raised on the 28th when a Labour frontbencher, Robin Cook, explicitly named Cazenove's as accomplices in the Guinness scandal. However, a statement next day by Cazenove's declared that an inquiry by the solicitors Simmons & Simmons had found no evidence of wrongdoing; and over the coming weeks and months, Mayhew himself remained in place, with no evidence that the Bank tried to persuade the two joint senior partners, John Kemp-Welch and Anthony Forbes, otherwise. Soon the headlines moved elsewhere, but few imagined that the Guinness affair would quietly die away, certainly not once the arrests began. Between April and October 1987 there were five (Saunders, Parnes, Lyons, Ronson and Seelig), prompting the *FT*'s Richard Lambert to observe with a certain relish that 'not since the South Sea Bubble in the early eighteenth century had so many top British financiers faced so many serious charges arising from a single event'.[4]

In January 1987, with the scandal unfolding amidst almost daily revelations, the same paper's David Lascelles reported that 'the Guinness affair has plunged the City into a mood of gloom, anxiety and even, in some corners, despair'. He added that 'people with long memories say they cannot recall a time when the City's reputation has been so badly battered by scandal, or when the threat of political repercussions has loomed so large'. Predictably, even though it was barely two months since the Takeover Panel had rebuked Hill Samuel and Cazenove's for not dissimilar share buying during the early autumn battle to prevent the British engineering company AE being taken over by Turner & Newall, all the City's instincts were to close ranks and deny that Guinness had been anything more than a one-off operation. Over a decade later Spens spoke feelingly on television:

> I felt rather as though one had put one's head above the parapet and had it shot off. The failure by people to stand up and be counted was stunning. The City retreated into a shell and started to go into a denial mode and say, 'We never did this, we never had anything to do with any of these practices' – it was astonishing, because they all had been.
> *Everyone had been doing this?*
> Everyone, absolutely everyone.

Nor did the publication in February 1987 of the Neill Report on Lloyd's improve City morale, as it spelled out that institution's endemic conflicts of interest (including the baby syndicates aspect) and recommended that henceforth its Council should have a majority of outside members. 'The power of insiders to control the market in their own interest was thus finally eroded', Adam Raphael noted some years later in his coruscating study of Lloyd's. 'It was the end of a shameful era at Lloyd's which, more than anything else, buried the myth that "utmost good faith" still held sway.' Altogether, with the Conservative Party chairman, Norman Tebbit, having recently made an uncomfortable comparison – 'We cleaned up the trades union movement and we'll clean up the City too' – these were awkward times for the Bank's governor, Robin Leigh-Pemberton. Interviewed in February, he accepted that standards were coming 'under greater strain', and that it was 'inevitable' that 'we are going to have to have more bodies, more rules, and more law'. Not surprisingly, his interviewers pushed him on whether the emerging dispensation, essentially of practitioner regulation within a statutory framework, could work 'if people aren't concerned about public censure and the old City club atmosphere no longer exists'. The governor's reply would not have dismayed any of his predecessors: 'I think that people are still very sensitive to public censure and the vast majority are proud of their standards.'[5]

Undeterred by a sharp decline in the number of takeover bids, the bull market roared on, especially during March 1987, either side of Lawson's expansive, pre-election Budget. The FTSE 100 (increasingly the benchmark of market sentiment) rose above 2000 shortly before Lawson announced his tax cuts – double the level at which it had started just over three years earlier. That summer was in retrospect the apogee of both Thatcherism and the mid-decade City boom. On the day of the general election, 11 June, many of LIFFE's traders sported stickers proclaiming 'We all say yes to Maggie', and the electorate obliged.[6] On 16 July the FTSE 100 peaked at 2443.4 (and the FT 30-Share Index at 1926.2). The next few weeks saw a faltering, followed by a strong recovery through into early October.

Few saw the great crash coming, which at first took literal form. On the morning of Friday 16 October, those living in the south-east of England woke up to a scene of devastation following a hurricane-force storm. Telephone lines were down, trees lay across roads, trains were not running. In the City, the north end of Bishopsgate was cordoned off; the bowling green at Finsbury Circus was crushed by a huge tree; and the ongoing demolition of Lee House in London Wall spontaneously proceeded apace. Many City workers abandoned the struggle to get in, with the result that the London clearing system was suspended, thereby halting all payments between Britain's banks; trading on the Stock Exchange barely functioned; and several other exchanges failed to open at all. The can-do exception was LIFFE, hailed by *The Times* as 'irrepressible'. Altogether it was a bad day for the City, made worse towards the end by the ominous news that Wall Street, which had been steadily on the slide since the 6th, was losing a further hundred points or more, representing a fall of almost 5 per cent. Over the weekend, therefore, it was natural that many felt some queasiness about the prospects for the coming week – but no one imagined the scale of what was about to happen. As Sir David Scholey of Warburgs memorably put it, the train that hit the buffers was travelling flat out and fully loaded.[7]

The crash of '87 – the most sensational event in the world's financial markets for over half a century – took place on Monday the 19th and Tuesday the 20th.[8] 'I've never seen so much business in all my life', Nigel Briggs, an equity trader, recalled about the London market on the Monday morning. 'Thousands and thousands of bargains. Every phone ringing. People clamouring to sell. It was absolute bedlam.' The selling continued for the rest of the day – however low the prices were put – and by the end the FTSE 100 had sustained a record 249.6 fall. 'Panic Hits The City' was the *Standard*'s headline, if anything understated. There was far worse to come on this 'Black Monday', for on Wall Street the Dow Jones Index then fell by 508 points, or 22 per cent. 'If it wasn't a meltdown it was certainly as hot as I want it to be,' said John Phelan, chairman of the New York Stock Exchange.[9] Tuesday began with a veritable rout in the Far East – the Nikkei Index in Tokyo dropping by 12 per cent, the Ordinary Index in Australia by 25 per cent and the Hang Seng in Hong Kong by 33 per cent – and in London the FTSE fell by another 250.7 points. Over the two days it had dropped from 2301.9 to 1801.6, a 23 per cent fall.

At BZW, one of the City's biggest trading houses, where a particularly bullish book in equities was being run, losses amounted to £75m, which at least had the effect of moving risk management systems up the agenda. There were also some big losses at LIFFE – 'I know one who's £130,000 adrift', one trader told the *Standard* about another – but for the exchange as a whole the crash was good news, with huge volumes being traded and, at least as important, a continuous market being provided, unlike its Chicago rivals or even arguably the Stock Exchange. Fortunes were made, of course, as well as lost. 'The 1987 crash was terrific for us, we made a lot of money because we were a fixed-interest house and not an equity house', Ross Jones of Gerrard & National remembered fondly some years later:

> On the night of Black Monday there was a dinner at the Savoy Hotel, the Lord's Taverners' Annual Dinner, and we had a table. Roger Gibbs [chairman of Gerrards] came in and said something like, 'Wall Street's down seven hundred points.' We rubbed our hands and said, 'Terrific. Suits our book' . . . The next morning the money supply figures were really bad and the gilt market fell further. The equity markets were nervous and going down. A member of our board phoned up and said, 'For God's

sake, buy everything you can. They're going to slash interest rates.' We bought everything we could get our hands on. Within an hour and a half the American bond market had gone up five points, the gilt market had gone up three points. It was very exciting.

Jones added an evocative tailpiece: 'I was driving back along the Embankment in the rush hour that night with a colleague – I had an XJS Convertible – and a German car came up alongside and wound down the window and shouted, "You yuppies, you are all finished. It serves you right." He thought it was the funniest thing. We just sat there roaring with laughter.'[10]

Meanwhile, the words '*force majeure*' were coming under scrutiny.[11] The week before the crash had seen the government's biggest privatisation issue to date – £7.25bn of British Petroleum shares, the world's largest-yet equity offering – fully underwritten. As markets plunged, with BP going down in two days from 350p to 286p, way below the underwriting price of 330p, Lawson was soon under heavy pressure (particularly from North American underwriters) to pull the issue. He believed that this would be not only morally wrong, in that the generally well-remunerated under-writing system was supposed to protect against precisely something like a stock market slump, but that pulling would also damage London's reputation as a trustworthy international financial centre. At first he was supported by the Bank of England, in the person of George Blunden; but over the next week or so, leading up to the 30th when dealing in the new shares was due to begin, it seems that the Bank was persuaded otherwise by the silky-tongued Michael Richardson of Rothschilds, who spoke for the underwriting group. On the 29th, just hours before Lawson was due to tell the Commons how he proposed to resolve this intensely invidious situation, he received the Bank's advice: its first preference was to pull the issue; if that was deemed impossible, its second preference was for Lawson to institute a buy-back arrangement that would save the underwriters roughly three-quarters of the £1bn that they stood to lose. Thoroughly unimpressed, Lawson rejected both options and announced a far more robust compromise, by which the issue went ahead but with a much less generous buy-back (or 'floor') arrangement. He was strongly supported by Thatcher, who had become (in Lawson's words) 'increasingly outraged that the Bank had given so little weight in its deliberations to the sanctity of contract and the reputation of the City of London'. Lawson's scheme proved a resounding success – so much so that in his memoirs he would even allege, fairly or unfairly, that in the immediate aftermath the Bank attempted to claim the kudos, something that he found a bit rich. As for Richardson, there was no doubt truth in his rather plaintive remark after it was all over: 'I was the nut in the nutcracker.'[12]

Had the crash itself vindicated London's new market structure? The

Stock Exchange's own report, published the following February, argued strongly that it had, and Goodison took the line that if the old jobbing system had still been in operation on 19 and 20 October, it would have seized up under the weight of selling orders and precipitated a financial crisis. On the much-discussed question of the difficulties that investors had experienced in dealing because of the market makers' failure to answer their telephones, the belief that they had not wanted to be forced to deal in a plunging equity market was categorically dismissed as implausible; the alternative explanation was that if investors failed to get through to market makers, this was simply an inevitable result of the unprecedented volumes of trading. 'An exercise in self-congratulation rather than self-criticism' was the view of Labour's spokesman on the City, Tony Blair, and the press on the whole agreed. One equity trader, Mike Smith, was frank enough on television almost a decade later, as he recalled the Monday morning: 'All the phones were flashing. We didn't answer them. No, bugger that . . . Because if you didn't do that, you'd end up up to your eyeballs long of stock you didn't want.'[13]

There was also much agitated discussion in the immediate aftermath of the crash as to whether, in the new world of electronic, globally seamless markets, it heralded an era of permanent financial instability. The long, reassuring view was taken by Henry Grunfeld, still at the age of eighty-three a daily presence at Warburgs. Speaking to the *FT* in November – in his first ever press interview – he conceded there were some things that did worry him. They included the complexity of financial instruments, widely traded by people who did not understand them properly; the hunger for market share, in the context of 'too many people trying to do the same thing and not doing it very well'; and the fact that markets were increasingly dominated by a generation that had never lived through a prolonged bear market. However, he saw no likelihood of a repeat of the events of the late 1920s and early 1930s, on the grounds that 'the degree of co-operation between governments and central banks is totally different today – it just won't happen'. After noting, with implicit reference to Warburgs and its bigger rivals, that 'capital follows brains, but brains don't necessarily follow capital', he returned at the end to his overriding theme:

> I just don't believe governments won't stick together and keep control. I think we have learned our lesson. I look back over 65 years and conclude that things could have turned out very, very much worse. I retain my optimism in this respect. In the end, common sense will prevail.[14]

Happily, the October 1987 crash did indeed prove less momentous than the Wall Street crash of October 1929. Nevertheless, it severely affected financial confidence – and abruptly halted the often mindless optimism, sometimes taking the form of an arrogant masters-of-the-universe syndrome, that had characterised much of the City during the mid-1980s. Equity turnover in the Stock Exchange in 1988 was down by one-third on the previous year, while in the late 1980s trading in gilts remained thin against the background of unprecedented (for modern times) budget surpluses and an absence of new gilt issues. 'Big Bang: Big Bust, Big Lessons' was a headline in March 1989 in *Business Week*, which estimated that 'the City's major players have lost a staggering $2 billion since Britain's ballyhooed Big Bang of 1986'. Eight months later *Institutional Investor* went one better, as it looked back on a year of redundancies, readjustments and much-reduced profits, and asked apocalyptically, 'Will the City ever recover?' In October 1991 the highly respected economist Stephen Lewis estimated total City job losses during the five years since Big Bang at 60,000, of which 10,000 had been in the securities industry. That year, however, saw the end of loss-making at most securities firms; the following year the equity market responded powerfully to the double stimulus of another Conservative election victory and the enhanced prospects for growth following Britain's enforced departure from the ERM; and in 1993 there was jam all round, as the UK equity market rose by 20 per cent and turnover was up by almost 35 per cent.[15] The City, in short, *had* recovered.

For the merchant banks, though, few imagined after Big Bang that the glory days would ever return. In 1988 there were two ritually symbolic moments: the end of the Accepting Houses Committee and Hambros' sale of its Bishopsgate home to a Japanese development company. Charles Hambro, talking to the *FT*, noted that it was only a few years previously that he had had to check whether Nomura was creditworthy, whereas now Japan's most powerful securities house – an increasingly potent force in the Eurobond market – had a market capitalisation of £30bn. 'Sometimes', he added wryly, 'I wonder whether we have been so clever after all.' Certainly there was a widespread assumption that the Japanese, on the back of the booming Tokyo stock market, were about to become a well-nigh irresistible force. 'Now the City is on the brink of a new era where Japanese, not American, money is moving in', the *Independent on Sunday*'s Peter Koenig asserted in February 1990. 'Japanese bankers will almost certainly prove as brutal, combative and relentless as the Americans.' Later that year Nomura apparently sealed its intentions by moving to the newly named Nomura House, the former General Post Office in St Martin's le Grand. The leading figures in the Japanese houses in the City seldom gave interviews to the press or sought publicity, but in February 1992 one executive director at the City branch of a Japanese bank did speak frankly (if anonymously) to the sociologist Junko Sakai:

The City, now, only has its own tradition and past legacy. The City will survive, but British houses will not remain at all. Most of them are now being taken over or becoming weak. There are many English merchant banks, but now they are called 'museums'.[16]

At Lloyd's, meanwhile, the problems were becoming severe.[17] From the late 1980s the market there was sustaining heavy losses: by 1990 and 1991 as much as £2bn each year. The main causes were catastrophes (notably the Piper Alpha oil rig disaster of 1988 and Hurricane Hugo the following year), a sharp rise in US pollution liabilities (especially relating to asbestos) and sheer incompetence on the part of the market's so-called professionals. Following the semi-cleansing of the Augean stables in the mid-1980s, it was undoubtedly a less corrupt market than it had been, but that did not prevent a revolt of the external, non-working Names as the losses mounted up. By 1988 there were as many as 32,000 Names, following a high-powered recruitment campaign through that avaricious decade that had often bordered on the mendacious, and over the next few years many of those in the most seriously affected syndicates became fiercely litigious. 'Out there, the revolt of the shires is in earnest', the novelist Julian Barnes memorably wrote in the *New Yorker* in 1993. 'The Names have witnessed negligence, fraud, complacency, and sardonic uncaringness; they have discovered the realities of money, how it works, and how those who live off it work.' Names under the financial cosh by the mid-1990s included, according to *Time* magazine figures, Camilla Parker Bowles (estimated potential exposure of $561,000), Sir Edward Heath ($1.4m), Frances Shand Kydd ($1.3m), Jeffrey Archer ($2m) and Ronald Ferguson ($1m). By the end of 1994 the 20,000 litigating Names were still refusing to be bought off, despite a £900m offer by Lloyd's.

Since 1992, a new team had been in place, with David Rowland as chairman and Peter Middleton as chief executive, grappling to ensure the institution's very survival. They published their first business plan in April 1993, and managed to introduce £800m in corporate capital, thereby beginning the process of reducing the market's reliance on individual Names. Nevertheless, as the journalist (and litigating Name) Adam Raphael observed soon afterwards in his account, *Ultimate Risk*, 'the biggest financial smash this century is a possibility that cannot be ruled out'.[18] Once the City's most arrogant institution, against fairly severe competition, Lloyd's now found itself in an astonishing plight.

There was still – in the public perception at least – a whiff of scandal about Lloyd's, though that was nothing unusual during these years after Big Bang. Another scandal whose endgame was laboriously being played out was that of Guinness.[19] By autumn 1987 five of those involved had been arrested; while Spens and Mayhew were arrested in spring 1988. The first Guinness trial – involving Saunders, Ronson, Parnes and Lyons

– took place during summer 1990 at Southwark Crown Court and lasted 107 days. On 27 August, bank holiday Monday, all four were found guilty, between them convicted on twenty-eight charges of conspiracy, theft and false accounting. Three of them received prison sentences, while Lyons eventually escaped jail on the grounds of ill health. 'The danger is that when men are hell-bent for victory, greed is in the saddle and ordinary commercial probity and respect for the law are thrust aside and the individual voice of conscience will not be heard', Mr Justice Henry declared before passing sentence. Inevitably this outcome, following the revelations about the share-support operation that had come out during the trial, damaged the City's reputation, though as Riley tartly commented in the *FT*, 'the City has always tended to have a much more starry-eyed impression of its own honesty than has the public at large'. The fact was, though, that of the guilty quartet only Parnes – whose success fee, as agreed by Saunders, had been a tidy £3.35m – was a real City person. In the event, perhaps regrettably, there never was a real 'City' trial. The second Guinness trial, involving Spens and Seelig, got under way in autumn 1991, but had made pitifully slow progress by the following February when it collapsed, largely on account of the judge's concern about the mental strain on Seelig, who had insisted on conducting his own defence. 'The whole of my working life I gave to Morgans and I made a significant contribution to the house', he told the *FT* on the eve of the trial's collapse. 'And it's a matter of deep feeling that not only were they not prepared to stand by me but they actually tried to make me a scapegoat.' A few weeks later the trial of Spens was also ended, again on health grounds. There was supposed to have been a third Guinness trial, of Seelig and Mayhew, but the prosecution decided not to proceed – apparently because, as Spens had forcibly pointed out during his trial, the secret indemnifying of purchases of shares in a bid situation had also been done in 1986 in the Turner & Newall/AE battle, when the Takeover Panel had ruled that such an arrangement was compatible with the Takeover Code.[20]

For those still interested, there ensued a long wait (over five years) before the eventual publication of the DTI report, painstakingly compiled by the QCs David Donaldson and Ian Watt. 'Three features still shine disturbingly through,' they concluded, 'firstly, the cynical disregard of laws and regulation; secondly, the cavalier misuse of company monies; thirdly, a contempt for truth and common honesty: all these in a part of the City which was thought respectable.'[21]

Other scandals came to light in the early 1990s. A striking sequence began in July 1991 when the Bank of England, acting in concert with bank regulators in other countries, managed to get closed down the fraudulent, money-laundering BCCI, the creation of a charismatic

Pakistani called Agha Hasan Abedi. BCCI's collapse broke all records, with depositors and investors losing at least $5bn and maybe as much as $20bn, and the Bank of England was severely criticised for having been too complacent for too long. The Bank could justifiably retort that it did not have global supervisory responsibilities for BCCI, but the episode did not enhance either its own or the City's reputation.[22] The next scandal, by contrast, was unalloyed City – the resignation in October 1991 of Mark Blundell, the youthful, ambitious chief executive at the London Futures and Options Exchange (FOX), after it emerged that he had apparently indemnified brokers in order to encourage them to trade on some of the exchange's less popular property and commodities contracts, thereby artificially inflating the overall trading volumes. The sums involved were peanuts compared to the BCCI affair, but the temptation to which Blundell had seemingly succumbed accurately reflected the intense competition that now existed between rival exchanges.[23]

Blundell, however, was only a bit-player in the pageant, quite unlike Robert Maxwell, whose sudden death in November 1991 – and the subsequent revelations of his theft of £400m or more from the pension funds for which he had a fiduciary responsibility – put the City uncomfortably in the spotlight.[24] As Tom Bower's exhaustive researches would make clear, such an eminent merchant banker as Sir Michael Richardson had been among those in Maxwell's corner during his last, financially increasingly troubled years; while no individual bank had done more to keep the great bully afloat than Goldman Sachs. 'I took it on faith that Robert Maxwell was an honest person', Eric Sheinberg of Goldmans subsequently said of the man who, when he hit the water, owed his various bankers no less than £2.8bn. 'Now he turned out to be a crook, I can't help it – I didn't know.' No doubt there is some truth in that and similar retrospective self-justifications. Nevertheless, Richard Lambert surely has it right. 'Maxwell generated enormous fees for those who undertook his wheeling and dealing', he observed in the *FT*'s end-of-century gallery of financial rogues. 'To their lasting discredit, enough people were prepared to hold their nose and take their money.'[25]

*

In November 1988 Nigel Lawson sent Thatcher a memorandum proposing 'to give statutory independence to the Bank of England, charging it with the statutory duty to preserve the value of the currency, along the lines already in place and of proven effectiveness for the US Federal Reserve, the National Bank of Switzerland, and the Bundesbank'. It was not, Lawson stressed subsequently, that he had any 'illusion that the Bank of England possesses any superior wisdom'. Instead, the benefit lay in 'the logic of the institutional change itself', through which an independent central bank would necessarily enjoy a far greater degree of market credibility than a government ever could; and 'this extra market credibility is what would make the successful conduct of monetary policy less difficult'. Thatcher was appalled, and faced by her insistence that the control of inflation was ultimately a political problem, not amenable to institutional solutions, Lawson was compelled to let his secret proposal rest.[26]

Less than a year later, however, the genie was out of the bottle, as Lawson's resignation speech of October 1989 gave him the opportunity to launch the proposal publicly. Immediate City reaction, as represented by its economists, was positive. 'It is an excellent idea', Giles Keating of CSFB told *Euroweek*. 'The credibility of the anti-inflationary policy would be much greater. Also, the markets would be far more inclined to regard sterling as a hard currency.'[27] Leigh-Pemberton claimed that if there had been an independent Bank in 1987–8, it would have been able to act more quickly to dampen down the Lawson boom – a boom that, ironically, had done much to tarnish Lawson's reputation while simultaneously enhancing the case for taking monetary policy out of the hands of politicians.

It was Lawson's successor, John Major, who in October 1990 – the dying weeks of the Thatcher era – at last took Britain into the exchange rate mechanism (ERM) of the European monetary system. Less than two years later, on 16 September 1992, it all unravelled horribly, as Britain was forced out amidst humiliating scenes for the Major government, which had effectively staked its credibility on the non-devaluation of sterling. Even by 8.30 a.m., when Major refused the request of his Chancellor, Norman Lamont, to put up interest rates, there was heavy selling of the pound, by both speculators (such as George Soros) and institutions (including banks and pension funds). If the pound was to be defended, that left no alternative to massively expensive intervention by the Bank of England. 'It was incredible', Mark Clarke, a foreign exchange dealer at the Bank of America, recalled of the atmosphere that morning. 'Obviously you can hear what's going on in the market, and you can hear wave after wave of selling hitting the market, being met with resistance and support by the Bank of England. They were buying such a phenomenal amount of pounds.' The Bank's deputy governor, Eddie George, subsequently explained the thinking: 'We decided that as the London market came in we would intervene, on a scale which would make it quite clear that we were intervening, and that's what we did.'

At eleven o'clock a belated rise in interest rates (from 10 per cent to 12 per cent) failed to do the trick, with the markets scenting blood; and by late morning, with the Bank spending Britain's currency reserves at the alarming rate of £2bn per hour, both George and Lamont reckoned that the game was up and that British membership of the ERM would have to be suspended immediately. Major, however, decided on a final throw of the dice, and at 2.15 p.m. interest rates went up to 15 per cent – prompting the cry in one dealing room, 'Anyone want to buy a house?' Again the move was viewed by the markets as a sign of weakness, not strength, and after sterling had staged a tiny, flickering rally the Bank was soon buying pounds again. 'That afternoon,' Soros recollected, 'it became a veritable avalanche of selling.' Kenneth Clarke, one of the ministers close to Major, graphically evoked the sense of impotence at the other end of town: 'We had no power. The markets and events had taken over. It became increasingly obvious as the day went on that we were merely flotsam and jetsam, being tossed about in what was happening.' At about four o'clock, by which time the Bank had spent no less then £15bn in support of sterling, it was agreed to let it go. From a dealer's perspective, Mark Clarke remembered that moment, a cardinal one in the relationship between the nation state and the financial markets:

> At four o'clock suddenly the Bank of England wasn't supporting pounds. Instead of a load of noise coming out of the voice brokers and everything and around the dealing room, everyone sat in stunned silence, for almost two seconds or three seconds, and all of a sudden it erupted, and sterling just free-fell. That sense of awe, that the markets could take on a central bank and actually win. I couldn't believe it.[28]

Three and a half hours later Lamont stood outside the Treasury and announced to the television cameras that UK membership had been suspended – a de facto devaluation.

It had been an extraordinary day. As it drew to an end, Mark Clarke candidly told *Channel 4 News* that his team had made £10m. That sounded a lot, but it would soon emerge that Soros had netted a staggering $1bn on his day's work. For those of a patriotic bent, it was not a day that did much for the City's image. The *Sunday Telegraph*'s Trevor Fishlock vividly described how the government's 'Black Wednesday' was 'Delirium Day' in the Square Mile:

> With the pound falling with each second it was a chaotic day on the currency trading floors, a day of shrieking, bellowing and swearing as dealers shouted into telephones and kept half an eye on screens which showed the pound's deteriorating cardiogram trace. Men with glistening faces and staring eyes leaped to their feet, punched buttons and shouted themselves hoarse from 7 a.m. until late in the evening. Tens of millions of pounds passed through their fingers in moments. To an outsider the sheer energy and noise of an exchange floor, the rapid-fire jargon, the evident enthusiasm and passion, the animal aggression, combine in a dizzying, exciting and baffling spectacle. You soon learn that a man who shouts 'five quid' means £5 million.
>
> At the London International Financial Futures Exchange, the institutional or wholesale market [by this time a purpose-built market at Cannon

Bridge], dealers crammed the sweltering, paper-littered dealing pits, shouting their offers and bids at the tops of their voices, signalling in fast tic-tac semaphore. Their bright striped blazers made the exchange floor a teeming mass, like Henley gone berserk. On Wednesday the exchange traded a record 886,000 contracts worth £254 billion.

The *Daily Mirror*'s headline was 'SOLD down the river', but no amount of moral indignation could alter the underlying lesson of the day: the balance of power had shifted irrevocably towards the markets.[29]

*

Driven by record low dollar interest rates, together with a rapidly expanding range of the financial instruments that were now being called by the umbrella term 'derivatives', 1993 was a bonanza year in the world's financial markets, particularly for the big trading houses. 'It is thought that the City created at least 250 millionaires,' the *Daily Telegraph*'s Neil Collins noted afterwards, 'and the most *junior* partner at Goldman Sachs was paid a $5m bonus.' For the first time since the crash, the good times were indubitably back. They seemed likely to roar on well into 1994, until on 4 February Alan Greenspan at the Fed threw the markets (above all the world bond markets) into first turmoil and then gloom by raising interest rates by a half per cent. As he sought to counter inflationary dangers, there were five more interest rate rises over the next ten months. For houses like Goldman Sachs or Salomons, the consequences were not far short of catastrophic: the latter's London office, for example, lost $400m through proprietary trading in the course of the year. In early October there were shock warnings from both Warburgs and Hambros of sharply reduced profits; and although later that month there was a fillip to the City in the announcement by Deutsche Bank (which had bought Morgan Grenfell in 1989) that it intended to make London, not Frankfurt, the hub of its international investment banking operations, the mood as Christmas approached was far from festive. 'Thousands of City workers could see their Christmas bonuses slashed to as little as £10,000 this year – less than 5 per cent of what many took home last year', the *Guardian* reported on 5 December to a presumably distraught readership.[30]

Just under three months later, on Saturday 25 February 1995, the news broke to an astonished world that Barings – after an impeccable, blameless 105 years – was once again deep in trouble.[31] At this stage little more was publicly known than that a Barings trader operating from the Singapore futures exchange (SIMEX) had run up huge, fraudulent losses, probably of at least £400m. Instead, over a long weekend, it was very much behind closed doors – just as in 1890 – that the City collectively addressed the question of whether Barings could be saved. Significantly 'the City' still meant, in the eyes of the Bank of England which convened the emergency meetings, only the British banks, with the American, European and Japanese banks all excluded. The deadline set for any rescue was 10 p.m. on the Sunday, before the Japanese market, on which most of Barings' positions were open, began trading again.

That Sunday, with most of the outside world confidently expecting a rescue, though unaware that the latest estimate of losses had risen to £650m, there were several acutely piquant moments at the Bank. At one point Peter Norris of Barings, in a notably unapologetic presentation of his bank's financial position, elicited audible gasps by revealing that in two days' time Barings intended to pay bonuses for 1994 of no less than £84m, even though its pre-tax profit for that year (excluding the profits from Singapore that were now realised to be fictitious) was only £83m. Under questioning, it also emerged from Norris, again to collective astonishment, that as much as £800m had been transferred from London to support the requirement for margin in SIMEX – a staggering piece of information that instantly made nonsense of the claim by Barings' chairman, Peter Baring, that his bank had been powerless to prevent the fraud.

Nevertheless, it was not a sudden distaste for Barings that caused the rescue talks to fail, but three specific factors. First, Eddie George – who had become governor in June 1993 – took the view (unlike Lidderdale in 1890) that if, however regrettably, Barings went to the wall, there was unlikely to be any systemic threat to the banking system as a whole; therefore there was no justification for asking the government to sanction the use of public money to bale out the City's oldest but no longer most important merchant bank. Second, the Bank was unable in time to find a buyer for Barings, with neither Merrill Lynch nor the Sultan of Brunei coming through in the end. And third, although the other banks were willing, at a suitable rate of interest, to lend £640m to Barings, thereby enabling it to recapitalise itself under new management, no way could be found of putting a cap on further losses that might arise from the positions still open in the Far East. It did not help that the very word 'derivatives' had such a fear-inducing ring, following some spectacular trading debacles in America the previous year, nor that so few of those around the table properly understood them. 'It is perhaps salient to observe', one of those present noted immediately afterwards, 'that there was a glaring lack of knowledge about this type of business and the inherent risks among a representative cross-section of leading British bankers.'[32] It was thus announced shortly after 10 p.m. that there would be no rescue package and that Barings was to be placed in administration. Such a resonant name, such a sudden demise – it was perhaps the most memorable, sad, blood-quickening moment yet in the City's peacetime history.

'They all want to read about the bank that's gone phut' was how my newsagent explained to me next morning at seven-thirty the absence of any copies of the *FT*. The story dominated the day's papers, and as William Rees-Mogg vividly put it in *The Times*, 'For those of us who can remember the Second World War, the loss of Barings has something of the same impact as the sinking of the *Hood*. At one moment in time it is unthinkable; at the next it has happened.'

By this time the trader who had managed to run up such crippling losses had been identified as Nick Leeson. He was twenty-eight, and had grown up in a council house in Watford, where his family still lived. He had disappeared from Singapore the previous Thursday, and no one knew where he was. That Monday morning, two particularly striking *Evening Standard* placards appeared all over London: 'Manhunt as the Pound Dives' and 'Bank Crash Savages Markets'. In fact, although a 6.6 per cent fall in Tokyo's Nikkei Index had pushed Barings' losses on its contracts up to £880m, the FTSE 100 lost only 12.4 points (closing at 3,025.3) and the pound recovered much of the ground it had lost earlier in the day. This relative steadiness came as a huge relief to both governor and Chancellor. George talked of the importance of keeping the concept of 'moral hazard' in the banking system, while though Kenneth Clarke conceded to the Commons that 'this failure is of course a blow to the City of London', he emphasised that 'it appears to be a specific incident unique to Barings centred on one rogue trader in Singapore'.[33] The phrase would stick, as the image of the rogue trader who had brought down the mighty Barings became one of the most compelling of the era.

Tuesday the 28th at last saw the first photographs of Leeson – fresh-cheeked, slightly chubby-faced, smiling, balding, wearing his navy-and-gold trader's jacket. The *FT* carried an interview with Peter Baring, who claimed that Barings had been running a low-risk business until 'the fraud', and speculated that Leeson might have been in a systematic conspiracy with an unknown partner in order to bankrupt the bank.[34] Meanwhile the administrators, Ernst & Young, had begun negotiations with parties interested in buying different bits of Barings. During Tuesday and Wednesday, with Leeson still evading his pursuers, there was growing evidence that Barings had known at least something of what was going on but had failed to act, provoking widespread ridicule for Peter Baring's conspiracy theory. Leeson was held early on Thursday 2 March at Frankfurt airport, where he had hoped to change to a London flight; and by that evening a buyer, the Dutch bank ING, had been found for the whole of Barings, priced at an attractive £1. The next day Leeson, wearing his iconic baseball cap and clutching a Tom Clancy thriller, was remanded in custody by a Frankfurt court. For all concerned, even at the periphery, it had been an unforgettable week. That Friday afternoon I took part in a television discussion on the Barings crash and its implications. The venue was the English Speaking Union in Mayfair's Charles Street, and we sat in a large, elegant room on the first floor – amazingly, the drawing-room of the first Lord Revelstoke's London home, where in November 1890 he had sweated out what would now for ever be known as the first Barings crisis.

Most commentators had a view. Rees-Mogg thundered on the Tuesday about 'the grotesque timidity' of the Bank of England, arguing that it had 'avoided risking at most a few hundred million pounds', whereas 'the credit of London, which has been put in jeopardy, may be an unquantifiable asset, but it must be measured in hundreds of billions of pounds of Britain's future earning power'. He concluded gravely: 'The Bank of England exists to protect British credit. In this instance, it has failed in its prime duty.' On Wednesday, however, the *FT*'s John Plender, arguably unrivalled among financial journalists for his grasp of the big picture, persuasively countered the Bank's critics:

> It is, of course, a case of mistaken identity. A City whose good name has been so dreadfully traduced no longer exists. London's competitive advantage in international finance has little, if anything, to do with the older cohorts of the merchant banking fraternity who financed world trade in the 19th century. For the best part of two decades the powerhouse of financial innovation has been located largely in the foreign banking and securities community.

Moreover, he added, 'in the absence of a club, successful lifeboats are not easily launched'. By the end of the week there was widespread agreement that George had got it right. 'The external impact of the crisis has so far been successfully contained, vindicating the decision not to rescue Barings', the *Independent* noted on Saturday, while next day the *Sunday Telegraph*'s Bill Jamieson argued that 'if the impression got around that domestic banks could be counted on to be baled out by their central bank, that would suggest a playing field so tilted as to drive out every non-resident bank'. And, he asked rhetorically, 'where would the City be then?'[35]

By this stage the agenda had moved on to the question of how much Barings – and, indeed, the Bank – were to be blamed for not having acted earlier, before the situation became so critical. 'Fingering Leeson alone is like blaming a lance-corporal for the outcome of the First World War', a senior banker declared. 'It is ridiculous.' The head of treasury at a large merchant bank, who could not get over how Barings had transferred more than £400m from London to Singapore in the final six weeks, without apparently any effective controls being in place, agreed: 'Even Colombian drug barons don't throw that sort of money around without a few signatures.'

To Jeff Randall in the *Sunday Times* it was all crystal clear: 'Leeson, the oik from Watford, looked the perfect fall-guy.' Already there was quite a lot of sneaking admiration felt in the City for 'the man with lots of balls but no Barings', as a broker in a City bar on the Friday evening had told a journalist.[36] As for his former employers, an adage that apparently had been circulating in the City for some years never seemed truer: 'You can tell a Barings man anywhere, but you can't tell him much.'

Nick Leeson was never really 'a Barings man'. He had gone to Baring Securities in 1989 as a book-keeper, and was sent to Singapore three years later to run its new futures office. Although responsible for settlement, he would also, as he had long wanted, have a chance to trade – a blurring of traditionally distinct functions apparently justified by the smallness of the office.[37] Unfortunately he proved from the start a more or less hopeless trader, but so dreaded being ignominiously recalled to London that he began to hide his losses in a secret account – the infamous error account no. 88888. Within three months, by October 1992, the secret losses amounted to £4.5m, and Leeson saw no alternative but to go on trading, hoping to get the money back. By summer 1993, against the background of favourable market conditions, he had almost retrieved the situation – only to go on trading, make new losses, again hide them in the secret account and again hope to trade out of them. By the end of the year he was sleeping badly and hiding losses of £25m.

Back in London there had been a palace revolution at Baring Securities. Christopher Heath, famous in the late 1980s as the UK's highest-paid man, seemed to lose his golden touch in the early 1990s, as the Japanese stock market plunged; and in March 1993 the deputy chairman of Barings, Andrew Tuckey, engineered Heath's resignation as chairman of Baring Securities. Ironically, as it would turn out, their main policy disagreement was that Heath wanted the resources to enable him to engage in larger-scale proprietary trading, in both the cash and derivative markets of the Far East, whereas Tuckey was concerned that this would make the Baring group as a whole too exposed to the performance of the securities business. He also, as a merchant banker, wanted much tighter control over the securities arm.

In fact a mixture of benign markets in mid-1993 and healthy (but in reality fictitious) profits coming from Singapore meant that Baring Securities appeared to flourish in the post-Heath era, so much so that when in September 1993 Peter Baring paid a routine visit to Brian Quinn, the Bank of England's head of banking supervision, the note of their meeting recorded that, in relation to Baring Securities, 'the recovery in profitability had been amazing, leaving Barings to conclude that it was not actually very difficult to make money in the securities business'. 'Derivatives need to be well controlled and understood,' Peter Baring declared a few weeks later, 'but we believe we do that here.' Certainly that competence was not questioned by Christopher Thompson, the Bank of England's supervisor with direct responsibility for Barings, for soon afterwards he gave it a so-called 'informal concession', in effect enabling it to use as much of its capital as it wished in sending margin payments to the Singapore office, where Leeson was claiming to be acting on behalf of an in fact non-existent client and, contrary to the belief of his superiors in London, had none of his futures offset. Thompson's action, or rather non-action, was 'staggering', Stephen Fay justly observes in his authoritative account of the whole debacle, being 'more in keeping with the way the Bank of England was run more than a generation ago, when there were no written rules and assent was given on a nod and a wink'.[38]

So it went on. Between January and July 1994 the proprietary trading being done by Leeson apparently produced profits for Baring Securities of £30m, although by the time an internal, London-authorised audit in late summer had failed to uncover anything amiss, Leeson's secret losses were over £100m. By the end of the year the fake profits (immortalised by Peter Baring's description of them as 'pleasantly surprising') had become ever bigger; Baring Securities had gone on sending out the lethal financial bullets, amounting to some three-quarters of Barings' capital; Leeson's secret losses were in the order of £160–£200m; and video footage of the SIMEX floor showed him staring blankly ahead, completely out of it.[39]

After a Christmas break away, Leeson did not want to return to Singapore in the New Year, but his wife Lisa – completely ignorant of what he had been up to – persuaded him that it would be crazy to forsake the imminent prospect of a £450,000 bonus. On 17 January, a week after his return, the Kobe earthquake and its violent impact on the Japanese financial markets drove Leeson into a final, utterly reckless frenzy of speculation, during which he made almost all the wrong trading decisions possible. His real losses were as much as £144m in a day, his declared profits as much as £10m in a day, and Barings blindly went on sending the margin payments, even after it had on 24 January gone over its overdraft limit with Citibank. Mary Walz, the head of equity derivatives trading, and Ron Baker, her boss, then tried to get a grip on Leeson's increasingly bizarre explanations of his trading. They found it impossible and Baker groaned, 'All this work just drives me nutty. I just want to retire.'[40] At last, from about 17 February, the people in London started to apprehend something of the enormity of what Leeson had been doing and the position they were in. The charming, amoral, chameleon-like trader did his bolt on Thursday the 23rd, and the next day Peter Baring went round to the Old Lady to break the awkward news.

A month later the ensuing smash was already passing into history. Leeson would spend the next four and a bit years in jail, mainly in Singapore. His autobiography, inevitably called *Rogue Trader*, was published in 1996 to mixed reviews. For Tom Bower, seldom a friend of those in high places, it made 'a good case' for the view that Leeson had been 'the victim of the stupidity and greed of his superiors'. But the journalist Bryan Appleyard, noting that Leeson's victim image had already been 'shored up by a pathetically soft television interview with David Frost', called it a 'vile and mendacious' account, whose 'emotional and factual dishonesty glares at you from every page'. At his press conference at Heathrow Airport in July 1999, following his release, Leeson made an explicit apology: 'I did wrong. I am not proud of my activities as a trader with Barings Bank in Singapore. I was foolish and very much regret what happened. But I have done my time.' A few months later it emerged that he had been offered a job as a trader. 'You would have thought that was inconceivable, wouldn't you?' he observed to a journalist.

The real losers were the people – many of them elderly, living far from the City and investing their life savings – who late in 1994 had subscribed to a £100m perpetual loan at 9.25 per cent issued by Barings in order to raise funds to send its star trader. 'We do quite a lot in the village and the income from this investment was to allow us to carry on', Edward Pease-Watkin, a retired headmaster living in Herefordshire, told the *Evening Standard* in July 1995. 'It will be a lot harder now . . . The money they paid out in bonuses would have repaid the bondholders but I think they see us as people who really don't matter very much.' Not long afterwards, Fay offered a crushing verdict: 'Had there been any real gentlemen left at Barings, they would have donated their bonuses to the bondholders; but there weren't.'[41]

It had been a story without heroes, a story that killed off the last whiff of romance about the money machine. 'Much more than money was lost to London with Barings', Christopher Fildes, a veteran observer of the City scene and broadly sympathetic to its activities and inhabitants, wrote in sorrow as well as anger a year afterwards. 'Credit was lost, honour was lost. Leeson, the agent of this downfall, was greedy, ignorant and panicky by turns, and crooked too. But his panic, ignorance and greed were no more than a symptom of Barings' own. The house had been betrayed by what was false within.'[42] Traditionally, before the 1980s, the City had been viewed as stuffy, boring and unimaginative, but essentially honest and competent. In many ways it was a place that had been given a cumulative benefit of the doubt by outsiders who neither knew much about it nor wanted to. The events of the 1980s had significantly altered those perceptions; and now, after February 1995, the last illusions had been stripped. Never again, it seemed reasonable to assume, would the City be able to claim the moral high ground.

*

The broad picture between 1995 and 2000 was of the City flourishing, both in itself and as an international financial centre relative to others. 'The City of London: Why It's the Center of Global Finance' boomed *Business Week* in March 1998. Trading in international equities, forex trading, cross-border loans – in these, as by other familiar yardsticks, London still led the way. However, the magazine's Stanley Reed argued, there was something more interesting going on:

> The charge is being led by US banks and investment houses [the so-called 'bulge bracket' firms], which are using their record profits on Wall Street to pave the way for aggressive expansion abroad. Followed closely by European institutions that see their future in investment banking, these financial giants are bringing a massive infusion of capital and technology . . .
>
> The City's reawakening is part of a seismic shift in European economic, social, and political attitudes. A new equity culture is developing across Eastern and Western Europe as citizens realise that their cash-strapped governments will no longer be able to provide for their retirements. That change will mean a surge in demand for mutual funds and other investments for City firms to create and manage. A new generation of profit-driven managers and activist shareholders, meanwhile, is demanding that European corporations improve their performance. To do so, corporations are searching for cheaper and more creative sources of financing. That means huge new quantities of equity and debt for City firms to underwrite.

Just over a year later, some four months after the launch (without Britain) of the European single currency, a survey by *Institutional Investor* found no hard overall evidence of Frankfurt managing to claw back London's considerable lead in the European time zone: 'London's critical mass is vast, and its gravitational pull seems to be increasing as a result of the single currency, technology and globalisation. Barring unforeseen new developments, the City will continue to prosper – and be the envy of financial center wannabes the world over.'[43]

For most of these five years the markets were bullish (for example the FTSE 100, having been just over 3,000 at the start of 1995, was well over 5,000 at the start of 1998 and by the end of summer 2000 was in the 6,600 region), but there was a nasty blip in 1998 as Russia defaulted and then the giant American hedge fund Long Term Capital Management virtually collapsed. Nearer home, there were – for the historically minded – moments of resonant irony during the general election campaign of April 1997. 'We accept, and indeed embrace, the new global economy', Tony Blair declared in a speech at the Corn Exchange. 'I accept the need for economic discipline and embrace the role of free enterprise in the economy. There will be no retreat from any of that.' On the eve of the election, with opinion polls correctly predicting a Labour landslide, share prices soared to new heights. It was a reflection of how much not only Labour, but also the City, had fundamentally changed in character.[44]

On 6 May 1997, only five days after the election, the new Chancellor, Gordon Brown, surprised and pleased the City by announcing that he was handing over responsibility to the Bank of England to set the interest rates that would seek to ensure the meeting of the government's inflation target. The nine-member Monetary Policy Committee (MPC), charged with doing the business, was to comprise the governor and two deputy governors (all appointed by the government), four members ('recognised experts', in Brown's phrase) appointed by the government from outside the Bank, and two Bank nominees. Press reaction was mainly positive, though *The Economist* did observe that 'much as the chancellor and Eddie George might deny it, the Bank will be engaged in the highly political task of choosing how many jobs to sacrifice in order to hit the inflation target quickly rather than slowly'. Looking ahead optimistically to 'a Bank of England that is more distant from the "gentlemanly capitalist" culture of the financial system than any we have so far experienced', Will Hutton argued that such a Bank, as part of a modernised British state, would finally lay to rest the ghost of Montagu Norman.[45] It was an appropriate invocation of the great man's name, for the new Chancellor knew his Labour history probably better than anyone else in the Cabinet and was well aware of how the 1931 financial crisis had destroyed an earlier Labour government – not to mention, of course, all those problems with the City that had so bedevilled the subsequent administrations of Attlee, Wilson and Callaghan. Brown presumably believed in the economic arguments for removing monetary policy from the temptations of the electoral cycle; but almost certainly there was also a political motive at work, a motive that was essentially defensive, even buck-passing.

As it turned out, the new arrangements were soon under widespread attack, as during much of 1998 the inflation-busting MPC kept interest rates high, despite the evident damage inflicted on the British economy by a strong pound. The Bank was uncomfortably exposed to forceful, at times even vicious, attacks – from both sides of industry, from columnists and cartoonists, even from demonstrators gathered by the Duke of Wellington's statue outside the Royal Exchange. George came under particular fire in October when he gave the impression in an interview that job losses in the north were a price worth paying to curb inflation in the south. By spring 1999 the storm had abated, with one commentator, Gavyn Davies of Goldman Sachs, looking back in May on the economy's pleasantly soft landing and praising as crucial 'the professional skills of Eddie George and a committee dominated by genuine monetary policy experts, instead of the businessmen and trade unionists who could so easily have been appointed'.[46] There was also by this time, adding to the plaudits, an increasingly drawn contrast between the relative openness and accountability of the central bank in London and the opaqueness of its European counterpart in Frankfurt. Nevertheless, the pound remained high, the north–south divide continued to widen and, entering the new century, the notion that monetary policy did not involve political – in the broadest sense of the word – judgements seemed wishful thinking. The shame was that elected politicians were no longer ultimately responsible for making those judgements.

The granting to the Bank of quasi-independence over monetary policy in May 1997 had been accompanied by the transferring from the Bank to the Treasury of day-to-day management of the gilts market. That same month, exactly a fortnight later, the Bank's role was further narrowed when Brown announced that it was to lose its responsibility for banking supervision, as part of a new system of financial services regulation that would see not only the supervision of banks, securities firms and fund managers, but also the regulation of the financial markets, brought under a single roof. The thinking behind the new regulatory arrangements was fairly obvious: the Bank's reputation for banking supervision had suffered from the BCCI and Barings episodes; more generally, there had been a plethora of financial scandals during the decade since the Financial Services Act, most recently (in September 1996) a fund management scandal at Morgan Grenfell; even New Labour had little sympathy for the concept of practitioner self-regulation, albeit within a statutory framework; and the increasing complexity of financial markets and financial instruments made the continuing existence of nine separate regulatory bodies seem too inflexible and too liable to turf wars.

The new super-regulator, named in September 1997 as the Financial Services Authority (FSA), was to be run by Howard Davies, who had been deputy governor at the Bank; and in due course he found himself at Canary Wharf with some 2,000 budding regulators under him. Initially there was widespread support for the broad sweep of the changes – 'not only is the present system hopelessly bureaucratic,' Lex commented the day after Brown's announcement, 'but self-regulation was never a terribly credible basis for public confidence in the first place' – but as the eventual Financial Services and Markets Bill began to make its ponderous way through Parliament, opposition from both inside and outside the City started to build up. 'No person or body should ever act as prosecutor, judge and jury combined', the *Daily Telegraph* declared in July 1999, while the following spring a right-wing think tank, the Centre for Policy Studies, branded the FSA as one of the most powerful and least accountable institutions created since the Second World War. The City itself lobbied hard, and by summer 2000 the FSA's draconian powers had been significantly diluted, though in many eyes there remained the problem of inadequate accountability. More than a quarter of a century after the secondary banking crisis it was still a moot point whether all the ensuing regulatory legislation and heartache had rendered the City a fundamentally cleaner place – not least in the ever-vexed area of frequently perpetrated, infrequently prosecuted insider dealing, still the classic white-collar crime.[47]

The Bank of England was not the only 'pillar' to find itself, in City terms, a diminished force. That certainly applied to Lloyd's, even though under David Rowland's leadership it did survive its life-threatening crisis, at last in summer 1996 managing to buy off the great majority of the Names who were threatening to take legal action, largely on the grounds of alleged fraud. Shortly afterwards, in a packed Room, Rowland rang the Lutine bell an unprecedented three times. 'Mr Rowland told the sea of underwriters, brokers and guests who lined the shiny metal galleries and stationary escalators', the *FT* reported, 'that the three rings of the bell symbolised the suffering of Names who have borne losses totalling more than £8bn, the implementation of the [£3.2bn] recovery plan, and the start of work to restore international competitiveness.' Integral to Rowland's strategy was that the underwriting capacity of Lloyd's should increasingly come from corporate capital rather than that of individual Names; and over the next few years that indeed became the case, so that by the new century corporate members accounted for more than four-fifths of the market's capacity.

That change, although perhaps inevitable, was not necessarily all gain. 'The old Lloyd's died in the process, leaving a skeleton to be fleshed out to form a new trader to compete in a global market' was how Graham Searjeant in May 1997 persuasively interpreted Rowland's achievement and its likely legacy. 'This will lose the cost advantage of unlimited liability and rely on marketing, City finance and the concentration of expertise among surviving underwriters and brokers. Like the Stock Exchange, it will be in London rather than of London, dominated by large international interests.'[48]

The 'third pillar' was the Stock Exchange itself, where John Kemp-Welch, having done much to steer Cazenove's through the Big Bang era and its immediate aftermath, was chairman for almost six years from July 1994. Increasingly the Stock Exchange was trying to turn itself into a freestanding business, as opposed to an institutional club, and by the end of Kemp-Welch's chairmanship the member firms had voted almost unanimously to demutualise. No longer a monopoly provider, the Stock Exchange was conscious that it would survive only if it provided an efficient marketplace, and in July 1996, after a thorough strategic review, it published a business plan outlining how it intended to 'deliver the highest-quality services at the most competitive prices'. It did so in the comforting knowledge that its new trading system, SEQUENCE, was on the verge of successful completion. Moreover, in Ranald Michie's words, 'with the introduction of SEQUENCE the Stock Exchange had at its disposal an electronic platform that would support either a continuance of a quote-driven market, with competing market makers, or an order-driven market, for the automatic execution of orders'.[49]

The new chief executive from August 1996 was Gavin Casey, under whom the new order-driven system, SETS (Stock Exchange Trading Service), able to handle 3,000 transactions a minute, was introduced fourteen months later. Would it deliver the goods? 'Cheaper, more transparent trading conditions are good news for the London market', the Lex column claimed. 'It will increase participation by those who previously kept their distance, such as US institutional investors, and quantitative and derivative style traders who require the greater automation which SETS provides.' There was, accordingly, the prospect of rising volumes, falling costs, and 'a virtuous spiral of liquidity'. The euphoria did not last long. By December SETS was accounting for only 40 per cent of trades in the stocks it covered, and the *Independent*'s Jeremy Warner frankly called it 'a disaster', especially in terms of its ability to 'distort share prices and disadvantage small investors'. A few months later the consultants Tempest carried out a comprehensive survey of Britain's largest companies and leading institutional fund managers, leading to the unambiguous conclusion that 'on most criteria, the centralised dealing desks give SETS a massive thumbs-down'. Volatile pricing was undoubtedly a serious problem. However, after two years most of the teething difficulties had been ironed out, and Casey was able to claim in January 2000 that 53 per cent of trades by value were being executed automatically through the SETS system, rather than through firms acting as principals. Altogether, it was a hybrid system of trading that had evolved, but on the whole it worked well.

There still awaited, however, a day of technological humiliation. On Wednesday 5 April 2000 – the last day of the tax year – the Stock Exchange's computer systems crashed and trading in UK equities did not start until mid-afternoon. 'Third World nightmare on Old Broad Street' and 'The day London's Stock Exchange died' were the headlines in one broadsheet, but perhaps the most apposite comment came from the veteran market maker Brian Winterflood: 'This is the IT world for you. You drop your calculator and the battery falls out and suddenly you haven't got a brain.'[50]

*

In October 1997 – in the wake of a two-and-a-half-year period in which Warburgs had been bought by Swiss Bank Corporation, Kleinwort Benson by Dresdner Bank, and Smith New Court by Merrill Lynch, while more recently BZW had abandoned its ambition to be the City's 'national champion' integrated house – Christopher Fildes was moved to write an obituary in the *Daily Telegraph*:

> I am sorry to announce the demise of the City of London. It is part of our history, it has been with us ever since the legendary days of King Lud and the giants Gog and Magog, but all good things come to an end. As from today, it is being relaunched as Hong Kong West . . .
>
> Already, two out of every five people working in the former City are employed by companies in foreign ownership. Now these foreign owners must see their way clear. They can build up their stake to 51pc and declare their takeover bid unconditional . . .
>
> The apologists are standing by to tell us that ownership is not important. What matters is to have the business here, with all that it contributes to the British economy, and British exports, and all the places where the bankers spend their bonuses. The money that goes home is just a residual.
>
> Stanislas Yassukovich, who arrived with the new markets [i.e. the Euromarkets] 30 years ago, is not so sure. The real threat, he says, is a lack of commitment. The new masters come and go on short postings, with barely time to buy a house in the Boltons and sell it again. They have no stake in the place and no reason to concern themselves with its cause or its values. It will be the poorer for that.
>
> To me, the City's genius has always been to reinvent itself. So Hong Kong West is just its latest invention. It is the first, though, in which its players have conceded that they cannot keep up with the game and must live by providing a playground for others. That must limit their scope and put their future into pawn. For all the City's faults, I cannot think of Hong Kong West as an improvement on it. I shall miss it.[51]

Over the next three years the debate rumbled on, with no shortage of apologists for the economic blessings of a predominantly foreign-owned City. There was, however, an illuminating episode in March 2000 as Deutsche Bank, about to take over Dresdner Bank, apparently threatened to close down Dresdner's London investment banking arm, Dresdner Kleinwort Benson. In the end the takeover did not happen, largely because of the problem of what to do about Kleinworts, but that did not invalidate Andreas Whittam Smith's reading of the larger implications:

> The Square Mile has survived many crises in the past 300 years: the South Sea Bubble; the Napoleonic wars; the banking crises of the Victorian era; the First World War, which ended the supremacy of the pound sterling in world trade, and the severe restrictions on financial markets that lasted from 1940 until 1960. There is always a new threat on the horizon to replace the one most recently overcome.
>
> I confess, however, to a bit more unease than usual. For in effect we have given the keys of the City of London to its global competitors. They could, if they chose, on grounds of national rivalry rather than pure

commercial calculation, set about dismantling it. The threat is there, even if distant and, in many people's opinions, improbable. It could be the stuff of nightmares.[52]

To which the obvious rebuttal was that, in the age of globalisation and economic interdependence, such crude economic nationalism was long dead, certainly on the part of sophisticated international investment bankers. It was in itself a plausible assumption. But then, there had been a similarly plausible assumption, a similarly great illusion, almost a hundred years earlier – an illusion destroyed for the next half-century and more by the guns of August 1914.

Of course, one much-touted, supra-national threat was the coming of the euro. As early as September 1996, more than two years ahead of the eventual launch, George insisted that whether Britain was in or out of a single currency, the City would thrive. 'The euro is just a bigger Deutschmark', he declared. 'We have seemed to do perfectly satisfactorily handling the mark, just as we have the dollar and yen. I am sure that the City will cope.' Few observers then or later believed that George himself was an enthusiast for British participation in economic and monetary union – the prospect of the Bank of England becoming a branch office of the European Central Bank was hardly likely to enchant a Threadneedle Street man – while generally in the late 1990s there developed no coherent, overall 'City view' about what British policy should be. What did emerge quite clearly, however, after January 1999 was that the City was, if anything, benefiting from being outside the eurozone. In November that year the outgoing Lord Mayor, Lord Levene, who some months earlier had been publicly warning against Britain staying out, conceded that so far London had 'done more than hold its own', as well as specifically asserting that Britain's membership of the euro was not the key factor in whether foreign banks and financial institutions continued to do business in London. The following month saw similar remarks from George, tempting the economic commentator Hamish McRae to argue that just as the City back in the 1960s had reinvented itself on an essentially offshore basis, so at the turn of the century it could do the same in relation to the distinctly onshore, heavy-of-foot euro. By April 2000 the bald fact was that the City was handling more international euro-denominated transactions than Paris and Frankfurt put together.[53]

Nevertheless, it was arguable that if the City genuinely did face a threat to its future, that threat came not so much from questions of ownership or currencies, as from more intangible, internal causes. This view was seldom articulated, but Yassukovich expressed it eloquently in the *Spectator* in September 1999:

Complacency, loss of distinct corporate culture, fragmented leadership, excessive bureaucracy, poor service, lower ethical and quality standards, lack of collective motivation; all of these diseases sap the strength of the once-healthy enterprise, and even an apparently overwhelming competitive advantage collapses. In one form or another these illnesses are all evident in the City.

Yassukovich was also concerned about increasingly inflexible, bureaucratic regulation; a lack of leadership from the Bank of England, suffering a loss of authority after the stripping of its supervisory function; and the way in which the spread of an unhealthy bonus culture had 'undermined corporate loyalty and diminished collective responsibility for standards'.[54] The analysis was brilliant, but ironically it was as if Yassukovich – who had played his full part in breaking up the club – was now calling for a return to club rules, or at least those that were not flagrantly uncompetitive. That this was almost certainly a vain hope was more obvious than whether, as a result, the City would ultimately perish from within.

In 1997 a middle-aged stockbroker remarked to me that when he came to the City in the late 1960s, people there felt rather sorry for those working in industry on large factory floors; but that now, as he and his colleagues sat behind row after row of screens on vast dealing floors, it was as if the positions had been reversed. The City was becoming a duller, blander, less flavoursome place. It was somehow apt that in summer 1998 the demise of tea auctions, a prime symbol of the traditional City, coincided almost exactly with the decision to abandon the pits at the 'fourth pillar', LIFFE, an equally prime symbol of the new City.

The sparkiness was also reduced by changing recruitment patterns, particularly post-Leeson. A leading trader, with some twelve years' experience, was asked in July 1996 what it took to be a foreign exchange dealer:

> When I started in money broking, the best traders were like East End barrow boys. They had gut instinct, a quick mind and a real flair for the market. The guys who succeed today need to have a first-class Oxbridge Honours degree, super dealing skills and an outstanding mathematical mind to understand highly complex markets and equipment – computers, screens, telecom lines and new information systems. Besides concentrating on all the movement in front of you, you've got to work closely with senior dealers, financial engineers, risk managers, analysts and position keepers who keep traders up to date with long and short positions.[55]

Barrow boy or graduate, stockbroker from Surrey or foreigner on a two-year secondment to London, the prevailing culture was workaholic. 'The new City values have bred some hideously topsy-turvy thinking', the banker-turned-novelist John McLaren reflected in November 1999:

In March I talked to a young Englishman who works for a big American investment bank. Proudly he told me how three times his plans to go skiing had been cancelled . . . To be fair, his approach may have been key to survival in that bank. A month later one of his colleagues was called in to be fired. The executioner began: 'Michael, how many weekends have you worked this year? Need I say more?'

The long hours, the pressure to perform, the unpleasant working environment, the job insecurity – it was no wonder that many City workers found release in drink. Damien McCrystal, diarist for *Sunday Business*, reported from the front line in autumn 1999. After commending the Corney & Barrow behind the Royal Exchange as 'one of the few pleasant places remaining', and noting that two of Walbrook's bars, Deacon's and the Slug & Lettuce, were 'characterised by booming music, neon lights and crowds spilling on to the streets' and were 'to be avoided at all costs', he pinpointed the most important change since the 1960s:

> When I first started drinking in the Square Mile, virtually all pubs were closed by 8 p.m. Now the City is a drinking destination after work. The modern bars stay open and the music blares until 11 p.m. and beyond . . . The last train home to Essex from Liverpool Street is known as the Vomit Comet. It is not a pretty sight, though it is, in a way, reassuring to the traditionalists.[56]

It gave no pleasure even to traditionalists that occasionally the pressure – or perhaps the meaninglessness – got too much and the time-honoured, ultimate exit was taken. Amschel Rothschild was a gentle, insecure, attractive character who should have been an archaeologist or a farmer or something to do with the arts, but in his early thirties he bowed at last to family pressure and joined the family bank. Although not a natural, he worked hard and in 1993 became executive chairman of Rothschild Asset Management. The business, though, fared indifferently (certainly in comparison to rival asset-management operations like that of Schroders), and by summer 1996 he may well have felt under pressure to produce better results; he may also have been becoming increasingly anxious about the expectation that he would eventually succeed to the chairmanship of N. M. Rothschild as a whole. On a Sunday night in July, staying at the Hotel Bristol in Paris, he hanged himself in his £500-a-night room. The cause of death was originally given as a heart attack, but the shocking truth emerged later in the week. 'I don't think he would ever have gone into the City if he hadn't been a Rothschild', a colleague said after it had come out. Amschel was forty-one.[57]

For most in the City, certainly the young and ambitious, it was the prospect of the crock of gold that, more than anything, drove them on. Given the material rewards that were on offer, it could hardly have been otherwise. 'The million-pound City man is back', the *Independent* reported in June 1996. 'After several years of modest earning levels – in Square Mile terms at least – hundreds of top investment bankers, analysts and dealers are again enjoying salaries and bonuses of at least £1m this year.' And it quoted a headhunter to the effect that by the end of the year there would be at least 1,000 dollar millionaires in the City, and probably many more. 'I do sometimes sit down and think: "Can this be right?"' one investment banking millionaire confessed at this time to the *FT* about the City windfall in general. 'My answer is that it is not wrong.'[58]

In 1999 City bonuses again hit the headlines, partly on the back of the huge number of merger and acquisition deals. There were no definitive figures, but the probability was that up to 500 bankers and dealers each received £1m or more, with a handful picking up something over £3m. As the good times continued into 2000, so expectations continued to rise about what constituted a just wage. 'We are having problems with our young recruits, new graduates who traditionally work 60- or 70-hour weeks devising clever corporate deals', a merchant banker with one of the most respected City firms confided in April to the journalist Kevin Rafferty. 'Now they won't do it unless we guarantee them packages worth £1 million over two or three years.' Rafferty himself, who had recently spent three years at the World Bank, could not refrain from offering a global perspective: 'A cool £1 million by the age of 26 or 27 – guaranteed – that's more than senior World Bank staff can dream of in a life's work. As for the peasants of Bangladesh, Bolivia, India, Ivory Coast, Zimbabwe, they'd be happy with work that would allow them enough money to afford to eat and provide a safe shelter to raise their children.'[59]

In June 1999 the City had a day to remember, as the 'Carnival against Capitalism' turned into a six-hour riot on the part of several thousand protesters – a riot forcibly repelled by LIFFE traders, and during which David Barnett of Cazenove's deliberately wore a stiff collar in defiance of advice from police to keep a low profile – but what was significant was that the initial protest did not take place even remotely within the political mainstream. By the end of the 1990s the question of the specific culpability of the City – for the state of British industry, for the state of world poverty – seemed to be hardly on the agenda at all. Recalling that there had once been 'a long-running, ill-tempered and inconclusive debate over what was called the City–industry divide', Graham Searjeant observed in December 1999 that that debate had now been stilled. 'He who pays the piper calls the tune, so the City's view prevailed; industry had to shut up and play it their way.' It was, in sum, a case of 'City cultural supremacy'.[60] Nor, he could have added, was it a supremacy solely exercised over industry: in all sorts of ways (short-term performance, shareholder value, league tables) and in all sorts of areas (education, the NHS and the BBC, to name but three), bottom-line City imperatives had been transplanted wholesale into British society. In an age of weak nation states, discredited systems of representative democracy and infinitely mobile, infinitely amoral international capital, the City had – almost by default – won the arguments and was calling the shots.

Was that all there was to look forward to in the twenty-first century? 'Money: A Valediction' was the optimistic title of the final chapter of James Buchan's 1997 inquiry into the meaning of money, *Frozen Desire*, and he ended with an inspiriting vision:

> One day, who knows, the human race might stir. My heroes and heroines wake from their sleep and rub their eyes. Honour pushes credit away with an indescribable grimace of disgust. Charity runs shrieking from the Charity Ball and virtue and solvency discuss a separation, which becomes permanent. Liberty puts down her shopping-bag and rests her bunioned feet. The owl of Minerva opens one eye, then the other, and extends her tattered wings for flight. And as these dreams dissolve, the Age of Money, which came after the Age of Faith, will itself draw, as all things under the sun, to an end.[61]

Notes

Addis   Papers of Sir Charles Addis (School of Oriental and African Studies Library)

AHC   Records of Accepting Houses Committee (London Metropolitan Archives)

Barclays   Barclays Group Archives: Bank of Liverpool records, Langton Papers

BB   Baring Brothers & Co. Archives (at ING Barings)

BBJB   Journal of Joshua Bates, Baring Brothers & Co. Archives (at ING Barings)

BM   *Bankers' Magazine*

BoE   Bank of England Archives

Bolton   Unpublished autobiography of Sir George Bolton (at Bank of England Archives)

Brand   Papers of Lord Brand (Bodleian Library, Oxford)

Brandt   Records of Wm Brandt, Sons & Co. (Nottingham University Library)

BS   Records of Brown, Shipley & Co. (London Metropolitan Archives)

BSP   Papers of Sir Henry Babington Smith (Trinity College, Cambridge)

BW   Records of Balfour, Williamson & Co. (University College London)

Cairncross   Diary of Sir Alec Cairncross (University of Glasgow Archives)

CCJ   *Chamber of Commerce Journal*

Churchill   Diaries of Charles Churchill, Snr and Charles Churchill, Jnr (London Metropolitan Archives)

CL   Cathy Courtney and Paul Thompson, *City Lives* (1996)

CP   *City Press*

DBB   David J. Jeremy (ed), *Dictionary of Business Biography* (1984–6)

FN   *Financial News*

FRBNY   Federal Reserve Bank of New York Archives

FT   *Financial Times*

Gibbs   Records of Antony Gibbs & Sons (London Metropolitan Archives)

Grey   Grey Papers (University of Durham Library)

Hambros   Records of C. J. Hambro & Sons (London Metropolitan Archives)

Hamilton   Diaries of Sir Edward Hamilton (British Library)

Harcourt   Harcourt Papers (Bodleian Library, Oxford)

HSBC   HSBC Group Archives

IHA   Records of Issuing Houses Association (London Metropolitan Archives)

IR   *Investors' Review*

JF   Records of John Foster & Sons (Brotherton Library, Leeds)

JIB   *Journal of the Institute of Bankers*

JM   Records of Jardine Matheson & Co. (Cambridge University Library)

JS   Centre for Metropolitan History, 'The Jobbing System of the London Stock Exchange: An Oral History' (at British Library National Sound Archive)

Kleinwort   Records of Kleinwort, Sons & Co. (London Metropolitan Archives)
LCC   Records of London Chamber of Commerce (London Metropolitan Archives)
Lloyds   Lloyds TSB Group Archives
LMA   London Metropolitan Archives
McLean   Letter books of David McLean, 1875–89, at the School of Oriental and African Studies Library, London (SOAS Ms 380401/13)
Macmillan   Diary of Harold Macmillan (Bodleian Library, Oxford)
Martin   Diaries of Sir Richard Biddulph Martin and John Biddulph Martin (the Holland-Martin family archives)
MC   (Macmillan) Committee on Finance and Industry: Report and Minutes of Evidence (Parl Papers, 1930–1, Cmd 3897)
Meyer   Letters of Sir Carl Meyer (family archives)
MG   Records of Morgan, Grenfell & Co. (at Deutsche Bank)
Midland   Midland Bank Archives (at HSBC Group Archives)
Milner   Papers of 1st Viscount Milner (Bodleian Library, Oxford)
Morgan   Records of J. S. Morgan & Co. (London Metropolitan Archives)
ND   Records of National Discount Company (London Metropolitan Archives)
NLSC   National Life Story Collection (at British Library National Sound Archive)
NW   National Westminster Bank Archives (at the Royal Bank of Scotland Archive)
Overstone   D. P. O'Brien (ed), *The Correspondence of Lord Overstone* (Cambridge, 1971)
PP   Parliamentary Papers
PRO   Public Record Office (now National Archives)
RAL   N. M. Rothschild & Sons Archives (London)
Rathbone   Records of Rathbone Bros & Co. (Liverpool University Library)
RBS   The Royal Bank of Scotland Archive (London)
Sambourne   Diary of Roy Sambourne (at Kensington Public Library)
Sayers   R. S. Sayers, *The Bank of England, 1891–1944* (Cambridge, 1976, two volumes and appendixes)
SE   Records of London Stock Exchange (at Guildhall Library up to 1954)
SSA   Records of Smith, St Aubyn & Co. (London Metropolitan Archives)

The place of publication is London, unless stated otherwise.

CHAPTER ONE

1. Kenneth Garlick and Angus Macintyre (eds), *The Diary of Joseph Farington* (1979), vol VI, pp 2253–4; *Public Characters of 1803–1804* (1804), p 387; *John Julius Angerstein and the Woodlands* (Woodlands art gallery, Greenwich, 1974); *Select Committee on Marine Insurance* (PP 1810, IV), p 67.

2. J. Leighton-Boyce, *Smiths the Bankers, 1658–1958* (1958), pp 130–5.

3. *Annual Register* (1810), pp 403–5; *Gentleman's Magazine* (Oct 1810); S. R. Cope, 'The Goldsmids and the Development of the London Market during the Napoleonic Wars' in *Economica* (1942); L. Alexander, *Memoirs of the Life of Benjamin Goldsmid* (1808), p 95; *Cobbett's Weekly Political Register*, 3 Oct 1810.

4. Charles Buxton (ed), *Memoirs of Sir Thomas Fowell Buxton* (1849), pp 288–9; Stanley Chapman, *N.M. Rothschild, 1777–1836* (1977); Lord Rothschild, *The Shadow of a Great Man* (1981); Richard Davis, *The English Rothschilds* (1983); RAL, XI/82/10; RAL, T29/364; RAL, T31/1/5.

5. Van Akin Burd (ed), *The Ruskin Family Letters* (1973), vol I, pp 54–6, 64; Tim Hilton, *John Ruskin: The Early Years* (1985), pp 1–12; Wolfgang Kemp, *The Desire of My Eyes: The Life and Work of John Ruskin* (1991), pp 3–11.

CHAPTER TWO

1. J. M. Price, 'What Did Merchants Do? Reflections on British Overseas ⌐ 1660–1790' in *Journal of Economic History* (1989).

2. S. D. Chapman, 'The International Houses: The Continental Contribu... .ɔ British Commerce, 1800–1860' in *Journal of European Economic History* (1977), pp 9–10; Stanley Chapman, *The Rise of Merchant Banking* (1984), p 9.

3. Hugh Barty-King, *The Baltic Exchange* (1977), pp 28–9; Bryant Lillywhite, *London Coffee Houses* (1963), pp 20–1.

4. S. W. Dowling, *The Exchanges of London* (1929), pp 4–5.

5. S. E. Fairlie, 'The Anglo-Russian Grain Trade, 1815–1861' (London PhD, 1959), pp 262–3.

6. T. S. Ashton, *An Economic History of England: The 18th Century* (1955), p 140; David Kynaston, *Cazenove & Co.* (1991), pp 11–12; Stanley Chapman, *N. M. Rothschild, 1777–1836* (1977), p 4.

7. Philip Ziegler, *The Sixth Great Power: Barings, 1762–1929* (1988), pp 17–19; Kenneth Garlick and Angus Macintyre (eds), *The Diary of Joseph Farington* (1979), vol VI, p 2060; Ziegler, p 51.

8. K. F. Dixon, 'The Development of the London Money Market, 1780–1830' (London PhD, 1962), p 80; S. D. Chapman, 'British Marketing Enterprise: The Changing Roles of Merchants, Manufacturers and Financiers, 1700–1860' in *Business History Review* (1979), pp 217–25.

9. D. E. W. Gibb, *Lloyd's of London: A Study in Individualism* (1957); S. D. Chapman, 'Hogg Robinson: The Rise of a Lloyd's Broker' in Oliver M. Westall (ed), *The Historian and the Business of Insurance* (Manchester, 1984); *Select Committee on Marine Insurance* (PP1810, IV), pp 64, 76, 42.

10. Sir John Clapham, *The Bank of England: A History* (Cambridge, 1944), vol I; Michael C. Lovell, 'The Role of the Bank of England as Lender of Last Resort in the Crises of the Eighteenth Century' in *Explorations in Entrepreneurial History* (1957–8); Stanley Chapman, *Merchant Enterprise in Britain: From the Industrial Revolution to World War I* (Cambridge, 1992), p 56.

11. D. M. Joslin, 'London Private Bankers, 1720–1785' in *Economic History Review* (1954–5); P. W. Matthews and A. W. Tuke, *History of Barclays Bank Limited* (1926), p 35; Roger Fulford, *Glyn's, 1753–1953* (1953), pp 2–6; Joslin, p 181; L. S. Pressnell, *Country Banking in the Industrial Revolution* (Oxford, 1956), Dixon; 'Money Market'.

12. Perry Anderson, 'The Figures of Descent' in *New Left Review* (Jan/Feb 1987), p 31; E. Victor Morgan and W. A. Thomas, *The Stock Exchange: Its History and Functions* (1962), W. J. Reader, A *House in the City: A Study of the City and of the Stock Exchange Based on the Records of Foster and Braithwaite, 1825–1975* (1979); S. R. Cope, 'The Stock Exchange Revisited: A New Look at the Market in Securities in London in the Eighteenth Century' in *Economica* (1978); Larry Neal, *The Rise of Financial Capitalism: International Capital Markets in the Age of Reason* (Cambridge, 1990); S. R. Cope, 'The Stock-Brokers Find a Home: How the Stock Exchange Came to be Established in Sweetings Alley in 1773' in *Guildhall Studies in London History* (1977); Anon (J. Lancaster?), *The Bank – The Stock Exchange – The Bankers – The Bankers' Clearing House – The Minister, and the Public* (1821), p 7.

13. P. G. M. Dickson, *The Financial Revolution in England: A Study in the Development of Public Credit, 1688–1756* (1967), p 493; Lucy Sutherland, 'Samson Gideon: Eighteenth-Century Jewish Financier' in Lucy Sutherland, *Politics and Finance in the Eighteenth Century* (1984).

14. Philanthropos (Thomas Mortimer), *Every Man His Own Broker* (1761), pp 79–81.

15. A. Heertje, 'On David Ricardo' in *Transactions of the Jewish Historical Society*

(1970–3); Piero Sraffa (ed), *The Works and Correspondence of David Ricardo* (Cambridge, 1952), vol VI, pp 150–1.

16. Lancaster, p 9; *Rules and Regulations Adopted by the Committee for General Purposes of the Stock-Exchange* (1812), p 46.

17. Dixon, 'Money Market', p 24; S. R. Cope, 'The Goldsmids and the Development of the London Market during the Napoleonic Wars' in *Economica* (1942), p 182; S. R. Cope, *Walter Boyd: A Merchant Banker in the Age of Napoleon* (1983), p 2; Elizabeth Gaskell, *Cranford* (Oxford, 1972 edn), pp 12, 187; George and Pamela Cleaver, *The Union Discount: A Centenary Album* (1985), pp 33–4; Martin Daunton, 'London and the World' in Celina Fox (ed), *London – World City, 1800–1840* (1992), pp 21–33.

18. Dr William Fleetwood, *A Complete Collection of the Sermons* (1737), p 732; George Birkbeck Hill and L. F. Powell (eds), *Boswell's Life of Johnson* (Oxford, 1934), vol III, p 353.

19. M. Dorothy George, *Hogarth to Cruikshank: Social Change in Graphic Satire* (1967), p 77; Diana Donald, '"Mr Deputy Dumpling and Family": Satirical Images of the City Merchant in Eighteenth-century England' in *Burlington Magazine* (Nov 1989); Peter Pindar, *The Fat Knight and the Petition; or, Cits in the Dumps* (1815), p 29; Clive Trebilcock, *Phoenix Assurance and the Development of British Insurance*, vol 1 (Cambridge, 1985), pp 50–1; Ziegler, p 36.

20. P. J. Cain and A. G. Hopkins, 'The Political Economy of British Expansion Overseas, 1750–1914' in *Economic History Review* (1980), p 469; P. J. Cain and A. G. Hopkins, 'Gentlemanly Capitalism and British Expansion Overseas: I. The Old Colonial System, 1688–1850' in *Economic History Review* (1986), p 513; Nicholas Rogers, 'Money, Land and Lineage: The Big Bourgeoisie of Hanoverian London' in *Social History* (1979); *Boswell's Life of Johnson*, vol II, p 126; Cain and Hopkins, 'Gentlemanly Capitalism', p 514.

21. H. V. Bowen, 'Investment and Empire in the Later Eighteenth Century: East India Stockholding, 1756–1791' in *Economic History Review* (1990); Sutherland, 'Samson Gideon'; J. Leighton-Boyce, *Smiths the Bankers, 1658–1958* (1958), p 129; Ziegler, p 51; Jane Austen, *Sense and Sensibility* (Oxford, 1980 pbk edn), p 145; Rogers, 'Money, Land and Lineage'; Lucy Sutherland, 'The City of London in Eighteenth-Century Politics' in Sutherland, *Politics and Finance*; *Diary of Joseph Farington*, vol VI, p 2059.

22. Barry Supple, *The Royal Exchange Assurance* (Cambridge, 1970), pp 76–8; Chapman, *Merchant Enterprise*, pp 55–6.

23. James C. Riley, *International Government Finance and the Amsterdam Capital Market, 1740–1815* (Cambridge, 1980), pp 195–204; S.R. Cope, 'Bird, Savage & Bird of London: Merchants and Bankers, 1782–1803' in *Guildhall Studies in London History* (1981).

24. F. M. L. Thompson, *English Landed Society in the Nineteenth Century* (1963), p 63; Walter Bagehot, *Lombard Street: A Description of the Money Market* (1873), p 161.

25. Gibb, pp 71–2; John M. Sherwig, *Guineas and Gunpowder: British Foreign Aid in the Wars with France, 1793–1815* (Cambridge, Mass., 1969), pp 263–4; S. D. Chapman, 'The Establishment of the Rothschilds as Bankers' in *Jewish Historical Studies* (1985–6), pp 179–81; Cope, 'Goldsmids', p 191; Cope, *Walter Boyd*; Ziegler, p 58; Ralph W. Hidy, *The House of Baring in American Trade and Finance: English Merchant Bankers at Work, 1763–1861* (New York, 1949), p 53; Cope, 'Goldsmids', pp 204–6; Norman J. Silberling, 'Financial and Monetary Policy of Great Britain during the Napoleonic Wars, II' in *Quarterly Journal of Economics* (1924).

26. Dixon, 'Money Market', pp 21–137, 220–9.

27. Chapman, *Merchant Enterprise*, chs 2 and 5; Chapman, *Merchant Enterprise*, p 56.

28. Anthony Webster, 'The Political Economy of Trade Liberalization: The East India Company Charter Act of 1813' in *Economic History Review* (1990).

CHAPTER THREE

1. *The Post-Office Annual Directory for 1815*, p 241.
2. Richard Rush, *Memoranda of a Residence at the Court of London* (Philadelphia, 1833), pp 77–8.
3. Jon Lawrence,'From Counting-House to Office: The Evolution of London's Central Financial District, 1693–1871' (ESRC End of Award report, *c.*1993); Edmund Sheridan Purcell, *Life of Cardinal Manning* (1895), vol I, p 3; Philip Ziegler, *The Sixth Great Power: Barings, 1762–1929* (1988), p 48; Lawrence, 'Counting-House'.
4. J. H. Dunning and E. V. Morgan, *An Economic Study of the City of London* (1971), p 34; Roger Fulford, *Glyn's, 1753–1953* (1953), p 101; John Arthur Gibbs, *The History of Antony and Dorothea Gibbs* (1922), p 202; W. Marston Acres, *The Bank of England from Within* (1931), vol II, p 351; Charles Duguid, *The Story of the Stock Exchange* (1901), p 93.
5. *The Picture of London, for 1815* (sixteenth edn, 1815), pp 183, 192; *Leigh's New Picture of London* (1818), p 294.
6. Robert Hawker, *The Royal Exchange* (*c.*1808), pp 3–6.
7. Philip Ziegler, *The Sixth Great Power: Barings, 1762–1929* (1988), pp 80–5.
8. Stanley Chapman, *The Rise of Merchant Banking* (1984), p 83.
9. D. C. M. Platt, *Foreign Finance in Continental Europe and the United States, 1815–1870* (1984), pp 8–10; Chapman, *Merchant Banking*, pp 83–4.
10. *Commercial Chronicle*, 16 Jan 1817; *Select Committee on the Expediency of the Bank Resuming Cash Payments* (PP1819, III), pp 53, 158.
11. SE, Ms 14,600, vol 9, 26 Nov 1821–24 Dec 1821.
12. On all these episodes, see Frank Griffith Dawson, *The First Latin American Debt Crisis: The City of London and the 1822–25 Loan Bubble* (1990).
13. Dawson, pp 39–40; *Morning Chronicle*, 12 Oct 1822, 18 Oct 1822, 25 Oct 1822.
14. RAL, T42/4; Richard Davis, *The English Rothschilds* (1983), p 33; RAL, T3/230; Chapman, *Merchant Banking*, pp 18, 48.
15. Lord Rothschild, *The Shadow of a Great Man* (1982), p 14, quoting *The Times*, 3 Aug 1836; RAL, T27/219; Chapman, *Merchant Banking*, p 40.
16. Nina L. Kay Shuttleworth, *A Life of Sir Woodbine Parish* (1910), p 201.
17. RAL, T5/164; BoE, G8/21, 18 June 1823; Davis, p 37.
18. Ziegler, pp 94, 76.
19. Richard Roberts, *Schroders: Merchants & Bankers* (1992), pp 32–40; C. Amburger, 'Wm Brandt and the Story of His Enterprises' (typescript, *c.*1937, University of Nottingham Library); Georgina Meinertzhagen, *A Bremen Family* (1912), pp 251–2.
20. Anon, *Cook's of St Paul's* (1957), pp 4–5; Richard Gatty, *Portrait of a Merchant Prince: James Morrison, 1789–1857* (Northallerton, ?1977), p 23.
21. SE, Ms 17,957, vol 22; M. C. Reed, *A History of James Capel and Co.* (1975), pp 1–4, 19–21; Roberts, pp 356–8; David Kynaston, *Cazenove & Co.* (1991), pp 15–16; Stanley D. Chapman, *Raphael Bicentenary, 1787–1987* (1987), pp 5–13.
22. Dawson, p 40; *Morning Herald*, 5 Nov 1824.
23. *Cash Payments*, p 178; K. F. Dixon, 'The Development of the London Money Market, 1780–1830' (London PhD, 1962), pp 200–4; L. S. Pressnell, *Country Banking in the Industrial Revolution* (Oxford, 1956), p 103.
24. Dixon, 'Money Market', pp 220–34.

CHAPTER FOUR

1. Samuel Thornton, *Yearly Recollections* (1891), p 196; Francis Bamford and the Duke of Wellington (eds), *The Journal of Mrs Arbuthnot* (1950), vol I, p 382; Frank Whitson

Fetter, *Development of British Monetary Orthodoxy, 1797–1875* (Cambridge, Mass., 1965), pp 111–13.

2. K. F. Dixon, 'The Development of the London Money Market, 1780–1830' (London PhD, 1962), pp 178–9, 181.

3. *Morning Chronicle*, 14–15 Dec 1825.

4. Walter Bagehot, *Lombard Street: A Description of the Money Market* (1873), pp 51–2; Liverpool papers (British Library), Add Ms 38, 371, fo 77.

5. *Mrs Arbuthnot*, vol I, pp 426–7.

6. *Morning Chronicle*, 17 Dec 1825; *Macmillan's Magazine* (Dec 1874), p 157; *Mrs Arbuthnot*, vol I, p 428.

7. Philip Ziegler, *The Sixth Great Power: Barings, 1762–1929* (1988), p 98.

8. Thomas Love Peacock, *Paper Money Lyrics, and Other Poems* (1837), pp 26–8.

9. Frank Griffith Dawson, *The First Latin American Debt Crisis: The City of London and the 1822–25 Loan Bubble* (1990), pp 128–9.

10. A German Prince, *Tour in Germany, Holland and England* (1832), vol III, pp 43, 59–63.

11. G. Duckworth Atkin (ed), *House Scraps* (1887), p 150.

12. This paragraph is largely drawn from Frank Whitson Fetter, *Development of British Monetary Orthodoxy, 1797–1875* (Cambridge, Mass., 1965), pp120–64 and Boyd Hilton, *Corn, Cash, Commerce: The Economic Policies of the Tory Governments, 1815–1830* (Oxford, 1977), pp 232–68.

13. *Committee of Secrecy on the Bank of England Charter* (PP1831–2, VI), qq 3689, 4946.

14. W. T. C. King, *History of the London Discount Market* (1936), pp 35–101; Dixon, 'Money Market', pp 186–204; W. M. Scammell, *The London Discount Market* (1968), pp 133–49.

15. K. F. Dixon, *Alexanders Discount Company Limited, 1810–1960* (1960), p 4.

16. Charles Harvey and Jon Press, 'The City and Mining Enterprise: The Making of the Morris Family Fortune' in *Journal of the William Morris Society* (1990).

17. Dixon, 'Money Market', p 195.

18. Augustus Hare, *The Gurneys of Earlham* (1895), vol II, pp 238–9; Hare, vol I, p 241.

19. *Circular to Bankers*, 9 Oct 1835; *A Portion of the Journal Kept by Thomas Raikes, Esq from 1831 to 1847* (1856), vol II, pp 221–2.

20. George Otto Trevelyan, *The Life and Letters of Lord Macaulay* (1881 edn), p 160; A. Aspinall (ed), *The Correspondence of Charles Arbuthnot* (1941), p 136; *Mrs Arbuthnot*, vol II, p 200; BoE, G23/53, 4 Dec 1830.

21. Ralph W. Hidy, *The House of Baring in American Trade and Finance: English Merchant Bankers at Work, 1765–1861* (New York, 1949), p 84; Ziegler, p 123; Hidy, p 83; Ziegler, p 123.

22. BBJB, 31 Dec 1832.

23. This paragraph is wholly drawn from Hidy, pp 124–50.

24. Hidy, p 150; Ziegler, p 150.

25. Ziegler, pp 136,134; JM, II.A.1.10, reel 291, no 795, reel 292, no 889.

26. *Morning Chronicle*, 4 Feb 1831; Ziegler, p 114; BBJB, 21 Aug 1831; Place Papers (British Library), Add Ms 3 5,149, fo 107.

27. *Despatches, Correspondence, and Memoranda of Field Marshal Arthur Duke of Wellington* (1880), vol VIII, p 308; BBJB, 24 May 1832.

28. Anon, *The History of Goad, Rigg & Company* (1952).

29. W. Heseltine, *A Family Scene during the Panic at the Stock Exchange, in May 1835* (second edn, Canterbury, 1848), pp 22–3, 27–9.

30. Barclays, 25/265 (104); BBJB, 31 May 1835.

31. P. L. Cottrell, *Industrial Finance, 1830–1914: The Finance and Organization of English Manufacturing Industry* (1983 pbk edn) is the fullest guide to the overall theme; M. C.

Reed, *A History of James Capel and Co.* (1975), pp 28–32; *Circular to Bankers*, 23 Oct 1829; R. S. Sayers, 'Ricardo's Views on Monetary Questions' in T. S. Ashton and R. S. Sayers (eds), *Papers in English Monetary History* (Oxford, 1953), p 94; M. J. Daunton, '"Gentlemanly Capitalism" and British Industry, 1820–1914' in *Past and Present* (Feb 1989), p 138.

32. *Circular to Bankers*, 26 Feb 1836; Barclays, 25/265 (120); Jack Simmons (ed), *The Birth of the Great Western Railway: Extracts from the Diary and Correspondence of George Henry Gibbs* (Bath, 1971), p 78; T. R. Gourvish, *Railways and the British Economy, 1830–1914* (1980), pp 16–17.

33. Stanley Chapman, *The Rise of Merchant Banking* (1984), pp 39–42; *Select Committee on Manufactures, Commerce and Shipping* (PP1833, VI), qq 2009, 2014–5; JM, II.A.1.10, reel 292, no 1,021; Barclays, 25/265 (68); Richard Gatty, *Portrait of a Merchant Prince: James Morrison, 1789–1857* (Northallerton, ?1977), pp 156–8.

34. Chapman, *Merchant Banking*, pp 109–11; Michael Greenberg, *British Trade and the Opening of China, 1800–1841* (Cambridge, 1951), pp 168–9; Barclays, 25/265 (185).

35. BBJB, 25 July 1836; RAL, T23/148; *Morning Chronicle*, 9 Aug 1836; *Circular to Bankers*, 5 Aug 1836; Heseltine, pp 53–6.

CHAPTER FIVE

1. BB, HC1.20.1.2C; BBJB, 17 Sept 1836; BoE, G8/29, 26 Oct 1836; BBJB, 13 Nov 1836.
2. Barclays, 25/265 (286, 278, 286).
3. BoE, G4/59, 21 March 1837.
4. Muriel Emmie Hidy, *George Peabody: Merchant and Financier, 1829–1854* (New York, 1978), p 84; Morrison Cryder records (LMA), Ms 11,720, folder 1, 21 May 1837; Barclays, 25/265 (289, 290); BoE, G4/60, 30 May 1837; Richard Gatty, *Portrait of a Merchant Prince: James Morrison, 1789–1857* (Northallerton, ?1977), p 164; Barclays, 25/265 (292).
5. BoE, G4/60, 1 June 1837; Barclays, 25/265 (293).
6. Barclays, 25/265 (297); Morrison Cryder, Ms 11,720, folder 1, 9 June 1837; BBJB, 20 Aug 1837.
7. Churchill, Ms 5,762, vol 16, week ending 13 Jan 1838; Gresham Committee Repertories, Report of the Special Committee of Enquiry into the Destruction of the Exchange by Fire, 18 Jan 1838.
8. Sir John Clapham, *The Bank of England: A History* (Cambridge, 1944), vol II, pp 167–8; Stanley Chapman, *The Rise of Merchant Banking* (1984), p 165; BBJB, 20 July 1839.
9. Overstone, vol I, p 245; BBJB, 4 June 1842; Chapman, *Merchant Banking*, p 42; S. D. Chapman, 'The International Houses: The Continental Contribution to British Commerce, 1800–1860' in *Journal of European Economic History*, p 29; Hidy, *George Peabody*, is the best book on Peabody.
10. Richard Davis, *The English Rothschilds* (1983), pp 58, 80, 129–30; Chapman, *Merchant Banking*, p 165; J. R. Freedman, 'A London Merchant Banker in Anglo-American Trade and Finance, 1835–50' (London PhD, 1969).
11. T. E. Gregory, *The Westminster Bank Through a Century* (1936), vol I, p 255.
12. J. Leighton-Boyce, *Smiths the Bankers, 1658–1958* (1958), p 271; George Chandler, *Four Centuries of Banking*, vol I (1964), p 301.
13. Lloyds, A12/1D/7; Barnett, Hoares & Co., private letter book, 1840–71.
14. Mrs Grote, *The Personal Life of George Grote* (1873), p 141; Davis, p 70; Charles Stuart Parker (ed), *Sir Robert Peel from His Private Papers* (1899), vol II, pp 570–1.
15. BB, HC1.20.8.
16. *Circular to Bankers*, 27 Oct 1843; A. C. Howe, 'Free Trade and the City of London, c.1820–1870' in *History* (1992), pp 397–8; BBJB, 22 Dec 1843.

17. J. Horsley Palmer, *The Causes and Consequences of the Pressures upon the Money-Market* (1837); S. J. Loyd, *Reflections Suggested by a Perusal of Mr J. Horsley Palmer's Pamphlet* (1837), pp 45–6; M. C. Reed, *A History of James Capel and Co.* (1975), p 47; Daniel Hardcastle, Jnr, *Banks and Bankers* (1842), p 164.

18. *Hansard*, 6 May 1844, col 750; Lytton Strachey and Roger Fulford (eds), *The Greville Memoirs, 1814–60* (1938), vol V, p 173; *The Economist*, 18 May 1844; *The Times*, 14 May 1844; Anon (David Morier Evans), *The City; or, The Physiology of London Business; with Sketches on 'Change, and at the Coffee Houses* (1845), p 9.

19. *Sir Robert Peel*, vol III, p 140; *Circular to Bankers*, 14 June 1844; *The Economist*, 15 June 1844; BoE, M5/206 (item 65); *Circular to Bankers*, 14 June 1844; *The Economist*, 15 June 1844.

20. S. J. Loyd, *Thoughts on the Separation of the Departments of the Bank of England* (July 1844 edn), p 55.

CHAPTER SIX

1. *The Economist*, 25 Oct 1845; *Punch*, 22 Nov 1845.

2. *The Economist*, 4 Oct 1845 (estimated from market reports); Benjamin Disraeli, *Endymion* (1881), p 356; BBJB, 25 April 1845.

3. G. Duckworth Atkin (ed), *House Scraps* (1887), p 109; Judy Slinn, *Linklaters & Paines: The First One Hundred and Fifty Years* (1987), pp 10, 16; Charles Duguid, *The Story of the Stock Exchange* (1901), pp 148–9.

4. *Bankers' Magazine* (April 1845), p 53; Overstone, vol I, p 378.

5. Churchill, Ms 5,762, vol 29, 29 April 1847; Overstone, vol I, p 383; Frank Whitson Fetter, *Development of British Monetary Orthodoxy, 1797–1875* (Cambridge, Mass., 1965), pp 206–8.

6. NW, 11,521, Prescotts committee minutes, 19 Aug 1847.

7. JM, II.A.1.10, reel 300, no 3,128.

8. Sir John Clapham, *The Bank of England: A History* (Cambridge, 1944), vol II, pp 198–204; W. T. C. King, *History of the London Discount Market* (1936), p 142; Fetter, pp 209–10.

9. BoE, M5/517.

10. *Morning Chronicle*, 23 Oct 1847; Overstone, vol I, p 397; *Secret Committee on Commercial Distress* (PP1847–8, VIII.I), q 1600.

11. David Kynaston, *The Chancellor of the Exchequer* (Lavenham, 1980), p 134.

12. Overstone, vol I, p 403.

13. Philip Ziegler, *The Sixth Great Power: Barings, 1762–1929* (1988), p 137.

14. D. C. M. Platt, *Foreign Finance in Continental Europe and the United States, 1815–1870* (1984), p 13.

15. *Morning Chronicle*, 11 April 1848 (two separate reports).

16. SE, Ms 14,600, vol 20, 10 April 1848; *Morning Chronicle*, 11–12 April 1848.

CHAPTER SEVEN

1. BBJB, 10 Oct 1852; E. J. Hobsbawm, *Industry and Empire* (1969 Pelican edn), pp 139–40; G. A. Fletcher, *The Discount Houses in London: Principles, Operations and Change* (1976), p 17; E. Victor Morgan and W. A. Thomas, *The Stock Exchange: Its History and Functions* (1962), p 88; Hobsbawm, p 119.

2. BBJB, 10 Oct 1852, 9 June 1860; Stanley Chapman, *The Rise of Merchant Banking* (1984), p 108.

3. SE, Mss 14,600, vol 21, 30 June 1851, vol 24, 12 April 1858, vol 22, 5 Jan 1852.

4. P. W. Matthews and A. W. Tuke, *History of Barclays Bank Limited* (1926), p 45; Overstone, vol II, p 475.

5. Edward Nevin and E. W. Davis, *The London Clearing Banks* (1970), p 68; Sir Albert Feavearyear, *The Pound Sterling: A History of English Money* (Oxford, 1963 edn), p 288; BoE, M5/209.

6. W. T. C. King, *History of the London Discount Market* (1936), pp 182–5; W. F. Crick and J. E. Wadsworth, *A Hundred Years of Joint Stock Banking* (1936), p 30.

7. Philip Ziegler, *The Sixth Great Power: Barings, 1762–1929* (1988), p 162; BBJB, 12 June 1853, 5 Nov 1853, 9 Dec 1855, 3 Jan 1857.

8. Ziegler, p 180; Richard Davis, *The English Rothschilds* (1983), p 139.

9. John Francis, *Characters and Chronicles of the Stock Exchange* (1855 edn), p 308.

10. Stanley D. Chapman, *Raphael Bicentenary, 1787–1987* (1987), p 15; Richard Roberts, *Schroders: Merchants & Bankers* (1992), pp 43–61, 79, 85–6.

11. S. J. Diaper, 'The History of Kleinwort, Sons & Co. in Merchant Banking, 1855–1961' (Nottingham PhD, 1983), pp 1–49; Bo Bramsen and Kathleen Wain, *The Hambros* (1979), pp 250–1, 262, 298–300.

12. Franklin Parker, *George Peabody: A Biography* (Nashville, 1971), pp 39, 51–3; Ralph W. Hidy, *The House of Baring in American Trade and Finance: English Merchant Bankers at Work, 1763–1861* (New York, 1949), pp 305, 341; BBJB, 31 July 1853, 25 Oct 1862.

13. Hidy, pp 300, 340; Kathleen Burk, *Morgan Grenfell, 1838–1988: The Biography of a Merchant Bank* (Oxford, 1989), pp 16–18.

14. Burk, pp 20–3, gives the fullest account of this episode; Parker, p 94; BBJB, 21 Nov 1857, 26 March 1862.

15. Nathaniel Hawthorne, *The English Notebooks* (1941), pp 282, 287, 604–7.

16. *The Education of Henry Adams: An Autobiography* (1918 edn), p 73; NW, 11,525, Prescotts committee minutes, 13 July 1865; *The Times*, 17 Nov 1857.

17. *The Economist*, 7 April 1860.

18. BoE, M5/457, M6/65.

19. Thomas J. Spinner, Jnr, *George Joachim Goschen: The Transformation of a Victorian Liberal* (Cambridge, 1973) is the best book on Goschen.

20. This paragraph is culled from A. C. Howe, 'From "Old Corruption" to "New Probity": The Bank of England and its Directors in the Age of Reform' in *Financial History Review* (1994), as are some of the earlier points in this chapter.

21. John Morley, *The Life of William Ewart Gladstone* (1905 two vol edn), vol I, p 518; Howe, 'Bank of England'; Richard Shannon, *Gladstone, 1809–1865* (1984 pbk edn), p 319; Overstone, vol II, pp 912, 936; Morley, vol I, p 686.

22. Lloyds, file 4553 (Sayers notes); BoE, M6/65.

23. NW, 11,432, Alliance Bank, letter book of Frank Wilde 8–10 Aug 1864.

24. *The Times*, 15 July 1865; King, pp 239–40; NW, 11,525, Prescotts committee minutes, 13 July 1865; John Stephen Flynn, *Sir Robert N. Fowler* (1893), p 150; *The Economist*, 15 July 1865; *Bankers' Magazine* (Aug 1865), pp 905–9; SE, Ms 14,600, vol 29, 18 Aug 1865.

25. Bertram Wodehouse Currie, *Recollections, Letters and Journals* (Roehampton, 1901), vol I, p 61; JM, II.A.1.10, reel 320, no 8,429; *The Times*, 10 May 1866; Martin (R), 10 May 1866; RBS, GM/600/3; JM, II.A.1.10, reel 320, no 8,448.

26. *Bankers' Magazine* (Jan 1870 supplement), p 3; King, p 247; Ziegler, p 182.

27. *The Times*, 11 May 1866; Churchill, Ms 5,762, vol 42; Martin (R), 11 May 1866; NW, 11,525, Prescotts committee minutes, 11 May 1866; *The Economist*, 19 May 1866; *The Times*, 12 May 1866; RAL, RFamC/21,12 May 1866.

28. Norman St John Stevas (ed), *The Collected Works of Walter Bagehot*, vol XIII (1986), p 608; H. C. G. Mathew (ed), *The Gladstone Diaries*, vol VI (Oxford, 1978), p 436; Sir

Notes

John Clapham, *The Bank of England: A History* (Cambridge, 1944), vol II, p 264; Martin (R), 12 May 1866.

29. *The Economist*, 22 Sept 1866; Walter Bagehot, *Lombard Street: A Description of the Money Market* (1873), pp 169–70; Sir Albert Feavearyear, *The Pound Sterling: A History of English Money* (Oxford, 1963 edn), p 305; Frank Whitson Fetter, *Development of British Monetary Orthodoxy, 1797–1875* (Cambridge, Mass., 1965), pp 272–5.

CHAPTER EIGHT

1. *Quarterly Review* (Jan 1872), p 120; Baron E. B. d'Erlanger, *My English Souvenirs* (1978), pp 103–4; Youssef Cassis, *La City de Londres, 1870–1914* (Paris, 1987), p 40.

2. Ranald C. Michie, *The City of London: Continuity and Change, 1850–1990* (1991), pp 72–3.

3. G. M. Young, *Victorian Essays* (1962), p 126; Walter Bagehot, *Lombard Street: A Description of the Money Market* (1873), pp 4, 19–20, 40–2, 71–4.

4. Norman St John Stevas (ed), *The Collected Works of Walter Bagehot*, vol XIII (1986), p 642; R. S. Sayers, *Central Banking after Bagehot* (Oxford, 1957), p 9; Rathbone, files of general correspondence 1851–73, XXIV.I.24 (51–113), 17 Oct 1873, 21 Oct 1873.

5. *Blackwood's Edinburgh Magazine* (Sept 1876), p 310; Rathbone, files of general correspondence 1851–73, XXIV.I.19, 18 March 1868, XXIV.I.23 (43–90), 22 Oct 1872; *Fraser's Magazine* (Oct 1876), pp 493–503.

6. *Hansard*, 20 March 1877, cols 209, 216, 237; *The Economist*, 24 March 1877; *The Times*, 21 March 1877.

7. *Commission appointed to inquire into the Origin, Objects, Present Constitution, &c, of the London Stock Exchange* (PP1878, XIX), pp 19–27; *The Times*, 17 Aug 1878; *The Economist*, 7 Sept 1878.

8. T. H. S. Escott, *England: Its People, Polity, and Pursuits* (1879), vol II, pp 39–42.

9. Rathbone, files of general correspondence 1851–73, XXIV.I.19, 3 Jan 1868; Mary Cathcart Borer, *The City of London: A History* (1977), p 288; Philip Ziegler, *The Sixth Great Power: Barings, 1762–1929* (1988), p 204; S. J. Diaper, 'The History of Kleinwort, Sons & Co. in Merchant Banking, 1855–1961' (Nottingham PhD, 1983), p 348; D. T. A. Kynaston, 'The London Stock Exchange, 1870–1914: An Institutional History' (London PhD, 1983), p 116.

10. *Civil Service Inquiry Commission* (PP1875, XXIII), qq 8779–80; Lloyds, file 4553 (Sayers notes), 22 May 1878.

11. Youssef Cassis, *Les banquiers de la City à l'époque Edouardienne* (Geneva, 1984), p 35; Bertram Wodehouse Currie, *Recollections, Letters and Journals* (Roehampton, 1901), vol I, p xi; Roger Fulford, *Glyn's, 1753–1953* (1953), pp 199–203; John Orbell, *Baring Brothers & Co., Limited: A History to 1939* (1985), between pp 42–3; Currie, vol I, p 44, vol II, p 8.

12. Kurt Grunwald, '"Windsor-Cassel" – The Last Court Jew' in *Leo Baeck Institute, Year Book* (1969); *DBB*, P. Thane, 'Sir Ernest Joseph Cassel', vol 1, pp 604–14; Anthony Allfrey, *Edward VII and his Jewish Court* (1991), p 137.

13. Richard Roberts, 'What's in a Name? Merchants, Merchant Bankers, Accepting Houses, Issuing Houses, Industrial Bankers and Investment Bankers' in *Business History* (1993); Aytoun Ellis, *Heir of Adventure: The Story of Brown, Shipley & Co., Merchant Bankers, 1810–1960* (1960), pp 102–3; Ziegler, pp 202–4; Kathleen Burk, *Morgan Grenfell, 1838–1988: The Biography of a Merchant Bank* (Oxford, 1989), p 38.

14. Stanley Chapman, *The Rise of Merchant Banking* (1984), pp 106, 124–5; Diaper, pp 155, 180, 72.

15. *The Economist*, 30 Jan 1869.

16. Burk, pp 32–3, 43–6.

17. Niall Ferguson, *The World's Banker: The History of the House of Rothschild* (1998), p. 1042; Ziegler, p 376; Burk, p 264; Richard Roberts, *Schroders: Merchants & Bankers* (1992), pp 75, 107; Gibbs, Ms 19,880; Youssef Cassis, *La City de Londres, 1870–1914* (Paris, 1987), p 141; Richard Meinertzhagen, *Diary of a Black Sheep* (1964), p 19.

18. Chapman, *Merchant Banking*, p 44; Roberts, *Schroders*, p 528; Ziegler, p 376; Burk, p 264.

19. Roberts, *Schroders*, pp 110–11.

20. Ferguson, *Rothschild*, pp 808–11; NW, 4,337, vol 1, Union Bank of London; Chapman, *Merchant Banking*, p 53; Dolores Greenberg, *Financiers and Railroads, 1869–1889: A Study of Morton, Bliss & Company* (Newark, 1980).

21. Roberts, *Schroders*, p 358; RAL, Tn/67; Alfred Wagg, 'Autobiography' (unpublished typescript, c.1958, held by Schroders), p 15.

22. R. C. Michie, *The London and New York Stock Exchanges, 1850–1914* (1987), pp 9, 19; *The Times*, 25 Dec 1874; *Financial News*, 14 Nov 1902.

23. Walter Bagehot, *Economic Studies* (1905 edn), pp 197–8.

24. O'Hagan, vol II, p 335; Elizabeth Hennessy, *Stockbrokers for 150 Years: A History of Sheppards and Chase, 1827–1977* (1978), p 27.

25. *London Stock Exchange*, qq 3435, 3438, 3447–59 plus App VI, 3491–3 (Branch), 8419, 8495–6, 8500–4, 8486, 8491, 8493 (Medley).

26. SE, Ms 14,609, vol 2, 11 May 1904. The argument in this paragraph owes much to Daunton, 'Financial elites', pp 136–8.

27. Kynaston, 'London Stock Exchange', p 99; W. J. Reader, *A House in the City: A Study of the City and of the Stock Exchange based on the Records of Foster and Braithwaite, 1815–1975* (1979), pp 61–2; RAL, RFamC/21, 28 July 1874, 31 July 1874; Reader, p 82. Jehanne Wake, *Princess Louise: Queen Victoria's Unconventional Daughter* (1988), pp 274, 288, gives the poignant story of what happened subsequently to Lord Walter's City career.

28. F. C. Carruthers Gould, 'Draft Autobiography' (House of Commons Library manuscript collection), pp 73–7.

CHAPTER NINE

1. T. H. S. Escott, *England: Its People, Polity, and Pursuits* (1879), vol I, pp 190, 193–4.

2. R. C. Michie, *The London and New York Stock Exchanges, 1850–1914* (1987), pp 145–7.

3. G. A. Fletcher, *The Discount Houses in London: Principles, Operations and Change* (1976), p 30; *The Economist*, 5 Dec 1874; *Bankers' Magazine* (Jan 1875), pp 5–7.

4. L. S. Pressnell, 'Gold Reserves, Banking Reserves, and the Baring Crisis of 1890' in C. R. Whittlesey and J. S. G. Wilson (eds), *Essays in Money and Banking* (Oxford, 1968), pp 186–9, Fletcher, pp 32–3; BoE, M6/28, p 5; W. T. C. King, *History of the London Discount Market* (1936), pp 295–6.

5. Martin (J), review of 1878; R. S. Sayers, *Lloyds Bank in the History of English Banking* (Oxford, 1957), p 246; Martin (J), review of 1878.

6. Pressnell, p 189; Michael Collins, *Banks and Industrial Finance in Britain, 1800–1939* (1991), p 42.

7. A. R. Holmes and Edwin Green, *Midland: 150 Years of Banking Business* (1986), pp 50, 64, 81; Sayers, *Lloyds*, pp 247–8; R. S. Sayers, *Gilletts in the London Money Market, 1867–1967* (Oxford, 1968), p 192.

8. *Statist*, 17 Jan 1885; Martin (J), review of 1884.

9. Dudley W. R. Bahlman (ed), *The Diary of Sir Edward Walter Hamilton, 1880–1885* (Oxford, 1972), vol II, p 774; Robert Blake, *Disraeli* (1969 pbk edn), pp 581–7; Lord

Rothschild, *'You Have It, Madam': The Purchase, in 1875, of Suez Canal Shares by Disraeli and Baron Lionel de Rothschild* (1980), p 22; Iddesleigh papers (British Library), Add Ms 50,017, 19 Feb 1876; Alfred Wagg, 'Autobiography' (unpublished typescript, *c*.1958, held by Schroders), p 11; George Earl Buckle, *The Life of Benjamin Disraeli, Earl of Beaconsfield*, vol V (1920), p 448; Stephen Gwynn and Gertrude M. Tuckwell, *The Life of the Rt Hon. Sir Charles W. Dilke* (1917), vol I, p 285; *The Times*, 27 Nov 1875; Overstone, vol III, p 1285.

10. This account is indebted to B. R. Johns, 'Business, Investment, and Imperialism: The Relationship between Economic Interests and the Growth of British Intervention in Egypt' (Exeter PhD, 1982), A. G. Hopkins, 'The Victorians and Africa: A Reconsideration of the Occupation of Egypt, 1882' in *Journal of African History* (1986).

11. Wilfred Scawen Blunt, *Secret History of the English Occupation of Egypt* (1907), p 240; *The Economist*, 17 June 1882; *The Times*, 27 June 1882; 6 July 1882; *The Economist*, 8 July 1882.

12. *The Economist*, 15 July 1882, 22 July 1882; *Bankers' Magazine* (Aug 1882), p 606.

13. Andrew Porter, '"Gentlemanly Capitalism" and Empire: The British Experience since 1850' in *Journal of Imperial and Commonwealth History* (1990), pp 282–5.

14. Frederic Harrison, *National and Social Problems* (1908), pp 199, 218–19, 114.

15. BS, Ms 20,111, vol 2, 28 Oct 1882.

16. Edwin J. Perkins, *Financing Anglo-American Trade: The House of Brown, 1800–1880* (Cambridge, Mass., 1975), pp 222–3; Stanley D. Chapman, *Raphael Bicentenary, 1787–1987* (1987), p 23.

17. Stanley Chapman, *The Rise of Merchant Banking* (1984), pp 88, 158.

18. Miriam Rothschild, *Dear Lord Rothschild: Birds, Butterflies and History* (1983), pp 10–12; *DBB*, S. D. Chapman, 'Nathan Meyer Rothschild, 1st Lord Rothschild of Tring, Hertfordshire', vol 4, pp 946–53; Letters of Sir Carl Meyer (unpublished), 11 March 1886; *DBB*, P. Thane, 'Sir Ernest Joseph Cassel', vol 1, pp 604–14; Pat Thane, 'Financiers and the British State: The Case of Sir Ernest Cassel' in *Business History* (1986); Meyer, 10 Aug 1886.

19. *Independent*, 15 Dec 1990; David Kynaston, *Cazenove & Co.* (1991), pp 76–7; Wedd Durlacher brochure (*c*.1984).

20. H. Panmure Gordon, *The Land of the Almighty Dollar* (1892), p 4; *DBB*, David Kynaston, 'Harry Panmure Gordon', vol 2, pp 611–13; Frank H. H. King, *The History of the Hongkong and Shanghai Banking Corporation*, vol I (Cambridge, 1987), p 545; Vivian Nickalls, *Oars, Wars and Horses* (1932), p 81.

21. *The Economist*, 22 Nov 1884.

22. SE, Ms 14,609, vol 2, 11 May 1904; *City Press*, 4 March 1885.

23. Charles Duguid, *The Story of the Stock Exchange* (1901), p 303; this and the next paragraph are almost entirely taken from G. Duckworth Atkin (ed), *House Scraps* (1887), pp 12–17.

24. W. A. Morgan (ed), *The Stock Exchange Christmas Annual, 1925–6* (1925), pp 64–7.

CHAPTER TEN

1. McLean, 27 June 1884; John Stephen Flynn, *Sir Robert N. Fowler* (1893), pp 315–16; *City Press*, 3 April 1886.

2. Youssef Cassis, 'Bankers in English Society in the Late Nineteenth Century' in *Economic History Review* (1985), p 211; David Kynaston, *The Chancellor of the Exchequer* (Lavenham, 1980), p 130; R. F. Foster, *Lord Randolph Churchill* (1981), p 277; Hamilton, Add Mss 48,649, 21 Aug 1888, 48,642, 4 Dec 1885, 48,647, 31 Aug 1887, 48,650, 18 April 1889.

3. Andrew Porter, 'Which City? What Empire? Shipping, Government, and the Limits of Co-operation, 1870–1914' in R. V. Turrell and J. J. Van-Helten (eds), *The City and the Empire* (Collected Seminar Papers no 35, Institute of Commonwealth Studies, University of London, 1985), p 61.

4. Cassis, 'Bankers', p 227.

5. Significant contributions to the debate include: W. D. Rubinstein, 'Wealth, Elites and the Class Structure of Modern Britain' in *Past and Present* (1977); Geoffrey Ingham, *Capitalism Divided: The City and Industry in British Social Development* (Basingstoke, 1984); José Harris and Pat Thane, 'British and European Bankers, 1880–1914: An "Aristocratic Bourgeoisie"?' in Pat Thane, Geoffrey Crossick and Roderick Floud (eds), *The Power of the Past* (Cambridge, 1984); M. Lisle-Williams, 'Beyond the Market: The Survival of Family Capitalism in the English Merchant Banks' in *British Journal of Sociology* (1984); Cassis, 'Bankers'; S. D. Chapman, 'Aristocracy and Meritocracy in Merchant Banking' in *British Journal of Sociology* (1986); P. J. Cain and A. G. Hopkins, 'Gentlemanly Capitalism and British Expansion Overseas: I. The Old Colonial System, 1688–1850' in *Economic History Review* (1986); P. J. Cain and A. G. Hopkins, 'Gentlemanly Capitalism and British Expansion Overseas: II. New Imperialism, 1850–1945' in *Economic History Review* (1987); Perry Anderson, 'The Figures of Descent' in *New Left Review* (Jan/Feb 1987); Youssef Cassis, 'Merchant Bankers and City Aristocracy' in *British Journal of Sociology* (1988); S. D. Chapman, 'Reply to Youssef Cassis' in *British Journal of Sociology* (1988); M. J. Daunton, '"Gentlemanly Capitalism" and British Industry, 1820–1914' in *Past and Present* (1989); Porter, '"Gentlemanly Capitalism" and Empire'; H. L. Malchow, *Gentlemen Capitalists: The Social and Political World of the Victorian Businessman* (1991); W. D. Rubinstein, *Capitalism, Culture, and Decline in Britain, 1750–1990* (1993); P. J. Cain and A. G. Hopkins, *British Imperialism* (2 vols, 1993).

6. Daunton, '"Gentlemanly Capitalism"', p 119.

7. E. C. Grenville Murray, *Side-Lights on English Society* (1881), vol II, pp 163–4; David Cannadine, *The Decline and Fall of the British Aristocracy* (1990), pp 406–20.

8. Dudley W. R. Bahlman (ed), *The Diary of Sir Edward Walter Hamilton, 1880–1885* (Oxford, 1972), vol II, p 880; Roger Fulford, *Glyn's, 1753–1953* (1953) p 198; *Hamilton*, vol II, p 839; Hamilton, Add Mss 48,644, 27 May 1886, 48,649, 16 July 1888.

9. W. D. Rubinstein, 'The Victorian Middle Classes: Wealth, Occupation and Geography' in *Economic History Review* (1977).

10. *Statist*, 31 March 1894–21 July 1894, 21 Nov 1896.

11. Youssef Cassis, *Les Banquiers de la City a l'époque Edouardienne* (Geneva, 1984), pp 242–5, 121–9.

12. Cassis, *Banquiers*, pp 265–8; Clive Trebilcock, *Phoenix Assurance and the Development of British Insurance*, vol I (Cambridge, 1985), p 702; *DBB*, P. Thane, 'Sir Ernest Joseph Cassel', vol I, pp 604–14; Stanley Chapman, *The Rise of Merchant Banking* (1984), p 153; M. J. Daunton, 'Inheritance and Succession in the City of London in the Nineteenth Century' in *Business History* (1988), p 279.

13. R. G. G. Price, *A History of Punch* (1957), pp 91–2; *Hamilton*, vol II, p 899; Harris and Thane, 'British and European Bankers', p 226.

14. Hamilton, Add Mss 48,645, 12 Dec 1886, 48,649, 21 Aug 1888; Fulford, p 208.

15. Hamilton, Add Ms 48,651, 17 Oct 1889; S. J. Diaper, 'The History of Kleinwort, Sons & Co. in Merchant Banking, 1855–1961' (Nottingham PhD, 1983), pp 66–70; Richard Roberts, *Schroders: Merchants & Bankers* (1992), p 113; Chapman, 'Aristocracy and Meritocracy'; A. C. Howe, 'From "Old Corruption" to "New Probity": The Bank of England and its Directors in the Age of Reform' in *Financial History Review* (1994); RAL, RFamC/21, 17 Sept 1869.

16. *The Economist*, 21 May 1887; *Statist*, 2 March 1889; the role of the City is examined in S. D. Chapman, 'Rhodes and the City of London: Another View of Imperialism' in

Historical Journal (1985), Charles Harvey and Jon Press, 'The City and International Mining, 1870–1914' in *Business History* (1990); *The Economist*, 4 Feb 1888; Max Karo, *City Milestones and Memories* (1962), p 3.

17. Robert V. Kubicek, *Economic Imperialism in Theory and Practice: The Case of South African Gold Mining Finance, 1886–1914* (Durham, NC, 1979), pp 87–90.

18. Colin Newbury, 'The Origins and Function of the London Diamond Syndicate, 1889–1914' in *Business History* (1987); Robert Vicat Turrell, '"Finance . . . The Governor of the Imperial Engine": Hobson and the Case of Rothschild and Rhodes' in Rob Turrell (ed), *The City and the Empire* (Collected Seminar Papers no. 36, Institute of Commonwealth Studies, University of London, 1986), p 88.

19. Philip Ziegler, *The Sixth Great Power: Barings, 1762–1929* (1988), pp 199–201, gives a full account of the Guinness episode; Hamilton, Add Ms 48,645, 23 Oct 1886, 27 Oct 1886; G. Duckworth Atkin (ed), *House Scraps* (1887), p 123.

20. Hamilton, Add Ms 48,645, 23 Oct 1886; Ziegler, pp 201–2; *Bankers' Magazine* (June 1888), p 609.

21. Youssef Cassis, 'The Emergence of a New Financial Institution: Investment Trusts in Britain, 1870–1939' in J. J. van Helten and Y. Cassis (eds), *Capitalism in a Mature Economy: Financial Institutions, Capital Exports and British Industry, 1870–1939* (Aldershot, 1990), pp 140–1; Fulford, p 163; A. R. Hall, *The London Capital Market and Australia, 1870–1914* (Canberra, 1963), p 55; Stanley D. Chapman, 'Venture Capital and Financial Organisation: London and South Africa in the Nineteenth Century' in Stuart Jones (ed), *Banking and Business in South Africa* (1988).

22. Frank Harris, *My Life and Loves* (1966 Corgi edn), p 518; Morgan Grenfell records (LMA), Ms 21,799, fo 79.

23. Letters of Sir Carl Meyer (unpublished), 25 Jan 1890; Hamilton, Add Ms 48,652, 16 Feb 1890.

24. Hamilton, Add Ms 48,647, 7 Jan 1888; RBS, GM/7, 11 Jan 1888; Hamilton, Add Ms 48,647, 18 Jan 1888.

25. *The Economist*, 17 March 1888; Hamilton, Add Ms 48,649, 18 Oct 1888.

26. Hamilton, Add Ms 48,650, 16 Jan 1889–13 Feb 1889; S. R. B. Smith, 'British Nationalism, Imperialism and the City of London, 1880–1900' (London PhD, 1985), p 147.

27. Charles Duguid, *The Story of the Stock Exchange* (1901), p 315; SE, Ms 14,600, vol 57, 13 Jan 1890; *Rialto*, 4 Oct 1890.

28. M. C. Reed, *A History of James Capel and Co.* (1975), p 68; *Bankers' Magazine* (Oct 1890), p 1638; *Blackwood's Edinburgh Magazine* (Dec 1894), p 786.

CHAPTER ELEVEN

1. Rathbone, IX.8.12, 15 Oct 1889.

2. *Statist*, 1 Dec 1888; *Bankers' Magazine* (June 1888), p 609.

3. Helpful accounts of the Baring crisis include: Sir John Clapham, *The Bank of England: A History* (Cambridge, 1944), vol II, pp 326–39; L. S. Pressnell, 'Gold Reserves, Banking Reserves, and the Baring Crisis of 1890' in C. R. Whittlesey and J. S. G. Wilson (eds), *Essays in Money and Banking* (Oxford, 1968), pp 192–207; Philip Ziegler, *The Sixth Great Power: Barings, 1762–1929* (1988), pp 235–66; John Orbell, 'When Croesus Stumbled and the City Shook' in *Independent on Sunday*, 4 Nov 1990.

4. Hamilton, Add Ms 48,654, 8 Oct 1890; Arthur D. Elliot, *The Life of George Joachim Goschen, First Viscount Goschen* (1911), vol II, p 169; Bertram Wodehouse Currie, *Recollections, Letters and Journals* (Roehampton, 1901), vol I, p 90.

5. Imperial Ottoman Bank records (LMA), Ms 23,993, vol 2, 24 Oct 1890.

6. BoE, G15/191, f.176, G15/189, f.15A.

7. Pressnell, p 191; Hamilton, Add Ms 48,654, 8 Jan 1891; BB, HC3.52.8; Pressnell, p 169.

8. Pressnell, p 169; Hamilton, Add Ms, 48,653, 9 Aug 1890; BoE, G15/192, f.176; Elliot, vol II, pp 170–1; Hamilton, Add Ms 48,654, 10 Nov 1890.

9. Elliot, vol II, pp 171–2.

10. Ziegler, pp 247–8; Hamilton, Add Ms 48,654, 12 Nov 1890; BoE, G15/192, f.183.

11. BoE, G15/192, f.177; Clapham, vol II, pp 330–1.

12. BoE, G15/192, f.179, G15/189, f.15A.

13. Currie, vol I, pp 92–3; Hamilton, Add Ms 48,654, 15 Nov 1890.

14. BoE, Gi 5/189.

15. *Financial Times*, 15 Nov 1890; Stanley D. Chapman, *Raphael Bicentenary, 1787–1987* (1987), p 31; RAL, Ti 5/44; Hamilton, Add Ms 48,654, 16 Nov 1890; RAL, XI/109/127.

16. *Financial Times*, 17 Nov 1890; Maurice Brett (ed), *Journals and Letters of Reginald Viscount Esher* (1934), vol I, p 145; Gibbs, Ms 11,040, vol I, 19 Nov 1890; George Chandler, *Four Centuries of Banking*, vol I (1964), pp 333–4.

17. Ziegler, pp 251–2, 265; *Punch*, 8 Nov 1890.

18. Norman and Jeanne Mackenzie (eds), *The Diary of Beatrice Webb*, vol 1 (1982), p 349; BoE, G15/189, f.29A; R. S. Sayers, *Lloyds Bank in the History of English Banking* (Oxford, 1957), pp 213–14.

CHAPTER TWELVE

1. P. Villars, *London and its Environs: A Picturesque Survey of the Metropolis and the Suburbs* (1888), pp 49–50; H. G. de Fraine, *Servant of this House* (1960), pp 128–9; *Rialto*, 10 Sept 1892 (cuffs); Villars, p 7; Hurford Janes, *de Zoete & Gorton: A History* (?1963), pp 39, 47.

2. *Building News*, 6 Sept 1889; Harold P. Clunn, *The Face of London: The Record of a Century's Changes and Development* (1932), p 37; George and Pamela Cleaver, *The Union Discount: A Centenary Album* (1985), p 30; W. J. Loftie, *London City* (1891), pp 279–80.

3. De Fraine, p 9; Alfred Wells, 'Fifty Years in a Lawyer's Office' (unpublished, c/o Freshfields), p 13; Villars, pp 7–8; Wells, p 12; Sir Francis Oppenheimer, *Stranger Within* (1960), p 64.

4. Stanley Jackson, *The Sassoons* (1968), p 84; diary of Edward Clodd (family papers), 1 July 1890.

5. Ranald C. Michie, *The City of London: Continuity and Change, 1850–1990* (1992), p 14; de Fraine, p 130.

6. Youssef Cassis, *City Bankers, 1890–1914* (Cambridge, 1994), pp 5–6.

7. Michie, *City*, pp 16–17.

8. Michie, *City*, p 34.

9. Michie, *City*, p 39.

10. James Salmon, *Ten Years' Growth of the City of London* (1891), p 101; Edgar Jones, *Accountancy and the British Economy, 1840–1980* (1981), p 43.

11. Laurie Dennett, *Slaughter and May: A Century in the City* (Cambridge, 1989), pp 1–37, 56–70, 86.

12. D. E. W. Gibb, *Lloyd's of London: A Study in Individualism* (1957), pp 152, 157.

13. Andrew Brown, *Cuthbert Heath* (Newton Abbot, 1980), pp 61–2.

14. Brown, *Heath*, pp 61–2; *DBB*, Oliver M. Westall, 'Cuthbert Eden Heath', vol 3, pp 136–41; S. D. Chapman, 'A History of Insurance Broking' in Roderick Clews (ed), *A Textbook of Insurance Broking* (2nd edn, 1987), p 8.

15. Most of this paragraph is derived from R. S. Sayers, *The Bank of England, 1891–1944*

(Cambridge, 1976), vol 1, p 8, Ranald C. Michie, 'The Myth of the Gold Standard: An Historian's Approach' in *Revue Internationale d'Histoire de la Banque* (1986), pp 177–9, and Tessa Ogden, 'An Analysis of Bank of England Discount and Advance Behaviour, 1870–1914' in James Foreman-Peck (ed), *New Perspectives on the Late Victorian Economy: Essays in Quantitative Economic History, 1860–1914* (Cambridge, 1990), p 333; Hamilton, Add Ms 48,654, 8 Jan 1891.

16. Hamilton, Add Ms 48,656, 19 Nov 1891; Welby Collection on Banking and Currency (London School of Economics), vol VII, fos 374–97; L. S. Pressnell, 'Gold Reserves, Banking Reserves, and the Baring Crisis of 1890' in C. R. Whittlesey and J. S. G. Wilson (eds), *Essays in Money and Banking in Honour of R. S. Sayers* (Oxford, 1968), p 213.

17. *JIB*, Dec 1891, p 620; Hamilton, Add Ms 48,655, 30 Jan 1891; Bertram Wodehouse Currie, *Recollections, Letters and Journals* (Roehampton, 1901), vol II, p 212.

18. *JIB*, Dec 1891, pp 622–39; Hamilton, Add Ms 48,656, 2 Dec 1891; *FT*, 3 Dec 1891; Welby Collection, vol VII, fo 419.

19. Hamilton, Add Mss 48,656, 18 Dec 1891, 48,657, 19 Dec 1891; Currie, vol II, p 216; Hamilton, Add Mss 48,615 A, 21 Dec 1891.

20. *BM*, Jan 1891, p 8, Feb 1891, pp 243–5; *JIB*, March 1892, pp 150–2; Hamilton, Add Ms 48,657, 24 Jan 1892; RBS, A4/4/18.

21. Pressnell, p 219; A. R. Holmes and Edwin Green, *Midland: 150 Years of Banking Business* (1986), p 99; Sir Albert Feavearyear, *The Pound Sterling: A History of English Money* (Oxford, 1963 edn), pp 330–1.

22. *BM*, March 1892, p 378; RBS, GM/7.

23. Marcello de Cecco, *Money and Empire: The International Gold Standard, 1890–1914* (Oxford, 1974), p 95. My emphasis on this rivalry owes much to de Cecco's pioneering analysis.

CHAPTER THIRTEEN

1. Norman Mackenzie (ed), *The Letters of Sidney and Beatrice Webb: Volume I, Apprenticeships, 1873–1892* (Cambridge, 1978), p 396.

2. For the fullest discussion of the controversy, see: E. H. H. Green, 'Rentiers Versus Producers? The Political Economy of the Bimetallic Controversy, *c.*1880–1898' in *English Historical Review* (July 1988); A. C. Howe, 'Bimetallism, *c.*1880–1898, a Controversy Re-opened?' in *English Historical Review* (April 1990); E. H. H. Green, 'The Bimetallic Controversy: Empiricism Belimed or the Case for the Issues' in *English Historical Review* (July 1990). See also P. J. Cain and A. G. Hopkins, *British Imperialism: Innovation and Expansion, 1688–1914* (1993), pp 151–3; Youssef Cassis, *City Bankers, 1890–1914* (Cambridge, 1994), pp 299–301.

3. Hamilton, Add Ms 48,657, 12 May 1892; *BM*, June 1892, p 889; Harcourt, Dep 166, fo 43; Hamilton, Add Ms 48,658, 20 Aug 1892; Harcourt, Dep 166, fo 46.

4. Hamilton, Add Ms 48,658, 31 Aug 1891; Welby Collection on Banking and Currency (London School of Economics), vol V, fo 18; Harcourt, Dep 166, fos 59, 87.

5. Gibbs, Ms 11,021, vol 25, 7 Oct 1891; Harcourt, Deps 221, fos 163, 40–2, 45–6.

6. Harcourt, Dep 387, fos 86–7.

7. Meyer, 27 Nov 1892; *BM*, Jan 1893, pp 38–40; Bertram Wodehouse Currie, *Recollections, Letters and Journals* (Roehampton, 1901), vol II, p 239; BSP, HBC 15, 1 Dec 1892.

8. Harcourt, Deps 167, fos 5–6, 11–14, 26 and 388, fo 57.

9. Welby Collection, vol V, fos 73–4; Harcourt, Dep 389, fo 23.

10. R. S. Sayers, *The Bank of England, 1891–1944* (Cambridge, 1976), vol 1, p 17.

11. Hamilton, Add Mss 48,615 B, 19 Sept 1893, 23 Sept 1893.

12. *BM*, Dec 1889, pp 1490–1, Dec 1893, p 807.

13. Hamilton, Add Ms 48,661, 12 Nov 1893.

14. Harcourt, Dep 170, fo 55.

15. *FT*, 3 Jan 1894.

16. In general, see: Anthony Howe, 'From "Old Corruption" to "New Probity": The Bank of England and its Directors in the Age of Reform' in *Financial History Review* (1994); Elizabeth Hennessy, 'The Governors, Directors and Management of the Bank of England' in Richard Roberts and David Kynaston (eds), *The Bank of England: Money, Power and Influence, 1694–1994* (Oxford, 1995).

17. Hamilton, Add Ms 48,654, 8 Jan 1891; Currie, vol II, p 278; Harcourt, Dep 170, fos 62–3; Bo Bramsen and Kathleen Wain, *The Hambros* (1979), pp 332–6; Hamilton, Add Ms 48,662, 25 Jan 1894.

18. BoE, G15/139; Bramsen and Wain, p 335.

19. *FN*, 6 Oct 1893.

20. *Rialto*, 3 Feb 1894; Harcourt, Dep 401, fos 35–6; *FT*, 5 March 1894.

21. *The Economist*, 22 Sept 1894.

22. *Investors' Chronicle*, 12 March 1949; Max Karo, *City Milestones and Memories* (1962), p 4; *FN*, 3 Feb 1920; Alan Jenkins, *The Stock Exchange Story* (1973), p 104; Robert V. Kubicek, 'The Randlords in 1895: A Reassessment' in *Journal of British Studies* (1972), p 99. Geoffrey Wheatcroft, *The Randlords* (1985) gives a convincing portrait of Barnato; *FN*, 12 Jan 1895.

23. *Citizen*, 16 March 1895.

24. *Evening News*, 20 March 1895; *FN*, 21–3 March 1895; SE, Ms 14,600, vol 63, 21–2 March 1895; Gibbs, Ms 11,040, vol 2, 22 March 1895; Charles Duguid, *The Story of the Stock Exchange* (1901), p 336.

25. Thomas J. Spinner, Jnr, *George Joachim Goschen: The Transformation of a Victorian Liberal* (Cambridge, 1973), pp 182–3; Hamilton, Add Ms 48,666, 14 Feb 1895; *City Times*, 16 Feb 1895.

26. *FT*, 4 April 1895; RBS, A9/3/3.

27. RBS, A9/3/3.

28. RBS, A9/3/3; Currie, vol I, pp 104–8; RBS, A9/3/3.

29. Harcourt, Dep 163, fos 79–83.

30. Harcourt, Dep 163, fos 84–98; RBS, A9/3/3.

31. *JIB*, Dec 1895, p 552; RBS, GM/180/24/13, GM/180/24/1.

32. In general re this loan, see: David McLean, 'The Foreign Office and the First Chinese Indemnity Loan, 1895' in *Historical Journal* (1973); Frank H. H. King, *The History of the Hongkong and Shanghai Banking Corporation* (vol II, Cambridge, 1988), pp 164–72.

33. PRO, FO 17/1253.

34. *FT*, 8–9 July 1895; Roberta Allbert Dayer, *Finance and Empire: Sir Charles Addis, 1861–1945* (1988), p 36.

35. Pat Thane, 'Financiers and the British State: The Case of Sir Ernest Cassel' in *Business History* (1986), pp 83–5.

36. *FT*, 3 July 1895; the two best biographical accounts are: Kurt Grunwald, '"Windsor-Cassel" – The Last Court Jew' in *Leo Baeck Institute, Year Book* (1969); *DBB*, P. Thane, 'Sir Ernest Joseph Cassel', vol 1, pp 604–14.

37. Anthony Allfrey, *Edward VII and his Jewish Court* (1991), p 137; S. Japhet, *Recollections from My Business Life* (1931), p 130.

38. *The Economist*, 17 Aug 1895.

39. J. W. McCarty, 'British Investment in Overseas Mining, 1880–1914' (Cambridge PhD, 1961), p 87; Robert V. Kubicek, *Economic Imperialism in Theory and Practice: The Case of South African Gold Mining Finance, 1886–1914* (Durham, NC, 1979), pp 121–2.

40. *City Recorder*, 31 Aug 1895.

41. *FT*, 3 Sept 1895; Kubicek, *Economic Imperialism*, p 122.

42. *The Economist*, 14 Sept 1895; Hamilton, Add Ms 48,667, 1 Oct 1895; *FT*, 4 Oct 1895; *Statist*, 12 Oct 1895; Kubicek, *Economic Imperialism*, p 68; *FT*, 19 Oct 1895; *The Economist*, 26 Oct 1895.

43. Hamilton, Add Ms 48,668, 7 Nov 1895; *The Times*, 8 Nov 1895.

44. Richard Meinertzhagen, *Diary of a Black Sheep* (1964), pp 217–19.

CHAPTER FOURTEEN

1. *Mammon*, 22 Nov 1893; *FN*, 23 Nov 1895.

2. *FT*, 15 Jan 1896; Robert V. Kubicek, *Economic Imperialism in Theory and Practice: The Case of South African Gold Mining Finance, 1886–1914* (Durham, NC, 1979), p 122, and 'The Randlords in 1895: A Reassessment' in *Journal of British Studies* (1972), pp 99–100; *FN*, 1 Aug 1896; *Citizen*, 22 Feb 1896.

3. Hamilton, Add Ms 48,669, 7 May 1896; R. R. Mabson, *The Statist's Mines of the Transvaal* (3rd edn, 1904), p 11; *FN*, 17 Oct 1896; *Citizen*, 3 Oct 1896 (Nickalls), 20 March 1897; Meyer, 16 June 1897.

4. *FT*, 15 Nov 1895; SSA, Ms 14,894, vol 5, 15–16 Nov 1895; *BM*, May 1895, pp 713–15.

5. BoE, G15/39. On the 'competitive' theme, see Sayers, vol 1, pp 17–22.

6. Esther Madeleine Ogden, 'The Development of the Role of the Bank of England as a Lender of Last Resort, 1870–1914' (London PhD, 1988), pp 376, 378; Midland, M 153/45.

7. *FT*, 10 June 1896; P. W. Matthews and A. W. Tuke, *History of Barclays Bank Limited* (1926), pp 8–9; *DBB*, P. E. Smart, 'Frederick Crauford Goodenough', vol 2, pp 603–6; *BM*, June 1896, p 819.

8. Midland, M 153/47/4.

9. Sayers, vol 1, p 18; BoE, G15/39; Sayers, vol 1, p 61.

10. Richard Meinertzhagen, *Diary of a Black Sheep* (1964), pp 311, 314.

11. *Statist*, 5 Sept 1896; L. E. Jones, *Georgian Afternoon* (1958), p 133.

12. Meinertzhagen, pp 328, 336–40.

13. C. L. Currie, *Bertram Wodehouse Currie: A Memorial* (1897), pp 8–9; Bertram Wodehouse Currie, *Recollections, Letters and Journals* (Roehampton, 1901), vol II, p 357; Hamilton, Add Ms 48,670, 30 Dec 1896; Roger Fulford, *Glyn's: 1753–1953* (1953), p 218.

14. *IR*, 24 June 1898.

15. Ruth Dudley Edwards, *The Pursuit of Reason: The Economist, 1843–1993* (1993), pp 403–4.

16. See Dilwyn Porter, '"A Trusted Guide of the Investing Public": Harry Marks and the *Financial News*, 1884–1916' in *Business History* (1986).

17. Jamie Camplin, *The Rise of the Plutocrats: Wealth and Power in Edwardian England* (1978), p 65; *The Times*, 28 July 1898.

18. *The Times*, 8 Nov 1898, 3 Nov 1898, 15 Nov 1898.

19. Hamilton, Add Ms 48,673, 18 Nov 1898; *National Review*, Dec 1898, pp 574–84.

20. Meyer, 6 Feb 1899, 25 Aug 1899, 28 Aug 1899; *FT*, 6 Sept 1899; Gibbs, Ms 11,040, vol 3, 26 Sept 1899.

21. Charles Duguid, *The Story of the Stock Exchange* (1901), p 384; *Citizen*, 14 Oct 1899.

22. G. K. Chesterton, *Autobiography* (1936), p 113; J. A. Hobson, *Imperialism: A Study* (1902), p 359.

23. P. J. Cain and A. G. Hopkins, *British Imperialism: Innovation and Expansion, 1688–1914* (1993), pp 373–4.

24. J. W. McCarty, 'British Investment in Overseas Mining, 1880–1914' (Cambridge PhD, 1961), p 91.

25. A helpful overview is Robert Vicat Turrell, "'Finance . . . The Governor of the Imperial Engine": Hobson and the Case of Rothschild and Rhodes' in Rob Turrell (ed), *The City and the Empire*, Volume 2 (Collected Seminar Papers no. 36, Institute of Commonwealth Studies, University of London, 1986), pp 85–6, part of a paper subsequently published in *Journal of Southern African Studies* (1987).

26. Both the quotations and the argument derive from Andrew Porter, 'The South African War (1899–1902): Context and Motive Reconsidered' in *Journal of African History* (1990).

27. Richard Davis, *The English Rothschilds* (1983), pp 217–19.

28. *JIB*, Dec 1899, pp 533–4, 538–9.

29. *BM*, Feb 1900, p 313; *JIB*, May 1900, pp 255, 258–9.

30. Midland, M 153/67/2; PRO, T 168/87; Hamilton, Add Ms 48,676, 26 Feb 1900.

31. Norman Mackenzie (ed), *The Letters of Sidney and Beatrice Webb: Volume II, Partnership, 1892–1912* (Cambridge, 1978), p 125.

32. PRO, T 168/87.

33. PRO, T 168/87; R. S. Sayers, *The Bank of England, 1891–1944* (Cambridge, 1976), vol I, p 16; Hamilton, Add Ms 48,676, 16 March 1900, 28 April 1900.

34. Heather Gilbert, *The End of the Road: The Life of Lord Mount Stephen, Volume 2, 1891–1921* (Aberdeen, 1977), p 181; *FT*, 21 May 1900.

35. BoE, G23/88; Hamilton, Add Ms 48,676, 24 July 1900.

36. Kathleen Burk, *Morgan Grenfell, 1838–1988: The Biography of a Merchant Bank* (Oxford, 1989), pp 115–18.

37. Hamilton, Add Ms 48,676, 2 Aug 1900.

38. *Statist*, 11 Aug 1900; Meyer, 7 Aug 1900; *FT*, 8 Aug 1900; Hamilton, Add Ms 48,676, 8 Aug 1900.

39. Milner, Dep 177, fos 155–6.

40. In general for the two 1901 war loans, see Burk, *Morgan Grenfell*, pp 118–21.

41. BB, 200241, 23 Jan 1901; Milner, Dep 214, fo 40; Hamilton, Add Mss 48,614, 6 Feb 1901.

42. Hamilton, Add Ms 48,677, 11 Feb 1901; *FT*, 13 Feb 1901.

43. Hamilton, Add Ms 48,678, 28 March–19 April 1901; PRO, T 168/89; BoE, G23/88; Midland, M 153/67/2.

44. *FT*, 23 April 1901; PRO, T 168/89.

45. Meyer, 5–6 May 1901.

46. Vincent P. Carosso, *Investment Banking in America: A History* (Cambridge, Mass., 1970), pp 110–11; Meyer, 8 May 1901.

47. *FT*, 10 May 1901; *FN*, 10 May 1901.

48. *BM*, June 1901, p 897; SE, Ms 14,600, vol 71, 23 May 1901; Kleinwort, Ms 22,033, vol 1, fo 90.

49. Anthony Allfrey, *Edward VII and his Jewish Court* (1991), p 195.

50. George R. Sims (ed), *Edwardian London* (1990 Village Press reprint of *Living London*), vol 1, pp 199–202.

51. Ranald Michie, 'Dunn, Fischer & Co. in the City of London, 1906–14' in *Business History* (1988), pp 195–6.

52. David Kynaston, *Cazenove & Co.* (1991), p 82.

53. S. J. Diaper, 'The History of Kleinwort, Sons & Co. in Merchant Banking, 1855–1961' (Nottingham PhD, 1983), p 368; Heseltine, Moss & Co. records (consulted at 3 Trump Street *c.*1980).

54. *Quarterly Review*, July 1912, p 94.

55. George and Pamela Cleaver, *The Union Discount: A Centenary Album* (1985), pp 42–5.

56. David Wainwright, *Government Broker: The Story of an Office and of Mullens & Co.*

(1990), p 54; Frank H. H. King, *The History of the Hongkong and Shanghai Banking Corporation* (vol 2, Cambridge, 1998), p 587; Richard Roberts, *Schroders: Merchants & Bankers* (1992) p 122; Diaper, p 356.

CHAPTER FIFTEEN

1. Milner, Deps 213, fo 161, 214, fo 45, 215, fo 60, 216, fo 36.
2. Richard Roberts, *Schroders: Merchants & Bankers* (1992), pp 122, 526.
3. Stanley Chapman, *The Rise of Merchant Banking* (1984), pp 169–81 gives a critical assessment of 'performance', including p 172 on the specific missed opportunities.
4. This thesis is propounded by Michael Lisle-Williams, 'Beyond the Market: The Survival of Family Capitalism in the English Merchant Banks' in *British Journal of Sociology* (1984).
5. Philip Ziegler, *The Sixth Great Power: Barings, 1762–1929* (1988), p 303; Chapman, *Merchant Banking*, p 88 on 'the mutual insurance system'.
6. This is the analysis at the core of Youssef Cassis, *City Bankers, 1890–1914* (Cambridge, 1994), including p 59 for a table showing merchant bank representation on the boards of joint-stock banks.
7. Chapman, *Merchant Banking*, p 62.
8. Richard Roberts, 'What's in a Name? Merchants, Merchant Bankers, Accepting Houses, Issuing Houses, Industrial Bankers and Investment Bankers' in *Business History* (1993), pp 19–31.
9. Morgan, Ms 21,795, vol 12, 8 Jan 1907; Roberts, 'Name', p 31.
10. Roberts, *Schroders*, p 151.
11. Ziegler, p 377; Roberts, *Schroders*, p 149.
12. Roberts, *Schroders*, p 115.
13. Roberts, *Schroders*, p 131.
14. These imponderables are brought out in Youssef Cassis, 'Merchant Bankers and City Aristocracy' in *British Journal of Sociology* (1988).
15. Milner, Dep 214, fo 42.
16. Morgan, Ms 21,800, vol 1, 1 Nov 1901 (related by Dawkins); Ziegler, p 285; Hamilton, Add Ms 48,683, 5 Sept 1905. Also see: Chapman, *Merchant Banking*, pp 22–5; *DBB*, S. D. Chapman, 'Nathan Meyer Rothschild, 1st Lord Rothschild of Tring, Hertfordshire', vol 4, pp 946–53.
17. Hamilton, Add Ms 48,680, 1 Oct 1902; Alfred Wagg, 'Autobiography' (unpublished typescript, *c.*1958, held by Schroders), p 13; Blanche E. C. Dugdale, *Arthur James Balfour* (1936), vol II, p 135; Hamilton, Add Ms 48,681, 25 Sept 1904.
18. Walter's life is sympathetically narrated in Miriam Rothschild, *Dear Lord Rothschild: Birds, Butterflies and History* (1983), including pp 220–2, 229–31 on the financial disaster.
19. John Vincent (ed), *The Crawford Papers: The Journals of David Lindsay Twenty-seventh Earl of Crawford and Tenth Earl of Balcarres 1871–1940 during the Years 1892 to 1940* (Manchester, 1984), p 105.
20. For fuller characterisations of Revelstoke, see: *DBB*, John Orbell, 'John Baring, 2nd Lord Revelstoke', vol 1, pp 164–7; Ziegler, pp 268–72.
21. Hamilton, Add Ms 48,678, 4 Oct 1901; Christopher Sykes, *Nancy: The Life of Lady Astor* (1972), p 103.
22. Ziegler, p 272.
23. Ziegler, p 281; BB, Deps 33.8, 11 Oct 1904.
24. This paragraph is largely based on Kathleen Burk, *Morgan Grenfell, 1838–1988: The Biography of a Merchant Bank* (Oxford, 1989), including pp 58–9 on Dawkins.

25. In general on Norman, see: Sir Henry Clay, *Lord Norman* (1957); Andrew Boyle, *Montagu Norman: A Biography* (1967); *DBB*, Michael Moss, 'Montagu Collet Norman, Lord Norman of St Clere', vol 4, pp 447–58.

26. Aytoun Ellis, *Heir of Adventure: The Story of Brown, Shipley & Co. Merchant Bankers, 1810–1960* (1960), pp 121–2.

27. Clay, p 65.

28. On the relative decline of Glyn Mills and Martins, see Roger Fulford, *Glyn's: 1753–1953* (1953), pp 220, 224-8; George Chandler, *Four Centuries of Banking*, vol 1 (1964), p 412; *JIB*, May 1903, pp 267–8.

29. Youssef Cassis, *La City de Londres, 1870–1914* (Paris, 1987), pp 29–30.

30. *FN*, 23 July 1901.

31. Youssef Cassis, 'Financial Elites in Three European Centres: London, Paris, Berlin, 1880s–1930s' in *Business History* (1991), p 55.

32. *BM*, March 1901, pp 423–7; *DBB*, Youssef Cassis, 'Sir Felix Otto Schuster', vol 5, pp 77–82.

33. Hamilton, Add Ms 48,679, 11 March 1902.

34. NW, 4905, Union Bank of London, 12 July 1902; *BM*, Feb 1905, p 233, March 1901, p 423.

CHAPTER SIXTEEN

1. Hamilton, Add Ms 48,679, 13 Feb 1902; *FT*, 21 March 1903.

2. The larger context to Chamberlain's campaign is lucidly outlined in Scott Newton and Dilwyn Porter, *Modernization Frustrated: The Politics of Industrial Decline in Britain Since 1900* (1988), pp 1–22.

3. Ruth Dudley Edwards, *The Pursuit of Reason: The Economist, 1843–1993* (1993), pp 452–3; *FN*, 18 May 1903; *FT*, 18 May 1903; Hamilton, Add Ms 48,681, 3–5 July 1903; Julian Amery, *Joseph Chamberlain and the Tariff Reform Campaign* (1969), p 301; *BM*, Sept 1903, p 405; *CCJ*, Aug 1903, p 179.

4. *FT*, 19 Sept 1903; *FT*, 9 Oct 1903.

5. *BM*, Jan 1904, pp 50–1; P. J. Cain and A. G. Hopkins, *British Imperialism: Innovation and Expansion, 1688–1914* (1993), p 220; Roland Quinault, 'Joseph Chamberlain: A Reassessment' in T. R. Gourvish and Alan O'Day (eds), *Later Victorian Britain, 1867-1900* (1988), pp 71–3; *JIB*, Dec 1904, p 534; *BM*, March 1904, p 380.

6. Stimulating discussions of the new dispositions include: Geoffrey Ingham, *Capitalism Divided? The City and Industry in British Social Development* (1984), pp 152–3, 159–62, 169; Newton and Porter, pp 22–9; E. H. H. Green, 'The Influence of the City over British Economic Policy, c.1880–1960' in Youssef Cassis (ed), *Finance and Financiers in European History, 1880–1960* (Cambridge, 1992), p 200; Cain and Hopkins, pp 214–24.

7. Beatrice Webb, *Our Partnership* (1948), p 269; W. J. Ashley, *The Tariff Problem* (1903), pp 112–13.

8. *BM*, Dec 1903, pp 696–8, March 1904, p 476.

9. *BM*, July 1920, p 43; *FT*, 21 June 1906; *BM*, March 1904, pp 381–2, 383.

10. Sir John Clapham, *The Bank of England: A History* (Cambridge, 1944), vol II, p 379.

11. Sayers, vol 1, pp 60–3.

12. *JIB*, Dec 1904, p 533; L. S. Pressnell, 'Gold Reserves, Banking Reserves, and the Baring Crisis of 1890' in C. R. Whittlesey and J. S. G. Wilson (eds), *Essays in Money and Banking in Honour of R. S. Sayers* (Oxford, 1968), p 224.

13. *FN*, 23 Jan 1904; *The Economist*, 5 March 1904; *DBB*, David T. A. Kynaston, 'Ferdinand Faithfull Begg', vol 1, pp 249–50; *City Punch Bowl*, 13 March 1897; *FN*, 16 March 1904; *The Economist*, 26 March 1904.

14. *The Economist*, 5 Nov 1904; *FN*, 6–8 Dec 1904.

15. D. T. A. Kynaston, 'The London Stock Exchange, 1870–1914: An Institutional History' (London PhD, 1983), pp 66, 73.

16. Kynaston, 'Stock Exchange', pp 61–3.

17. Kynaston, 'Stock Exchange', pp 63–4; *The Economist*, 26 Nov 1904, 6 May 1905; R. C. Michie, *The London and New York Stock Exchanges, 1850–1914* (1987), pp 81–2, offers a partial defence of the managers, mainly on the international side.

18. SE, Mss 19,297, vol 17, 3 Feb 1904, 17 Feb 1904, 14,608, vol 3, 17 April–23 July 1907, 14,601, vol 1, 5 Nov 1908–8 June 1909, 14,600, vol 89, 6 Nov 1911, 19.297, vol 17, 21 Sept 1904.

CHAPTER SEVENTEEN

1. BB, 200164, 9 June–9 Oct 1905, 100143, 14 Oct 1905, Dep 33.9, 17 Oct 1905.

2. BB, 200164, 22–31 Oct 1905, 100243, 7 Nov 1905.

3. Toshio Suzuki, *Japanese Government Loan Issues on the London Capital Market, 1870–1913* (1994), pp 117–27.

4. *FT*, 28–9 Nov 1905.

5. RAL, XI/130A/0, 1 Jan 1906.

6. BB, Dep 33.10, 13 Feb 1906; *The Economist*, 27 Jan 1906, 24 Feb 1906; Robert V. Kubicek, *Economic Imperialism in Theory and Practice: The Case of South African Gold Mining Finance, 1886–1914* (Durham, NC, 1979), p 78.

7. *IR*, 3 March 1906.

8. On this loan, see Philip Ziegler, *The Sixth Great Power: Barings, 1762–1929* (1988), pp 313–14.

9. BB, 200214, 11 May 1906.

10. *BM*, July 1906, pp 64–6.

11. Morgan, Ms 21,802, vol 11, 13 July 1906; RAL, XI/130A/0, 16 July 1906; BB, 200214, 20 July 1906; SSA, Ms 14,894, vol 16, 19 July 1906.

12. BB, Dep 33.10, 3 Aug 1906, 200214, 5 Sept 1906.

13. RAL, XI/130A/1, 16 Jan 1907; SSA, Ms 14,894, vol 17, 31 Jan 1907.

14. *FT*, 14–15 March 1907.

15. BB, 200216, 12 June 1907.

16. Sayers, vol 1, pp 57–9 is the best guide to the events between August and December 1907.

17. Grey, 202/3, 12 Oct 1907.

18. RAL, XI/130A/1, 23 Oct 1907.

19. *FT*, 29 Oct 1907; RAL, XI/130A/1, 29 Oct 1907; *FT*, 31 Oct–1 Nov 1907.

20. Sayers, vol 1, p 59; *FT*, 5 Nov 1907; RAL, XI/130A/1, 4 Nov 1907; *FT*, 6–7 Nov 1907.

21. Grey, 202/3, 7 Nov 1907; *FT*, 8 Nov 1907; RAL, XI/130A/1, 7 Nov 1907; *FT*, 8 Nov 1907.

22. Morgan, Ms 11,795, vol 13, 13 Nov 1907; *FT*, 16 Nov 1907; Grey, 202/3, 18 Nov 1907; SSA, Ms 14,894, vol 17, 18 Nov 1907; *FT*, 19 Nov 1907; Sayers, vol 1, p 59.

23. Grey, 102/3, 15 Nov 1907.

24. ND, Ms 18,211.

25. *Statist*, 20 Jan 1906.

26. *FT*, 15 Jan 1906.

27. *Investor's Monthly Manual*, Jan 1910, p 2.

Notes

CHAPTER EIGHTEEN

1. On Lloyd's in 1908, see: D. E. W. Gibb, *Lloyd's of London: A Study in Individualism* (1957), pp 190–6; Andrew Brown, *Cuthbert Heath* (Newton Abbot, 1980), pp 98–104. On the Stock Exchange and the capacity question in 1908/9, see two detailed, broadly compatible accounts: R. C. Michie, *The London and New York Stock Exchanges, 1850–1914* (1987), pp 14–27, 84–5; D. T. A. Kynaston, 'The London Stock Exchange, 1870–1914: An Institutional History' (London PhD, 1983), pp 236–62.

2. *The Times*, 17 July 1908.

3. *FT*, 5 Nov 1908; *The Times*, 6 Nov 1908.

4. SE, Ms 14,600, vol 81, 27 Jan–3 Feb 1908.

5. Kynaston, 'Stock Exchange', pp 256–7.

6. *Morning Post*, 23 March 1908; *FT*, 27 June 1908, 15 Jan 1908; BB, 200243, IX Dec 1905.

7. *IR*, 27 June 1908; Henry Lowenfeld, *All About Investment* (1909), p 241; Kynaston, 'Stock Exchange', p 220; SE, Ms 14,600, vol 83, 1 March 1909. On Williams, see also Donald Read, *The Power of News: The History of Reuter's, 1849–1989* (Oxford, 1992), pp 114–15.

8. Peter Clarke, 'Churchill's Economic Ideas, 1900–1930' in Robert Blake and Wm Roger Louis (eds), *Churchill* (Oxford, 1993), p 87.

9. *BM*, March 1908, p 454; LCC, Ms 16,647, 16 Dec 1908, 13 Jan 1909, 10 Feb 1909, 8 July 1909.

10. *JIB*, Dec 1909, pp 612–15.

11. Midland, Acc 150/1, 23 March 1909; *Statist*, 4 April 1908; R. P. T. Davenport-Hines, 'Lord Glendyne' in R. T. Appleyard and C. B. Schedvin (eds), *Australian Financiers: Biographical Essays* (Melbourne, 1988), p 194; *The Economist*, 18 April 1908.

12. RAL, XI/130A/3, 17 March 1909; *The Times*, 1 April 1909.

13. Kurt Grunwald, '"Windsor-Cassel" – The Last Court Jew' in *Leo Baeck Institute, Year Book* (1969), pp 149–50; Maurice V. Brett (ed), *Journals and Letters of Reginald, Viscount Esher* (1934), vol 2, p 295; Morgan, Ms 21,795, vol 14, 23 March 1909.

14. John Grigg, *The Young Lloyd George* (1973), p 202; RAL, XI/130A/3, 4 Jan 1909; *BM*, March 1909, p 462; Meyer, 27 April 1909.

15. *FN*, 30 April 1909; RAL, XI/130A/3, 3 May 1909; Grey, 202/5, 5 May 1909; RAL, XI/130A/3, 10 May 1909; Asquith Papers (Bodleian Library), Ms Asquith 12, fos 34-5; Alan Sykes, *Tariff Reform in British Politics, 1903–1913* (Oxford, 1979), p 186; John Buchan, *Francis and Riversdale Grenfell: A Memoir* (1920), p 138.

16. *FT*, 24 June 1909.

17. *FT*, 25 June 1909; RAL, XI/130A/3, 25 June 1909.

18. G. R. Searle, *Corruption in British Politics, 1895–1930* (Oxford, 1987), p 246 (Speyer); *DBB*, John P. Scott, 'John Wynford Philipps, 1st Viscount St Davids of Lydstep Haven', vol 4, p 666; Searle, p 148 (Kleinwort); José Harris and Pat Thane, 'British and European Bankers, 1880–1914: An "Aristocratic Bourgeoisie"?' in Pat Thane, Geoffrey Crossick and Roderick Floud (eds), *The Power of the Past: Essays for Eric Hobsbawm* (Cambridge, 1984), p 225; Morgan, Ms 21,795, vol 16, 30 Nov 1909.

19. *Hansard* (House of Lords), 22 Nov 1909, cols 795–9, 23 Nov 1909, cols 868–9, 29 Nov 1909, col 1153, 30 Nov 1909, col 1277.

20. RAL, XI/130A/3, 1 Dec 1909; *FN*, 6 Jan 1910.

21. Sykes, p 186.

22. The answer given here follows the persuasive analysis in P. J. Cain and A. G. Hopkins, *British Imperialism: Innovation and Expansion, 1688–1914* (1993), pp 220–1.

23. SE, Ms 14,600, vol 87, 28 Nov 1910; Richard Davis, *The English Rothschilds* (1983), p 240; *FN*, 12 Aug 1911; Roy Jenkins, *Asquith* (1964), pp 539–42.

CHAPTER NINETEEN

1. SSA, Ms 14,894, vol 20, 16 Aug 1911; *The Economist*, 19 Aug 1911; Foster & Braithwaite records, consulted *c.*1980 at 22 Austin Friars, letter by John Braithwaite dated 1 Sept 1911.

2. BS, Ms 20,111, vol 4, 4 Oct 1911, 21 Nov 1911; Sir Henry Clay, *Lord Norman* (1957), pp 56–8, 70.

3. The implications of the inquiry are explored in Paul M. Kennedy, 'Strategy versus Finance in Twentieth-Century Great Britain' in *International History Review* (1981).

4. PRO, CAB 16/18A.

5. *JIB*, Feb 1912, pp 50–83.

6. Duff Hart-Davis (ed), *End of an Era: Letters and Journals of Sir Alan Lascelles, 1887–1920* (1986), pp 109–20; H. Osborne O'Hagan, *Leaves from My Life* (1929), vol II, p 335; Baron E. B. d'Erlanger, *My English Souvenirs* (1978), p 268. Also on Bevan, see *DBB*, R. P. T. Davenport-Hines, 'Gerard Lee Bevan', vol 1, pp 321–4.

7. *Lascelles*, pp 122–3; *FN*, 16 April 1912.

8. *FN*, 17 April 1912; Ron Chernow, *The House of Morgan* (1990), p 146 (Smith); Jehanne Wake, *Kleinwort Benson: The History of Two Families in Banking* (Oxford, 1997), p 272; SE, Ms 19,297, vol 11, 8 May 1912; *FN*, 18–20 April 1912; *DBB*, Oliver M. Westall, 'Sir Edward Mortimer Mountain', vol 4, p 362; RAL, XI/130A/6, 16 April 1912; *Lascelles*, p 123.

9. *Lascelles*, p 125.

10. In general on the Marconi Scandal, see: Frances Donaldson, *The Marconi Scandal* (1962); G. R. Searle, *Corruption in British Politics, 1895–1930* (Oxford, 1987), pp 172–200; Bentley Brinkerhoff Gilbert, 'David Lloyd George and the Great Marconi Scandal' in *Historical Research* (1989).

11. Donaldson, p 21; Robert Speaight, *The Life of Hilaire Belloc* (1957), p 15.

12. RAL, XI/130A/7, 25 March 1913; *The Economist*, 3 May 1913.

13. *Select Committee on Marconi's Wireless Telegraph Company, Limited* (PP1913, VII), qq 3671–4425.

14. RAL, XI/130A/7, 10 April 1913.

15. SE, Mss 14,600, vols 92–3, 9 Oct–10 Nov 1913; *The Economist*, 15 Nov 1913.

16. *FN*, 6 June 1912; RAL, XI/130A/6, 2–3 Oct 1912; *The Economist*, 5 Oct 1912, 15 Feb 1913; SE, Ms 19,297, vol 22, 19 March 1913; *The Economist*, 27 Dec 1913.

17. MG, private letter book, no. 10, 18 Oct 1913.

18. Richard Roberts, *Schroders: Merchants & Bankers* (1992), pp 363–4.

19. On Norman in 1913, see: Sir Henry Clay, *Lord Norman* (1957), pp 71–5; Andrew Boyle, *Montagu Norman: A Biography* (1967), pp 90–5.

20. BS, Mss 20,111, vol 4, 23 Dec 1912, 4 April 1913, 20,120, vol 1, 12 Nov 1913; Clay, pp 72–3.

21. LCC, Ms 16,648, 7 May 1913.

22. LCC, Ms 16,648, 7 May 1913.

23. LCC, Ms 16,648, 11 June 1913, 18 June 1913.

24. On this background, see Marcello de Cecco, *Money and Empire: The International Gold Standard, 1890–1914* (Oxford, 1974), pp 70–5.

25. *Royal Commission on Indian Finance and Currency: Minutes of Evidence, Volume I* (PP1914, XIX), qq 3348, 3351, 3429, 3463, 3465–9.

26. *BM*, Sept 1913, p 318.

27. LCC, Ms 16,648, 12 Nov 1913.

28. *DBB*, R. P. T. Davenport-Hines, 'Walter Cunliffe, 1st Lord Cunliffe', vol 1, pp 861–5.

29. Morgan, Ms 21,795, vol 14, 10 Nov 1908; BoE, G15/111.

CHAPTER TWENTY

1. RAL, XI/130A/8, 29 June 1914; *FT*, 30 June 1914.

2. RAL, XI/130A/8, 14 July 1914; *FT*, 18 July 1914.

3. MG, private letter books, no. 12, 20 July 1914; *FT*, 21–2 July 1914; BB, Dep 33.15, 21 July 1914; *FT*, 23 July 1914; RAL, XI/130A/8, 22 July 1914.

4. Ellis T. Powell, *The Mechanism of the City* (1910), pp 1, 4; *The Economist*, 11 Jan 1913; Ranald C. Michie, *The City of London: Continuity and Change, 1850–1990* (1992), p 14.

5. Hartley Withers, *Stocks and Shares* (1910), pp 234–5; Georgiana Blakiston (ed), *Letters of Conrad Russell, 1897–1947* (1987), p 17.

6. For elaboration, see: Marcello de Cecco, *Money and Empire: The International Gold Standard, 1890–1914* (Oxford, 1974), pp 104–6; Richard Roberts, *Schroders: Merchants & Bankers* (1992), p 115; Michie, pp 42–4, 64–5, 73–5, 78–9, 109–10.

7. Helpful accounts of the 1914 financial crisis include: de Cecco, pp 141–70; 'Sir John Clapham's account', reproduced in Sayers, *Bank*, appendices, pp 31–45; Sayers, *Bank*, vol 1, pp 70–4; Teresa Seabourne, 'The Summer of 1914' in Forrest Capie and Geoffrey E. Wood (eds), *Financial Crises and the World Banking System* (1986).

8. RAL, XI/130A/8, 24 July 1914; MG, private letter books, no. 12, 24 July 1914; SSA, Ms 14,894, vol 24, 24 July 1914; *FT*, 25 July 1914; SSA, Ms 14,894, vol 24, 25 July 1914; BB, Dep 33.15, 7 Aug 1914; Heseltine, Powell & Co. records (LMA), Ms 23,267, vol 2, 26 July 1914.

9. *FT*, 27–8 July 1914; SSA, Ms 14,894, vol 24, 27 July 1914.

10. *FT*, 29 July 1914.

11. *FT*, 30 July 1914; BS, Ms 20,112, vol 16, 29 July 1914; SSA, Ms 14,894, vol 24, 29 July 1914.

12. *Pall Mall Gazette*, 29 July 1914; BB, Dep 33.15, 7 Aug 1914; de Cecco, pp 142–3; LCC, Ms 16,648, 29 July 1914.

13. *FT*, 31 July 1914; RAL, XI/130A/8, 30 July 1914; SE, Ms 14,600, vol 94, 30 July 1914.

14. SE, Ms 14,600, vol 94, 31 July 1914; SSA, Ms 14,894, vol 24, 31 July 1914; *FT*, 1 Aug 1914.

15. Gibbs, Ms 11,115, vol 2, 31 July 1914; RAL, XI/130A/8, 31 July 1914; Roberts, p 153, analyses the position facing some of the accepting houses; RAL, XI/130A/8, 31 July 1914.

16. Elizabeth Johnson (ed), *The Collected Writings of John Maynard Keynes: Volume XVI, Activities, 1914–1919* (1971), p 3; Ronald Knox, *Patrick Shaw-Stewart* (1920), p 99.

17. PRO, T 170/14.

18. BB, Dep 33.15, 7 Aug 1914; SSA, Ms 14,894, vol 24, 3 Aug 1914; MG, private letter books, no 12, 3 Aug 1914.

19. PRO, T 170/14.

20. SSA, Ms 14,894, vol 24, 4 Aug 1914; MG, private letter books, no 12, 4 Aug 1914 (reply to Huth Jackson); PRO, T 170/55.

21. D. E. Moggridge, *Maynard Keynes: An Economist's Biography* (1992), pp 238–9.

22. Semi-defences include Sayers, *Bank*, vol 1, pp 72–3; Seabourne, pp 96–101.

23. RAL, XI/130A/8, 30 July 1914; *War Memoirs of David Lloyd George, I* (1933), pp 111–12.

24. *FT*, 29 July 1914; *The History of The Times* (vol IV, part I, 1952), p 208; *Lloyd George*, p 65; Ruth Dudley Edwards, *The Pursuit of Reason: The Economist, 1843–1993* (1993), pp 537–8.

25. *Lloyd George*, pp 65–6; *FT*, 4 Aug 1914; RAL, XI/130A/8, 4 Aug 1914.

26. BB, Dep 33.15, 7 Aug 1914; Hartley Withers, *War and Lombard Street* (1915), p 1; Anthony Allfrey, *Edward VII and his Jewish Court* (1991), pp 267–8; Baron E. B. d'Erlanger, *My English Souvenirs* (1938), p 238; David Kynaston, *The Financial Times: A Centenary History* (1988), p 75.

CHAPTER TWENTY-ONE

1. ND, Ms 18,130, box 2, 20 Jan 1915.

2. Accounts of the crisis and its resolution include: Richard Roberts, *Schroders: Merchants & Bankers* (1992), pp 152–5; Sayers, pp 66–78; Teresa Seabourne, 'The Summer of 1914' in Forrest Capie and Geoffrey E. Wood (eds), *Financial Crises and the World Banking System* (1986).

3. *FT*, 14 Aug 1914.

4. Stephen McKenna, *Reginald McKenna, 1863–1943: A Memoir* (1948), p 235; *War Memoirs of David Lloyd George, I* (1933), p 111.

5. Cameron Hazlehurst, *Politicians at War* (1971), p 173.

6. The fullest treatment of this episode is in John Peters, 'The British Government and the City–Industry Divide: The Case of the 1914 Financial Crisis' in *Twentieth Century British History* (1993).

7. PRO, T 170/28, 26 Aug 1914, T 172/128, 9 Sept 1914; BoE, G 15/59, 25 Aug 1914.

8. PRO, T 170/56, 5 Aug 1914, T 170/57, 6 Aug 1914, T 170/28, 15 Aug 1914, T 172/162 (Grenfell); *Hansard*, 26 Aug 1914, col 71.

9. Addis, 14/175, 9 Aug 1914; BB, Dep 33.15, 14 Aug 1914.

10. *Economic Journal*, Sept 1914, p 484; Kathleen Burk, 'Money and Power: The Shift from Great Britain to the United States' in Youssef Cassis (ed), *Finance and Financiers in European History, 1880–1960* (Cambridge, 1992), p 362.

11. Sayers, pp 79, 81, for details.

12. Roberts, *Schroders*, p 160.

13. MG, private letter books, no 12, 7 Aug 1914; *Lord Riddell's War Diary, 1914–1918* (1933), p 72; Derek Wilson, *Rothschild* (1988), pp 329–30; records of Morgan, Grenfell & Co. (LMA), Ms 21,799, fo 79.

14. Kathleen Burk, 'A Merchant Bank at War: The House of Morgan, 1914–18' in P. L. Cottrell and D. E. Moggridge (eds), *Money and Power* (Basingstoke, 1988).

15. Philip Ziegler, *The Sixth Great Power: Barings, 1762–1929* (1988), pp 328–32; BB, 204071.

16. MG, letter book of E. C. Grenfell, 21 Jan 1915; *Riddell*, p 60; *War Memoirs of David Lloyd George, I*, p 114; *Riddell*, p 370.

17. *Riddell*, p 94; A. J. P. Taylor (ed), *Lloyd George: A Diary by Frances Stevenson* (1971), p 53.

18. John Ramsden (ed), *Real Old Tory Politics: The Political Diaries of Sir Robert Sanders, Lord Bayford, 1910–35* (1984), p 20; Robert Skidelsky, *John Maynard Keynes: Volume One, Hopes Betrayed, 1883–1910* (1983), p 306; Lady Cynthia Asquith, *Diaries, 1915–1918* (1968), p 457; J. A. Gere and John Sparrow (eds), *Geoffrey Madan's Notebooks* (1981), p 27; Lord Beaverbrook, *Politicians and the War, 1914–1916, Volume I* (1928), p 155. In general on McKenna, see also: Stephen McKenna, *Reginald McKenna, 1863–1943: A Memoir* (1948); *DBB*, Edwin Green, 'Reginald McKenna', vol 4, pp 33–7.

19. MG, Grenfell, 24 Aug 1915; Stephen McKenna, p 237; Kathleen Burk, *Morgan Grenfell, 1838–1988: The Biography of a Merchant Bank* (Oxford, 1989), p 130; MG, Grenfell, 14 Jan 1916; Beaverbrook, p 153.

20. Sayers, pp 89–91.

21. HSBC, 158/20, 29–30 Nov 1915, 3 Dec 1915, 8 Dec 1915.

22. Andrew Boyle, *Montagu Norman: A Biography* (1967), p 103; BS Ms 20,111, vol 4, 17 Sept 1917; Boyle, pp 104–5.

23. Strong Papers at Federal Reserve Bank of New York: Diary of European Visit, 1916.

24. Kenneth Moure, 'The Limits to Central Bank Co-operation, 1916–36' in *Contemporary European History* (1992), p 262.

25. BW box 10, 11 Feb 1915.

26. BB, Dep 33.16, 9 Feb 1915, Dep 33.18, 7 Sept 1917; Ranald Michie, 'Dunn, Fischer & Co. in the City of London, 1906–14' in *Business History* (1988), p 212; Edgar Jones, *True and Fair: A History of Price Waterhouse* (1995), p 110.

27. Sayers, p 616; BB, Dep 33.16, 11 June 1915; Frank H. H. King, *The History of the Hongkong and Shanghai Banking Corporation: Volume II* (Cambridge, 1988), p 598; BW, box 10, 12 May 1916, box 11, 11 April 1918.

28. Sir William Nott-Bower, *Fifty-Two Years a Policeman* (1926), pp 271–3; SSA, Ms 14,894, vol 27, 13 June 1917; MG, Grenfell, 19 June 1917.

29. Siegfried Sassoon, *Memoirs of an Infantry Officer* (1965, pbk), pp 207–8.

30. SSA, Ms 14,894, vol 27, 7 July 1917; Addis, 14/35, 7 July 1917; MG, Grenfell, 7 July 1917; BB, Dep 33.17, 11 July 1917.

31. BB, Dep 33.15, 7 Aug 1914; *FT*, 12 May 1915, *FN*, 8 May 1915; *FT*, 14 May 1915; Ronald Palin, *Rothschild Relish* (1970), pp 94–5.

32. Addis, 14/33, 25 Feb 1915, 14/34, 21 Sept 1916; Roberts, *Schroders*, pp 363–6; Morgan Grenfell, Ms 21,799, fo 108; Roberts, *Schroders*, p 156.

33. Sir Almeric Fitzroy, *Memoirs* (1925), vol II, p 569; *FT*, 21 May 1915; Kurt Grunwald, '"Windsor-Cassel" – The Last Court Jew' in *Leo Baeck Institute, Year Book* (1969), p 160; Jamie Camplin, *The Rise of the Plutocrats* (1978), p 290.

34. BoE, ADM 34/4, 30 May 1916, 6–7 June 1916, 27 June 1916.

35. BoE, ADM 34/4, 24 Oct 1916, 8 Nov 1916, 17–18 Nov 1916, 22 Nov 1916.

36. BoE, M 6/64, 10 Nov 1916, ADM 34/4, 29 Nov 1916; Skidelsky, *Keynes*, vol 1, p 335; *FT*, 12 Dec 1916; BoE, ADM 34/5, 12 Jan 1917; *FT*, 9 Jan 1917; *FN*, 12 Jan 1917; Robert C. Self (ed), *The Austen Chamberlain Diary Letters* (Cambridge, 1995), p 41.

37. MG, Grenfell, 30 June 1916; BB, 204071; Addis, 14/35, 29 March 1917; Sayers, pp 93–4.

38. BB, Dep 33.17, 30 May 1917.

39. Sayers, pp 99–109 gives the authoritative account of the quarrel.

40. Sayers, p 105; BoE, G 15/31, fos 34–42.

41. BoE, ADM 34/5, 12 Sept 1917, 10 Oct 1917, 18 Oct 1917; Morgan Grenfell, Ms 21, 799, fo 121; BoE, ADM 34/5, 20 Nov 1917, 12 Dec 1917.

42. BoE, ADM 34/6, 27 Feb 1918, 22 March 1918; Morgan Grenfell, Ms 21, 799, fos 121, 123.

43. Brand, file 12, 3 Oct 1918; BW, box 11, 5 Oct 1918.

CHAPTER TWENTY-TWO

1. R. P. T. Davenport-Hines, *Dudley Docker* (Cambridge, 1984), esp. chapters 5–7; Scott Newton and Dilwyn Porter, *Modernization Frustrated* (1988), chapter 2.

2. *Round Table*, Dec 1916, pp 52–6, 62–3; *Economic Journal*, Dec 1917, pp 518–19.

3. Sayers, pp 597, 628–31; Elizabeth Hennessy, 'The Governors, Directors and Management of the Bank of England' in Richard Roberts and David Kynaston (eds), *The Bank of England* (Oxford, 1995), pp 194–5.

4. BoE, G 15/31, fo 95c, G 15/111, fos 5, 7a, 11, 13, 21.

5. Elizabeth Johnson (ed), *The Collected Writings of John Maynard Keynes: Volume XVI* (1971), p 31.

6. *Daily Express*, 4 Feb 1918.

7. *The Times*, 17 July 1918.

8. *Edinburgh Review*, July 1918, pp 44, 48.

9. The classic account of the Cunliffe Report and all that derived from it remains D. E. Moggridge, *British Monetary Policy, 1924–1931: The Norman Conquest of $4.86* (Cambridge, 1972). See also, on the Cunliffe Report specifically: R. Boyce, 'Creating the

Myth of Consensus: Public Opinion and Britain's Return to the Gold Standard in 1925' in P. L. Cottrell and D. E. Moggridge (eds), *Money and Power* (Basingstoke, 1988), pp 174–5; Ross E. Catterall, 'Attitudes to and the Impact of British Monetary Policy in the 1920s' in *Revue internationale d'histoire de la banque* (1976), pp 29–42.

10. Sayers, Appendixes, p 58; *The Times*, 30 Oct 1918; Boyce, 'Creating the Myth', p 175.

11. *The Times*, 31 Oct 1918.

12. BB, 101951, 4 Jan 1918; Philip Ziegler, *The Sixth Great Power: Barings, 1762–1929* (1988), pp 323–4; *Economic Journal*, Dec 1918, p 386; Roberta Allbert Dayer, *Finance and Empire: Sir Charles Addis, 1861–1945* (Basingstoke, 1988), p 85; *Economic Journal*, Dec 1918, p 397.

13. *FT*, 9 May 1945; Addis, 14/36, 11 Nov 1918; Bryher, *The Heart to Artemis* (1963), p 190.

14. C. H. Rolph, *London Particulars* (Oxford, 1980), pp 151, 153, 197–9.

CHAPTER TWENTY-THREE

1. BB, Dep 33.20, 9 April 1919; Susan Howson, *Domestic Monetary Management in Britain, 1919–38* (Cambridge, 1975), p 10.

2. *Sunday Express*, 16 Jan 1930. In general on Hatry, see: P. S. Manley, 'Clarence Hatry' in *Abacus* (June 1976), pp 49–60; *DBB*, David Fanning, 'Clarence Charles Hatry', vol 3, pp 110–14; *Banker*, May 1985, pp 78–9.

3. SSA, Ms 14,894, vol 29, 29 Sept 1919; S. J. Diaper, 'The History of Kleinwort, Sons & Co. in Merchant Banking, 1855–1961' (Nottingham PhD, 1983), p 376.

4. BB, 101953, 12 Jan 1920; BoE, G 35/1, 16 Jan 1920; *Punch*, 14 Jan 1920.

5. RAL, XI/111/101, 29 April 1919.

6. The definitive overview is John Atkin, 'Official Regulation of British Overseas Investment, 1914–1931' in *Economic History Review* (1970).

7. Brand, file 12, 26 May 1919, file 16, 27 May 1919; BoE, ADM 34/9, 29 Jan 1920.

8. Roberta Allbert Dayer, *Finance and Empire: Sir Charles Addis, 1861–1945* (Basingstoke, 1988), chapter 5.

9. Brand, file 12, 10 June 1919; Addis, 14/36, 24 Dec 1918; BB, 200256, 7 Jan 1925.

10. Sir Charles Petrie, *The Life and Letters of the Right Hon. Sir Austen Chamberlain* (1940), vol 2, p 141.

11. Susan Howson, 'The Origins of Dear Money, 1919–20' in *Economic History Review* (1974), pp 90–2.

12. Brand, file 16, 6 Sept 1919; PRO, CAB 27/72, 25 Sept 1919.

13. SSA, Ms 14,894, vol 29, 6 Nov 1919; BoE, G 35/1, 6 Nov 1919; *FN*, 31 Jan 1920; *FT*, 24 July 1919; Robert C. Self (ed), *The Austen Chamberlain Diary Letters* (Cambridge, 1995), p 128; Sayers, p 117.

14. PRO, T 172/1384, 25 Feb 1920; Self, p 130. In general on the rise to 7 per cent and immediate aftermath, see Howson, 'Origins', pp 100 ff.

15. Robert Skidelsky, *John Maynard Keynes: Volume Two, The Economist as Saviour, 1920–1937* (1992), p 40; *FT*, 16 July 1920; BoE, G 3/176, 17 July 1920.

16. Addis, 14/37, 11 Nov 1919, 14/38, 1 April 1920, 14/40, 27 Sept 1922.

17. Émile Moreau, *The Golden Franc* (Boulder, Col., 1991), p 51; Marguerite Dupree (ed), *Lancashire and Whitehall: The Diary of Sir Raymond Streat* (1987), vol 1, pp 32–4; *Lloyds Bank Review*, April 1968, pp 33–4.

18. Addis, 14/38, 15 July 1920, 14/454, 28 Sept 1926. In general on the ending of the two-year tradition, see Sayers, pp 647–8.

19. BoE, G 35/3, 17 Feb 1922, 13 March 1922, 31 Oct 1922; Addis, 14/41, 5 Nov 1923, 20 Nov 1923; BoE, ADM 34/13, 20 Feb 1924.

20. L. E. Jones, *Georgian Afternoon* (1958), pp 122–3.

CHAPTER TWENTY-FOUR

1. Andrew Boyle, *Montagu Norman: A Biography* (1967), p 152.

2. BoE, G 3/179, 26 Feb 1923; Robert Skidelsky, *John Maynard Keynes: Volume Two, The Economist as Saviour, 1920–1937* (1992), pp 123–4.

3. Frank C. Costigliola, 'Anglo-American Financial Rivalry in the 1920s' in *Journal of Economic History* (1977), pp 911–34; Gyorgy Peteri, 'Central Bank Diplomacy: Montagu Norman and Central Europe's Monetary Reconstruction after World War I' in *Contemporary European History* (1992), pp 248–9.

4. Brand, file 37, 2 Jan 1923, 4 Jan 1923.

5. BoE, G 35/2, 5 Jan 1921; Sayers, Appendixes, p 75.

6. Peteri, pp 239–40; Costigliola, p 918.

7. BoE, ADM 34/13, mid-Jan 1924; Richard Roberts, *Schroders: Merchants & Bankers* (1992), pp 198–9.

8. Sayers, pp 174–83, gives a helpful overview of the City and Germany during these years.

9. BoE, G 30/9, 30 May 1922, G 35/4, 9 April 1923, G 3/180, 10 Jan 1924. On Schacht generally, see John Weitz, *Hitler's Banker: Hjalmar Horace Greeley Schacht* (New York, 1998).

10. BoE, G 3/180, 31 March 1924.

11. Peteri, pp 254–7; Costigliola, pp 919–20.

12. Peteri, p 254; BoE, G 3/180, 2 June 1924.

13. BB, Dep 33.22, 8 July 1924; BoE, ADM 34/13, 7 Oct 1924; Addis, 14/42, 1 Oct 1924; *FT*, 1 Oct 1924, 14 Oct 1924; BB, Dep 33.23, 14 Oct 1924; *FT*, 16 Oct 1924.

14. BoE, G 3/177, 14 May 1921; Brand, file 53, 30 May 1922; BoE, ADM 34/13, 9 July 1924.

15. *FT*, 4 July 1919; *FN*, 22 Jan 1934. Ranald C. Michie, *The London Stock Exchange: A History* (Oxford, 1999) provides the most authoritative survey of the interwar market.

16. Ranald C. Michie, *The City of London: Continuity and Change, 1850–1990* (Basingstoke, 1992), p 104; BoE, ADM 34/14, 15 April 1925, ADM 34/9, 2 Feb 1920; David Wainwright, *Government Broker: The Story of an Office and of Mullens & Co.* (1990), pp 64–5, 68.

17. *Sociological Review*, Jan 1924, p 10; Nicholas Davenport, *Memoirs of a City Radical* (1974), p 18.

18. BB, Dep 33.21, 18 Nov 1922; H. W. Phillips, *Modern Foreign Exchange and Foreign Banking* (1926), pp 54–5; Bolton; Roberts, *Schroders*, p 187; *FT*, 30 Jan 1920; Martin Gilbert, *Winston S. Churchill: Volume V Companion, Part I* (1979), p 28.

19. Phillips, pp 67-8, 70.

20. Phillips, p 69; BS, Mss 20,118, vol 2, 4 April 1921, 20,110, vol 1, 22 April 1921, 20,118, vol 2, 25 Aug 1922, 20,110, vol 1, 30 Aug 1922.

21. Roberts, *Schroders*, pp 371–2; W. Lionel Fraser, *All to the Good* (1963), p 71.

22. Wallis Hunt, *Heirs of Great Adventure* (1960), vol II, p 142.

23. Michie, *City*, p 45; P. J. Cain and A. G. Hopkins, *British Imperialism: Crisis and Deconstruction, 1914–1990* (1993), pp 31–48.

24. Cecil Beaton, *The Wandering Years: Diaries, 1922–1939* (1961), pp 59–60.

25. Significant versions and/or interpretations of this narrative include: Sidney Pollard (ed), *The Gold Standard and Employment Policies between the Wars* (1970); D. E. Moggridge,

British Monetary Policy, 1924–1931: The Norman Conquest of $4.86 (Cambridge, 1972), pp 37–97; Sayers, chapters 6 and 7; R. Boyce, 'Creating the Myth of Consensus: Public Opinion and Britain's Return to the Gold Standard in 1925' in P. L. Cottrell and D. E. Moggridge (eds), *Money and Power* (Basingstoke, 1988); Skidelsky, chapters 5 and 6.

26. BoE, G 3/176, 6 Sept 1920; Sir Henry Clay, *Lord Norman* (1957), p 292; BoE, ADM 34/9, 28 Dec 1920, ADM 34/10, 2 Nov 1921.

27. *Journal of the Institute of Bankers*, Dec 1921, pp 382–3, 386; Brand, file 62, 25 Aug 1922.

28. Philip Snowden, *An Autobiography* (1934), vol 1, pp 613–15; BoE, G 3/180, 30 Jan 1924; MG, private letter books, no. 30, 2 April 1924.

29. *The Times*, 22 Jan 1925, 30 Jan 1925, 7 Feb 1925, 28 Jan 1925; Martin Gilbert, *Winston S. Churchill, Volume V: 1922–1939* (1976), p 96.

30. Gilbert, *Churchill, Volume V*, p 96; Addis, 14/43, 23 Feb 1925; PRO, T 176/13, part 1, 4 March 1925.

31. *Daily Express*, 12 March 1925; PRO, T 176/13, part 1, 12 March 1925; Sir Frederick Leith-Ross, *Money Talks* (1968), p 95.

32. LCC, Ms 16,623, vol 2, 6 March 1925; *Round Table*, March 1925, pp 259, 262, 270.

33. P. J. Grigg, *Prejudice and Judgement* (1948), pp 182–4; Skidelsky, p 200; BoE, ADM 34/14, 19–20 March 1925; Addis, 14/43, 20 March 1925.

34. Gilbert, *Churchill, Volume V*, p 100.

35. *Nation and Athenaeum*, 21 Feb 1925.

36. *Economic Journal*, June 1924, p 169.

37. Stanley Chapman, *The Rise of Merchant Banking* (1984), p 179. However, in BoE, G 3/194, 14 Feb 1929, Cecil Lubbock puts the total of London acceptances at year-end 1928 significantly higher, at around £260m.

38. Andrew Boyle, *Montagu Norman: A Biography* (1967), p 197; Brand, file 78, 29 Oct 1926; BoE, G 3/187, 23 Oct 1926, ADM 34/15, 13 Dec 1926.

39. See Cain and Hopkins for a sophisticated treatment of City and Empire in the 1920s; BoE, G 3/191, 15 Feb 1927.

40. Philip Ziegler, *The Sixth Great Power: Barings, 1762–1929* (1988), p 351.

41. Roberts, *Schroders*, pp 194–6; BB, COF/05/14/4, 13–23 Sept 1926.

42. Stefanie Diaper, 'Merchant Banking in the Interwar Period: The Case of Kleinwort, Sons & Co.' in *Business History* (1986), p 64; John Orbell, *Baring Brothers & Co., Limited: A History to 1939* (1985), p 78; NW, 7442, 26 Feb 1929.

43. See especially Sayers, pp 183–9; Kenneth Mouré, 'The Limits to Central Bank Co-operation, 1916–36' in *Contemporary European History* (1992), pp 265–73.

44. BoE, G 3/184, 9 Sept 1925; Sayers, pp 337–41; BoE, G15/241, 30 April 1960 (Kershaw).

45. BoE, G 3/191, 23 June 1927.

46. BB, 202040, 18 Feb 1929; BoE, G 3/195, 7 March 1929; BB, 101961, 10 May 1928.

47. Ziegler, pp 356–7.

48. BB, 202040, 28 Feb 1929, 8 March 1929, 200729, 13 April 1929, 202040, 16 April 1929; Ziegler, p 357.

CHAPTER TWENTY-FIVE

1. BoE, G 1/511, 19 April 1929; Addis, 14/47, 19 April 1929; BB, 200427, 17 May 1929.

2. Sayers, pp 360–3, gives the background.

3. *FN*, 4 Oct 1929.

4. Peter Clarke, *The Keynesian Revolution in the Making, 1924–1936* (Oxford, 1988), p 104.

5. BB, 200427, 23 July 1929; Oliver M. Westall, *The Provincial Insurance Company, 1903–38* (Manchester, 1992), p 360.

6. *FN*, 24–5 Oct 1929, 29–30 Oct 1929.

7. Sidney Pollard, *The Development of the British Economy: 1914–1980* (1983 edn), p 141; Robert Skidelsky, *John Maynard Keynes: Volume Two, The Economist as Saviour, 1920–1937* (1992), p 343; MG, Ms 21,799, fo 136; BB, 200427, 13 Dec 1929; BS, Ms 20,110, vol 2, 30 Jan 1930; Frank Holt letter courtesy Davina Walter (granddaughter); David Kynaston, *Cazenove & Co.* (1991), p 125.

8. BoE, G 1/503, 16 Jan 1930, ADM 34/19, 25 Jan 1930.

9. Sayers, pp 352–9 covers fully the foundation and early years of BIS.

10. BoE, G 15/7, 4 Sept 1929, G 3/197, 6 March 1930, 13 March 1930.

11. In general on UDT and its impact, see Sue Bowden and Michael Collins, 'The Bank of England, Industrial Regeneration, and Hire Purchase between the Wars' in *Economic History Review* (1992). Stimulating discussions of the City and industrial rationalisation are to be found in: William H. Janeway, 'The Economic Policy of the Second Labour Government, 1929–31' (Cambridge PhD, 1971); Steven Tolliday, *Business, Banking and Politics: The Case of British Steel, 1918–1939* (Cambridge, Mass., 1987); J. H. Bamberg, 'The Rationalization of the British Cotton Industry in the Interwar Years' in *Textile History* (1988); W. R. Garside and J. I. Greaves, 'The Bank of England and Industrial Intervention in Interwar Britain' in *Financial History Review* (1996), 'Rationalisation and Britain's Industrial Malaise: The Interwar Years Revisited' in *Journal of European Economic History* (1997).

12. BoE, G 3/196, 8 Jan 1930; Sir Henry Clay, *Lord Norman* (1957), pp 326–7; Sayers, p 326; John Vincent (ed), *The Crawford Papers* (Manchester, 1984), p 531.

13. BoE, SMT 2/53, 22 Feb 1930, 5 March 1930.

14. For a fuller analysis of Norman's response, see: Sayers, pp 230–2; Susan Howson, *Domestic Monetary Management in Britain, 1919–38* (Cambridge, 1975), pp 66–7.

15. Roberta Allbert Dayer, *Finance and Empire: Sir Charles Addis, 1861–1945* (1988), p 211.

16. BoE, G 3/197, 1 Oct 1930; BB, 200534, 8 Oct 1930. In general on the growing sense of crisis during the closing months of 1930, see Philip Williamson, *National Crisis and National Government: British Politics, the Economy and Empire, 1926–1932* (Cambridge, 1992), pp 133–42.

17. BoE, SMT 9/1, 17 Nov 1930; MG, private letter books, no 42, 27 Dec 1930; W. N. Medlicott, *Contemporary England: 1914–1964* (1976, pbk), pp 245, 249.

18. BoE, ADM 34/20, 26 Jan 1931, G 3/198, 27 Jan 1931; Brand, file 30, 30 Jan 1931.

19. BoE, G 1/143, 2 Feb 1931.

20. Robert W. D. Boyce, *British Capitalism at the Crossroads, 1919–1932* (Cambridge, 1987), p 300.

21. On Booth and/or the early history of unit trusts, see: BoE, ADM 3 3/24; Duncan Crow, *A Man of Push and Go: The Life of George Macaulay Booth* (1965), especially pp 175–8; Sayers, pp 535–6; Adrienne Gleeson, *People and their Money: 50 Years of Private Investment* (1981); Karin Newman, *Financial Marketing and Communications* (Eastbourne, 1984), pp 143–6; *DBB*, R. P. T. Davenport-Hines, 'George Macaulay Booth', vol 1, pp 380–3.

22. SE, Ms 14,600, vol 125, 6 May 1931.

23. BoE, G 3/198, 30 April 1931, OV 32/7, 5 May 1931.

CHAPTER TWENTY-SIX

1. NW, 7387, 7 Jan 1931; BB, Dep 22.XXIII.

2. Accounts of the Credit Anstalt failure and its impact on the City include: Sir Henry Clay, *Lord Norman* (1957), pp 375–7; Sayers, p 389; Robert W. D. Boyce, *British Capitalism*

at the Crossroads, 1919–1932 (Cambridge, 1987), pp 332–3; Diane B. Kunz, *The Battle for Britain's Gold Standard in 1931* (Beckenham, 1987), pp 46–8, 54–9; P. L. Cottrell, 'The Bank of England in its International Setting, 1918–1972' in Richard Roberts and David Kynaston (eds), *The Bank of England* (Oxford, 1995), pp 95–9; Niall Ferguson, *The World's Banker: The History of the House of Rothschild* (1998), pp 993–5.

3. Cottrell, p 99; Kunz, p 48; NW, 7387, 28–9 May 1931; BoE, ADM 33/25.

4. For further detail about the City and Germany in 1931, including the Standstill Agreement, see: Clay, pp 377–83, 448; Sayers, pp 503–7; Stefanie Diaper, 'Merchant Banking in the Interwar Period: The Case of Kleinwort, Sons & Co.' in *Business History* (1986), pp 67–70; Boyce, pp 334–9, 344; Richard Roberts, *Schroders: Merchants & Bankers* (1992), pp 250–7; Jehanne Wake, *Kleinwort Benson: The History of Two Families in Banking* (Oxford, 1997), pp 242–4.

5. Sayers, p 503.

6. BoE, G 15/7, 18 June 1931, 25 June 1931, 29 June 1931.

7. The most authoritative assessment is Peter Clarke, *The Keynesian Revolution in the Making, 1924–1936* (Oxford, 1988), pp 212–18. See also, on the identification of the 'Macmillan gap', Richard Coopey and Donald Clarke, *3i: Fifty Years Investing in Industry* (Oxford, 1995), pp 9–10.

8. BoE, G 1/425, 23 June 1931, 26 June 1931; Brian Griffiths, 'Two Monetary Inquiries in Great Britain: Comments' in *Journal of Money, Credit, and Banking* (Feb 1974), pp III–12.

9. MC, pp 161–74; *FT*, 15 July 1931.

10. *FT*, 15–16 July 1931.

11. Wake, p 244; Roberts, *Schroders*, pp 265, 252–7; Laurie Dennett, *Slaughter and May: A Century in the City* (Cambridge, 1989), p 184.

12. There is an extensive literature on the 1931 financial crisis. Important contributions include: Clay, pp 383–98; Sayers, pp 391–415; Philip Williamson, 'A "Bankers Ramp"? Financiers and the British Political Crisis of August 1931' in *English Historical Review* (1984); Forrest Capie, Terence C. Mills and Geoffrey E. Wood, 'What Happened in 1931?' in Forrest Capie and Geoffrey E. Wood (eds), *Financial Crises and the World Banking System* (Basingstoke, 1986); Boyce, pp 339–66; Kunz, pp 77–146; Kathleen Burk, *Morgan Grenfell, 1838–1988: The Biography of a Merchant Bank* (Oxford, 1989), pp 148–56; Philip Williamson, *National Crisis and National Government: British Politics, the Economy and Empire, 1926–1932* (Cambridge, 1992), pp 259–424; William H. Janeway, 'The 1931 Sterling Crisis and the Independence of the Bank of England' in *Journal of Post Keynesian Economics* (winter 1995–6).

13. Kunz, p 77; Robert Skidelsky, *John Maynard Keynes: Volume Two, The Economist as Saviour, 1920–1937* (1992), p 393; Kenneth Young (ed), *The Diaries of Sir Robert Bruce Lockhart, Volume One* (1973), p 178.

14. Kunz, p 82.

15. Kunz, p 107.

16. BoE, ADM 34/20, 29 July 1931; PRO, 30/69/260 (MacDonald Papers), 30 July 1931.

17. Sayers, p 395; Williamson, 'Bankers Ramp', p 773.

18. Norman and Jeanne MacKenzie (eds), *The Diary of Beatrice Webb: Volume Four* (1985), p 249; Addis, 14/49, 5 Aug 1931; PRO, 30/69/260, 5 Aug 1931.

19. Sayers, p 395; BoE, G 3/210, 6 Aug 1931, ADM 34/20, 6 Aug 1931.

20. BB, 200489, 11 Aug 1931.

21. *FT*, 13 Aug 1931; Addis, 14/49, 12 Aug 1931; BoE, G 3/210, 12 Aug 1931, 17 Aug 1931.

22. *FT*, 21 Aug 1931; BoE, G 3/210, 20 Aug 1931; Burk, p 150.

23. Addis, 14/49, 22 Aug 1931.

24. *Beatrice Webb*, p 253; Burk, p 153.

25. Burk, p 152; *DBB*, John Orbell, 'Sir Edward Robert Peacock', vol 4, pp 565–6.

26. Addis, 14/49; *FT*, 25 Aug 1931.
27. Francis Williams, *Nothing So Strange* (1970), p 101.
28. Such is the persuasive interpretation put forward in Williamson, 'Bankers Ramp'.
29. Samuel Brittan, *The Treasury under the Tories, 1951–1964* (1964), p 308.
30. *FT*, 12 Sept 1931; *FN*, 14 Sept 1931.
31. *FN*, 16 Sept 1931, 18 Sept 1931; Williamson, *National Crisis*, pp 413–15.
32. Kunz, p 135; PRO, PREM 1/97, 18 Sept 1931, fos 84–9.
33. *FN*, 21 Sept 1931; *The Times*, 21 Sept 1931.
34. MG, private letter books, no. 44, 21 Sept 1931; Skidelsky, p 397; Anne Olivier Bell (ed), *The Diary of Virginia Woolf: Volume 4* (1982), p 45.
35. Sonia Orwell and Ian Angus (eds), *The Collected Essays, Journalism and Letters of George Orwell: Volume I* (1968), pp 93–4.

CHAPTER TWENTY-SEVEN

1. Robert Thorne, 'The Setting of St Paul's Cathedral in the Twentieth Century' in *London Journal* (1991), p 117; Richard Trench, *London Before the Blitz* (1989), pp 4, 12, 142, 163–4. Trench's book is a marvellously evocative – and poignant – reconstruction of the pre-1940 City.
2. *FN*, 22 Jan 1934.
3. John Summerson, 'The Victorian Rebuilding of the City of London' in *London Journal* (1977), p 164.
4. W. J. Reader and David Kynaston, *Phillips & Drew* (1998), pp 10–11.
5. BoE, E 1/5.
6. Ronald Palin, *Rothschild Relish* (1970), p 63; Michael Bonavia, *London Before I Forget* (Upton-upon-Severn, 1990), pp 108–9.
7. *CL*, p 60; Jehanne Wake, *Kleinwort Benson: The History of Two Families in Banking* (Oxford, 1997), pp 245–6, 296.
8. BB, 200606.
9. M. C. Reed, *A History of James Capel and Co.* (1975), p 83; Reader and Kynaston, p 11; Berry Ritchie, *A Touch of Class: The Story of Austin Reed* (1990), pp 67–73.
10. BB, 200463, 31 Dec 1924, 5–6 Jan 1925.
11. Stephen Graham, *Twice Round the London Clock* (1933), p 20.
12. George and Pamela Cleaver, *The Union Discount: A Centenary Album* (1985), pp 66–7.
13. Brian Johnston, *It's Been a Lot of Fun* (1974), pp 52–4.
14. In general on Eliot and the City, see: Lyndall Gordon, *Eliot's Early Years* (Oxford, 1977), pp 99–100; J. R. Winton, *Lloyds Bank, 1918–1969* (Oxford, 1982), pp 38–40; Robert Crawford, *The Savage and the City in the Work of T. S. Eliot* (Oxford, 1987), p 44.
15. Valerie Eliot (ed), *The Letters of T. S. Eliot: Volume I, 1898–1922* (1988), pp 164, 168; Michael Holroyd, *Lytton Strachey: Volume II* (1968), p 365; Eliot (ed), *Letters, Volume I*, p 597; Andy Bull, 'In Retreat from the Unreal City', *Independent*, 19 May 1990.
16. Herman Melville, *Israel Potter* (1925 edn), p 255; J. B. Priestley, *English Journey* (1934), p 204.
17. Charles F. G. Masterman, *England after War: A Study* (1922), pp 51–2.
18. The source for much of this and the next paragraph is Ranald C. Michie, *The London Stock Exchange: A History* (Oxford, 1999).
19. Financial News, *The Stock Exchange: An Investor's Guide* (1933), p 22.
20. F. E. Armstrong, *The Book of the Stock Exchange* (1934), p 167.
21. Michie.
22. Unpublished reminiscences of Sir George Aylwen; Donald Cobbett, *Before the Big Bang: Tales of the Old Stock Exchange* (Portsmouth, 1986), p 34; W. J. Reader, *A House in*

the City: A Study of the City and of the Stock Exchange Based on the Records of Foster & Braithwaite, 1825–1975 (1979), p 176.

23. Reader and Kynaston, pp 2–3; SE, Ms 14,600, vol 135, 19 Dec 1938; David Kynaston, *The City of London, Volume I* (1994), p 282.

24. E. W. Swanton, *Gubby Allen: Man of Cricket* (1985), pp 58, 142, 230.

25. *The Collected Writings of John Maynard Keynes: Volume VII* (1973), pp 155–6; JS, no 37.

26. David Wainwright, *Government Broker: The Story of an Office and of Mullens & Co.* (1990), pp 79, 68, 70, 72; JS, no. 21.

27. Wake, pp 231–6.

28. Lord Rothschild, *Meditations of a Broomstick* (1977), p 17. See Niall Ferguson, *The World's Banker: The History of the House of Rothschild* (1998), pp 995, 1009–13 on Rothschilds during these three decades.

29. Paul Morand, *A Frenchman's London* (1934), pp 282–4.

30. Hugh Barty-King, *The Baltic Exchange* (1977), pp 342–6.

31. *Banker*, Oct 1933, pp 29–30.

32. MG, private letter books, no. 31, 6 Feb 1925; Denzil Sebag-Montefiore, *The Story of Joseph Sebag and Co. and its Founding Families* (1996), p 42; BoE, ADM 34/21, 2 Feb 1932, G 3/199, 4 March 1932; L. E. Jones, *Georgian Afternoon* (1958), pp 142–3.

33. Reed, p 75; Roger Fulford, *Glyn's, 1753–1953* (1953), p 231; A. C. Pointon, *Wallace Brothers* (Oxford, 1974), p 66; HSBC, S. E. Franklin, 'Samuel Montagu & Co.: A Brief Account of the Development of the Firm' (1967 typescript).

34. Andrew Lycett, *Ian Fleming* (1995), p 60; MG, private letter books, no. 40, 14 Oct 1929.

35. Philip Ziegler, *The Sixth Great Power: Barings, 1762–1929* (1988), p 358; BB, 200832, 2 July 1937.

36. *DBB*, John Orbell, 'Sir Edward Robert Peacock', vol 4, pp 559–67; Daphne Pollen, *I Remember, I Remember* (1983), p 229.

37. Peter Brackfield, 'Singer & Friedlander Limited' in *Bowring Magazine* (summer 1978); personal information.

38. There have been three major biographical studies of Warburg: Jacques Attali, *A Man of Influence: Sir Siegmund Warburg, 1902–82* (1986); Ron Chernow, *The Warburgs: A Family Saga* (1993), esp chapters 28, 33, 38–40, 42–9; Niall Ferguson, *High Financier: The Lives and Time of Siegmund Warburg* (2010). See also *FT*, 20 Oct 1982.

39. Sebag-Montefiore, p 52; BoE, ADM 34/23, 15 Oct 1934. On Sir Albert Stern, see *The Times*, 3 Jan 1966; there is also much about his younger years in Shirley Nicholson, *An Edwardian Bachelor: Roy Sambourne, 1878–1946* (1999).

40. *FT*, 11 Jan 1945, 15 Jan 1945; Chernow, pp 548–9; *FT*, 23 Nov 1987; interview with Henry Grunfeld, 2 Feb 1989.

41. Morand, pp 286–7.

42. *DBB*, Geoffrey Jones and Margaret Ackrill, 'Sir Charles Lidbury', vol 3, pp 783–5; Marguerite Dupree (ed), *Lancashire and Whitehall: The Diary of Sir Raymond Streat* (1987), vol 1, pp 143–4.

CHAPTER TWENTY-EIGHT

1. Sambourne, 22 Sept 1931.

2. *Sunday Express*, 27 Sept 1931; John Maynard Keynes, *Essays in Persuasion* (1931), p ix.

3. Philip Williamson, *National Crisis and National Government: British Politics, the Economy and Empire, 1926–1932* (Cambridge, 1992), pp 497–9.

4. Tim Rooth, 'The Political Economy of Protectionism in Britain, 1919–32' in *Journal of European Economic History* (1992), pp 87–95.

5. *FT*, 5–6 Feb 1932.

6. For helpful accounts of the creation of the EEA, see: Susan Howson, *Domestic Monetary Management in Britain, 1919–38* (Cambridge, 1975), pp 80–8; Williamson, pp 499–500.

7. *Midland Bank Monthly Review*, Jan–Feb 1932, pp 1–4; *FT*, 21 April 1932.

8. On the creation of the sterling area, see: Sir Henry Clay, *Lord Norman* (1957), pp 409–11; P. J. Cain and A. G. Hopkins, *British Imperialism: Crisis and Deconstruction, 1914–1990* (1993), pp 79–82.

9. Sayers, p 449; Donald Moggridge (ed), *The Collected Writings of John Maynard Keynes: Volume XXIV* (1979), p 162.

10. On the coming of cheap money, see: Sayers, pp 423–5, 429–30; Howson, pp 86–8.

11. BoE, ADM 33/34, 11–12 Feb 1932.

12. *FT*, 1 July 1932.

13. Accounts include Clay, pp 457–8, Sayers, pp 430–47.

14. *FT*, 1 July 1932; BoE, ADM 34/21, 6–7 July 1932.

15. Robert Skidelsky, *John Maynard Keynes: Volume Two, The Economist as Saviour, 1920–1937* (1992), p 433. For an interpretation downplaying the conversion operation in terms of its impact on long-term interest rates, see Forrest H. Capie, Terry C. Mills and Geoffrey E. Wood, 'Debt Management and Interest Rates: The British Stock Conversion of 1932' in *Applied Economics* (1986).

16. These commentators include: Howson, pp 88–9; Shekhar Das, 'The 1932 War Loan Conversion Con Trick' in *Investors Chronicle*, 23 Dec 1983.

17. BoE, G 3/198, 16 Oct 1931; NW, 9338, 2 June 1932. In general on the renewal of Standstill in 1932, see Sayers, pp 507–8; Richard Roberts, *Schroders: Merchants & Bankers* (1992), p 257.

18. BB, 200551, 6 Sept 1932, 11 Nov 1932.

19. Andrew Boyle, *Montagu Norman: A Biography* (1967), p 280; Roberta Allbert Dayer, *Finance and Empire: Sir Charles Addis, 1861–1945* (Basingstoke, 1988), p 309.

20. BoE, ADM 34/21, 2 Feb 1932.

21. BoE, ADM 34/21, 12 July 1932, ADM 34/22, 22 March 1933, G 3/201, 8 March 1934.

22. William M. Clarke, *Inside the City* (1979), p 175; *Exco International News*, July 1989, Nov 1990.

23. Bolton; Richard Fry (ed), *A Banker's World* (1970), pp 20–1; Richard Roberts, 'The Bank of England and the City' in Richard Roberts and David Kynaston (eds), *The Bank of England* (Oxford, 1995), p 172.

24. BoE, ADM 25/11, 27 Oct 1936.

25. Sayers, p 470; Susan Howson, *Sterling's Managed Float: The Operations of the Exchange Equalisation Account, 1932–39* (Princeton, 1980), p 46.

26. *Futures*, Feb 1985, p 66.

27. BoE, G 3/202, 27 April 1935, 29 May 1935, ADM 23/1, 8 June 1935, ADM 34/24, 16–31 Dec 1935, G 3/203, 16 Jan 1936.

28. Sayers, p 470.

29. Michael Moran, 'Finance Capital and Pressure-Group Politics in Britain' in *British Journal of Political Science* (1981), pp 394–5.

30. Sayers, pp 556–7. In general on commercial banking in the 1930s, see: A. R. Holmes and Edwin Green, *Midland: 150 Years of Banking Business* (1986), chapter 8; Michael Collins, *Money and Banking in the UK: A History* (1988), chapters 7–8; Duncan M. Ross, 'Commercial banking in a market-oriented financial system: Britain Between the Wars' in *Economic History Review* (1996).

31. BoE, ADM 34/21, 21 Oct 1932; Elizabeth Hennessy, *A Domestic History of The Bank*

of England, 1930–1960 (Cambridge, 1992), p 196; Sayers, pp 250–2; Roger Fulford, *Glyn's, 1753–1953* (1953), p 234.

32. Stefanie Diaper, 'Merchant Banking in the Interwar Period: The Case of Kleinwort, Sons & Co.' in *Business History* (1986), pp 67–75.

33. Roberts, *Schroders*, pp 268–9.

34. Roberts, *Schroders*, pp 188, 267; Diaper, p 73.

35. BB, 200641, 23 Oct 1936; MG, miscellaneous business offered files, no. 20, 6 May 1937.

36. Duncan M. Ross, 'The Clearing Banks and Industry – New Perspectives on the Interwar Years' in J. J. van Helten and Y. Cassis (eds), *Capitalism in a Mature Economy* (Aldershot, 1990), p. 57.

37. BoE, ADM 34/22, 31 May 1933; Kathleen Burk, *Morgan Grenfell, 1838–1988: The Biography of a Merchant Bank* (Oxford, 1989), pp 162–6; Bo Bramsen and Kathleen Wain, *The Hambros* (1979), p 395.

38. *DBB*, Robert Murphy, 'Isidore Ostrer', vol 4, pp 492–6.

39. *DBB*, John King, 'Leo Frederic Alfred d'Erlanger', vol 2, pp 80–3.

40. On the Lewis story, see: E. R. Lewis, *No C.I.C.* (1956); *DBB*, Jenny Davenport, 'Sir Edward Roberts Lewis', vol 3, pp 757–60; T. Jackson, *The Origin and History of the Drayton Group* (Croydon, 1991), p 37.

41. NW, 7320, 14 Feb 1933.

CHAPTER TWENTY-NINE

1. In general on the City and Germany in the 1930s, important accounts include: Sayers, pp 507–12, 561–71; Neil Forbes, 'London Banks, the German Standstill Agreements, and "Economic Appeasement" in the 1930s' in *Economic History Review* (1987); Scott Newton, 'The "Anglo-German Connection" and the Political Economy of Appeasement' in *Diplomacy and Statecraft* (1991); Richard Roberts, *Schroders: Merchants & Bankers* (1992), pp 257–62; P. J. Cain and A. G. Hopkins, *British Imperialism: Crisis and Deconstruction, 1914–1990* (1993), pp 93–105; Scott Newton, *Profits of Peace: The Political Economy of Anglo-German Appeasement* (Oxford, 1996), chapters 3–5; *FN*, 31 Jan 1933; *FT*, 31 Jan 1933.

2. BB, 200631, 21 March 1933, 24 March 1933.

3. BB, 200641, 30 March 1933; *FT*, 18 May 1933, 19 June 1933.

4. HSBC, 30/194, 27 Feb 1933; Roberts, *Schroders*, pp 258–9.

5. BoE, G 3/200, 30 Sept 1933.

6. W. N. Medlicott, *Contemporary England: 1914–1964* (1976, pbk), p 338; BoE, G 3/201, 23 Jan 1934, 4 July 1934; Ron Chernow, *The House of Morgan* (New York, 1990), p 394; BoE, G 3/201, 23 Aug 1934.

7. *Banker*, Feb 1935, p 107; NW, 7410, 19–20 April 1934.

8. *FT*, 9–11 March 1936.

9. On the tantalising question of Germany and sterling, there is suggestive evidence in BoE, G 3/202, 20 Nov 1935' fo 652, 23 Dec 1935, fo 747, ADM 34/25, 10 Jan 1936, G 3/203, 15 Jan 1936, fo 50.

10. NW, 9339, 7 May 1936; Brand, file 191, c.18 May 1936.

11. BoE, G 3/203, 11 Aug 1936, 2 July 1936.

12. Records of Heseltine, Powell & Co. (LMA), Ms 23,267, vol 3, Aug 1936.

13. JM, semi-official correspondence, London to Hong Kong, 4 Sept 1936; Jehanne Wake, *Kleinwort Benson: The History of Two Families in Banking* (Oxford, 1997), pp 249–54; Sambourne, 7 Dec 1936, 9–10 Dec 1936; Kenneth Young (ed), *The Diaries of Sir Robert Bruce Lockhart, Volume One* (1973), p 361; BB, 200641, 11 Dec 1936.

14. Bolton.

15. Sayers, pp 567–8.

16. Bolton; BoE, G 3/204, 20 Oct 1937.

17. BoE, ADM 26/9, 25 Feb 1938, 28 Feb 1938; Addis, 14/56, 4 March 1938.

18. *The Private Diaries of Sydney Moseley* (1960), p 371; Andrew Boyle, *Montagu Norman: A Biography* (1967), p 304; BoE, G 3/205, 31 Aug 1938.

19. *FT*, 9 Sept 1938, 16 Sept 1938; *New Statesman*, 24 Sept 1938; Sambourne, 23 Sept 1938.

20. NW, 9341; Accepting Houses Committee, Ms 29,295, vol 4, 28 Sept 1938; *FT*, 29 Sept 1938.

21. *FT*, 29–30 Sept 1938; Sambourne, 29 Sept 1938; *FT*, 30 Sept 1938, 1 Oct 1938; Sambourne, 30 Sept 1938; Addis, 14/56, 30 Sept 1938.

22. *FT*, 3–4 Oct 1938; Chernow, p 434.

23. BoE, G 3/205, 7 Nov 1938, G 1/418; Ron Chernow, *The Warburgs: A Family Saga* (1993), p 484; Paul Einzig, *World Finance, 1938–1939* (1939), p 250; BoE, G 3/205,19 Dec 1938.

24. John Harvey (ed), *The Diplomatic Diaries of Oliver Harvey, 1937–1940* (1970), pp 234–5; *FN*, 4 Jan 1939; *Harvey*, p 235.

25. The main sources on Norman's visit to Berlin are: BoE, G 1/419, ADM 34/28, 4–6 Jan 1939; PRO, FO 371/23000 (Pinsent reports).

26. PRO, FO 371/23000, fos 245–6.

27. BoE, G 3/206, 18 March 1939.

28. Lloyds, HO/GM/Par.4, 31 Jan 1939.

29. *FT*, 16–17 March 1939, 20 March 1939.

30. *FT*, 1 April 1939.

31. Stefanie Diaper, 'Merchant Banking in the Interwar Period: The Case of Kleinwort, Sons & Co.' in *Business History* (1986), p 71; Forbes, p 585; Roberts, *Schroders*, p 262; NW, 7465, 10 May 1939.

32. Wake, p 255; Paul Einzig, *In the Centre of Things* (1960), pp 186–94.

33. *FT*, 5 June 1939, 31 July 1939.

34. On these preparations, see: Sayers, pp 567–71, 575–81; Elizabeth Hennessy, *A Domestic History of the Bank of England, 1930–1960* (Cambridge, 1992), pp 83–9.

35. BoE, G 1/505, 25 April 1939 (Holland-Martin memo); Bolton.

36. Bolton; BoE, ADM 33/6, 19 Sept 1974.

37. Lloyds, HO/GM/Par.4, 8 Aug 1939; *FT*, 17–18 Aug 1939.

38. Records of Gillett Brothers & Co. (LMA), Ms 24,693, 29 Aug 1939; *FT*, 30–1 Aug 1939; Sambourne, 31 Aug 1939; *FN*, 1 Sept 1939.

39. BoE, G 3/206, 2 Sept 1939; Boyle, p 309.

CHAPTER THIRTY

1. BoE, G 3/206, 8 Sept 1939.

2. Sayers, pp 584–8, gives an accessible overview. For the definitive treatment of war finance, however, see his *Financial Policy, 1939–45* (1956).

3. BoE, G 1/506, 11 Oct 1939, G 1/69, 2 Nov 1939.

4. D. E. Moggridge, *Maynard Keynes: An Economist's Biography* (1992), pp 629–34; BoE, G 1/15 (press cuttings).

5. For details of the Bank's implementation of exchange control during the war, see Sayers, pp 570–1; Elizabeth Hennessy, *A Domestic History of the Bank of England, 1930–1960* (Cambridge, 1992), pp 85–107.

6. Keith Middlemas, *Power, Competition and the State: Volume I* (Basingstoke, 1986), pp 26–7.

7. Hennessy, p 90; BoE, G 15/650, 'Notes by Lord O'Brien', *c*.1987.

8. BoE, G 1/69, 26 Sept 1939, G 15/7, fo 74, ADM 20/29, 28 Feb 1940.

9. Lloyds, HO/GM/Par.2, 6 March 1940.

10. BoE, ADM 20/29, 1 March 1940, 9 May 1940, 31 May 1940.

11. Richard Roberts, *Schroders: Merchants & Bankers* (1992), p 274.

12. BoE, ADM 34/28, 31 Oct 1939.

13. Brand, file 198, 3 May 1940; BoE, G 1/15, 9 May 1940.

14. Andrew Boyle, *Montagu Norman: A Biography* (1967), p 311; *FT*, 14 May 1940; Sambourne, 14 May 1940, 22 May 1940, 28 May 1940, 18 June 1940, 20 June 1940.

15. BB, 200820, 28 Aug 1940; Sambourne, 3 Sept 1940.

16. Richard Trench, *London Before the Blitz* (1989) is a wonderful account of the City during (as well as before) the Blitz.

17. Trench, p 24; BoE, G 1/510, 18 Sept 1940.

18. Charles Short, *Morgan Guaranty's London Heritage* (1986), p 57; J. R. Winton, *Lloyds Bank, 1918–1969* (Oxford, 1982), pp 100–1; Jehanne Wake, *Kleinwort Benson: The History of Two Families in Banking* (Oxford, 1997), pp 259, 317.

19. BoE, G 1/510, 24 Oct 1940; Hennessy, p 15.

20. Anne Olivier Bell (ed), *The Diary of Virginia Woolf: Volume 5* (1984), p 351; Trench, pp 122, 27; Leo Townsend, 'The Morning After' in Ian Norrie (ed), *The Book of the City* (1961), p 191.

21. *Evening News*, 30 Dec 1940; Philip Ziegler, *London at War, 1939–45* (1995), p 144; *Evening News*, 10 Jan 1941.

22. Ziegler, p 170; Nigel Nicolson (ed), *Harold Nicolson: Letters and Diaries, 1939–45* (1967), p 142.

23. Brand, file 197, 28 March 1941; Hennessy, pp 15–16.

24. Sonia Orwell and Ian Angus (eds), *The Collected Essays, Journalism and Letters of George Orwell: Volume II* (1968), pp 104–5.

25. Trench, p 28; Sambourne, 19 April 1941.

26. Duncan Crow, *A Man of Push and Go: The Life of George Macaulay Booth* (1965), p 167; BoE, ADM 34/30, 5 Sept 1941, 8 Sept 1941.

27. Paul Bareau, 'The Financial Institutions of the City of London' in The Institute of Bankers, *The City of London as a Centre of International Trade and Finance* (1961), p 16; Sayers, p 602.

28. BoE, G 15/7, 9 Oct 1941, G 1/510, 31 Oct 1941, ADM 34/30, 22 Dec 1941, ADM 20/31, 15 Jan 1942.

29. BoE, G 15/7, 18 March 1942, 16 Dec 1942; Marguerite Dupree (ed), *Lancashire and Whitehall: The Diary of Sir Raymond Streat* (Manchester, 1987), vol 2, p 144.

30. SE, Mss 14,600, vol 139, 16 March 1942, 20 April 1942, 11 May 1942, 14 May 1942, vol 140, 14 Dec 1942.

31. Wake, p 256; BB, 202800/22; Bo Bramsen and Kathleen Wain, *The Hambros* (1979), pp 399–400; BoE, ADM 34/32, 15 Oct 1943, ADM 20/31, 8 Dec 1942; Kathleen Burk, *Morgan Grenfell, 1838–1988: The Biography of a Merchant Bank* (Oxford, 1989), pp 168–9; BoE, ADM 34/32, 18 Jan 1943, 25 Jan 1943.

32. BoE, ADM 34/30, 2 Dec 1941, ADM 20/31, 15 April 1942, 8 Sept 1942, 10 Sept 1942, 2 Oct 1942, 23 Oct 1942, ADM 34/32, 21 Jan 1943, 10 Aug 1943; Roberts, p 277.

33. In general on the City and reconstruction, see: Middlemas, pp 73, 98; Scott Newton and Dilwyn Porter, *Modernisation Frustrated* (1988), pp 104–6.

34. Robert Rhodes James, *Bob Boothby: A Portrait* (1991), p 312; BoE, ADM 34/32, 23 Feb 1943.

35. BoE, ADM 14/8, 11 Dec 1941; John Kinross and Alan Butt-Philip, *ICFC, 1945–1961* (1985), pp 7, 9–10.

36. John Fforde, *The Bank of England and Public Policy, 1941–1958* (Cambridge, 1992), p 710; BoE, SMT 2/308, 7 Jan 1944. There are three principal accounts of the formation of ICFC: Kinross and Butt-Philip, pp 7–59; Fforde, pp 704–27; Richard Coopey and Donald Clarke, *3i: Fifty Years Investing in Industry* (Oxford, 1995), pp 13–28.

37. Kinross and Butt-Philip, p 22; Coopey and Clarke, p 22; Kinross and Butt-Philip, pp 314–23.

38. Important contributions to the literature include: L. S. Pressnell, *External Economic Policy Since the War, Volume I: The Post-War Financial Settlement* (1986), pp 66–261; Fforde, pp 31–73; Moggridge, pp 670–795; P. J. Cain and A. G. Hopkins, *British Imperialism: Crisis and Reconstruction, 1914–1990* (1993), pp 270–2; P. L. Cottrell, 'The Bank of England in its International Setting, 1918–1972' in Richard Roberts and David Kynaston (eds), *The Bank of England* (Oxford, 1995), pp 110–13.

39. Fforde, p 37; BoE, G 1/510, 3 Dec 1941; Fforde, p 44; Moggridge, p 676.

40. John Barnes and David Nicholson (eds), *The Empire at Bay: The Leo Amery Diaries, 1929–1945* (1988), p 762; Moggridge, p 734.

41. See the account in Sayers, pp 653–4.

42. BoE, ADM 34/33, 7 Jan 1944.

43. Boyle, pp 322–4; BoE, Norman to Stapley, 14 April 1944, G 15/241, 30 April 1960 (Kershaw).

44. *Thomas Sivewright Catto, Baron Catto of Cairncatto: A Personal Memoir and a Biographical Note* (Edinburgh, 1961), p 119; *Lancashire and Whitehall*, p 245; *Thomas Sivewright Catto*, p 118.

45. BoE, G 15/650, 'Notes by Lord O'Brien', c.1987; Philip Geddes, *Inside the Bank of England* (1987), p 36; Brand, file 198, 18 Jan 1945.

46. BoE, ADM 14/14, 15 June 1944; Brand, file 197, 12 Aug 1944.

47. *FT*, 24 July 1944; *FN*, 25 July 1944; Lloyds, HO/GM/Par.2, 9 Aug 1944, 25 Sept 1944; BoE, G 18/3, 20 March 1945.

48. BoE, SMT 2/308, 8 May 1944; Kinross and Butt-Philip, pp 324–7; John Kinross, *Fifty Years in the City* (1982), p 116.

49. Kinross and Butt-Philip, p 51.

50. *Committee on Company Law Amendment: Evidence and Minutes* (PP, 1944–5, Cmd 6659), qq 2512, 5306; Judy Slinn, *Linklaters & Paines: The First One Hundred and Fifty Years* (1987), pp 175–6.

51. W. T. C. King, *The Stock Exchange* (1947), pp 78–9; *FT*, 4 May 1945.

52. Judy Slinn, *A History of Freshfields* (1984), p 157; James Lees-Milne, *Prophesying Peace* (1984, pbk), p 174; W. Lionel Fraser, *All to the Good* (1963), p 172; BB, 200861, 23 March 1945; John Colville, *The Fringes of Power* (1985), p 597; *FT*, 9 May 1945.

53. BB, 200861, 28 July 1945; John Gale, *Clean Young Englishman* (1988, pbk), p 84.

CHAPTER THIRTY-ONE

1. Jehanne Wake, *Kleinwort Benson: The History of Two Families in Banking* (Oxford, 1997), pp 320–1; Richard Roberts, *Schroders: Merchants & Bankers* (1992), p 313; *Exco International News*, Nov 1990; London Trust Co. records at University College London Archives, E 4/2.

2. The best guide is Ranald C. Michie, *The City of London* (Basingstoke, 1992), pp 18–19, 35–8, 44–8.

3. Michie, *City*, pp 18, 35–6.

4. P. J. Cain and A. G. Hopkins, *British Imperialism: Crisis and Deconstruction, 1914–1990* (Harlow, 1993), pp 265–81.

5. Denzil Sebag-Montefiore, *The Story of Joseph Sebag and Co.* (1996), p 23.

6. Full biographical treatments of Warburg are: Jacques Attali, *A Man of Influence* (1986); Ron Chernow, *The Warburgs* (1993); Niall Ferguson, *High Financier* (2010).

7. *Institutional Investor*, March 1980, pp 50–2, 55, 193.

8. Attali, pp 168, 190.

9. BB, 200861, 2 Nov 1945.

10. Jim Tomlinson, 'Attlee's Inheritance and the Financial System' in *Financial History Review* (1994), pp 154–5; Nicholas Davenport, *Memoirs of a City Radical* (1974), pp 72, 149.

11. See Jim Tomlinson, 'The Attlee Government and the Balance of Payments, 1945–51' in *Twentieth Century British History* (1991), pp 59–60.

12. John Fforde, *The Bank of England and Public Policy, 1941–1958* (Cambridge, 1992), pp 73–87; L. S. Pressnell, *External Economic Policy since the War, Volume I* (1986), pp 262–341; D. E. Moggridge, *Maynard Keynes: An Economist's Biography* (1992), pp 796–820. *Fighting for Britain*, the final volume of Robert Skidelsky's biography of Keynes, appeared after I had completed my draft.

13. Moggridge, p 811; *FT*, 14 Dec 1945; Moggridge, p 821; John Barnes and David Nicholson (eds), *The Empire at Bay: The Leo Amery Diaries, 1929–1945* (1988), pp 1052–3.

14. Accounts of the Bank's nationalisation include: Fforde, pp 4–30; Elizabeth Hennessy, *A Domestic History of the Bank of England, 1930–1960* (Cambridge, 1992), pp 207–12; Ben Pimlott, *Hugh Dalton* (1985), pp 457–61; Susan Howson, *British Monetary Policy, 1945–51* (Oxford, 1993), pp 110–17.

15. BoE, G 15/7, 1 Aug 1945.

16. Philip Geddes, *Inside the Bank of England* (1987), p 37; BoE, G 18/2, 27 Feb 1946.

17. BB, 200884, 5 Jan 1947; *Banker*, June 1947, p 139.

18. On Dalton and cheap money, see: Hugh Dalton, *High Tide and After* (1962), pp 124–5, 160–7, 178–84, 230–1; Pimlott, pp 461–5; Fforde, pp 330–57; G. A. Fletcher, *The Discount Houses in London* (1976), pp 65–7; Howson, pp 121–52, 166–76, 193–9; Alec Cairncross, *Years of Recovery* (1985), pp 427–40.

19. Pimlott, p 462; BB, 200861, 15 May 1946.

20. Dalton, pp 162–6.

21. *The Economist*, 19 Oct 1946; David Kynaston, *The Financial Times* (1988), p 177; *Banker*, Nov 1946, pp 67–71.

22. BB, 200884, 13 Feb 1947, 5 March 1947; *Banker*, June 1957, p 380.

23. *Banker*, April 1947, pp 1–2; Kynaston, *Financial Times*, p 177; James Lees-Milne, *Caves of Ice* (1984, pbk), p 189; Dalton, p 184; Fforde, p 359.

24. Pimlott, p 521; BB, 200884, 30 Nov 1947.

25. On credit policy in 1948–9, see: Fforde, pp 359–70; Howson, pp 223–38; Alec Cairncross, 'Prelude to Radcliffe' in *Rivista Di Storia Economica* (1987), pp 2–8.

26. Alec Cairncross (ed), *The Robert Hall Diaries, 1947–53* (1989), p 38.

27. BoE, G 3/100, 8 Dec 1948; Fforde, pp 367–8.

28. *Hall*, p 84.

29. BoE, G 3/100, 8–10 Dec 1948, G 1/514, 14 Feb 1953; Pimlott, p 557; *Banker*, April 1949, p xxi.

30. Fforde, pp 170–219, tells the story.

31. Fforde, pp 213, 181; *Institutional Investor*, March 1980, p 210.

32. Kynaston, *Financial Times*, p 230; Fforde, pp 304–12.

33. On monetary policy during the final year of the Labour government, see: Fforde, pp 380–94; Howson, pp 288–98.

34. Philip M. Williams (ed), *The Diary of Hugh Gaitskell, 1945–1956* (1983), p 227.

35. Read, Hurst-Brown & Co., *Monthly Letter*, 4 Oct 1951; SE, Ms 14,600A, vol 9, 22 Oct 1951; BoE, G 1/71, 22 Oct 1951; Kynaston, *Financial Times*, p 211.

Notes

CHAPTER THIRTY-TWO

1. BoE, G 1/71, Nov 1951 (Maguire), 22 Oct 1951.

2. Ranald C. Michie, *The City of London* (Basingstoke, 1992), p 26.

3. For a helpful long-run perspective on the City in the 1950s, see Richard Roberts, 'The City of London as a Financial Centre in the Era of the Depression, the Second World War and Post-war Official Controls' in Richard Roberts (ed), *Global Financial Centres* (Aldershot, 1994), pp 13–25.

4. Michie, *City*, pp 35–8, 54–5, 94, 164–9.

5. Jacques Attali, *A Man of Influence* (1986), p 201; Ron Chernow, *The House of Morgan* (New York, 1990), p 515.

6. For overviews of the clearing banks and their policies in the 1950s, see: Duncan M. Ross, 'British Monetary Policy and the Banking System in the 1950s' in *Business and Economic History* (1992); Francesca Carnevali and Leslie Hannah, 'The Effects of Banking Cartels and Credit Rationing on U.K. Industrial Structure and Economic Performance since World War Two' in Michael D. Bordo and Richard Sylla, *Anglo-American Financial Systems* (Burr Ridge, Ill., 1995).

7. Anthony Sampson, *The Money Lenders* (1981), p 121; Alex Danchev, *Oliver Franks* (Oxford, 1993), p 154.

8. A. W. Tuke and R. J. H. Gillman, *Barclays Bank Limited, 1926–1969* (1972), p 114.

9. The authoritative account of this episode is Kathleen Burk, *The First Privatisation* (1988). See also: John Fforde, *The Bank of England and Public Policy, 1941–1958* (Cambridge, 1992), pp 733–43; David Kynaston, *Cazenove & Co.* (1991), pp 209–11.

10. BoE, G 3/4, 1 Nov 1951.

11. BoE, G 3/6, 20 Nov 1953, G 3/7, 25 Feb 1954, G 3/111, 13 April 1954.

12. A helpful account is Richard Roberts, 'Regulatory Responses to the Rise of the Market for Corporate Control in Britain in the 1950s' in *Business History* (January 1992).

13. Charles Gordon, *The Two Tycoons* (1984), p 42; David Clutterbuck and Marion Devine, *Clore* (1987), p 69.

14. *Banker*, May 1954, p 241; BoE, G 3/7, 28 Sept 1954, 12 Nov 1954; *FT*, 1 Jan 1955.

15. Accounts of the monetary policy dramas of 1955 include: Fforde, pp 630–53; Alec Cairncross, 'Prelude to Radcliffe' in *Rivista Di Storia Economica* (1987), pp 14–18.

16. Fforde, pp 631–2; PRO, T 230/384, 9 March 1955; BoE, G 3/8, 1 April 1955, 7 April 1955.

17. Cairncross, 'Prelude', p 14; BoE, G 1/73, 18–19 April 1955; Alec Cairncross (ed), *The Robert Hall Diaries, 1954–61* (1991), p 33.

18. *FT*, 21–2 April 1955; Read, Hurst-Brown & Co., *Monthly Letter*, 12 May 1955.

19. PRO T 230/384, 9 Aug 1955.

20. BoE, G 3/8, 4 Nov 1955, 10 Nov 1955.

21. Macmillan, dep d. 26, 21 July 1956, fo 123.

22. BoE, G 3/115, 6 Jan 1956; Macmillan, dep d. 25, 12 Jan 1956, fos 11–12.

23. Macmillan, dep d. 26, 4 May 1956, fo 24, 4 July 1956, fos 94–5, dep d. 27, 24 July 1956, fo 4.

24. Generally on the Bank of England and the Suez Crisis, see Fforde, pp 549–64.

25. *FT*, 28 July 1956; JS, no. 7, p 6; BoE, LDMA 1/10, 2 Nov 1956.

26. *FT*, 15 Dec 1956; BoE, G 1/74, 20 Dec 1956.

27. PRO, T 171/478, 28 Dec 1956, 31 Dec 1956.

28. Richard Fry (ed), *A Banker's World* (1970), p 28.

29. Cairncross (ed), *Hall*, p 94.

30. BoE, G 3/115, 25 June 1956, G 3/116, 23 Nov 1956; Richard Roberts, *Schroders: Merchants & Bankers* (1992), p 349.

31. BoE, G 3/8, 12 Aug 1955, G 3/116, 16 Oct 1956, G 3/9, 7 Nov 1956.

32. The fullest scholarly account (including bringing out developments during the two years before 1957) is Catherine R. Schenk, 'The Origins of the Eurodollar Market in London: 1955–1963' in *Explorations in Economic History* (1998). See also Gary Burn, 'The State, the City and the Euromarkets' in *Review of International Political Economy* (summer 1999), pp 229–35.

33. Fry, p 28; Paul Einzig, *The Euro-Dollar System* (1964), p 35; *Euromoney*, June 1984, p 64.

34. George G. Blakey, *The Post-War History of the London Stock Market* (Didcot, 1994 pbk edn), pp 41–2.

35. An excellent account of the phenomenon is John Littlewood, *The Stock Market* (1998), pp 120–8.

36. W. J. Reader and David Kynaston, *Phillips & Drew* (1998), pp 62–3; Edward du Cann, *Two Lives* (Upton-upon-Severn, 1995), pp 60–5.

37. HSBC, 192.152, 1957/8.

38. SE, Ms 14,600A, vol 11, 11 May 1953; BoE, G 3/119, 12 May 1958, 23 May 1958; SE, Council, 13 Oct 1958.

39. Fforde, pp 670–1, 689–91; A. R. Holmes and Edwin Green, *Midland* (1986), p 226.

40. BoE, G 1/76, 27 June 1958.

41. Richard Spiegelberg, *The City* (1973), p 107; *FT*, 23 July 1958; Spiegelberg, p 106.

42. Holmes and Green, pp 222–30, cover his arrival and impact.

43. Holmes and Green, pp 224–5; BoE, G 1/77, 16–17 Oct 1958, G 3/120, 24 Oct 1958.

44. Fforde, pp 595–605.

45. Andrew Shonfield, *British Economic Policy Since the War* (1958), pp 153–9; BoE, G 3/119, 9 May 1958.

CHAPTER THIRTY-THREE

1. Accounts of the Aluminium War include: 'How Reynolds Brought off Its British Coup' in *Fortune*, June 1959, pp 112–15, 230, 235–40; Paul Ferris, *The City* (1960), pp 87–90; Lionel Fraser, *All to the Good* (1963), pp 236–41; William Davis, *Merger Mania* (1970), pp 32–7; Jacques Attali, *A Man of Influence* (1986), pp 210–16; George David Smith, *From Monopoly to Competition* (Cambridge, 1988), pp 322–6; Richard Roberts, 'Regulatory Responses to the Rise of the Market for Corporate Control in Britain in the 1950s' in *Business History* (Jan 1992), pp 192–3; John Fforde, *The Bank of England and Public Policy, 1941–1958* (Cambridge, 1992), pp 743–9; Ron Chernow, *The Warburgs* (1993), pp 647–53.

2. BoE, G 1/179, 26 Nov 1958.

3. Macmillan, dep d. 33, 2 Dec 1958, fo 114; BoE, G 1/179, 1–2 Dec 1958; PRO, CAB 129/95, C (58), 247, 3 Dec 1958; BoE, C 160/30, 2 Dec 1958, G 1/179, 9 Dec 1958.

4. *The Times*, 16 Dec 1958, 6 Dec 1958; *The Economist*, 10 Jan 1959; *The Times*, 20 Dec 1958.

5. BoE, G 1/179, 15 Dec 1958, 19 Dec 1958.

6. David Kynaston, *Cazenove & Co.* (1991), pp 235–6.

7. BoE, G 1/179, 22 Dec 1958; Macmillan, dep d. 34, 27 Dec 1958, fos 16–17.

8. BoE, C 160/130, 31 Dec 1958, G 1/179, 31 Dec 1958.

9. *London Evening Standard*, 1 Jan 1959.

10. BoE, G 1/179, 1 Jan 1959.

11. BoE, G 1/179, 2 Jan 1959; Roberts, p 192; BoE, G 1/179, 2 Dec 1958.

12. *Church Times*, 9 Jan 1959.

13. Macmillan, dep d. 34, 5 Jan 1959, fo 27, 7 Jan 1959, fo 32.

14. *The Times*, 12 Jan 1959; *FT*, 13 Jan 1959; BoE, G 3/12, 13 Jan 1959; *The Times*, 21 Jan 1959, 20 Jan 1959.
15. BoE, G 15/19; Attali, p 214; *CL*, p 154; *Institutional Investor*, March 1980, pp 193–4.
16. Edmund de Rothschild, *A Gilt-Edged Life* (1998), pp 182–3.
17. The best overall guide is Ranald C. Michie, *The City of London* (Basingstoke, 1992), chapter 2.
18. Michie, *City*, pp 17–18; Charles Gordon, *The Two Tycoons* (1984), p 153.
19. Records of Tribble, Pearson & Co. (LMA), Mss 18,223, box 2, 5 Feb 1953, box 1, 16 March 1954, box 2, 11 Oct 1955, box 3, 7 Jan 1957, box 2, 6 May 1958, 13 May 1958.
20. *The Times*, 24 Aug 1945.
21. C. H. Holden and W. G. Holford, 'The New Plan for the City of London' (July 1946), p 6; *The City of London: A Record of Destruction and Survival* (1951), pp 44–6, 231, 256. See also Gordon E. Cherry and Leith Penny, *Holford* (1986), and Richard Trench, *London Before the Blitz* (1989), pp 184–5, for an enthusiastic evaluation of the Holden/Holford plan.
22. SE, Council, 23 May 1955; Leslie Thomas, *In My Wildest Dreams* (1984), p 276.
23. Nikolaus Pevsner, *The Buildings of England: London 1: The Cities of London and Westminster* (1957), pp 199, 238, 103–5.
24. Judy Slinn, *Linklaters & Paines* (1987), p 212; *City Press*, 16 Jan 1959, 10 July 1959, 13 Nov 1959.
25. W. J. Reader and David Kynaston, *Phillips & Drew* (1998), pp 136–43.
26. M. C. Reed, *A History of James Capel and Co.* (1975), p 93; Ronald Palin, *Rothschild Relish* (1970), p 185; Reader and Kynaston, p 130; *The Times* (Tim Congdon), 8 July 1996.
27. Michael Burns, 'Reminiscences of a Stockbroker's Clerk, or Whatever Happened to Ross-Munro, Duff & Co.?' (private papers).

CHAPTER THIRTY-FOUR

1. Anthony Sampson, *Anatomy of Britain* (1962), p 351.
2. David Kynaston, *Cazenove & Co.* (1991), pp 178–243.
3. Andrew Lycett, *From Diamond Sculls to Golden Handcuffs: A History of Rowe & Pitman* (1998), pp 77–80; Kynaston, *Cazenove*, pp 248–9; *Independent*, 26 Oct 1996; Kynaston, *Cazenove*, p 249.
4. *Director*, Oct 1987, p 118; *CL*, p 78; *Stock Exchange Journal*, Nov 1957, p 46; JS, no. 13, p 15; John Gapper and Nicholas Denton, *All That Glitters* (1996), p 65; Paul Thompson, 'The Pyrrhic Victory of Gentlemanly Capitalism' in *Journal of Contemporary History* (1997), p 434.
5. Ranald C. Michie, *The London Stock Exchange* (Oxford, 1999), pp 393–4; *FT*, 15 Jan 1988 (John Colegrave letter), 24 Sept 1965; SE, Council, 13 Aug 1962, 22 July 1963.
6. JS, no. 14 (Angus Ashton), pp 7, 26, no. 34 (Norman Whetnall), pp 6–7, no. 3 (Gerald Lederman), p 7, no. 6 (Tony Jenkins), pp 11, 41–2, no. 9 (Brian Winterflood), p 15.
7. *FT*, 1 July 1960, 26 Sept 1961; Edmund de Rothschild, *A Gilt-Edged Life* (1998) pp 181–2, Richard Kellett, *The Merchant Banking Arena* (1967), pp 100–1; *Queen*, 2 Aug 1961. See also Kathleen Burk, *Morgan Grenfell, 1838–1988* (Oxford, 1989), pp 157, 189.
8. Hugh Thomas (ed), *The Establishment* (1959), pp 12–13; NLSC, C 409/133, p 33; Thompson, 'Pyrrhic Victory', p 296.
9. Victor Sandelson, 'The Confidence Trick' in Thomas (ed), *Establishment*, p 148.
10. Macmillan, dep d. 34, 17 Feb 1959, fo 94; Keith Middlemas, *Power, Competition and the State: Volume 1* (Basingstoke, 1986), p 384.
11. BoE, G 3/12, 29 May 1959, 19 June 1959, 24 July 1959, 29 July 1959.

12. In general about the takeovers controversy during 1959, see Richard Roberts, 'Regulatory Responses to the Rise of the Market for Corporate Control in Britain in the 1950s' in *Business History* (Jan 1992), pp 193–5.

13. BoE, G 3/12, 19 May 1959.

14. Discussions of the Radcliffe Report include: Brian Griffiths, 'Two Monetary Inquiries in Great Britain' in *Journal of Money, Credit and Banking* (Feb 1974); G. A. Fletcher, *The Discount Houses in London* (1976), pp 77–9; Alec Cairncross, 'The Bank of England' in Gianni Toniolo (ed), *Central Banks' Independence in Historical Perspective* (Berlin, 1988), pp 63–5.

15. *The Economist*, 22 Aug 1959; BoE, G 3/84, 17 Aug 1959.

16. For other discussions, see: Michael Moran, *The Politics of Banking* (Basingstoke, 1984), p 25; Robert Elgie and Helen Thompson, *The Politics of Central Banks* (1998), pp 57–8.

17. Generally on Bolton, see: Richard Fry (ed), A *Banker's World* (1970); *DBB*, R. P. T. Davenport-Hines, 'Sir George Lewis French Bolton', vol 1, pp 364–9. Bolton's papers are now lodged at the Bank of England Archives. He awaits a biographer.

18. PRO, PREM 11/3758, 19 Dec 1960; Fry, p 78.

19. On the Eurodollar market between 1959 and 1964, see (in addition to my chapter 32 references to Einzig, Schenk and Burn) Stefano Battilossi, 'Banking with Multinationals: British Clearing Banks and the Euro-Market Challenge, 1958–74' in Stefano Battilossi and Youssef Cassis (eds), *European Banks and the American Challenge, 1950s–1970s* (Oxford, 2001).

20. *The Times*, 24 Oct 1960; *Banker*, June 1961, pp 395–404.

21. Paul Einzig, *The Euro-Dollar System* (1964), p 8; *Banker*, June 1961, p 400.

22. Accounts of the origins and early years of the Eurobond market are to be found in: Ian Kerr, *A History of the Eurobond Market* (1984); Kathleen Burk (ed), 'Witness Seminar on the Origins and Early Development of the Eurobond Market' in *Contemporary European History* (1992); Peter Shearlock and William Ellington, *The Eurobond Diaries* (Brussels, 1994); Gary Burn, 'The State, the City and the Euromarkets' in *Review of International Political Economy* (Summer 1999).

23. Kerr, p 17; Shearlock and Ellington, pp 8–11.

24. Kerr, p 17; Jacques Attali, *A Man of Influence* (1986), pp 223–4.

25. BoE, C 160/154, 6 June 1962, 11 July 1962, G 3/96, 23 July 1962.

26. Attali, p 224; BoE, C 160/173.

27. Ian Fraser, *The High Road to England* (Wilby, 1999), pp 259–62, provides the fullest account of the Autostrade issue. See also: Burk, 'Witness Seminar', p 69; Richard Roberts, 'Birthday of the Bond that Carried London to the Top', *The Times*, 14 Jan 1993; Peter Spira, *Ladders and Snakes* (1997), pp 115–17.

28. *The Times*, 14 May 1963; *Banker*, June 1963, p 377.

29. *FT*, 2 July 1963.

30. Ron Chernow, *The House of Morgan* (1990), p 540; *Wall Street Journal*, 22 July 1963.

31. BoE, ADM 13/6, 23 Aug 1963, G 3/138, 27 Nov 1963.

32. For a helpful discussion, see Richard Sylla, 'US Banks and Europe: Strategy and Attitudes' in Battilossi and Cassis, *European Banks*.

33. Sir Fred Warner, *Japan and the City of London* (Oxford, 1988), p 16; *Banker*, June 1971, pp 631–3; Duncan M. Ross, 'Cooperation versus Competition: Consortia and Clubs in European Banking' in Battilossi and Cassis, *European Banks*.

34. *The Times*, 5 Feb 1963; BoE, ADM 13/6, 14 March 1963; *CL*, pp 94–5.

35. BoE, ADM 13/5, 25 Sept 1962, 5 Dec 1962; Milton Gilbert, *Quest for World Monetary Order* (New York, 1980), p 65.

36. BoE, LDMA 1/13, 1 Nov 1963; Cairncross, DC 106/10/3, 21 Nov 1963.

37. SE, Council, 2 Sept 1963; BoE, G 3/139, 20 Jan 1964; BB, 210085, 7 Feb 1964.
38. PRO, PREM 11/4772, 26 Feb 1964; Cairncross, DC 106/10/3, 3 March 1964; PRO, PREM 11/4771, 24 July 1964.
39. John Littlewood, *The Stock Market* (1998), p 118.
40. PRO, PREM 11/4777, 1–2 Oct 1964.
41. BoE, LDMA 1/14, 9 Oct 1964, G 3/242, 15 Oct 1964; *FT*, 6 Oct 1964.

CHAPTER THIRTY-FIVE

1. FRBNY, C 261 England, 19 Oct 1964; Barbara Castle, *The Castle Diaries, 1964–1970* (1984), p xiii; Michael Clarke, *Fallen Idols* (1981), pp 45–6; Stephen Fay, *Portrait of an Old Lady* (1987), p 100; David Kynaston, *The Financial Times* (1988), p 329. More generally on the widespread assumption (especially as fostered by the press) that strong pound = strong Britain, see David Blaazer, '"Devalued and Dejected Britons": The Pound in Public Discourse in the Mid 1960s' in *History Workshop* (spring 1999), pp 121–40. See also, for a useful outline of events (by Kathleen Burk) in the three years from autumn 1964 and a stimulating discussion, 'Symposium: 1967 Devaluation' in *Contemporary Record* (winter 1988), pp 44–53.
2. *Sunday Telegraph*, 15 Nov 1964; *FT*, 13 Nov 1964; BoE, G 1/260, 13 Nov 1964.
3. PRO, PREM 13/261, 24 Nov 1964; Harold Wilson, *The Labour Government, 1964–1970* (1971), p 36.
4. PRO, PREM 13/237, 21 Dec 1964; FRBNY, 'Contingency Planning Silver/Gold Market, 1964–1973' (microfilm – roll UN), 28 Dec 1964; PRO, PREM 13/237, 23 Dec 1964.
5. Kynaston, *Financial Times*, pp 323–4; *Sunday Telegraph*, 20 Dec 1964; *Sunday Times*, 20 Dec 1964.
6. BoE, G 1/260, 10 March 1965, LDMA 1/14, 26 March 1965.
7. BoE, LDMA 1/14, 9 April 1965; John Littlewood, *The Stock Market* (1998), pp 145–7.
8. *The Cecil King Diary, 1965–1970* (1972), p 27.
9. Kenneth O. Morgan, *Callaghan* (Oxford, 1997), p 226; *Banker*, Oct 1965, p 648.
10. BB, 210091, 24 Feb 1966.
11. James Callaghan, *Time and Chance* (1987), p 195; BoE, G 15/650, 'Notes by Lord O'Brien', *c*.1987; information from Christopher Fildes; Alec Cairncross, *The Wilson Years* (1997), p 134. For a helpful (if perhaps too generous) assessment of O'Brien's character and career, see Keith Middlemas, 'Lord O'Brien of Lothbury', *Independent*, 27 Nov 1995.
12. *King*, pp 74–5.
13. Accounts of the July 1966 sterling crisis include: Alec Cairncross, *Managing the British Economy in the 1960s* (1996), pp 150–4; Morgan, pp 240–7.
14. PRO, PREM 13/853, 12 July 1966; *FT*, 15 July 1966.
15. PRO, PREM 13/853, 15 July 1966; Wilson, p 251.
16. Leslie O'Brien, *A Life Worth Living* (1995), p 65; BoE, LDMA 1/15, 21 July 1966.
17. Kathleen Burk (ed), 'Witness Seminar on the Origins and Early Development of the Eurobond Market' in *Contemporary European History* (1992), pp 74–5, 84, 81.
18. For the regulatory background in the 1960s, see Richard Roberts, 'How the City Put its House in Order', *FT*, 5 Nov 1989.
19. Richard Spiegelberg, *The City* (1973), pp 172–4; BoE, G 3/266, 7 July 1967; Jehanne Wake, *Kleinwort Benson: The History of Two Families in Banking* (Oxford, 1997), pp 392–3; *The Times*, 18 July 1967; BoE, G 3/266, 24 July 1967.
20. Jonathan Aitken, *The Young Meteors* (1967), pp 291–4. On how stockbroking changed from the mid-1960s, see the discussion in Littlewood, chapter 23.
21. For plentiful detail about life at Warburgs in the 1960s, see a trio of memoirs: Peter

Spira, *Ladders and Snakes* (1997), chapter 7; Ian Fraser, *The High Road to England* (Wilby, 1999), chapters 15–16; Peter Stormonth Darling, *City Cinderella* (1999), chapters 1–7.

22. NLSC, C 409/134, p 63; Stormonth Darling, pp 51, 19; Paul Ferris, *Gentlemen of Fortune* (1984), p 199; Stormonth Darling, pp 63, 59.

23. Stormonth Darling, p 59.

24. Spira, p 146; Stormonth Darling, p 33; *FT*, 20 Oct 1982; Ron Chernow, *The Warburgs* (1993), pp 670–2. BoE, ADM 13/7, 19 Nov 1964, suggests that rivalry between London and New York houses in the Eurobond market may also have played a part in the divorce from Kuhn Loeb.

25. Stormonth Darling, pp 43, 55, 250–1, 35–6; Spira, pp 259–60.

26. There have been two main accounts of Slater's career: Charles Raw, *Slater Walker* (1977); Jim Slater, *Return to Go* (1977).

27. *Sunday Telegraph*, 3 March 1963, 26 May 1963; Raw, pp 95–7.

28. Peter Walker, *Staying Power* (1991), p 67; Raw, pp 116–17.

29. *FT*, 31 Oct 1964; Slater, p 61; Raw, p 117; Slater, pp 62–3.

30. *The Times*, 4 Feb 1965; Raw, pp 124–5.

31. Raw, chapters 10–13; Nigel Broackes, *A Growing Concern* (1979), pp 229–30; *Observer*, 15 Jan 1967.

32. Raw, pp 191–2; *Sunday Times*, 27 Aug 1967; Aitken, p 186.

33. Aitken, pp 294–5; Godfrey Hodgson, *Lloyd's of London* (1984), pp 35, 113; Adam Raphael, *Ultimate Risk* (1995 Corgi edn), pp 75–6.

34. BoE, LDMA 1/16, 15 Sept 1967; Cairncross, *Wilson Years*, p 236.

35. 'Symposium: 1967 Devaluation' (Cairncross); Callaghan, p 218, Morgan, pp 268–9; O'Brien, p 72. In general on the November 1967 sterling crisis and devaluation, see: Cairncross, *Managing*, pp 184–91; Morgan, pp 268–77.

36. *The Times*, 8 Nov 1967; Morgan, pp 269–70; O'Brien, p 72; Callaghan, pp 220–1; Morgan, p 271.

37. Morgan, p 271; *King*, pp 155–6; Morgan, pp 272–3.

38. *The Times*, 18 Nov 1967.

39. Morgan, p 274; Stormonth Darling, p 71.

40. *Daily Telegraph*, 22 Nov 1967; John Fforde, *The Bank of England and Public Policy, 1941–1958* (Cambridge, 1992), p 300.

CHAPTER THIRTY-SIX

1. BoE, LDMA 1/16, 15 Dec 1967; *The Cecil King Diary, 1965–1970* (1972), pp 163, 170; BoE, LDMA 1/16, 19 Jan 1968; *King*, p 181; BoE, LDMA 1/16, 8 March 1968; Alec Cairncross, *Managing the British Economy in the 1960s* (1996), p 204; *King*, p 181.

2. *King*, p 183; Timothy Green, *The New World of Gold* (1985 edn), p 130; PRO, PREM 13/2051, 15 March 1968.

3. Alec Cairncross, *The Wilson Years* (1997), p 289; PRO, PREM 13/2051, 17 March 1968; BoE, G 3/268, 29 Aug 1968.

4. BoE, G 3/287, 19 March 1968; Roy Jenkins, *A Life at the Centre* (1991), p 231; *FT*, 20 March 1968; BoE, LDMA 1/16, 22 March 1968; Cairncross, *Wilson Years*, p 292.

5. *King*, pp 189, 191; PRO, PREM 13/2017, 9 May 1968; *Daily Mirror*, 10 May 1968; Leslie O'Brien, *A Life Worth Living* (1995), pp 58–9.

6. *FT*, 1 July 1985; Sir Gordon Newton, *A Peer Without Equal* (1997), p 127.

7. *King*, p 210.

8. BB, 202955, credit department's report for 1967; Cairncross, *Wilson Years*, p 319; BoE, G 3/290, 31 Oct 1968; William Clarke, 'The City's Movement Towards a Eurocurrency

Standard', *The Times*, 10 Nov 1976; C. R. Schenk, 'International Financial Centres 1958–71: Competitiveness and Complementarity' in Stefano Battilossi and Youssef Cassis (eds), *European Banks and the American Challenge, 1950s–1970s* (Oxford, 2001).

9. Schenk, 'International Financial Centres'.

10. The growth of the secondary banks is covered in Margaret Reid, *The Secondary Banking Crisis, 1973–75* (1982), chapter 4; *Banker*, Sept 1968, p 804.

11. *Euromoney*, Nov 1971, p 59; *Banker*, July 1969, p 619, Oct 1969, p 1085.

12. *Banker*, Oct 1969, p 1085; *Euromoney*, June 1994, p 50.

13. *Banker*, Oct 1969, pp 1063–71.

14. *Euromoney*, Dec 1970, pp 13–15.

15. *King*, p 307; O'Brien, p 97; *The Times*, 3–4 June 1970.

16. John Littlewood, *The Stock Market* (1998), pp 173–4; Jenkins, p 308.

17. Simon Bradley and Nikolaus Pevsner, *The Buildings of England: London 1: The City of London* (1997), pp 316–17; *The Times*, 23 Sept 1970; George and Pamela Cleaver, *The Union Discount* (1985), p 106; Stephen Fay, *Portrait of an Old Lady* (1987), p 20; Philip Ziegler, *The Sixth Great Power: Barings, 1762–1929* (1988), p 362; Littlewood, p 271; David Kynaston, *Cazenove & Co.* (1991), p 276.

18. NLSC, C 408/009, pp 151–4; SE, Council, 8 May 1973.

19. Littlewood, pp 442, 159–63; Andrew Lycett, *From Diamond Sculls to Golden Handcuffs: A History of Rowe & Pitman* (1998), p 92; Laurie Dennett, *Slaughter and May: A Century in the City* (Cambridge, 1989), pp 229–30, 236–40; Edgar Jones, *True and Fair: A History of Price Waterhouse* (1995), pp 257, 271–3.

20. Richard Whitley, 'Commonalities and Connections among Directors of Large Financial Institutions' in *Sociological Review* (Nov 1973), pp 613–32; Richard Spiegelberg, *The City* (1973), pp 131–2; Martin Vander Weyer, *Falling Eagle: The Decline of Barclays Bank* (2000), pp 67, 111; *Independent*, 25 Jan 1993.

21. *The Times*, 22 June 1971; *CL*, p 175; *Naked City*, BBC2, 23 Oct 1996, testimony of Susan Shaw; JS, no 13, p 18.

22. *FT*, 31 Oct 1987 (Riley); Spiegelberg, pp 21–4, 245.

23. City-oriented accounts include: A. R. Holmes and Edwin Green, *Midland* (1986), pp 274–6; Kathleen Burk, *Morgan Grenfell, 1838–1988* (Oxford, 1989), pp 198–200.

24. HSBC, 373/4, 13 Nov 1970; O'Brien, pp 107–8; *King*, p 54; Anthony Sampson, *The New Anatomy of Britain* (1971), p 478; FRBNY, C 261 England, 5 Feb 1971; HSBC, Acc 346, Rolls-Royce, 1970–3, inc Thompson memo, 16 Feb 1971.

25. *Banker*, March 1971, p 236.

26. Harold Evans, *Vickers* (1978), pp 159–69; *Investors Chronicle*, 19 March 1971.

27. O'Brien, pp 111–12; *Banker*, Dec 1971, p 1571; Burk, pp 195–8, Dominic Hobson, *The Pride of Lucifer* (1990), pp 128–37; *Euromoney*, March 1971, pp 6–7.

28. *Management Today*, Oct 1972, p 29, Aug 1971, pp 68–9.

29. David Kynaston, *LIFFE* (Cambridge, 1997), p 9; Keith Middlemas, *Power, Competition and the State: Volume 2* (Basingstoke, 1990), p 334; O'Brien, p 124.

30. HSBC, Acc 346, file re Bank of England, 28 Feb 1973; Janet Kelly, *Bankers and Borders* (Cambridge, Mass., 1977), pp 59–60; Adrienne Gleeson, *London Enriched* (1997), pp 87–8.

31. Timothy Green, *The New World of Gold* (1985 edn), pp 132–4.

32. The full story is told in Donald Read, *The Power of News: The History of Reuters, 1849–1989* (Oxford, 1992), pp 301–7.

33. Read, p 303.

34. *The Times*, 2 Aug 1996; Junko Sakai, *Japanese Bankers in the City of London* (2000), pp 31–3; *International Insider*, 27 June 1977, 6 March 1978; *Euromoney*, June 1989, special supplement.

35. Martin Vander Weyer, *Falling Eagle: The Decline of Barclays Bank* (2000), pp 56–7.

See also David Rogers, *The Big Four British Banks* (Basingstoke, 1999), pp 72–5, for his analysis of Barclays and international overreach.

36. Rogers, pp 128–9; *British Empires*, Channel 4, 9 Jan 2000; *Management Today*, Sept 1972, p 30.

37. *Daily Mail*, 10 May 1972.

38. *King*, p 206.

39. Reid, pp 48–52, offers a balanced overview of the supervisory relationship between the Bank and the secondaries.

40. Middlemas, p 344; *Spectator*, 23 May 1987 (Jock Bruce-Gardyne); FRBNY, C 261, England, 9 Nov 1972.

41. SE, Council, 13 Nov 1972; *FT*, 25 Nov 1972.

42. Ian Fraser, *The High Road to England* (Wilby, 1999), pp 314–16, discusses the insider dealing question during his three years (1969–72) at the Takeover Panel.

43. *The Times*, 3 Feb 1973, 7 Feb 1973; *Daily Telegraph*, 7 Feb 1973; *Sunday Times*, 29 April 1973.

44. Littlewood, p 193; Jim Slater, *Return to Go* (1977), pp 174–6, *Daily Mail*, 25 Jan 1973; *Investors Guardian*, 6 March 1973; Paul Bazalgette, *Musings of a Market Man* (1983), March 1973.

45. Middlemas, p 345; *King*, pp 271, 279; BoE, C 160, 7 March 1973. On the question of why O'Brien retired in 1973, he himself insisted in his memoirs (*A Life Worth Living*, p 134) that the decision was simply fulfilling the agreement he had reached with Barber prior to the start of his second term in 1971.

46. Tom Bower, *Tiny Rowland* (1994 Mandarin edn), chapters 5–6.

47. Bower, p 252 (Heath); *King*, p 278.

48. HSBC, Acc 141, no 13 ('Capital Structure'), July 1973; *Investors Chronicle*, 8 June 1973.

49. *King*, p 318; NLSC, C 409/009, p 121.

50. Reid, p 69; HSBC, Acc 141, no 13 ('Capital Structure'), July 1973.

51. Reid, p 79; John Campbell, *Edward Heath* (1993), p 530.

52. David McClintick, 'The Decline and Fall of Lloyd's of London', *Time*, 21 Feb 2000.

CHAPTER THIRTY-SEVEN

1. Keith Middlemas, *Power, Competition and the State: Volume 2* (Basingstoke, 1990), p 380; Ron Chernow, *The House of Morgan* (New York, 1990), pp 606–8.

2. John Littlewood, *The Stock Market* (1998), p 201.

3. James Lees-Milne, *Ancient as the Hills* (1997), p 110; Littlewood, p 202.

4. Littlewood, p 202; HSBC, 373/5, 21 Dec 1973; Edward du Cann, *Two Lives* (Upton-upon-Severn, 1995), pp 134–5.

5. HSBC, Acc 141, no 19, 19 Dec 1973; Margaret Reid, *The Secondary Banking Crisis, 1973–75* (1982), p 91 (Cornhill).

6. Reid, p 11.

7. Stephen Fay, *Portrait of an Old Lady* (1987), p 62.

8. *Banker*, Feb 1974, pp 151–5.

9. *Banker*, Dec 1973, p 1433; HSBC, 200/766, 2 Oct 1973 (transcript of Wilson's speech); Littlewood, p 205.

10. *Independent on Sunday*, 5 April 1992; Denis Healey, *The Time of My Life* (1989), pp 374–5.

11. *The Cecil King Diary, 1970-1974* (1975), p 350.

12. *FT*, 25 May 1974.

13. *International Insider*, 15 July 1974, 22 July 1974; Reid, p 117; *Euromoney*, Nov 1977,

p 85 (Nicholas Faith); Richard Roberts, *Take Your Partners: Orion, the Consortium Banks and the Transformation of the Euromarkets* (Basingstoke, 2001), pp 78–9, 178–9.

14. Littlewood, p 209; BoE, C 160/164, 4 Sept 1974.

15. *Investors Chronicle*, 18 Oct 1974.

16. For another account of the 'Lever Bank', see Richard Coopey and Donald Clarke, *3i: Fifty Years Investing in Industry* (Oxford, 1995), pp 123–7.

17. *Sunday Times*, 15 Sept 1974; *The Times*, 22 Sept 1974.

18. *FT*, 21 Oct 1974; HSBC, 74 (MC boxes), 23 Oct 1974, 8 Nov 1974, Acc 141, no 46, 28 July 1975; Michael Moss, *Standard Life, 1825–2000* (Edinburgh, 2000), pp 283–4.

19. *Investors Chronicle*, 25 Oct 1974; Rowe & Pitman, *Market Report*, Nov 1974.

20. *Investors Chronicle*, 22 Nov 1974; George G. Blakey, *The Post-war History of the London Stock Market* (Didcot, 1994), p 166; *Investors Chronicle*, 1 Nov 1974; *Banker*, Dec 1974, pp 1515–19; Jim Slater, *Return to Go* (1977), p 204.

21. *CL*, p 198.

22. Accounts include: John Plender, *That's the Way the Money Goes* (1982), pp 53–5; Laurie Dennett, *A Sense of Security: 150 Years of Prudential* (Cambridge, 1998), pp 338, 418; Moss, p 284.

23. Littlewood, p 218; *The Times*, 18 Dec 1974; *FT*, 24 Dec 1988 (Heather Farmbrough); *Sunday Telegraph*, 30 Aug 1998 (Winterflood profile); Moss, p 284.

24. Blakey, p 171; *FT*, 7 Jan 1975; Littlewood, p 218; *International Insider*, 6 Jan 1975.

25. Rowe & Pitman, *Market Report*, Feb 1975; Littlewood, p 223; the most detailed account of this stage of the secondary banking crisis is Margaret Reid, *The Secondary Banking Crisis, 1973–75* (1982), chapters 10–12.

26. Edmund Dell, *A Hard Pounding* (Oxford, 1991), p 135; Rowe & Pitman, *Market Report*, May 1975.

27. HSBC, 373/7, 4 April 1975; SE, Council, 29 April 1975.

28. Kathleen Burk, 'Symposium: 1976 IMF Crisis' in *Contemporary Record* (Nov 1989), p 39; HSBC, 200/554, 10 June 1975, 200/766, June 1975.

29. *FT*, 25 Oct 1975. In general on the Slater Walker endgame, see: Charles Raw, *Slater Walker* (1977), chapter 22; Slater, chapters 16–19; Slater, p 219; *Daily Telegraph*, 25 Oct 1975.

30. *Institutional Investor*, Dec 1976, p 45; *International Insider*, 19 Jan 1976.

31. Accounts of the March 1976 sterling crisis include: Fay, pp 73–6; Kathleen Burk and Alec Cairncross, *'Goodbye, Great Britain': The 1976 IMF Crisis* (1992), pp 21–33.

32. Fay, p 74.

33. *The Times*, 5 March 1976, 9 March 1976; *FT*, 9 March 1976; *International Insider*, 15 March 1976; Denis Healey, *The Time of My Life* (1989), p 427.

34. *The Times*, 6 March 1976.

35. *The Times*, 17 March 1976; David Kynaston, *The Financial Times* (1988), p 430.

36. Accounts of the sterling/IMF crisis between April and December 1976 include: Burk, 'Symposium'; Dell, *Hard Pounding*, pp 212–91; Burk and Cairncross; Edmund Dell, *The Chancellors* (1996), pp 422–38; Kenneth O. Morgan, *Callaghan* (Oxford, 1997), pp 528–54.

37. HSBC, 74 (MC boxes), 7 April 1976; Morgan, *Callaghan*, p 523.

38. Burk, 'Symposium', p 45.

39. HSBC, 200/554, 27 July 1976.

40. *New Statesman*, 28 Feb 2000.

41. Morgan, *Callaghan*, p 535; Healey, p 429.

42. *Euromoney*, Dec 1976, p 54; Jacques Attali, *A Man of Influence* (1986), pp 288–9; Kathleen Burk, 'The House of Morgan Redivivus?: The Abortive Morgan International 1972–73' in *Business History* (July 1991), pp 194–5.

43. Littlewood, pp 233–43; Paul Bazalgette, *Musings of a Market Man* (1983), Oct 1977.

44. SE, 1978 *Annual Report*; Rowe & Pitman, *Market Report*, Sept 1978.

45. Middlemas, p 140; Fay, p 69; Morgan, *Callaghan*, pp 508–9; Middlemas, p 526; Bernard Donoughue, *Prime Minister* (1987), p 102.

46. The fairly complex story is told in: Michael Moran, *The Politics of Banking* (Basingstoke, 1984), pp 118–30; Fay, pp 86–97.

47. For the background, see *FT*, 9 March 1978 ('Policing the markets').

48. SE, 4 March 1975, 11 Nov 1975; *FT*, 9 March 1978, 12 Oct 1978.

49. Michael Clarke, *Fallen Idols* (1981), p 232; *FT*, 21 July 1978; *The Economist*, 30 Sept 1978; *FT*, 20 Oct 1978; Clarke, *Fallen Idols*, p 202.

50. *Euromoney*, Oct 1995, p 67.

51. *The Economist*, 31 March 1979.

52. Charles Meynell, 'The Rothschild dilemma' in *Euromoney*, Oct 1977, pp 121–33. See also: Cary Reich, 'Inside the Rothschild Feud' in *Institutional Investor*, July 1980, pp 49–62; Niall Ferguson, *The World's Banker: The History of the House of Rothschild* (1998), p 1021.

53. *Institutional Investor*, Feb 1977, p 33; *Spectator*, 27. July 1985; *Banker*, July 1977, p 64. Also on BMB, see Martin Vander Weyer, *Falling Eagle: The Decline of Barclays Bank* (2000), pp 63–5.

54. On Lloyd's by the late 1970s, see: Godfrey Hodgson, *Lloyd's of London* (1984), chapters 4, 7, 9; Adam Raphael, *Ultimate Risk* (1995 Corgi edn), chapter 4.

55. *Time*, 21 Feb 2000.

56. Hodgson, p 218.

57. NLSC, C 409/015 (Sir Peter Miller), pp 109–10; Raphael, pp 91–2.

58. BoE, C 160.

59. *London Evening Standard*, 11 April 1979, 1 May 1979, 3 May 1979.

60. Bazalgette, *Musings*, May 1979.

CHAPTER THIRTY-EIGHT

1. SE, Council (appendixes), 4 Nov 1980; Peter Spira, *Ladders and Snakes* (1997), p 239.

2. John Littlewood, *The Stock Market* (1998), p 316.

3. *FT*, 2 April 1983; Rowe & Pitman, *Market Report*, June 1983.

4. On government/Bank relations in the early 1980s, see: William Keegan, *Mrs Thatcher's Economic Experiment* (1985 Penguin edn), chapter 5; Stephen Fay, *Portrait of an Old Lady* (1987), chapter 7; Keith Middlemas, *Power, Competition and the State: Volume 3* (Basingstoke, 1991), pp 243–59; Nigel Lawson, *The View from No. 11* (1992), chapters 7–8; Robert Elgie and Helen Thompson, *The Politics of Central Banks* (1998), pp 61–3.

5. Geoffrey Howe, *Conflict of Loyalty* (1994), p 139; Lawson, p 71.

6. The succession process is discussed in Fay, pp 126–7.

7. *FT*, 29 Dec 1982.

8. Accounts of the early privatisations include: Lawson, chapters 18–19; Jehanne Wake, *Kleinwort Benson: The History of Two Families in Banking* (Oxford, 1997), pp 416–17; Littlewood, pp 361–5.

9. *FT*, 31 Oct 1981.

10. *Daily Telegraph*, 3 March 1993.

11. *Institutional Investor*, March 1980, pp 155–6.

12. Margaret Reid, *All-Change in the City* (Basingstoke, 1988), p 244; *The Times*, 18 July 1981.

13. *The Times*, 5 Jan 1998 (obituary of Gower); SE, Council (appendixes), 27 Oct 1981; Michael Moran, 'Power, Policy and the City of London' in Roger King (ed), *Capital and Politics* (1983), p 64.

14. Neil Osborn, 'What's Ailing Lloyd's of London?', *Institutional Investor*, March 1980, pp 81–92.

15. *Time*, 21 Feb 2000; Godfrey Hodgson, *Lloyd's of London* (1984), p 318.

16. Ian Hay Davison, *Lloyd's* (1987), pp 6, 59; *Naked City*, BBC2, 6 Nov 1996.

17. Richard Roberts, 'Setting the City Free: The Impact of the UK Abolition of Exchange Controls' in *Journal of International Financial Markets* (Aug 2000), p 136. This is a valuable article about a subject that, granted its generally recognised importance, has received surprisingly little scholarly attention.

18. *FT*, 3 May 1980; David Rogers, *The Big Four British Banks* (Basingstoke, 1999), pp 32–3; Fay, pp 132–5; Reid, pp 140–6.

19. Martin Vander Weyer, *Falling Eagle: The Decline of Barclays Bank* (2000), pp 81–8.

20. *Euromoney*, July 1981, pp 141–7; *Independent*, 17 June 1992 (Hamish McRae); Tom Bower, *Maxwell: The Outsider* (1988), chapter 12.

21. *Daily Mail*, 26 April 1980; Edward du Cann, *Two Lives* (Upton-upon-Severn, 1995), p 142; *Independent*, 28 Feb 1989; *The Times*, 12 Dec 1997 (obituary of Kissin).

22. Ron Chernow, *The Warburgs* (1993), pp 703–5; Peter Stormonth Darling, *City Cinderella* (1999), p 115.

23. George and Pamela Cleaver, *The Union Discount* (1985), pp 111–12; *Spectator*, 16 Jan 1982.

24. David Kynaston, *LIFFE* (Cambridge, 1997), chapters 1–3.

25. Spira, pp 253–7; NLSC, C 409/046, pp 362–5; *Investors Chronicle*, 10 June 1983.

26. Reid, p 36; SE, Council (appendixes), 25 Nov 1980; NLSC, C 408/009, p 179; Michael David Kandiah, 'The October 1987 Stock Market Crash' in *Contemporary British History* (Spring 1999), p 127; *Independent on Sunday*, 11 Feb 1990.

27. Ian J. Fraser, 'Sir Anthony Lincoln', *Independent*, 14 Aug 1991; Reid, pp 42–3.

28. Fay, p 27.

29. Kandiah, pp 111–12; Lawson, pp 398–400.

30. Reid, pp 47–8.

31. SE, Council, 21–2 July 1983.

32. *The Economist*, 23 July 1983; *The Times*, 26 July 1983; Kandiah, p 112.

CHAPTER THIRTY-NINE

1. *FT*, 25 Oct 1983, 4 Nov 1983, John Plender and Paul Wallace, *The Square Mile* (1985), pp 53–7.

2. Alan Clark, *Diaries* (1993), p 34.

3. *Banker*, Nov 1983, pp 97–8.

4. *Banker*, Nov 1983, pp 98–100; Andrew Lorenz, *BZW: The First Ten Years* (1996), p 13; W. J. Reader and David Kynaston, *Phillips & Drew* (1998), p 188; Plender and Wallace, p 109; Andrew Lycett, *From Diamond Sculls to Golden Handcuffs: A History of Rowe & Pitman* (1998), pp 117–19, 136; *Wall Street Journal*, 29 Sept 1983.

5. *FT*, 4 Nov 1983, 8 Nov 1983.

6. *FT*, 15 Nov 1983.

7. *FT*, 17 Dec 1983.

8. *FT*, 28 Dec 1983.

9. SE, Markets Committee, 23 Jan 1984, Council, 7 Feb 1984; Maximilian Hall, *The City Revolution* (Basingstoke, 1987), p 19.

10. John Littlewood, *The Stock Market* (1998), pp 342–3; David Kynaston, *LIFFE* (Cambridge, 1997), pp 131–3.

11. Littlewood, p 342; SE, Council, 20 March 1984; *FT*, 23 March 1984; *Daily Telegraph*, 24 March 1984.

12. *Daily Telegraph*, 24 March 1984.

13. Dominic Hobson, *The Pride of Lucifer* (1990), pp 214–18; Reader and Kynaston, pp 189–90; *Wall Street Journal*, 6 Nov 1984.

14. Littlewood, pp 330–2; *Euromoney*, Feb 1984, p 35, Dec 1984, p 73.

15. Accounts of the BT flotation include: *CL*, pp 74–6; Jehanne Wake, *Kleinwort Benson: The History of Two Families in Banking* (Oxford, 1997), pp 417–18; Littlewood, pp 365–70.

16. Nigel Lawson, *The View from No. 11* (1992), p 222; Elroy Dimson and Paul Marsh, *Cases in Corporate Finance* (Chichester, 1988), p 222.

17. *Spectator*, 11 Aug 1984, 18 Aug 1984; SE, Markets Committee, 10 Dec 1984.

18. Plender and Wallace, pp 49–50.

19. *FT*, 18 June 1985; *The Economist*, 22 June 1985; *Banker*, July 1985, p 5; *Euromoney*, Sept 1985, p 58; *FT*, 27 Oct 1986.

20. *The Economist*, 6 July 1985.

21. *FT*, 21 Nov 1985; *Banker*, June 1986, p 69; *The Times*, 14 Oct 1986; *Banker*, Sept 1986, p 95; *FT*, 22 Sept 1986, 29 Sept 1986.

22. *The Times*, 17 Oct 1986; *Guardian*, 20 Oct 1986; *The Times*, 20 Oct 1986; NLSC, C 408/009, p 201.

23. *Spectator*, 18 Oct 1986.

24. *FT*, 25 Oct 1986; *Today*, 25 Oct 1986.

25. Godfrey Hodgson, *Lloyd's of London* (1984), pp 297–8; Simon Bradley and Nikolaus Pevsner, *The Buildings of England: London 1: The City of London* (1997), pp 313–14; *Spectator*, 26 April 1986.

26. *Spectator*, 4 May 1985; *Banker*, July 1985, p 33.

27. *FT*, 11 Jan 1992.

28. Jon Ashworth, 'Planner Who Built His Name on Controversy', *The Times*, 31 Dec 1996.

29. On the Broadgate development, see: Alastair Ross Goobey, *Bricks and Mortals* (1992), pp 50–6, 70–5; Bradley and Pevsner, pp 434–8.

30. *Futures World*, 17 Jan 1985; *FT*, 30 June 1986; *Time*, 25 Aug 1986.

31. *Listener*, 20 March 1986; Hobson, p 191; *Observer Magazine*, 5 Sept 1982.

32. *Observer Magazine*, 5 Sept 1982; Paul Ferris, *Gentlemen of Fortune* (1984), p 181.

33. *The Economist*, 20 July 1985; *Wall Street Journal*, 13 Aug 1985.

34. *Listener*, 20 March 1986; *Spectator*, 15 March 1986; *Institutional Investor*, June 1986, p 118; Margaret Reid, *All-Change in the City* (Basingstoke, 1988), p 69; Hobson, p 191.

35. *Nice-Matin*, 3 Nov 1982; Anthony Sampson, *The Changing Anatomy of Britain* (1982), pp 295–7.

36. Ferris, p 180; David Lazar, *Markets and Ideology in the City of London* (Basingstoke, 1990), pp 63, 75, 90, 110–11.

37. *New Statesman*, 24 Oct 1986; *Daily Express*, 27 Oct 1986.

CHAPTER FORTY

1. *FT*, 28 Oct 1986; *Business Week*, 12 Jan 1987.

2. George G. Blakey, *The Post-War History of the London Stock Market* (Didcot, 1994 pbk edn), p 277; *The Economist*, 29 Nov 1986; John Littlewood, *The Stock Market* (1998), pp 371–2; *FT*, 15 Sept 1987.

3. *Observer*, 7 Dec 1986; *FT*, 31 Dec 1986. For an account of how Guinness was becoming a 'scandal', see Dominic Hobson, *The Pride of Lucifer* (1990), chapter 11.

4. *London Evening Standard*, 21 Jan 1987; *Observer*, 25 Jan 1987; *FT*, 17 Oct 1987.

5. *FT*, 16 Jan 1987; *The Mayfair Set*, BBC2, 1 Aug 1999; Adam Raphael, *Ultimate Risk* (1995 Corgi edn), pp 125–7; *The Times*, 21 Jan 1987; *Independent*, 11 Feb 1987.

6. David Kynaston, *LIFFE* (Cambridge, 1997), p 174.

7. *Sunday Telegraph*, 18 Oct 1987; *The Times*, 17 Oct 1987; Littlewood, p 380.

8. Accounts include: Peter Pugh, *The City Slicker's Handbook* (1988), pp 100–7; Blakey, pp 208–9; Littlewood, pp 379–84; Michael David Kandiah, 'The October 1987 Stock Market Crash' in *Contemporary British History* (Spring 1999), pp 133–65.

9. *Naked City*, BBC2, 6 Nov 1996; *London Evening Standard*, 19 Oct 1987; *FT*, 20 Oct 1987.

10. Ian Fraser, *The High Road to England* (Wilby, 1999), p 358; *London Evening Standard*, 23 Oct 1987; Kynaston, *LIFFE*, p 177; *CL*, p 146.

11. Accounts of the BP flotation include: Nigel Lawson, *The View from No. 11* (1992), pp 757–75; Littlewood, pp 384–5; Kandiah, pp 160–4.

12. Lawson, p 771; *Business*, Dec 1987, p 78.

13. *FT*, 11 Feb 1988; *Naked City*, BBC2, 6 Nov 1996.

14. *FT*, 23 Nov 1987.

15. Littlewood, p 394; Richard Roberts, 'The Bank of England and the City' in Richard Roberts and David Kynaston (eds), *The Bank of England* (Oxford, 1995), pp 169–70; *Business Week*, 6 March 1989; *Institutional Investor*, Nov 1989, pp 50–8; *The Times*, 28 Oct 1991; Littlewood, p 438; *The Times*, 28 May 1992; *Euromoney*, June 1994, 'The 1994 Guide to World Equity Markets', p 32.

16. *FT*, 25 June 1988; *Independent on Sunday*, 11 Feb 1990; Junko Sakai, *Japanese Bankers in the City of London* (2000), p 48. In general, see Sakai, chapter 2, for a helpful discussion about the muted impact of the Japanese houses.

17. For a detailed account of Lloyd's during the late 1980s and early 1990s, see Adam Raphael, *Ultimate Risk* (1995 Corgi edn), chapters 7–12. See also the review of Raphael in *TLS*, 20 May 1994 (J. H. C. Leach).

18. *Independent*, 28 April 1994 (Hamish McRae); *New Yorker*, 20 Sept 1993; *Time*, 21 Feb 2000, p 43; Raphael, p 372.

19. The fullest account is Jonathan Guinness, *Requiem for a Family Business* (1997).

20. *FT*, 29 Aug 1990, 1 Sept 1990; Department of Trade and Industry, *Guinness PLC: Investigation under Sections 432 (2) and 442 of the Companies Act 1985: Report by David Donaldson QC and Ian Watt QC* (Nov 1997), p 302 (Parnes fee); *FT*, 12 Feb 1992; Guinness, *Requiem*, pp 330–2.

21. DTI, p 309.

22. Richard Roberts, *Inside International Finance* (1998), pp 203–6; Robert Pringle, 'The Bank of England and Central Bank Co-operation' in Roberts and Kynaston, p 143.

23. *FT*, 10 Oct 1991; Nicholas Bray, 'outFOXed', *GQ*, June 1992, pp 70–3.

24. The key account is Tom Bower, *Maxwell: The Final Verdict* (1996), following on from his *Maxwell: The Outsider* (1988).

25. Lisa Endlich, *Goldman Sachs* (1999), p 142; *FT*, 1 Jan 2000.

26. Lawson, pp 789–91, 1059–60, 868–9; Margaret Thatcher, *The Downing Street Years* (1993), p 706.

27. *Euroweek*, 3 Nov 1989.

28. The eye-witness quotations in this account of Black Wednesday derive from *Black Wednesday*, BBC1, 16 Sept 1997. The house-buying inquiry is from *The Major Years*, BBC1, 18 Oct 1999.

29. *Independent*, 18 Sept 1992; *Sunday Telegraph*, 20 Sept 1992; Kynaston, *LIFFE*, pp 257–9.

30. *Daily Telegraph*, 5 Oct 1994; Endlich, p 201; *Guardian*, 5 Dec 1994.

31. Four books about the Barings drama were published within two years: Judith Rawnsley, *Going for Broke* (1995); Stephen Fay, *The Collapse of Barings* (1996); Nick Leeson, *Rogue Trader* (1996); John Gapper and Nicholas Denton, *All That Glitters* (1996). Fay, together with Gapper and Denton, are the main sources for this account.

Notes

32. Fay, p 216.

33. *The Times*, 27 Feb 1995; Fay, photo opp p 150; *FT*, 28 Feb 1995.

34. *FT*, 28 Feb 1995.

35. *The Times*, 28 Feb 1995, 1 March 1995; *FT*, 1 March 1995; *Independent*, 4 March 1995; *Sunday Telegraph*, 5 March 1995.

36. *Sunday Times*, 5 March 1995.

37. Fay, p 78.

38. Fay, pp 109–10; *The Economist*, 4 March 1995 (Peter Baring quotations); Fay, p 113.

39. Rawnsley, p 135; *Inside Story Special*, BBC1, 12 June 1996.

40. Gapper and Denton, p 300.

41. *The Times*, 24 Feb 1996; *Independent*, 23 Feb 1996, 5 July 1999; *FT*, 4 Dec 1999; *London Evening Standard*, 17 July 1995; Fay, pp 232–3.

42. *Daily Telegraph*, 24 Feb 1996.

43. *Business Week*, 23 March 1998; *Institutional Investor*, May 1999, pp 32–40.

44. *Independent*, 8 April 1997; *Daily Mail*, 23 Oct 1997.

45. Treasury Committee, *First Report: Accountability of the Bank of England* (1997–8), Appendixes, pp 1–5; *Economist*, 10 May 1997; Will Hutton, *The State We're In* (1995), p 291; *Guardian*, 7 May 1997.

46. *Daily Telegraph*, 22 Oct 1998; *Independent*, 17 May 1999.

47. *FT*, 21 May 1997; *Daily Telegraph*, 1 July 1999; *The Times*, 11 April 2000; Martin Dickson, 'City Regulation Farce Threatens to Turn into Tragedy', *FT*, 1 April 2000; *FT*, 11 Sept 2000.

48. *FT*, 5 Sept 1996; Stephen Fay, *The Global Powerhouse* (Corporation of London, Jan 2000), p 19; *The Times*, 15 May 1997.

49. London Stock Exchange, *Marketplace to the World* (August 1996), p 1; Ranald C. Michie, *The London Stock Exchange* (Oxford, 1999), p 614. On another significant development a year earlier, the launch of AIM (Alternative Investment Market), see Michie, pp 619–20.

50. *FT*, 20 Oct 1997; *Independent*, 13 Dec 1997; *Guardian*, 30 April 1998; *FT*, 18 Jan 2000; *Independent*, 6 April 2000; *Daily Telegraph*, 6 April 2000. In general on SETS, see Michie, pp 614–18.

51. *Daily Telegraph*, 6 Oct 1997.

52. *Independent*, 13 March 2000.

53. *The Times*, 17 Sept 1996; *Daily Telegraph*, 9 Nov 1999; *Independent*, 16 Dec 1999, 18 April 2000.

54. *Spectator*, 18 Sept 1999.

55. *London Evening Standard*, 15 July 1996.

56. *Daily Telegraph*, 6 Nov 1999; *Independent on Sunday*, 31 Oct 1999; *Spectator*, 18 Sept 1999.

57. *London Evening Standard*, 11 July 1996. See also: James Fergusson, 'Amschel Rothschild', *Independent*, 11 July 1996; Martin Amis, *Experience* (2000), pp 223, 225–6.

58. *Independent*, 13 June 1996; *The Times*, 16 Jan 1997; *FT*, 1 Feb 1997.

59. *The Times*, 29 Nov 1999; *Independent*, 9 Dec 1999; *Tablet*, 6 May 2000.

60. *The Times*, 16 Dec 1999.

61. James Buchan, *Frozen Desire* (1997), pp 281–2.

Acknowledgements

The following kindly allowed me to reproduce material, including copyright material: the Bank of England; Barclays Bank; the British Library National Sound Archive; James Buchan; Michael Burns; Cazenove & Co.; the Centre for Metropolitan History; Alan Clodd; Deutsche Morgan Grenfell; Sir Edward du Cann; Mrs Valerie Eliot (Lines from T. S. Eliot's *The Waste Land* taken from *Collected Poems* © The Estate of T. S. Eliot and reproduced by kind permission of Faber & Faber); the Federal Reserve Bank of New York; University of Glasgow Archives and the Estate of Sir Alec Cairncross; David Higham Associates (*London Particulars*); the Holland-Martin family archives; HSBC Holdings; ING Barings; the Joint Grand Gresham Committee; University of Liverpool; Lloyds TSB Group; the London Investment Banking Association; the London Stock Exchange; Matheson & Co.; R. R. Meinertzhagen; Sir Anthony Meyer; Brian Peppiatt; N. M. Rothschild & Sons; the Royal Bank of Scotland Group; the School of Oriental and African Studies and the Addis family; Schroders; Slaughter and May; Peter Spira; Peter Stormonth Darling; Davina Walter; A. P. Watt Ltd on behalf of Mrs Lavinia Hankinson, the Hon. Mrs David Erskine and Duff Hart-Davis (Sir Alan Lascelles journals); Gillian Wyatt.

I would also like to thank my agent Deborah Rogers and her assistant Mohsen Shah for helping to make this edition happen; Liz Cowen for her copy-editing; Vicki Robinson for compiling the index; and at Random House (where it was a pleasure to be again), Rachel Cugnoni, Parisa Ebrahimi, Clara Farmer, Rowena Skelton-Wallace, and of course Jenny Uglow (who edited the four volumes and has had oversight of this). My greatest debt, though, is to David Milner. At the outset it seemed an impossible task to reduce well over a million words to under 300,000, but he has risen to the challenge with a mixture of tactful delicacy and brute vigour – the editorial equivalent perhaps of the late cut followed by a hoist over mid-wicket – and I am grateful indeed for his expertise.

Index

Abedi, Agha Hasan 586
Aberdare Holdings 486
Abrahams, Leopold A. 406
acceptance business/accepting houses 5–6,
9, 11, 21, 68, 263, 293, 335–6, 338, 370,
371, 380, 386–7, 507
Accepting Houses Committee 386–7, 420,
446, 509, 561, 583
accountancy firms (19th century) 146
accounting machines 351
Adams, Henry 75
Addis, Sir Charles 166–7; and World War I
273, 282, 286, 293; on Carl Meyer 283;
on bank amalgamations 291–2; on US
politicians 299; and Norman 301, 302–3,
305, 338; and Dawes Loan 308; urges
return to gold standard 313–14, 318; and
Bank rate 316; and Revelstoke's death
323; and financial crisis 339, 340, 341;
on anti-German sentiments 371; and
Chamberlain 385
Addison, Joseph 10, 11
Adeane, Sir Robert 495
AE 578, 585
Aiken, Conrad 352
Aitken, Jonathan 486–7, 491, 492, 541
Akass, Jon 575
Akroyd, Geoffrey 461
Akroyd, John 113, 192
Akroyd, Swainson 113, 192
Akroyd & Smithers 309, 437, 560, 562
Alcoa *see* Aluminium Company of America
Aldenham, Lord 435
Alexander, Ann 34, 41
Alexander, George William 34, 41
Alexander, Henry 473

Alexander, William 21, 34
Alexander & Co. 34, 41
Alexanders and Robarts 165
Allcard, John 21
Allen, G. O. ('Gubby') 356
Allen, Maurice 483, 496, 498
Alley, John 54
Alliance Insurance Co. 146
Althorp, John Spencer, Viscount 43
Aluminium Company of America (Alcoa)
446–52
American Express 540, 571
Amery, Leo 246, 336, 410, 424
Amory, Derick Heathcoat 443, 444, 451,
467
Amsterdam 11, 14, 19–20, 21, 274
Anderson, Sir Alan 385
Anderson, Arthur 448
Anderson, Sir John 410, 411, 414
Andreae, Herman 358
Angell, Norman 241–2; *The Great Illusion*
241
Angerstein, John Julius 3–4, 11–12, 19, 20
Anglo-American Telegraph and Com-
mercial Cable Companies 210
Anglo-German Fellowship 382
Anglo-German houses 123, 232, 283–4,
370–71, 391
Anna, Empress of Russia 3
Anspacher (Henry) & Co. 577
Anti-Aggression League 110
Anti-Corn Law League 58
anti-Semitism 5, 17, 19, 28–9, 190, 248, 259,
359–60, 379, 405–6
Appleyard, Bryan 595
Arab-Israeli War 520, 524